THE
realfood
COOKBOOK

Consultant Editor **Valentina Harris**

DUNCAN BAIRD PUBLISHERS

LONDON

THE REAL FOOD COOKBOOK

First published in the United Kingdom and
Ireland in 2011 by Duncan Baird Publishers Ltd
Sixth Floor, Castle House
75–76 Wells Street
London W1T 3QH

Conceived, created and designed by
Duncan Baird Publishers

ISBN: 978-1-84483-957-5

Typeset in Filosofia
Colour reproduction by Colourscan, Singapore
Printed in China by Imago

Publisher's Note
While every care has been taken in compiling the
recipes for this book, Duncan Baird Publishers, or any
other persons who have been involved in working on
this publication, cannot accept responsibility for any errors
or omissions, inadvertent or not, that may be found in the
recipes or text, nor for any problems that may arise as a
result of preparing one of these recipes. If you are pregnant
or breastfeeding, or have any special dietary requirements
or medical conditions, it is advisable to consult a medical
professional before following any of the recipes contained
in this book.

Notes on the Recipes
Unless otherwise stated:
Use medium eggs, fruit and vegetables
Use fresh ingredients, including herbs and chillies
Do not mix metric and imperial measurements
1 tsp = 5ml 1 tbsp = 15ml 1 cup = 250ml

Philip Lowery's Acknowledgements
I am enormously grateful to all of those people who have been
so instrumental in bringing this book together, especially
all the chefs and producers who have contributed their
recipes so generously. Particular thanks must go to Valentina
Harris without whom this book would never have got off the
starting blocks. Valentina is a talented chef in her own right
and has managed our Chef Theatre at the Festival every year.
Her experience with recipes and her incredible charm and
patience dealing with everyone has made what could have
become a very difficult process a pleasure! As a new boy to
the world of publishing, having my hand held so effectively
by Grace Cheetham from Duncan Baird Publishers has been
crucial, and our editor Katey Mackenzie's patience has been
a marvel to behold. I would also like to thank Manisha Patel
and Allan Sommerville for their inspired work designing
this book. It looks just as good as real food tastes.

Additional Photography
Duncan Baird Publishers would like to thank Billingsgate and
New Covent Garden markets for allowing us to photograph
fresh produce. Special thanks to Paul Murphy at Chef's
Connection for giving us access to his stock of fruit and
vegetables. The publisher would also like to thank Jane Baxter,
Cyrus Todiwala, Raymond Blanc, Giorgio Locatelli, Willie
Harcourt-Cooze, and Sophie Conran for their permission
to use the chef photographs on pages 36, 37, 68, 69, 112, 113,
138, 168, 169 and 200; Real Food Festival for their permission
to use Jason Ingram's photograph on page 106; and Getty for
their permission to use Jean-Paul Nacivet's photograph on
page 169.

Contents

Introduction

Philip Lowery *Founder of The Real Food Festival*

A few years ago in Italy, I had one of the best meals of my life. It wasn't in a fancy restaurant and the food, while really excellent, wouldn't have won any Michelin stars. It was a balmy evening in Piedmont, and I had been invited to join the family of someone with whom we had been working on our first Festival. Sitting on the terrace with a family of three generations was special in itself. But sharing their meal and their conversation over three or four hours created an atmosphere that would have been impossible without food.

Each course was simple rustic food from the local area. A raw sausage – cruda di Bra Piedmont – made from veal, spices and bacon was delicious; a fricando stew cooked in Barolo wine was full of rich, deep flavours from hours of cooking; and the dessert of panna cotta was unlike anything I had experienced anywhere else. Local food prepared with love by the grandmother of the house, made to a recipe that was utterly of the place and enjoyed by the whole family – a combination that I couldn't help but feel should be accessible to more people.

> **"** *Sharing their meal and their conversation created an atmosphere that would have been impossible without food.* **"**

Over the last decade or so, the idea of 'real food' has started to develop a resonance with more and more people who want to gain a greater understanding of where and how their food is produced. But we still have a long way to go. The industrialization of our food culture over the last 60 or 70 years has radically changed our relationship with food. Not so long ago every household had someone who cooked (usually a woman) and food production was invariably pretty local. Since then, however, we have become entirely comfortable with eating almost anything, anytime, as long as it involves little or no effort to actually cook it.

Bad for our bodies and for our planet, the industrialization of our food system has led inexorably to the degradation of our diets and the exploitation of our environment. Industrial production systems are responsible for massive environmental damage and they are also to blame for some of the worst conditions imaginable for large numbers of the workers employed by these global companies. And because we have become so disconnected with the way our food is produced, we never get to see the appalling conditions to which billions of animals reared for our table are subjected.

We should have a proper connection with our food. More than simple fuel, it brings us together as families and friends. It is a way of expressing our culture and identity, and of course it can be a huge pleasure – one that we can take part in each and every day.

It's hard to concisely and clearly define what 'real food' actually means. For me, the simplest definition is food and drink that taste great and

that are sustainably and ethically produced. In the case of processed food, I agree with Michael Pollan who argues that real food should generally contain less than five ingredients, and ideally those that you can pronounce and are identifiable outside a science lab. But inevitably this definition starts to raise a whole host of further questions...who decides how great it tastes? What do you mean by sustainable? And how ethical does it need to be to qualify?

The answers to these questions should be answered by each one of us, but this can't happen unless we reconnect and engage much more with our food. Cooking is the most practical and effective way of doing this. The simple act of shopping and cooking gives us a better understanding of ingredients, quality, seasonality and availability. When we cook we have more control over what we eat, which can encourage us to choose healthier food and to pay more attention to the quality of its ingredients.

A key factor in being able to assess how 'real' your food is, is to wherever possible buy direct from the people who actually produce your food. It's probably the only way to really trust your source. If this is not always feasible, then the next best thing is to aim for independent retailers who are more likely to have a personal relationship with their suppliers. By supporting these local businesses, more of your money will go back into your community: local suppliers supported by local people.

Back in 2007 we launched the Real Food Festival in London because we sensed that things were changing. It was obvious that people were becoming more interested in the provenance of their food: how it was produced and by whom. Inspiration came from a visit to Slow Food's

Salone del Gusto in Turin (in the region of Piedmont, of course, which brought me to that amazing dinner). There in Turin, more than 1,000 mostly small artisan producers gather to show some of the most amazing ingredients you could hope to find to more than 150,000 enthusiastic visitors.

> **" The simplest definition of 'real food' is food and drink that taste great and that are sustainably and ethically produced. "**

There are thousands of artisan producers in the UK creating wonderful food and drink, all of whom not only have a passion for what they do, but also expertise and huge enthusiasm. However, life is tough for this sector of the food industry. The Real Food Festival was created to help these producers find a channel to sell their food and drink and to continue a process of reconnecting us with the sources of our food. With real livestock on show, it is a tangible connection that can be seen (and smelt), and we bring together more than 400 mostly small producers to celebrate the very best food and drink we can find.

A key part of the Real Food Festival is the Chef Theatre where we have been exceptionally lucky to have been able to present some of today's most inspiring chefs. All of the chefs who have taken part represent cooking at its most real. They are

passionate about their ingredients and work with local and seasonal produce where possible, and all of them champion the idea of supporting artisanal food production. The Chef Theatre is so important because it is a place to find real inspiration – having an abundance of wonderful ingredients is one thing, knowing what to do with them is another.

The Real Food Cookbook is really an extension of this. It is a distillation of that inspiration from all the chefs who have taken part over the last few years, and importantly also includes recipes from some of the true heroes of real food, our small producers. There is a wonderful diversity of recipes in this book, from meals that take minutes and a few pence to create, to dishes that could grace any dinner party table, but the idea behind all of them is that they can, and should, be cooked at home using the best

quality ingredients you can find. Hopefully, these recipes will not only help you create your own version of that dinner I had in Piedmont, but also remind you of the simple pleasure and enjoyment of real food.

I sincerely hope that you find this book as useful and as inspirational as I have and that it encourages you to develop your passion for real food. It is really encouraging to realise that we are not alone in this as more and more people begin to get caught up in the pleasure and understanding of what real food can bring to their lives. We are changing our lives for the better because of it.

STARTERS & SALADS

Courgette and Mint Soup

Spicy Tomato Soup

Chickpea and Rosemary Soup

Aubergine Pâté

Chicken Liver Parfait

Duck Confit and Morbier Croque

Grilled Oysters

21st Century Prawn Cocktail

Mini Rarebits

Trotter Toast

Garden Salad of Raw Vegetables and Herbs

Hot-Smoked Salmon Salad with Garlic Shoots and a Chilli
    Lemon Dressing

Grilled Courgettes, Tomato and Bean Salad with a Basil Dressing

Speck and Fresh Goat's Cheese Salad with Balsamic Vinegar

Puy Lentil, Spelt Grain, Bean and Vegetable Salad

Asian Coleslaw with Peanuts and Chilli

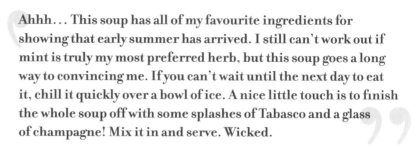

"Ahhh... This soup has all of my favourite ingredients for showing that early summer has arrived. I still can't work out if mint is truly my most preferred herb, but this soup goes a long way to convincing me. If you can't wait until the next day to eat it, chill it quickly over a bowl of ice. A nice little touch is to finish the whole soup off with some splashes of Tabasco and a glass of champagne! Mix it in and serve. Wicked."

Arthur Potts Dawson & The People's Supermarket

Courgette and Mint Soup

SERVES 6

1 tbsp sunflower oil
250g/9oz onions, peeled and chopped
450g/1lb potatoes, peeled and chopped
1 litre/35fl oz/4 cups vegetable stock
650g/1lb 7oz courgettes, chopped
2 round lettuces, shredded
250ml/9 fl oz/1 cup double cream
small bunch of mint, chopped
sea salt and freshly ground black pepper

1 Heat the oil in a large saucepan and sweat the onions and potatoes over a gentle heat for 5 minutes.

2 Season well with salt and pepper, and add the stock. Simmer for about 10 minutes, or until the potatoes are tender.

3 Add the courgettes and lettuce and simmer gently for another 10 minutes. Add the cream, and heat but do not boil the soup. Take off the heat and add the mint.

4 Using a blender, liquidize until smooth. Pour into a bowl, cover and chill in the fridge overnight. Serve cold.

We started making Jamaican hot chilli pepper jelly in our kitchens nearly 10 years ago, using a friend's recipe. Now we chop more than half a ton of Scotch bonnet chillies every year to keep up with demand and, yes, they are very, very hot. The chilli jelly really lifts the flavour of this amazing soup, and the crème fraîche adds just the right note of sourness.

Jules & Sharpie La La Ltd

Spicy Tomato Soup

SERVES 4

50g/1¾oz butter
2 medium onions, peeled
    and finely chopped
1 garlic clove, finely chopped
1 celery stick, finely chopped
700g/1lb 9oz tomatoes (the
    riper the better) peeled
    and roughly chopped
2 medium cooked beetroots,
    roughly chopped
750ml/26fl oz/3 cups chicken
    or vegetable stock
2 tbsp chilli jelly
2 tbsp crème fraîche
small basil leaves, to garnish
sea salt and freshly ground
    black pepper

1 Gently melt the butter in a saucepan over a medium heat then cook the onions, garlic and celery until they're soft.

2 Add the tomatoes and beetroot, and season with salt and pepper. Cook for about 5 minutes.

3 Add the stock and cook for about another 15 minutes.

4 Add the chilli jelly, then pour into a blender. Process until smooth, then sieve into another saucepan.

5 Reheat on a low heat and stir the crème fraîche through just before serving. Garnish with a small basil leaf.

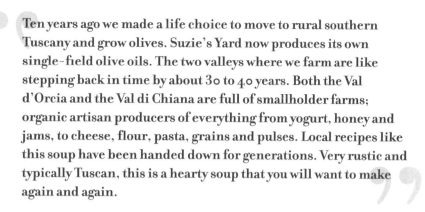

"Ten years ago we made a life choice to move to rural southern Tuscany and grow olives. Suzie's Yard now produces its own single-field olive oils. The two valleys where we farm are like stepping back in time by about 30 to 40 years. Both the Val d'Orcia and the Val di Chiana are full of smallholder farms; organic artisan producers of everything from yogurt, honey and jams, to cheese, flour, pasta, grains and pulses. Local recipes like this soup have been handed down for generations. Very rustic and typically Tuscan, this is a hearty soup that you will want to make again and again."

Suzie's Yard

Chickpea and Rosemary Soup

SERVES 4

250g/9oz/heaped 1 cup dried chickpeas
3 tbsp extra virgin olive oil, plus extra to serve
1 rasher unsmoked pancetta, cut into 5 pieces
2 garlic cloves
2 rosemary sprigs
sea salt and freshly ground black pepper

1 Soak the chickpeas in a bowl of water overnight. Drain off the liquid and then bring them to the boil in a pan of fresh water. Cook until you can easily pierce the chickpeas with a fork. This takes about 1½ hours, or 1 hour in a pressure cooker.

2 Heat the olive oil in a saucepan over a low heat. Then add the pancetta, garlic cloves and rosemary sprigs and sauté for a few minutes. This will flavour the oil.

3 Drain the chickpeas, reserving the liquid for later use. Add the chickpeas to the pan and coat them in the oil for 5 minutes to flavour them, then add enough of the reserved liquid to more than cover them. Season with salt and simmer over a low heat for 30 minutes. Add more of the liquid as you go along if needed. Taste for salt, adding more if necessary.

4 Remove the rosemary and pancetta and liquidize the remaining ingredients using a blender, leaving a few of the chickpeas whole. Serve hot, seasoned with ground pepper and a drizzle of a good extra virgin olive oil.

"This aubergine pâté is a wonderful summer treat to be tasted with a glass of chilled white wine under the swaying olive branches. As with most Italian recipes, the quality of the ingredients is paramount. The cooking is very simple and rests on the meticulous choice of the prime ingredients: choose homegrown summer ripened aubergines (not the tasteless, glasshouse, grown all-year-round kind) and a fresh, grassy olive oil with some spiciness in the back of your throat, juicy organic lemons and fresh, absolutely fresh parsley."

Oliodivino

Aubergine Pâté

SERVES 4

2 large aubergines
4 tbsp good quality olive oil
juice of 1 lemon
1 small garlic clove
a pinch dried chilli flakes
1 tsp chopped parsley
sea salt
crusty bread or crackers,
   to serve

1 Preheat the oven to 200°C/400°F/Gas 6. Put the whole aubergines on a baking sheet in the hot oven and let them cook until they are soft and slightly burnt. Turn them over once or twice during the cooking to make sure that they cook evenly on both sides.

2 When they are done, let them cool a little before peeling them – the skin will slip right off. Place the pulp in a colander and gently squeeze out the excess liquid.

3 Place the pulp in a food processor or blender with the olive oil, lemon and garlic. Add salt, chilli and parsley and adjust to your taste. Purée everything to a smooth mayonnaise-like paste. Spoon into a bowl, cover and chill in the fridge until needed.

4 Serve spread on fresh crusty bread or crackers.

Growing up in our family home, fittingly called 'Faraway' as it was lost in the Welsh mountains, with such amazingly creative and fun cooks as my mother, Margaret, who founded Patchwork Pâté with Jenny, was always an adventure. They preferred to recreate their own favourite delicacies rather than be served anyone else's. When they periodically announced they would be making Chicken Liver Parfait, I could never hide my excitement.

Patchwork Pâté
Chicken Liver Parfait

SERVES 4

300g/10½oz unsalted butter
2 tbsp port
2 tbsp brandy
2 tbsp madiera
2 shallots, finely chopped
1 bay leaf
2 thyme sprigs
250g/9oz fresh chicken livers
2 eggs
3 tbsp double cream
pinch of grated nutmeg
sea salt and freshly ground
   black pepper

1 Melt a knob of the butter in a large frying pan until it goes frothy. Add the port, brandy, madiera, shallots and herbs and then season with salt and lots of pepper.

2 Sauté over a low heat until the alcohol is almost dry and the shallots are soft. Put to one side to allow to cool.

3 In another pan, melt the rest of the butter, then allow to cool but remain liquid.

4 Preheat the oven to 140°C/275°F/Gas 1. Whiz the chicken livers in a blender until smooth. Add the shallot mix from the first pan and the melted butter, then add the eggs, cream and nutmeg and blend again.

5 Pass the whole mixture through a fine sieve, the finer the better.

6 Pour the mixture into an ovenproof terrine and put it in an oven tray filled with hot water that will cover the terrine dish to about half way up the sides. Place in the preheated oven and cook for 45 minutes, or until a knife comes out clean when inserted into the middle.

7 Allow to cool in the fridge overnight before serving. If you want to preserve the parfait longer in the fridge, cover the top with melted, slightly salted butter.

> This will make a double round of sandwiches for each person. I usually make a large quantity, and when I take them from the oven I cut them into fingers and serve them as a warm canapé on winter evenings. If you take care to remove the duck skin from the duck confit in one piece you can put it between two sheets of greaseproof paper and bake in the oven at 180°C/350°F/Gas 4 between two baking sheets for about 20 minutes to make some rather moreish duck crackling.

Henry Harris & Racine

Duck Confit and Morbier Croque

SERVES 4

2 legs duck confit
2 cloves of garlic, peeled
16 slices Pain Poilâne or
   sourdough bread
8 slices of Morbier or Gruyère
   cheese, cut to the thickness
   of 2 matches
2 tsp Dijon mustard
soft unsalted butter
sea salt and freshly ground
   black pepper

1　Preheat the oven to 180°C/350°F/Gas 4. Remove the duck meat from the legs, coarsely shred with a fork and place in a large mixing bowl.

2　Using the back of a knife, purée the garlic with a pinch of salt and mix well into the duck meat. Season generously with black pepper.

3　Pair the bread slices. Spread the duck mixture onto one side and then top with the Morbier. Spread the second slice with a healthy smear of Dijon mustard. Place the second slice on top and press together firmly.

4　Preheat the oven to 140°C/275°F/Gas 1. Lightly butter the outside of the sandwiches.

5　Place the sandwiches in batches in the pan and fry to toast and colour both sides.

6　Transfer to a baking sheet and bake in the preheated oven for about 5 minutes, or until piping hot. Remove from the oven, slice into pieces and serve immediately.

> The oysters are gratinated with a crisp mix of fresh herbs, savoury biscuit crumbs and Jersey Blue cheese. The creamy and slight tangy taste accentuates the salty ozone flavour of the Jersey oysters. This recipe also uses a continental-style blonde ale as the base for a refreshing dressing.

Liberation Brewery
Grilled Oysters

SERVES 4

12 fresh oysters
100g/3½oz classic herd organic Jersey Blue cheese (or similar blue veined brie)
1 tsp finely chopped chives
1 tsp finely chopped chervil
40g/1½oz water biscuits or plain crackers, crushed
2 tbsp chopped parsley

FOR THE DRESSING
2 shallots, finely chopped
2 tbsp white wine vinegar
2 generous pinches of cayenne pepper
60ml/2 fl oz/¼ cup blonde ale

1 If you have a friendly fishmonger you can ask him to open your oysters for you before taking them home to cook and serve. If not you first need to carefully open your oysters with a strong small knife and then loosen them from their shells. Set each opened oyster down on a small mound of rock salt, on a baking tray.

2 Remove the rind from the cheese, then finely dice the cheese. Pile the cheese equally on each oyster. Mix the herbs with the biscuit crumbs and sprinkle onto the cheese-topped oysters.

3 To make the dressing, simmer the shallots in a small pan with the white wine vinegar, cayenne and 2–3 tablespoons water until the shallots start to soften but retain a little bite. Cook until almost all of the liquid has evaporated, then allow to cool and chill briefly in the fridge. When cold, add in the blonde ale.

4 Preheat the grill to medium. Grill the oysters for 3–4 minutes until the cheese starts to bubble and the crumb mix browns.

5 Serve topped with a little dressing and the chopped parsley, and with the remaining dressing on the side.

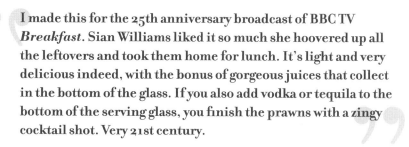

I made this for the 25th anniversary broadcast of BBC TV *Breakfast*. Sian Williams liked it so much she hoovered up all the leftovers and took them home for lunch. It's light and very delicious indeed, with the bonus of gorgeous juices that collect in the bottom of the glass. If you also add vodka or tequila to the bottom of the serving glass, you finish the prawns with a zingy cocktail shot. Very 21st century.

Glynn Christian

21st Century Prawn Cocktail

SERVES 4

225–250g/8–9oz large
  cooked, peeled prawns
3 tsp sweet chilli sauce
juice of 1 lime
12 small plum tomatoes or
  12 large cherry tomatoes
2 garlic cloves, very thinly
  sliced
1 thyme sprig
1 rosemary sprig
2–3 bay leaves
4–6 tbsp extra virgin olive oil
1 large buffalo mozzarella,
  drained
4 shots vodka or tequila,
  optional
up to ½ iceberg lettuce,
  sliced thinly
handful of pea shoots or
  small rocket leaves
sea salt and freshly ground
  black pepper

1 Preheat the oven to 140°C/275°F/Gas 1. Mix the prawns with the chilli sauce and lime juice. Cover and keep chilled.

2 Slice the tomatoes about halfway through and put slivers of garlic into the slit. Arrange the tomatoes in a single layer in a baking pan, then sprinkle with the herbs and the olive oil. Season lightly with salt and pepper.

3 Roast in the preheated oven for about 1½ hours, basting with the oil a couple of times, until the tomatoes are concentrated and wrinkly but not collapsed (but it doesn't matter if you forget, and they are).

4 Slice the mozzarella ball into eight slices and then cut those into fingers the long way.

5 If you are including vodka or tequila, put a shot or less into the base of tall glasses, which are all the better if they've been chilled in the refrigerator. Add the lettuce, which MUST be iceberg. Mix the tomatoes and their oil gently into the prawn mixture, and then add the mozzarella fingers, trying not to break them up.

6 Lightly add some pea sprouts or rocket leaves, or use them only to strew on top as the fancy takes you. Pile the prawn cocktail into the glasses.

7 You get a sweeter taste from the marinated prawns, and thus much greater contrast with the chilli and lime sauce, if you take the mixture from the refrigerator 20 minutes or so before serving. But only mix everything together just before serving.

When I was a boy at school there was a rule that the pupils were only allowed to bring back one jar of homemade jam or marmalade at the beginning of term, but there was no such rule governing mustard. My father had made the first wholegrain mustard available in the UK in 1970, so I grew up around the pungent smell of this firey condiment and loved nothing more than to smother a piece of toast with a thick spread of his deliciously tasty wholegrain mustard. Consequently I used to arrive at school with my trunk bursting with jars and jars of mustard. To this day I can't think of a starter or canapé that I'd rather have while I'm enjoying a pint with my Pa.

Tracklements
Mini Rarebits

SERVES 4

4 slices white bread
15g/½ oz butter
2 tbsp plain flour
125ml/4fl oz/½ cup milk
1 egg yolk
80g/2¾oz Cheddar cheese, grated
1 tbsp wholegrain mustard
lettuce leaves, to serve

1   Using a pastry cutter, cut two rounds out of each piece of white bread. Lightly toast the 8 resultant discs.

2   Over a medium heat, melt the butter in a saucepan, then add the flour. Stir until all the butter is soaked up. Slowly add the milk, whisking constantly.

3   Bring to the boil and then whisk in the egg yolk. Add the cheese and the mustard. Stir until the cheese has just melted.

4   When the mixture has thickened up, divide equally on top of the 8 circles of toast and serve piping hot with crisp green lettuce leaves.

> "Many people will find the whole idea of eating pig's trotters too hard to take, but in my opinion, one should eat all of the animal if one is to be a carnivore, wasting nothing at all if possible, so that the animal has not died in vain. This is one of the principles of being a real cook – one who is in tune with the provenance of ingredients as much as with the seasons. Apart from the ethical issues, this is a truly delicious, extremely cheap and very simple recipe that honestly deserves a place in this collection."

Oliver Rowe

Trotter Toast

SERVES 4

2 pig trotters, washed and any hair scraped or burnt off
250ml/9fl oz/1 cup crisp dry white wine
4 bay leaves
2 onions, chopped
2 celery sticks, chopped
2 carrots, chopped
2 garlic cloves, finely chopped
4 thyme sprigs
10 black peppercorns
½ teaspoon fennel seeds
8 juniper berries
4 slices good sourdough bread
2 tbsp unsalted butter
1 shallot, finely chopped
2 tbsp finely chopped parsley
sea salt and freshly ground black pepper

FOR THE MAYONNAISE
1 egg yolk
½ tsp wholegrain mustard
1 tbsp cider vinegar
350ml/12fl oz/1½ cups grapeseed or sunflower oil
2 tbsp cornichons, finely diced
1 tbsp capers, finely diced
2 pickled walnuts, finely diced

1 Preheat the oven to 170°C/325°F/Gas 3. Place the trotters in a large baking dish and add the wine, bay leaves, vegetables, garlic, 2 sprigs of thyme, peppercorns, fennel seeds, juniper berries and enough water to almost cover the trotters.

2 Wet and crumple a large piece of baking parchment. Unfold it and drape it over the dish with the edges hanging out. Cover with foil and tightly seal the dish. Place in the middle of the oven for 4–5 hours until the skin on the trotters is spoon-soft. Remove from the oven and take off the foil and paper. Strain off and reserve the liquid. Discard the vegetables and herbs. Put the liquid in a jug in the fridge.

3 When just cool enough to handle, pull apart the trotters and carefully pick out and discard the bones. Keep the fat, skin and any meat. Roughly chop these, place in a clean bowl and season with salt and pepper.

4 Take the jug out of the fridge and skim off the fat. Pour the liquid into a pan and bring to the boil over a medium heat. Reduce the liquid until slightly tacky to the touch. Use a little of this liquor to moisten the trotter pickings. Tip them into a cling film-lined terrine and spread out. Pour 3–4 tablespoons of the liquor over the top and put in the fridge to set.

5 Make the mayonnaise: put the egg yolk, mustard and vinegar in a food processor and drizzle in the oil in a very thin stream. Stir the cornichons, capers and walnuts into the mayonnaise. Add 1 teaspoon tepid water and spoon into a small bowl.

6 Preheat a grill to very hot. Toast the bread and spread it with butter and mayonnaise. Arrange a thin layer of the trotter mix on the toast. Grill until the trotter mix is soft, bubbly and starting to brown. Trim off any burnt bits. Chop the remaining thyme and mix together with the shallot and parsley. Cut the toast into small pieces, sprinkle with the herb mix and away you go.

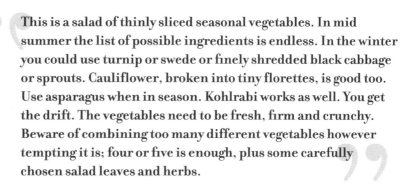

This is a salad of thinly sliced seasonal vegetables. In mid summer the list of possible ingredients is endless. In the winter you could use turnip or swede or finely shredded black cabbage or sprouts. Cauliflower, broken into tiny florettes, is good too. Use asparagus when in season. Kohlrabi works as well. You get the drift. The vegetables need to be fresh, firm and crunchy. Beware of combining too many different vegetables however tempting it is; four or five is enough, plus some carefully chosen salad leaves and herbs.

Barny Haughton

Garden Salad of Raw Vegetables and Herbs

SERVES 4

handful of freshly podded
   broad beans and/or peas
2 courgettes
2 carrots, peeled
1 fennel bulb, trimmed
4 baby beetroot, scrubbed
big handful of peppery salad
   leaves, such as rocket,
   watercress, pea shoots
   or mustard leaves
small bunch of mixed fresh
   herbs, such as mint, basil,
   tarragon and parsley
150g/5½oz feta or goat's
   cheese, crumbled (optional)
baked potatoes or crusty
   bread, to serve

FOR THE DRESSING
juice of 1 lemon
1 tbsp white wine vinegar
½ tsp salt
5 tbsp olive oil

1 Drop the freshly podded broad beans into a bowl and cover with boiling water. Leave to stand for 1 minute, then drain and pop them out of their skins, revealing the bright green bean within.

2 Mix the dressing ingredients together in a big salad bowl. Pour a little of this dressing into a smaller bowl for the beetroot.

3 Using a very sharp knife or mandolin, slice the courgettes, carrots and fennel into thin ribbon lengths. If you are including peas rather than broad beans, you can either leave them raw or blanch them in boiling water with a pinch of sugar for 3–4 minutes to soften and sweeten them.

4 Transfer the vegetables to the big bowl. Slice the beetroot as thin as the petals of a rose and transfer to the small bowl. Toss the vegetables in the dressing in the larger bowl, then add the leaves and herbs and toss gently together.

5 Tuck the slices of beetroot prettily into the salad – do this at the last minute so that the beetroot doesn't stain the other vegetables.

6 Crumbled feta or goat's cheese on top is lovely, but the dish is complete without. Serve with baked potatoes or some good crusty bread.

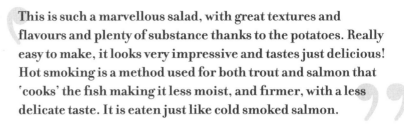

"This is such a marvellous salad, with great textures and flavours and plenty of substance thanks to the potatoes. Really easy to make, it looks very impressive and tastes just delicious! Hot smoking is a method used for both trout and salmon that 'cooks' the fish making it less moist, and firmer, with a less delicate taste. It is eaten just like cold smoked salmon."

The Really Garlicky Co.

Hot-Smoked Salmon Salad with Garlic Shoots and a Chilli Lemon Dressing

SERVES 8

250g/9oz new potatoes, scrubbed and halved
100g/3½oz garlic shoots
125g/4½oz mixed salad leaves, including watercress or rocket
small bunch of parsley, leaves picked and roughly chopped
small bunch of mint, leaves picked and roughly chopped
70g/2½oz radishes, thinly sliced
4 hot-smoked salmon steaks, skin removed

FOR THE DRESSING
3 tbsp lemon juice
125ml/4 fl oz/½ cup olive oil
1 tsp wholegrain mustard
2 red chillies, deseeded and finely chopped
sea salt and freshly ground black pepper

1 Whisk together all the dressing ingredients in a bowl, season with salt and pepper to taste.

2 Boil the potatoes in salted water for 10 minutes until tender, adding the garlic shoots for the final 2 minutes of cooking. Drain and place in a large mixing bowl, pour on half the dressing and gently mix to coat the potatoes. Leave to cool.

3 When cool, add the salad leaves, herbs and radishes. Mix carefully and turn out onto a large serving platter.

4 Break the hot-smoked salmon into large chunks and scatter over the salad. Finish by pouring the remaining dressing over the top.

At the Riverford Field Kitchen — the farm restaurant based at the box scheme — seasonality is key as our job is to showcase the produce that is grown in the fields around the kitchen. I feel very strongly that good food should be accessible and affordable, as well as being tasty.

Jane Baxter

I started cooking while I was studying at Leeds University for a degree in Agronomy in the early 80s. I quickly decided this would become my chosen career path, so I wrote to some top restaurants and managed to secure a place for the last two months of my degree at George Perry Smith's Helford restaurant, Riverside. This led to working under Joyce Molyneux at the Carved

Angel in Dartmouth. Joyce's unpretentious, tasty, generous food has influenced my own cooking style ever since. Along with the first pioneers of her time, Joyce used local and seasonal ingredients effortlessly; something that I always try to emulate in my own recipes.

I then went on to work with Rose and Ruthie at the River Café in London, where I couldn't help but be irrevocably influenced by their love of Italian food, and also the art of cooking vegetables simply.

Later, while travelling around the South Pacific, I needed in various jobs to use the local ingredients, which were often limited, in an inventive way. For instance, substituting the slippery cabbage of the Solomon Islands for spinach to make an Italian rotolo!

Now I am the chef at the Riverford Field Kitchen, where the food is cooked freshly each day. There is no choice in what is served here, it's simply the best of the day's produce, cooked and served in an informal dining environment.

I'm always actively looking for small local meat producers to support and showcase and I am a passionate supporter of rose veal. Having said that, the meat is a very small part of the dining experience at Riverford, as the focus is on the vegetables, which I try to prepare in an

imaginative way. I'm a firm believer that the Asian style of eating, where meat makes up a small part of the meal, is the way forward, by which I mean eating meat in moderation, for ethical and health reasons. But you kind of need to forget about the health aspect when it comes to the pudding trolley!

I find it quite challenging to cook seasonally on a day-to-day basis, certain vegetables such as cauliflower, leeks and cabbage seem to appear for most of the year, but when they do disappear, they are often mourned! But there is always an excitement when the first artichoke, broad beans and soft fruit appear.

&& *Good food brings people together; it's much better than sitting in front of the TV with a tray on your knee.* &&

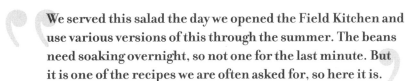

Jane Baxter & Riverford Organic

Grilled Courgettes, Tomato and Bean Salad with a Basil Dressing

SERVES 4

400g/14oz/2 cups dried cannellini or haricot beans
about 6 tbsp extra virgin olive oil
2 courgettes
250g/9oz cherry tomatoes
sea salt and freshly ground black pepper

FOR THE DRESSING
1 bunch of basil leaves
½ garlic clove
100ml/3½fl oz/scant ½ cup extra virgin olive oil

1 Soak the beans overnight. Drain and rinse the beans, then cover them with fresh water and simmer in a large pan of boiling water for 45–50 minutes until tender. Drain, season with salt and pepper and dress with 2 tablespoons of the extra virgin olive oil. Preheat the oven to 180°C/350°F/Gas 4.

2 Slice the courgettes into thick ribbons. Coat them with olive oil and cook on either a hot griddle pan or under a hot grill until softened and lightly browned.

3 Drizzle the cherry tomatoes with the remaining olive oil and roast them in the preheated oven for 10 minutes.

4 To make the dressing, blend all the ingredients in a food processor and season with salt to taste.

5 Gently mix the cooked beans, courgettes and tomatoes together in a large bowl. Add the basil dressing to taste and season with salt and pepper, if necessary.

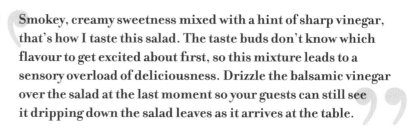

Smokey, creamy sweetness mixed with a hint of sharp vinegar, that's how I taste this salad. The taste buds don't know which flavour to get excited about first, so this mixture leads to a sensory overload of deliciousness. Drizzle the balsamic vinegar over the salad at the last moment so your guests can still see it dripping down the salad leaves as it arrives at the table.

Arthur Potts Dawson & The People's Supermarket

Speck and Fresh Goat's Cheese Salad with Balsamic Vinegar

SERVES 6

1 head of lollo rosso lettuce
1 head of oak leaf lettuce
1 head of frisée lettuce
16 slices of speck
250g/9oz soft goat's cheese
6 radishes, thinly sliced
4 large beetroots cooked,
  peeled and sliced thinly
2 marigold flowers, freshly
  picked
125ml/4fl oz/½ cup extra
  virgin olive oil
2 tbsp aged balsamic vinegar
6 nasturtium flowers, freshly
  picked
sea salt and freshly ground
  black pepper

1 Fill a sink up with lots of cold water and pick the lettuce into it, making sure you get rid of any soft, brown or damaged leaves. Gently wash the leaves together, then spin dry them in a salad spinner. Don't throw the lettuce washing water away – water the garden with it!

2 Arrange 2 slices of speck and a little of the salad leaves on each of six plates, then place a teaspoon of the cheese, some radish, salt and pepper and one slice of the beetroot.

3 Slice the remaining speck into thin strips and mix with the remaining salad leaves. Layer the ingredients onto the plates as before, finishing with salad leaves. Drizzle with the olive oil and balsamic vinegar.

4 Pick the petals from the flowers and let them rest where they fall on the plate. If there is any remaining cheese or radish, scatter delicately around each plate and serve.

"This is a really great salad with all sorts of different flavours and textures going on, which make every mouthful special. It is a wonderfully substantial salad for a summer lunch. One of the most interesting and 'in vogue' ingredients used here is also one of the most humble and ancient of all foodstuffs: spelt grain. This variety of wheat tends to be less of a problem for those suffering from a wheat intolerance, as the structure of the gluten contained within is different to that of modern day wheat grains, and it also has a wonderfully chewy texture and a deep nutty flavour that makes it perfect as a base for salads, soups and as a spelt version of risotto."

Barny Haughton

Puy Lentil, Spelt Grain, Bean and Vegetable Salad

SERVES 6

100g/3½oz/½ cup dried
   puy lentils
6 bay leaves
100g/3½oz/½ cup spelt grain
100g/3½oz/½ cup dried
   borlotti beans, soaked in
   cold water for 24 hours
4 tbsp olive oil
2 tbsp raisins
1 aubergine, cut into 2cm/
   ¾in dice
2 red peppers, deseeded and
   cut into 2cm/¾in pieces
2 courgettes, cut into 2cm/
   ¾in dice
2 garlic cloves, finely sliced
big bunch parsley, coarsely
   chopped
sea salt and freshly ground
   black pepper

FOR THE DRESSING
1 tbsp vinegar
1 tbsp soy sauce
3 tbsp olive oil

1 Wash and simmer the lentils with a couple of bay leaves in a saucepan filled with as little water as you can get away with but always enough to cover. After about 40 minutes when cooked (don't undercook; they should be firm but absolutely not crunchy), leave to cool, then drain, reserving the liquor for soup and discarding the bay leaves.

2 Cook the spelt and beans, separately, in the same way. Mix the lentils, spelt and beans together with half the olive oil and season with salt.

3 Meanwhile, soak the raisins in water for about 15 minutes until plump but still firm, then drain and set aside.

4 Season the aubergine, peppers and courgettes with salt and pepper. Heat the remaining olive oil in a frying pan over a medium-high heat and fry the aubergine, peppers and courgettes until they are a good colour, but are still a little crunchy. Remove the vegetables from the pan and then add the garlic and fry until nutty brown.

5 Mix the dressing ingredients together in a salad bowl, then toss all the other elements into the dressing and serve.

One of my favourite dishes ever is *som tam* or green papaya salad, which is from northern Thailand and is a daily staple in that region. I often try to emulate it with the humble cabbage and carrot for staff meals here at the farm. Here is my version of the recipe.

Jane Baxter & Riverford Organic

Asian Coleslaw with Peanuts and Chilli

SERVES 4

FOR THE SALAD
2 tbsp unsalted peanuts
½ white cabbage, finely shredded
3 carrots, coarsely grated
2 apples, grated
1 red pepper, deseeded and thinly sliced
2 handfuls of beansprouts
1 large handful of sliced mushrooms
4 tomatoes, chopped

FOR THE DRESSING
1 garlic clove, crushed
½ onion, finely sliced
1 chilli, chopped
3 tsp fish sauce
1½ tbsp brown sugar
3 tbsp lemon juice
1 tbsp sweet chilli sauce

1 Combine all the dressing ingredients together, either in a pestle and mortar or whisked together in a bowl. Set aside.

2 Toast the peanuts briefly in a hot pan over a medium-high heat until smelling aromatic and looking lightly golden. Place them in a pestel and mortar and pound them enough to just break them up, or blitz for a few seconds in a food processor.

3 Mix all the raw vegetables together in a large bowl and toss them with the dressing. Pile onto a serving plate and sprinkle with the roasted peanuts.

FISH & SEAFOOD

Battered Salmon Tails with Split Walnut, Honey and
    Balsamic Dressing

Salmon with Sweet and Sour Seasonal Vegetables

Red Mullet with Orange and Cardamom Potatoes

Trout Fillets with Dill and Bacon

Roast Cod with Brown Shrimps, Crispy Asparagus and Sea Purslane

Pan-Fried Sea Bass with Artichokes and Broad Beans

Celery and Lemon Marinated Sea Bass Fillets

Confit of Pollack with Clam Chowder

Hay-Smoked Mackerel, Pickled Lemon and Pea Shoots

Black Cod Marinated in Coffee with Broccoli Purée

Mussels in Thai Broth

Crab Spaghetti with Orange Olive Oil

Kerala Crab Masala

Ragoût of Scallops, Asparagus and Wilted Greens

King Scallops on Beetroot Salsa

Scallops with Chorizo, Chestnut Purée and Rocket

Oysters and Spiced Sausages

Slow-Stewed Octopus with Cep Mushrooms, Onions and
    Green Asparagus

Linguine with Clams and Cider

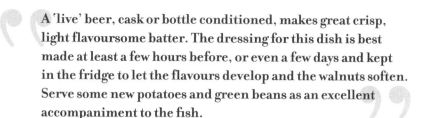

A 'live' beer, cask or bottle conditioned, makes great crisp, light flavoursome batter. The dressing for this dish is best made at least a few hours before, or even a few days and kept in the fridge to let the flavours develop and the walnuts soften. Serve some new potatoes and green beans as an excellent accompaniment to the fish.

Liberation Brewery

Battered Salmon Tails with Split Walnut, Honey and Balsamic Dressing

SERVES 4

4 x 200–225g/7–8oz salmon tails (ask your fishmonger to skin them)
seasoned flour, for dredging
vegetable oil or sunflower seed oil, for deep-frying
4 chervil sprigs, to garnish
sea salt and freshly ground black pepper

FOR THE DRESSING
85g/3oz/¾ cup walnuts
2 tbsp good quality balsamic vinegar
2 tbsp runny honey
55ml/1¾fl oz/scant ¼ cup extra virgin olive oil
1 thyme sprig
1 piece of lemon zest, pith removed
juice of 1 lemon

FOR THE BATTER
125g/4½oz/1 cup self-raising flour
1 egg, at room temperature
300ml/10½fl oz/scant 1¼ cups pale ale, at room temperature

1 To prepare the dressing, place all the ingredients in a heavy-based saucepan and heat on the gentlest setting available. When the mixture begins to simmer remove it from the heat and set aside to infuse. The dressing can be made in advance and then stored for 2 weeks in a tightly sealed container in the fridge. Simply bring up to room temperature before use.

2 Place the salmon tails in the seasoned flour and gently shake off any excess.

3 Next make the batter. Sift the self-raising flour into a large bowl and season well with salt and pepper. Beat in the egg and ale until the mixture is smooth and the texture of thick double cream. Correct the thickness of the mixture with a little extra flour or water, if necessary. The ingredients are best used at room temperature as this gives a very crisp batter.

4 Heat the oil for deep-frying, either in a deep pan or a deep-fat fryer. The oil needs to reach 190°C/375°F – if you're using a pan, this is when a small piece of bread dropped into the oil sizzles instantly. Coat the salmon in batter mix and gently shake off any excess. Deep-fry for approximately 8 minutes, turning once during cooking. The salmon should be light golden brown. Remove and drain on kitchen paper.

5 To serve, place on warm plates and dribble the dressing around the salmon. The dressing should split slightly into pools of oil and dark rich sweet balsamic. Serve garnished with a little chervil.

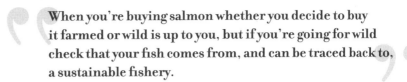

'When you're buying salmon whether you decide to buy it farmed or wild is up to you, but if you're going for wild check that your fish comes from, and can be traced back to, a sustainable fishery.'

Allegra McEvedy

Salmon with Sweet and Sour Seasonal Vegetables

SERVES 2

2 pieces of salmon fillet (about 150g/5½oz each), and from middle to head half, not tail half, if possible
4 tbsp extra virgin olive oil
1 small, firm aubergine, diced
2 garlic cloves, thinly sliced
1 fat thumb fresh ginger, trimmed but not peeled, cut into matchsticks
1 red pepper, cut into bite-size pieces
1 yellow pepper, cut into bite-size pieces
125ml/4fl oz/½ cup white wine vinegar
150ml/5fl oz/scant ⅔ cup vegetable or chicken stock
1 carrot, cut into ribbons with a vegetable peeler
2 tbsp sweet chilli sauce
1–2 tsp lime juice
small handful of dill, roughly chopped, plus extra to finish
lime wedges, to serve
sea salt and freshly ground black pepper

1 Preheat the oven to 180°C/350°F/Gas 4. Give the salmon a quick rinse in cold water and then sit it on some kitchen roll and pat dry.

2 Put a large frying pan over a high heat and add 2 tablespoons of the olive oil. Allow to heat until smoking, then add the aubergine dice and stir. You may want to add a splash more oil, as aubergines are notoriously spongy. The aubergine should be frying rather than sticking and looking unhappy.

3 Add the garlic to the aubergine along with the ginger. Once you can really smell the ginger and garlic, add the pepper pieces and stir again. Bring to good sizzle before adding the white wine vinegar, followed a minute later by the stock. Leave on a high heat to simmer, uncovered until it reaches a saucey consistency.

4 Meanwhile, put a frying pan on a high heat to warm up ready for the salmon. Season the fillets generously with salt and pepper. Pour the remaining 2 tablespoons of extra virgin olive oil into the hot pan. The oil should instantly move around very freely and start to smoke. Gently lay the salmon pieces in the oil, skin side down, and give them a quick press with a palette knife to get the skin flat against the surface of the pan. When you can see that the fish is just beginning to brown along the edge of the skin, move the pan into the preheated oven for 8 minutes.

5 Add the carrot ribbons to the rest of the vegetables, then add the sweet chilli sauce and salt and pepper, to taste, and give it a good stir. Take off the heat once the carrots have softened.

6 Take the salmon out of the oven and transfer to warm plates. Tip all the vegetables into the ex-salmon pan and stir, watching them sizzle while the liquid reduces. Add the lime juice and dill to the vegetables. Adjust the lime if necessary. Serve the vegetables with the salmon and a wedge of lime. Scatter with the last of the dill leaves.

My daughter, Lucy, developed this recipe when working at a wine bar in Portsmouth during the time she was studying for her degree. She says the trick is to make sure you don't make the layer of potatoes too thick or they won't become nice and crispy.

Kitchen Garden

Red Mullet with Orange and Cardamom Potatoes

SERVES 4

8 red mullet fillets
2 tbsp olive oil
salt and freshly ground
  black pepper

FOR THE ORANGE AND
CARDAMOM DRESSING
juice of 1 orange
¼ tsp sea salt
½ teaspoon lightly crushed
  cardamom seeds

FOR THE POTATOES
500g/1lb 2 oz baby new
  potatoes
200ml/7 fl oz/scant 1 cup
  olive oil
8 cloves garlic, sliced
1 large red onion, sliced
2 tbsp capers, rinsed

1 Mix together the dressing ingredients in a bowl and leave them to infuse for 30 minutes.

2 Preheat the oven to 180°C/350°F/Gas 4. Boil the potatoes in a saucepan of salted water for 15–20 minutes until tender.

3 Drain the cooked potatoes, tip them into an ovenproof dish, then toss them in the olive oil. Using your thumb, press the potatoes down to crush them a bit but without breaking them into small pieces. Add the garlic, red onion and capers to the potatoes and mix together.

4 Generously cover the mix with the orange and cardamom dressing then put in the preheated oven for 20 minutes, turning the potatoes occasionally.

5 Place the fish in an ovenproof dish, season lightly with salt and pepper, and drizzle with olive oil. Increase the heat of the oven to 200°C/400°F/Gas 6 and roast in the oven (along with the part-roasted potatoes) for 10–15 minutes, until the flesh flakes easily when tested with the tip of a knife.

6 Serve the crispy potatoes with the roasted mullet fillets.

> We had been curing, cooking and eating bacon at Denhay for about 12 years, before I learnt the trick of uncurling streaky bacon! Lesley had invited me to her wonderful cookery school and we were preparing a version of this recipe; she took a rasher from the pack and started to flatten it out with the wide side of a knife. The bacon almost doubled in length, which let it wrap smoothly round the fillets. This ensures that you can really impart the flavour of the bacon into the trout.

Lesley Waters & Denhay Farms

Trout Fillets with Dill and Bacon

SERVES 4

8 small trout fillets, skinned
1 small bunch dill or tarragon
juice of 1 lemon
12 rashers dry-cured streaky
  bacon, stretched by scraping
  on a board using the back
  of a knife
freshly ground black pepper

TO SERVE
4–5 tbsp half fat crème fraîche
2–3 tbsp beer mustard or mild
  English mustard
1 small country-style loaf or
  ciabatta, sliced into 4
115g/4oz salad leaves
2 lemons, cut into wedges

1 Preheat a barbecue, grill or griddle pan to hot. Take 4 of the trout fillets and cover each of them generously with dill leaves. Squeeze over a little lemon juice and season with black pepper. Top with the remaining 4 fillets and then wrap each one in 3 of the streaky bacon rashers.

2 Lightly oil the barbecue rack, grill or griddle pan and cook the fish for 5 minutes on each side until the bacon is crisp.

3 Combine the crème fraîche and mustard in a bowl. Place the cut bread on the barbecue, grill or griddle to toast. Pile the salad leaves onto the toasted bread, top with the wrapped trout and finish with a drizzle of the mustard sauce and some lemon wedges. Serve at once with large napkins!

"This is a lovely dish. Try to get the cod from a sustainable source, such as Alaska, and you can usually get the cooked brown shrimps from a fishmonger. If peeled, cooked brown shrimps prove elusive, you could use potted shrimps instead, removing as much of the butter as possible, or small cooked prawns. Sea purslane can be found on salt marshes throughout the year and can be picked at any time. I prefer the smaller leaves and use them sparingly when a salty back note is required. Larger leaves can be blanched in boiling water or wilted down in cream or butter. An alternative could be samphire or even large leaf spinach. The key to this dish is having superb cod and ensuring your butter has reached the right 'nut brown' stage."

Ben Tish & Salt Yard

Roast Cod with Brown Shrimps, Crispy Asparagus and Sea Purslane

SERVES 4 as a sharing tapa,
or 2 as a main course

2 x 100g/3½oz cod fillets
3–4 tbsp olive oil, for cooking
100g/3½oz unsalted butter
80g/2¾oz sea purslane (or
    samphire, large leafed
    spinach, or 1 tbsp salted
    capers, rinsed well and
    chopped finely)
80g/2¾oz peeled pre-cooked
    brown shrimps, or potted
    shrimps
2–3 tsp flat-leaf parsley,
    chopped
1–2 tsp lemon juice
500ml/17fl oz/2 cups
    vegetable oil
8 thin asparagus
sea salt and freshly ground
    black pepper

FOR THE BATTER
300ml/10½ fl oz/scant
    1¼ cups sparkling water
small pinch baking powder
80g/2¾oz/scant ⅔ cup plain
    flour, sifted

1   Incorporate all the batter ingredients together and mix well until smooth. Cover and rest until required.

2   Season the cod well with salt and pepper. Heat a non-stick frying pan over a high heat and add enough olive oil to cover the base. Once smoking, add the cod, skin-side down, and cook the fillets for 3–4 minutes until the skin is crisp and golden brown. Turn the fish over and cook for a further 2 minutes.

3   Add the butter and then cook for 2–3 minutes until the butter turns a golden brown. (Too less and the flavour will lack, too much and it will burn.) As soon as the butter is right, add the purslane, shrimps, parsley and the lemon juice to the pan. Cook for a further 1 minute, then remove the cod from the pan and keep it warm. Turn off the heat and season the butter with salt and pepper to taste.

4   Heat the vegetable oil in a high-sided saucepan to about 170°C/325°F. A cube of bread should brown instantly at this temperature. Dip the asparagus in the batter and then fry in the hot oil for 1–2 minutes until crisp and golden. Remove from the oil, drain well on kitchen paper and season.

5   Spoon the butter sauce onto serving plates, top with the cod and the crispy asparagus and serve immediately.

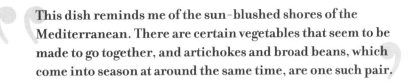

This dish reminds me of the sun-blushed shores of the Mediterranean. There are certain vegetables that seem to be made to go together, and artichokes and broad beans, which come into season at around the same time, are one such pair.

James Walters & The Arabica Food & Spice Company

Pan-Fried Sea Bass with Artichokes and Broad Beans

SERVES 4

2 sea bass fillets
1 tbsp olive oil

FOR THE ARTICHOKE AND
BROAD BEAN SALAD
200g/7oz/1 cup broad beans
4 whole cooked artichoke
hearts
1 preserved lemon
2 spring onions
½ garlic clove
3 tbsp extra virgin olive oil
1 tsp sumac
sea salt and freshly ground
black pepper

1. To pod the broad beans, drop them into a pan of simmering water for 2 minutes, drain and refresh in cold water. Then peel off their thin skins using either your thumbnail or a small sharp knife.

2. Trim the bases of the artichoke hearts slightly. Cut the preserved lemon into quarters, remove the flesh with a sharp paring knife and discard and then finely slice the zest.

3. Finely slice the green parts of the spring onions so you end up with lots of tiny discs. Discard the white parts.

4. Put the garlic in a pestle and mortar, sprinkle with a pinch of sea salt and black pepper and purée, gradually adding the olive oil. Gently mix the preserved lemon zest slices, spring onions, broad beans and sumac with the garlic infusion, then gently toss through the artichoke.

5. Wash and pat dry the sea bass fillets and portion them into 4 even pieces. Sprinkle the skin of the fish with a pinch of sea salt. Heat the olive oil in a heavy-based, non-stick frying pan, and once it's nice and hot add the fish, skin-side down. Cook for 2 minutes until the skin becomes crispy, then turn the fillets over and cook for a further minute.

6. Place one seabass fillet in the centre of each plate and spoon over the dressed broad beans and artichokes.

We first made our living on Anglesey as a fish and game wholesaler, and one of the most popular fish was wild sea bass. I used to alternate cooking it with ginger and garlic and then with celery salt, little dreaming that one day I would have my own business and end up blending my own celery salt. This dish is quick, healthy, and tastes delicious.

Anglesey Sea Salt Company
Celery and Lemon-Marinated Sea Bass Fillets

SERVES 4

6 tbsp extra virgin olive oil
finely grated zest and juice
  of 1 lemon
1 tbsp freshly chopped
  tarragon
4 x 175–200g/6–7oz sea
  bass fillets
½ tsp sea salt
¼ tsp organic celery seeds
15g/½oz unsalted butter
freshly ground black pepper

1 In a large shallow dish combine the olive oil, lemon zest and juice and tarragon. Season with pepper, mixing well.

2 Using a very sharp knife, lightly score the skin of the sea bass, making sure you don't cut right through the skin. This will prevent the skin from curling up when it is pan-fried.

3 Add the sea bass fillets to the marinade, making sure they are coated well. Cover and leave the fish to marinate in the fridge for at least 2 hours but ideally overnight.

4 Mix together the sea salt and celery seeds. Remove the sea bass from the marinade and sprinkle the skin side with half of the sea salt mix.

5 Pour a little of the remaining marinade into a large non-stick frying pan, add the butter and heat until the oil is very hot and the butter foaming.

6 Add the sea bass fillets to the pan, skin-side down in one layer. Fry over a medium heat for 3–4 minutes, without moving the fish, until the skin is very crispy and the fish is cooked two-thirds of the way through. While cooking the fish, sprinkle the uppermost flesh side of the fillets with the remaining salt and celery seed mix. Carefully turn the fish fillets over and cook for a further 1–2 minutes or until cooked through. Serve at once.

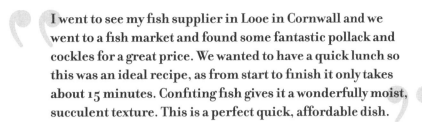

I went to see my fish supplier in Looe in Cornwall and we went to a fish market and found some fantastic pollack and cockles for a great price. We wanted to have a quick lunch so this was an ideal recipe, as from start to finish it only takes about 15 minutes. Confiting fish gives it a wonderfully moist, succulent texture. This is a perfect quick, affordable dish.

Jun Tanaka & Pearl

Confit of Pollack with Clam Chowder

SERVES 4

600g/1lb 5oz clams, well
    soaked
400g/14oz pollock fillet
500ml/17fl oz/2 cups olive oil,
    plus 2 tbsp to drizzle
1 thyme sprig
100g/3½oz smoked bacon,
    diced
1 large potato, peeled and
    diced
1 celery stick, diced
1 garlic clove, sliced
1 leek, finely chopped
½ tbsp plain flour
500ml/17fl oz/2 cups
    chicken stock, hot
2 tbsp crème fraîche
juice of ½ lemon
1 tbsp chopped parsley
toasted ciabatta, to serve
freshly ground black pepper

1 First clean and check the clams. Discard any that do not close at once when tapped sharply on the work surface.

2 To confit the pollock, season the fish with pepper and leave it to stand for 10 minutes. Gently warm the olive oil in a pan with the thyme. Place the fish in the oil and leave for 8–10 minutes, off the heat.

3 Meanwhile, make the chowder. Drizzle 1 tablespoon olive oil in a frying pan, add the bacon and cook together for 1 minute. Add the diced potato, celery, garlic and leek and cook them for a further 4 minutes. Add the flour, cook for 1 minute, and then add the clams and chicken stock.

4 Cover with a lid and boil for 4 minutes until the clams open. Discard any that fail to open. Add the crème fraîche, squeeze in the lemon juice and sprinkle with the parsley.

5 Serve the chowder in bowls with flakes of the pollock and some toasted ciabatta on the side.

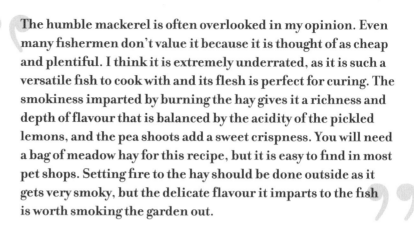

> The humble mackerel is often overlooked in my opinion. Even many fishermen don't value it because it is thought of as cheap and plentiful. I think it is extremely underrated, as it is such a versatile fish to cook with and its flesh is perfect for curing. The smokiness imparted by burning the hay gives it a richness and depth of flavour that is balanced by the acidity of the pickled lemons, and the pea shoots add a sweet crispness. You will need a bag of meadow hay for this recipe, but it is easy to find in most pet shops. Setting fire to the hay should be done outside as it gets very smoky, but the delicate flavour it imparts to the fish is worth smoking the garden out.

Ashley Palmer-Watts & The Fat Duck

Hay-Smoked Mackerel, Pickled Lemon and Pea Shoots

SERVES 2–4 (as a main course or a substantial starter)

4 mackerel fillets, with the skin on
450ml/16fl oz/scant 2 cups olive oil
40g/1½ oz pea shoots
sea salt and freshly ground black pepper

FOR THE PICKLED LEMONS
100ml/3½ fl oz/⅓ cup + 2 tbsp chardonnay vinegar
50g/1¾oz/scant ¼ cup caster sugar
2 Amalfi lemons (or large unwaxed lemons)

FOR THE MACKEREL CURE
2½ tbsp table salt
50g/1¾oz/scant ¼ cup unrefined caster sugar
5 tsp grated lemon zest
4 tsp grated lime zest
2 tsp coriander seeds

1. To make the pickled lemons, gently heat 150ml/5 fl oz/scant ⅔ cup water, the vinegar and the sugar together in a pan. When the sugar has dissolved, remove from the heat and allow to cool.

2. Thinly slice the lemons, discarding the seeds, and place them into the pickling liquid. Transfer to a bowl, cover and place in the fridge for at least 48 hours before serving.

3. To mix the mackerel cure, put the salt, sugar, lemon and lime zest and coriander seeds in a food processor and blend to a fine powder. Sprinkle the resulting mix onto a tray and lay the fillets on top, flesh side down. Put in the fridge for 30 minutes.

4. Rinse the fillets under cold running water to remove the salt mix and drain well on kitchen paper.

5. To smoke the mackerel, line a barbecue fish clamp with meadow hay. Place the fillets in a single layer on the hay and cover with more hay before closing the clamp. Either place onto a lit barbecue or set the hay alight and allow to burn.

6. Remove the fillets from the hay, cleaning off as much of the hay as possible, and set aside.

7. Drain the lemon slices, reseving the liquid, and place them in the centre of each plate. Arrange the mackerel fillets on top and season with black pepper.

8. In a small bowl, combine 150ml/5 fl oz/scant ⅔ cup of the pickling liquid with the olive oil and mix well. Dress the pea shoots with this mixture, season with salt and black pepper and serve alongside the mackerel.

Surprisingly, the coffee in this dish adds a very subtle flavour making the cod richer, which is then enhanced by the slight sweetness from the sugar and honey. The coffee also tenderizes the cod, so it almost melts in your mouth. The broccoli florets add texture, and along with the purée, complements the beautiful flavours from the fish.

Carlo Cracco & Ristorante Cracco

Black Cod Marinated in Coffee with Broccoli Purée

SERVES 4

160g/5¾oz/¾ cup caster sugar
80g/2¾oz instant coffee powder
650g/1lb 7oz black cod fillet (regular cod will also work), cut into 3cm/1¼in cubes
8 tsp Acacia honey
800g/1lb 12oz broccoli tips
160ml/5¼ fl oz/²⁄₃ cup extra virgin olive oil
4 garlic cloves, crushed
2 bay leaves
sea salt

1 Heat 80ml/16½fl oz/2 cups water with the sugar and the instant coffee over a medium heat and stir until dissolved. Let it cool down and pour the liquid into a container large enough to hold the cod cubes. Place the cod in the marinade and leave in the fridge for 5 hours.

2 Drain the fish cubes and place them in a sieve or small colander over a pan of simmering water. Cover tightly with a lid and steam for about 6 minutes, or until the fish is opaque and flakes easily when pierced with a fork.

3 Preheat the grill to its maximum setting. Remove the skin and any remaining bones from each cube, then coat with the honey. Place the cubes on a baking tray and grill them for 4 minutes, turning once. Season to taste with salt.

4 Blanch the broccoli tips in salted water for 4 minutes. Drain, reserving 2 tablespoons of cooking water, and cool down in iced water. Keeping 8 small broccoli tips aside, blitz the rest in a blender along with the reserved cooking water and 2 tablespoons of the oil. Season well with salt.

5 Warm the remaining oil, with some salt, the crushed garlic and bay leaves in a small pan. Add the reserved broccoli tips to the pan and heat through.

6 Serve the cod cubes with a quenelle of the broccoli purée and garnish with the dressed broccoli tips.

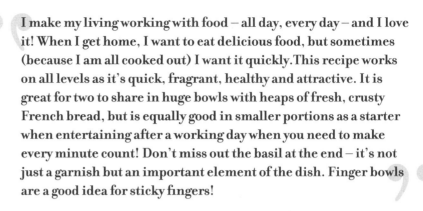

'I make my living working with food – all day, every day – and I love it! When I get home, I want to eat delicious food, but sometimes (because I am all cooked out) I want it quickly. This recipe works on all levels as it's quick, fragrant, healthy and attractive. It is great for two to share in huge bowls with heaps of fresh, crusty French bread, but is equally good in smaller portions as a starter when entertaining after a working day when you need to make every minute count! Don't miss out the basil at the end – it's not just a garnish but an important element of the dish. Finger bowls are a good idea for sticky fingers!'

Henshelwoods Fine Foods
Mussels in Thai Broth

SERVES 4

1kg/2lb 4oz fresh, live
   mussels, scrubbed
   and beards removed
2 garlic cloves
2 ½ long red chillies, deseeded
   and thinly sliced
½ tsp sea salt
2 tbsp rapeseed or
   sunflower seed oil
500ml/17fl oz/2 cups
   chicken stock
2 tbsp chilli jam (optional)
handful of basil leaves,
   thinly sliced, to garnish
French bread, to serve

1 Discard any mussels that do not close at once when tapped sharply on the work surface or are unusually heavy (they will be filled with mud!). Rinse the rest under cold running water.

2 Pound the garlic, 2 of the chillies and salt in a pestle and mortar to produce a paste. Alternatively, you can whiz them for 30 seconds in a food processor.

3 Heat a wok or large frying pan until hot, then add the oil, garlic and chilli paste. Cook for 1 minute and then add the stock, chilli jam, if you're using it, and mussels.

4 Cover and cook for about 8 minutes, or until all the mussels have opened. Discard any that fail to open after this time.

5 Serve the mussels and their broth in deep bowls scattered with chopped basil and the remaining chilli slices. Serve at once with French bread to soak up every last drop of the fabulous broth.

> My mum was a proper '60s feminist and she made absolutely sure I grew up doing my fair share in the kitchen and knowing how to cook. One of the plus sides of this was that I got to hang out with my mum a lot. Following the old lady's lead, I'm always roping my older daughter, Rosie, into helping me cook. She's five and our most recent adventure was shelling a crab. Half anatomy lesson, half cooking lesson and nearly half eaten by Rosie before we were finished. Anyway, this recipe is a brilliant combination of crab and orange oil. If you can't be bothered to shell the crab yourself, your fishmonger will do it for you. But make sure you buy the crab already cooked, as the fishmonger will be better at killing it swiftly (ie humanely) than you.

Jason Gibb & Nudo: Adopt An Olive Tree

Crab Spaghetti with Orange Olive Oil

SERVES 4

1 crab – a 550g/1lb 4oz crab gives about 200g/7oz of flesh
350g/12oz spaghetti
3 tbsp orange infused olive oil (you can also use ordinary un-infused olive oil)
1 garlic clove, finely chopped
1–2 fresh red chillies, halved
80ml/2½ fl oz/⅓ cup white wine
3–4 tbsp chopped flat-leaf parsley
sea salt and freshly ground black pepper

1 Find a sharp knife and a hammer (Rosie enjoyed this bit, eagerly hunting down the toolbox). Turn the crab belly-side up. Pull off the triangular-shaped belly flap, which is actually its abdomen. Turn it over and pull off the shell by inserting your thumb between the body and shell at the back of the crab and pulling the shell up, or use a knife with a similar manoeuvre.

2 Scoop what you can out of the shell and then crack it in half, if necessary, to get the rest out. Now twist off the legs and work your way carefully through the body compartments, cutting it up where necessary to get to the good bits. Make sure to discard the spongy gills and any bits of gristle and membrane. Use the hammer to crack open the leg shells and scoop out the nice bits.

3 Bring a large pan of salted water to the boil, feed in the spaghetti and cook for about 10 minutes, or according to the packet instructions, stirring occasionally to stop it sticking.

4 Meanwhile, gently heat the orange olive oil in a large frying pan, add the garlic and chillies and fry for 1 minute. Add the crabmeat to the pan with the wine, season with salt and pepper and cook off some of the wine, but not all of it.

5 Drain the spaghetti and tip it into the crab mixture. Toss in the parsley and serve immediately.

Sourcing ethically, cooking ethically and working as ethically as is possible are the ways in which we work at Café Spice Namasté. The environmental philosophy of food is also key. These are very similar principles to those held by The Real Food Movement — our beliefs are the same.

Cyrus Todiwala

At Café Spice Namasté we have in place some of the most robust environmental policies. Even before the others jumped onto the bandwagon we were at the forefront of good practice. Coming from India, and being very frugal on wastage, prompted us to put several measures in place. We nurture the environment around us by trying our hardest to come as close to a zero total waste operation as is possible. We have very good measures in place on recycling too.

Our cuisine is primarily Indian, however the produce we use is normally local. One often gets tempted to buy other produce, but if one delves deeper into local produce you realize that anything is possible. Selection is key and understanding the effects of certain spicing on local produce is key to that selection, as is understanding how and what works, and accepting what does not. Our fresh meat comes from local suppliers and imported produce is used only if the ingredient is either unavailable locally or not of the desired quality. Flavour, quality, family business survival, continuity and community are important to us, and we bring the best to our customers, many of whom are unaware of the great produce available in our own country. Over and above all else, you can really taste it.

The advantage of having a changing speciality menu means that we can make the most of seasonal ingredients. Yet, the one thing I do miss when it's not in season is asparagus. But, having made 50 kilos of pickle this year from asparagus means my guests will be eating it for a few months after its departure from the market.

But there is always so much to look forward to: quinces, apples, game, mutton, vegetables like purple sprouting broccoli, and of course, great organic, bio-dynamic tomatoes, which are truly wow.

Our recipes are handed down over generations. My great grandma's Parsee Lamb Curry recipe for instance, calls for 750g/1lb 10oz of pure homemade ghee for 2kg/4lb 8oz of mutton! That would be considered far too unhealthy nowadays. I have adapted most of these recipes, except where classical masalas are required, so as to make them easier for the modern day diner to digest and enjoy. We do not cook with ghee at all, for example, only cold pressed extra virgin rapeseed oil or cold pressed extra virgin sunflower seed oil. We still get the best flavours possible, but have had to juggle some recipes. Having grown up with a family-owned oil mill, the aromas of cold pressed oils take me back many years.

Cooking traditional Indian food has got to be slow and painstaking, but modern technology helps the chef to produce quality in less time. At Café Spice Namasté we will buy anything and put it on the menu if we think we can make it work to suit the intended flavours, and that really separates us from the masses as well as allowing us to open up a wider repertoire for our customers.

> **❝ Small producers play a major role in the food on our menu and sustainability of the raw material is paramount. Above all else, you can really taste the difference. ❞**

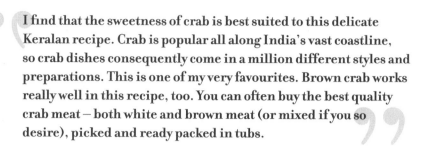

> I find that the sweetness of crab is best suited to this delicate Keralan recipe. Crab is popular all along India's vast coastline, so crab dishes consequently come in a million different styles and preparations. This is one of my very favourites. Brown crab works really well in this recipe, too. You can often buy the best quality crab meat – both white and brown meat (or mixed if you so desire), picked and ready packed in tubs.

Cyrus Todiwala & Café Spice Namasté
Kerala Crab Masala

SERVES 4

300–400g/10½–14oz white
   crab meat
2 tbsp sunflower oil
2 tsp mustard seeds
2½cm/1in root ginger,
   peeled and grated
2 garlic cloves, finely crushed
6–8 fresh curry leaves,
   finely shredded
2 slender green chillies,
   deseeded and chopped
1 dried red chilli, soaked in
   water for 10 minutes and
   finely shredded
2–3 small shallots, finely
   chopped
150–200g/5½–7oz, fresh
   coconut, grated
1 heaped tsp red chilli powder
½ tsp turmeric powder
2 small plum tomatoes,
   deseeded and finely diced
2 tbsp chopped coriander
sea salt

1 Check the crab meat to ensure that there are no hidden pieces of shell or cartilage in the meat.

2 Pour the oil into a wok or frying pan and heat until it forms a haze. Add a couple of mustard seeds to check to see if they crackle immediately. If the oil is ready, add all the mustard seeds and cover the pan with a lid for a few moments to prevent the seeds from flying all over the place and hitting your face.

3 As soon as the crackling dies down and you can smell a roasted aroma, add the ginger, garlic, curry leaves and the green and red chillies.

4 As soon as the garlic turns golden, but not deep in colour, add the shallots and sauté them until soft. Add the grated coconut and sauté for 3–4 minutes and then add the red chilli powder and turmeric.

5 Sauté for about 30 seconds, then add the crab meat, tossing well for about a minute. Add the diced tomato and coriander and check the seasoning, adding salt if needed.

6 Serve with some plain Goan or Keralan-style coconut curry and rice or some steamed rice dumplings. Alternatively, serve as a filling for thick savoury Indian pancakes.

Andrew Baird & Longueville Manor

Ragoût of Scallops, Asparagus and Wilted Greens

SERVES 4 (as a subsantial
starter or as a light lunch)

50g/1¾oz basil leaves
3½ tbsp olive oil
600g/1lb 5oz ripe sweet
   plum tomatoes, roughly
   chopped
12 asparagus spears, trimmed
12 diver caught scallops,
   cleaned
2 heads of pak choy
2 heads of bok choy
200g/7oz baby spinach
sea salt

FOR THE SQUID INK PASTA
500g/1lb 2oz '00' pasta flour
2 tsp salt
4 egg yolks, beaten
2 whole eggs, beaten
20g/¾oz squid ink
2 tbsp olive oil
6 tbsp water

1   First make some basil-scented oil. Heat the basil leaves with
    4 tablespoons of water until it withers. This will only take a
    moment. Purée it in a bowl using a hand blender, then add the
    olive oil and blitz again. Pass through a sieve and leave to settle.
    It will gradually clear, leaving a bright green basil scented oil.

2   Place any bits left in the sieve in a large bowl, then add the plum
    tomatoes and a good pinch of salt. Blitz for a minute with the hand
    blander and you will end up with a foaming pink purée. Place this
    in a muslin cloth, tie it up and hang it over a bowl in the fridge.
    (Ideally this should be done the day before.) The resulting clear
    liquid, or nage, has a refreshing tomato taste which will keep for
    up to 3 days in the fridge.

3   To make the squid ink pasta, place the flour in a bowl and make a
    well. Pour the eggs and egg yolks into the well along with the other
    pasta ingredients and mix well. After a few minutes it will bind
    together. Don't worry if the dough feels slightly dry at this stage.
    Wrap it in clingfilm in the fridge for at least 2 hours.

4   After resting, let the dough reach room temperature before
    kneading it again. Roll the dough out using a pasta machine set
    to the finest setting, then cut with the linguine, tagliatelle or
    spaghetti cutter. Bring a pan of water to the boil and add a splash
    of olive oil. Boil the pasta for 2 minutes then drain.

5   Using either a layered steamer or a colander set over a pan of
    water (with a lid), steam the asparagus for 3 minutes, then add the
    scallop meat with the bok choy, pak choy and spinach and steam
    for a further 3 minutes. Meanwhile, heat the clear plum tomato
    nage in a pan over a low heat.

6   Remove the greens from the steamer and place on 4 warm plates
    with the squid ink pasta. Top with the scallops, spoon over the
    warm nage, finish with the scented basil and serve.

> We use local organic beetroot. It's not all about crinkle cut and pickled you know! If you are put off by the colour that I find so gorgeous, (not everyone likes their hands getting stained), you can find golden or white beetroot in the shops and markets at certain times of the year – with all the flavour, just not the bright purple colour.

Jacqueline O'Donnell & The Sisters

King Scallops on Beetroot Salsa

SERVES 4 as a starter or 2 as a main course

8 king scallops, cleaned
4 tsp rapeseed oil
salad leaves, to serve

FOR THE SALSA
400g/14oz beetroot
½ tbsp olive oil
½ tsp cumin seeds, plus extra to flavour
1 heaped tbsp finely chopped coriander
1 heaped tbsp finely chopped chervil
1 heaped tbsp finely chopped chives
1 tbsp finely chopped shallot or red onion
sea salt and freshly ground black pepper

1 Preheat the oven to 180°C/350°F/Gas 4. Wrap each beetroot in foil, leaving the skin and stalk on so none of the flavour leaks out during the cooking. Rub them with olive oil and sprinkle a pinch of cumin seeds over each beetroot, before wrapping, just to add flavour. Bake the wrapped beetroot in the preheated oven for 45 minutes, or until tender.

2 Once the beetroot are cooked, remove from the oven and leave to cool. Once cool enough to handle, remove the foil and peel the beetroot, then cut them into dice and place in a bowl.

3 Warm the cumin seeds by placing them in a dry frying pan over a medium heat until they release their aroma. Add them to the beetroot.

4 Mix in the remaining salsa ingredients and set aside (if you have a wee scone cutter you can press the beetroot into the ring and sit the scallops on top when it comes to serving).

5 Leave the scallops out of the fridge for about 10 minutes before cooking. (Since you only lightly sear the scallops it's best not to start with them too cold.)

6 Heat either a good non-stick pan or a cast iron griddle pan until very hot. Rub each scallop with rapeseed oil and place in the pan for 1–2 minutes on each side until lightly seared.

7 Serve the scallops with the beetroot salsa, some salad leaves and most of all a knife and fork.

Scallops embody all that is perfect about seafood – a subtle, slightly sweet flavour of saltwater, a succulent, fleshy texture and health benefits galore. Scallops are a good source of vitamin B12, which can benefit cardiovascular health so they can make both your tastebuds and heart happy.

Turnham Green

Scallops with Chorizo, Chestnut Purée and Rocket

SERVES 4

100g/3½oz fresh chestnuts, scored (prepared chestnuts will also work)

75–100ml/2½-3½ fl oz/⅓ cup vegetable stock

2 tbsp rapeseed oil

150g/5½oz chorizo, sliced

1 red pepper, deseeded and finely sliced

1 tbsp capers, chopped

1 garlic clove, crushed

3 tbsp good quality tomato ketchup

8 scallops, cleaned

55g/2oz rocket, chopped

1 Preheat the oven to the lowest possible setting. Prepare the chestnuts by boiling them in the stock for 10–15 minutes until soft. Top up with boiling water to cover the chestnuts, if necessary. When cooked, drain the chestnuts (but reserve the stock) and peel. If you are using prepared chestnuts, go straight to step 2.

2 Blitz the chestnuts in a food processor, slowly adding the stock, until you have a smooth purée with the texture of mayonnaise. Place the purée in a covered ovenproof dish in the warm oven.

3 Gently heat the oil in a heavy-based frying pan. Add the chorizo and pepper and gently fry, stirring occasionally, for 2 minutes. Add the capers and garlic and fry for a further 2 minutes.

4 Add the tomato ketchup and thoroughly mix with the other ingredients. Remove from the pan and place in a covered dish in the oven.

5 Keeping the hob heat quite high, add the scallops to the same pan and cook for 1–2 minutes on each side, or until they are just cooked through.

6 Stir the rocket through the chorizo sauce. Divide the reserved chestnut purée between 4 warm plates. Spoon the sauce on top of the chestnut purée and then crown each plate with 2 scallops and serve.

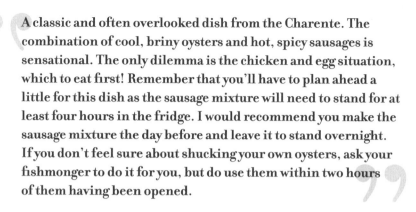

A classic and often overlooked dish from the Charente. The combination of cool, briny oysters and hot, spicy sausages is sensational. The only dilemma is the chicken and egg situation, which to eat first! Remember that you'll have to plan ahead a little for this dish as the sausage mixture will need to stand for at least four hours in the fridge. I would recommend you make the sausage mixture the day before and leave it to stand overnight. If you don't feel sure about shucking your own oysters, ask your fishmonger to do it for you, but do use them within two hours of them having been opened.

Henry Harris & Racine

Oysters and Spiced Sausages

SERVES 4

FOR THE SPICED SAUSAGES
350g/12oz lean lamb mince
250g/9oz lean pork mince
juice and zest of 1 lemon
1 garlic clove, finely chopped
1 tsp harissa
¼ tsp coriander seeds, lightly
   toasted and ground
2 tbsp parsley leaves, finely
   chopped
2 tbsp chives, finely chopped
a generous amount of freshly
   ground black pepper
½ tsp sea salt
1–2 tbsp rapeseed or olive oil

FOR THE OYSTERS
4 handfuls of seaweed, washed
   (optional)
24 oysters, shucked
2 lemons

1 Place all the ingredients for the sausages, except the oil, in a large bowl and mix until well combined. Set aside in the fridge and leave for at least 4 hours to let the flavours develop.

2 Take small quantities of the sausage mixture and shape into 24 little patties. Place them on a tray and keep in the fridge until required, but take them out 30 minutes before you cook them.

3 Heat a large, heavy-based frying pan over a medium heat, add a splash of oil and cook the little patties for a couple of minutes on each side. Set aside and keep warm.

4 Take 4 large plates and, if you're using it, arrange a handful of seaweed on each one. Place 6 oysters on each plate.

5 Cut off the top and bottom of each lemon, then halve them horizontally. (Topping and tailing gives a stable base, preventing the lemon from leaving the plate!) Serve the oysters with the spiced sausages and lemon halves

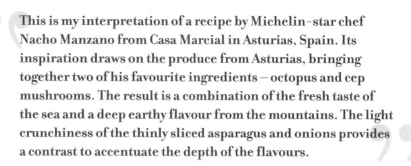

This is my interpretation of a recipe by Michelin-star chef Nacho Manzano from Casa Marcial in Asturias, Spain. Its inspiration draws on the produce from Asturias, bringing together two of his favourite ingredients – octopus and cep mushrooms. The result is a combination of the fresh taste of the sea and a deep earthy flavour from the mountains. The light crunchiness of the thinly sliced asparagus and onions provides a contrast to accentuate the depth of the flavours.

Santiago Guerrero & Iberica

Slow-Stewed Octopus with Cep Mushrooms, Onions and Green Asparagus

MAKES 10 portions

3½kg/7lb 14oz whole octopus
1 bay leaf
1 onion, thinly sliced
100ml/3½fl oz/scant ½ cup white wine
5 whole black peppercorns
15 green jumbo asparagus, sliced thinly with a mandolin
100ml/3½fl oz/scant ½ cup extra virgin olive oil, plus extra to dress
sherry vinegar, to dress
1 tsp of smoked pimentón dulce
1 onion, sliced thinly with a mandolin
sea salt

FOR THE CEP MUSHROOMS
2 tsp extra virgin olive oil
500g/1lb 2oz cep mushrooms, cleaned and halved
1 garlic clove, chopped
1 thyme sprig
1 rosemary sprig

1 Wash the octopus thoroughly to ensure that it is does not have any dirt or gelatine on the tentacles. Cut off the tentacles from the base of the head and discard the head. Place the tentacles in a wide heavy-based pan, then add the bay leaf, onion, white wine and black peppercorns.

2 Place the pan on a low heat and cover with a lid. Leave the octopus to gently simmer for 40 minutes. The octopus will release its juices and slowly cook. Check it every 10 minutes to ensure that it is not boiling too quickly or sticking to the pan.

3 After 40 minutes check again to ensure that the octopus is cooked – stick a skewer into the thickest part of the tentacle (you should feel some kind of resistance but not too much). Replace the lid, remove from the heat and allow to cool.

4 Take the tentacles out of the pot and cut them into 6cm/2½in pieces. Place the octopus back into the cooking stock, covered with the cooking liquor.

5 To serve, warm the octopus in the pan with its cooking liquor. Meanwhile, in a separate pan, heat the oil over a medium high heat and fry the cep mushrooms with the garlic, thyme and rosemary. Remove them from the pan and drain.

6 Dress the green asparagus with some olive oil and a little bit of sherry vinegar. Mix together the pimentón and olive oil, then toss with the onion. Place the octopus on a plate, then the mushrooms on top and finish with the asparagus and the onions. Drizzle a little bit of the warm cooking liquor on top of the whole salad and serve.

> *This great recipe is best eaten in autumn when the cider pressing season really gets going. We source our clams from the pristine waters of a local bay, and raid the chillies from a neighbouring farm. It's important to use the best dry cured bacon available. Fortunately we have some local farmers who can be relied upon to always produce quality bacon.*

Heron Valley

Linguine with Clams and Cider

SERVES 4

3kg/6lb 8oz fresh clams
1 tbsp olive oil
1 onion, peeled and chopped
3 fat garlic cloves, chopped
3 mild chillies, deseeded
  and chopped
8 rashers smoked streaky dry
  cured bacon, finely chopped
425g/15oz linguine
500ml/17fl oz/2 cups dry cider
4 tbsp chopped flat-leaf
  parsley leaves
freshly ground black pepper

1 Make sure the clams are fresh and fragrant when you cook them. They should be firmly closed and have a fresh, sweet smell of the sea. Discard any that remain open. To keep the clams fresh, put them in a bowl and cover with fresh salted water until required.

2 Heat the olive oil in a wide casserole dish over a medium heat and fry the onion, garlic, chillies and bacon, stirring occasionally, until the onion has softened and the bacon is slightly crisp.

3 Meanwhile, cook the linguine in a large pan of boiling, salted water for 8–10 minutes, or according to the packet instructions.

4 Add the clams to the casserole dish and stir them into the onion and bacon mixture. Add the cider, put on the lid and leave to cook for another couple of minutes until all the shells have opened (discard any that remain closed after this time), giving the clams a stir once or twice. Stir in the parsley and season with pepper.

5 Drain the linguine, then toss it into the clam and cider sauce. Serve immediately.

POULTRY, GAME & MEAT

Crunchy Pistachio and Spiced Sea Salt Chicken

Palestinian Maftoul with Za'atar Chicken

Pomegranate Chicken

Chicken Bhoona

Really Garlicky Chicken

Duck Breast Strips in Merlot Reduction Sauce

Quail Marinated in Plum Wine and Barley Miso

Rabbit with Olives

Venison, Fennel and Honey in an Elderberry Wine Glaze

Slow-Cooked Oriental Crispy Pork Belly

Roast Pork Loin with Apple Compote and Roast Fennel, Potatoes and Onions

Marinated 'Secreto' Pork Loin with Spicy Pimentón and Piquillo Peppers

Pork Loin Olives Wrapped in Black Forest Ham

Pasta alla Carbonara

Pappardelle with Wild Boar and Venison Ragù

Chorizo with Vegetables and Baked Eggs

Buffalo Chilli con Carne

Braised Beef in Red Wine with Jabugo Ham

Grilled Beef Bavette with Crispy Artichokes, Shallots and Horseradish

Rose Calf's Liver with Marsala and Sage

Rose Veal Chops with Smoky Corn Salad

Grilled Aubergine, Caramelized Onion and Lamb Shish Kebab

Lamb Tagine

Cannon of Liquorice Lamb, Ratatouille and Fondant Potatoes

This deliciously different way to serve chicken drumsticks would be perfect for a supper dish, served with a baked potato and salad, or as part of a lunchbox. When my children were younger it used to be their Friday school treat, with celery sticks, cherry tomatoes and Little Gem lettuce hearts. Now it's a popular picnic item in our house, as much at home in our annual Henley hamper when we go to watch our middle son rowing, or as an excuse for a spur-of-the-moment trip out to a local beach on a sunny day.

The Anglesey Sea Salt Company
Crunchy Pistachio and Spiced Sea Salt Chicken

SERVES 4

115g/4oz/¾ cup shelled pistachio nuts
1 tsp, plus 2 tbsp plain flour
1 tbsp sea salt mixed with 1 tsp organic spices – try a mixture of any of the following: cinnamon, nutmeg, ginger, coriander, cumin, sweet paprika, cayenne pepper, coarsely ground black pepper
1 large egg, beaten
1 tbsp milk
8 free range organic chicken drumsticks, skin removed
3 tbsp vegetable oil

1 Preheat the oven to 220°C/425°F/Gas 7. In a food processor or blender, combine the pistachio nuts, 1 teaspoon of flour and 1 tablespoon of sea salt and process together until finely chopped and well mixed. Transfer this mixture to a plate.

2 On a second plate combine the remaining 2 tablespoons of flour and 1 teaspoon of sea salt mix, and in a third bowl combine the beaten egg and milk.

3 Toss the chicken into the seasoned flour, making sure each drumstick is well coated before tapping off any excess.

4 Dip the flour-coated chicken into the egg until lightly coated and again tap off any excess. Finally roll each drumstick in the chopped nut mixture until well coated.

5 Arrange the drumsticks on a sheet of greaseproof paper on a baking tray and drizzle with the vegetable oil.

6 Cook in the preheated oven for 10 minutes, then remove the tray from the oven and turn the drumsticks over, using tongs. Return to the oven and cook for a further 10 minutes, or until very crisp and golden. Serve either hot or cold, as preferred.

> My mother taught me to cook, but she, like her mother before her, never wrote anything down, committing every recipe she knew to memory – a prodigious task, knowing, as she did, some hundred ways to cook meat, fish and vegetables. It was during one of her many summers spent with me in London that I realized all these recipes would be lost if I did not record them. So for me, the summer she spent with me was a delicious reawakening to the tastes and aromas of my youth. This recipe uses za'atar, a Middle Eastern herb mix of wild thyme, sesame seeds and sumac – a delicious combination for making one of my favourite chicken recipes from my mother's repertoire. This dish can also be made using garlic-infused olive oil.

L'ailOlive

Palestinian Maftoul with Za'atar Chicken

SERVES 4

4 tbsp za'atar
4 skinless chicken breasts
6 tbsp olive oil
1 large white onion, finely
   diced
1 tsp dill seeds
1 green pepper, deseeded
   and chopped finely
250g/9oz maftoul (large-
   grained, hand-rolled
   couscous) or ordinary
   couscous
200ml/7fl oz/scant 1 cup
   chicken or vegetable stock
100g/3½oz/²⁄₃ cup blanched
   almonds, chopped coarsely
juice and zest of 1 lemon
1 tsp ground cumin
handful of coriander leaves or
   flat-leaf parsley

1 Preheat the oven to 180°C/350°F/Gas 4. Sprinkle the za'atar liberally over the chicken breasts, put in an ovenproof dish and drizzle with about 2 tablespoons of the olive oil. Put into the oven and roast for about 30 minutes, until the chicken is cooked through, basting frequently.

2 Fry the onion in a large pan in 1 tablespoon of the olive oil until golden, then add the dill seeds and green pepper. Add the dry maftoul to the pan and stir well so that it is coated with the oil and seasonings. Add 150ml/5fl oz/scant ²⁄₃ cups of the stock and leave on the heat until the liquid is absorbed and the maftoul is plump and soft (add more stock if needed).

3 Heat 1 tablespoon of the olive oil in a frying pan and fry the chopped almonds for 2 minutes until golden, then drain and set aside.

4 Mix the remaining 2 tablespoons of the olive oil with the lemon juice, cumin and herbs. Stir into the maftoul.

5 Slice the chicken breasts and serve on top of the maftoul. Sprinkle with the lemon zest and toasted almonds.

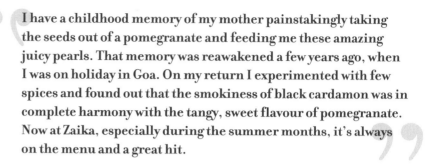

"I have a childhood memory of my mother painstakingly taking the seeds out of a pomegranate and feeding me these amazing juicy pearls. That memory was reawakened a few years ago, when I was on holiday in Goa. On my return I experimented with few spices and found out that the smokiness of black cardamon was in complete harmony with the tangy, sweet flavour of pomegranate. Now at Zaika, especially during the summer months, it's always on the menu and a great hit."

Sanjay Dwivedi & Zaika

Pomegranate Chicken

SERVES 4

5 garlic cloves
1cm/½ inch fresh ginger, peeled
3 tbsp vegetable oil
4 skinless corn-fed chicken breasts
juice of ½ lemon
sea salt and freshly ground black pepper

FOR THE MARINADE
200ml/7 fl oz/scant 1 cup pomegranate juice
50g/1¾oz dried pomegranate seeds, optional
3 tsp yogurt
1 tsp black cardamom seeds
3 tbsp vegetable oil
1 tsp red Kashmiri chilli powder

FOR THE SALAD
100ml/3½fl oz/scant ½ cup extra virgin olive oil
1½ tbsp white wine vinegar
1½ pomegranate paste
100g/3½oz pea shoots
100g/3½oz rocket leaves

TO SERVE
100ml/3½fl oz/scant ½ cup pomegranate juice
pomegranate seeds, to garnish

1 Blitz the garlic, ginger and oil to a fine paste in a blender. Cut each chicken breast into 4 and season with salt and lemon juice. Rub 1 teaspoon of the ginger and garlic paste over each piece of chicken breast and set aside in the fridge, covered, until required.

2 Reduce the pomegranate juice by a quarter by boiling it in a wide pan. Soak the dried pomegranate seeds (if you're using them) for 15 minutes in water, then blitz in a blender with the yogurt and reduced pomegranate juice. Pass the mixture through a fine sieve.

3 Blitz the black cardamom seeds in a grinder. Warm the vegetable oil and gently cook the Kashmiri chilli powder for a few minutes, then add the ground black cardamoms and a pinch of salt. Remove from the heat and cool, then mix with the pomegranate and yogurt mixture and rub into the chicken. Put the chicken back into the fridge, covered, to marinate until required – overnight if you wish.

4 Meanwhile make the salad dressing. Mix the oil, vinegar and pomegranate paste and season to taste with a little salt.

5 Reduce the pomegranate juice for the garnish to a quarter by boiling in a small pan – it should reach the consistency of a very thick glaze.

6 Cook the marinated chicken on the barbecue or in a tandoor, making sure you turn it at least once. Depending on the heat, it should take approximately 5–8 minutes.

7 To serve, paint the reduced pomegranate juice glaze onto one half of each plate, and decorate with pomegranate seeds.

8 Dress the pea shoots and rocket with the vinaigrette and place them next to the pomegrate seeds. Arrange the cooked chicken pieces next to the salad and serve.

"I've worked in the hospitality industry since 1986 and have had the pleasure of working with marvellous chefs, picking up ideas and secret tips. This recipe is one of my favourites and can be made mild, medium or hot simply by adding yogurt or chilli powder. Three teaspoons of chilli powder will give Madras strength; five teaspoons will give vindaloo strength. Once cooked, the dish should have the same flair and flavour as you would get served in a restaurant cooked by a professional chef."

Mr Huda
Chicken Bhoona

SERVES 4

2 onions, peeled
5 cherry tomatoes, quartered
½ small green pepper, deseeded and chopped
8–10g/¼ oz fresh ginger, peeled and sliced
1–2 green chillies, deseeded and chopped
3 garlic cloves, peeled
a few sprigs of coriander, chopped
1 tsp ground turmeric
6 tbsp vegetable or olive oil
3 or 4 cardamom pods
2 bay leaves
6 tsp curry paste
½ tsp chilli powder
500g/1lb 2oz skinless chicken, diced
250ml/9fl oz/1 cup chicken stock
sea salt and freshly ground black pepper

1   Quarter 1 onion and put it in a small pan with 3 of the tomatoes, the green pepper, ginger, chilli, 1 chopped garlic clove and half the coriander. Add the turmeric, 4 tablespoons of the oil, a pinch of salt and about 200–250ml/7–9fl oz/about 1 cup of warm water. Cover the pan with a lid and cook gently until the vegetables are soft, about 15–20 minutes, stirring occasionally. When cooked, place them in a blender and blitz to a purée.

2   Heat the remaining 2 tablespoons of oil on a moderate heat in a medium-sized saucepan. Add the cardamoms, bay leaves and remaining garlic cloves and slowly fry until the garlic is golden.

3   Finely slice the remaining onion, add to the pan with a pinch of salt and cook gently, stirring regularly. Add the curry paste, chilli powder and the rest of the quartered tomatoes and cook for 1–2 minutes, stirring continuously.

4   Add the chicken and stock to the pan with 100–125 ml/3½–4fl oz/ about ½ cup of warm water and bring to the boil. Leave to simmer gently for 15–20 minutes, or until the required texture is reached. (Add more water if you prefer more sauce, or cook on a higher heat for slightly longer, with the lid half open, if you like your sauce thicker).

5   Once the cooking time is nearly over, add the rest of the coriander. Leave the curry to settle for 10–15 minutes, and skim off any excess oil from the surface before serving.

This dish is traditionally known as chicken with forty cloves of garlic. Cooked in this way the garlic becomes mild and sweet, with a smooth, buttery texture. Serve it with creamy mashed potatoes to soak up the garlicky juices.

The Really Garlicky Company
Really Garlicky Chicken

SERVES 4

4 tbsp extra virgin olive oil
1 onion, chopped
1 celery stick, chopped
3 tbsp mixed fresh herbs,
    such as flat-leaf parsley,
    tarragon, chervil, thyme
    or basil, chopped
1 small free range chicken,
    weighing 1.2–1.3kg/2lb
    12oz–3lb
40 garlic cloves
1 lemon
150ml/5fl oz/scant ⅔ cup
    dry white wine
sea salt and freshly ground
    black pepper

1   Preheat the oven to 180°C/350°F/Gas 4. Heat 1 tablespoon of olive oil in a large, heavy-based casserole dish over a medium heat, then add the onion and celery. Cook until just beginning to soften, then add half of the fresh herbs.

2   Lay the chicken on the herby mixture and scatter the garlic cloves around the chicken. (Don't worry about peeling the 40 cloves, part of the fun of eating this dish is squishing the juicy cloves from the skins).

3   Pare the zest from the lemon using a potato peeler and add it to the dish along with the juice. Pour in the white wine and the rest of the olive oil. Scatter on the rest of the fresh herbs and season with salt and pepper.

4   Cover the casserole dish and place in the preheated oven for 1 hour. Uncover the casserole and put it back into the oven for a further 20 minutes to brown the chicken. Remove from the oven, carve and serve.

This is a favourite for impromptu winemaker dinners at Château Haut Garrigue, accompanied by organically grown Merlot. The wine reinforces the spices and dark fruit and goes really well with the duck.

Château Haut Garrigue

Duck Breast Strips in Merlot Reduction Sauce

SERVES 4

2 duck breasts, sliced in half
2 tbsp plain flour
a pinch of cinnamon
a pinch of nutmeg
1 tbsp olive oil
240ml/8fl oz/scant 1 cup
    Merlot red wine
4 tsp dark fruit jam, such as
    plum, cherry or blackberry
mashed potatoes, to serve
chopped flat-leaf parsley,
    to serve
sea salt and freshly ground
    black pepper

1   Ideally buy your duck breast already cut into strips (called 'aiguillettes' in France), but if you can't do this, cut them into strips yourself. Roll the strips in a mix of flour, cinnamon, nutmeg, salt and black pepper until they are lightly covered.

2   Heat the olive oil in a frying pan over a medium to high heat. Add the duck strips and fry for 3 minutes until tender, taking care not to overcook them – medium rare is ideal.

3   Remove the duck strips and keep them warm, then deglaze the hot pan with the Merlot (pour it in, then boil on a high heat, stirring all the time). Add the jam, stirring until it has melted, then season with salt and pepper to taste.

4   Serve the duck and sauce with some mashed potato sprinkled with chopped parsley and pepper.

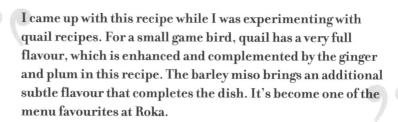

I came up with this recipe while I was experimenting with quail recipes. For a small game bird, quail has a very full flavour, which is enhanced and complemented by the ginger and plum in this recipe. The barley miso brings an additional subtle flavour that completes the dish. It's become one of the menu favourites at Roka.

Nic Watt & Roka

Quail Marinated in Plum Wine and Barley Miso

SERVES 4

4 large quails, boned
200ml/7fl oz/scant 1 cup
   plum wine
1 tbsp umeboshi plum paste
2 tsp soy sauce
1½ tsp sesame oil
2 tsp barley miso
1 tsp garlic paste
1 tsp ginger paste
4 umeboshi plums
sea salt and ground black
   pepper

1 Ask your butcher to spatchcock the quails, discarding the carcass but leaving the breast and legs attached.

2 To make the marinade, put the plum wine, plum paste, soy sauce, sesame oil, barley miso, garlic paste and ginger paste into a mixing bowl and whisk together to incorporate. Add the quails, stir to coat with the marinade, cover and leave to marinate for 4 hours in the fridge.

3 When ready to cook the quails, preheat the grill. Grill the quails skin side down first, basting each side with the marinade 3 or 4 times while cooking. Cook for about 3 minutes on each side.

4 While the quails are cooking, remove the stones from your umeboshi plums and chop the flesh roughly.

5 To serve, season the cooked quails with sea salt and black pepper. Serve with a spoonful of chopped pickled plums and a final fine pinch of sea salt.

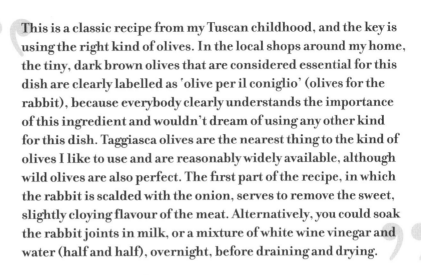

This is a classic recipe from my Tuscan childhood, and the key is using the right kind of olives. In the local shops around my home, the tiny, dark brown olives that are considered essential for this dish are clearly labelled as 'olive per il coniglio' (olives for the rabbit), because everybody clearly understands the importance of this ingredient and wouldn't dream of using any other kind for this dish. Taggiasca olives are the nearest thing to the kind of olives I like to use and are reasonably widely available, although wild olives are also perfect. The first part of the recipe, in which the rabbit is scalded with the onion, serves to remove the sweet, slightly cloying flavour of the meat. Alternatively, you could soak the rabbit joints in milk, or a mixture of white wine vinegar and water (half and half), overnight, before draining and drying.

Valentina Harris

Rabbit with Olives

SERVES 4

1¾kg/4lb rabbit, jointed
1 onion, finely chopped
5 tbsp olive oil
1 tsp sea salt
2 tender sticks of celery,
    finely chopped
3 garlic cloves, finely chopped
1 sprig of rosemary
2 small sprigs of thyme
3 tbsp Cognac
455ml/16fl oz/scant 2 cups
    dry red wine
200g/7oz/2 cups Taggiasca
    olives
500g/1lb 2oz fresh ripe
    tomatoes, peeled, deseeded
    and coarsely chopped
250ml/9fl oz/1 cup chicken
    stock, if required

1 Wash the rabbit joints, dry them carefully and place them in a saucepan with the onion and 2 tablespoons of the oil. Cover thoroughly with the salt and place the pan over a lively flame.

2 Allow the rabbit to exude all its liquid, turning it frequently, then remove from the heat. Pour away the liquid and rinse all the joints carefully. Discard the onion.

3 In a separate pan over a medium heat, fry the celery, garlic, rosemary and thyme in the remaining oil for 1 minute, then add the rabbit joints to the pan and thoroughly seal all over until well browned. Add the Cognac and flame briefly for a couple of minutes.

4 Add the wine and boil quickly for 2 minutes to evaporate the alcohol. Add the olives and the tomatoes, stir together thoroughly and cover with a lid.

5 Lower the heat and simmer for about 55 minutes, stirring occasionally, or until the rabbit is tender. Add the stock only if the casserole appears to be drying out. Serve hot.

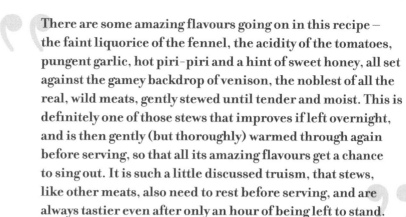

"There are some amazing flavours going on in this recipe – the faint liquorice of the fennel, the acidity of the tomatoes, pungent garlic, hot piri-piri and a hint of sweet honey, all set against the gamey backdrop of venison, the noblest of all the real, wild meats, gently stewed until tender and moist. This is definitely one of those stews that improves if left overnight, and is then gently (but thoroughly) warmed through again before serving, so that all its amazing flavours get a chance to sing out. It is such a little discussed truism, that stews, like other meats, also need to rest before serving, and are always tastier even after only an hour of being left to stand."

Cairn O'Mohr

Venison, Fennel and Honey in an Elderberry Wine Glaze

SERVES 4

1 tbsp olive oil
1 celery stick, finely chopped
1 large onion, finely chopped
2 garlic cloves, finely chopped
1kg/2lb 4oz stewing venison, cubed
2 tbsp chopped fennel fronds
piri-piri sauce, to taste
2 tbsp flour
1 glass elderberry wine (or medium-dry, fruity red wine)
1 tbsp honey
1 x 400g/14oz canned chopped tomatoes
sea salt and freshly ground black pepper

1 Heat the oil in a heavy-based pan over a medium heat and brown the celery, onion and garlic.

2 Add the venison to the pan along with the fennel. Season with salt, pepper and piri-piri sauce.

3 Sprinkle on the flour and stir well. Add the elderberry wine and honey and cook to reduce the sauce slightly. Add the tomatoes and stir again.

4 Bring the mixture to the boil, then either lower the heat and simmer for 2½ hours or transfer to a covered casserole and cook in the oven at 180°C/350°F/Gas 4 for 2 hours. Serve with pasta or new potatoes, and curly cabbage.

> "This recipe was inspired by a love of oriental cooking and many happy visits to good Chinese restaurants. The wonderful combination of lusciously soft pork with crunchy crackling, and rice mixed with a delicious sauce, all then topped with fiery chilli oil, keeps me returning to the recipe again and again."

David's Chilli Oil

Slow-Cooked Oriental Crispy Pork Belly

SERVES 4

1.5kg/3lb 5oz pork belly, scored
1 tbsp chilli oil, plus extra to serve
5 garlic cloves, peeled and finely chopped
5cm/2in fresh ginger, finely chopped
2 tbsp light soy sauce
1 tbsp dark soy sauce
1 tsp tomato purée
1 tbsp red wine vinegar
1 tbsp sugar or honey
1 tsp five spice powder
a handful of coriander leaves, to serve
a handful of sliced spring onions, to serve
sea salt and freshly ground black pepper

1 Preheat the oven to 140°C/275°F/Gas 1. Place the pork belly in the sink and pour a whole kettle of boiling water all over the skin. Dry the pork with a clean tea towel, then rub a small handful of sea salt all over the fat.

2 Put all the other ingredients, except the ones for serving, into a roasting dish, add a dash of water and stir well. Add the pork belly, being careful not to touch the skin with the sauce mixture. Roast in the preheated oven for 2½ hours.

3 Check the pork every 30 minutes or so, adding a little more water to the tray if it seems necessary. You don't want the sauce to dry up!

4 Finally, slip the dish under a preheated medium to hot grill for about 8 minutes to achieve nice crispy skin.

5 Serve with steamed, roasted or stir-fried vegetables, accompanied by noodles or steamed rice. Sprinkle with coriander leaves and spring onions, and add more chilli oil once plated.

"A good piece of nicely cooked pork with crispy skin and juicy flesh is a joy to behold. Apple, bay, fennel and pork are all wonderful autumnal flavours that sit very happily on a plate together. If you want to add a delicious and truly seasonal touch, you can throw a couple of handfuls of elderberries into the apple compote."

Oliver Rowe

Roast Pork Loin with Apple Compote and Roast Fennel, Potatoes and Onions

SERVES 4–6

3 garlic cloves
8 juniper berries
6 black peppercorns
1 tsp wholegrain mustard
1.3kg/3lb organic, free range, fatty pork loin, boned
4 onions
2 large potatoes, peeled and cut into large dice
2 fennel bulbs, trimmed and cut into wedges
4 tsp cold-pressed rapeseed oil
¼ tsp fresh thyme leaves
570ml/20 fl oz/scant 2⅓ cups of light ale or cider
a pinch of coriander seeds
2 cooking apples, such as Bramley, peeled, cored and roughly chopped
200g/7oz elderberries, (optional)
1 bay leaf
2 tbsp golden caster sugar
sea salt and freshly ground black pepper

1 Crush the garlic with a good pinch of salt, the juniper berries and the peppercorns. When you have achieved a smooth paste add the mustard. Score the skin of the pork loin, just fat deep, with the cuts as close together as you can make them. Turn the pork over and rub in the marinade. Turn the loin back over again and rub the skin with fine salt and then liberally and evenly sprinkle with a little more. After 20–30 minutes wipe off the liquid and any excess salt. Tie the pork with cook's string to help it keep its shape during roasting.

2 Preheat the oven to 250°C/500°F/Gas 9. Slice 2 of the onions and toss them with the potatoes and fennel in a large bowl with a couple of teaspoons of the rapeseed oil, salt, pepper, thyme and coriander seeds. Spread them out on a baking tray and drizzle a bit more oil on top.

3 Quarter the remaining onions and put them, cut side up, on another baking tray. Put the pork loin on top.

4 Put the pork and vegetables in the oven. Don't open the oven door too much – it needs to be blisteringly hot. Turn the vegetables once to make sure they colour evenly. When the pork skin is crispy and bubbly (about 25 minutes), pour the ale or cider into the baking tray. Remove the vegetables and keep warm. Turn the oven down to 180°/350°F/Gas 4 and cook the pork for a further 20–30 minutes. You may need to top it up with a little water. Remove from the oven and leave to rest, uncovered, for 10 minutes.

5 Put the apples and elderberries in a heavy-based saucepan with 150ml/5fl oz/scant ⅔ cup water, the bay leaf and sugar. Cover and cook on a high heat for 10 minutes, then set aside.

6 Drain off any excess pork fat from the baking tray, then pour the liquid into a small pan with a few of the onions. Heat over a medium heat until reduced to a loose gravy.

7 Cut the pork into finger thick slices and serve with the gravy.

> The thing that left a lasting impression on me when I worked in the south of Spain was just how much meat is marinated prior to cooking. This dish takes inspiration from that marinating, and especially Adobo, which is a pimentón marinade from Andalucia. I'm using a special cut between the shoulder and the loin of the Iberico pig, called Secreto Iberico, that is really succulent and full of flavour, and I've made the Adobo with a slight sweetness that really compliments the flavour of the pork. The marinade works best if left on for at least 24 hours to allow the meat to absorb as much flavour as possible.

Santiago Guerrero & Iberica

Marinated 'Secreto' Pork Loin with Spicy Pimentón and Piquillo Peppers

SERVES 4

80g/2¾oz spicy pimentón
80g/2¾oz/⅓ cup sugar
1 tsp ground cumin
2 garlic cloves, chopped
1 tsp chopped flat-leaf
   parsley
80ml/2½fl oz/⅓ cup dark
   soy sauce
1½ tsp olive oil, plus extra
   for frying
1½ tsp white wine vinegar
1kg/2lb 4oz Secreto Iberico
   pork loin

TO SERVE

450g/1lb jarred piquillo
   peppers, drained
2–3 tbsp olive oil
sea salt

1   Mix the pimentón, sugar and cumin together in a bowl with the garlic and parsley. Add the soy sauce, oil, vinegar and 1 tablespoon of water, and stir to make a paste.

2   Slice the pork loin into 4 pieces and coat each one with the paste. Allow to marinate for 24 hours in the fridge.

3   Heat the olive oil in a hot frying pan and sear the pork on both sides. If you prefer, you can also sear the pork in a hot griddle pan until medium rare. Don't worry if the marinade turns black. Once the pork has been turned over, lower the heat to allow the pork to cook for 2 more minutes.

4   In another frying pan, shallow fry the piquillo peppers with 2–3 tablespoons olive oil until they are heated through and have taken on a little colour. Serve the pork hot with a couple of piquillo peppers for each person, and sprinkled with salt.

> "As a 15 year old in the midst of the summer school holiday, I bravely decided to take a cookery course. Did it bother me that I was the only boy in the class? You bet it did! I prayed that none of my friends spotted me sneaking into the cookery school building. It became a pivotal moment in my life. On weekly trips to the market with my mother I discovered 'strange' vegetables au naturelle, which previously I had seen only in cans. So freshness became my mantra on my way to learning about cooking. This recipe, a family favourite, requires a little planning. To get the most out of red cabbage, start with the recipe the day before. Your palate will thank you and your opinion of this colourful, yet humble cabbage will change for the better."

Dan Schinkentanz & De Gustibus

Pork Loin Olives Wrapped in Black Forest Ham

SERVES 4

FOR THE RED CABBAGE
2 heads red cabbage, tough stalks removed and cut into quarters
40g/1½oz/¼ cup brown sugar
150ml/5fl oz/scant ⅔ cup red wine
100ml/3½fl oz/scant 1 cup apple juice
55ml/1¾fl oz/¼ cup red wine vinegar
60g/2¼oz goose fat
1 onion, chopped
1 eating apple, such as Cox, peeled, cored and chopped
1 tsp ground cloves
1cm/½in of cinnamon stick
1 tbsp juniper berries, crushed
1 tbsp black peppercorns
2 bay leaves
sea salt and freshly ground black pepper

FOR THE NOODLES (*spätzle*)
300g/10½oz/heaped 2⅓ cups plain flour
a pinch of salt
5 eggs
small knob of butter, to serve

1 To prepare the red cabbage, start the night before (or as far ahead on the day as you can manage). Slice the cabbage thinly, using a mandolin or by hand, and place in a large bowl. Add the brown sugar, red wine, apple juice and red wine vinegar, then place a smaller bowl inside to weigh the cabbage down. Leave overnight. Drain the red cabbage, reserving the marinade.

2 Heat the goose fat in a heavy-based pan over a medium heat then add the onion and apple. When they are transparent, add the red cabbage and continue to cook gently until soft.

3 Add the reserved marinade along with the cloves, cinnamon stick, juniper berries, peppercorns and bay leaves (a handy tip is to buy a tea-brewing 'ball' that you can put these bits in, allowing you to remove them easily before serving the dish). Cook for 1 hour, adding a little water, if needed, and season with salt and pepper.

4 To make the noodles, mix the flour with a pinch of salt. Fold in the eggs along with about 250ml/9fl oz/1 cup water. You're aiming for a smooth batter with the consistency of good, thick custard, so add or reduce the water accordingly. Leave to stand for at least 30 minutes.

5 Bring a large pot of water to the boil and add plenty of salt. Using a potato ricer (or colander), squeeze the batter in streams into the water and boil until the noodles float to the surface and are warmed through. Drain the noodles and reserve in a bowl. To serve, reheat them in a pan with a small knob of butter.

FOR THE PORK

4 butterflied pork loin steaks
4 tbsp mustard of your choice
4 tbsp Quark or fromage frais
2 carrots, grated and 1 carrot,
    chopped
3 leeks, trimmed and sliced
12 slices Black Forest ham or
    Parma ham
1 onion, peeled
90g/3¼oz unsalted butter
100ml/3½fl oz/scant ½ cup
    white wine
100ml/3½ fl oz/scant ½ cup
    whipping cream

6 Preheat the oven to 180°C/350°F/Gas 4 and put a roasting tin in to heat up. Lay the pork steaks between 2 sheets of clingfilm and pound flat, to around 5mm/¼in thick. Mix the mustard with the Quark or fromage frais and brush over the meat. Divide the grated carrot and leeks evenly between the pork steaks and roll them up, starting from the thin end.

7 You need 3 slices of Black Forest ham for each pork roll. Lay the 3 slices flat on a board so that they overlap and fit the overall width of one of the pork rolls. Now take the pork roll, place it on the ham, seam side down, and wrap it up in the ham, to create an attractive package. Repeat with the rest of the ham and pork rolls.

8 Put the remaining carrot and onion into the heated roasting tin along with the butter. Place the pork and ham rolls in the roasting tin (seam-side down) and cook in the preheated oven for 10 minutes. Add the white wine, return to the oven and allow to reduce for a further 10 minutes. Pour the whipping cream into the roasting tin and cook in the oven for a final 5 minutes.

9 When the pork comes out of the oven, put the rolls to one side so that they can rest for a few minutes. Blend the remaining ingredients in the tin to make a sauce. You can either stir them together with a spoon or use a handheld blender for a smoother consistency. Slice the pork rolls at an angle and pour the sauce over the slices. Serve along with the noodles and red cabbage.

> Italians are adamant about their 'sacred' recipes and spend hours discussing the right way to do this or that dish. Carbonara is among the classics of Roman cuisine, and in my family we would be scandalized if anyone wanted to use cream in it – as I believe most Romans would be. However, in the north of Italy some people have been known to breach this rule. The story is that carbonara was eaten by the Carbonari, the members of a secret political society in the early 19th Century in Italy, as a fast and filling meal. In fact it is an ideal last-minute meal decision.

Oliodivino
Pasta alla Carbonara

SERVES 4

1 onion, chopped
3 tbsp good quality olive oil
120g/4¼oz pancetta, cut into small strips
4 eggs
abundant Parmesan and Pecorino cheese, grated (about 60g/2¼oz of each)
400g/14oz pasta of your choice, I prefer rigatoni
½ tbsp chopped flat-leaf parsley
½ tsp chilli powder
sea salt

1 To begin with, put a large pan of water on a high heat – in the time it takes for the water to boil, the rest will be ready.

2 In a large frying pan (the pasta will be tossed in it at the end), gently fry the onion with 2 tablespoons of the olive oil and the pancetta until the onion just starts to brown and the pancetta is crisp. With a spoon, remove a little of the excess oil (mostly due to the pancetta fat) from the bottom of the pan and replace with the remaining olive oil. This will give a fresher flavour to your carbonara. Set aside.

3 Beat the eggs well in a large bowl and incorporate the grated cheeses. The mixture will become very creamy.

4 When the water comes to a rolling boil, stir in the pasta (the 'right' shape is rigatoni). Cover the pan until the water boils again, then leave uncovered. Stir occasionally so that the pasta doesn't stick together while cooking. As soon as the pasta has lost the white uncooked line in the middle it is 'al dente'. This will be about the time written on the pack but check it one minute before the end to make sure you agree with the recommended timing. I generally salt the water towards the end of the cooking time so that it coats the pasta rather than putting salt all through the pasta.

5 Just before the pasta is ready, put the frying pan with the onion and pancetta over a gentle heat. Drain the pasta and then, while still hot, mix it with the beaten egg and cheese mixture. Stir well, then pour the mixture into the frying pan and turn up the heat. Toss rapidly over the heat until cooked to your liking: ideally the egg should be cooked but creamy.

6 Sprinkle with chopped parsley and chilli powder. As with all hot pasta dishes, the carbonara now needs to be eaten immediately! Your guests should already be seated.

> The roots of this recipe lie in Tuscany in central Italy, a region well known for the contrasts of its food, which mirrors its beautiful landscape. Mountains on one side and seaside on the other make the region one of the most interesting culinary provinces of Italy. Pappardelle are a great match for this deep-flavoured game meat ragù, being just the right size to cope with the meatiness and richness of such a sauce.

The Fresh Pasta Company

Pappardelle with Wild Boar and Venison Ragù

SERVES 4–6

FOR THE PASTA
500g/1lb 2oz/4 cups '00' type
   flour, plus extra for rolling
5 eggs, at room temperature
1 tsp extra virgin olive oil
a pinch of salt

FOR THE RAGÙ
750ml/26fl oz/3 cups red wine
500g/1lb 2oz wild boar
   shoulder, cut into cubes
500g/1lb 2oz venison haunch,
   cut into cubes
2 garlic cloves, halved
2 carrots, peeled and finely
   chopped
2 celery stalks, finely chopped
1 onion, finely chopped
2 rosemary sprigs
2 sage sprigs
½ stick cinnamon
zest of ½ orange
3 tbsp olive oil
pinch of chopped red chilli
1 tbsp tomato purée
500ml/17fl oz/scant 2½ cups
   tomato passata
200g/7oz grated Pecorino or
   Parmesan cheese, to serve
sea salt and freshly ground
   black pepper

1 To make the pasta, put the flour in a mound on your work surface. Make a dip in the centre and add the eggs, olive oil and salt. Incorporate the flour into the eggs bit by bit, using your fingertips – this is always better than using a fork or spoon. Continue to bring the flour from the sides of the well into the eggs until you have incorporated it all. Knead the dough for 15 minutes, or until you achieve a smooth plasticine-like ball. The pasta dough is ready when you are left with a clean and dry work surface. While kneading, you might need to use extra flour to avoid the pasta sticking to your work surface, but remember that the flour absorption will depend on the type of flour used as well as on the ambient humidity. So if you have some flour left or indeed use a bit more than expected, do not worry.

2 The pasta can also be made using a food processor. If you do this, I recommend finishing the pasta by hand, as this is the best way to check if the pasta is ready.

3 Cover the dough and let it rest for at least 30 minutes. You can keep it for up to a day in the fridge. To turn the dough into pappardelle, roll it out on a floured surface with a rolling pin until translucent, then cut into thumb-wide strips. Alternatively, use a pasta machine to achieve a smooth, fine, elastic sheet of dough and then use the pappardelle cutter on your machine to cut the dough into the right shape.

4 To make the ragù you need to marinate the meat. Pour 500ml/17fl oz/2 cups of the wine into a pan and bring to a simmer. Cook the wine for no more than 10 minutes and leave to cool.

5   Place the meat in a bowl and pour over the cooled wine. Add
    1 garlic clove, half the carrot, celery and onion, 1 sprig of
    rosemary, 1 sprig of sage, the cinnamon stick and half the orange
    zest. Cover and leave to marinate in the fridge for at least 12 hours,
    and 24 hours if possible.

6   Remove the meat from the marinade and let it reach room
    temperature. Strain the marinade and reserve the liquid.

7   Heat the olive oil in a heavy wide-based saucepan and add the
    remaining carrot, celery and onion, the remaining herbs, garlic
    and orange zest and the chilli, stirring all the time to avoid
    colouring for about 5 minutes. Add the meat to the pan, making
    sure that it covers the base, and season with salt and black pepper.
    Cook for 5 minutes. Do not move the meat until seared. Stir the
    meat and vegetables and leave to cook for another 10 minutes.
    The meat will start to stick to the bottom of the pan – once you see
    this happening, it is time to add the reserved marinade and let it
    reduce completely. Add the tomato purée and cook for 2 minutes,
    stirring all the time, then add the passata with an equal amount
    of water and simmer for 1½ hours, adding more water if needed.
    Cook until you achieve a thick sauce and the meat is falling apart.

8   Bring a large pan of salted water to the boil. Add the pappardelle
    and cook for about 3 minutes until al dente, then drain, reserving
    250ml/9fl oz/1 cup of the cooking water.

9   Toss the pappardelle with the ragù. If the mixture looks too thick,
    add a bit of the cooking water. To serve, put some pasta on each
    plate and finish with grated Pecorino or Parmesan.

This recipe came from a good friend Keith Dalton and his wife, Encarna. The couple live in southern Spain, in the foothills of the Sierra Nevada. Keith used to help out at the Bath Pig, offering free advice, comment and the occasional family recipe. This one is based on a very traditional Spanish recipe of baked eggs and ham called Huevos a la Flamenca, and I have adapted it to use chorizo instead of ham, with delicious consequences.

Bath Pig
Chorizo with Vegetables and Baked Eggs

SERVES 4

500g/1lb 2oz ripe tomatoes
80ml/2½fl oz/⅓ cup olive oil
350g/12oz new potatoes,
    peeled and cut into cubes
1 red pepper, deseeded and
    cut into strips
1 red onion, chopped
150g/5½oz thin asparagus,
    trimmed
120g/4¼oz/scant 1 cup fresh
    or frozen peas
120g/4¼oz baby green beans,
    sliced
3 tablespoons tomato purée
15g/½oz butter, for greasing
4 free range eggs
1 chorizo, thinly sliced (use
    a good sharp knife)
2 tbsp chopped flat-leaf
    parsley
sea salt and freshly ground
    black pepper

1   Score the base of each tomato, place in a bowl of boiling water for 10 seconds, then remove with a slotted spoon and plunge into cold water. This will make it easier to remove the skins. Roughly chop the skinned tomatoes.

2   Heat the oil in a large heavy-based frying pan and fry the potatoes over a medium heat until golden brown. Remove and set aside. Reduce the heat, add the pepper and onion, and stir-fry until soft.

3   Preheat the oven to 180°C/350°F/Gas 4. Reserve 4 asparagus spears and add the rest to the pan with the peas, beans, tomatoes and tomato purée. Stir in 125ml/4fl oz/½ cup of water and season with salt and pepper. Return the potatoes to the pan, cover, and cook over a low heat for 10 minutes, stirring occasionally.

4   Grease a large ovenproof dish with the butter and put in the vegetable mixture. Make 4 deep, evenly spaced wells in the mixture and crack the eggs into the indentations, without breaking the yolks. Top with the reserved asparagus and the chorizo slices. Sprinkle with parsley and bake in the preheated oven for about 20 minutes, or until the egg whites are just set. Serve warm.

"Farming for me starts in the soil, if you have healthy soil, it creates healthy grass which in turn provides healthy food for your animals and ultimately yourself. Our animals feast on pastures with 31 different herbs, clovers and grasses, so they get a diverse diet – we should all think about what food the animals are given that we eat! We have various breeds of cows, sheep, pigs and chickens at Laverstoke, but my biggest love is the buffalo; we have some 2000 of them. Water buffaloes are the least developed bovines – they produce a rich, creamy milk and a finely textured meat very similar to beef. This Chilli con Carne is best when made 24 hours in advance and reheated very slowly. It freezes well, so why not make a double batch?"

Laverstoke Park Farm
Buffalo Chilli con Carne

SERVES 4

2 tbsp olive oil
1 large onion, finely diced
2 rashers of streaky bacon, smoked or green, roughly chopped
500g/1lb 2oz buffalo mince, or beef mince if you prefer
1 garlic clove, crushed
2 tbsp tomato purée
1 tsp chilli powder (or more, depending on how hot you like it)
145ml/4¾fl oz/scant ⅔ cup beef stock
400g/14oz canned chopped tomatoes
400g/14oz canned red kidney beans, drained and rinsed in boiling water
sea salt and freshly ground black pepper

1 Heat half the olive oil in a large heavy-based frying pan over a medium-high heat and sauté the onions, bacon and mince until the meat is well browned. Put the remaining olive oil into a separate, smaller pan and fry the garlic, tomato purée and chilli powder. Combine the contents of the two pans and fry together for 1 minute, stirring.

2 Add the beef stock and canned tomatoes and stir thoroughly. Add salt and pepper to taste, then cover the pan and cook on a low heat for 1 hour.

3 Add the kidney beans, stir, cover and cook gently for another 30 minutes. Turn off the heat and either serve immediately or cover the pan and leave to cool. Once cooled, put into the fridge and leave overnight.

4 Two hours before you want to eat the chilli, remove it from the fridge and gently reheat it in a pan over a very low heat over the next 2 hours. If it is too thick, add a little boiling water.

At Le Manoir aux Quat' Saisons we grow as much of our own vegetables, salad leaves and fruit as we can, and we try hard to source as much of our produce locally as possible. As our name states, we are totally seasonal in our menus, and we take our ethical responsibilities seriously – we know our suppliers, and we know how they grow and raise the food we buy from them.

Raymond Blanc

As a child my family was not well off, but even in post-war France we ate beautifully, because we were completely connected to our bit of earth. Maman Blanc's vegetable garden provided a constant supply of fresh green vegetables, tomatoes and salad things in their seasons, and preserved vegetables in the cold months. Neighbouring farms supplied wonderful big chickens, we kept our own rabbits, and there were brown trout in the nearby streams. Like all red meat, beef was

more of a treat. It had to be bought from the butcher, but it was honest, grass-fed beef that had never been near a feedlot. Saturday lunch was always beefsteak with chips made from our own potatoes and vegetables from the garden.

My home town was only 30 miles from Burgundy and my recipe for Braised Beef in Red Wine with Jabugo Ham is really a refinement of the classic boeuf bourguignon. Now that you can buy ox cheek at some supermarkets, you can make this dish using this wonderful moist cut,

❝ *I try hard to reconnect what I put on my guests' tables with the land.* ❞

or indeed other economical cuts such as shin or blade. Blade of beef has an excellent flavour and there is no waste.

This hearty dish will do very well with a wonderful robust red wine, such as a shiraz, pinot noir or cabernet sauvignon, rather than a red burgundy. Real burgundy is far too expensive for this dish, and the flavour is actually improved by using a more full-bodied red. In any case, the real trick is to boil the wine for five minutes to evaporate the alcohol before marinating the beef in it. On the other hand, to accompany this dish, any great quality red burgundy will celebrate this dish very well.

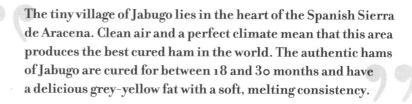

> The tiny village of Jabugo lies in the heart of the Spanish Sierra de Aracena. Clean air and a perfect climate mean that this area produces the best cured ham in the world. The authentic hams of Jabugo are cured for between 18 and 30 months and have a delicious grey-yellow fat with a soft, melting consistency.

Raymond Blanc & Le Manoir aux Quat' Saisons
Braised Beef in Red Wine with Jabugo Ham

SERVES 4

1.2kg/2lb 10oz ox cheek, shin
  or blade, trimmed of sinew,
  cut into 2cm/¾in steaks
2 tbsp plain flour
2 tbsp clarified butter
300ml/10½fl oz/1 cup plus
  3 tbsp water
sea salt and freshly ground
  black pepper

FOR THE MARINADE
750ml/26fl oz/3 cups full bodied
  red wine, such as Shiraz or
  Cabernet Sauvignon
2 carrots, cut into 2cm/¾in slices
1 celery stick, cut into 1cm/½in
  slices
2 baby onions, quartered,
  root left on
6 garlic cloves
8 whole peppercorns,
1 bouquet garni (a few parsley
  stalks, 4 bay leaves, 6 sprigs
  of thyme, tied together)

FOR THE GARNISH
1 tbsp unsalted butter
320g/11¼ oz button mushrooms,
  wiped and trimmed
100g/3½oz Jabugo ham,
  finely sliced
1 tbsp chopped flat-leaf parsley

1 To make the marinade, first boil the red wine in a saucepan for 5 minutes to remove the alcohol. Then allow to cool. Pour into a large dish containing the carrots, celery, baby onions, garlic, peppercorns and bouquet garni. Add the beef and cover with clingfilm. Put in the fridge and leave to marinate for 24 hours.

2 Put the beef mixture in a colander over a bowl to drain. Leave for at least 1 hour. Separate the beef, vegetables and herbs and pat dry with kitchen paper. Reserve the marinade.

3 Preheat the oven to 200°C/400°F/Gas 6. Spread the flour on a baking tray and cook in the oven for 8–10 minutes, until pale brown. Reduce the oven temperature to 110°C/225°F/Gas ½.

4 Season the beef with 4 pinches of salt. Heat the clarified butter in a heavy-based casserole on a high heat, and colour the beef in it for 5–7 minutes. Transfer the beef to a plate. Add the vegetables and herbs to the casserole. Lower the heat to medium high and cook for 5 minutes until lightly coloured.

5 Spoon out the fat; add the toasted flour to the casserole and stir for a few seconds. Then add the wine from the marinade little by little, whisking constantly to incorporate it into the flour. The sauce should be smooth and thick enough to coat the back of a spoon. Add the beef pieces, bring the sauce to the boil and skim. Cover and cook in the preheated oven for 3 hours, adding water if the meat seems to be drying out.

6 Place a colander over a large saucepan and drain the beef and vegetables through it. Put the saucepan on the heat and boil until the sauce has reduced by half. Taste the sauce and adjust the seasoning. Put the beef pieces back into the sauce.

7 Over a high heat in a non-stick frying pan, heat the butter and cook the mushrooms until lightly caramelized. Season with salt and pepper. Mix the Jabugo ham and mushrooms into the beef, sprinkle with the parsley and serve piping hot.

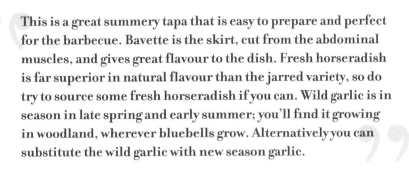

This is a great summery tapa that is easy to prepare and perfect for the barbecue. Bavette is the skirt, cut from the abdominal muscles, and gives great flavour to the dish. Fresh horseradish is far superior in natural flavour than the jarred variety, so do try to source some fresh horseradish if you can. Wild garlic is in season in late spring and early summer; you'll find it growing in woodland, wherever bluebells grow. Alternatively you can substitute the wild garlic with new season garlic.

Ben Tish & Salt Yard

Grilled Beef Bavette with Crispy Artichokes, Shallots and Horseradish

SERVES 4 (as a tapa)

6 baby artichokes
2 tbsp wholemeal flour, for dusting
125ml/4fl oz/½ cup olive oil, for frying
300g/10½oz beef bavette (skirt)
2 handfuls baby red chard
6 leaves of wild garlic, cut into strips
3 shallots, finely sliced
5cm/2in piece of fresh horseradish, peeled
sea salt and freshly ground black pepper

FOR THE VINAIGRETTE

5 tsp sugar
100ml/3½fl oz/scant ½ cup Pedro Ximénez vinegar
200ml/7fl oz/scant 1 cup extra virgin olive oil

FOR THE POACHING LIQUOR

200ml/7fl oz/scant 1 cup water
200ml/7fl oz/scant 1 cup white wine
200ml/7fl oz/scant 1 cup white wine vinegar or cider
150ml/5fl oz/scant ⅔ cup olive oil
2 lemons, halved and lightly squeezed

1 Put the poaching liquor ingredients into a large pan.

2 Now prepare your artichokes. Remove and discard the outer leaves until you reach the white leaves in the centre. Using a vegetable peeler, remove the hard, woody skin on the stem. Trim the top off the leaves. As each artichoke is done, put it into the pan of cold poaching liquor.

3 Place the pan on a medium-high heat and bring to a simmer. Cook until the artichokes are al dente, about 10 minutes. Remove from the liquor and leave to cool.

4 Cut the artichokes into quarters and dust them with the wholemeal flour. Heat the olive oil in a heavy-based frying pan over a medium-high heat, add the artichokes, and fry until golden brown.

5 To make the vinaigrette, put the sugar and a pinch of salt and vinegar in a small pan over a medium-high heat and boil vigorously until reduced by half. Whisk in the olive oil.

6 Preheat the grill until smoking hot. Grill the beef for 3 minutes on each side until medium rare. Be careful of overcooking it, as bavette can get quite tough if overcooked. Leave to rest for 3 minutes.

7 Slice the beef thinly, and top with a salad consisting of the baby artichokes, red chard, garlic leaves and shallots, dressed in the Pedro Ximénez vinaigrette.

8 Finely grate some horseradish over the top and sprinkle with sea salt to serve.

An Italianish recipe, but using liver from British veal calves – usually called rose or rosé veal. Unlike traditional veal, the animals are raised to high welfare standards in social groups, with proper bedding and a diet that includes a higher proportion of fibrous food.

Lucas Hollweg

Rose Calf's Liver with Marsala and Sage

SERVES 4

500g/1lb 2oz rose calf's
  liver, trimmed
2 tbsp butter
2 tbsp olive oil
150ml/5fl oz/scant ⅔ cup
  marsala
2 tbsp red wine vinegar
250ml/8fl oz/1 cup chicken
  stock
6 fresh sage leaves, finely
  shredded
4 tbsp double cream or
  crème fraîche
salt and freshly ground
  black pepper
mashed potato, to serve

1 If the liver is unsliced, cut it horizontally using a sharp knife – each slice should be about 5mm/¼in thick. You may also need to cut the pieces in half lengthways.

2 Heat the butter and oil in a large heavy-based frying pan over a medium heat. When they start to bubble, add the liver in two batches and cook for about 1–1½ minutes each side – it should feel just firm to the touch. Don't be tempted to cook it longer or it will toughen. Season with salt and pepper and remove to a plate and keep warm.

3 Turn up the heat and pour the marsala into the pan. Using a spatula, scrape up any savoury bits stuck to the bottom and bubble for a couple of minutes or so until the liquid has reduced by half.

4 Add the vinegar and bubble for a minute or so, then pour in the chicken stock and cook until things start to thicken.

5 Remove the pan from the heat, then add the sage and cream or crème fraîche and stir until mixed. Return the pan to a gentle heat and warm through.

6 Divide the liver between four plates and pour over the sauce. Mash would be my preference to serve on the side.

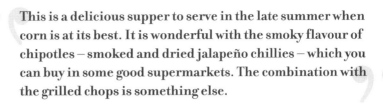

This is a delicious supper to serve in the late summer when corn is at its best. It is wonderful with the smoky flavour of chipotles – smoked and dried jalapeño chillies – which you can buy in some good supermarkets. The combination with the grilled chops is something else.

Thomasina Miers & Wahaca

Rose Veal Chops with Smoky Corn Salad

SERVES 4

4 rose veal chops
juice of 1 lemon
3½ tbsp olive oil
5 sprigs of oregano or
    marjoram
25g/1oz butter
225g/8oz baby spinach leaves
4 tbsp crème fraîche, to serve
grated Parmesan cheese,
    to serve
sea salt and freshly ground
    black pepper

FOR THE CORN SALAD
4 corn on the cob
1 tbsp olive oil
25g/1oz butter
1 onion, finely chopped
1 tsp chipotles en adobo or
    2 red chillies, deseeded
    and finely chopped
2 garlic cloves, chopped
2 big pinches allspice
a handful of chopped
    coriander leaves
a handful of chopped
    mint leaves
juice of 1–2 limes

1   Take the chops out of the fridge at least 30 minutes before you are ready to cook so that they can reach room temperature. Place the veal chops in a dish with the lemon juice, 2 tablespoons of the olive oil, the oregano or marjoram and plenty of salt and pepper. Set aside to marinate.

2   To make the corn salad, sit the cobs up in a bowl and scrape a knife down along the cob at a 45 degree angle to shave off the kernels into the bowl.

3   Heat the oil and butter in a frying pan over a medium heat and when it is gently sizzling add the onion, corn and chipotles. Cook for at least 5 minutes, or until the onion has turned translucent without colouring, then add the garlic and allspice and season with salt and pepper. Turn up the heat to high and cook for another 5–10 minutes until the corn starts to take on some colour and caramelize.

4   Pour over the lime juice and keep warm until the chops are ready.

5   Heat a large, heavy frying pan or a griddle pan over a high heat until it is smoking hot and season the veal generously on both sides with salt and pepper. Add the butter and 1 tablespoon of the olive oil to the pan and cook the steaks for 4–5 minutes each side (depending on their thickness and how you like them cooked) and then leave to rest in a warm place for 10 minutes.

6   Warm the spinach leaves in a saucepan with the remaining olive oil, salt and pepper for a minute until slightly wilted. Stir into the corn salad mix with the chopped coriander and mint. Put on plates and top with the veal chops, a scoop of crème fraîche and a sprinkling of the Parmesan cheese.

> *This is a tasty barbecue option, mixing a few different influences, and is fantastic served with a grilled vegetable couscous salad and followed by a sweet mint tea to aid digestion. It is best cooked on a barbecue grill as skewers, although it can just as easily, and satisfactorily, be made into burger-style patties.*

Fabio Diu & Real Food Festival

Grilled Aubergine, Caramelized Onion and Lamb Shish Kebab

SERVES 4

450g/1lb lamb mince
1 egg, beaten
1 onion, very finely chopped
2 garlic cloves, very finely
    chopped
1 red chilli, deseeded and
    finely chopped
1 tsp ground cumin
1 tsp garam masala
1 tbsp tomato purée or
    sweet chilli sauce
1 tbsp Worcestershire sauce
1 tsp sea salt
1 tbsp olive oil

FOR THE WRAP FILLING
125ml/4fl oz/½ cup olive oil
2 large onions, sliced
1 tsp brown sugar
1 tsp sea salt
1 tbsp garam masala
1 large aubergine, thickly
    sliced into discs
4 pitta breads (preferably
    large round ones)
4 tomatoes, thickly sliced
a few sprigs of flat-leaf parsley

1 Heat the barbecue grill to hot. Mix together the lamb and egg, then add the onion and garlic, chilli, spices, tomato purée and Worcestershire sauce. Season with a little salt. Blend together thoroughly using your hands.

2 Lightly wet your hands, then take a handful of the mixture and wrap it round skewers, rotating and pressing it into even sausage shapes. You will need 8 skewers. If you're using wooden skewers, soak them in water first. Brush the lamb with olive oil and place over the hot grill until nicely browned, turning them occasionally.

3 To make the wrap filling, heat about half the olive oil in a heavy-based frying pan over a moderate heat, add the onions, sugar, salt and garam masala. Leave to caramelize on a low heat for a good 20 minutes, until the onions are translucent and soft.

4 Brush the aubergine discs with the remaining olive oil and salt. Grill (on the barbecue, if using) until lightly browned and soft to the touch all the way through. Cut the tomatoes into 1cm/½in slices.

5 Place the pitta breads on the grill for literally just a few moments, to heat and lightly toast them. Remove the kebabs from the skewers. Open up pitta breads and insert a couple of slices of tomato, followed by a couple of sprigs of parsley, a slice of grilled aubergine, a dollop of caramelized onion and finally the kebab. Wrap it all up and enjoy!

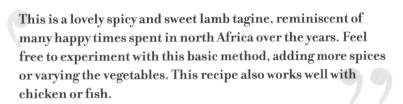

This is a lovely spicy and sweet lamb tagine, reminiscent of many happy times spent in north Africa over the years. Feel free to experiment with this basic method, adding more spices or varying the vegetables. This recipe also works well with chicken or fish.

Valentina Harris
Lamb Tagine

SERVES 4

55g/2oz/ ¹/₃ cup dried
 apricots, halved
2 tbsp olive oil
500g/1lb 2oz diced leg of lamb
1 onion, finely chopped
1 garlic clove, thinly sliced
¹/₂ tsp ground cumin
¹/₂ tsp ground coriander
¹/₂ tsp ground cinnamon
200g/7oz canned tomatoes
300ml/10¹/₂fl oz/1¹/₄ cup
 lamb stock
small pinch of saffron threads
2 tbsp ground almonds
2 large courgettes, cut into
 large pieces
200g/7oz butternut squash or
 pumpkin, peeled and diced
2 tomatoes, skinned and
 quartered
1 tsp harissa
2 tbsp chopped flat-leaf
 parsley leaves
sea salt and freshly ground
 black pepper
steamed couscous, to serve

1 Place the apricots in a small bowl and just cover them with boiling water. Leave to soak for an hour. Preheat the oven to 180°C/350°F/Gas 4.

2 Heat the olive oil in a flameproof casserole and brown the lamb in batches all over, then lift out with a slotted spoon and set aside.

3 Add the chopped onion to the casserole and cook gently for 10 minutes until soft and golden. Add the garlic and spices and cook them for a further 2 minutes, then return the lamb to the casserole.

4 Add the apricots and their soaking liquid, the canned tomatoes and the stock. Stir in the saffron and ground almonds and season with sea salt.

5 Heat to simmering point, then cover the casserole and cook in the oven for 1 hour. Add the courgettes, squash, tomatoes and harissa, with a little extra water if necessary. Put the lid back on and return the casserole to the oven for a further 30 minutes.

6 Season with salt and pepper, adding extra harissa if desired, then stir in the parsley and serve with steamed couscous.

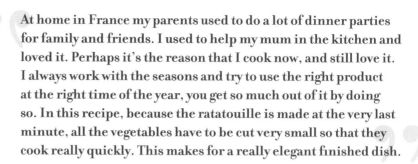

"At home in France my parents used to do a lot of dinner parties for family and friends. I used to help my mum in the kitchen and loved it. Perhaps it's the reason that I cook now, and still love it. I always work with the seasons and try to use the right product at the right time of the year, you get so much out of it by doing so. In this recipe, because the ratatouille is made at the very last minute, all the vegetables have to be cut very small so that they cook really quickly. This makes for a really elegant finished dish."

Daniel Galmiche & The Vineyard
Cannon of Liquorice Lamb, Ratatouille and Fondant Potatoes

SERVES 4

4 sticks of fresh liquorice root
1 red pepper
1 yellow pepper
4 plum tomatoes
2 courgettes
1 aubergine
4 x 115g/4oz loin of spring lamb
2 garlic cloves
small bunch of parsley
sprig of thyme
3 tbsp olive oil
25g/1oz butter

FOR THE FONDANT POTATOES
12 small Ratte potatoes, peeled
150g/5½oz clarified butter

1   Take the liquorice and cover it with warm water to soften, this may take up to 20 minutes. Once soft, peel it and cut the roots into 4 or 5 strips, then set aside. Discard the water.

2   Blanch the peppers in a pan of boiling water for 1 minute, then peel off the skin. Blanch and skin the tomatoes in the same way, then cut them into segments and remove the seeds. Cut the peppers, tomatoes, courgettes and aubergine into very thin strips, then turn them sideways and cut again, producing tiny cubes that are 1–3mm/about ⅛in or less per side. Remove the kernel from the centre of the garlic cloves.

3   Using the tip of a sharp knife, pierce the lamb here and there and push the liquorice strips into the meat. Wrap in clingfilm to keep the shape and put in the fridge for about 30 minutes.

4   Meanwhile, using a sharp knife, shape the potatoes into neat ovals, like miniature rugby balls. Gently heat the clarified butter in a pan. Put the potatoes into the clarified butter and cook, basting frequently, until golden all round, making sure they are not overcooked – this should take about 20 minutes.

5   Preheat the oven to 220°C/425°F/Gas 7. While the potatoes are cooking, heat 1 tablespoon olive oil and the butter in a large ovenproof frying pan over a medium-high heat. Add the lamb to the hot pan, turning to seal the meat on all sides. Transfer to the preheated oven for 8–10 minutes. Remove from the oven, and rest until required.

6   Cook the ratatouille in a pan with the remaining olive oil; first the pepper, then the courgette, aubergine and finally the tomato, herbs and garlic. Cook for 5 minutes until al dente.

7   Flash the lamb into the oven for a couple of minutes and serve it with the ratatouille and potatoes. Bon appétit!

VEGETARIAN

Onion Tart

Runner Bean and Watercress Quiche

Celeriac and Chestnut Pie

Omelette with Comté

Fennel Gratin with Beetroot, Bitter Leaves and
    Walnut Salad

Fresh Egg Tagliolini with Summer Vegetables

Mushroom and Basil Tart

Arancini and Special Salad

Pear, Parmesan and Rocket Risotto

Risotto of Summer Truffles

Lemon, Pea and Mint Risotto

Simple Curry

Masala Bhaat

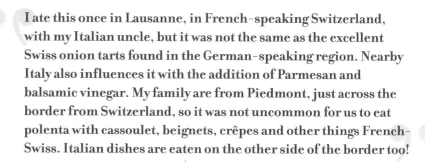

> I ate this once in Lausanne, in French-speaking Switzerland, with my Italian uncle, but it was not the same as the excellent Swiss onion tarts found in the German-speaking region. Nearby Italy also influences it with the addition of Parmesan and balsamic vinegar. My family are from Piedmont, just across the border from Switzerland, so it was not uncommon for us to eat polenta with cassoulet, beignets, crêpes and other things French-Swiss. Italian dishes are eaten on the other side of the border too!

Franchi Seeds (1783)

Onion Tart

SERVES 4–6

15g/½oz butter, plus extra for greasing
250g/9oz ready-made shortcrust pastry
flour, for rolling
300g/10½oz onions, finely sliced
2 tbsp balsamic vinegar
2 large eggs
150ml/5fl oz/scant ⅔ cup single cream, plus a little extra just in case
80g/2¾oz Swiss Gruyère cheese or Cheddar, grated
3 tbsp freshly grated Parmesan cheese
pinch of celery salt
sea salt and freshly ground black pepper

1 Preheat the oven to 170°C/325°F/Gas 3. Butter a 23cm/9in flan case. Roll out the pastry on a lightly floured surface until it fits the case, cutting off any extra bits and using them to plug any gaps. Remember that pastry shrinks a bit when cooked, so trim it to leave about 2mm/¹⁄₁₆in of pastry above the edge of the flan case.

2 Put a sheet of greaseproof paper on top of the pastry and fill with baking beans. I didn't have any the first time I made this dish so I used dried peas – they did the trick! Put the flan case into the oven and bake for 12 minutes.

3 In the meantime, cook the onions in a pan with the butter for 5 minutes over a medium to low heat. Add the balsamic vinegar and turn the heat to low. Beat the eggs in a bowl and stir in the cream, Gruyère and 2 tablespoons of the Parmesan. (If you don't have any Gruyère you can use Cheddar cheese, which is an excellent cheese for cooking and superb for this dish.) Season with salt and pepper.

4 Remove the tart from the oven and turn the temperature up to 200°C/400°F/Gas 6 if you are going to cook the tart straight away. Alternatively, you can put it into the fridge and cook it later. Take out the greaseproof paper and baking beans, then put in the onions and spread them out evenly. Sprinkle with celery salt and pour over the egg and cream mixture. If you don't have enough liquid, don't add another egg but do add some more cream – your dish might be a little bigger or deeper, for example. If you add another egg it will just be eggy, though still nice to eat of course.

5 Sprinkle the top with the remaining Parmesan, or use some good mountain cheese like Fontina, Toma or Gruyère, as this is a mountain dish. Put it into the oven for 25–30 minutes until golden. Once cooked, you can serve it hot or cold – it makes a nice picnic dish.

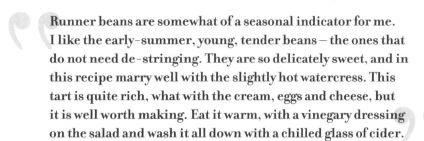

Runner beans are somewhat of a seasonal indicator for me. I like the early-summer, young, tender beans – the ones that do not need de-stringing. They are so delicately sweet, and in this recipe marry well with the slightly hot watercress. This tart is quite rich, what with the cream, eggs and cheese, but it is well worth making. Eat it warm, with a vinegary dressing on the salad and wash it all down with a chilled glass of cider.

Arthur Potts Dawson & The People's Supermarket

Runner Bean and Watercress Quiche

SERVES 4–6

butter, for greasing
½ tbsp flour, for dusting and rolling
350g/12oz shortcrust pastry, homemade or bought
450g/1lb runner beans
2 large eggs
5 tbsp cream
5 tbsp milk
200g/7oz Cheddar cheese, grated
1 bunch of watercress, leaves picked
sea salt and freshly ground black pepper

1   Preheat the oven to 200°C/400°F/Gas 6. Grease a 26cm/10½in flan dish and dust it with flour. Roll out the shortcrust pastry on a lightly floured surface and line the flan dish with it. Place it in the refrigerator and chill for 30 minutes.

2   Slice the runner beans into strips, discarding the stringy bits. Boil for 5 minutes in a pan of boiling salted water, drain and put aside.

3   Take the flan dish out of the refrigerator and line the pastry with greaseproof paper. Fill with dried beans to prevent the pastry from rising, and bake in the oven for 15 minutes. Take the flan dish out of the oven and turn the oven temperature down to 150°C/300°F/Gas 2.

4   Mix together the eggs, cream, milk and three quarters of the grated cheese, seasoning with salt and pepper. Place the runner beans and watercress in the pastry case and pour the egg mixture over, then sprinkle the rest of the cheese on top.

5   Bake in the middle of the oven for 40 minutes until well risen and golden brown. Serve with a side salad.

This recipe is based on one that Joyce Molyneux used to cook as a vegetarian main course at the Carved Angel in Dartmouth when I was lucky enough to work there. It has developed over the years by the increasing addition of celeriac when celery was not around. Every year when I go home to Sunderland for Christmas, I make this for the turkey stuffing but with a little sausage meat added and extra booze so as not to be too virtuous. The dish is lifted when served as a veggie main with Cumberland sauce on the side.

Jane Baxter & Riverford Organic
Celeriac and Chestnut Pie

SERVES 6–8

1 tbsp groundnut oil
1 small onion, chopped
1 celery stick, chopped
½ celeriac, peeled and cut
    into very small cubes
1 garlic clove, chopped
175g/6oz/1¼ cups peeled
    chestnuts
2–3 tbsp chopped walnuts
2–3 tbsp chopped cashew
    nuts or brazils or almonds
1 egg, plus extra beaten egg,
    for brushing
½ tsp thyme
½ tsp marjoram
1 tbsp brandy
zest of ½ orange, finely grated,
    about ½ teaspoon
pinch of salt
¼ tsp cayenne pepper
350g/12oz ready-made
    shortcrust pastry
flour, for rolling
2 tsp olive or rapeseed oil,
    for greasing
good quality Cumberland
    sauce, to serve

1 Heat the oil in a frying pan over a medium to low heat, then sweat the onion, celery, celeriac and garlic for 5–10 minutes until soft. Remove from the heat and add the chestnuts, walnuts and cashews. Mix in the egg, herbs, brandy, orange zest, salt and cayenne pepper.

2 Roll out the pastry on a lightly floured surface to form a large oblong, 5mm/¼in thickness. Lift carefully onto a greased baking sheet. Trim to even up the edges. Pile the filling down the centre of the oblong and then brush the edges of the pastry with beaten egg and bring them together over the filling, to enclose completely. Pinch the edges of the pastry to seal firmly. Trim off any excess and use the trimmings to decorate, if you like.

3 Cover loosely with clingfilm and transfer the pie to the fridge for 30 minutes. Meanwhile, heat the oven to 220°C/425°F/Gas 7. Remove the pie from the fridge, brush with beaten egg and bake in the preheated oven for 10 minutes. Reduce the heat to 160°C/300°F/Gas 2 and cook for a further 20 minutes.

4 Serve hot, sliced thickly, with Cumberland sauce.

> The real secret of a great omelette is not just the eggs, nor the size of the pan, but actually the butter. The famous Omelette de la Mère Poulard from Normandy boasts whisking the yolks and whites separately and adding crème fraîche to the yolks as you cook them, prior to adding the whisked whites. But it is the copious amounts of the famous Normandy unsalted butter that really brings it all together. The butter of Jean-Yves Bordier is still hand-formed with traditional wooden paddles in his St Malo production unit, and the richness, together with the flavour, is really special. Making an omelette is an art, and one to be taken seriously.

Patricia Michelson & La Fromagerie
Omelette with Comté

SERVES 1 (as a main course)

3 large, very fresh, free-range organic eggs
2–3 lumps, or at least 85g/3oz, Brittany or Normandy unsalted butter
1 tbsp double crème fraîche
handful, or at least 115g/4oz, grated aged Comté cheese
2 tsp finely chopped soft herbs, such as chervil, chives, thyme or flat-leaf parsley
coarse sea salt and freshly ground white pepper

1 Whisk up the eggs using a balloon whisk and preferably a copper bowl – this is really worth investing in. Add the salt by grinding it between your forefinger and thumb – 2 or 3 good pinches should do it.

2 Heat a 20cm/8in non-stick omelette pan, and when hot but not searing, add the butter in pieces and let it melt. When it is foaming but not turning brown, add the eggs. Swirl around the pan to evenly distribute, then with your spatula gently ease the edges to release the loose egg mixture in the middle so that it can travel to the sides.

3 When still soft and runny, add the crème fraîche and the cheese and pat down. When the cheese is starting to melt with the eggs, add the herbs and a little white pepper. As soon as you can, before the egg becomes set, use your spatula to flip or fold the omelette in half.

4 Slide the omelette onto a plate and serve immediately.

This fantastically simple but utterly delicious meal is a wonderful healthy autumn supper, with the bitter, crispy salad balancing out the cream. At The Duke of Cambridge we only use field-grown, local, seasonal vegetables, so being able to substitute ingredients is essential. Getting what we want is not always possible – as with real life! So, swap the fennel with Jerusalem artichoke, or make it simply with potato. Bitter leaves come in so many varieties; chicory bulb or leaves will work best, but play around with what seasonal field-grown vegetables you can find. Young spinach would be scrumptious, for example.

Geetie Singh & Sara Berg & The Duke of Cambridge Organic Pub

Fennel Gratin with Beetroot, Bitter Leaves and Walnut Salad

SERVES 4

2 fennel bulbs, washed and trimmed
2 large potatoes, scrubbed
100g/3½oz crème fraîche
150ml/5fl oz/scant ⅔ cup double cream
juice of ½ lemon
100g/3½oz salty ewe's or goat's cheese
50g/1¾oz breadcrumbs
50g/1¾oz butter, plus extra for greasing
sea salt and freshly ground black pepper

FOR THE SALAD

1 large beetroot, peeled
a handful flat-leaf parsley
100g/3½oz bitter leaves or 2 heads of chicory, washed
2 to 3 tbsp freshly shelled walnuts
1½ tbsp walnut oil
1½ tbsp olive oil
3 tbsp balsamic vinegar

1 Preheat the oven 200°C/400°F/Gas 6. Slice the fennel and potatoes into 5mm/¼in slices. Butter a 20 x 10cm/8 x 4in oven dish. Layer the fennel and potatoes in the dish, seasoning with salt and pepper between each layer.

2 Mix together the crème fraîche, cream, lemon juice, half the cheese and spread out on top of the fennel and potatoes.

3 Sprinkle over the remaining cheese and the breadcrumbs. Dot the butter evenly on top.

4 Place in the preheated oven for about 40 minutes. Test that it's ready by inserting a fork in the centre. It should sink into the gratin with a tiny bit of resistance.

5 While this is cooking, make the salad. Finely slice the beetroot, preferably with a mandolin and put it in a salad bowl.

6 Pick the leaves off the parsley and add them, with the bitter leaves and walnuts, to the salad bowl.

7 Gently whisk together the walnut oil, olive oil and balsamic vinegar, and season with salt and pepper. Pour over the salad and toss. Serve with the piping hot gratin.

There's so much talk today about seasonality — I never used to bother about any of this! In Italy, we only ever used to eat what was in season and easily available. Whatever was in season, if it was good, just went on the menu. It was as simple as that, and that is how it should always be!

Giorgio Locatelli

I grew up in my village in Italy, in the family restaurant. My first steps, in terms of my career, involved daily contact with the various producers who supplied the restaurant — the fishermen, the fruit farmers, the rice grower — everybody was part of the family, and thus part of the whole process of creating the menu and then cooking it. We were just the last step

in a long line of production. But this all felt completely natural, it was and should be the most normal way to create a menu. It was only later, when I went on to work in Switzerland and later landed in London that I realized there were middle men involved, and that there were prices to be negotiated and so on.

At home, I had always felt completely involved in the process — for example it was my job to wash out the box that the fish was always delivered in, just so that it would be clean and ready to use again when the fisherman came to deliver again the next day. The whole basis of Italian cuisine is about linking the production of the food, and the producer, to the food on the plate. The Real Food Festival helps to create the same sort of links for all those who attend the festival, even just for one day. I know it is really hard for some people to avoid shopping in the supermarkets, because that is what they can afford, but I believe that just by going along to the Real Food Festival for one day could help consumers make better choices, even in their local supermarket.

In Italy, everybody you talk to believes absolutely that what he or she produces, grows or makes is the very best there is. I believe it is

« I like to be able to put a face to the names of the people supplying my food. »

really important that producers in this country should develop that same sort of pride, and get properly recognized for their excellence — the Real Food Festival helps to promote that kind of pride, it inspires people to try new tastes and gives the producers a voice.

I do like to source my food locally, it makes me feel better, as though I am connected to the whole process rather than being a part of a system that is exploiting nature. People come to my restaurant for my Italian food of course, and yet I source 90 per cent of my ingredients here in the UK. I cheat a little bit, in so far as I bring my seeds for my rocket over from Italy, for example, and then I get somebody to grow it for me over here, but by and large I am proud to use the best local produce for the best of Italian cuisine, which is a style of cooking that is always adaptable.

One of my most popular dishes currently on my menu at La Locanda is a Saffron Aspretto with Scallops — for me this is a perfect example of a great combination of ingredients — King Scallops with a slightly sour, very Italian dressing. We only ever have Queenie Scallops in Italy, so these big, juicy, meaty scallops are very special for us Italians, and not what we are used to! But what is interesting to me is that practically every single Italian customer who comes to the restaurant orders this dish, even though the basic ingredient is so very British — so does this make my dish really, truly Italian? Or isn't this just about using local produce and treating it with due care and respect?

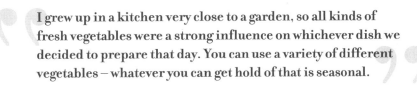

I grew up in a kitchen very close to a garden, so all kinds of fresh vegetables were a strong influence on whichever dish we decided to prepare that day. You can use a variety of different vegetables – whatever you can get hold of that is seasonal.

Giorgio Locatelli & Locanda Locatelli

Fresh Egg Tagliolini with Summer Vegetables

SERVES 4

FOR THE PASTA
500g/1lb 2oz/4 cups '00' flour,
    plus extra for drying the pasta
a pinch of sea salt
3 large eggs
2 large egg yolks
2 tsp olive oil

FOR THE VEGETABLES
2 courgettes
2 carrots, peeled
5 asparagus spears
3 tomatoes
a handful of fresh peas
a handful of young broad beans
4 tbsp extra virgin olive oil
2 garlic cloves, finely chopped
1 spring onion, thinly sliced
6 tbsp white wine
10 sugar snap peas, sliced
    thinly on the bias
4 courgette flowers
3 tbsp finely chopped flat-leaf
    parsley
3 tbsp grated Parmesan cheese
sea salt

1 Sieve the flour onto a clean work surface and make a well in the centre with your fist. Sprinkle the salt into the well, then crack in the eggs and add the egg yolks and olive oil. Break the yolks with the fingertips of one hand, and then move your fingers in a circular motion, gradually incorporating the flour, until you have worked in enough to start bringing it together in a ball. Knead the dough for 10 minutes, then divide it into 2 balls, cover with clingfilm, and leave to rest for 1 hour before use.

2 Roll the dough in a pasta machine until smooth then, using the tagliolini cutter, put the flattened dough through the machine. Spread the pasta out on a floured surface to dry.

3 Cut the outer green layer of the courgettes into strips the same width and thickness as the tagliolini. Cut the carrots and asparagus into similar size strips. Put the strips in a colander, season with salt and leave for 15 minutes until soft.

4 Bring a large saucepan of salted water to the boil. Blanch the tomatoes for 1 minute, then skin, quarter, deseed and cut them into wedges. Blanch the shelled peas for 2 minutes, then refresh in cold water. Do the same with the broad beans. Keep the water boiling, as you will use it for the pasta.

5 Heat the oil in a large, heavy-based frying pan over a medium heat. Add the garlic and spring onion and fry for 2 minutes until soft. Turn up the heat to high and add the vegetable strips. Pour in the wine and add the sugar snap peas, blanched tomatoes, peas and broad beans. Cook for a further 2 minutes, then set aside.

6 Add the tagliolini to the boiling water and cook for 2 minutes until just tender. Drain, reserving a little of the cooking water. Tip the pasta into the sauce. Add the courgette flowers, parsley and Parmesan and pour in a little of the reserved cooking water. Cook for 1–2 minutes, stirring continuously, then serve.

As the official UK Pesto Pioneers, we truly love basil, the one herb that should always be used fresh. This is a recipe that uses wild mushrooms that, in the spirit of Real Food you may well have foraged for yourself, or you could possibly use a jar of wild mushrooms preserved in olive oil (known in Italy as *Funghi sott'olio*) that you might have in your storecupboard. Either way, it is a simple tart that takes only minutes to put together, tastes heaps better than many of the ready-made varieties that are available and has an unmistakable Italian twist. Real food is about homemade food, (even if you do cheat a little by buying the ready-made puff pastry), however simple and easy the recipe might be. This is a lovely homemade treat to serve as a starter, a quick lunch or supper dish, or as an impromptu snack.

Sacla'

Mushroom and Basil Tart

SERVES 4

375g/13oz packet of ready
    rolled puff pastry
1 tbsp of Dijon mustard
300g/10½oz wild mushrooms
    (fresh or preserved, drained
    of oil)
3 large ripe vine tomatoes,
    sliced
a handful of fresh basil leaves,
    torn
75g/2½oz Gorgonzola cheese,
    thinly sliced
sea salt and freshly ground
    black pepper

1   Preheat the 'oven' to 190°C/375°F/Gas 5. Unroll your pastry onto a large baking sheet and score a border 1cm/½in from the edge.

2   Simply spread the mustard up to the border of the pastry and arrange the mushrooms, tomatoes and basil artfully on top.

3   Scatter the Gorgonzola cheese over the whole lot before seasoning with salt and pepper.

4   Bake for 20–25 minutes, or until the pastry has risen around the edges and turned golden.

5   Cut into squares and serve. A tomato and red onion salad makes an excellent accompaniment.

> "All over Sicily, even in the tiniest of little cafés, Arancini are offered as an anytime snack. They also work well as a light meal with a salad, as shown here. The name means 'little oranges', and they are typical of a whole range of Sicilian dishes that are one thing, but are named after something else. Sicilian cooks have obviously, and uniquely, always been into representative cooking, which is really confusing for the rest of us."

Valentina Harris & Arancini Brothers
Arancini and Special Salad

SERVES 4

1 onion, finely chopped
75g/2½oz unsalted butter
500g/1lb 2oz/2¼ cups risotto rice (preferably Vialone Nano)
1.5 litres/52fl oz/about 6 cups best-quality chicken or meat stock, or very flavoursome vegetable stock, kept hot
6–7 tbsp freshly grated Parmesan cheese
5 tbsp cooked peas
5 tbsp diced mozzarella
4 tbsp chopped mushrooms, sautéed in butter or oil
55g/2oz Parma ham, chopped
3 tbsp plain flour
3 eggs, beaten
5 tbsp fine dried white breadcrumbs
sunflower oil for frying, or olive oil for brushing prior to baking
sea salt and freshly ground black pepper

FOR THE SPECIAL SALAD
3 blood oranges (if unavailable, use regular oranges)
4 tbsp sugar
2 star anise
1 cinnamon stick
3 cloves
pinch of dried chilli flakes
½ cup pecan nuts
4 chicory heads, sliced
2 avocados, stone removed and sliced
3 tbsp extra virgin olive oil

1 First you need to make a risotto. Fry the onion in half the butter for about 10 minutes over a very low heat, or until it is soft but not coloured. Stir in the rice and toast the grains thoroughly on all sides, so that they are opaque but not coloured.

2 Add the first ladleful of hot stock and stir it in. Continue to add the stock gradually, letting the rice absorb the liquid and all its flavour, stirring constantly.

3 When the rice is almost completely soft and creamy, take it off the heat and stir in the cheese and the rest of the butter. Season with salt and pepper, then cover and let it rest for about 3 minutes. Transfer to a bowl and leave it to cool down.

4 When the risotto is cold, stir in the peas, mozzarella, mushrooms and Parma ham. Shape the mixture into balls about the size of satsumas. Roll them in flour, beaten egg and dried breadcrumbs.

5 Shallow-fry the arancini in sunflower oil until crisp and golden, then drain on kitchen paper. Alternatively, put them on an oiled baking sheet, brush gently with olive oil, and bake for 10 minutes at 180°C/350°F/Gas 4 until crisp and golden.

6 To make the salad, peel the zest from the oranges, then cut them into thin slices. Pour 250ml/9fl oz/1 cup of water into a small pan with the sugar and spices and bring to the boil. Simmer for 1 minute, then add the orange slices. Reduce the heat to low and poach for 5 minutes, then leave to cool.

7 Cut the pecans in half and toast them in a dry pan for a few minutes. Add a pinch of salt after the heat is turned off.

8 Drain the poached oranges, reserving the juice. Arrange the chicory, avocados and oranges on a plate with the warm arancini.

9 Dress with the olive oil and a little of the orange poaching water. Season with salt and pepper and serve immediately.

"I get a kick out of coming up with new Italy-inspired recipes and testing them out on my partner, Cathy. Those that pass the discerning Cathy taste test are then, sometimes, released to the wider public – friends, blogs and even the odd book. It's great to hear feedback from people who've tried these recipes themselves. For the first time, recently I experienced a new, more direct form of feedback: we went round to some friends for lunch and found they'd cooked one of my risotto recipes. I was flattered and a bit nervous. It was a bit like hearing your own voice on an answer machine for the first time. The less self conscious younger members (my two kids, Rosie and Sorrel) gulped down the lot without looking back. That's proper feedback."

Jason Gibb & Nudo: Adopt an Olive Tree

Pear, Parmesan and Rocket Risotto

SERVES 4

2 tbsp olive oil
25g/1oz unsalted butter
1 onion, finely chopped
½ celery stick, finely chopped
350g/12oz/heaped 1½ cups
  risotto rice
1.5litres/52fl oz/6 cups chicken
  or vegetable stock
185ml/6fl oz/¾ cup white wine
55g/2oz Parmesan cheese,
  grated
100g/3½oz rocket
2 ripe pears, unpeeled, cored
  and cut into small cubes
sea salt and freshly ground
  black pepper

1 Put the olive oil and butter into a heavy-based pan and place over a low heat. Once the butter has melted, add the onion and celery and cook them nice and slowly for around 15 minutes until soft but not coloured.

2 Now add your rice and fry over a moderate heat while you warm up your stock. When the rice starts looking translucent it means that the creamy starch is ready to be released, so add the wine in one go and keep stirring until it has been absorbed.

3 Turn down the heat a bit and add the hot stock one ladleful at a time, allowing most of it to be absorbed before you add the next one.

4 Cook until the rice is tender but still has some bite. Add a couple of pinches of salt and lots of pepper. Stir in the grated Parmesan cheese, then the rocket, and then, at the last minute, the pear. Serve immediately.

> In the chef world, truffles are regarded as one of the most respected and prestigious products around. They are something that is not often used at home or outside the professional kitchen. So I thought I'd share this truffle recipe with you, as it's a quick and easy way to use these amazing little gems! Truffles come in all different shapes, colours, varieties and sizes, available all year round. The summer and autumn truffles are by far the most reasonable in price, so are ideal to use in this recipe. The white truffles are often found in Alba, and are regarded by many as the king of truffles. In 2007 a truffle weighing 1½kg was sold at auction for £161,000; I'm sure that would have made a great risotto!

Marcus Eaves & L'Autre Pied
Risotto of Summer Truffles

SERVES 4

1.5 litres/52fl oz/6 cups white chicken stock
3 tbsp olive oil
2 shallots, finely chopped
350g/12oz/heaped 1½ cups arborio risotto rice
3 garlic cloves, finely chopped
160ml/5¼fl oz/⅔ cup Noilly Prat vermouth
20g/¾oz summer truffles, finely chopped
120g/4¼oz Parmesan cheese
120g/4¼oz/½ cup crème fraîche
120g/4¼oz softened butter
a small handful finely chopped soft herbs, such as parsley or chervil
2 medium summer truffles, to shave over the risotto just before serving
sea salt and freshly grond black pepper

1 Bring the chicken stock to the boil, then turn off the heat.

2 Warm a saucepan on a medium heat, add the olive oil and shallots, and heat until they start to cook but without browning. Now add the risotto rice and garlic. Keep stirring over a medium heat until the garlic and shallots are tender. The rice will become translucent around the edges.

3 Add a generous pinch of salt, then pour in the vermouth and cook until it has all evaporated. Add the hot chicken stock little by little; as the rice soaks up the stock, slowly add a little more. Add the chopped truffles and continue cooking until the rice is tender. You may not have to use all the stock.

4 Finally add the Parmesan, crème fraîche and butter, stirring continuously. Season with salt and pepper, then at the last second add the finely chopped herbs. Shave the remaining truffles over the top of the risotto, using a truffle slicer or sharp mandolin, and serve.

"This risotto is a firm favourite in our house. My husband doesn't like cheesy risottos, having had one portion too many once, so this is the ideal antidote for him. It's fabulously creamy despite the lack of dairy, rich in flavour but light. It provides a magical risotto for dairy intolerant vegetarians and vegans, but is delicious no matter what your dietary preference. Our daughters, Sophia and Ellie, love it too. At seven and five years respectively they are the ultimate gourmets thanks to the three course French lunch in school everyday (at less than four they could already tell the difference between brie and camembert). This recipe is perfect matched with a sauvignon blanc or sauvignon blanc/semillon blend."

Château Haut Garrigue

Lemon, Pea and Mint Risotto

SERVES 4

200g/7oz/1⅓ cup frozen
   peas, lightly cooked
1 litre/35fl oz/4 cups
   vegetable stock
1 onion, finely chopped
1 garlic clove, finely chopped
olive oil, for frying
450g/1lb/scant 2 cups
   risotto rice
125ml/4fl oz/½ cup Sauvignon
   Blanc white wine
1 tbsp lemon juice
zest of 2 lemons or limes
1 tbsp finely chopped mint

1 Bring a small pan of water to the boil, add the peas and simmer for 3–5 minutes until defrosted.

2 Meanwhile, put the stock into a large pan and heat slowly. Fry the onion and garlic in olive oil in a large saucepan over a low heat, turning a few times, for 10 minutes until cooked but not brown. Add the rice and keep stirring and gently cooking for another 5 minutes until translucent.

3 Add the wine and let it reduce until absorbed, then gradually add your hot stock, a couple of ladlefuls at a time, waiting until it has absorbed before adding the next ladleful, and stirring all the time.

4 Finally stir in the peas, lemon juice and grated lemon or lime zest. Serve sprinkled with the finely chopped mint.

This is an easy curry to make, and can yield very good results if you stick with the basics. The original recipe would have originated from the Nizam of Hyderabad's kitchen. I have no doubt given it a more modern touch for cooks who may not have much time or are afraid of more intricate dishes. It is not only simple to make but also has the delicate yet lush texture that you can enjoy. It is great served with rice, but you can also add potatoes, chickpeas, or any mixture of vegetables.

Cyrus Todiwala & Café Spice Namasté
Simple Curry

SERVES 7–10

1–2 tbsp sunflower oil
1 onion, thinly sliced
1 long, slender green chilli,
    cut into small pieces
10 curry leaves
200g/7oz/1½ heaped cups
    coconut flour
½ tbsp chilli powder
½ tbsp ground cumin
¾ tbsp ground coriander
3–4 garlic cloves
2½cm/1in fresh ginger,
    peeled
½ tsp ground turmeric
250g/9oz canned tomatoes
sea salt
steamed rice, to serve

1 Heat the oil in a deep saucepan and gently fry the onion over a medium heat with the chilli pieces and curry leaves. It is important not to allow the onions to brown, so keep the heat on medium and stir regularly. Remove from the heat and allow to cool.

2 Put the cooled onion mixture and all the other ingredients into a blender. Pour in 750ml/26fl oz/3 cups water (more if needed) and whiz until smooth. Make certain that the ginger and garlic in particular are thoroughly puréed.

3 Transfer the purée mix from the blender to the saucepan and bring slowly to the boil, stirring. It is essential at this stage to stir regularly, as the coconut may thicken at the bottom and give the curry a burnt flavour. Simmer gently for about 15 minutes, then season with salt and remove from the heat. Serve with steamed rice.

> The name of this recipe translates as masala rice, but this Maharashtrian speciality is much more than that. I grew up eating several versions in several different homes, each friend's mother claiming to have the best grandma's recipe. How could I not say to them all that each one was the best? After all, I was getting a feast and each one was truly spectacular. Masala bhaat is a type of vegetable pulao with a flavoursome combination of spices and nuts. It is best eaten with a thin daal, and of course a good pickle or chutney. The preparation may look daunting and the list of ingredients immense, but, believe me, it is worth a try. The tindli looks like a small marrow or gherkin and has a very sticky sap. If you cannot find any, use a courgette instead.

Cyrus Todiwala & Café Spice Namasté
Masala Bhaat

SERVES 4

5–6 black peppercorns
3–4 cloves
2–3 heaped tbsp desiccated coconut
1 stick of cinnamon or piece of cassia bark
1 tbsp coriander seeds
1 heaped tsp sesame seeds
1 heaped tsp cumin seeds
4–5 tbsp sunflower oil or ghee
½ tsp black mustard seeds
large pinch of asafoetida
10–12 curry leaves
8–10 tindlis, topped and tailed and cut into 4 lengthways, or 1 courgette, cubed
4–5 heaped tbsp podded green peas
1 medium aubergine, cubed, sprinkled with salt, rinsed and dried
2 medium potatoes, peeled and cubed
3–4 green chillies, slit into 4 lengthways
200g/7oz/1 cup good quality basmati rice
½ tsp ground turmeric
1 heaped tbsp chopped cashew nuts
2–3 heaped tbsp skinned raw peanuts
2 tbsp butter or ghee
5–6 tbsp chopped coriander
freshly grated coconut, to serve
salt

1 In a wok or frying pan dry roast the peppercorns, cloves, desiccated coconut, cinnamon, coriander seeds, sesame seeds, and half the cumin. Make sure you do this over a low heat so as not to burn anything. Once roasted, cool then grind everything in a coffee or spice grinder. (You could also roast the spices in a preheated oven at 150–160°C/300–315°F/Gas 2–3 for about 30 minutes, then cool and grind.)

2 Pour the oil or ghee into a wide casserole and heat to a slight haze. Add the mustard seeds, and as soon as they start to crackle add the remaining cumin seeds and the asafoetida. As soon as the crackling stops, add the curry leaves and all the vegetables, including the chillies.

3 Sauté for 4–6 minutes, then add the rice and turmeric and mix well. Sauté for a further 3–5 minutes, then add the roasted ground spices, the cashew nuts and the peanuts.

4 Preheat the oven to 130°C/250°C/Gas 1. Spread everything out evenly in the casserole and add enough water to cover the rice to a depth of about 2½cm/1in. Season with salt. Once the water comes to the boil, reduce the heat to low, cover the casserole with a lid and cook for 20 minutes, or until the rice is fully cooked and no liquid remains. Place the casserole in the oven for 20 minutes.

5 Remove the rice from the oven and spoon the butter or ghee on top, add the coriander and mix together gently but thoroughly. Serve sprinkled with the freshly grated coconut.

DESSERTS

Dulce de Leche

Puff Candy Meringue

Clementine and Cranberry Clafoutis

Individual Vanilla Baked Alaskas with Spiced
    Rhubarb and Rhubarb Consommé

Baked Apple and Almond Tart

Peaches with Roses

Chestnut, Walnut and Chocolate Cake

Tasha's Apple Pavlova or Apple Mess

Black Forest Cocktail

Raspberry and Earl Grey Jellies

Dairy-Free White Chocolate Ice Cream

Rhubarb and Orange-Flower Ice Cream

> About 90 per cent of the Italians in Argentina originate from Piedmont, where my family comes from. Those early settlers found themselves with plenty of milk, but no refrigerators, so they had to be creative when it came to preserving this delicate resource. There are so many Piemontesi with relatives in Argentina that sometimes a reverse culture follows, with recipes coming back home from immigrants. Dulce de leche is not caramel, and has a lovely milk flavour with a honey sweetness and a thick consistency that complements a whole raft of desserts, especially tart fruits in pies, stewed fruits – from rhubarb and pears to plums and apples – and any soft fruit. It goes a long way – you only need one dessertspoon per person.

Franchi Seeds (1783)
Dulce de Leche

MAKES 750ML/26FL OZ/3 CUPS

2 litres/70fl oz/8 cups
   whole milk
500g/1lb 2oz/heaped
   2 cups sugar
1 tsp sea salt
2 vanilla pods

1 Pour the milk into a large non-stick pan over a medium heat. Add the sugar and salt.

2 Split the vanilla pods lengthways, scrape the seeds from the pods, then add the seeds and pods to the milk. Turn the heat to medium high, and whisk or stir the mixture constantly until it comes to a full boil. Turn the heat down to a bare simmer and continue to cook, uncovered, for 2–3 hours until you see the dulce de leche reduce and become thicker. If in doubt, move the pan to your smallest ring once the milk is at simmering point and use your lowest heat to keep it turning over very gently. If the heat is too high, your milk will boil over and develop a rough skin on top, which won't dissolve no matter how much you whisk later. Whereas if the heat is too low you'll just have to cook it longer, no harm done.

3 Check the consistency after about 2 hours and remove the vanilla pods. Continue to simmer if necessary – the consistency you are looking for is a loose caramel, remembering that the mixture will thicken more as it cools. My last batch took just over 3 hours to reach the consistency I like.

4 When it gets there, whisk it until smooth, using a balloon whisk. Pour into small jars and allow to cool. When completely cold, seal the jars with lids and keep in the fridge for up to a month. If you hermetically seal the jars, they will keep (unopened) in a larder for up to a year.

"This dish is an adapted version of a pudding my Grannie used to make me and is also where my love of food began. I was always told to pull the rhubarb in the garden which she would turn into rhubarb candy crumble. I was only allowed into the kitchen when Grampa had gone to sit down ('for peace and quiet') however I was quite happy sat out on the back garden step with my prize stalk of rhubarb to dip in a wee poke of sugar. So then I was brought in to the kitchen to watch my Gran make puff candy. At 4 years old, and even now, it had such a wow factor! I love the look on people faces when we make this. It must have given my Grannie great pleasure to see me so excited, if only she knew now…"

Jacqueline O'Donnell & The Sisters
Puff Candy Meringue

SERVES 6–8

FOR THE PUFF CANDY
250g/9oz/heaped 1 cup
    granulated sugar
2½ tbsp golden syrup
2½ tbsp bicarbonate of soda

FOR THE MERINGUES
4 egg whites
100g/3½oz/scant ½ cup
    caster sugar

FOR THE BUTTERSCOTCH SAUCE
100g/3½oz/scant ½ cup
    granulated sugar
100g/3½oz unsalted butter
100ml/3½fl oz/scant ½ cup
    double cream

good quality vanilla ice cream,
    to serve

1   To make the puff candy, boil the sugar and syrup together until light golden, then remove from the heat. Quickly whisk in the bicarbonate of soda, until the mixture is frothy, then pour onto a greased baking tray. Leave to cool until required.

2   To make the meringues, preheat the oven to 150°C/300°F/Gas 3 and lay some greaseproof paper on a baking sheet. Whisk the egg whites, adding the sugar gradually, until they form soft peaks (you can fold some crushed puff candy through the whisked egg whites before baking if you like).

3   Drop spoonfuls of the mixture about 6cm/2½ inches in diameter on to the greaseproof paper, spaced well apart. Put in the hot oven and bake for 40 minutes. You want these meringues to be chewy in the middle. Remove them from the baking sheet with a spatula and lay them on a wire cooling rack until required.

4   To make the sauce, boil the sugar and butter until dark golden brown. Carefully add the double cream and simmer for 2 minutes Use a high-sided pan, as this mixture will boil up quite a long way. Cool and store in an airtight container in the fridge. It will keep for 3–4 weeks, if you can resist it for that length of time.

5   To serve, place a meringue in each bowl, add some good quality vanilla ice cream and a large spoonful of crushed puff candy. Pour the butterscotch sauce over the top and serve.

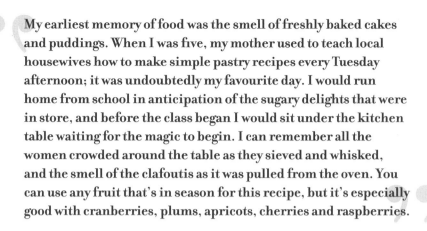

"My earliest memory of food was the smell of freshly baked cakes and puddings. When I was five, my mother used to teach local housewives how to make simple pastry recipes every Tuesday afternoon; it was undoubtedly my favourite day. I would run home from school in anticipation of the sugary delights that were in store, and before the class began I would sit under the kitchen table waiting for the magic to begin. I can remember all the women crowded around the table as they sieved and whisked, and the smell of the clafoutis as it was pulled from the oven. You can use any fruit that's in season for this recipe, but it's especially good with cranberries, plums, apricots, cherries and raspberries."

Jun Tanaka & Pearl

Clementine and Cranberry Clafoutis

SERVES 6

25g/1oz unsalted butter, softened
120g/4¹⁄₄oz/¹⁄₂ cup caster sugar, plus a little for the dish
150ml/5fl oz/scant ²⁄₃ cup double cream
150ml/5fl oz/scant ²⁄₃ cup whole milk
2 eggs
3 egg yolks
1 tbsp plain flour
8 fresh clementines, peeled and segmented
50g/1³⁄₄oz fresh cranberries
icing sugar, for dusting

1 Preheat the oven to 180°C/350°F/Gas 4. Butter a 20cm/8in diameter shallow ovenproof dish and sprinkle it with some caster sugar.

2 Pour the cream and milk into a pan and bring to the boil. Remove from the heat.

3 Cream the eggs, yolks and sugar together using a balloon whisk. Add the flour and finally whisk in the cream and milk, straining if necessary to remove any skin that might have formed on the surface in the interim.

4 Arrange the clementines and cranberries on the bottom of the dish, pour in the batter mix and cook in the preheated oven for 30 minutes.

5 Remove from the oven, dust with icing sugar and serve warm.

"Baked Alaska is an old favourite of mine; it was one of the first desserts I ever put on my menu. I have fantastic memories of making it and coming up with new flavour combinations, trying different ice creams and sorbets to put inside. Baked Alsaka is originally a French dessert also known as 'omelette a la norvegienne' devised in the Victorian era. So I guess this dessert is an absolute classic, and the great thing about classics is that they always stand the test of time."

Marcus Eaves & L'Autre Pied

Individual Vanilla Baked Alaskas with Spiced Rhubarb and Rhubarb Consommé

SERVES 4

FOR THE FINANCIERS
(ALMOND SPONGE)
220g/7¾oz unsalted butter
90g/3¼oz/¾ cup plain flour
90g/3¼oz/¾ cup ground
    almonds
120g/4¼oz/scant 1 cup
    icing sugar
5 tbsp runny honey
6 large egg whites

FOR THE VANILLA ICE CREAM
500ml/17fl oz/2 cups milk
500ml/17fl oz/2 cups double
    cream
1 vanilla pod
10 large egg yolks
220g/7¾oz/1 cup caster sugar

FOR THE SWISS MERINGUE
3 large egg whites
200g/7oz/heaped 1½ cups icing
    sugar

FOR THE RHUBARB CONSOMMÉ
2 tbsp sugar syrup
1 vanilla pod
2 star anise
1kg/2lb 4oz rhubarb, sliced
a few drops of lemon oil,
    to serve

1 To make the financiers, preheat the oven to 180°C/350°F/Gas 4. Melt the butter over a low heat in a heavy-based pan until pale brown and with a pronounced nutty smell, making sure that it doesn't burn. The butter will separate into butterfat and milk solids. The milk solids will sink to the bottom of the pan and begin to brown. When they reach a toasty hazelnut colour remove the pan from the heat. This is called beurre noisette.

2 Beat the flour, ground almonds, icing sugar, honey and beurre noisette together in a bowl until they form a smooth paste. Beat the egg whites in a separate bowl, then beat them into the financier mixture until it becomes smooth.

3 Place 4 sheets of baking paper, each about 10 x 5cm/4 x 2in, on a baking sheet, then spread a thin layer of the paste over each sheet using a palette knife. Place the baking sheet in the preheated oven and bake for 6 minutes until golden brown. Cool the sheets on wire cooling racks. Leave the financiers on the baking paper and store in an airtight container.

4 To make the vanilla ice cream, pour the milk and cream into a stainless steel pan. Split the vanilla pod and add the seeds to the liquid, bring to the boil for 30 seconds. Take the pan off the heat. Cover the top of the pan with clingfilm to prevent a skin forming. Leave to cool completely, then strain into a bowl or fresh pan.

5 Whisk the egg yolks with the sugar until pale, then gradually whisk in the milk and cream. Heat gently, stirring all the time, then leave to cool. Churn in an ice cream maker according to the manufacturer's instructions. Once the ice cream is churned, transfer it to the freezer to solidify. Place the now firm ice cream on top of the financiers and freeze.

FOR THE SPICED YORKSHIRE
  RHUBARB
10g/¼oz unsalted butter
120g/4¼oz rhubarb, sliced
1 tbsp caster sugar
1 star anise
½ vanilla pod

6   To make the Swiss meringue, whisk the egg whites until they
    become fluffy. Add the icing sugar and continue whisking until
    the meringue is stiff and firm to the touch. Chill until required.

7   To make the rhubarb consommé, put the syrup, vanilla pod, star
    anise and rhubarb into a large pan and bring to the boil over a low
    heat. Cover with a lid and cook until the rhubarb begins to split.
    Take off the heat and leave to infuse for 15 minutes. Pass the liquid
    through a fine sieve lined with muslin. Press the pulp gently, but
    don't force it or the consommé will become cloudy. Set aside.

8   Finally, to make the spiced Yorkshire rhubarb, cook all the
    ingredients together gently until they form a compote. Set aside.

9   To assemble the four Baked Alaska portions, use a 4cm/1½in
    cutter and cut out four neat ice cream cylinders on their biscuit
    base. Fill a piping bag with Swiss meringue and snip off the
    end to give a 5mm/¼in hole. Pipe lines of meringue over the
    top and down the sides of the ice cream, leaving no gaps. To
    achieve a finish that makes the outside of each Alaska look like a
    'hedgehog', touch the meringue with a fingertip and pull outwards
    to make small points.

10 The Alaskas are now ready to bake, but it's best to return them
    to the freezer for 1 or 2 hours before baking and serving. When
    you are ready to bake them, preheat the oven to 250°C/500°F/
    Gas 9. Stand the four Alaskas on a cold baking tray and bake for
    4 minutes, until the surface is light brown.

11 To serve, place a spoonful of the rhubarb compote in the centre of
    a bowl. Stand a Baked Alaska on top of the compote. Pour a quarter
    of the rhubarb consommé around the outside and finish with
    drops of lemon oil. Repeat with the remaining Baked Alaskas.

Flour Power City Bakery
Baked Apple and Almond Tart

SERVES 4–6

2 large cooking apples,
  such as Bramley
a good pinch of cinnamon
2 tbsp brown sugar
juice of 1 lemon
2 tbsp flaked almonds
2–3 tsp granulated sugar
single or double cream,
  to serve

FOR THE SWEET PASTRY
350g/12oz/heaped 2¾ cups
  unbleached plain flour
175g/6oz butter
zest of 1 lemon
80g/2¾oz/scant ⅔ cup
  icing sugar
1–2 eggs

FOR THE FRANGIPANE
120g/4¼oz butter
120g/4¼oz/½ cup caster sugar
2 large eggs, beaten
120g/4¼oz/1 cup ground
  almonds
1 tbsp plain white flour

1 To make the pastry, put the flour, butter, lemon zest and icing sugar into a large bowl and work the mixture with your fingertips until you achieve a consistency like sand. Add an egg and use your fingertips to bind the mixture – if you need more liquid, add another egg or a drop of water. It should have an even texture, like soft clay.

2 Form the pastry into a smooth ball, working it as little as possible. Flatten it on a plate and pop it into the fridge while you prepare the apples.

3 Preheat the oven to 180°C/350°F/Gas 4. Peel and dice the apples, then sprinkle them with cinnamon, brown sugar and lemon juice.

4 Remove the pastry from the fridge and roll out on a lightly floured base until it is large enough to line a 25cm/10in tart tin. Prick the pastry with a fork. Spread the apples evenly over the base.

5 To make the frangipane, cream the butter and sugar together using a wooden spoon in a bowl. Gradually add the eggs. Finally, blend in the ground almonds and flour. Cover the apples with the frangipane mix and top with flaked almonds and the sugar. It's best to do this when the frangipane has just been made, so that it spreads easily.

6 Bake the tart in the preheated oven for 45–50 minutes until golden brown. Allow to cool and serve with pouring cream.

> This is such a delicate way to serve a peach. At the end of the season, when peaches are starting to become more woolly, losing all their mid-summer juicy sweetness as their season draws to a close, it is by far better to enjoy them cooked. Part of being a real cook is tuning into the passing of the seasons and realizing how so many ingredients change in taste, texture and cooking requirements. This recipe makes the most of precious peaches and somehow lets them extend their season of glory.

Choi Time
Peaches with Roses

SERVES 4

4 large ripe peaches
3–4 tbsp elderflower cordial
2–3 tbsp vanilla sugar, to taste
8–10 Damask rose tea buds
vanilla ice cream, vanilla
 yogurt or crème fraîche,
 to serve

1 Wash the peaches and put them into a large saucepan. Pour in about 1 litre/35 fl oz/4 cups of water, enough to just cover the peaches. Pour in the elderflower cordial and add at least 2 tablespoons of vanilla sugar, or more to taste.

2 Bring to the boil, then turn down the heat, add the roses and leave to simmer gently for about 30 minutes, until the peaches are completely tender, keeping the lid on to make sure the liquid does not evaporate.

3 Add a little more sugar if the syrup is not quite sweet enough. Remove the tea buds with a slotted spoon, then turn off the heat and leave the peaches to cool in their syrup. When they are cold, chill thoroughly.

4 Serve one peach per person and place them in shallow bowls. Pour some of the chilled syrup on top and serve with vanilla ice cream, vanilla yogurt or crème fraîche, if you like.

If you want to make chocolate, you've got to roast your own beans because that's where the secret is. Everyone has their own approach to making chocolate, and other people are very slick and produce a very good-quality product, but there is a uniformity to it. I prefer mine to have a slight roughness. I try to enhance the flavours that are there. Having said that, it's easier for me to do because I'm just a small producer.

Willie Harcourt-Cooze

The Real Food Festival is about the foundations of food. There is no place where you have such a gathering of so many small producers who are so passionate about their products. Real food is about good honest ingredients. I am a small producer of fine chocolate on an adventure, sourcing my beans from around the world on the merits of flavour. My discovery was no different from the explorers who first made chocolate in the 19th century – I am just reminding people of cacao. It's a drug, a pick-me-up, a vitamin punch based on flavour that was developed before price became so important.

To source the beans I use for my chocolate, I travel wherever I need to in order to get the finest flavours. This often takes me to places such as Sierra Leone and Colombia. I judge the bean on its intrinsic qualities, not on what it looks like, and I try to connect with people growing the beans. In Colombia, I work with a farmer called Marlena in Santa Rosa. She lived under the rule of the FARC rebels for 30 years and was growing coca (which is not the same as cacao!) to produce cocaine for the rebels. Against all the odds, Marlena has torn out the coca and replaced it with cacao. Six years later, she is now growing Trinitario, a fine bean originally from Trinidad, which thrives on Colombia's beautiful Caribbean coast. Her transformation is an inspiration to me, and I hope it shows in my chocolate.

> **❝** *I strive to do direct trade with farmers to put money directly in their hands, cutting out the middle man.* **❞**

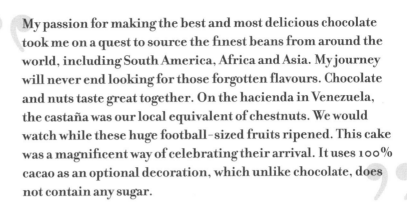

> *My passion for making the best and most delicious chocolate took me on a quest to source the finest beans from around the world, including South America, Africa and Asia. My journey will never end looking for those forgotten flavours. Chocolate and nuts taste great together. On the hacienda in Venezuela, the castaña was our local equivalent of chestnuts. We would watch while these huge football-sized fruits ripened. This cake was a magnificent way of celebrating their arrival. It uses 100% cacao as an optional decoration, which unlike chocolate, does not contain any sugar.*

Willie Harcourt-Cooze
Chestnut, Walnut and Chocolate Cake

SERVES 8–10

3 tbsp raisins
4 tbsp walnut liqueur, rum
　or Cognac
100g/3½oz salted butter,
　plus extra for greasing
100g/3½oz/scant ½ cup
　unrefined granulated
　or caster sugar
5 large eggs, separated
400g/14oz/scant 2 cups
　vacuum-packed cooked
　chestnuts
1 tsp vanilla extract
120g/4¼oz chocolate, 72%
　cocoa solids, chopped into
　small pieces
4–5 tbsp walnuts, roughly
　chopped
50g/1¾oz 100% cacao,
　for decoration (optional)

1　Soak the raisins in the walnut liqueur for 48 hours.

2　Preheat the oven to 180°C/350°F/Gas 4 and butter and line a 28cm/11in cake tin with baking parchment. Beat the butter, sugar and egg yolks in a mixer for a few minutes until light and fluffy.

3　Meanwhile, blend the chestnuts in a food processor until they are slightly coarser than ground almonds. Add them to the butter mixture along with all the other ingredients except for the egg whites and decoration chocolate.

4　Whisk the egg whites in a clean bowl until quite stiff, then gently fold them into the butter and chestnut mixture.

5　Tip the mixture into the prepared cake tin and bake in the preheated oven for 25 minutes, or until set. Allow to cool, then turn the cake out of the tin and grate the 100% cacao over the top to decorate, if you like. Delicious eaten warm on the day it's made.

> "Our chickens seem to have a feast or famine approach to egg laying – this is a great way to use up egg whites in the 'feast' times, when we've run out of ideas for egg recipes and are making vats of mayonnaise. The meringues keep well, and are always a great favourite. For a crunchier meringue, omit the cider vinegar and cornflour (these will also keep better in an airtight tin). However, I love the gooeyness of the meringue recipe below, particularly if you make an Apple Pavlova instead of the Apple Mess!"

Heron Valley

Tasha's Apple Pavlova or Apple Mess

SERVES 6

10 sharp eating apples, such as Braeburn, peeled, cored and cut into medium-size chunks
140ml/4½ fl oz/generous ½ cup apple juice
580ml/20¼fl oz/2⅓ cups double cream
2 or 3 handfuls of toasted hazelnuts, skins rubbed off

FOR THE MERINGUE
6 large free range egg whites
350g/12oz/1½ cups caster sugar
2 tsp cornflour
1 tsp cider vinegar
1 tsp vanilla essence

1 Preheat the oven to 150°C/300°F/Gas 2. To make the meringue, whisk the egg whites in a very clean bowl until they form soft peaks, then whisk in half the caster sugar. Gently fold in the remaining caster sugar along with the cornflour, cider vinegar and vanilla essence.

2 Line a baking sheet with greaseproof paper. Pour the meringue mixture onto the sheet and, using a palette knife, spread it out to about 4cm/1½ inches thick.

3 Bake in the preheated oven for 50 minutes until set but still marshmallowy inside. Allow to cool to room temperature.

4 Heat the apples and juice in a pan and simmer over a low heat until the apples have softened to a chunky, squidgy consistency (very technical term!), with not too much liquid. Allow them to cool. Lightly whip the double cream in a separate bowl.

5 To make Apple Pavlova, put a layer of the whipped cream on top of the meringue base. Pour on the cooled apple, then chop the hazelnuts and scatter them liberally on top. Cut into big squares and serve.

6 Alternatively, to make Apple Mess, break the meringue into largish chunks and put into a big serving bowl, being careful not to over-handle the gooey marshmallowy bits. Add the whipped cream and the cooked apples and very gently fold all three ingredients together. Chop the toasted hazelnuts, liberally scatter them on top of the mess and serve.

"This is a great simple dish with flavours that hark back to my childhood, done in a slightly more refined way using the very finest ingredients, including Valrhona chocolate and fresh dairy cream. It also uses Griottines – French cherries sold in jars of delicious syrup. They have quite a kick when eaten by themselves. This dessert would be great for anything from a Sunday lunch to a dinner party, and makes a great alternative to Christmas pudding."

Andrew Baird & Longueville Manor
Black Forest Cocktail

SERVES 8

FOR THE CHOCOLATE SPONGE
butter, for greasing
125g/4½oz/1 cup plain flour
½ tsp baking powder
1 tbsp cocoa powder, 100%
   (extra bitter)
5 eggs, separated
140g/5oz/⅔ cup caster sugar

FOR THE CHERRY FILLING
1 tbsp cornflour
150ml/5fl oz/scant ⅔ cup
   griottine syrup, or cherry
   cordial
100g/3½oz griottine cherries,
   stoned

FOR THE CHOCOLATE MOUSSE
100g/3½oz dark chocolate
   (Valrhona 66% Caraibe is
   our choice)
1 egg white
50g/1¾oz/¼ cup caster sugar
100ml/3½fl oz/ ⅓ cup + 2 tbsp
   whipping cream

FOR THE KIRSCH CREAM
1 tbsp caster sugar
200ml/7fl oz/scant 1 cup
   whipping cream
Kirsch, to taste

1 First make the chocolate sponge. Preheat the oven to 190°C/375°F/Gas 5 and thoroughly grease a 20cm/8in cake tin. Sieve the flour, baking powder and cocoa powder into a bowl.

2 Whisk the egg yolks with 100g/3½oz of the sugar until they turn pale. Whisk the egg whites with the remaining sugar until they hold stiff peaks. Gently add the chocolate powder mix to the egg yolk mix. Then fold the egg white mix into the chocolate mix.

3 Carefully pour into the cake tin and bake in the preheated oven for 15 minutes. Once cooked, leave to cool in the tin and then turn out onto a cooling rack until cold.

4 Next make the griottine cherry filling. In a small bowl, mix the cornflour with 3 tablespoons of water. Mix the griottine syrup with the slaked cornflour, tip into a small pan and bring to a simmer, stirring all the time. Leave to cool and then add the whole griottine cherries. Set aside until required.

5 Now make the chocolate mousse. Melt the chocolate in a bowl set over a pan of simmering water. Do not let the water boil and take care not to let the bowl touch the water.

6 Meanwhile, whisk the egg whites and sugar in a bowl until they hold stiff peaks. Whisk a third of the whipping cream separately until it peaks. Carefully but quickly fold and mix all the chocolate mousse ingredients together, including the remaining cream. Set aside to cool, then cover and put into the fridge.

7 Finally, make the Kirsch cream. Whisk the sugar and cream together until thick, adding a good splash of Kirsch.

8 Once all the ingredients are ready, layer them in a cocktail glass and decorate as far as your imagination will take you before serving or chilling until required.

"I grew up on a fruit farm so every summer was a soft fruit bonanza. Nothing can compare to fruit freshly picked and eaten in the field. Good food was central to our household with lots of recipe books and cooking going on. We always ate well and soft fruit was always on the menu. We had a fruit for cream arrangement with a local farmer who had a herd of Jersey cows, so we always had an abundant supply of delicious cream to accompany the fruit. Of course, we always had a freezer full of fruit to use in the winter. This recipe is perfect for frozen raspberries as well as fresh, and will bring the flavours of summer flooding back into the kitchen during the cold, dark days of winter."

Bellevue Tea

Raspberry and Earl Grey Jellies

SERVES 6

450g/1lb ripe fresh
   raspberries (or good quality
   frozen ones)
150g/5oz/²/3 cup caster sugar
4 sheets leaf gelatine
3 Earl Grey tea bags
juice of ½ lemon
double cream, to serve
   (optional)

1 Put the raspberries and sugar into a bowl and mash to a juicy pulp. Set aside for 30 minutes, stirring occasionally, so the sugar can dissolve, then rub through a sieve into a jug. You will have a delicious raspberry liquid. Discard anything left in the sieve.

2 Half fill a bowl with cold water and lay the gelatine sheets in it to soften them.

3 Drop the Earl Grey tea bags into a large measuring jug and pour in enough boiling water to bring the level up to 300ml/10½fl oz/ scant 1¼ cups. Leave the tea bags in for a few minutes, removing them while the tea is still hot

4 Scoop the gelatine out of its water bath, squeeze out the excess water and stir the gelatine into the steaming tea. Add the lemon juice and pour in the raspberry liquid. Pour into 6 x 120ml/ 4fl oz/½ cup moulds, champagne flutes or small wine glasses.

5 Leave to cool, then put into the fridge to set for 5–6 hours. Turn out the jellies onto serving plates if you have made them in cup moulds, or serve in the champagne flutes or wine glasses. Accompany with whipped double cream, if desired.

Many of our customers for our dark chocolate powders are dairy intolerant and were asking us for a white chocolate powder for easy use in cooking, so I decided to develop a dairy-free version. It would lack the milk notes that can often overpower the more delicate cocoa notes in white chocolates, plus if it was going to be dairy-free, then why not gluten and soya-free too? My chocolatier husband, Adrian, suggested that West African cocoa butter would give the best result. He became especially interested in helping once he and our girls had tasted a white chocolate cheesecake made with an early attempt! The final version gives a wonderful, rich, creamy flavour to any white chocolate recipe.

Mortimer Chocolate Company
Dairy-Free White Chocolate Ice Cream

SERVES 4

100g/3½oz white couverture powder
200ml/7fl oz/scant 1 cup coconut cream
2 eggs, separated
3 heaped tbsp caster sugar

1 Heat the couverture powder in a bowl set over a pan of simmering water. Take care not to let the bowl touch the water. Stir the white chocolate couverture powder until melted and smooth.

2 Put the coconut cream into a separate bowl and stir until smooth, then add the melted couverture and stir well.

3 Beat the egg yolks with the sugar in a large bowl until pale and thick, then beat in the coconut mixture.

4 Whisk the egg whites in a separate bowl until they form firm peaks. Beat 1 tablespoon of the egg white into the coconut mixture, then fold in the rest using a large metal spoon.

5 Freeze, preferably overnight, to allow the flavours to develop. Move to the fridge for 20 minutes before serving so that the ice cream can soften.

> *More than 20 years after I first gave this super simple ice cream recipe on BBC TV Breakfast I still get grateful letters and emails about it. You'll never make an ice cream custard again; as the combination of sweetened condensed milk and double cream whips up to give the perfect freezing mixture that never goes icy. This is an exotic summer version that's wonderful with strawberries or raspberries, but I'm looking forward to serving it with winter's crumbles and pies, too.*

Glynn Christian

Rhubarb and Orange-Flower Ice Cream

SERVES 4–6

200ml/7fl oz/scant 1 cup
  sweetened condensed milk
200ml/7fl oz/scant 1 cup
  double cream
1–1½ tsp orange-flower water
250–300g/9–10½oz
  unsweetened cooked
  rhubarb, puréed
shortbread or other dessert
  biscuits, to serve

1 Pour the condensed milk into a suitable container and put it into the freezer for several hours, then remove from the freezer and mix it in a bowl with the double cream. Beat until it thickens to a texture like whipped cream. Mix in the orange-flower water.

2 Fold in the rhubarb purée evenly, or swirl it to make contrasting colours and textures.

3 This ice cream does not become icy but can freeze very hard. Take it out of the freezer and leave it on the worktop an hour before you intend to eat it. Serve it with some shortbread or other dessert biscuits.

BAKING

f

CHAPTER SIX

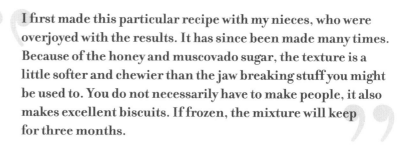

I first made this particular recipe with my nieces, who were overjoyed with the results. It has since been made many times. Because of the honey and muscovado sugar, the texture is a little softer and chewier than the jaw breaking stuff you might be used to. You do not necessarily have to make people, it also makes excellent biscuits. If frozen, the mixture will keep for three months.

Sophie Conran
Gingerbread Families

MAKES **about 4–6 families (mummy, daddy, little boy and little girl)**

350g/12oz/heaped 2¾ cups plain flour, plus extra for dusting
1 tsp bicarbonate of soda
100g/3½oz butter, straight from the fridge, cut into 1cm/½in cubes
2 tsp ground ginger
2 tsp ground cinnamon
175g/6oz/scant 1 cup dark muscovado sugar
1 egg, beaten
4 tbsp runny honey
writing icing and tiny silver sugar balls, to decorate

1 Preheat the oven to 200°C/400°F/Gas 6. Put the flour, bicarbonate of soda, butter and spices into a large bowl, then rub the butter into the flour between your thumb and fingers (this is a perfect job for a 6-year-old) until you have a mixture that looks like breadcrumbs. Stir in the sugar.

2 Mix together the egg and honey in a small bowl, and pour into the flour and butter crumbs. Mix with your hands (a lovely, sticky job) to make a dough. Form into 2 large, fat sausages. Wrap them in clingfilm and pop them into the fridge for an hour to chill.

3 Dust a work surface with flour and roll out one of the sausages to 3mm/⅛in thick, leaving the other in the fridge until needed. Cut out your gingerbread families, rerolling as necessary, and gently place on a non-stick baking sheet. Repeat with the second sausage of gingerbread dough. Bake in the preheated oven for 10 minutes, or until golden brown.

4 Remove to a wire tray to cool before adding faces and fabulous outfits with squeezy icing and any other decorations you fancy.

Cocoa is unsweetened, so these nibs give these biscotti something very special – chocolate flavour, but without the sweetness. They never really melt as they have not been blended with cocoa butter and sugar like chocolate. You can of course buy biscotti but try making them yourself and see just how easy it is to do, and what delicious results you'll very quickly achieve! Once you've got the hang of the basic method, you can add nuts, spices, dried fruit or anything you fancy. They make excellent Christmas presents too.

L'Artisan du Chocolat
Cocoa Nibs Biscotti

SERVES 4

50g/1¾oz salted butter
100g/3½oz/heaped 1 cup
  flaked almonds
250g/9oz/2 cups self-raising
  flour
100g/3½oz/scant ½ cup
  demerara sugar
100g/3½oz cocoa nibs
3 eggs

1 Preheat the oven to 190°C/375°C/Gas 5. Melt the butter in a small pan over a low heat and leave it to cool.

2 Lay the flaked almonds on a baking sheet and put them in the oven to roast, then leave to cool (or you can buy flaked almonds already roasted).

3 In a large bowl, sift the flour, then add the sugar, almonds and cocoa nibs. Beat the eggs and cooled melted butter together, then add them to the dry ingredients. Work the mixture into a slightly sticky dough.

4 Shape the dough into a flattened log shape, about the length of your hand and slightly deeper, and lay it on a lightly greased baking sheet. Bake in the preheated oven for 20 minutes. Remove from the oven and leave to cool on the tray for 30 minutes.

5 Cut the log into individual biscotti. Place them on a baking sheet and return to the oven for a further 15 minutes.

6 Remove from the oven with a spatula and cool on wire racks. Either serve at once, or keep in an airtight container until needed. They will keep very well for about a month.

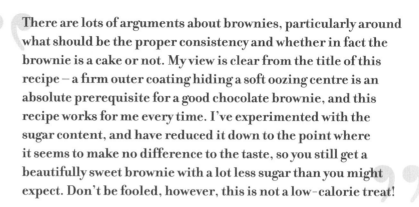

"There are lots of arguments about brownies, particularly around what should be the proper consistency and whether in fact the brownie is a cake or not. My view is clear from the title of this recipe – a firm outer coating hiding a soft oozing centre is an absolute prerequisite for a good chocolate brownie, and this recipe works for me every time. I've experimented with the sugar content, and have reduced it down to the point where it seems to make no difference to the taste, so you still get a beautifully sweet brownie with a lot less sugar than you might expect. Don't be fooled, however, this is not a low-calorie treat!"

Philip Lowery & Real Food Festival
Soft, Oozing Triple-Chocolate Brownies

MAKES 12

275g/9¾oz plain chocolate, 70% cocoa solids, the best quality you can find
100g/3½oz milk chocolate
275g/9¾oz unsalted butter, cut into cubes, plus extra for greasing
175g/6oz/scant 1½ cups plain flour
1 tsp baking powder
4 large eggs
100g/3½oz white chocolate
2 tsp vanilla extract
250g/9oz/1 cup caster sugar

1 Preheat the oven to 170°C/325°F/Gas 3. Lightly grease some greaseproof paper with butter and use it to line a baking tin measuring about 30cm x 20cm/12in x 8in. It will help the paper sit in the tin better if you make a diagonal cut into the paper at each corner.

2 Break the plain and milk chocolate into chunks. In a heatproof glass bowl set over a pan of simmering water, melt the plain chocolate with the milk chocolate and butter.

3 Meanwhile, sieve the flour and baking powder into a large bowl. Whisk the eggs in a glass jug. Chop up the white chocolate into small chunks.

4 When the chocolate and butter have melted, stir in the eggs, vanilla extract and sugar. Add to the bowl of flour and baking powder and fold into the mixture. Drop in the white chocolate chunks and mix them in, then scrape the mixture into your prepared baking tin. Smooth the surface, then bake in the preheated oven for 20–30 minutes, depending upon how soft and gooey you prefer your brownies to be.

5 The surface of the brownies should be crisp and the inside soft, so check before taking them out of the oven. Once out, leave to cool in the baking tin – the mixture will continue cooking for a while, so don't leave it in the oven until the inside is too dry as your brownies will turn into a chocolate cake!

6 Once cooled, turn out and cut into squares. For a real indulgence these brownies are gorgeous with a dollop of clotted cream.

> Chocolate has always been my passion. I love working with it every day, while listening to the gentle sound of the conche and refiner mixing and griding the cocoa beans. I trained as a chef and pastry chef, but always found working with chocolate in a professional kitchen frustrating because of the lack of space, high humidity and strong smells from adjacent sections. These days my cooking with chocolate is reserved for my pleasure and the pleasure of my friends and guests at home. After a long week working making all sorts of chocolates and truffles, I like to relax at home, work in the garden and bake with the highest quality chocolate. These indulgent, intense, melt-in-the-mouth chocolate chip cookies are one of my favourite recipes.

L'Artisan du Chocolat
Chocolate Chip Cookies

MAKES 12 TO 16

250g/9oz/2 cups plain flour
¾ teaspoon bicarbonate of soda
½ teaspoon salt
150g/5½oz butter, at room temperature
200g/7oz/heaped 1 cup brown sugar
100g/3½oz/scant ½ cup granulated sugar
1 egg and 1 yolk, at room temperature
300g/12oz/10½ cups chocolate chips

1 Sift the flour, bicarbonate of soda and salt in a mixing bowl.

2 In a second bowl, cream the butter with the brown and white sugar until fluffy. Beat in the egg and yolk, one at a time.

3 Add the flour mixture to the bowl and fold in. Stir in the chocolate chips. Cover with clingfilm and put into the fridge for 2 hours.

4 Preheat the oven to 170°C/325°F/Gas 3. Form the dough into balls and place on a baking tray lined with baking parchment, leaving enough space between them to allow for spreading.

5 Bake in the oven for about 10 minutes. For soft cookies, take them out of the oven as soon as they are golden brown around the edges. Lift the cookies and paper off the tray and set them to cool on a wire rack before serving.

> "Baking is a fantastic but understated profession, which requires a vast skill set and plenty of passion. Twenty-five years into the trade, I am still learning and experimenting. My obsession for baking has led my kids to award me the title 'Baking Anorak'! This recipe makes the most fantastic light-textured, full flavoured panettone – so much nicer than the pre-packaged, long-life versions. If you make it by hand, you will experience working with dough that evolves from a firm, heavy, bread consistency to a very soft, sticky, stretchy organized mess! The beauty of mastering this technique is that you will be more than capable of making any other bread dough. Make sure you have a cappuccino to hand to accompany your finished result."

Paul Barker & Cinnamon Square

Panettone

MAKES 26

1.2kg/2lb 11oz/9½ cups strong white flour
2 tsp salt
a few drops of vanilla essence
70g/2½oz fresh yeast
360ml/12fl oz/about 1½ cups fresh milk
8 eggs, beaten, plus 1 egg, beaten, for glazing
3 egg yolks
215g/7¾oz/scant 1 cup caster sugar
480g/1lb 1oz unsalted butter, softened
540g/1lb 3oz California raisins
grated zest of 2 oranges
butter, for greasing moulds
50g/1¾oz flaked almonds

1   Put the flour, salt, vanilla essence, yeast, milk and beaten eggs into a bowl and knead by hand until a smooth, firm dough has formed. Leave to rise in a warm place, covered, for 40 minutes.

2   Mix the egg yolks and sugar together, then add to the dough and keep kneading until the dough is smooth and soft. Add the butter in three portions, mixing well between each addition. The dough will become very sticky and requires a slapping and stretching action to incorporate the butter, rather than the kneading method used earlier. A scraper is useful to remove the sticky dough from the table. This will take a while but will eventually give you a very soft stretchy dough. Leave to rise for 40 minutes, as before.

3   Add the raisins and orange zest to the dough and knead gently until evenly distributed. Cut the dough into pieces weighing around 125g/4½oz each, roll them into balls and leave to rest for 10 minutes. Reroll the balls and place them in paper cases in small, greased panettone moulds or greased dariole moulds. You will need 26 in total.

4   Leave to rise again in a warm place for 30 minutes, or until doubled in size, then brush with beaten egg and sprinkle with flaked almonds. Meanwhile, heat the oven to 180°C/350°F/Gas 4.

5   Bake the panettone in the preheated oven for around 15 minutes, or until golden brown. Remove from the oven and set the panettone, still in their moulds, on a wire cooling rack to cool.

Our family celebrations and occasions are always centred around food, whether it's an elaborate family meal or a get together with coffee and cake. This recipe is the first cake I remember making with my mum as a little girl of about 7 or 8, about the time I discovered my passion for baking. It was my job to mix the cinnamon and sugar together, ready to be sprinkled over the apples. I can smell it now and the thought brings back the memory of the cake coming out of the oven all spicy and buttery.

Nutty Tarts
Apple Cake

SERVES 6

175g/6oz/scant 1½ cups
    self-raising flour
85g/3oz/heaped ⅓ cup
    caster sugar
1 tsp baking powder
1 egg, beaten
6–7 tbsp milk
50g/1¾oz unsalted butter,
    melted

FOR THE TOPPING
50g/1¾oz unsalted butter
a handful sultanas (optional)
2 cooking apples, such as
    Bramley, peeled, cored
    and thinly sliced
85g/3oz/⅓ cup caster sugar
1 tsp cinnamon

1   Preheat the oven to 200°C/400°F/Gas 6. Line the bottom of a 20 x 24cm/8 x 9½in cake tin with greaseproof paper.

2   Beat all the cake ingredients together in a big bowl until light and fluffy. Spoon the mixture into the prepared cake tin.

3   Melt the butter for the topping in a small saucepan over a medium heat. Pour it over the top of the cake and sprinkle with the sultanas. Arrange the apple slices on top. Mix the sugar and cinnamon together in a small bowl, then sprinkle over the apples.

4   Bake in the preheated oven for about 35 minutes, or until an inserted skewer comes out clean. Leave to cool, then remove from the tin. You can store the cake in an airtight container for up to 5 days.

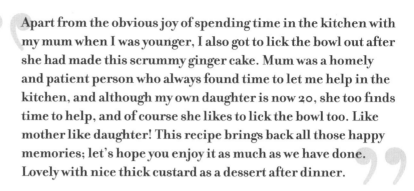

Apart from the obvious joy of spending time in the kitchen with my mum when I was younger, I also got to lick the bowl out after she had made this scrummy ginger cake. Mum was a homely and patient person who always found time to let me help in the kitchen, and although my own daughter is now 20, she too finds time to help, and of course she likes to lick the bowl too. Like mother like daughter! This recipe brings back all those happy memories; let's hope you enjoy it as much as we have done. Lovely with nice thick custard as a dessert after dinner.

Hambleden Herbs
Scrummy Ginger Cake

SERVES 6

100g/3½oz unsalted butter,
   plus extra for greasing
3 tbsp caster sugar
1 tbsp marmalade
200ml/7fl oz/scant 1 cup
   golden syrup
200g/7oz/heaped 1½ cups
   self-raising flour
1 tsp ground ginger
¼ tsp bicarbonate of soda
1 tsp mixed spice
a pinch of salt
2 large eggs, beaten
6 tbsp milk

1 Preheat the oven to 180°C/350°F/Gas 4. Grease and line an 18cm/7in round tin or a 20cm/8in loaf tin. Put the butter, sugar, marmalade and golden syrup into a non-stick pan and cook on a low heat until melted. Leave to cool.

2 Sift the flour, ginger, bicarbonate of soda, mixed spice and salt together in a bowl. Gradually add the sifted flour and spice mixture, beaten eggs and milk to the mixture in the pan, carefully whisking out any lumps.

3 Pour the mixture into the prepared cake or loaf tin and bake in the preheated oven for about 45 minutes, or until firm to the touch and golden brown.

4 Remove the cake from the oven and leave to cool in the tin, then turn out. Cut into slices to serve. It will keep for up to 1 week in an airtight container.

> **I may seem a little old-fashioned in that I don't use a mixer but make my cake in a big mixing bowl – most modern mixers aren't big enough to accommodate the ingredients of a big Christmas cake anyway, and it's such a pain washing them. Our children have always liked to be included in any cake making – it's the thrill of taking lots of different things and creating something else. And indeed how else will they learn to cook? I use an Aga, so I just pop the cake in the bottom oven and leave it to cook for 2½ or 3 hours, then I take it out and test it by sticking a knitting needle into the cake.**

The Spencerfield Spirit Company
Christmas Cake

MAKES 1 x 20cm/8in cake

350g/12oz/2¾ cups raisins (the soggy moist sort)
350g/12oz/2¾ cups sultanas (as above)
175g/6oz/heaped 1½ cups glacé cherries (the inexplicably more expensive and undyed sort are a nicer colour), rinsed, dried and halved
115g/4oz whole almonds
115g/4oz hazelnuts
150ml/5fl oz/scant ⅔ cup malt whisky, such as Sheep Dip, plus another 150ml/5fl oz/scant ⅔ cup closer to Christmas
280g/10oz/1½ cup soft brown sugar
280g/10oz butter, plus extra for greasing
6 large free-range eggs
225g/8oz/heaped 1¾ cups self-raising flour
225g/8oz/heaped 1¾ cups ground almonds
grated zest of 2 oranges
grated zest of 2 lemons
juice of 1 lemon
175g/6oz whole blanched almonds, to decorate

1 The night before, put the fruit and nuts into a bowl, spoon over 6 large tablespoons of the whiskey and breathe in deeply… aaaahhhh! Cover with a tea towel (the mix, not the cook), and allow to steep and swell overnight.

2 The next day, preheat the oven to around 170°C/325°F/Gas 3. Butter a 20cm/8in square cake tin (or 23cm/9in round tin) and line it with a double thickness of greaseproof paper. Take a big bowl and beat the sugar and butter together with a wooden spoon until the mixture becomes pale and fluffy. Whisk the eggs together in a separate bowl, then add to the mixture bit by bit, with a sprinkling of flour each time. Using a big metal spoon, fold in the rest of the flour and the ground almonds. Add all the soaked fruit and nuts, the citrus zest and lemon juice and mix them until evenly distributed.

3 Put the mixture into the cake tin, level the surface and arrange the blanched almonds lightly on top in a pretty pattern. Bake in the preheated oven for 2½ hours, or until a skewer can be inserted into the cake and come out clean. If not cooked, pop it back in the oven for a half hour or so and retest. Repeat until cooked.

4 When cooked, leave the cake to cool for half an hour. Once cooled, feed the cake by pouring over the rest of the whiskey… aaaahhhh!!

5 Double wrap the cake in greaseproof paper, then leave it to mature in an airtight container. Feed again a month later, depending on the baking date. The result is a moist, sumptuous cake with a fantastic aroma, but lighter and crumblier than traditional Christmas cake. Highly recommended with an obligatory glass of whiskey.

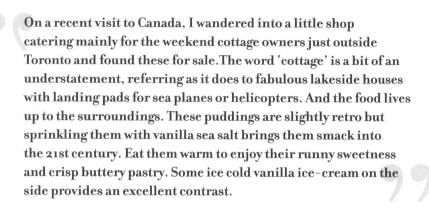

On a recent visit to Canada, I wandered into a little shop catering mainly for the weekend cottage owners just outside Toronto and found these for sale. The word 'cottage' is a bit of an understatement, referring as it does to fabulous lakeside houses with landing pads for sea planes or helicopters. And the food lives up to the surroundings. These puddings are slightly retro but sprinkling them with vanilla sea salt brings them smack into the 21st century. Eat them warm to enjoy their runny sweetness and crisp buttery pastry. Some ice cold vanilla ice-cream on the side provides an excellent contrast.

The Anglesey Sea Salt Company
Anglesey Butter Tarts

MAKES 12–18

butter or oil, for greasing
340g/12oz shortcrust pastry, homemade or ready-made
plain flour, for dusting
250g/9oz/2 cups raisins, soaked in about 4 tbsp boiling water or Cointreau, or 250g/9oz chopped candied orange and lemon peel
250g/9oz unsalted butter
250g/9oz/1⅓ cups light brown sugar
250ml/9fl oz/scant 1 cup golden syrup
2 large eggs, lightly beaten
1 tsp vanilla extract
flaky sea salt or sea salt with vanilla
good quality vanilla ice cream, to serve

1 Preheat the oven to 190°C/375°F/Gas 5 and grease a tray of muffin tins. Roll the pastry out evenly on a lightly floured surface and cut it into circles to fit the tins. Line the tins with the pastry, but do not prick the base. This amount of filling is enough for about 12–18 tins, depending on their depth.

2 Drain the soaked raisins, if using. Arrange the raisins, or the candied orange and lemon peel, in the pastry cases.

3 Mix together the butter, sugar and golden syrup in a large bowl. Add the beaten eggs and vanilla essence and mix until just combined.

4 Spoon into the unbaked pastry cases to come two-thirds of the way up (any fuller and they will overflow) and bake in the preheated oven for 15–18 minutes, or until golden brown and set.

5 Remove the tarts from the oven, sprinkle the tops with sea salt, and serve slightly warm with some good quality vanilla ice cream.

> I think it's a shame that you can buy hot cross buns all year round. They are such a treat – but more so when they are only around at Easter. There is something wonderful about making your own – rich in spice and fruit and a little sticky to the touch. I like to make a big batch and freeze some so that I don't run out.

Richard Bertinet & The Bertinet Kitchen
Hot Cross Buns

MAKES 20

FOR THE CROSS PASTE
100g/3½oz/heaped ¾ cup plain
   flour
a pinch of salt
1 tsp vegetable oil

FOR THE BUNS
½ tsp mixed spice
80g/2¾oz/⅓ cup mixed peel
180g/6¼oz/¾ cup currants
   or sultanas
250ml/9fl oz/1 cup full-fat milk
3 large eggs
60g/2¼oz unsalted butter, diced
500g/1lb 2oz/4 cups strong
   bread flour, plus extra for
   dusting
2 tbsp caster sugar
20g/¾oz fresh yeast
¼ tsp salt

FOR THE RUM SUGAR SYRUP GLAZE
100g/3½oz/scant ½ cup sugar
100ml/3½fl oz/scant ½ cup
   water
2 tbsp dark rum

1 First make the cross paste. Sift the flour into a bowl. Add the salt and oil, then add 4 tablespoons water, a little at a time, to form a paste that can be piped. Set aside until required.

2 To make the buns, put the mixed spice, mixed peel and currants or sultanas into a bowl and set aside. Tip the milk and 1 egg into a mixer with the dough hook attached. Add the butter, flour, sugar, yeast and salt and mix on a slow speed for 5 minutes, or until the mixture forms a dough. Increase the speed to medium for 6–8 minutes, or until the dough comes cleanly away from the sides of the bowl. Add the spice and fruit mix on a slow speed for 1–2 minutes.

3 Turn the dough onto a worktop dusted wiith flour and form it into a ball. Put it back into the bowl, cover with a clean tea towel and leave it to rest in a draught-free place for an hour.

4 When the dough has risen and nearly doubled in size, carefully tip it out on to your work surface and divide it into satsuma-size balls. Roll each piece into a tight ball and place them on a buttered baking tray, close to each other.

5 Make an egg wash by beating the remaining 2 eggs with a pinch of salt. Brush each bun with a little egg wash and place in a warm place for about 1½ hours, until risen.

6 Preheat a fan oven to 190°C/375°F/Gas 4. If you don't have a fan oven, adjust the temperature according to your oven manufacturer's instructions. Brush the buns again with the egg wash and pipe a cross on top of each one, using the cross paste. Bake in the preheated oven for 18–20 minutes. Remove the buns from the oven and transfer to wire racks to cool.

7 For the rum sugar syrup glaze, mix the sugar and 100ml/ 3½fl oz/½ cup water in a small saucepan. Bring to the boil for 4 minutes, then add the rum. Brush over the top of the cooled buns. Serve immediately, or store in an airtight container for up to 3 days. Alternatively freeze and defrost at room temperature before serving.

I was brought up in the English countryside with an abundant vegetable garden and chickens, pigs and sheep. So from an early age I learnt to appreciate the excellent flavours of real food and the difference that good seasonal ingredients, sourced as locally as possible if not home-grown, make to any dish.

Sophie Conran

My mother is a food writer and my father a restaurateur, so food was a central feature of my childhood – my siblings and I were always being sent off to pick things from the garden, either for my mother's recipe testing or for one of our many big family dinners. We were always welcomed into the kitchen and given

jobs to do, mine were mainly chopping garlic, salad spinning and helping to lay and decorate the table.

These days I have a vegetable garden that I nurture lovingly with my own compost. Last year I was a little bit disappointed with the results of all my efforts, but it was only my first year and I have since learned a lot along the way. This year has been so much better, especially for my cabbages! I can't think I've ever been so excited about a vegetable, but when you grow something yourself, you have such a wondrous sense of anticipation. Even a simple cabbage can be something so special, and it makes you want to get really creative in thinking up recipes.

In an ideal world I would eat only things I have grown myself, but sadly this is not really practical. Quality, care and provenance all play

" *I believe we should celebrate ingredients as they come into season.* "

a vital role in the way the food tastes and has a huge environmental impact. I like to have as much variety as possible, and it's fantastic that you can get such diversity when it comes to the range of ingredients.

I love to cook seasonally. In autumn I'm always excited to have wild mushrooms to forage for, and keep an abundance of tomatoes from my little vegetable patch to play with in my kitchen. I pick lots of wild blackberries from the hedgerows and have frozen bags of the extras to enjoy in crumbles and smoothies, and I also make jam, so we can continue to enjoy the sweet taste of summer all year round.

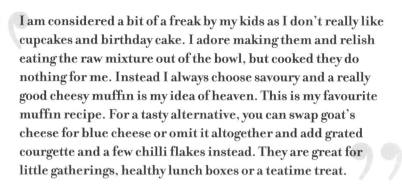

I am considered a bit of a freak by my kids as I don't really like cupcakes and birthday cake. I adore making them and relish eating the raw mixture out of the bowl, but cooked they do nothing for me. Instead I always choose savoury and a really good cheesy muffin is my idea of heaven. This is my favourite muffin recipe. For a tasty alternative, you can swap goat's cheese for blue cheese or omit it altogether and add grated courgette and a few chilli flakes instead. They are great for little gatherings, healthy lunch boxes or a teatime treat.

Sophie Conran

Goat's Cheese and Herb Muffins

MAKES 16

250g/9oz/2 cups plain flour
1 tsp baking powder
½ tsp salt
100g/3½oz butter, straight from the fridge, cut into 1cm/½in cubes
150g/5½oz Cheddar cheese, grated
2 tsp chopped thyme leaves
a handful of basil, chopped
50g/1¾oz/heaped ⅓ cup pumpkin seeds
150ml/5fl oz/scant ⅔ cup milk
3 eggs
135g/4¾oz goat's cheese, cut into 1cm/½in cubes

1 Preheat the oven to 170°C/325°F/Gas 3 and line a muffin tray with paper cases. You will need 16 cases in total. Combine the flour, baking powder and salt in a bowl, then rub in the butter between your fingers and thumbs, until the mixture resembles fine breadcrumbs.

2 Mix in the grated cheese, chopped herbs and pumpkin seeds.

3 Whisk the milk and eggs together in a separate bowl, using a fork. Pour into the flour and mix to a chunky paste. Gently stir in the goat's cheese.

4 Half fill the muffin cases and pop them into the preheated oven on the middle shelf for 20–25 minutes, checking that the middle of each muffin is cooked by poking with a skewer or toothpick (when it comes out clean the muffins are done).

5 Leave the muffins in their tins until cool enough to handle, then transfer them carefully onto a wire cooling rack to finish cooling. Serve warm or cold.

Despite the name, these north Staffordshire oatcakes are thoroughly real bread. Though in his dictionary south Staffordshire lad Dr Johnson dismissed oats as animal fodder, after trying a 'potteries pancake' when visiting the lexicographer in Lichfield, his biographer James Boswell wrote 'It was pleasant to me to find, that "Oats," the "food of horses," were so much used as the food of the people in Dr Johnson's own town.' Great value, healthy and simple to make, a Tunstall tortilla is an excellent alternative to an additive-laden, long-life factory flatbread and ideal for making wraps. Avoid instant/fast-acting/easy yeast unless you know it is additive-free. To find out, read the label.

Chris Young & The Real Bread Campaign
Staffordshire Oatcakes

MAKES **about 5**

100g/3½oz/1 cup porridge oats
100g/3½oz/¾ cup stoneground wholemeal wheat flour
½ tsp salt
½ tsp dried yeast (or 1 tsp fresh yeast), or 2½ tbsp liquid sourdough starter (see below)
350ml/12fl oz/1½ cups milk, water, or a mixture of the two
a little oil, for greasing

1 Put the oats, flour, salt and yeast into a bowl and stir in the milk and/or water. The batter should be loose enough to ladle, but not as thin as cream.

2 Cover the bowl with clingfilm and leave to ferment for about 30–60 minutes, or until bubbles form at the surface.

3 Lightly oil a griddle or heavy-bottomed frying pan (ideally about 25–30cm/10–12in diameter) and place over a medium heat. Ladle in the batter and swirl around to form a pancake about 3mm/⅛in thick.

4 Cook for 3–4 minutes until the batter sets and bubbles pop through the surface like those in a crumpet or pikelet.

5 Flip the pancake over with a spatula or fish slice and cook for about a minute more.

6 Use these as you'd use a pancake, tortilla, chapatti or other flatbread – flat, rolled or folded with the filling of your choice. They're best hot. If you want to store your oatcakes, put them on a wire cooling rack covered with a clean tea towel until they are cool. Sealed in a bag or container, they will keep in the fridge for a day or two, and for 2 months in the freezer.

I remember vividly the first time I tasted a scone. It was within days of first arriving in the UK some 25 years ago and they were served, in the time honoured fashion, with clotted cream and good jam. It was a novelty and a revelation! I've been making scones ever since and I (just like all bakers) am pretty convinced that my scones are better than anyone elses! This recipe is for a cheese scone which adds a bit of variety and is delicious with some thick cut ham.

Richard Bertinet &
The Bertinet Kitchen
Cheese Scones

MAKES 12–15

600g/1lb 5oz/4²⁄₃ cups plain flour, plus extra for dusting
150g/5¹⁄₂oz salted butter, roughly chopped
100g/3¹⁄₂oz/scant ¹⁄₂ cup caster sugar
2 tbsp baking powder
250g/9oz good-quality mature Cheddar or other flavoursome hard cheese, coarsely grated
170ml/5¹⁄₂fl oz/²⁄₃ cup double cream
170ml/5¹⁄₂fl oz/²⁄₃ cup full-fat milk
1 egg, beaten
a pinch of salt

1 Preheat the oven to 200°C/400°F/Gas 6. Put the flour into a mixing bowl and rub in the butter. Add the sugar and baking powder, then add the cheese and mix until it is evenly distributed.

2 Add the cream and milk, then mix with a knife until all the ingredients are bound together. Lightly dust a work surface with flour and turn the dough out on to it.

3 Press the dough down, then fold it in half. Press it down again, fold it again the opposite way, and then repeat until you have a rough square. Flour the top and bottom of the dough, cover with a clean tea towel and leave to rest in a cool place for 15 minutes.

4 Lightly flour the work surface again and roll out the dough to 2¹⁄₂–3cm/1–1¹⁄₄in thick. Brush off any excess flour. Using a sharp knife, cut the dough into scones about 6 x 6cm/2¹⁄₂ x 2¹⁄₂in square.

5 Lay the scones on a baking tray, making sure they are not too close together. Roll out any leftover scraps and cut out more scones until you have used all the dough.

6 Beat the egg with a pinch of salt and brush it over the tops of the scones. Wait 2 minutes, then repeat.

7 Place the scones into the preheated oven using the middle and top shelves (if you used 2 trays), then reduce the heat to 180°C/350°F/ Gas 4. You should always heat your oven to a higher temperature than you want – usually about 20°C above is fine – to compensate for the heat you loose when you open the door. You may need to swap the trays over halfway through baking. Bake the scones for 20 minutes, or until they are well risen, and the tops and undersides are golden brown. Remove from the oven and set on a wire cooling rack to cool.

> *This is based on an old recipe for scones, which before the introduction of baking powder in the mid-1800s, would have been made with barm (yeast from real ale brewing) or a natural leaven. There are many similar recipes to be found across south-west England, with various names, including cut rounds, splits, chudleys (or chudleighs) and tuff buns. As well as arguing whether scone should rhyme with gone or cone, I'll also leave it up to you to decide which should go on first — the jam or cream.*

Chris Young & The Real Bread Campaign
Yeasted Scones

MAKES 10–12, depending on size

290ml/10fl oz/1 cup plus 2 tbsp milk, plus extra for brushing
1 tsp caster sugar
30g/1oz fresh yeast
450g/1lb/scant 3⅔ cups white flour
1 tsp salt
30g/1oz lard, diced
clotted cream, to serve
strawberry jam, to serve

1 Warm the milk in a small saucepan, but not so hot that you can't dip your finger into it. Mix the sugar and yeast together in a cup, then stir them into the milk.

2 Sieve together the flour and salt in a mixing bowl. Gently rub in or fork in the lard to make fine crumbs, then add the yeast mixture.

3 Mix thoroughly, but knead only lightly to keep the finished scones quite 'short'. Even so, these won't be quite as crumbly as modern scones made with baking powder.

4 Leave the dough to rise until about doubled in volume, then fold it over on itself to deflate it but don't knock the living daylights out of it and lose all the gas you've built up.

5 You can then either cut the dough into equal-sized pieces (even better to use scales) and roll them into balls, or roll the dough out to about 1½cm/¾in thick and then cut out circles with a pastry cutter.

6 Lightly grease a baking tray. Place the dough pieces on it and cover with a damp tea towel or a used (but clean) plastic bag, making sure the dough has space to rise without touching the covering. Leave to prove for a further 30–45 minutes.

7 Preheat the oven to 220°C/425°F/Gas 7. Brush the top of the scones with milk and bake in the oven for about 15 minutes until golden brown.

8 Best served when only just cooled, spread with butter or clotted cream and jam. If you have any scones left by the next day, in which case you have more self-restraint than me, split them in half and toast lightly before serving.

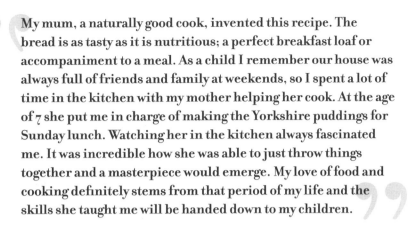

"My mum, a naturally good cook, invented this recipe. The bread is as tasty as it is nutritious; a perfect breakfast loaf or accompaniment to a meal. As a child I remember our house was always full of friends and family at weekends, so I spent a lot of time in the kitchen with my mother helping her cook. At the age of 7 she put me in charge of making the Yorkshire puddings for Sunday lunch. Watching her in the kitchen always fascinated me. It was incredible how she was able to just throw things together and a masterpiece would emerge. My love of food and cooking definitely stems from that period of my life and the skills she taught me will be handed down to my children."

Lovedean
Granola Bread

MAKES 1 loaf

2 tsp dried yeast
2 tbsp dark brown sugar
½ tsp sea salt
500g/1lb 2oz/3⅓ cups good strong plain wholemeal flour
1 tsp melted butter, margarine or lard
8 tbsp granola
1 tbsp melted butter

1 Place the yeast, sugar and salt in a large bowl. Pour on 350ml/ 12fl oz/scant 1½ cups warm water (making sure it is not too hot) and cover with a cloth. Leave in a warm place until frothy (this may take up to an hour).

2 Add the flour, melted fat and granola and mix it all together using a wooden spoon. When it begins to form a dough begin to knead it by hand.

3 Knead by hand or for about 5 minutes in a bread mixer, then shape into 2 round loaves. Place them on a greased tray, cover with a damp cloth and leave to rise in a warm place.

4 Preheat the oven to 200°C/400°F/Gas 6. When the dough has doubled in size, put it into the oven and bake for about 25 minutes, or until firm and crisp. Brush with melted butter and leave to cool. Serve with butter, jam or other spreads.

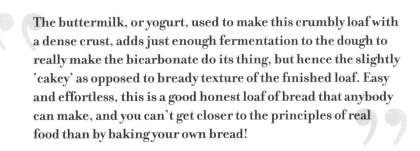

The buttermilk, or yogurt, used to make this crumbly loaf with a dense crust, adds just enough fermentation to the dough to really make the bicarbonate do its thing, but hence the slightly 'cakey' as opposed to bready texture of the finished loaf. Easy and effortless, this is a good honest loaf of bread that anybody can make, and you can't get closer to the principles of real food than by baking your own bread!

Flour Power City Bakery
Irish Soda Bread

MAKES 1 small loaf

125g/4½oz/scant 1 cup wholemeal flour, plus extra for dusting
125g/4½oz/1 cup strong white flour
1 tsp salt
1 tsp bicarbonate of soda
200ml/7fl oz/scant 1 cup buttermilk (natural yogurt is a good alternative)
1 tbsp honey
1 tbsp black treacle

1 Preheat the oven to 200°C/400°F/Gas 6. Sift the dry ingredients together in a large bowl. Add the buttermilk, honey and treacle and bring together as a homogenous mix, taking care to mix as little as possible.

2 Place on a very lightly oiled baking sheet and dust lightly with wholemeal flour. Cut a cross on the top.

3 Bake for about 30 minutes until brown and crisp on the outside but still soft on the inside. The delicious aromas from the oven are the best way to know when things are ready.

I started baking this magnificent bread as a student because it was easy and cooks on an oven tray – I didn't own a bread tin at the time. The cottage loaf is one of those iconic bread shapes that has been made by generations of artisan and domestic bakers over hundreds of years. In 1978 I set up Doves Farm Foods with my husband and we've been growing organic cereals and milling specialist flours and grains ever since. As you might imagine baking my own bread is one of my passions because it is so simple, fun and healthy, allowing you to control mixing bowl ingredients to suit your needs and tastes. Why not double up these recipe quantities and gift a cottage loaf to a friend or pop it in the freezer for another day.

Doves Farm
Cottage Loaf

MAKES 1 500g/1lb 2oz loaf

500g/1lb 2oz/4 cups strong white bread flour or white spelt flour, plus extra for dusting
½ tsp salt
1 tsp dried quick yeast
1 tsp caster sugar
1 tbsp vegetable oil, plus extra for greasing

1   In a large bowl, mix together the flour, salt, yeast and sugar. Add 300ml/10fl oz/scant 1¼ cups warm water and roughly mix. While the dough is still lumpy, add the vegetable oil, then knead well until it feels smooth and pliable.

2   Leave the dough in a draught-free place, covered with a clean tea towel for about 1 hour.

3   Turn the dough out onto a floured surface and knead it firmly for several minutes. Cut off two-thirds of the dough, roll it into a ball and place on an oiled baking tray. Roll the remaining dough into a smaller ball and place it on top of the first one.

4   Press down through the middle of both dough balls with your thumb and leave to rise, covered with the tea towel, until roughly doubled in size.

5   Meanwhile preheat the oven to 220°C/425°F/Gas 7. Once the dough has risen, bake it for 35–40 minutes until brown.

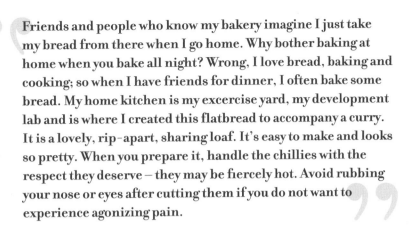

Dan Schinkentanz & De Gustibus

Chilli, Ginger and Coriander Flatbread

MAKES 1 medium loaf

400g/14oz/heaped 3 cups strong white bread flour, plus extra for kneading
1½ tsp dried easy-bake yeast
1 tsp sea salt
2 small red chillies, deseeded and finely chopped
a bunch of coriander, chopped
320ml/11fl oz/scant 1⅓ cups warm water
2 tbsp olive oil, for brushing and drizzling, plus extra to grease
1 tbsp peeled and grated root ginger

1 Place all the dry ingredients, plus half the chillies and half the coriander in a mixer with a dough hook attached. Pour in the water and mix to a soft dough. Then turn onto a floured board and knead for 10 minutes.

2 Shape the dough into a circle. Place on a greased baking sheet, brush with olive oil and boldly dimple the surface with your fingertips. Do not worry about ripping the dough, it will be fine.

3 Sprinkle with the remaining chillies and coriander, then scatter with the ginger. Cover with a tea towel and leave to prove until doubled in size, which will take about an hour.

4 Preheat the oven to 190°C/375°F/Gas 5. Bake the risen circle of dough for 25 minutes. Remove the flatbread from the oven, drizzle with olive oil and serve warm.

Contributors

Anglesey Sea Salt Company
Halen Môn began in a saucepan on the Aga of the Lea-Wilson family kitchen. Today this Welsh sea salt sensation has caught the attention of chefs and food lovers with their organically certified sea salt and flavoured spiced salts making their way onto the menus of top international restaurants.

Arancini Brothers
Arancini Brothers produce their own vegetarian, gluten-free, antipodean version of the Sicilian street food classic, arancini. Their homemade arancini deep fried risotto balls are full of fresh herbs, cheeses, onion, garlic and a hint of citrus, and have won them an ever-growing legion of fans on the London market circuit.

L'Artisan du Chocolat
L'Artisan du Chocolat produce luxury handmade chocolates with exceptional craftsmanship and individuality. Their range includes couture chocolates, chocolate truffles, salted caramels, mints, pearls, hot chocolate and bars.

Andrew Baird
Andrew Baird has been head chef at Longueville Manor in Jersey for more than 17 years, despite stating that he feels he has only been at the hotel for 2 minutes. His inspired cooking makes the most of Jersey's rich waters, with oysters and fresh fish star-studding his menus. Andrew and his dedicated kitchen try to source produce either from Longueville Manor's own walled kitchen garden and restored Victorian hot houses or from the fields and shores of Jersey.

The Arabica Food & Spice Company
Founders Jordanian Jad Al Younis and Londoner James Walters have travelled extensively through Syria, Lebanon, Jordan, Palestine and Israel to procure the finest Levantine produce. Their range boasts a culinary kaleidoscope of delicacies, epitomizing the breadth of flavour of one of the world's finest food cultures.

Bath Pig
Tim French and Matthew 'Mash' Chiles launched The Bath Pig in 2009 to make a British Chorizo – the traditional spicy cured pork sausage from Spain – with British meat. Using outdoor reared, free range and RSPCA freedom food approved pork, The Bath Pig supports British pig farmers and provides a low-carbon and high-welfare alternative to the Spanish equivalent.

Jane Baxter
Imaginative and with an obsession for fresh, seasonal food, Jane previously worked at the River Café, has cooked on TV and has an award winning cookbook to her name. She now heads the acclaimed Field Kitchen, the onsite restaurant at Riverford Organic and twice winner of the Observe Food Monthly UK Best Ethical Restaurant award. The Riverford Organic box scheme began when Guy Watson started delivering vegetables

locally to 30 friends in Devon. Driven by the belief that people want to understand where their food comes from, and care how it is produced, Riverford has created a viable and rewarding alternative to the supermarket grocery shop. Today they deliver around 47,000 boxes a week to homes around the UK from their regional sister farms.

Bellevue Tea
A love affair with tea that started 25 years ago in Calcutta, India, led Clare Jones to start Bellevue Tea, sourcing only the best teas possible from Sri Lanka, South Africa and Kenya to produce a high quality tea bag tea for everyday drinking. Clare takes the time to visit the estates where her tea is grown, and to meet the people at the factory where it is packed.

Richard Bertinet
Originally from Brittany in north west France, Richard trained as a baker from the age of 14, both in Brittany and at the Grand Moulin de Paris. He has previously worked as Head Chef at the Rhinefield House Hotel in the New Forest and the Silver Plough at Pitton in Salisbury, where in 1990 he was awarded Egon Ronay, Pub of the Year and *American Express Magazine*, UK Pub of the Year. Richard now runs The Bertinet Kitchen, a cookery school in Bath which, among many other accolades, was awarded the South West Tourism Excellence Award for Best Tourism Experience 2008/9. He continues to champion the value of 'real' bread.

Raymond Blanc
When he came to the UK from France in 1972, Raymond Blanc started modestly as a waiter in a pub in Oxford. He is now recognized as one of the world's finest chefs and holds two Michelin stars at the highly acclaimed Le Manoir aux Quat' Saisons. He believes in 'good food being central to good living', is a long standing supporter of the organic movement and has been ambassador to the Real Food Festival since its very beginning.

Cairn O'Mohr
Cairn O'Mohr make award-winning Scottish fruit wines from berries, flowers and leaves that grow around their local farm in Perthshire. They claim to do 'nothing fancy, just the best and freshest ingredients we can get, grow or find, fermented in the traditional way' creating distinctive juicy and aromatic fruit wines.

Château Haut Garrigue
Chateau Haut Garrigue – also known as Wild Earth Vineyards – is in South West France along the Dordogne valley. The region offers excellent terroir, the right mix of grape varietals and old vines. These natural wines are created with artisan practices in the vineyard and minimal intervention in the winery. No animal products are used in the winemaking and the wines are thus

suitable for vegans. The wines are also certified organic and currently in conversion to biodynamics with Demeter.

Choi Time
Melissa Choi personally sources and selects her range of high quality Chinese loose leaf teas, including Jasmine-infused teas and flowering teas. Through Choi Time she offers the ritualistic and sensory experience central to traditional Chinese culture and part of her family heritage.

Glynn Christian
Best known in the UK as a BBC TV food traveller and food writer, Glynn Christian has been popular on UK television since the start of the 80s and the early days of celebrity chefdom making *A Cook's Tour*, the BBC's first cookery series shot on location. He also co-founded Mr Christian's in 1974, the cutting-edge deli just off Portobello Road in the Notting Hill area of London. He is the author of *Real Flavours – The Handbook of Gourmet and Deli Ingredients* and, more recently *How to Cook Without Recipes*.

Cinnamon Square
Founded and run by Paul and Tricia Barker, Cinnamon Square opened the store in their home town of Rickmansworth named after their signature patisserie, the US Cinnamon Square bun. They won a gold rating at the Great Taste Awards, an annual competition organized by The Guild of Fine Food, for their wheat and rye bread. Mr Barker understands that 'A lot of people have bread as a big part of their diet, so it should be as wholesome as possible.'

Sophie Conran
Food has never been far from Sophie Conran's world. As well as launching a highly successful tableware and kitchen range, she has created a popular range of gourmet pies. She is a regular food writer and has published several cookery books including *Pies* and *Soups and Stews*.

Carlo Cracco
Carlo Cracco's innovative style of blending various influences and playful combinations of textures and flavours while remaining rooted in the classic Italian tradition has won him huge international acclaim and a reputation as the supreme exponent of Italian cuisine. He has worked with Alain Ducasse and Gualtiero Marchesi – the first chef in Italy to be awarded 3 Michelin stars and considered to be the inventor of the Modern Italian Cuisine. He opened his own restaurant, Ristorante Cracco, which holds 2 Michelin Stars and was voted as one of the World's 50 Best Restaurants in *Restaurant Magazine*.

David's Chilli Oil
Made with chillies and extra virgin cold pressed rapeseed oil from the Cotswolds this chilli oil was created to enliven food with a delicious heat, perfect for drizzling over hot or cold food, cooking and marinating.

De Gustibus

Founders of De Gustibus, Dan and Annette Schinkentanz settled in Oxfordshire in 1990 and started the award winning bakery from a home baking business to become one of the leading artisan bakers in Britain.

Fabio Diu

Having worked in food journalism and for Slow Food International, Fabio is driven by a passion and interest in food from field to plate, conscious of how it shapes our lives and the world around us. This led him to graduate with a Masters in Gastronomic Sciences at the Slow Food University in Italy and to help launch the Real Food Festival.

Doves Farm

The Doves Farm story began at their farm near Hungerford in 1978 and they now offer a wide range of organic, fair trade, gluten-free flour and products. Doves Farm have always had a strong commitment to using the best quality ingredients by applying organic agricultural methods and avoiding added nutrients, enzymes, and GM material. By relying on sustainable and productive farming systems, such as crop rotation, an honest approach to food labelling and a nurtured partnership with suppliers, they have become a well respected and trusted name for organic flour.

Sanjay Dwivedi

Originally from Delhi, Sanjay mixes his knowledge of spices and Indian cuisine with his experience of the Western kitchen learnt in some of London's greatest kitchens (including The Caprice, The Atlantic, The Ivy and The Lanesborough), as well as delighting Mick Jagger's palate as touring chef on The Rolling Stones' 'Bridges of Babylon' world tour. Today, as chef patron of Zaika restaurant he creates his own unique interpretation of modern Asian cuisine and his innovative and sophisticated cuisine made Zaika one of the first Indian restaurants to gain a Michelin star.

Marcus Eaves

Marcus credits his father, a chef in a local country house hotel, as his main inspiration, teaching him the value of seasonal, fresh and local produce. His personal career as a young rising star saw him win Young Chef of the Year at Simpsons before working as Chef de Partie in the two Michelin stared Bath restaurant Lettonie and later, the Landmark Hotel in London working with two Michelin Star Chef John Burton Race. It was while working with Shane Osborne at Pied à Terre that he was introduced to modern cuisine, which led him to run his own kitchen in L'autre Pied which won a Michelin Star in 2008, just 14 months after opening.

Flour Power City

Matt Jones' passion for rustic, good quality 'real' bread has earned Flour Power City and its dedicated team of bakers an enviable reputation on the wholesale and retail market circuit for producing a wonderful range of artisan breads, pastries and cakes. The watchword at Flour Power City is 'quality', meaning a commitment to using only the finest ingredients such as organic Shipton Mill and a network of suppliers who specialise in 'free range' products and un-waxed fruit and vegetables which are grown without the use of pesticides, and additive-free foodstuffs.

Franchi Seeds (1783)

Franchi Seeds, run by Paolo Arrigo, have been established since 1783, and started by selling seeds around the market squares in Parma, Italy. They are now the oldest family-run seed company in the world. Throughout this time they have been maintaining and offering traditional, regional seed varieties of provenance. Franchi Seeds understand the value and importance of growing your own food and the joy and reward that can be derived from nurturing a heritage tomato variety, from seed to sauce.

The Fresh Pasta Company

The Fresh Pasta Company was founded in 2003 by Mark Garcia-Oliver who was born in Cambridge to an Italian mother and raised in Argentina. Argentinean food and culture has been informed and influenced a lot by the significant waves of Italian immigration to Argentina where a strong passion for good food and wine is a fully integrated part of daily life. On returning to England Mark had one purpose: to raise the standards of pasta in the UK, free from additives and made only from the finest ingredients. The Fresh Pasta Company make an award-winning premium range of fresh pasta by hand in Italy using "oo" flour, free range eggs and the most exquisite ingredients for the fillings.

Daniel Galmiche

Considered by many to be gastonomy's best kept secret, Daniel Galmiche has held a Michelin star for 20 years and is currently head chef at The Vineyard in Berkshire. Brought up on an organic farm in Eastern France, Daniel was born into a world of fresh produce. Taking up a 3-year apprenticeship with chef Ynes Lalloz after leaving school, Daniel further developed his skills in field-to-plate French food. Daniel's career has since taken him all over the world, holding responsible posts in Portugal, teaching at a cooking school in France, winning Master Chef of the Year in Scotland and receiving a Michelin Star at Harvey's in Bristol.

Jason Gibb for Nudo: Adopt An Olive Tree

Nudo are a collection of olive groves, mainly in the region of Le Marche, on the eastern coast of central Italy. They offer the rather unique opportunity to adopt an olive tree from which you then receive a yearly harvest of olive oil and in the process also help to support small scale, artisan farming.

Santiago Guerrero

Santiago is a rising talent of authentic Spanish cuisine. Before joining Iberica Food and Culture he worked as the Executive Sous-chef and acting Head Chef at the Melia White House's L'Albufera restaurant in London, voted best Spanish restaurant outside Spain by the Ministerio de Agricultura Caza y Pesca of Spain. Santiago aims to offer a lighter, modern version of many Spanish dishes that not only provide a healthy nutritional base, but also still respect the traditions of his homeland and its artisan producers.

Valentina Harris

Valentina Harris has hosted the Real Food Festival chef theatre from the festival's beginning and is one of the country's leading authorities on Italian Cuisine and gastronomy. As well as her many TV appearances, Valentina is a prolific author and has won many accolades for her cookery books and on the subject of the art of *mangiar bene*.

Hambleden Herbs

Hambleden Herbs only do organic teas, specialising in herbal varieties. They firmly believe that organic teas are all the better for the way they are grown and treated after harvesting. Hambleden Herbs are led by a desire to enhance, rather than dominate the surrounding environment and a belief that this benefits their organic teas in both their purity and flavour.

Willie Harcourt-Cooze

From his cocoa farm in Venezuela, Willie is pursuing his 15-year dream to introduce high quality 'real' chocolate (rather than the more commonly available 'chocolate confectionary' made with high quantities of sugar and fat) to the British public, as well promoting the use of cocoa as a versatile cooking ingredient.

Henry Harris

Head Chef/Patron Henry Harris's passionate enthusiasm for seasonality and the very best quality of ingredients has ensured his restaurant Racine's place as one of London's top French restaurants. Since it opened in 2002 it has been awarded *Time Out* Best New Restaurant, *Tatler* magazine's Most Consistently Excellent Award and ITV's Best French Restaurant of the Year. In a broad ranging career, he has been at the fore of the openings of Bibendum and Harvey Nichols Fifth Floor Restaurants, had various chef consultancies including Soho House. He has published his book *Harvey Nicholls Fifth Floor Cookbook*.

Barny Haughton

One of the pioneers of sustainable eating, Barny Haughton, founded the eco-friendly restaurant Bordeaux Quay in Bristol in 2006. The restaurant and deli is founded on ethical and environmental principles with the aim of creating a restaurant and food business committed to sustainable food practices, responsible energy use, zero waste and community education. Barny continues to be a strong advocate for the organic movement and is involved in food education and environmental work.

Henshelwoods Fine Foods

Lynn Henshelwood started making pickles, chutneys and jams when she owned and ran an award-winning delicatessen in York, where she was already known as a Rick Stein Food Hero. No wonder, as Henshelwoods only use the best seasonal ingredients with the minimum possible food miles, made in small batches, by hand, spiced and flavoured to their own recipes.

Heron Valley

Heron Valley organic drinks are a family business that has been making award winning organic juices and cider for nearly 15 years. They use the best organic whole fruit with no concentrates, water or sugars and hand wash, press and bottle each one. Many of their apples are also sourced from rare indigenous varieties from deepest Devon and their Devon Cider is made using Devon Cider apples fermented with natural yeasts and aged in oak.

Lucas Hollweg

Lucas Hollweg is a journalist turned cook with a regular recipe column in the *Sunday Times Style* magazine. His cooking is all about simple, seasonal food that's as doable as it is delicious.

Mr Huda

Mr Huda's authentic Indian sauces are prepared with fresh spices and herbs, naturally preserved in vegetable oil and ready blended for you to use at home.

Jules and Sharpie La La Limited

Julie Field and Frances Hopewell-Smith (aka Jules and Sharpie) decided to set up a business to indulge their love of chilli. They began with a batch of traditional Jamaican hot pepper jelly in Sharpie's kitchen. Seven years later, they've outgrown the kitchen and now make 12 spicy condiments. Their hand-prepared jellies, jams and chutneys are made with scotch bonnet chillies – last year they got through half a tonne!

Kitchen Garden

On the edge of the Cotswold Hills, in the heart of Gloucestershire, Barbara and Robin Moinet have been making top quality jams, chutneys, marmalades and condiments since 1989 when Barbara Moinet cooked up her first batch of blackberry and apple jam in her cottage kitchen. They continue to make their critically acclaimed preserves of uncompromising quality.

L'ailOlive

L'ailOlive is a wonderfully unique and versatile product; the result of a traditional South Asian recipe that has been passed down three generations of Salina's family while evolving though constant modifications and refinement. Different to the deep-fried garlic in vegetable oil, common in the Chinese kitchen, Salina first slowly bakes Isle of Wight garlic, before combining with, and infusing, extra virgin olive oil. Crispy and crunchy, beautifully sweet and fragrant with no trace of bitterness, L'ailOlive is an equally useful secret culinary weapon to flavour a pasta, salad or roast chicken.

Laverstoke Park Farm

Laverstoke Park Farm is a truly exceptional organic and biodynamic mixed farm, owned and run by former F-1 driver Jody Scheckter. It aims to become self-sufficient and self-sustaining, producing the best-tasting, healthiest food without compromise.

Liberation Ale

The Jersey Brewery (the home of Mary Ann beers and their flagship traditional, cask-conditioned Liberation Ale) in one form or another has been part of island life for well over a century, and the unique beers it produces can truly be called genuine Jersey products. The brewery's beers are part of Jersey's rich history and heritage. Brewing continued during the German occupation and the first World War, and by the 1970s Mary Ann beers were known as 'the beers that made Jersey famous'.

Giorgio Locatelli

Considered by many to be one of the best Italian chefs in the UK, Giorgio Locatelli's outstanding Michelin stared Locanda Locatelli serves traditional Italian dishes, emphasising the quality and freshness of the produce, as well as adding his own personal creative spirit. A Real Food Festival supporter from its inception, Giorgio has always promoted the value and importance of using the best ingredients possible while caring about those who produced it and how it was made.

Lovedean

After discovering a delicious homemade toasted cereal in the Alps, Lucy O'Donnell returned home and stated experimenting to create her own granola recipe. Spurred on by its popularity amongst friends and family, Lovedean was born, using premium jumbo oats, nuts and seeds, slowly toasted with oils including hemp and pumpkin and sweetened only with honey,

Allegra McEvedy

Allegra McEvedy worked in The Belvedere, The Groucho Club, River Café, The Cow and Robert De Niro's Tribeca Grill in New York before returning to London as Head Chef of the Tabernacle, a community restaurant in Notting Hill serving a two-course lunch every day for £5. This shunning of the Michelin allure and a belief that good healthy food should be eaten by one and all led her to open the award winning, healthy fast-food chain LEON with Henry Dimbleby and John Vincent. Allegra is currently chef in residence at the *Guardian*. Her TV work includes presenting *Economy Gastronomy*, and she has penned a series of cookbooks of her own including *Allegra McEvedy's Colour Cookbook* and *LEON: Ingredients & Recipes*.

Patricia Michelson, La Fromagerie

Patricia's love of cheese began up a mountain whilst she was skiing in Meribel. She returned to London with a wheel of Beaufort Chalet d'Alpage, which she sold from her garden shed, graduating to a stall in Camden market a year later. La Fromagerie now comprises two shops and a successful wholesale business along with Patricia's award winning first book *The Cheese Room* and, most recently, *Cheese* to her name.

Thomasina Miers

Thomasina attended the celebrated Ballymaloe Cookery School in Ireland before going on a trip to Mexico and starting an ongoing love affair with the country. After winning Masterchef she made

a couple of television programmes including *A Cook's Tour of Spain*, a wonderfully evocative food travelogue, before opening the first Wahaca restaurant in Covent Garden, a highly successful and growing restaurant group offering authentic Mexican street food. She is also author of a number of cookery titles including *Cook: Smart Seasonal Recipes* and *Mexican Food Made Simple*. She champions local markets and cooking seasonal food.

Mortimer Chocolate

Adrian Smith was once responsible for creating and managing the Galaxy and Maltesers brands of hot chocolate drinks at Masterfoods. Disillusioned with the homogenous and restrictive nature of working with such big brands he decided to start up Mortimer Chocolate Company, sourcing and producing fine quality chocolate from around the world, focusing on small growers. Chocolate is made from cocoa beans, which, just like coffee and wine, vary in flavour according to the soil, season and region in which they grow. So instead of blending to achieve consistency, Adrian selects directly from origin so that you can experience and understand the variety of different cocoa flavours from around the world. His 100% plain chocolate powder is made with no milk, no fats and no additives, just fine, pure, chocolate.

Nutty Tarts

Conceived as an alternative to the customary flowers and cards, Rachael and Deborah started Nutty Tarts to offer something different as a gift. They home bake their award-winning biscuits and cakes using the best ingredients.

Jacqueline O'Donnell

Chef at The Sisters restaurants, Jacqueline, together with her sister Pauline, runs two restaurants in the heart of Glasgow's West End at Kelvingrove and just off Crow Road at Jordanhill. The two Glasgow restaurants offer modern Scottish cooking using the best local ingredients they can find.

Oliodivino

Oliodivino is a truly divine artisan, organic, extra-virgin olive oil. Cultivated and produced in the small town of Castel Madam near Rome, the olives are picked late in November, at the season of 'invaiatura', when the olives are in their prime. Careful selection and treatment ensures that the olive oil retains its low acidity level and all the natural aromas and flavours.

Ashley Palmer-Watts

Ashley joined Heston Blumenthal at The Fat Duck in Bray in 1999, at which point it had been open for 4 years and just received its first Michelin star. Today it holds 3 Michelin stars, and has been awarded many accolades including 'Best Restaurant in the UK' with a 10/10 score (*Good Food Guide* 2008, 2009), and 'Second Best Restaurant in the World' (San Pellegrino Worlds 50 Best Restaurant Awards 2009, 2008,2007, 2006). Ashley became Sous Chef of The Fat Duck within 2 years and Head Chef in 2003. His eye for detail, formidable enthusiasm for research and creativity has seen him accomplish, with Heston Blumenthal, the historic British and multisensory dishes served at The Fat Duck.

Patchwork Pâté

Patchwork Pâté was established in 1982 by Margaret Carter, a talented, although untrained, home cook, who found herself divorced with three children to look after. With a start up cost of just £9.00, saved from the housekeeping, she began selling her homemade pâtés to pubs in nearby Llangollen. Today, Patchwork Pâté is a highly regarded and award-winning business still handmaking its delicious pâtés in small batches, without artificial colouring, additives or preservatives, to Margaret's original recipes.

Arthur Potts Dawson

Arthur can be said to be one of London's leaders in the crusade for eco-friendly restaurants and food retailing. After having worked as Head Chef at River Café and Fifteen Restaurant he was Executive Chef at Acorn House in King's Cross, which runs along a strong ethic of sustainability, producing far less waste than many domestic households. Arthur has now also launched the progressive People's Supermarket in London; a consumer owned cooperative food store that aims to reshape and rethink the way we buy food.

Real Bread Campaign

Bread is a fundamental part of our diet: 99% of UK households buy bread and 74% of us eat it at least once a day. Unfortunately, most of the bread we eat in Britain is made using methods that arguably have little regard for its nutritional qualities or the environmental and social impact of its production and distribution. Co-ordinated by the charity Sustain: the alliance for better food and farming, the Real Bread Campaign is a not-for-profit initiative that brings together bakers, independent millers, cereal growers, researchers, activists and anyone else who cares about the state of bread in Britain.

The Really Garlicky Company

From their farm at the foot of the Cawdor Hills in the Highlands of Scotland, The Really Garlicky Company are the only UK growers of Porcelain garlic. Closely related to wild garlic, it packs a sweet punch with plump cloves that are easy to peel and won't drive you mad in the kitchen.

Oliver Rowe

Oliver Rowe worked in restaurants in Italy and Greece, before returning to London to train under Sam and Sam Clarke at Moro. He climbed up the ranks to become Deputy-head Chef, then turned to French cuisine, cooking in an Anglo-French restaurant in Hammersmith, and for a period in France. In 2004 he set up a café serving European food. When a former pub came up for sale he set up a new restaurant, sourcing all ingredients from in and around Greater London, with the BBC programme *The Urban Chef* charting his mission.

Sacla'

For 70 years Sacla' have made their pesto sauces and foods with care, flair and love. A family business since 1939, the company has a respect for tradition, honouring the wisdom of age-old techniques in growing and preserving vegetables, following the seasons whenever possible. Sacla' develop and nurture supportive relationships with their farmers and growers, investing in quality and sustainability, avoiding the use of pesticides and other nasties, preferring to encourage a more organic approach to farming.

Geetie Singh

Geetie opened the Duke of Cambridge to be the UK's first organic gastropub, and it has been an outstanding success, regarded as one of the best places to eat out in London. Geetie was determined to combine her passion for pubs and food to set up a business that could thrive without harming the environment, bringing delicious organic food to its customers, and educating them about organics, sustainable living and seasonal eating.

The Spencerfield Spirit Company

The rather idiosyncratic name for their whisky, Sheep Dip, came about because British farmers would hide their barrels of homemade whisky marked as 'Sheep Dip' to avoid paying taxes. This masterfully blended tipple couldn't be further away from the chemical insecticide and fungicide treatment for sheep. Marrying together several single malt whiskies, they are then aged between 8 and 12 years in quality 'first fill wood', each adding unique characteristics to produce an exceptional product.

Suzie's Yard

Suzie's Yard is a small family-run farm in Val di Chiana in Tuscany. As well as producing their own olive oil they also have a mission to promote products from small farm producers of the Val di Chiana and the Val d'Orcia and select a range of organically certified and ethically produced products from the area with one fundamental pre-requisite: that they simply taste great.

Jun Tanaka

Jun Tanaka has headed up the kitchen at Pearl since its opening in 2004, during which time he has gained an excellent reputation for his modern French cuisine. Jun uses the very best seasonal ingredients, with the simple premise to enhance flavour, bringing out natural qualities and fresh, distinct tastes. Together with Mark Jankel, Jun is also involved in the Food Initiative, including a street kitchen and restaurant aiming to fully integrate sustainable practices from the build and running to food sourcing.

Ben Tish

Ben Tish is Executive Head Chef of the highly acclaimed Salt Yard in Fitzrovia and its sister restaurant Dehesa off Carnaby Street in London. Both restaurants express Ben's passion for Spanish and Italian flavours while sourcing their meat from small farms in Wales and the UK's south east. Ben also oversees The Blackfoot Butchers, which specialises in free range British meats, artisan charcuterie and cheese.

Cyrus Todiwala

Described by *Harper's Bazaar* as a 'Chef of Genius', Cyrus is a passionate campaigner for sustainability and buying locally – Café Spice Namasté's list of green awards includes two 'Environmental Best Practice' awards, The Green Point Award and most recently was Highly Commended in The Sustainable Food category of the Sustainable City Awards 2009. Cyrus was awarded an OBE by the Queen. Renowned for its innovative and fresh Indian cuisine, Café Spice Namasté is one of the most highly regarded Indian restaurants in the UK.

Tracklements

In 1970, William Tullberg started to make the first wholegrain English mustard. Since then, in the heart of the Wiltshire countryside, William, his son Guy and his growing family of co-workers have been making outstanding products. For more than 40 years Tracklements products have continued to be handmade in small batches to traditional recipes using only the best, natural ingredients resulting in products that taste as good as the best homemade.

Turnham Green

'Indulgence with a conscience' is Turham Green's guiding motto to which Nathalie, who left her job in the City to train as a chef and nutritionist, creates condiments from natural ingredients and preserving methods.

Lesley Waters for Denhay Farm

Appearing regularly on *Ready Steady Cook*, *Great Food Live* and *This Morning*, Lesley is a former Head Tutor of Leith's School of Food & Wine and author of several cookery books. Originally a Londoner, Lesley was charmed by Dorset where she now has a cookery school. Inspired by the quality of the local produce, such as Denhay Farm, she cooks simple, delicious seasonal food. Committed to quality, animal welfare and environmental sensitivity, Denhay Farm in west Dorset has an enviable reputation for producing the finest dry cured bacon and traditional farmhouse Cheddar cheese.

Nic Watt

Born in Sydney, Nic was drawn to Japan and Japanese food by his strong passion for quality seafood. After having worked in many of the finest restaurants around the world, including the Michelin stared Nobu in London, Nic is now Group Executive Chef at London's Roka, which in 2005 (less than a year after it opened) was awarded Best Oriental Restaurant.

Index

COLOR DRAWING

Design Drawing Skills and Techniques for Architects, Landscape Architects, and Interior Designers

THIRD EDITION

MICHAEL E. DOYLE

CommArts

BICENTENNIAL 1807 WILEY 2007 BICENTENNIAL

JOHN WILEY & SONS, INC.

To William Kirby Lockard, FAIA

For your kindness, mentorship, and support.
Drawing as a Means to Architecture spoke to me as a student,
late one night years ago, and changed my life.

CONTENTS

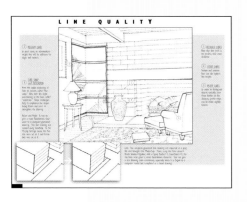

ACKNOWLEDGMENTS

This book would not have been accomplished without the presence of the many generous people in my life:

My wife, Ellen, for her love and wisdom.

The partners of CommArts—Janet Martin, Richard Foy, and Henry Beer—whom I thank for their continued and enthusiastic support.

The many designers and staff at CommArts, who freely gave their assistance: Melissa Britz, Taku Shimizu, Bryan Gough, Kristian Kluver, Jim Babinchak, Grady Huff, Patty Van Hook, and Gary Kushner. Keith Harley deserves special thanks for the graphic design of this book and its cover.

John Bacus, for his brilliance and wit—and for opening my eyes to the digital universe.

The Design Communication Association (DCA), for its support of both traditional and new design communication education. The DCA has given us a wonderful way to exchange ideas about how to more effectively communicate our design ideas.

James R. DeTuerk, professor emeritus, Department of Landscape Architecture, the Pennsylvania State University. I will be forever grateful for his inspiration.

Frank M. Costantino, Douglas E. Jamieson, Ronald J. Love, Thomas W. Schaller, AIA, and Curtis J. Woodhouse for their generosity in allowing me to publish their professional illustrations. Their words of encouragement were much appreciated.

Paul Stevenson Oles, FAIA, for his gentle insistence, through his work and his words, that value is the key to effective color illustration.

INTRODUCTION

The purpose of this book is to provide an approach to drawing in color during the early phases of your design process. As you become familiar with this approach, you will find your ability to draw in color considerably expanded and, as a result, you will be able to create your design studies more quickly and effectively. You will also find yourself selecting—and inventing—favorite ways of drawing in color. This is as it should be, as there is no one correct approach to creating these drawings. Rather, you will find that your approach keeps changing and adjusting, depending on the design communication task before you. Use the approach—or combination of approaches—that works best for each situation. A significant amount of new material on digital techniques has been added to this new edition, and the presentation of this material presumes the reader has a working knowledge of Photoshop. You may choose to incorporate some or all of these techniques into your approach to color drawing. Or you may choose not to use any of them. The utility of *Color Drawing*, third edition, does not depend on your understanding or use of digital drawing techniques.

Most of the step-by-step drawings in the book are in perspective, but begin with a completed line drawing. However, be assured that no amount of skill with color can help a drawing that has a poorly drawn underlying structure or one that demonstrates a lack of understanding of light, shade, and shadow. Perspective and shade and shadow are the universal language of design picture making. They form the link between you and those to whom you wish to communicate your conceptual ideas about form, space, and, ultimately, place. In order to help you review and recall the basic elements of design drawing, summary sheets on perspective, line quality, shade and shadow, and illumination have been added to the opening chapter.

If you are new to color design drawing, start at the beginning of the book, because it is organized in a way that builds skills one step at a time, with each succeeding chapter predicated on information supplied by those previous to it. On the other hand, if you are more familiar with this kind of drawing, you may wish to use the book more like a handbook, accessing materials, methods, and techniques as needed.

Part I is an overview of the basic phenomena, media, papers, and techniques that assist you in illustrating the various elements, materials, and finishes you propose to use to bring your ideas to life. You illustrate them to communicate them both to yourself and to others. Chapter 1 is an empirical introduction to the subject, presenting the phenomena of color and light that inform the effects and techniques used throughout the book. Chapter 2 discusses the media and papers that work best for color design drawing. Line media and color media—including pastels and alcohol-based markers—are introduced, as well as recommended palettes of markers, color pencils, and pastels. Ink-jet paper has been added to a list of papers that includes Canson paper and bond paper, all of which are compatible with this book's approach to color drawing. Chapter 3 shows a variety of techniques used to apply color media and to create impressions of materials, and now includes basic digital techniques. The "sketch/photo combo"—hand drawing with digital color, "hybrid" color drawing, and a new "retrocolor" technique that uses mylar are a particular focus. Chapter 4 uses these media, paper, and techniques to create an encyclopedia of step-by-step approaches to the illustration of elements, materials, and finishes that architects, landscape architects, and interior designers commonly use in practice. Chapter 5 shows how to draw scale elements in color, including unique approaches to drawing automobiles and a new way to illustrate human figures.

Part II shows how the basic skills found in Part I can be used to create a range of drawings for presentation purposes. In addition to looking *into* a drawing for design information, as Part I implicitly encourages, the designer is introduced to ways of looking *at* his drawings as a graphic composition and how to provide his drawings with visual organization and impact.

Chapter 6 shows how to consider your color design drawings as compositions in their own right. Color relationships are discussed in terms of contrasts, and unity, balance, proportion, and rhythm are introduced as compositional principles to be used as tools to evaluate your drawings as you prepare them for presentation. Chapter 7 shows step-by-step how to utilize the material covered in the first six chapters to create a variety of kinds of color design drawings—from quick sketches to finished presentation drawings. The first part of the chapter covers new ways to plan your drawings, with an emphasis on value composition as a means to creating dramatic impact. The rest of the chapter covers approaches for creating color design drawings on a variety of papers, including Bristol, bond, tracing paper, mylar, ink-jet paper, and toned papers such as Canson, using both traditional line drawings and different kinds of computer "setup" drawings. Additional layers of information found in design drawings are also discussed, including photographs and various ways of applying notes. The chapter closes with some recommendations for creating single-sheet and multiple-sheet presentations. Chapter 8 has been entirely redeveloped to introduce an approach to color drawing in which color is applied entirely by digital means.

A number of new tools and approaches to design communication have been developed during the last decade. Regardless of the ongoing development of hardware, software, and technique used to create illustrations, however, the knowledge and skills needed to do so effectively and efficiently remain unchanged. A designer still needs facility in the fundamentals of design drawing—perspective, light, value, color, and materials representation. Hopefully, you will find this new edition of *Color Drawing* helpful in developing these fundamentals.

Use what you can from this book as you create your own approach to a drawing-based design process—one that will, it is hoped, allow you access to the deepest reaches of your abilities. Like any tool, this book is a means to an end. Its ultimate purpose is to enable you, the designer, to make our built surroundings better than we could ever have dreamed possible.

COMMUNICATION

"**A**lthough draftsmanship is no longer the price of admission to a design career, those who master the language of drawing are likely to see, to think, and to communicate with more sophistication than those who only master the computer. Aside from this competitive advantage, however, there's a deeper satisfaction to be derived from drafts-manship: the thrill of vanquishing a monster-sized, fire-breathing design problem with nothing more than a small, sharpened stick."

| *Marty Neumeier*

INITIAL CONSIDERATIONS

Those who design places for use by others—architects, landscape architects, and interior designers—engage in a specialized form of communication. They first create images of their ideas about the three-dimensional forms and spaces that make these places, but they create them on two-dimensional surfaces.

To do this effectively, a designer must understand not only the visual phenomena on which these kinds of images are based, but also how to work with them to communicate these images to others. No amount of technique with color media can rescue a drawing that displays a lack of understanding of the basics of perspective, line quality, and light and shadow.

BEFORE COLOR SKILLS, ACQUIRE DRAWING BASICS

An unfortunate outcome of our computer-intensive system of design education has been our students' undereducation in design drawing fundamentals: perspective; line quality; the effective use of line weight, shade, and shadow; and illumination. While students and young professionals may know how these building blocks of drawing work, many have weak skills when it comes to actually using them easily, quickly, and confidently during the conceptual and schematic stages of the design process. They struggle to sketch an idea convincingly and are often embarrassed by the results. Consequently, many default entirely to the computer at an inappropriate point in the process—not to leverage skills, but to cover for their absence. This is a growing problem.

Professional design is a business. To be successful, designers must "work smart." This means applying the appropriate skills to the appropriate tasks. The quick generation of design ideas demands the ability to explore them fluidly. Usually, designers who can employ "eyeball" perspective and quick shade and shadow techniques with pencil and paper are able to sketch out numerous alternatives in the time it takes to generate a single computer-based study. Although building your drawing skills in perspective, shade and shadow, and illumination will most certainly take time at first, such skills will not only save you time later on, they will make you far more competitive in the professional design market, whether you are self employed or work for others.

If you are just beginning the study of design, you may be curious about the best sources of information to help in building these skills. There are many books on these subjects; all take different approaches to roughly the same subject matter: drawing for designers. William Kirby Lockard's books, such as *Drawing as a Means to Architecture* and *Design Drawing Experiences, 2000 Edition* have helped many students build their understanding and skills. *Design Graphics* by C. Leslie Martin is a classic, unparalleled even today in its explanation of shade and shadow construction. An annotated bibliography of the best of these books can be found in the back of this book.

Students of design must have more than "book knowledge," however, in order to build their skills to the point of usefulness. The best teacher of perspective, shade and shadow, illumination, and color is the world around you. Begin your study by starting to *see* that world instead of simply *looking* at it. The best way to see is to *draw*, to attempt—over and over—to represent the three-dimensional world on a two-dimensional surface. If you persist, especially if you can refrain from judging your product too harshly, your skills will progress. Improvement may happen imperceptibly, as drawing to visualize slowly becomes second nature. Your skill with free, easy, and nonjudgmental drawing will be an important ally on your way to becoming a better designer.

The pages that follow are intended as summary sheets of basic design drawing skills. They are not meant to serve as a complete course in design drawing; hopefully, they will refresh your memory and function as references for its basic steps and techniques. The drawings (with the exception of the computer drawings inset in figure 1-2) were created quickly, the way a designer typically works, and in the order shown. Common drawing media—tracing paper, a .5 mm graphite pencil, *Black* Prismacolor pencil, and a couple of gray markers—were used.

Perspective

Figure 1-1 shows the basic elements used to create a typical perspective drawing. An important component in this early stage is the "vision" sketch shown at the upper left. It is important to draw this nascent image—no matter how rough or crude—directly from your mind onto a sheet of paper. Work quickly. Do not worry about correct perspective, scale, or proportion. The only thing to concern yourself with at this point is getting as much of your idea—your "vision"—out of your mind and onto the page as possible. Use notes liberally; add other sketches and diagrams as necessary. You will most likely have plan diagrams, even crude ones, to help you pick viewpoints and organize your thinking. While it may seem self-evident, *it is only after you have your vision in front of you* that you can proceed to the next steps, evolving a drawing in an informed way. Then you can make a picture of your idea using your vision sketch as a guide. The first steps in making this picture are shown in the larger image.

The green lines show how the lines in the drawing relate to their vanishing points, while the red arrows point out the parts of the drawing being discussed. The numbers show roughly the order in which these parts of the perspective were considered and utilized.

Fig. 1-1 These studies show how an initial vision is cleaned up so that it is "in perspective" and makes perceptual sense. A border is drawn to clearly define the drawing area. Note how the design evolves with each successive version of the drawing.

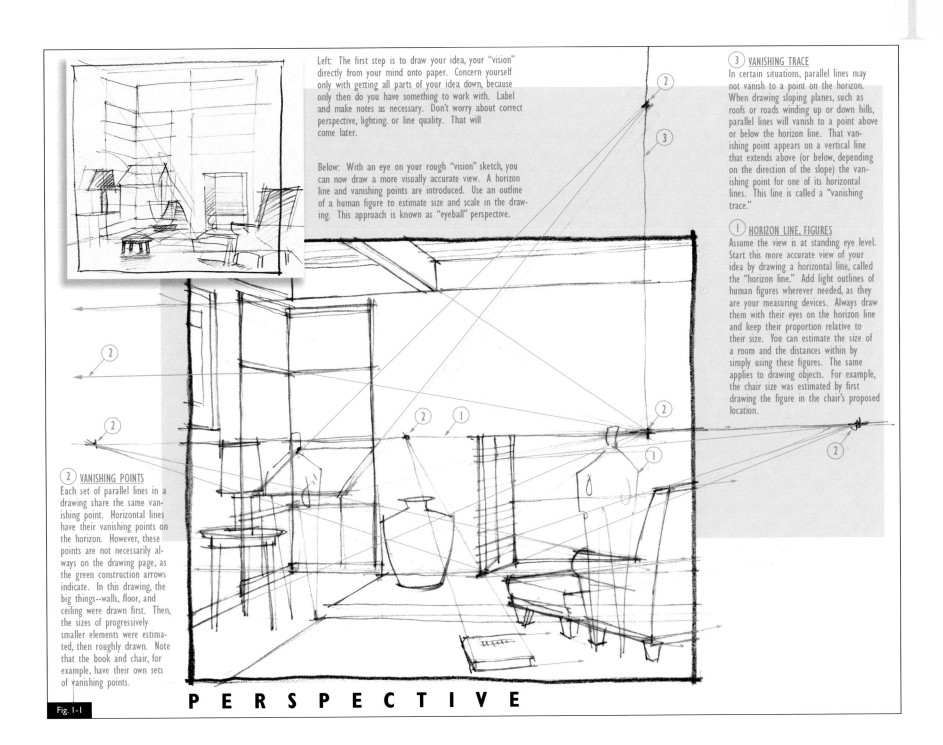

Left: The first step is to draw your idea, your "vision" directly from your mind onto paper. Concern yourself only with getting all parts of your idea down, because only then do you have something to work with. Label and make notes as necessary. Don't worry about correct perspective, lighting, or line quality. That will come later.

Below: With an eye on your rough "vision" sketch, you can now draw a more visually accurate view. A horizon line and vanishing points are introduced. Use an outline of a human figure to estimate size and scale in the drawing. This approach is known as "eyeball" perspective.

③ VANISHING TRACE
In certain situations, parallel lines may not vanish to a point on the horizon. When drawing sloping planes, such as roofs or roads winding up or down hills, parallel lines will vanish to a point above or below the horizon line. That vanishing point appears on a vertical line that extends above (or below, depending on the direction of the slope) the vanishing point for one of its horizontal lines. This line is called a "vanishing trace."

① HORIZON LINE, FIGURES
Assume the view is at standing eye level. Start this more accurate view of your idea by drawing a horizontal line, called the "horizon line." Add light outlines of human figures wherever needed, as they are your measuring devices. Always draw them with their eyes on the horizon line and keep their proportion relative to their size. You can estimate the size of a room and the distances within by simply using these figures. The same applies to drawing objects. For example, the chair size was estimated by first drawing the figure in the chair's proposed location.

② VANISHING POINTS
Each set of parallel lines in a drawing share the same vanishing point. Horizontal lines have their vanishing points on the horizon. However, these points are not necessarily always on the drawing page, as the green construction arrows indicate. In this drawing, the big things--walls, floor, and ceiling were drawn first. Then, the sizes of progressively smaller elements were estimated, then roughly drawn. Note that the book and chair, for example, have their own sets of vanishing points.

P E R S P E C T I V E

Fig. I-I

Line Quality

The drawing in figure 1-2 was created using a tracing paper overlay on the rough perspective view in figure 1-1. With the basics of perspective out of the way, the designer was free to focus on other issues. Generally, medium-weight lines are used for most of the drawing, with the designer exercising more control than in figure 1-1. Where lines intersect, the connection can be emphasized by slightly crossing the lines—called *extension*—and making the ends of the lines ever so slightly darker—called *line snap.* Somewhat heavier lines are used to emphasize distance between objects and the background where necessary; light lines are used to indicate materials, patterns, and distant objects.

Designers frequently draw directly on computer-generated wireframes, and there are ways to give computer line drawings a more hand-drawn character. This can reduce the distinction between the two types of lines and make the resultant "hybrid" drawing more coherent. In other words, if rough sketches can be used for presentation, you can avoid having to redraw the wireframe component of the drawing. The inset drawings in figure 1-2 show an easy way to "roughen" computer-generated lines.

Design drawings used for presentation that have a loose, hand-drawn character are more important during the conceptual and schematic phases than many designers realize. When shown to clients, their unfinished quality indicates that the ideas they represent are works in progress. Compared to a more polished illustration, they leave the impression that the design process is not yet closed, and they invite participation in that process.

An important but frequently overlooked point about freehand design drawing using tracing paper overlays is that while designer create these "picture views" of their ideas, their "design minds" are always working. Not only is the *picture* of the idea being refined, so are the design *ideas* represented in the view. For example, when you compare the drawings in figures 1-1 and 1-2, note how the furniture was refined, materials indicated, and patterns introduced in figure 1-2. As designers, our propensity to respond to three-dimensional views is why freehand perspective drawing is such a powerful design tool.

Fig. 1-2 The way lines are created in drawings not only helps communicate the drawing's content, it also communicates the attitudes and intentions of the designer. Note how this overlay refines the design by adding information about furniture detail, materials, and patterns—all while improving the drawing itself.

LINE QUALITY

② MEDIUM LINES

In most cases, an intermediate-weight line will be sufficient for edges and corners.

⑤ LINE SNAP and EXTENSION

Note the subtle darkening of lines at corners, called "line snap." Also, note the slight overcrossing of the lines, called "extension." These techniques help to emphasize the shapes being drawn and serve to strengthen the drawing

Below and Right: A way to give a more hand-drawn char-acter to a computer-generated drawing. This line drawing was created using SketchUp. In the Display Settings menu, the Pro-files were set at 3 and Exten-tion was set at 8.

① RELAXED LINES

Note that line work is not perfect, with some shakiness

④ LIGHT LINES

Texture and pattern lines use the lightest line weight.

③ HEAVY LINES

In order to distinguish objects spatially from those further in the distance, profile edges can be made slightly heavier

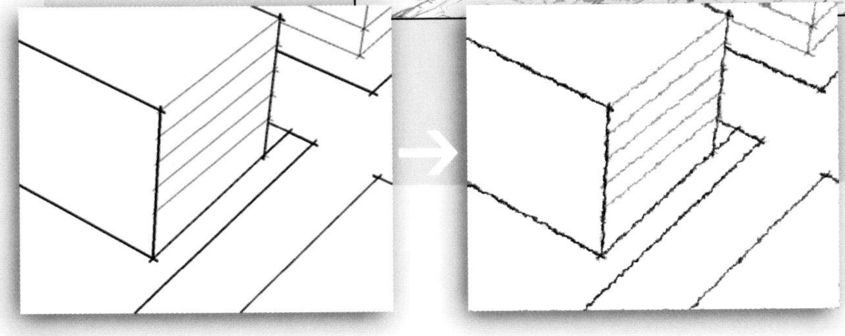

Left: The computer-generated line drawing was exported as a jpeg file and brought into Photoshop. There, using the Filter menu> Brush Strokes>Spatter, with a Spray Radius=7, Smoothness=9, the the lines were given a more hand-drawn character. This can give a line drawing more consistency, especially when it is begun as a computer model but completed as a hand drawing.

Fig. 1-2

Shade and Shadow

The term *shade* refers to those surfaces that face away from the sun. A *shadow* is an area without sunlight on a surface that would otherwise be illuminated by the sun. The shape of a shadow is determined by the form of the object that causes it. It is important for a designer to know how to approximate accurate shade and shadow three-dimensionally. Shade and shadow help reveal forms and spaces and make them appear real. They help convince the viewer of a drawing that these forms and spaces can indeed exist.

The rules for shade and shadow are few, and remain consistent no matter what the view. To best understand these rules, observe shade and shadow in your surroundings. Draw them when opportunities present themselves. You will be able to eyeball shade and shadow in a drawing sooner and more effectively than you may think possible.

Figure 1-3 shows a rough shade and shadow study done on a tracing paper overlay on the drawing in figure 1-2. First, analyze the view to consider where the sun is coming from, and from what angle. Your view may have a particular cardinal orientation that, in turn, tells you the sun direction. Likewise, there may be a particular time of day and season you want to illustrate. If your view is hypothetical, with no particular orientation, pick the sun direction and angle that will best reveal the forms and spaces in the drawing. This means the sun can come from either side, and the forms and spaces in your drawing will be partially sunlit and partially in shade.

Next, consider which surfaces are in shade (facing away from the sun) and which are sunlit. The edges that divide sunlit surfaces from shaded surfaces are known as the *casting edges*. They will determine the shape of the shadows. These edges may be visible in the drawing, or they may be partially or fully blocked by other objects. Think of your drawing as "see-through" in order to help you locate all the casting edges.

Pick a vertical casting edge and momentarily think of it as being a single, freestanding "flagpole." Recall your decision about general sun direction that helped you locate the casting edges, and decide where you want the shadow of the flagpole to fall. Remember that all the shadows (caused by the sun) of all the verticals in the drawing will fall in the same direction. In a plan of the view, they would all be parallel on the sheet. This means, of course, that in the perspective view, the shadows of all these verticals point to the same vanishing point. Once you have determined the direction of the verticals' shadows, decide how long

you want the shadow of your first flagpole to be. By taking a line from the top of your flagpole to the end of your flagpole's shadow, you will determine the sun angle. This angle can, of course, vary, depending on how high or low you want the sun, but it should remain consistent throughout the drawing (e.g., if the sun is coming from the left or right). If the sun is coming toward you or from behind you, its rays require a vanishing point (see Martin 1968). One final rule not illustrated in figure 1-3: The shadow of a vertical casting edge that falls on a vertical surface—such as a wall—is also vertical.

The shadows of horizontals cast shadows parallel to themselves, whether they fall on the ground or a nearby *parallel* vertical surface. Again, remember that all parallel lines point to a common vanishing point, whether they are an object or an object's shadow. The exception to this rule is if the nearby vertical surface is *perpendicular* to the direction of the horizontal shadow. Then, the shadow *resolves* back to its casting edge, as you can see in figure 1-3.

If you are unfamiliar with the rules of shade and shadow, these brief explanations may seem like a lot to absorb. However, most shade and shadow situations can be drawn using these few rules. Sometimes, of course, interpolation may be required, such as when a wall is neither parallel nor perpendicular to a horizontal shadow, but at an angle somewhere between the two. Spend some time studying these examples, as well as the more detailed examples shown in the references in the bibliography. Most importantly, look at the world around you and notice that its shades and shadows behave the same way as the rules describe. Spend some time observing shadows on a sunny day; try to figure out how their particular shapes are formed. Once you become familiar with these rules, you will be more comfortable using them in your design drawings. Create simple objects and spaces in perspective, pick a sun angle, and practice creating its shades and shadows using these rules. With adequate practice, drawing convincing shade and shadow will become second nature.

Fig. 1-3 This is a quick shade and shadow study on a tracing paper overlay. The study includes illumination responses to the light source. The green lines are shade and shadow construction lines; the red arrows point to shade and shadow issues; the blue arrows point to illumination issues.

① DETERMINE
CASTING EDGES

Determine, in general, where you want the sun coming from. That will tell you which edges are "casting edges" --those edges that form the boundary line between sunlit surfaces and those in shade. The casting edges determine the shape of the shadow/sunlit area.

② DETERMINE
SHADOW OF A VERTICAL

Think of vertical casting edges as freestanding "flagpoles," as Lockard calls them. Pick a direction you want this flagpole shadow to fall on the floor, away from the light source. Note that if you extend the flagpole shadow, it will eventually reach the horizon. All other shadows of verticals falling on horizontal surfaces will aim toward this same point on the horizon. This is because the shadows of all verticals in a drawing are parallel to one another. This is obvious when you look at a plan view with shadows.

Ⓐ BRIGHT AREAS

In addition to direct sunlight, bright areas in an interior are themselves light sources. The ambient light from outside, as well as the reflected sunlight on the wall and floor, all act as a diffuse source of light. The interior elements create shadows that correspond to this source

③ DETERMINE SUN ANGLE

Extend a line from the top of the "flagpole" until it meets its shadow on the floor. This line can be at any probable angle, but once chosen, should stay consistent throughout the drawing.

④ SHADOWS OF HORIZONTALS

Horizontal edges cast shadows parallel to themselves, so the shadow uses the same vanishing point. Note that you can locate where these shadows should be on the floor using the "flagpole method."

Ⓒ GRADIENTS

Note how gradients are employed to create the diffuse shadows. They are also subtly darkened toward the sunlit areas to make the sunlit areas appear brighter. Gradients can also give more interest and dynamism to a drawing.

HORIZON LINE

⑤ THE RESOLVE RULE

When the shadow of a horizontal "bumps into" a surface that is perpendicular to it, it "resolves" back to its casting edge along that surface. The green dashed line, where floor and wall planes meet, is where the horizontal turns into a resolve line. The similarity of the resolve line and sun angle in this drawing is a coincidence. Note how the shadow of the horizontal interacts with the vase as it resolves.

Ⓑ DIFFUSE SHADOWS

Bright areas and diffuse sources of light create diffuse shadows, with indistinct edges, that simply fall away from their source. Objects that "see" multiple sources of this kind of light respond with multiple shadows. These shadows are usually graded-- darker at their edge of origin.

SHADE and SHADOW
with ILLUMINATION

Fig. 1-3

Illumination

The term *illumination* is borrowed from engineering terminology and is introduced here, in the context of design drawing, to describe "nonsunlit" lighting. There has long been a need in the field of design drawing to address the best ways to represent this kind of lighting. It is especially important for interior architects and designers, since they must work with this kind of lighting far more frequently than those who design outdoor environments and building exteriors.

The illustration of interior illumination created by multiple sources can be a complicated task for the designer. However, you need not illustrate each and every source of light in an interior space. Instead, an interior drawing can be adequately illustrated by indicating just a few *general* lighting directions. By following the minimal number of rules about interior lighting, a successful interior illustration is quite achievable.

There are a few things to remember as you start an interior lighting study. First, consider whether your space has (or will have) major sources of daylight or artificial lighting, and use them as a starting point. Surfaces that face away from these sources will be in shade, so they will be relatively darker than those facing them. Surfaces more distant from major light sources will be dimmer than those near them. Remember that all of the larger surfaces in an interior are *gradients* of value and color; rarely do you find a larger surface of even, consistent illumination or color. How you manipulate these gradations in an interior drawing will create the visual cues that provide an overall sense of illumination and indicate its sources.

Second, interior shadows should not be as dark or have as much contrast as exterior shadows. Make them visible, but keep them subtle. You can always darken them later as necessary, but it is usually much more difficult to lighten a surface in a drawing that has become too dark. The edges of interior shadows are almost always diffuse because they are usually created by soft and indistinct sources of light, such as frosted lamps, lamp shades, and indirect light. You will notice that interior shadows are also usually gradients—they are darker at their edges of origin and get lighter as they move away from that edge.

As you add these shadows, notice how they "anchor" the objects to the surfaces they touch. Until subtle shade and shadow is added, objects in a drawing can seem to "float" on the page. For example, a diffuse shadow under a chair visually anchors that chair to the floor. Since interiors usually have multiple sources of illumination, an object responds by casting multiple, though subtle, shadows. Each set of shadows simply falls away from the general direction of the light source to which it corresponds.

Figure 1-4 illustrates illumination at night, while figure 1-3 shows that even interiors with direct sunlight will still respond to the rules of illumination.

The best way to build skills at representing interior illumination is to create numerous quick studies and, as with building other design drawing skills, observe and draw from life. Start first with small vignettes, sketching parts of interiors that catch your interest. Gradually, work up to quickly drawing the major part of an entire space. When you are comfortable with representing illumination on that scale, try your drawing skills on spaces of your own design.

Dynamic Perspective: Computer Modeling

Not so long ago, typical presentation requirements for a school architectural project consisted of providing plans, elevations, sections, and "a perspective view." The student usually left the perspective view for last, after the project had been "designed" via orthogonal, measured drawings. This view, in which isolated decisions coalesced, often sent the surprised designer scrambling in the wee morning hours to revise the orthogonal drawings and reflect new insights. Perspective has long been touted as a design tool because it gives the designer the advantage of experiencing the bounding planes of forms and spaces in a single view—something not afforded in the easily measured but two-dimensional world of plan, elevation, and section. While certainly useful, perspectives were somewhat inconvenient and slow to "set up." No longer.

The ubiquity of computer modeling has revolutionized how we practice design in architecture, interior design, and landscape architecture. Nascent ideas about form and space can be visualized quickly and easily. The designer can view, rotate, and "walk through" an idea in three dimensions—all to exact

Fig. 1-4 Using a .5 mm pencil with 2H lead, this quick illumination study on tracing paper over the line drawing reveals the approximate quality of light in a room. Studies like these are a useful guide for creating a more finished illustration.

ILLUMINATION

Fig. 1-4

① PRE-DARKEN SURFACES
Before you begin an illumination study, you know which surfaces will be darker because of where the light sources are located. You will save time by "predarkening" appropriate surfaces with markers. Here, the corner window was darkened with a gray 90% marker; the fireplace wall with a gray 70% marker.

④ USE GRADIENTS
The value and color of most every surface of an interior is a gradient. Thus, when one looks at an entire space, it is perceived as washes of interlocking gradients, all created by the same few rules of illumination. Gradients make a drawing more dynamic because they continually change over a surface.

⑥ CHARACTERISTIC PATTERNS
Observe and learn the few characteristic light-shadow patterns caused by familiar objects. Here, a lamp with an open-top shade throws a typical parabolic up-down pattern of light on the wall.

⑤ STRONG CONTRAST
In a drawing, luminosity is created by contrast in value. Here, the sources of light are perceivable because they are among the strongest light-dark contrasts in the room

② SHADOW CHARACTER
With interior lighting, shadows are more soft and subtle compared to those made by outdoor daytime lighting. These shadows simply fall away from the sources of light. They have diffuse edges and are gradients that are darkest at their edge of origin.

③ MULTIPLE SHADOWS
Objects in an interior frequently have multiple shadows because there are multiple sources of illumination. The darkest of these shadows are caused by the closest and strongest source.

scale—almost instantly. The amount of experiential feedback available early in the conceptual and schematic phases of a project has increased infinitely and with it, the potential for better design.

One of the best computer applications for use as a companion to design drawing is SketchUp, which quickly models three-dimensional ideas to scale (1-5). It is relatively inexpensive and available for trial and purchase online. Its tool palette is simple and its learning curve very short. While it is not the application of choice for highly complex form modeling, most typical forms and spaces can be developed quickly and easily. Its shade and shadow is dynamic: They follow the model as it is rotated, so no computer redraw or "render" time is necessary. Shade and shadow can be easily tuned to time of day and location. Predrawn components, such as human figures, vehicles, landscape materials, and furniture are available from drag-and-drop palettes, and these elements are automatically scaled properly; your own digital imagery can be used as well. For example, a

sketched floor plan can be imported, upon which the three-dimensional model can be quickly built.

Ironically, with the availability of applications like SketchUp, it is more important than ever for the designer to have a working knowledge of the basics of design *drawing*. Why? Our ability to flesh out basic computer models and wireframes into sketch "picture" views with adequate detail and contextual elements—views that help team members and clients make decisions—still depends on taking advantage of the speed and deftness afforded by skill in design *drawing* (1-6). Designers who can deploy the principles of perspective, create respectably proportioned human figures, apply shade, shadow, and illumination, as well as represent basic building and plant materials, can free themselves from the time-consuming constraints of the computer during the early phases of the design process.

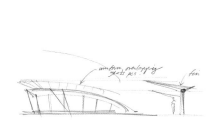

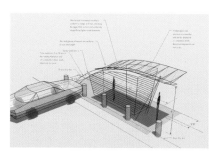

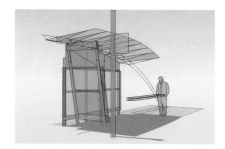

Fig. 1-5

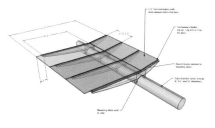

Fig. 1-5 The sketch in the upper left is the first hand-drawn "vision sketch" for an urban transit shelter, created during a design meeting. The other views are taken from subsequent SketchUp models of the idea. At the upper right is an early concept view; at the lower left, a view from the schematic design phase; and at the lower right, a schematic design study of the roof canopy.

Fig. 1-6 A SketchUp model was used to generate a series of very quick design drawings for an urban revitalization competition. The drawing at the upper right was used to show how a usable village green could be created on a sloping site. The study, left, was made on tracing paper over a printout view of the model, using a .5 mm graphite pencil

with 2H lead. Color pencil was applied on the back of the tracing paper. The drawing was scanned with the printout view of the model still behind it, avoiding the necessity of redrawing the lines of the contextual buildings, since the model's lines showed through the tracing paper. The image was imported into Photoshop. All but the area with color was selected. The gray lines were changed to the sepia color by adjusting the *Hue* slider (Image > Adjustments > Hue/Saturation > Colorize).

The study drawing at the lower right was also created on tracing paper over a model view, lower left. The scan of the drawing was colorized similarly to its counterpart, above. Notes were added to both drawings in Photoshop.

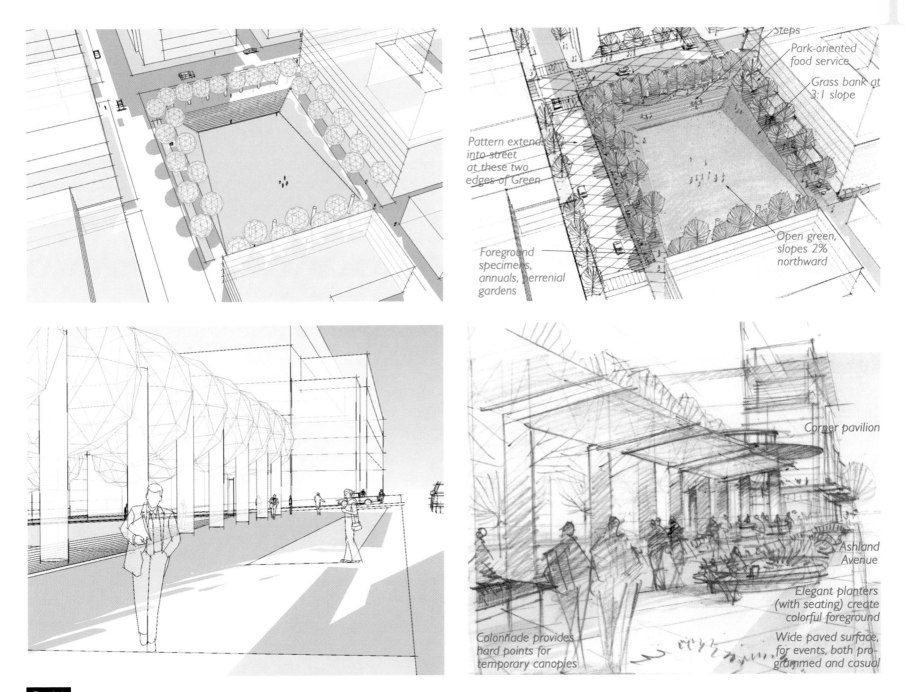

Steps

Park-oriented
food service

Grass bank at
3:1 slope

Pattern extends
into street
at these two
edges of Green

Foreground
specimens,
annuals, perrenial
gardens

Open green,
slopes 2%
northward

Corner pavilion

Ashland
Avenue

Elegant planters
(with seating) create
colorful foreground

Colonnade provides
hard points for
temporary canopies

Wide paved surface,
for events, both pro-
grammed and casual

Fig. 1-6

PHENOMENA OF COLOR AND LIGHT

To successfully illustrate design ideas, it is instructive—and, more to the point, necessary—to observe the color phenomena that surround you in your everyday life. Ten such basic phenomena are briefly discussed and illustrated here. You will discover more, but these 10 should help you to understand the relationship between what you see around you and the techniques shown later in the book. It is hoped that they will also inspire you to use the power of your own unique observations.

Local Tone

Every object has an intrinsic lightness or darkness, regardless of its illumination. This phenomenon is known as *local tone,* a term coined by artist and teacher Nathan Goldstein (1977). A typical brick, for example, has a much darker local tone than a block of white marble. When both are exposed to sunlight, each will have lighter and darker sides, but the illuminated faces of the brick will still be darker than the shaded faces of the marble (1-7).

When you create color drawings that illustrate various forms, whether buildings, landscapes, or interiors, each form will possess a local tone owing to your choice of its material. Each form will have lighter and darker surfaces, as in the preceding example, depending on the location of the light sources. The degree of lightness or darkness of these surfaces will be in proportion to the lightness or darkness of the local tones of the forms.

Chiaroscuro

The term *chiaroscuro* refers to the light-to-dark shading of an illustrated form in order to make it appear three-dimensional. Its use has a long history in art. Leonardo da Vinci said of chiaroscuro that "he who excels all others in that part of the art, deserves the greatest praise" (Birren 1965, 77).

In a black-and-white drawing, these shadings and shadows may range, of course, from light gray to black. However, this is not the case in color drawing. Gray to black shadings and shadows in a color drawing (unless on a gray form) will appear dull and lifeless. Instead, as figure 1-7 illustrates, you can see that the color of a surface in shade or shadow usually remains the same color as its illuminated sides, only darker, and that the degree of darkness depends on the local tone of the form.

Fig. 1-7

Fig. 1-7 Notice the sunlit and shaded/ shadowed surfaces of the pitcher, table, and floor. Each has shades or shadows whose degree of lightness or darkness corresponds to its local tone. For example, the side of the pitcher in shade is light, whereas the shadow of the pitcher on the table is quite dark. The medium-toned floor has a corresponding medium shadow.

Look closely at the colors of the shadows on the floor. They are not gray or black, but darker versions of the corresponding sunlit colors of the floor.

Color of Shade and Shadow

You can see, however, under certain conditions, that the shades and shadows on forms also take on subtle colorations other than only the darker versions of their illuminated surfaces.

This condition most commonly occurs when the shaded or shadowed surface faces a source of colored light. This source may be direct light, or it may be light reflected from a nearby form that is itself brightly illuminated. A common example of this phenomenon appears on the shaded surfaces of buildings on a clear day. These surfaces are illuminated by the bright blue "light source" of the sky, resulting in a surface that is a mixture of the building's surface material and the blue of the sky (1-8). The shaded face of a red brick building, for example, can have a purplish cast to it. This is because the resultant color falls somewhere on the color wheel between the red of the brick and the blue of the sky (see figure 1-18).

This effect is also readily apparent on neutral—white or gray—surfaces. Notice the colors of the shadows on snow, concrete, or worn (light gray) asphalt on a sunny day. The shadows on these surfaces appear bluish, so blue in fact that you can see yet another color phenomenon manifest itself. The sunlit portion of these surfaces will appear slightly "warm," or tinged with a pinkish orange. This effect, called *simultaneous contrast,* forms in our perception when we behold a color next to a neutral surface. We perceive the neutral surface as tinged with the color opposite on the color wheel, its *complementary color.* The more intense the color, the more it tends to tinge its neighbors with its complement. A red apple and its surrounding green leaves will appear particularly brilliant against one another.

Simultaneous contrast was written about as early as the sixteenth century. M. E. Chevreul was the first to study this effect in depth in the early nineteenth century, and the phenomenon was utilized extensively by the Impressionists in the late nineteenth and early twentieth centuries (Hope and Walch 1990). It is an established part of the visual language of artists and illustrators today. Color contrasts are discussed further in Chapter 6.

Fig. 1-8

Fig. 1-8 The surfaces in shade and shadow are alive with color. The pink stucco grades to purplish on the upper left-hand wall owing to its reflection of blue sky; the dark gray foreground floor and windowsill also reflect the blue sky.

The right-hand wall takes on an orange cast, reflected from the sunlit floor tile. Notice the reflected colors on the shaded and shadowed surfaces in the space beyond.

Gradation

Have you ever noticed that very few flat surfaces in your surroundings actually appear uniformly colored or illuminated? Most appear uneven, graduating from one color to another and one level of lightness or darkness to another. This effect is particularly easy to notice on large surfaces like walls, floors, and ceilings but occurs on most all surfaces if you look carefully (1-9).

Continuous surfaces *gradate* in appearance because of their proximity to sources of direct light and because of the light and colors reflected onto them (and into them) from nearby objects and surfaces. These *gradations* usually appear gradual on matte surfaces and become sharper with the increasing specularity or "polish" of a surface. A concrete or drywall surface will host more even color and light gradations than one of, say, brushed stainless steel. Polished wood or glass will exhibit much sharper boundaries between changes in light and color.

You will find gradations a useful tool in color illustration. They make surfaces appear more realistic and result in illustrations that are far more dynamic. For example, in a technique used by fine arts painters called *forcing the shadow,* a shadow is graded darker toward its boundary with the illuminated portion of the surface. The illuminated portion is graded lighter toward this same boundary. The result is an unexpectedly brilliant effect of illumination. The same technique is often employed between the colors of foreground and background elements in an illustration. A background element may gradually be darkened and cooled (made more bluish) in hue as it moves toward its boundary with a foreground element, whose treatment is just the opposite: It is lightened and warmed (made more reddish) in hue as it approaches the same boundary. This is a useful way to make forms appear more distinct. These effects are easy to create and impart activity and sparkle to an illustration.

Fig. 1-9 Gradations of color and tone occur on virtually every surface of this illustration as a result of illumination and reflected color. Gradations are particularly effective in making interior design illustrations appear vital and realistic.

Fig. 1-9

Multiplicity of Color

You see your surroundings in a variety of colors. A green tree, a wall of red brick, a brown rock, and yellow field grass are common objects whose colors are familiar to you. But most of the colors you see are really visual averages or mixtures of a multitude of colors. The clump of winter field grasses that look yellow from a distance are, upon closer inspection, made up of such colors as magentas, ochres, grays, and greens—as well as a variety of different kinds of yellow.

As you observe your surroundings more closely, you may find these subtle variations of color in natural and exterior architectural surroundings difficult to describe or illustrate satisfactorily. This is in part due to these visual averages, called *medial mixtures* (1-10). It is also because many natural materials *refract* light as a result of their water, mineral, and cellulose content, splitting the light into its component colors on a microscopic scale. As indicated earlier, both exterior and interior man-made materials are also rarely of a single, consistent color, because of gradations, the reflection of color, and the impacts of such phenomena as simultaneous contrast.

Close observation of your surroundings will lead you to see that your world literally scintillates with color. Impressionist painters Seurat, Signac, van de Velde, and many others utilized these observations in their paintings. At a distance the colors of their forms appear soft and subtle, but closer inspection reveals that each area of color is made up of many different colors. These colors are not mixed, but placed side by side with tiny brushstrokes, which imparts an incredible richness to the painting and allows the viewer, rather than the artist, to create the final colors of the images. You will explore similar approaches to color illustration later, in Part II, by *mingling* a variety of color media to create your color images, including marker, pastel, and color pencil.

Fig. 1-10

Fig. 1-10 The colors in this illustration are composed of a mingling of many different colors applied with marker, pastel, and color pencil—all on pale green Canson paper. The color of the foreground grasses, for instance, was made with three markers, two pastel colors, and five color pencils.

Atmospheric Perspective

Forms that recede into the distance undergo a color change. Generally, they become lighter, cooler (more bluish), and more grayed. This is due in part to the layers of humidity, dust, and pollutants that accumulate in proportion to the distance between the form and the viewer (1-11). This phenomenon is known as *atmospheric perspective.*[1]

Your subconscious conditioning through lifelong experience with atmospheric perspective may lie behind a related phenomenon. Cool colors—blue greens, blues, and purple blues—appear to *recede* from the viewer. Conversely, colors opposite on the color wheel, warm colors—reds, yellow reds, and yellows—tend to *advance* toward the viewer, particularly when used in conjunction with cool colors. Another explanation for our apparent spatial positioning of color may lie in how the lenses of our eyes refract color. Reddish colors focus at a point behind the retina, whereas bluish colors focus at a point in front of the retina. The lens becomes convex to focus on a reddish image, "pulling it nearer," and flattens to focus on a bluish image. This flattening of the lens "pushes the [bluish] image back and makes it appear smaller and farther away" (Birren 1965, 130).

Reflections

Reflective surfaces present the colors they "see" back to you. In most cases, however, on such surfaces as glass, water, and polished furniture the reflected colors are less intense than those of the objects reflected. When a reflective surface is darker than its surroundings, such as a window in a sunlit wall, notice that the colors it reflects are less intense *and* darker than those of the objects reflected.

Mirrored surfaces such as chrome and polished stainless steel usually distort the *shapes* of the objects reflected, but reflect their colors exactly (1-12).

1. The art world sometimes refers to this phenomenon as *aerial perspective.* The use of this term for our purposes would be confusing, since an aerial perspective in architecture and landscape architecture refers to a perspective view of a subject from above. Such views are also known as "birds-eye" views.

Fig. 1-11

Fig. 1-12

Fig. 1-11 In each successive layer of buildings and landforms, care was taken to lighten the colors, make them more bluish-to-pale purple, and make them weaker (more grayed). These color effects reinforce the diminution in size of the forms to create the illusion of distance. This effect was further enhanced by making the foreground elements warm (yellow-reddish) in color.

Fig. 1-12 The colors reflected into the window and glass tabletop are weaker than those of the objects reflected, but those reflected into the polished stainless-steel column are not. As windows in a building become higher and more oblique to the viewer's sight line, they progressively reflect more sky.

Note the forced shadow on the patio surface and the gradation of the wall color.

Luminosity

Light colors and strong, vivid colors appear to be illuminated, or to glow, when they are surrounded by darker values or applied to or seen against toned backgrounds. The darker the background, the more *luminous* the color appears (1-13). This phenomenon can be used to create the effects of illumination, as many of the illustrations throughout this book demonstrate (1-14).

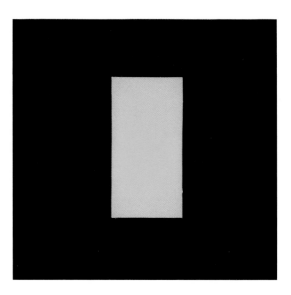

Fig. 1-13

Fig. 1-13 **Notice how the color of the rectangle appears progressively more luminous as its background becomes darker.**

WEST MARINE / EMBARCADERO VIEW
CommArts

PIERS
27·31
SAN FRANCISCO, CALIFORNIA

Fig. 1-14

Fig. 1-14 This illustration uses light, strong colors next to darker surroundings to create the sense of an illuminated interior. It was created to show an idea for a storefront proposed for an existing building. A digital (daytime) photograph of the building was printed and a line drawing of the proposed awnings, poles, flags, and figures was drawn with *Black* pencil on tracing paper placed over the printed image.

The building image was then imported into Photoshop. The line drawing was scanned and imported as another layer. The blending mode for the drawing layer was set to "Multiply," making the line drawing appear as if it had been drawn directly on the photographic image.

The building image was darkened (**Image > Adjustments > Brightness/ Contrast**) to create a dusklike level of ambient lighting. Color was added to the line drawing and in the windows as a separate layer; the gray tone on the people was yet another layer. That way, the brightness of the windows and people could be manipulated separately.

Color was applied using the *Pencil Tool* as well as the airbrush capability of the *Brush Tool*. The interior view seen through the window is actually an image scanned from the store's catalog.

Color and Light Level

Your perception of color depends on a different kind of reflection from those discussed earlier. The various colored objects and forms that make up your surroundings absorb certain wavelengths of light—that is, they absorb certain colors—and reflect others. You see these forms and objects as certain colors because those are the colors reflected. A banana in a bowl of fruit absorbs most other wavelengths of light *except* yellow, which it reflects back to you.

As the light level diminishes, it follows that the amount of light available for objects to reflect also diminishes. The banana appears less yellow and more neutral, but yellow nonetheless when compared with the colors of other fruit in the bowl: "We judge colors by the company they keep. We compare them to one another and revise according to the time of day, light source, memory" (Ackerman 1991, 252).

However, in near darkness or on a moonlit night, color seems to disappear altogether. Our only sources of color come from those objects and surfaces sufficiently illuminated to reflect light (1-15). A nighttime walk will encounter color only in such places as windows that allow a view into an illuminated interior, or beneath streetlights and in illuminated signs. Most other forms and surfaces reflect only enough light for you to perceive them as low levels of light and dark.

Fig. 1-15 In this nighttime lighting study, the buildings and surroundings have almost no local color. The exceptions are those elements that are either internally illuminated (sign, taillights, windows) or directly illuminated (uplighted trees and those areas directly beneath down-lights).

The image is a daytime photograph that was colorized in Photoshop (Image > Adjustments > Hue/Saturation). Once in the *Hue/Saturation* dialog box, the "*Colorize*" option was enabled, creating a duotone effect. The *Hue* slider was used to select an appropriate nighttime hue and the *Lightness* slider was adjusted downward to an appropriate level.

A layer was created to add color via the airbrush capability of the *Brush Tool* for the sign, taillights, trees (for which the *Pencil Tool* was also used), and site lighting. The window illumination color was added to another layer, so it could be manipulated independently.

Fig. 1-15

Arrangements of Light and Dark

There are a wide variety of tones in your surroundings, ranging from the brightest whites to the blackest of blacks. If you squint until your eyes are almost closed as you look around, you will notice fewer shadings of light to dark. In fact, every tonal group you see in the scene can fall into one of three categories: light, medium, or dark.

This way of viewing your surroundings is important because it provides a way to understand the underlying tonal arrangement of your surroundings and offers a way to approach strong tonal arrangements in your design communication illustrations as well. When the brilliant landscape illustrator Ted Kautzky prepared a scene, he first simplified it to three diagrammatic spatial planes of foreground, middle ground, and background. He assigned to each plane one of the three aforementioned tones—light, medium, or dark—which yielded six possible basic tonal arrangements (Kautzky 1947). This approach not only made his finished illustrations far more manageable to execute, but built into each one a surprising degree of impact. You will investigate tonal arrangements further in Chapters 6 and 7.

One of the most useful and powerful of these arrangements is frequently employed for illustrating evening and nighttime exterior views. Most of the background is illustrated as a medium tone, whereas the middle ground is the lightest—especially windows, as they are intended to be illuminated from within. When foreground elements, such as trees or figures, are made very dark, they appear to be in silhouette, further emphasizing the *brilliance* and luminosity of the middle ground (1-16).

Fig. 1-16

Fig. 1-16 This black-and-white illustration was created as a presentation tool for a hotel/condominium project in its early design stages. Note how the values are arranged so that one's attention gravitates toward the ground floor of the building. This is also where the starkest contrasts are located.

Begun as a line drawing using a *Black* pencil on white tracing paper, it was then scanned, and the tones added in Photoshop. The tones on the elements of the foreground, middle ground (the subject building), and background were generated as separate layers so they could be manipulated independently to maximize the sense of illumination. The reflections were created by copying the façades, inverting them, and reducing their opacity. The *Transform Tool* (Edit > Transform > Skew) was used to align the reflections' horizontal lines to the same vanishing points as those used to draw the façades themselves.

Once the image was flattened, the *Noise* filter (Filter >Noise >Add Noise) was used to soften the image.

THE DIMENSIONS OF COLOR

Certain groups and organizations, ranging from paint manufacturers to fashion designers, have descriptive names for colors that are commonly understood within a particular group. One may refer to a color as "Butterscotch," while another may refer to a similar color as "Goldenrod." Both names evoke an image of a yellow with perhaps a tinge of red, neither too light nor particularly vivid (1-17). Descriptive color names work well in instances where colors need only casual identification or when the user is attempting to summon particular associations or emotions in others, such as when these names are used for marketing purposes.

However, when asked to adjust a color or compare similar colors—like Butterscotch and Goldenrod—a designer must revert to a vocabulary capable of describing color in more accurate terms. He uses three dimensions to describe color, much the way he uses the dimensions of height, width, and depth to quantitatively describe form and space.

The term *hue* denotes the *name of a color,* such as "red," "yellow," or "blue green." When full-spectrum light, such as sunlight, is fractured into a rainbow by a cloud of water vapor or a prism, what you are seeing are the component colors that make up the light. You will see these colors blend or grade from one into another. Because the colors on either end of the rainbow are also related to each other, all the colors taken together form a circular relationship. This relationship is known as a *color wheel* or, more accurately, a *hue wheel,* inasmuch as most color wheels show only one representative color (usually vivid) for each hue (1-18). The terms *hue* and *color* are often confused. Hue is only one of the three dimensions required to make a color.

The degree of "darkness or lightness" of a color is known by the term *value.* The range of value of a color can extend from "very low" to "very high," that is, from very dark to very light. You may see other terms for value, such as *lightness* or *brightness,* used in other systems of describing color (1-19).

Fig. 1-17

Fig. 1-17 "Butterscotch" *(left)* **and "Goldenrod" are casually descriptive names for these colors, but the names are almost meaningless when used to compare one color with the other.**

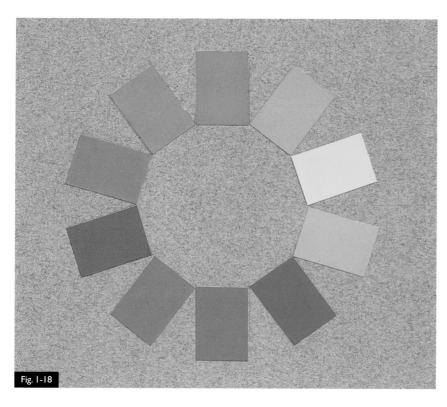

Fig. 1-18

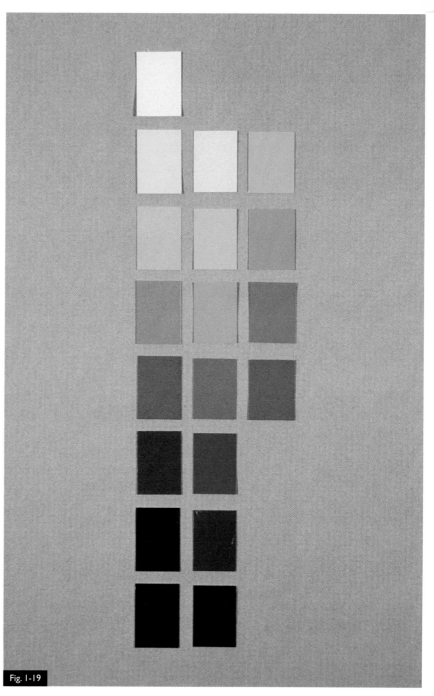

Fig. 1-19

Fig. 1-18 A hue wheel or "color wheel" shows the relationships of hues to one another.

Fig. 1-19 Red-purple and green-yellow colors arranged vertically according to value. **A corresponding neutral gray** scale appears on the left. **Note that** although the colors change in value in each vertical row, the chroma of the colors is the same.

The terms *vividness* and *grayness* are observations that describe the strength of a color. This quality is known as the *chroma* of a color and can range from "very weak" (grayish) to "very strong" (vivid). Other commonly used terms for chroma are *purity* and *saturation* (1-20).

In theory, each of these three dimensions of a color can be altered *without affecting the other two.* For example, a color's value can be changed without affecting its hue or chroma, or a color's hue can be changed from green to blue while its value and chroma remain the same.[2] Notice that the qualities of hue and chroma cannot exist by themselves; you cannot create an image with *only* hue or *only* chroma. However, you *can* create an image exclusively with value,

as you often do when making a black-and-white drawing or photograph. Although the terms *hue, value,* and *chroma* will be used to describe the dimensions of color throughout this book, your choice of terms for these dimensions is important only insofar as those with whom you communicate are familiar with them.

---

2. In reality, however, value and chroma are interrelated in strong-chroma colors. If you attempt to significantly change the value of a strong-chroma color, you find you must usually reduce its chroma to do so. This is because each hue reaches its strongest chroma at a particular value, called its *spectrum value.* For example, try to imagine a strong-chroma *dark* yellow. It is impossible to imagine, because the color does not exist. As a yellow becomes darker, its chroma grows weaker. Certain colors are simply not achievable.

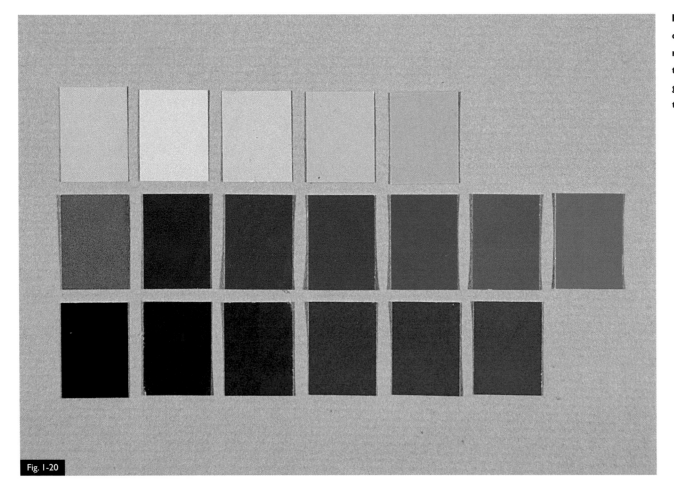

Fig. 1-20 In each horizontal row of colors, the hue and value of the colors remain constant. Only the chroma of the colors changes, progressing from gray on the left to stronger chroma on the right.

Fig. 1-20

Munsell Student Sets

A detailed knowledge of any particular organized system of color and the alphanumeric classifications of its colors is unimportant for the purposes of this book. What *is* important is that you have an understanding of the relationships between the dimensions of color and that you are able to identify and communicate the similarities and differences between colors that are intended to be seen together, as a composition.

You may find it worthwhile to purchase an inexpensive Munsell Student Set[3] to further explore the relationships between the dimensions of color. The set comes with a color wheel, value scale, chroma scale, 10 hue charts (one for each of the 10 hues of the color wheel), and packages of loose color chips. You must assemble the color wheel, scales, and hue charts by applying the color chips to their proper locations. During this process, each color chip must be evaluated according to its hue, value, and chroma, refining your ability to discriminate between the three color dimensions and to evaluate subtle differences within a particular dimension.

The student set can also be used to explore various combinations of color by arranging the loose color chips into small compositions, before they are adhered in their final locations on the scales and charts, similar to those in figures 6-4 and 6-11. Once you can visualize how a color's three dimensions can be manipulated, each independent of the others, it becomes easier to entertain the many possible relationships that can be established *between* colors. *Colors form relationships when their characteristics appear to affiliate or interact with one another.* Inasmuch as each and every color possesses the same three dimensions, it is the creative arrangement of the relationships between the dimensions of the colors in a composition that establishes the mood or expressive direction of the scheme. When these relationships are established, a perceptible order is introduced to the scheme. Color harmony is predicated on order, whether that color is arranged for a design idea for a place or for the *illustration* of an idea. For example, an exercise may explore the combination of five different hues with different chromas but all the same (or similar) values. You will notice that it is the similarity of the values of the colors that acts as the unifying agent of the composition. Such simple chip-arrangement exercises can help you build your skills in arranging colors in successful combinations, particularly with the guidance of Chapter 6.

Once a student set is assembled, it makes an excellent reference tool for evaluating and comparing the ranges of hues, values, and chromas of colors.

Simplified Color Descriptions

As you work with a Munsell Student Set, you will realize its value to the designer. However, its notation system, although simple, is of little value to the designer who wishes to describe a color to a client or colleague with more accuracy than the one-word names mentioned earlier. A typical *Munsell Student Chart* is shown with the numeric designations for value and chroma, accompanied by a verbal description of each (1-21). Thus, 5R 3/4 can be described verbally as a "low-value, weak-chroma red," whose relationship to all the other possibilities for red can be imagined from your mental picture of the chart. The verbal description lies between the very accurate description ("5R 3/4") and the casual description ("burgundy red"). Incidentally, you can see in figure 1-17 that Goldenrod is slightly more yellow red, lower in value, and of about the same medium-strong chroma as Butterscotch.

Computer Color Controls

Some of the most useful Photoshop color controls are shown in figure 1-22. When using Photoshop for illustrations in this book, most color selections were made solely using the *Color Picker* at the top. Hues were selected using the vertical *Hue* slider, then a color was chosen from the available colors in that hue using the blended color field, top left. A particular color is chosen by pointing and clicking on the field. Note the similarity in arrangement of value and chroma to that of the Munsell Student Chart in figure 1-21.

---

3. The New Munsell Student Color Set can be ordered from:
Fairchild Books
7 West 34th Street
New York, New York 10001
Telephone: (800) 932-4724 or (212) 630-3880. Fax: (212) 630-3868.
Or they can be ordered from Amazon.com.

Fig. 1-21 A Munsell Student Chart for the hue red (5.0 R) is accompanied by descriptions of the numeric indications for the increments of value and chroma. The descriptions are by the author.

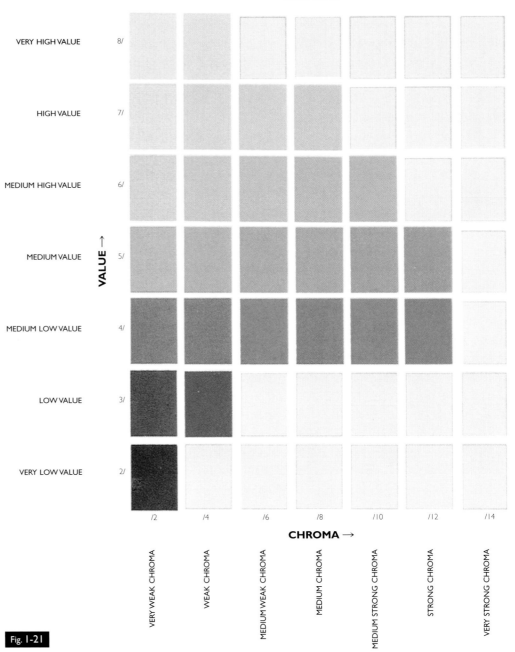

HUE 5.0 R

VERY HIGH VALUE   8/

HIGH VALUE   7/

MEDIUM HIGH VALUE   6/

VALUE →

MEDIUM VALUE   5/

MEDIUM LOW VALUE   4/

LOW VALUE   3/

VERY LOW VALUE   2/

/2   /4   /6   /8   /10   /12   /14

CHROMA →

VERY WEAK CHROMA

WEAK CHROMA

MEDIUM WEAK CHROMA

MEDIUM CHROMA

MEDIUM STRONG CHROMA

STRONG CHROMA

VERY STRONG CHROMA

Fig. 1-21

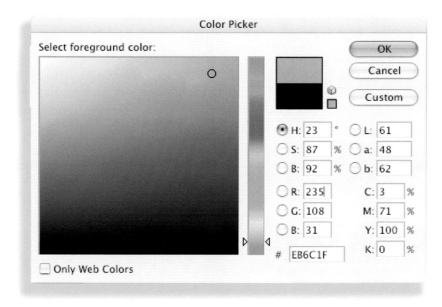

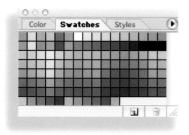

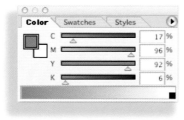

Fig. 1-22

Fig. 1-22 Typical Photoshop color controls. The *Color Picker* is shown at the top, while two versions of the *Color Palette* are shown at the bottom.

The *Color Picker* is activated by double-clicking on the *Foreground* or *Background* color swatch near the bottom of the toolbox. The *Color Picker* has a vertical *Hue* slider that is divided into 360 hues. Each hue can be displayed as a blended field of choices on the left. The field's brightness (or *value,* in Munsell terms) is divided into 100 units, top to bottom. Its saturation (or *chroma,* in Munsell terms) is divided into 100 units, side to side. Clicking on the field displays the numerical values of a particular color choice in the boxes on the right in terms of hue, saturation, and brightness, as well as **RGB** (additive color, as displayed on a monitor), **CMYK** (subtractive color, as in print), and **Lab** (used for color separation). All are linked, such that a change in any one setting produces corresponding changes in all the others.

The *Color Palette* is found in the *Window* drop-down menu along the menu bar at the top of the Photoshop window. If you click on the *Swatches* tab of the *Color Palette* the palette will appear at the lower left. This is the place to save colors you may use repeatedly in an illustration, such as when you want to return to a particular font color used for labeling. When you move the cursor over the desired color, it changes to an eyedropper. Click once, and the desired color becomes the *Foreground* swatch in the toolbox. The rightward-pointing button at the upper right also accesses preset colors from other color systems, such as the Pantone system.

The *Color Palette's Color* tab allows you to manipulate your selected colors, using sliders, relative to a chosen color mode, such as **RGB**, **CMYK** (shown), **Lab**, and **Web** colors.

CHAPTER 33

MEDIA AND PAPER

You are probably familiar with the various media and papers used in color drawing, as your first exposure to such color media as color pencils, pastels, and markers most likely happened during childhood. That children are exposed to these media early in life is a testament not only to their ease of use but also to their ability to assist the user in acting as a visceral connection between the observed (whether visually or in the imagination) and a resultant image made of that observation on a two-dimensional surface. In fact, the approach to color design drawing presented in this book is actually a refined "coloring book" approach, whereby once a line drawing is created, the colors are subsequently applied. So you perhaps have a longer history with this approach to illustration and these media than you thought. This chapter and the next are intended to refresh your memory.

MEDIA

The media discussed in this chapter have a number of advantages. They are, relatively speaking, inexpensive. For an initial expense of a few hundred dollars, you can purchase enough professional-quality color media to create illustrations of the type shown in this book. Many of these materials should last for years. These media are also forgiving. That is, most mistakes can be easily corrected or adjusted so the designer can stay focused on the pursuit of ideas. They are dry, so they will not buckle the papers most commonly used by design professionals during the conceptual and schematic design process. They are contiguous. These same color media can be used for all your design illustrations, from your earliest conceptual doodles to highly finished renderings.

In many design and presentation situations we at CommArts use hand media, rather than digital technologies, because they are faster, simpler, and offer a more direct way to create color design illustrations. In terms of person-hours, these illustrations are more cost-effective. Many effects and illusions can be created with only a few steps, as you will see later in this book. However, they are completely compatible with digital technologies. Hand drawings can be scanned and digitized for further manipulation on a computer—for editing and color adjustments, for importation of other imagery into the drawing, for inclusion into documents, for digital transmission, and even for billboard-size enlargement.

The emergence of high-quality color copy technologies has allowed designers to create color design drawings that are much smaller and, consequently, far more time-efficient than their predecessors. In the past an original drawing for a meeting or public presentation had to be created large enough to be visible across a room, often at a minimum of 24" x 36" to 30" x 42" in size. Now we can illustrate ideas at an 8½" x 11" to 11" x 17" size far more quickly, then use a number of widely available color photocopy techniques to enlarge them to a size suitable for a classroom-scale presentation. These techniques are discussed further in Chapter 8. The media and papers described in the following sections are widely used by designers at CommArts because their utility and versatility allows them to produce color drawing effects quickly and easily.

Line Media

Line is that "abstract necessity" used by all artists and designers to indicate the outlines and edges of shapes and forms. Lines do not really exist in your perceived reality; you use them as a convention to describe the skeletons of your ideas in the most economical way. When you are short on time, it is the line drawing—without tone or color—that serves as the minimum standard graphic device for the communication of ideas about places.

It is important to have a variety of widths of line media available as you create *design drawings,* and just about any with which you are comfortable will work. They should be capable of making very dark lines, reproduce well on photocopiers and diazo print machines, and, if possible, be sufficiently erasable so that their remnants do not detract from the finished drawing.

The line media we use extensively at CommArts are shown in figure 2-1. The Pigma Micron 005 and Micron 01 are excellent felt-tipped pens for small drawings that require fine linework, because when a drawing is enlarged, its lines *are enlarged in width* as well as in length. The Micron 005 has a line width of .20 mm, and the Micron 01 has a width of .25 mm. Their inks do not easily smear when water or marker is applied over them, and the lines erase fairly cleanly when a pink erasing strip is used in an electric eraser. Their one shortcoming is that they will clog when used to draw over color pencil.

Fig. 2-1

Fig. 2-1 A variety of useful line media for design drawing.

The Pilot Razor Point is an excellent all-purpose felt-tipped pen to use with the color media displayed in this chapter. Its line is slightly wider than that of the Micron 01. Although it is not waterproof (it will smear if wetted), it is markerproof and draws well over color pencil with a minimum of clogging. It is more difficult to eradicate with an electric eraser than the Micron pens, but its line can be partly eradicated with the use of a pink erasing strip. Line remnants can be hidden with color pencil during the coloring stage.

The "pointed nib" tip of the black Eberhard Faber Design Art Marker 229-LF makes it a good felt-tipped marker for making wider lines, adding small areas of black to a drawing, and creating rough conceptual diagrams. It should not be used over color pencil, because its solvent will dissolve and consequently smear the pencil. Like all markers, it should be capped immediately after each use because it can dry out very quickly.

One of the most versatile of the line media shown in figure 2-1 is the *Black Prismacolor pencil.* Its line is very dark and can, of course, vary in width. It is often used with a straightedge if its lines must be kept very thin. It reproduces well on a photocopier, especially as compared with graphite pencil lines made with pencils harder than an "H." It erases fairly well, though not entirely, when an electric eraser is used. It can make very even tones because of its slight waxiness and is particularly good for applying shade and shadow.

Color Media

Markers

Markers can apply a transparent color to paper that appears similar to watercolor. Most markers use a concentrated colorant, usually *aniline dye,* mixed with a carrier, typically a volatile solvent of xylene or alcohol. Their tips, once made from felt, are now made from proprietary plastics. However, most designers still refer to them as "felt-tipped" markers. Marker does not buckle paper the way water-based color media do, because the carrier evaporates quickly. This quality makes it an excellent color medium for designers, because it is compatible with the kinds of paper they most frequently use (2-2).

In our design work, we often use markers to create the "base," or underlying colors, for drawings that are subsequently modified by applying colored pencil, pastel, and sometimes line media to achieve the illusion of materials, patterns, and light. Many interesting effects can be created quickly and easily, as you will see

Fig. 2-2

Fig. 2-2 There are a variety of marker brands and types on the market. The Design 2 Art Marker, AD Marker Spectrum, and Prismacolor markers are all alcohol-based. The AD Marker and Design Art Marker are xylene-based.

throughout this book. You should note that some kinds of markers are incompatible with certain line media. Marker should not be used over color pencil. Not only will the pencil smear because of its dissolution by the marker's solvent, but the dissolved pencil color will adhere to the marker's tip, waiting to surprise you with a revised marker color, usually when you least want it. Moreover, *only alcohol-based markers should be used on black-and-white photocopies.* Xylene-based markers will dissolve and smear the black toner that creates the photocopy image. Alcohol-based markers can cause certain kinds of felt-tipped pen line and the lines of diazo prints to smear slightly *if applied with excessive hand pressure.* However, as a general rule of thumb, both alcohol- and xylene-based markers can be safely used over most felt-tipped pens, on diazo prints, on all papers, and even over each other with no ill effects, provided they are used with restraint.

Because marker colorant is aniline dye, it tends to fade with continuous exposure to ultraviolet light, even the small amounts found indoors. If you intend to display a color design drawing that uses marker, make a more lightfast color photocopy or bubble-jet copy of the illustration for display purposes. Store the original in the dark. Contemporary color reproduction methods, such as that of the *bubble-jet photocopier,* can provide an excellent rendition of your original.

Always use markers in a place that has adequate ventilation. The prolonged inhalation of marker solvents, particularly *xylene* (which has the stronger, more pungent odor of the two marker types), can cause headaches and nausea. This can also happen if you work with your face too close to the page, especially when your markers are new.

The largest-selling marker brands together have hundreds of colors from which to choose, but you can create most of your color design illustrations with a limited number. There are two basic *palettes* of markers recommended in this book: a palette of grays and a general color palette. Each palette is described in both alcohol-base and xylene-base in figures 2-3 and 2-4. They are recommended as minimum starting palettes for general color design drawing for architects, interior designers, and landscape architects. These palettes have evolved from the repeated marker choices made by designers at CommArts during our work in these areas. In your pursuit of design solutions for your particular design specialty, you may choose to substitute others or augment the number of colors shown here.

The most important is the palette of grays, because these markers are used most frequently (2-3). Gray can set the value of a color, whose hue and chroma can be determined later with subsequent applications of color pencil or pastel. *French grays* are slightly yellow reddish, *warm grays* slightly reddish, and *cool grays* a touch bluish in hue. The same observations apply to gray color pencils.

The markers shown in the general color palette (2-4) are derived from those we consistently select to illustrate frequently used natural and ubiquitous materials (wood, stone, metals, glass), those found on building exteriors, and landscape materials. Special marker colors, particularly for interiors, can be chosen in addition to the general palette for specific projects.

Xylene-based markers appear capable of delivering slightly richer, smoother color, particularly on diazo prints. They also usually last longer than alcohol markers. However, if you must choose one marker system, the best all-around system is the alcohol-based, inasmuch as it can be used on both diazo prints *and* photocopies. If you have a limited budget for drawing materials, purchase a palette of gray markers first, because the grays can set the values of colors and other less expensive color media can be used to bring up their hue and chroma, as you will see in Chapters 3 and 7.

Fig. 2-3 A recommended palette of gray markers. You can choose either the AD marker (xylene-based) or Prismacolor marker (alcohol-based) grays—or a range of each. It is not necessary to buy both kinds.

AD MARKER

PRISMACOLOR MARKER

WARM GREY #1

COOL GREY #1

FRENCH GREY 10%

COOL GREY 10%

WARM GREY #3

COOL GREY #3

FRENCH GREY 30%

COOL GREY 30%

WARM GREY #5

COOL GREY #5

FRENCH GREY 50%

COOL GREY 50%

WARM GREY #7

COOL GREY #7

FRENCH GREY 70%

COOL GREY 70%

WARM GREY #9

COOL GREY #9

FRENCH GREY 90%

COOL GREY 90%

Fig. 2-3

SUNSET PINK
(DECO PINK)

BUFF
(BRICK BEIGE)

NAPLES YELLOW
(EGGSHELL)

PALE INDIGO
(CLOUD BLUE)

SAPPHIRE BLUE
(LIGHT CERULEAN BLUE)

PINK
(BLUSH PINK)

PALE SEPIA
(GOLDENROD)

LIGHT IVY
(PUTTY + CREAM)

WILLOW GREEN
(LIME GREEN)

MAUVE
(GREYED LAVENDER)

FLESH
(SALMON PINK)

KRAFT BROWN
(LIGHT TAN)

SAND
(SAND)

YELLOW GREEN
(LIMEPEEL)

VIOLET LIGHT
(LILAC)

PALE CHERRY
(MINERAL ORANGE)

REDWOOD
(SIENNA BROWN)

BURNT UMBER
(DARK UMBER)

OLIVE
(OLIVE GREEN)

SLATE GREEN
(TEAL BLUE)

BRICK RED
(CHERRY)

BURNT SIENNA
(TERRA COTTA)

DELTA BROWN
(BLACK)

DARK OLIVE
(FRENCH GREY 80%)

DEEP EVERGREEN
(PEACOCK BLUE + DARK GREEN)

Fig. 2-4

Fig. 2-4 This is a palette of markers useful for general color tasks. The colors of the AD markers are reproduced here. The names of the closest corresponding matches in the Prismacolor markers are shown in parentheses. Where no close Prismacolor marker match was found for an AD marker, a mixture of two Prismacolor markers is indicated with a plus (+) sign between the two.

Color Pencils

Color pencils are the mainstay of the color drawings shown in this book. They are the most frequently used of the color media, the most flexible (they can be applied very lightly or quite heavily), and the most precise. On small drawings, marker is frequently less necessary as a color base, because small drawings require only a color medium that can be applied precisely to a given area but still be removed if the designer makes a mistake or changes her mind. In fact, color pencil is often the only color medium necessary to complete small drawings, particularly those that are highly detailed.

Sanford Prismacolor and Design Spectracolor pencils are two of the best brands of color pencil to use for the kind of color drawing discussed in this book. Both brands come in a wide variety of colors, are soft enough to apply easily and smoothly, and are able to impart a solid, brilliant color when necessary. The Bruynzeel design Fullcolor color pencils (Holland) and the Derwent Studio color pencils by the British company Rexel Cumberland are slightly harder than the Prismacolor and Spectracolor pencils, making it somewhat more difficult to create brilliant colors without indenting the paper surface. However, the Bruynzeel and Derwent pencils both offer colors that are unavailable in the American brands (2-5).

In this book, Prismacolor pencils are used for the drawings. Recommended palettes of grays and general colors are shown in figures 2-6 and 2-7. As with the recommended palette of markers, these pencils are not the only ones we use at CommArts. Rather, they are the pencils selected most frequently for a wide variety of illustration tasks.

Fig. 2-5

WHITE

FRENCH GREY 20%   COOL GREY 20%

FRENCH GREY 30%   COOL GREY 30%

FRENCH GREY 50%   COOL GREY 50%

FRENCH GREY 70%   COOL GREY 70%

Fig. 2-6

Fig. 2-5 These brands of high-quality color pencil are widely available, and each brand has many different colors.

Fig. 2-6 This palette of gray pencils is adequate for most every drawing task that requires their use.

Fig. 2-7 A general palette of Prismacolor pencils (and one Derwent pencil), useful for illustrating a wide variety of materials.

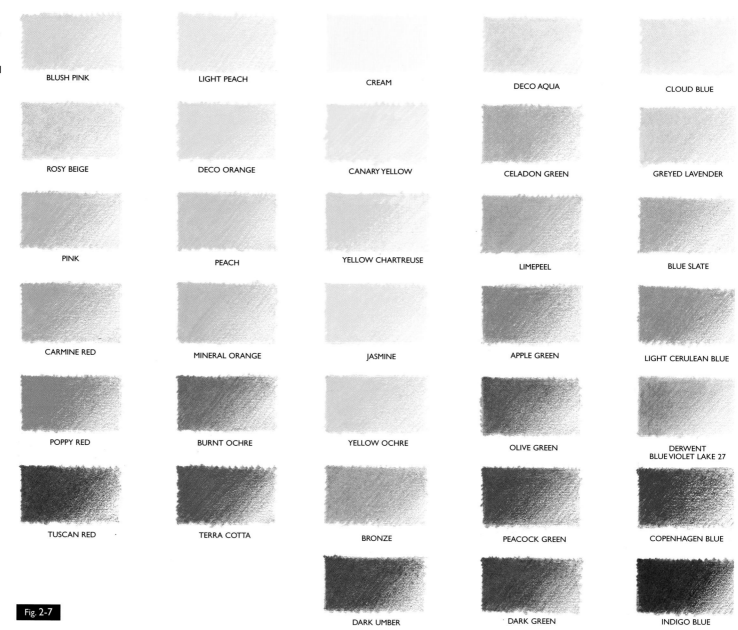

BLUSH PINK

LIGHT PEACH

CREAM

DECO AQUA

CLOUD BLUE

ROSY BEIGE

DECO ORANGE

CANARY YELLOW

CELADON GREEN

GREYED LAVENDER

PINK

PEACH

YELLOW CHARTREUSE

LIMEPEEL

BLUE SLATE

CARMINE RED

MINERAL ORANGE

JASMINE

APPLE GREEN

LIGHT CERULEAN BLUE

POPPY RED

BURNT OCHRE

YELLOW OCHRE

OLIVE GREEN

DERWENT
BLUE VIOLET LAKE 27

TUSCAN RED

TERRA COTTA

BRONZE

PEACOCK GREEN

COPENHAGEN BLUE

DARK UMBER

DARK GREEN

INDIGO BLUE

Fig. 2-7

Pastels

Pastels are the fastest and most directly manipulated (worked with the fingers) of the color media featured in this book. They are also the least controllable at the edges of shapes; that is, they tend to "go outside the lines" more than the other color media. They are meant to be used loosely, in order to apply very quick color to a *sketch* or study illustration. They blend extremely well and are most effective in "high key" schemes of color—those in the lighter ranges of value. They are especially well suited for creating very light, subtle colors.

A designer can produce very successful color illustrations without using pastels. However, larger areas of mixed media color illustrations (those using marker and colored pencil) can be colored quickly and easily with this medium. Skies and clouds in particular lend themselves to illustration in pastel.

Pastels are made by combining dry pigment with a methylcellulose binder. Because of their dry, powdery composition, they erase very easily and cleanly from most kinds of paper. Use a soft, high-quality stick pastel for large areas of color (2-8). These pastels are in the more expensive range, but are worth the cost inasmuch as cheap pastels tend to leave streaky deposits of color and do not blend well. The Rembrandt stick pastels can be found in most art supply stores and have been used for the illustrations that required pastel shown in this book.

If you want to use pastels on small drawings, use them in pencil form. These pastels are somewhat harder and more pointed than stick pastels, which enables the designer to color small areas of a drawing more easily and accurately. Streakiness is not usually a problem, owing to the small areas of color. Just as with stick pastels, use a high-quality pastel pencil. The Schwan Stabilo pastel pencils are widely available and are shown in various illustrations in this book.

If you wish to limit your initial exploration of pastel to a few colors, a useful palette to select from is shown in figure 2-9. If you are an architect or landscape architect, purchase at least the blue stick pastels for creating skies in your illustrations. These skies can take on the more dramatic qualities of a sunset with the help of subsequent additions of pastels in the pink and orange range. If you are an interior designer, you may first wish to test various pastel colors in the store to find a few colors you will tend to use in your work.

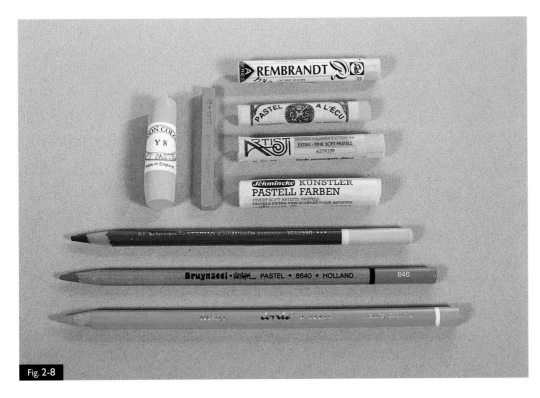

Fig. 2-8

Fig. 2-8 A variety of high-quality pastels. The stick pastels arranged horizontally are, from top to bottom: Rembrandt by Royal Talens (Holland), Pastel a l'Écu by Sennelier (France), Artisti by Maimeri (Italy), and Künstler Pastell Farben by H. Schmincke & Co. (Germany). The two stick pastels arranged vertically are the Conté stick by Conté a Paris *(right)* and Unison Colour, made in England *(left)*. The pencil pastels are, from top to bottom, Schwan Stabilo (Germany), Bruynzeel design pastel (Holland), and the Conté a Paris pastel (France). Note that the Conté a Paris pastel has a wider shaft diameter than most pencils and will not fit into many electric pencil sharpeners. It must be sharpened with a knife.

Fig. 2-9 A useful palette of both stick and pencil pastels. You may wish to revise or supplement these palettes, depending on your specific color design needs.

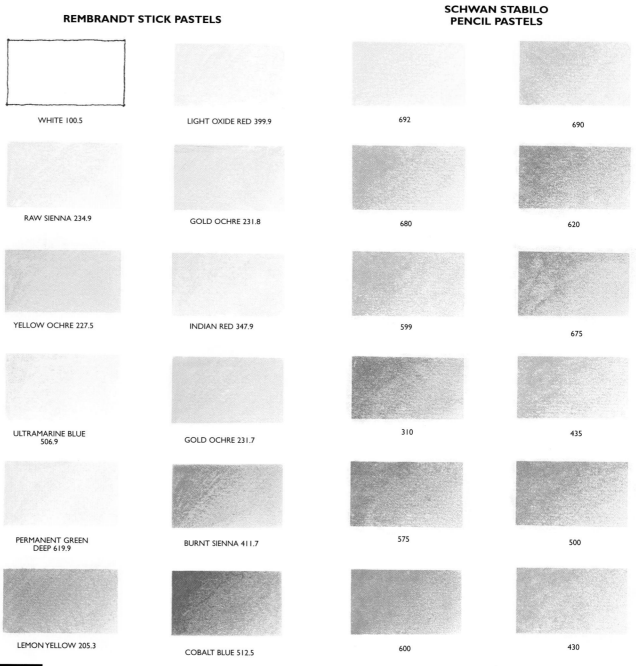

REMBRANDT STICK PASTELS

WHITE 100.5

LIGHT OXIDE RED 399.9

RAW SIENNA 234.9

GOLD OCHRE 231.8

YELLOW OCHRE 227.5

INDIAN RED 347.9

ULTRAMARINE BLUE
506.9

GOLD OCHRE 231.7

PERMANENT GREEN
DEEP 619.9

BURNT SIENNA 411.7

LEMON YELLOW 205.3

COBALT BLUE 512.5

**SCHWAN STABILO
PENCIL PASTELS**

692

690

680

620

599

675

310

435

575

500

600

430

Fig. 2-9

Pastel works well over marker and gives the marker a smoother appearance as it modulates its color. Color pencils also work well over pastels. However, avoid using felt-tipped media—pens and markers—over pastel, because the pastel will eventually clog them and tend to dry them out.

Once you have used pastels on part of a drawing, avoid touching that part. Pastel can lift, smear, and show fingerprints. If you must rest your hand on a part of a drawing where you have used pastel, place a piece of bond paper under your hand while you draw. When you are finished with your drawing, you may wish to apply a light coating of spray *fixative* to preserve the pastel, but this can somewhat deaden its luminous quality. If possible, avoid using fixative. Instead, make a good color copy of your drawing to use for presentation purposes and safely store the original between two sheets of clean paper.

Accents

You may frequently find yourself in a drawing situation where you need those "final touches" or accents that bring a design drawing to life (2-10). Touches of white *gouache* are good for effecting *highlights* or "sparkle" on chrome, water, polished stainless steel, and the edges of glass objects—anywhere a specular reflection may occur. A touch of gouache is also good for creating the illusion of an illuminated lamp in drawing light fixtures.

Touches of metallic gold or silver may also occasionally be necessary for a drawing. These can be easily added with pointed liquid marker pens; the highlights glisten convincingly when they catch the light. However, metallic pen accents work best as small touches or dots and should not be substituted for the designer's illustration of polished metals (see figures 4-69 through 4-72). Metallic pen accents will not copy effectively on a color photocopier or bubble-jet copier, so, when necessary, they must be added to each copy.

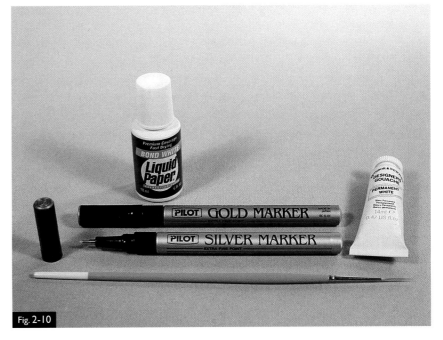

Fig. 2-10

Fig. 2-10 Media for creating accents in drawings. You will find a small tube of Windsor & Newton Permanent White gouache and a long, thin "lining brush" useful for applying both dots and lines of white accent. Dots can be applied full-strength, but lines require that the gouache be diluted slightly with water in a mixing tray. Liquid Paper correction fluid is a good "emergency" white accent medium when gouache is unavailable, but it can absorb and turn into a tint of the color of certain kinds of marker.

Pilot's Gold Marker and Silver Marker come in an extra-fine point, good for applying spots of metallic accent.

PAPER

The variety of paper types commonly used in the design professions can be successfully used for color design drawings. Each of these papers—even roll tracing paper—can be used to receive images from a black-and-white photocopier. This allows the easy transfer of line drawings from, say, tracing paper to Canson paper for a more finished color drawing. This capability also enables the designer to make more than one copy of a line drawing in case an illustration must be repaired or redone.

Tracing Paper

White roll tracing paper is the most frequently used paper in professional design offices for the illustration and development of ideas early in the design process (2-11). It can be used for drawings of many types, ranging from preconceptual doodles to finished color illustrations.

Tracing paper is an excellent surface for color design drawings. It takes all pencil, dry media, and felt-tipped line media well and erases cleanly. Markers bleed only slightly and appear muted—usually an advantage. Its translucency is less refined than that of mylar or vellum. This, too, is an advantage, because when color pencil is applied on the back of a line drawing on white trace, it appears softened, more even, and less mottled or streaky when viewed from the front. When toned paper is slipped behind a color illustration that is drawn on white trace, its lighter pencil colors appear more luminous. This quality, which is also imparted to color photocopies of this arrangement, is advantageous in creating lighting effects in both exterior and interior illustrations.

We usually use Bienfang brand, No. 106, white tracing paper in 12" or 18" rolls. One of the few disadvantages of white trace is that its thinness makes it somewhat fragile. It is susceptible to holes from electric erasure, particularly if the harder erasing strips are used. Because oils and perspiration from your hand can cause it to curl, use a piece of paper under your hand if you find you must rest it for any length of time on the tracing paper as you draw.

Fig. 2-11

Fig. 2-11 This view was created by using felt-tipped pen on tracing paper placed over a computer wireframe. Color was applied to the back of the drawing with marker. Note how the marker colors were blended.

The drawing was scanned and opened in Photoshop. Elements in the view were selected, copied, and flipped vertically using the *Transform* command (Edit > Transform > Flip Vertical). Where necessary, the reflected images were skewed (Edit >Transform > Skew) to conform them to the same vanishing points used by the reflected objects. The reflection layers were then linked and merged. Once merged, the opacity of the reflection layer was reduced. (Drawing: Taku Shimizu)

Toned Papers

One of the greatest advantages of *toned paper* is that it allows the designer to complete a color design drawing very quickly, as only the center of interest need be colored for the illustration to have a visual impact. This is because the greatest contrasts will most likely occur within the colored area. If the same is attempted on white paper, the strongest contrasts are often inadvertently created at the *edges* of the colored area, where, frequently, the marker stops and the white paper begins. This area competes with the center of interest. This is not to say that partially colored drawings on white paper are impossible, but the designer must take more care to fade from the colored area into the uncolored part of the drawing.

Toned papers also allow the designer to create dramatic effects very easily and efficiently. Highlights become vivid, and the colors of pastels and color pencils can be made to appear luminous with little effort. Darks can be added where necessary, and middle tones need only be lightly colored or even left uncolored. Far less effort is spent trying to adequately cover the white of the paper when illustrating medium- or low-key color schemes.

A common type of toned paper that works especially well with the color media discussed in this book is Canson paper. Ink-jet plotter paper, discussed below, can also become a form of toned paper in that background tones (including gradients) can be easily added to line drawings with Photoshop, creating an excellent drawing surface.

Canson Paper

The Mi-Tienes line of paper manufactured by Canson-Talens is called *Canson paper* in this book. It is a high-quality textured, toned art paper that comes in a wide variety of subtle colors as well as a number of different colors of gray. It provides an excellent background for color design drawings and accepts marker, color pencil, and pastel quite well (2-12). Canson paper has a more pronounced texture than the other papers described in this chapter, and this quality helps to mask errors and streakiness inherent in pencil application. In fact, the textural quality of the finished drawing is a unifying factor that helps tie the elements of the illustration together. You can see that the texture of the paper is slightly more pronounced on one side than on the other. Either side can be used.

Line drawings can be transferred to the lighter colors of Canson paper with the use of a light table, which is helpful particularly if you want to keep the lines very light. If line value is not an issue, a faster and easier way to make the transfer is by using a black-and-white photocopier. Once a line drawing is photocopied onto the Canson, it should be lightly sprayed with Krylon Crystal Clear, because the photocopier toner often does not fuse completely to the rough paper. This clear acrylic coating, which dries in a few minutes, will help prevent the lines from smearing with normal use. Remember to use only alcohol-based markers on photocopies.

Fig. 2-12

Fig. 2-12 This is a study of suggested modifications to an existing building. A line drawing was photocopied onto Canson paper, and color pencil was subsequently used to highlight the modifications.

White Paper

Bond Paper

During the design process, you will frequently want to add some quick color to a black-and-white copy of a line drawing or computer-generated drawing that has been reproduced on bond paper (figures 2-13 through 2-16). This paper, the most common white paper used in offices, is typically found in laser printers, plotters, and black-and-white photocopiers. It is inexpensive, durable, and has sufficient grain (or *tooth*) to allow effective use of color pencils and pastels. Markers can also be used successfully on bond paper, but they will tend to bleed more than on other papers described in this chapter, due to its greater absorbency (see figures 3-20 (a) and 3-20 (b)). Remember to use alcohol-based rather than xylol-based markers on these machine-produced images, as the xylol-based markers will smear the toner. If possible, use a high-quality, heavier weight bond paper (24 lb. and up) if it is compatible with your machines.

Fig. 2-13 A photocopy of a line drawing on ordinary 8½" x 11" bond paper was colored with alcohol markers, color pencil, and touches of white gouache.

Fig. 2-13 · PERSPECTIVE · LINEAR OASIS STUDY

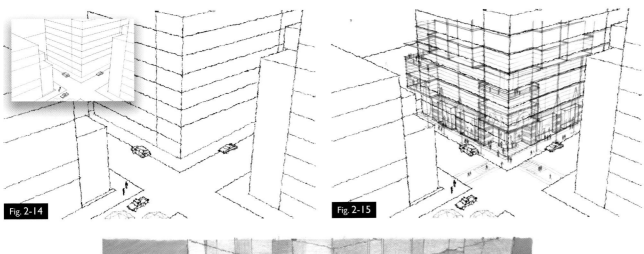

Fig. 2-14

Fig. 2-15

Fig. 2-16

Fig. 2-14 A line drawing was exported from SketchUp (inset) and opened in Photoshop. A filter was used to roughen the lines so it appeared more compatible with hand drawing (Filter > Brush Strokes > Spatter; Spray Radius = 7, Smoothness = 9).

Fig. 2-15 The roughened line drawing was laser printed on bond paper. *Black* pencil and a .5 mm graphite pencil using 2H lead were used to create the line drawing study of the building directly on the print.

Fig. 2-16 A black-and-white photocopy was made of the pencil drawing in figure 2-15 so the color media would not smear the lines. Marker and color pencil were applied directly to the copy to create this quick study. Notes were also added.

Bristol Paper

Bristol paper is a dense, high-quality paper that yields excellent results when used with the color media described in this book. It has the right amount of tooth to take pencil and pastel beautifully. Because of its density and makeup, markers bleed very little when applied to Bristol paper (2-17).

This versatile white paper can be run through many black-and-white photocopiers, and the toner usually fuses well to its surface. Because it is very translucent on a light table, drawings can be traced onto it quite easily. If you prefer the lines to be subtle, trace the original drawing onto the Bristol with .5 mm mechanical pencil using a 6H lead.

A number of high-quality Bristol papers are available in most art supply stores. Some of the best for color design illustration include the Strathmore Bristol, 100 lb., and Canson Bristol. Both are two-ply and have a *vellum finish*. The 11" x 14" pad size is adequate for most illustration tasks. Bristol paper, like toned Canson paper, has one side with a very slightly rougher texture than the other. Although either side can be used, the texture is so subtle that the rougher side is usually preferable.

Fig. 2-17 This design study of a combination sign and light fixture is drawn on Bristol paper with marker and color pencil. The shade of the light fixture is subtly colored with two colors of pastel that grade from warm to cool. Note also the subtle highlights of white gouache. (Drawing: Henry Beer)

Fig. 2-17

Ink-Jet Plotter Paper

There are a wide variety of papers available for ink-jet plotters. High-quality, heavy papers, such as Hewlett Packard's Heavyweight Coated Paper C6569C, take hand-applied line and color media—marker, color pencil, and pastel—beautifully. Ink-jet inks dry with a matte finish, so hand-applied color media can be used on plotted images to add color adjustments, detail, and nuance quickly (2-18, 2-19). These "hybrid" drawings can be presented as is or scanned to create a digital image. See Chapter 7 for more on hybrid color drawing.

Fig. 2-18

Fig. 2-18 This restaurant interior, shown here in partial view, was modeled and colored in Form•Z. It was then opened in Photoshop in order to filter it with the *Dry Brush* filter (Filter > Artistic > Dry Brush; Brush Size = 4, Brush Detail = 4, Texture =1). Remember, to use this filter, the mode must be set to "RGB" (Image > Mode > RGB Color). This filter softened the hard-edged quality of the Form•Z image, giving it a watercolor-like character. The image was then plotted at 11" x 17" and hand color was added with marker and color pencil. The use of hand color was a fast way to darken the foreground partition and add gradients to the partition, walls, and ceiling. The flowers, tile grout lines, plates, and touches of lighting sparkle were also added by hand, helping to both modify the drawing and further soften its character. (Illustration: Grady Huff)

Fig. 2-19

Fig. 2-19 This illustration began as an 11" x 17" line drawing on tracing paper, created with a *Black* pencil and a .5 mm pencil using a 2H lead. The completed line drawing was then scanned and opened in Photoshop.

Large gradients of transparent color were added to the image by setting the blending mode for each layer to "Multiply." This kept the lines of the drawing visible through the layers of color. The sky, the first layer created, transitions from pink on the right to dark blue on the left, simulating a dusk sky just after sunset. The middle-ground buildings and street were selected as another layer, which transitions from yellow red at the street level to blue green toward the tops of the buildings. Additional yellow red was lightly airbrushed (using the airbrush capability of the *Brush Tool*) over the street area on a different layer whose blending mode was kept on "Normal." This helped the illuminated street to "glow." The train tunnel and highway were similarly colored as a layer, as were the foreground trees and frontage road.

Once the line drawing had its large areas of color, it was plotted on heavy-weight coated paper. Color pencil was used to add much of the detail far more quickly than it could have been if the detail had been attempted by computer. It was also used to add the illuminated building windows, as well as the texture for the plant materials and trees. White gouache was applied for the sparkle of lighting at the street level and for the automobile headlights.

The drawing was then rescanned and opened in Photoshop to add the final touches—the glowing pylons, auto-mobile headlight washes on the pavement, red taillights, and the aircraft warning lights on the buildings. The background searchlight was the final accent added.

CHAPTER 53

TECHNIQUE

Designers usually work within time constraints. The reasons vary, ranging from tight fees to looming construction starts. This time pressure trickles down, of course, to all parts of the design process, including the illustration of design ideas.

The techniques discussed and illustrated in this chapter form the basis for the approach to color design drawing presented in this book. They have evolved because they help make the process of illustrating ideas during the evolution of a design—from conception to design development—efficient and effective.

If you are unfamiliar with the hand media, digital media, and paper introduced in Chapters 1 and 2, use this chapter as a springboard for experimenting with them. You will discover that there are few firm rules that govern their use as you become more familiar with them. While you will be introduced to the basic techniques for their use, feel free to modify these in ways that work best with your specific approach to illustrating your design ideas.

WAYS TO APPLY AND ADJUST COLOR

The techniques that follow show ways to apply a variety of color media. Once you familiarize yourself with them, you may wish to create variations that more closely meet your own approach to design drawing.

Color Washes

A *wash,* a term originally used in watercolor art, describes a deposit of color on paper. There are two kinds of color washes you will use continually in color design illustration—the *even* wash and the *graded* wash.

The Even Wash

An *even wash* is often used as the base color for many parts of a design illustration, such as a wall or sky. Certain media described in Chapter 2 lend themselves to even washes more than others. Markers, for example, usually leave a faint striped effect. Although this is not a problem in most illustrations, there are ways to minimize the effect when necessary (3-1). The faster you work with marker, the smoother the results, because the carrier (alcohol or xylene) remains fresher, allowing each successive swipe of color to blend more thoroughly with its neighbors.

Washes of pencil or pastel are easier to create, as these media do not "bleed" and are thereby more controllable (3-2 through 3-5). Although they alter a marker's color, they tend to smooth its appearance, as figure 3-21 shows.

Applying a very faint wash of color, often with pastel or pencil over marker, is referred to in this book as *flavoring* a color.

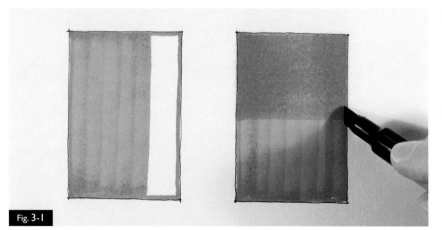

Fig. 3-1

Fig. 3-1 When you apply marker, first outline the shape of the area you intend to color using the marker's tip *(left).* When you subsequently fill in the shape with color, there is less chance that the color will stray beyond the lines. If the marker color must appear smoother than usual, apply a second marker coat by stroking the marker in a direction perpendicular to the first *(right).*

Fig. 3-2

Fig. 3-2 Use the side of the pencil point when applying a pencil wash to get a more even application. Stray pencil color can be easily removed with an electric eraser.

Fig. 3-3

Fig. 3-3 Use the side of a piece of stick pastel *(top)* or the side of a pastel pencil *(right)* to apply these media to paper. Maintain light hand pressure to avoid streakiness. You can also scrape the side of a stick pastel with a knife *(left)* to deposit the color onto a drawing.

Fig. 3-4a

Fig. 3-4b

Fig. 3-4c

Fig. 3-4 Once the pastel is deposited onto the drawing surface, there are a number of ways to distribute it. You can use your finger (a), which will give you the least smooth, though darkest, deposit of color. By wrapping a tissue over your finger, you can make your pastel color more even and somewhat lighter (b). The use of a piece of soft leather chamois (the kind used to polish cars) will make the pastel application even smoother and lighter (c). Chamois can be obtained at an auto supply store.

Fig. 3-5

Fig. 3-5 An electric eraser with a soft white erasing strip can be used to easily clean up the edges of an overextended pastel application.

The Graded Wash

A wash of color that progressively changes in color dimension over a surface is called a *graded wash*. A graded wash may change in hue, such as from red to yellow, in value from lighter to darker, or in chroma—for example, from grayed to saturated. In your surroundings, a surface often changes in more than one dimension at a time, as when a sky grades from a tint of violet at the horizon to a more saturated blue at its zenith.

Very few surfaces in your world appear evenly colored, owing usually to the play of direct and reflected light. You will see gradations of color everywhere, from the surfaces of the room that surrounds you to the way light influences the colors of a tree. Gradations of color make an illustration appear more realistic and far more dramatic. They can be used to build necessary contrasts subtly, almost unnoticeably. These washes can be made with marker, color pencil, and pastel (3-6).

Fig. 3-6 Graded washes of marker are usually made with the grays, inasmuch as their progressive value designations lend themselves to this kind of application (a). Dark-to-light applications are easiest.

It is important to work quickly. If, for example, you begin with a *Warm Grey #5* marker, briefly scrub the leading edge of the marker deposit you make with the next lightest marker to blend the edge between the two. Most likely, this will be *Warm Grey #3*. Continue with *Warm Grey #3* until you begin with *Warm Grey #1,* and repeat the process at the edge. If you want to grade back into the paper color, repeat the edge treatment at the edge of *Warm Grey #1* with a colorless blender marker. After you experiment with this kind of gradation, it becomes quite easy.

A graded wash with pencil (b) is best accomplished with the side of the pencil point. Here, Derwent *Blue Violet Lake #27, Mineral Orange,* and *Jasmine* pencils were progressively blended one into the other. Each color was extended far enough into the next to ensure a smooth gradation.

The pastel graded wash (c) was easily created by scraping the Rembrandt stick pastels *Permanent Green Deep 619.9* on the ceiling on the left, *Ultramarine Deep 506.9* in the center, and *Raw Sienna 234.9* on the right side. The three colors were distributed by finger, then evened and blended with a chamois.

Fig. 3-6a

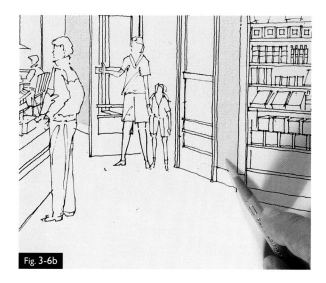

Fig. 3-6b

Fig. 3-6c

Digital Washes

Washes of color, whether uniform or gradient, can also be easily applied and manipulated using Photoshop. These washes can range from completely transparent to fully opaque. They can also range in size, covering very small areas or the entire illustration.

The illustrations shown in this book use Photoshop in a simple and direct way. Figures 3-7 and 3-8 show the menus, palettes, and selection and editing tools that were used most frequently to create them.

Any hand drawing you create, be it a simple line drawing or one with color already applied, may be colored or modified in Photoshop. The drawing must first be scanned to transform the physical image into a digital image. A drawing that ranges in size from letter to tabloid (8½" x 11" to 11" x 17")—the size of most of the drawings in this book—can be scanned at 150 dots per inch, or dpi. This will create an easy-to-manipulate file size and a print of sufficient resolution. Drawings that are intended to be wall-mounted and presented in meetings, at sizes between 24" x 36" to 36" x 42", should be scanned at between 220 dpi and 300 dpi.

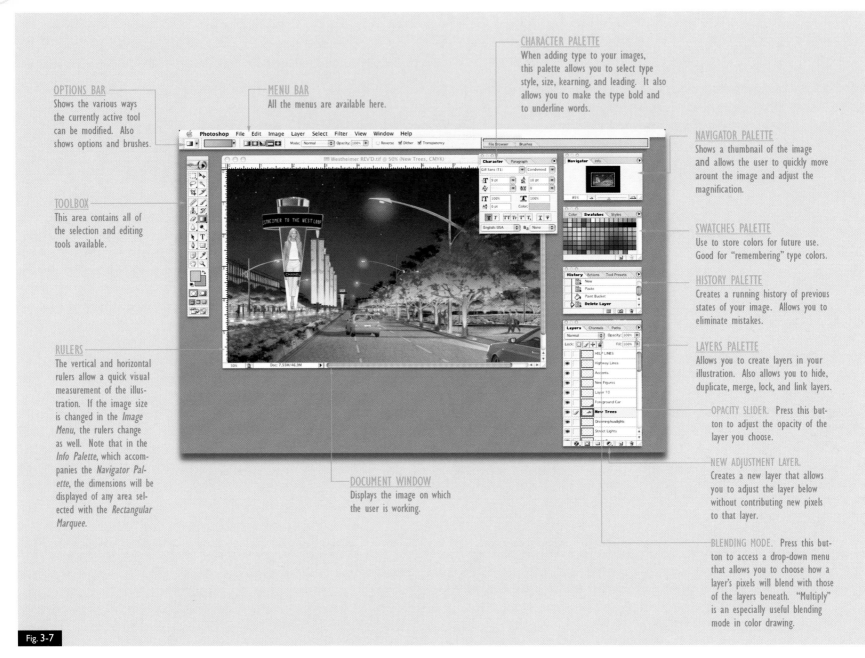

OPTIONS BAR
Shows the various ways the currently active tool can be modified. Also shows options and brushes.

MENU BAR
All the menus are available here.

CHARACTER PALETTE
When adding type to your images, this palette allows you to select type style, size, kearning, and leading. It also allows you to make the type bold and to underline words.

NAVIGATOR PALETTE
Shows a thumbnail of the image and allows the user to quickly move arount the image and adjust the magnification.

TOOLBOX
This area contains all of the selection and editing tools available.

SWATCHES PALETTE
Use to store colors for future use. Good for "remembering" type colors.

HISTORY PALETTE
Creates a running history of previous states of your image. Allows you to eliminate mistakes.

RULERS
The vertical and horizontal rulers allow a quick visual measurement of the illustration. If the image size is changed in the *Image Menu*, the rulers change as well. Note that in the *Info Palette*, which accompanies the *Navigator Palette*, the dimensions will be displayed of any area selected with the *Rectangular Marquee*.

LAYERS PALETTE
Allows you to create layers in your illustration. Also allows you to hide, duplicate, merge, lock, and link layers.

OPACITY SLIDER. Press this button to adjust the opacity of the layer you choose.

NEW ADJUSTMENT LAYER.
Creates a new layer that allows you to adjust the layer below without contributing new pixels to that layer.

DOCUMENT WINDOW
Displays the image on which the user is working.

BLENDING MODE. Press this button to access a drop-down menu that allows you to choose how a layer's pixels will blend with those of the layers beneath. "Multiply" is an especially useful blending mode in color drawing.

Fig. 3-7

Fig. 3-7 Shown here are the document window, toolbox, menu bar, and palettes most frequently used for color drawing in Photoshop.

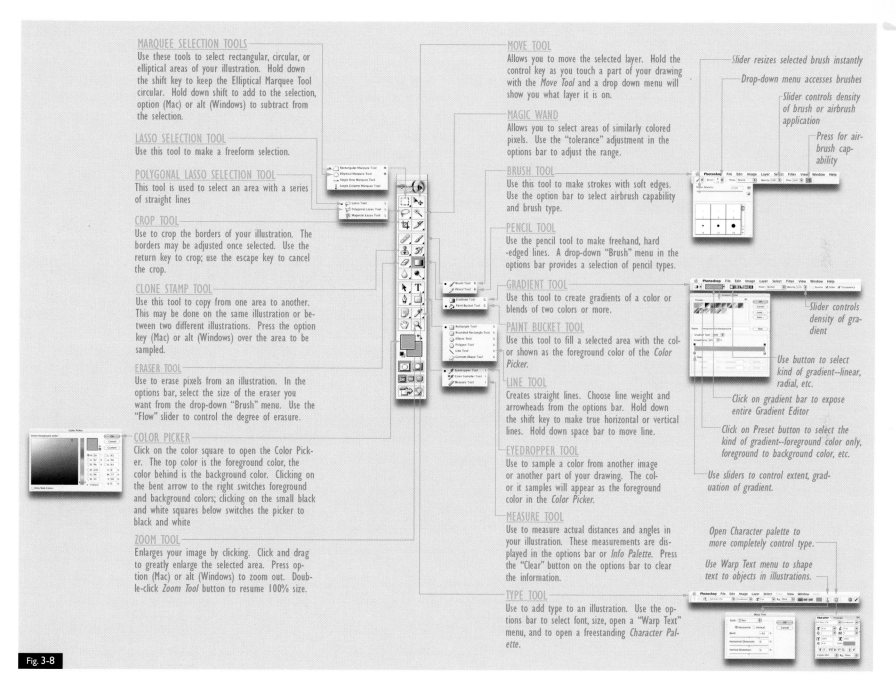

MARQUEE SELECTION TOOLS
Use these tools to select rectangular, circular, or elliptical areas of your illustration. Hold down the shift key to keep the Elliptical Marquee Tool circular. Hold down shift to add to the selection, option (Mac) or alt (Windows) to subtract from the selection.

LASSO SELECTION TOOL
Use this tool to make a freeform selection.

POLYGONAL LASSO SELECTION TOOL
This tool is used to select an area with a series of straight lines

CROP TOOL
Use to crop the borders of your illustration. The borders may be adjusted once selected. Use the return key to crop; use the escape key to cancel the crop.

CLONE STAMP TOOL
Use this tool to copy from one area to another. This may be done on the same illustration or between two different illustrations. Press the option key (Mac) or alt (Windows) over the area to be sampled.

ERASER TOOL
Use to erase pixels from an illustration. In the options bar, select the size of the eraser you want from the drop-down "Brush" menu. Use the "Flow" slider to control the degree of erasure.

COLOR PICKER
Click on the color square to open the Color Picker. The top color is the foreground color, the color behind is the background color. Clicking on the bent arrow to the right switches foreground and background colors; clicking on the small black and white squares below switches the picker to black and white

ZOOM TOOL
Enlarges your image by clicking. Click and drag to greatly enlarge the selected area. Press option (Mac) or alt (Windows) to zoom out. Double-click Zoom Tool button to resume 100% size.

MOVE TOOL
Allows you to move the selected layer. Hold the control key as you touch a part of your drawing with the Move Tool and a drop down menu will show you what layer it is on.

MAGIC WAND
Allows you to select areas of similarly colored pixels. Use the "tolerance" adjustment in the options bar to adjust the range.

BRUSH TOOL
Use this tool to make strokes with soft edges. Use the option bar to select airbrush capability and brush type.

PENCIL TOOL
Use the pencil tool to make freehand, hard-edged lines. A drop-down "Brush" menu in the options bar provides a selection of pencil types.

GRADIENT TOOL
Use this tool to create gradients of a color or blends of two colors or more.

PAINT BUCKET TOOL
Use this tool to fill a selected area with the color shown as the foreground color of the Color Picker.

LINE TOOL
Creates straight lines. Choose line weight and arrowheads from the options bar. Hold down the shift key to make true horizontal or vertical lines. Hold down space bar to move line.

EYEDROPPER TOOL
Use to sample a color from another image or another part of your drawing. The color it samples will appear as the foreground color in the Color Picker.

MEASURE TOOL
Use to measure actual distances and angles in your illustration. These measurements are displayed in the options bar or Info Palette. Press the "Clear" button on the options bar to clear the information.

TYPE TOOL
Use to add type to an illustration. Use the options bar to select font, size, open a "Warp Text" menu, and to open a freestanding Character Palette.

Slider resizes selected brush instantly

Drop-down menu accesses brushes

Slider controls density of brush or airbrush application

Press for airbrush capability

Slider controls density of gradient

Use button to select kind of gradient--linear, radial, etc.

Click on gradient bar to expose entire Gradient Editor

Click on Preset button to select the kind of gradient--foreground color only, foreground to background color, etc.

Use sliders to control extent, graduation of gradient.

Open Character palette to more completely control type.

Use Warp Text menu to shape text to objects in illustrations.

Fig. 3-8

Fig. 3-8 The tools in the Photoshop toolbox most frequently used for color drawing.

You will find using a pen tablet much easier than using a mouse when working in Photoshop for prolonged periods (3-9). Not only is it more comfortable, it allows you to make more precise hand-drawn movements more facilely as well. It also affords pressure-sensitive control when using the *Pencil Tool* and the *Brush Tool,* which has an airbrush capability.

The Paint Bucket Tool

Figures 3-10 through 3-17 show various ways an even wash of color can be applied using Photoshop. Figure 3-10 demonstrates how a color can be sampled from one image for use in another. The *Paint Bucket Tool* is used to apply the color. You can control the amount of opacity and transparency of the color by using the

Fig. 3-9

Fig. 3-9 Wacom's "Intuos3" 9" x 12" pen tablet (Courtesy: Wacom Technology Corporation)

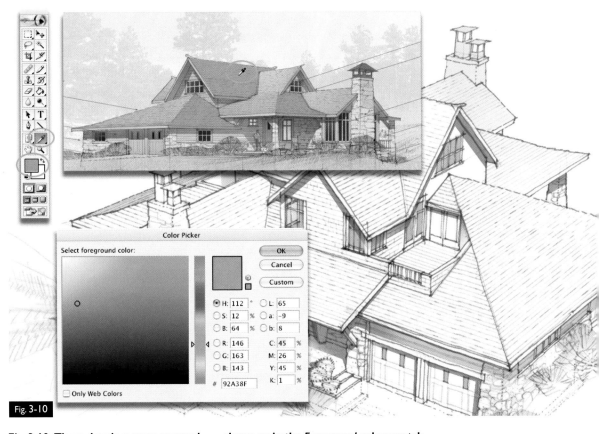

Fig. 3-10

Fig. 3-10 These drawings were scanned and opened in Photoshop. The roof color of the eye-level view of this duplex is shown being sampled to create the same color for the roof of the bird's eye view. When the *Eyedropper Tool* is selected from the toolbox and used to click on the roof color, it immediately shows up in the *Foreground* color swatch in the *Color Picker*. **By clicking on the *Foreground* color swatch, the entire *Color Picker* opens, showing where in the color field the selected color is located. You can modify the color here if you wish— this is just one of many ways the color can be modified.**

Opacity slider, shown in figure 3-12. If the blending mode of the layer is set to "Multiply," the entire layer becomes transparent, allowing the detail of the line drawing to show through the color layer (3-13). This creates a result very similar to that created by the use of transparent hand media such as markers, or by applying color to the back of a line drawing on tracing paper (3-55 and 3-56).

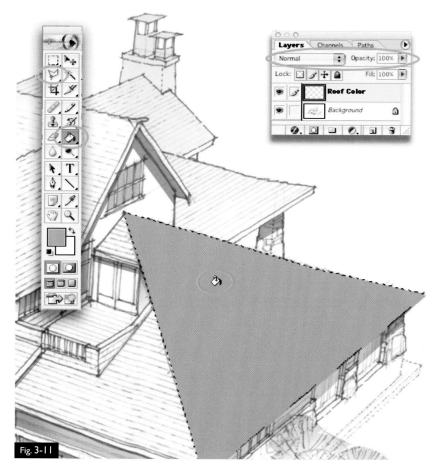

Fig. 3-11

Fig. 3-12

Fig. 3-11 Next, a new layer is created, called "*roof color.*" A destination area for the color is selected using the *Polygonal Lasso Selection Tool*, which limits the area the color can spread to the shape selected. The *Paint Bucket Tool* is then used to apply the color—the *Foreground* color showing in the *Color Picker*. Since the layer's blending mode is set to "Normal" and the opacity at 100%, the resultant color in the selected area is fully opaque.

Fig. 3-12 You can increase the transparency of the layer (or reduce its opacity) by clicking on the button to the right of the *Opacity Percentage* field to expose and manipulate the *Opacity* slider. You can also select and change the percentage number in the window to produce the same effect. When the opacity is reduced, the color becomes fainter and more background color shows through the applied color—in this case, white.

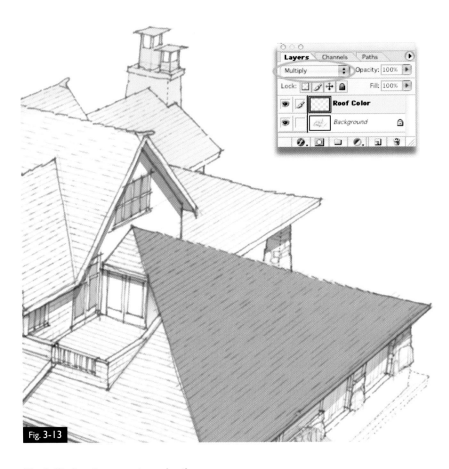

Fig. 3-13

Fig. 3-13 Another way to make the color layer transparent is to select "Multiply" from the drop-down menu after clicking on the blending mode button. This makes the active layer—in this case, the *"roof color"* layer—transparent, without reducing its color density. Of course, you can still further adjust the amount of color showing by using the *Opacity* slider.

The Gradient Tool

Large graded washes of color are easily made in Photoshop using the *Gradient Tool*. This tool can help you create simple gradients, such as one that transitions from a single color to transparency, or from one color to another. It also allows you to create gradients that transition through multiple colors.

Creating gradients over large areas, such as backgrounds and skies, may be easier to accomplish digitally than by hand, depending on the medium and the task. However, avoid the trap of trying to create gradients on many *small* areas of a drawing. They can be quite time consuming to handle digitally and are easier and faster to make by hand.

Figures 3-14 through 3-17 show how to use the *Gradient Tool* to create a graded wash of color across a sky. The *Gradient Editor,* accessed through the options bar, is used to manipulate the character and color of the gradient.

Fig. 3-14

Fig. 3-15

Fig. 3-14 A color gradient is begun by first determining which colors you want to use. Click on the *Foreground* color field in the toolbox. The *Color Picker* will open. You can select the hue from the vertical slider, then adjust the color in the color field. Or, you can use the *Eyedropper Tool* to select a color from a photograph or other image that is also open in Photoshop. Click on the *Background* color field and repeat the process.

Fig. 3-15 In the *Layers Palette,* a new layer called "*sky*" was created so the sky could be independently adjusted later, after other colors were applied to the illustration. The sky area was then selected. In this example, the *Rectangular Marquee Selection Tool* was used to select the entire sky area, then the forms of building and mountains were subtracted from it using the *Polygonal Lasso Selection Tool* and the *Rectangular Marquee Selection Tool*.

After the *Gradient Tool* is selected, its *Options Bar* opens (top). The blue arrow button beside the *Gradient* swatch was clicked to access the Foreground to Background button in the *Presets* drop-down menu. In addition, the linear gradient was specified from the black-and-white *Gradient Geometry* buttons.

Using the pen tablet (or mouse), the *Gradient Tool* was placed in the lower right of the selected area, clicked and dragged to the upper left, and released. The gradient filled in instantly.

Fig. 3-16 You can adjust the way the gradient transitions from one color to another. By clicking on the Gradient swatch in *the Options Bar,* the *Gradient Editor* will open. Note that the same *Presets* menu becomes available at the top.

At the lower part of the *Gradient Editor,* there are sliders at the top and the bottom of the gradient bar. The bottom sliders control the colors of the gradient, while the top sliders control the transparency of those colors. Click on either of the bottom sliders, called *color stops,* and a color midpoint control will appear. You can control the amount of either color showing in the gradient by moving the slider. In this example, the color midpoint was moved to the left, setting the gradient to 25% of the yellow red, leaving the sky 75% purple blue.

To modify the gradient, the sky was reselected (the selection had been saved) and the *Gradient Tool* was once again clicked and dragged from lower right to upper left. Once released, the revised gradient was applied.

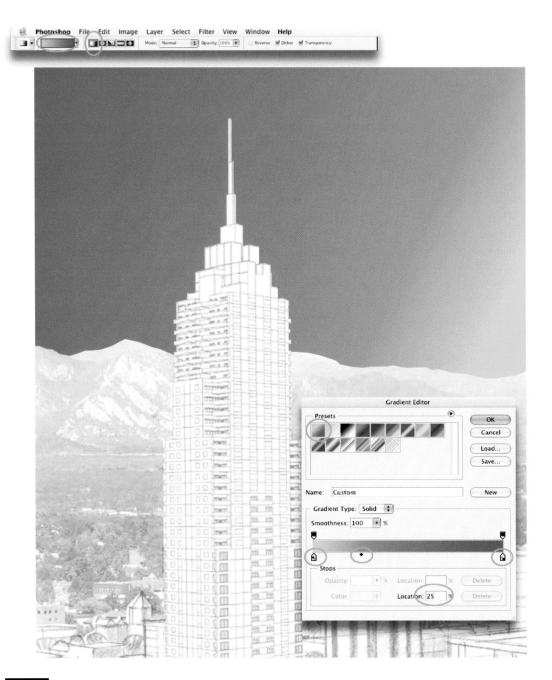

Fig. 3-16

Fig. 3-17

Fig. 3-17 Using the *Gradient Editor,* you can create a gradient that transitions between more than two colors.

In the example shown here, a click just below the gradient bar adds a color stop. Note that there are now *two* color midpoint controls available. Then, a click on the now-activated color bar opens the *Color Picker.* A hue in the red-purple range is selected on the vertical hue slider. On a color wheel, this hue is roughly between the yellow-red and purple-blue hues already in use in this example, ensuring a visually logical and smooth transition between these analogous hues. In the color field of the *Color Picker,* a weaker-chroma red purple is selected, so the sky does not become too intense.

Once the middle color is selected, the *OK* buttons on the *Color Picker* and *Gradient Editor* were clicked. The sky was again reselected, and the *Gradient Tool* dragged from lower right to upper left. When released, the three-color gradient was created.

Ways to Modify Colors by Hand

Design ideation is an iterative process. In most cases, you will find that once an idea initially bursts forth onto paper, you instantly begin a dialog with yourself: Move this here, shift that to there, add this, delete that. All those thoughts and feelings happen at lightning speed, without words and almost beneath notice.

Color is one of the elements in early design illustrations you will most certainly want to adjust easily. You will want to "massage" it, shift its dimensions, sometimes only slightly and at other times more significantly as your design effort progresses.

Any combination of color media, whether similar—such as pencil over pencil—or differing—such as pastel over marker, is legitimate for the purposes of color mixing and adjustment as long as the media are compatible. When you attempt to modify a color, you will achieve the best results when you use another color to do so. Extensive use of a *neutral color* (gray, black, or white) applied over chromatic colors to modify them can make your drawing dull or muddy.

Fig. 3-18 A *Deco Blue* pencil (a Munsell blue, *top left*) is applied over a *Pale Cherry* marker (a Munsell yellow red, *bottom left*). Because the colors are complements, the result is the gray shown on the right.

Fig. 3-18

Keep in mind that, in general, when two colors are mixed, the resulting color will be somewhere between the two. An exception to this precept applies to markers. Because marker applications are transparent, the darker markers will predominate and overwhelm lighter markers. But with most media, including markers of similar value, the rule of thumb holds. If, for example, a light red pencil is applied over a dark blue marker, the resulting color will be a medium-value purple. If a color pencil with a blue-green hue, such as *Deco Aqua,* is applied as a wash over a pencil color (of similar value) that is green-yellowish in hue, such as *Yellow Chartreuse,* the resultant color will be somewhere between the two, in the green hue range.

The further away the two colors are from each other on the color wheel, the more grayish the resultant hue. Refer to the color wheel in figure 1-18. If a *Deco Blue* pencil (a blue hue) is used to draw over its visual complement, a yellow-red hue made with a *Pale Cherry* marker, the result will yield a gray. This gray is a livelier, more interesting gray than a perfectly neutral gray, however, and much better suited for the purposes of color design drawing (3-18).

Although pencils and pastels can and should be blended with themselves to create more interesting colors, some less common combinations of color drawing media can also yield rich, though subtle, colors. Such combinations are discussed and illustrated in the following paragraphs.

Marker over Marker

The best way to begin a color illustration that requires marker is to apply a *marker base* color that most closely approaches the color you intend. If you want to modify it—adjust its hue, value, or chroma—you can do so by applying other marker colors, pastel, and/or color pencil over the original marker color (3-19 through 3-22). If your marker colors tend to "bleed" past their intended boundary, see figure 3-20 for ways to control them. Markers tend to bleed more on less dense papers, such as bond and diazo prints. This happens particularly when the markers are new, owing to an excess of the alcohol or xylene carrier. This problem will self-correct as you use your markers.

Fig. 3-19a

Fig. 3-19b

Fig. 3-19 Markers can be applied over other markers to create new colors. One of the most common uses of marker blends is to reduce the chroma of the underlying color. This can be done by using complementary marker colors. In example (a), a *Willow Green* marker is applied over a *Burnt Sienna* marker. Another way to achieve similar results is simply to apply a gray marker over the first color. In example (b), a *Warm Grey #3* marker is applied over the *Burnt Sienna*.

Fig. 3-20a

Fig. 3-20b

Fig. 3-20 Marker that "bleeds" past an edge can be controlled by gently blowing on the marker tip as you apply it near the edge (a). This accelerates the evaporation of the carrier solvent and reduces the spread of the dye.

If bleeding has already occurred, the edges of the marker colors can be "trimmed" with color pencils that are similar in color to the markers (b). The semiopaque pencils will cover the bleeding fairly well. In the example here, *Cloud Blue* pencil is applied with a straightedge where the *Sapphire Blue* marker meets the *Flesh* marker, and *Light Peach* pencil is used to cover areas where the *Sapphire Blue* has bled into the *Flesh*.

Pastel over Marker

Pastel can be applied over marker quite effectively. The resultant color is a visual mixture of the underlying marker color and the coating of pastel. The more pastel you apply, of course, the more the resultant color will shift toward that of the pastel (3-21).

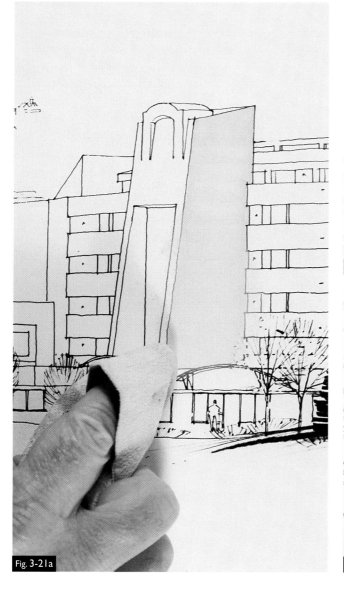

Fig. 3-21a

Fig. 3-21b

Fig. 3-21c

Fig. 3-21 Pastel smooths the streaked appearance of the marker base as it also shifts the dimensions of its color. In (a), a near-complementary *Permanent Green Deep 619.9* is applied over *Flesh* marker, resulting in a grayish green. As more pastel is wiped from atop the marker, the more the marker will show through.

Marker colors can be tinted with pastel. In (b), *White* pastel has been applied over the *Light Ivy* marker on the curved fascia to the right.

Pastel can be used to "bring up" color from gray, as in (c), where *Raw Sienna 234.9* pastel is applied over the graded wash of *Warm Grey* markers shown in figure 3-6a.

Pencil over Marker and Pastel

Color pencil works well over marker and pastel. It not only can shift the dimensions of the marker color, it can add texture while doing so (3-22). This is a benefit particularly in illustrating materials, as you will see in Chapter 4.

Fig. 3-22a

Fig. 3-22b

Fig. 3-22c

Fig. 3-22d

Fig. 3-22 Color pencil over marker can simultaneously shift the color of the marker as it creates texture and pattern. Figure 3-11 (a) shows *Celadon Green* pencil applied over *Mauve* marker. These near complements result in a lively gray. In (b) a graded wash of color pencil, from *Light Peach* to *Terra Cotta*, is applied over *French Grey 30% Prismacolor* marker. Although the grain of the paper causes the pencil to produce a texture, the underlying gray marker diminishes the impact of this texture. In (c) *Light Peach* pencil is used to apply the grain pattern to a beam initially colored with a *Kraft Brown* marker. *White* pencil is used over the pastel and *Warm Grey* marker in (d) to draw the grout joints of the tile floor.

Ways to Modify Colors Digitally

Once your drawings are in the form of digital files, whether these originate with a digital original from an illustration program or a scan of a hand-drawn original, you can use Photoshop to modify them in many different ways. To make these modifications, the Adjustment commands are used. These commands allow you to revise specific colors, change the brightness and contrast of an image, or confine your changes to the dark, middle, or light values of a drawing.

These commands are found under the *Image* menu on the menu bar at the top of the program window. Found in the *Adjustments* submenu (Image > Adjustments), the five most frequently used adjustments for color drawing are, in descending order, *Brightness/Contrast, Hue/Saturation, Color Balance, Levels,* and *Replace Color* (3-23).

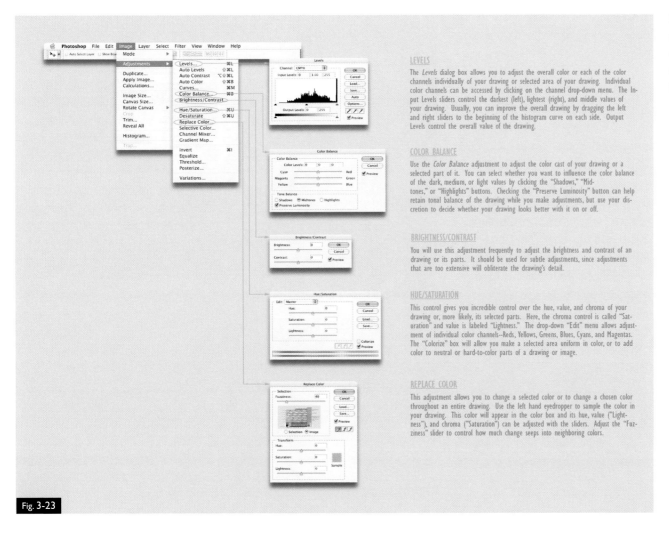

Fig. 3-23 These are the Photoshop color adjustments most frequently used for color drawing. Adjustment layers can be created to modify the color of your image without changing the image itself.

LEVELS

The *Levels* dialog box allows you to adjust the overall color or each of the color channels individually of your drawing or selected area of your drawing. Individual color channels can be accessed by clicking on the channel drop-down menu. The Input Levels sliders control the darkest (left), lightest (right), and middle values of your drawing. Usually, you can improve the overall drawing by dragging the left and right sliders to the beginning of the histogram curve on each side. Output Levels control the overall value of the drawing.

COLOR BALANCE

Use the *Color Balance* adjustment to adjust the color cast of your drawing or a selected part of it. You can select whether you want to influence the color balance of the dark, medium, or light values by clicking the "Shadows," "Midtones," or "Highlights" buttons. Checking the "Preserve Luminosity" button can help retain tonal balance of the drawing while you make adjustments, but use your discretion to decide whether your drawing looks better with it on or off.

BRIGHTNESS/CONTRAST

You will use this adjustment frequently to adjust the brightness and contrast of an drawing or its parts. It should be used for subtle adjustments, since adjustments that are too extensive will obliterate the drawing's detail.

HUE/SATURATION

This control gives you incredible control over the hue, value, and chroma of your drawing or, more likely, its selected parts. Here, the chroma control is called "Saturation" and value is labeled "Lightness." The drop-down "Edit" menu allows adjustment of individual color channels--Reds, Yellows, Greens, Blues, Cyans, and Magentas. The "Colorize" box will allow you make a selected area uniform in color, or to add color to neutral or hard-to-color parts of a drawing or image.

REPLACE COLOR

This adjustment allows you to change a selected color or to change a chosen color throughout an entire drawing. Use the left hand eyedropper to sample the color in your drawing. This color will appear in the color box and its hue, value ("Lightness"), and chroma ("Saturation") can be adjusted with the sliders. Adjust the "Fuzziness" slider to control how much change seeps into neighboring colors.

Fig. 3-23

Perhaps you made modifications to a drawing using the Adjustment commands, then saved and closed the drawing. Some time later, you open the drawing, evaluate it, and regret the adjustments you made earlier. You go to the *History Palette* in order to go back a few steps to reverse your actions. To your dismay, the *History Palette* has no record of your previous steps, since it clears each time you save and close an image: the modifications are permanent. To reverse your steps, you must go to the trouble of recreating and revising your previous modifications.

A better way to modify your color drawings in Photoshop is to use adjustment layers. An adjustment layer does not permanently change your drawing. Instead, it gives instructions to the pixels that comprise the image on the layer beneath it. Best of all, when you reopen a drawing, you can easily revise or eliminate the modifications you made previously. You can even have multiple adjustment layers that modify different characteristics of the same drawing.

You can create adjustment layers for four of the five adjustments most frequently used in color drawing: brightness/contrast, hue/saturation, color balance, and levels. An adjustment layer cannot be made for the *Replace Color* adjustment. The action cannot be revised; it must be redone.

To create an adjustment layer, select *New Adjustment Layer* from the *Layer* menu on the menu bar (Layer > New Adjustment Layer), then select the kind of adjustment you want to make. Or, at the bottom of the *Layers Palette,* click on the half-white, half-black circle icon (3-7), then select the kind of adjustment layer you want from the drop-down menu. Once you have created an adjustment layer, you can revise a modification by double-clicking on the adjustment layer icon for the appropriate adjustment layer in the *Layers Palette* (circled in 3-33). The *Adjustment* command will appear, and its sliders can be repositioned.

Brightness/Contrast

The simple *Brightness/Contrast* adjustment (3-24) is one of the most useful and powerful of all the Photoshop adjustments for color drawing. You can adjust the value and contrast of all or selected parts of a drawing, arranging and rearranging them to create an image with more impact and focus than perhaps you had first created (3-25, 3-26). Note that this adjustment can obliterate detail in a drawing if the sliders are moved too far in either direction. (See also Chapter 7.)

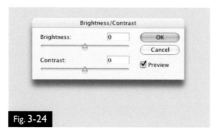

Fig. 3-24

Fig. 3-24 Use the sliders to adjust the brightness and contrast of an image. You can click the *Preview* button to compare the image before and after the adjustment.

Fig. 3-25

Fig. 3-25 This hand-drawn study for an atrium of an interior botanical garden focuses less on its subject than it could. It scatters the viewer's attention by including a number of elements that distract from the atrium itself: the figures to the left, the woman with the white bag, and the white flowers.

Hue/Saturation

The *Hue/Saturation* adjustment gives you control over the hues, values (using the *Lightness* slider), and chromas (using the *Saturation* slider) of the colors in an image or its selected areas (3-27). To simultaneously adjust all the colors in an image or a selected part of that image, keep the *Edit* button set on "Master."

By clicking the *Edit* button, a drop-down menu also provides you the opportunity to adjust any of the six color groups in an image independently. When you click on a particular color group—"Reds" in this example—note that sliders appear between the color strips at the bottom of the adjustment control box. By moving the rectangular sliders, you can enlarge or shrink the range of the color group you are adjusting. You can also control the transition between the changed and unchanged colors by moving the triangular sliders (3-28 through 3-30).

The *Hue/Saturation* adjustment can also be used to add simple color tints, as shown in figures 3-31 through 3-33.

Fig. 3-26

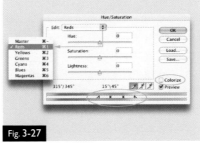

Fig. 3-27

Fig. 3-26 Since the purpose of the drawing is to showcase the character of the atrium idea, the foreground was used to further "set off" the atrium. First, the openings into the atrium were selected and the inverse of that selection was saved (Select > Inverse, then Select > Save Selection > *name the selection*). Everything was selected and saved *except* what could be seen through the openings.

Next, an adjustment layer was created by clicking on the half-black, half-white circle icon at the bottom of the *Layers Palette*. In the drop-down menu that appeared, the *Brightness/Contrast* adjustment was selected. The brightness and contrast adjustments were moved to the left, darkening the foreground and reducing its contrast, respectively.

The *Eraser Tool* was then selected, a 65-pixel brush chosen, and the *Flow* set at 15%. The *Eraser Tool* was then used to subtly erase some of the adjustment layer behind the bench shadow, making the floor lighter to account for the light from the skylight illuminating the floor.

Because the foreground figures were on independent layers, they could be further darkened and reduced in contrast. Since they were photographic images, they were also roughened using the *Filter* menu (Filter > Dry Brush; Brush Size = 0, Brush Detail = 0, Texture = 2) to give them a character more like that of the drawing.

By darkening and reducing the contrast of the foreground, the atrium becomes the focus of the drawing.

Fig. 3-27 The *Hue/Saturation* adjustment command displays the *Color Group* drop-down menu when the *Edit* button is clicked. When a color group within the menu is clicked, sliders at the bottom appear, allowing you to control the color group's range and transition. The *Colorize* button can be clicked to add monochromatic color to black-and-white images or selections within an image that resist being colored when attempting to use only the sliders.

Fig. 3-28 This is one of a series of color studies for the façade of a midrise, mixed-use building built in the early 1960s. It shows an analogous hue scheme as a gradient that transitions horizontally from yellow red to green yellow.

It was decided that the chroma of the green-yellow side of the scheme, on the left, should be more like that of the yellow red on the opposite side. To do this, the entire part of the facade with the color panels was first selected with the *Rectangular Marquee Tool.* Next, an adjustment layer was created (Layer > New Adjustment Layer > Hue/ Saturation . . . > *name the layer* > OK).

Fig. 3-29 The *Edit* button was clicked after the *Hue/Saturation* adjustment control appeared. Since the green yellows are in the yellow family, the "Yellow" group was selected from the drop-down menu. As soon as the "Yellow" group was selected, the eyedroppers and sliders at the bottom of the adjustment box were activated. The eyedropper on the left was used to sample the existing green-yellow panel color from the drawing. As the color was sampled, the sliders centered on its hue location.

The *Saturation* slider was moved to the right, and the entire selected area increased in chroma. The cursor was then centered between the two rectangular sliders. By clicking and dragging, all the sliders were moved together toward the greener side of the yellow-to-green gradient until only the green was stronger in chroma. By adjusting these sliders, along with the *Saturation* slider, the green side of the study was adjusted to about the same chroma as the existing yellow side.

Fig. 3-30 The facade color study, after the chroma of the green side of the scheme was strengthened.

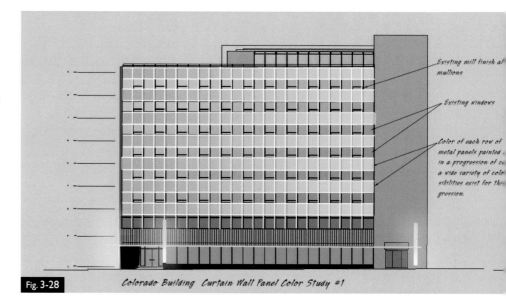

Fig. 3-28

Colorado Building   Curtain Wall Panel Color Study #1

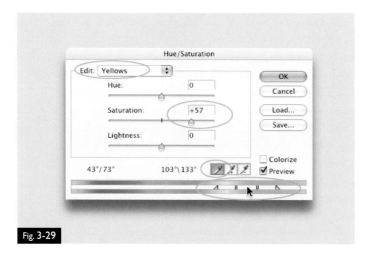

Fig. 3-29

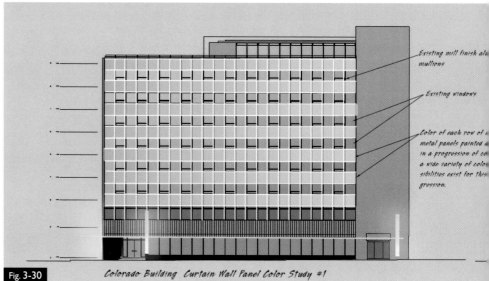

Fig. 3-30

Colorado Building   Curtain Wall Panel Color Study #1

Fig. 3-31

Fig. 3-32

Fig. 3-31 The *Hue/Saturation* adjustment can also be used to add areas of simple color tints, much like a watercolor wash. This study for a small church was drawn with *Black* pencil and .5 mm pencil with a 2H lead. It was scanned and opened in Photoshop. Shadows were added as a layer, with the layer's blending mode set to "Multiply." This enabled them to be made transparent. A background and sky was added as another layer, using a digital photograph taken from the proposed site. Once compiled, the image was flattened, then desaturated (Image > Adjustments > Desaturate), making it a uniform grayscale image.

A single selection was made that encompassed the building and foreground. The treetops were added to the selection by holding down the Shift key and using the *Magic Wand* (its tolerance adjustment in the options bar was set at 32). The selection was then saved.

Fig. 3-32 Once the selection was saved, a new hue/saturation adjustment layer was created. The sliders were adjusted to give a subtle yellow-red tint to the foreground. (If you try this and get no color, click on the *Colorize* button.) Once the foreground color was added, the selection was again loaded (Select > Load Selection . . . > *selection name*), then inverted (Select > Invert). A second hue/saturation adjustment layer was created. This time, the sliders were manipulated to create a subtle purple-blue tint that was darkened, enabling it to contrast in both hue and value with the foreground. This was an easy way to both create the effect of morning light and make the building slightly more dominant in the composition. Note that care was taken not to allow the newly added color to become too saturated, maintaining the delicacy of a watercolor wash.

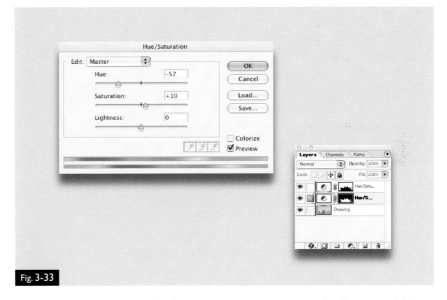

Fig. 3-33

Fig. 3-33 This *Layers Palette* for figure 3-32 shows its two hue/saturation adjustment layers, one for the foreground and one for the background. These layers can be readjusted in the future by clicking on the half-black, half-white icon (circled). The *Hue/Saturation* adjustment control will appear with its current settings displayed. You can also delete or turn off adjustment layers (click on the eye icon, left), which will take the adjusted part of the drawing back to its original state.

Color Balance

The *Color Balance* adjustment (3-36) can be used to change the general color cast of the light ("Highlights"), medium ("Midtones"), and dark ("Shadows") colors in an image independently (3-34, 3-35). Thus, if an image or some of its parts seems to have too much of a particular color, the sliders can be moved in the direction opposite to that color. For example, if an image has too much red, the *Red/Cyan* slider is moved toward the cyan end of the spectrum. Additionally, you may wish to experiment with moving the *Magenta/Green* slider toward the green end of the spectrum to see if that also helps the problem.

When checked, the *Preserve Luminosity* check box ensures that the relationships between the darkest and lightest values in the image are maintained as color balance adjustments are made. Experiment with your image to see if it looks better with this option enabled.

Fig. 3-34 This is a hand-drawn study of a small café (curved in plan) for a proposed university technical education building. Once scanned, the drawing's hue appeared too cool; the intention for the space's character had been warm and nontechnical, with wood finishes and incandescent lighting color temperatures.

Fig. 3-34

Figs. 3-35, 3-36 To fix the problem, a color balance adjustment layer was created (Layer > New Adjustment Layer > Color Balance . . . > *name the layer* > OK).

First, the *Highlights* button was chosen in the *Color Balance* adjustment control. The bottom slider was moved to add more yellow, and the top slider moved to add more red to the lightest values in the drawing. Next, the *Shadows* button was chosen and the sliders were again moved to add more yellow and red, this time to the darkest values in the drawing (fig. 3-36). However, when the same was done after the *Midtones* button was chosen, the drawing started to have the opposite problem—it became overly warm in character. Therefore, the sliders for the midtone values were moved to add more blue and cyan. While the drawing still appeared warmer, this balanced the color cast of the image.

After the color balance adjustments were made, the drawing needed some areas of complementary color to give it more hue balance. The distant window wall and the illuminated display cases were selected with the *Polygonal Lasso Selection Tool* and a second color balance adjustment layer was created. This time, the sliders were moved to add more cyan, green, and blue to emphasize the cool "glass" color of the cases and case lighting, as well as the cooler outdoor light of dusk seen through the window wall.

In addition, the back bar wall and the

blue accent lights along the soffit were selected and a hue/saturation adjustment layer was created. The saturation and lightness of these elements were increased to help them appear more luminous and to make the bar area the focal point of the drawing.

Fig. 3-35

Fig. 3-36 Shown here are the *Color Balance* slider settings for the dark values in figure 3-35.

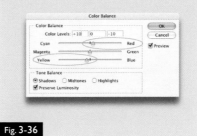

Fig. 3-36

Replace Color

The *Replace Color* adjustment lets you sample a color in a drawing and change the hue, value, and chroma of all similar colors in that drawing or its selected areas (3-37 through 3-40). The extent of the change can range anywhere from a slight adjustment to replacing the sampled color with a completely new color. The *Fuzziness* slider allows you to control the amount of transition between changed and unchanged areas of color.

While the *Replace Color* adjustment can save you the time of carefully selecting each area of similar color that you want to change, its effectiveness on scanned color drawings can sometimes be spotty. The adjustment may not change the intended colors completely; the fuzziness controls may include colors you do not want to change. However, the rough quality of the color changes afforded by the *Replace Color* adjustment may not only be sufficient, but a better fit with the character of a hand-drawn illustration.

Remember that the *Replace Color* adjustment is the only one of the five Adjustment commands discussed in this book that is not available as an adjustment layer. Once *Replace Color* adjustments are made, you have less ability to easily reverse the changes after the file is saved and reopened.

Fig. 3-37

Fig. 3-38

Fig. 3-37 This is a partial close-up view of a restaurant interior illustration created in Form•Z. The image was plotted, then color pencil was used to adjust the image. After it was rescanned, the chair seats were changed from blue to red. (Illustration: Grady Huff)

Fig. 3-38 The *Elliptical Marquee Tool* was used to quickly target the seats that were changing color. These selections limit the influence the *Replace Color* adjustment can have in the image, but are faster than selecting the complex shapes more precisely with the *Polygonal Lasso Tool*.

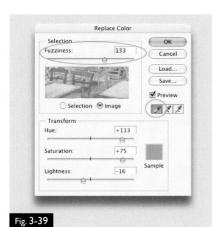

Fig. 3-39

Fig. 3-39 The eyedropper on the left was used to sample the color of a typical blue seat. Here, the second seat from the right was sampled. When it was clicked on with the eyedropper, its color immediately appeared in the *Sample* box. The *Hue, Saturation,* and *Lightness* sliders were then moved to achieve the desired red. The *Fuzziness* slider was adjusted until only the seat color remained—and nothing else changed—inside the selected areas.

Fig. 3-40

Fig. 3-40 The illustration after the *Color Replace* adjustment was used. Note that the replacement was not 100% effective, as certain pixel groups resisted replacement in the second seat from the left. This can happen with the *Color Replace* adjustment, especially with the less uniform, more fractured color of scanned color drawings, in which similar pixel groupings are not contiguous. However, the *Color Replace* adjustment is still a valuable tool—especially given how quickly the adjustment can be made—and using this "approximate" replacement on scanned drawings with a rougher, more spontaneous character will not usually detract from the drawing. If the replacement color does not reach certain critical areas, these areas may be "touched up" with the *Pencil Tool* or *Brush Tool*.

Levels

The *Levels* adjustment is unique in its ability to correct the tonal range of an image. You can give an image that appears washed out or too dark a full range of values, from black blacks to white whites (3-41 through 3-43). The *Input Levels* sliders allow you to adjust the light, middle, and dark values of the drawing—or selected areas of it—independently from one another.

When you open the *Levels* command, you will see a graph called a *histogram*. The histogram is a map of the value range of your drawing divided into 256 levels, ranging from pure black at level 0 on the left to pure white at level 255 on the right. The vertical range shows how many pixels are at each value. The histogram on the left in figure 3-43 is for all the colors in the drawing in figure 3-41. The values of most of the pixels in the image are below midrange, with no pure blacks, since the histogram is flat at the darkest end. There are some spikes in the histogram at the light end, which represent the two illuminated pyramidal lights and the car's headlights. When you click on the *Channel* button, you can also access *Levels* controls for each of the color groups that comprise the image (3-43, right).

When the sliders for the *Input Levels* are adjusted, as figure 3-42 shows, the tonal range of the drawing can be made more complete, resulting in a more dramatic, vivid drawing.

Fig. 3-41 **The line work for this study of a project entry was hand drawn, using .5 mm (with 2H lead) and *Black* pencils. The drawing was scanned and added as a Photoshop layer over a photograph of the proposed site of the entry.**

The background image's contrast was drastically reduced (Image > Adjustments > Brightness/Contrast…) and color was added to both the foreground and background as additional layers so the colors of each could be adjusted independently. The colors that appear transparent were added in layers whose blending mode was set to "Multiply." The type for the sign was created in Adobe Illustrator and imported into the image as a layer. When finished, a copy of the illustration was flattened and saved.

Fig. 3-41

Fig. 3-42 Sometimes, when you revisit an illustration and view it with a fresh eye, it may seem somewhat hazy and lack adequate "punch." The *Levels* adjustment may fix the problem.

A new levels adjustment layer was created (Layer > New Adjustment Layer > Levels . . .) which brought up the histogram with the sliders seen on the left in figure 3-43. The left slider was moved toward the right, approaching the base of the histogram. This darkened the image slightly, increased its contrast, and subtly enriched its color. Likewise, the right slider was moved toward the left, to keep the image from getting too dark. In addition, the *Channel* button was clicked, accessing the histograms of each of the individual color groups that combine to give the illustration its particular color. "Magenta" was selected in order to redden the image slightly. The left slider was moved slightly to the right, giving it a greater postsunset, reddish-purple cast.

Fig. 3-42

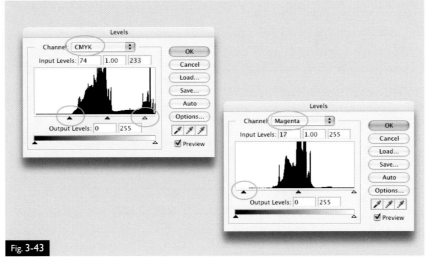

Fig. 3-43

Fig. 3-43 While adjusting the *Levels* adjustment on the left, all the colors in figure 3-41 changed, since the channel setting was "CMYK." The *Levels* adjustment on the right adjusted only the magenta hue in the image.

IMPRESSIONS OF MATERIALS

Many newcomers to color design drawing often feel overwhelmed when they attempt to create an illustration that shows a variety of different materials. This happens because they assume that each material must be illustrated in time-consuming detail to adequately communicate its character. But this is to confuse design illustration with photography.

Most of us have gained much of our impressions of the world through the photographic image—imagery whose every part is usually in sharp focus. It should come as no surprise, then, that beginning designers assume they must replicate a similar level of detail to communicate their ideas. However, this is not how we see.

Look up from this page and focus on something in your field of vision—near or far. Without moving your eyes from this object, notice that you perceive everything surrounding it *in much less detail.* In fact, as you fix your eyes forward, the very edges of your field of view are so indistinct that they are simply colorless blobs of light and dark. The average content of your field of view is far more impressionistic than a photograph.

One of your jobs in the early stages of the design process is to utilize the language of illustration to quickly assemble the many decisions about the form, space, proportion, scale, and *character* of a project into pictures—usually called studies or *sketches*—for feedback to yourself and review by others. Some of these pictures can be adequately communicated through line drawings. However, it is the visual communication of the additional information about the character of the space—color, light, materials, pattern, texture, and furnishings—that transforms a *space* into a *place.*

Because much of the way you see is impressionistic, your illustrations of previews of your ideas about places can be likewise impressionistic without seeming inappropriate. These impressions of materials can also be created far more quickly than detailed illustrations (3-44). Attempt to create impressions of materials that are easily understood by an untrained viewer.

Chapter 4 offers time-efficient approaches to illustrating a wide variety of materials commonly used by architects, landscape architects, and interior designers. Experiment with these approaches until you find those that work best for you.

Fig. 3-44a

Fig. 3-44b

Fig. 3-44c

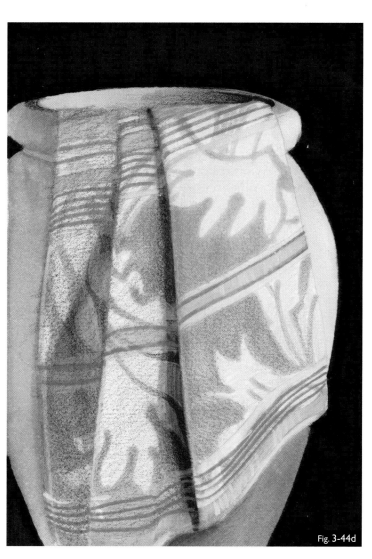

Fig. 3-44d

Fig. 3-44 Impressions of materials almost always begin with a line drawing to guide the color application. These line drawings can be quick and loose, because the color will more clearly define the images.

An impression of the stone in (a) has been drawn in (b) by rapidly mixing *Sand, Kraft Brown, Willow Green, Flesh,* and *French Grey 30%* markers. *Light Peach, Yellow Ochre, Celadon Green,* and *French Grey 30%* pencils were loosely washed over the marker. The shadow between the stones was applied last, with *Black* marker, to complete the illustration.

The fabric in (c) has been approximated in (d) by first drawing the diffuse shadows with *Cool Grey #1, #3,* and *#5* markers. The entire fabric surface was then washed with the lighter *Sapphire Blue* marker and the design approximated by delineating the negative spaces with a darker *Ice Blue* marker. *Celadon Green* and *Jasmine* pencils were used to add the colored stripes, and *Cool Grey 70%* pencil delineated the thin stripes. The shadows were softened further with *Indigo Blue* pencil, and the darker parts were washed lightly with the side of the *Cool Grey 70%* pencil.

CREATING THE EFFECTS OF LIGHT

In addition to creating successful impressions of materials, a designer can further communicate the character of proposed places by cultivating skills in the illustration of the effects of light. This is also the most convincing means of revealing the intended forms and spaces to the viewer of an illustration.

This book assumes that you understand the basics of how to illustrate and "cast" typical exterior and interior shade and shadow. This is a critical (but easily learned) skill for all designers of places, because a thorough understanding of how light works on forms and in spaces will, ultimately, influence your design decisions. As mentioned in Chapter 1, much can be learned about the behavior of light on forms and in spaces by carefully observing the world around you. Review figures 1-3 and 1-4 to refresh your memory about the basics of shade and shadow.

There are two important qualities you should understand about shade and shadow before you attempt to illustrate them in color. First, the shade and shadow should appear *transparent* (as opposed to "applied"), and, second, the *distinctness of the edges* of the shadows should be appropriate to the lighting conditions.

In drawings of exterior views, shadows usually have *distinct* edges, inasmuch as a sunlit condition is typically illustrated. In fact, the contrast at these edges can be intensified through the use of gradations of value. This is known as "forcing the shadow." Shadows in interior settings are often caused by diffused or indirect sources of light and have *indistinct* edges. Indistinct shadows can also be caused by reflected light from "secondary" light sources, such as sunlight reflected from a wall. *Interior shadows are generally more subtle* and have less contrast with their neighboring illuminated surfaces than exterior shadows. Interior objects often have multiple shadows, as interiors usually have multiple sources of light. Notice, too, that interior shadows appear to gradate in value more than exterior shadows, appearing darker at the base of the casting object and becoming lighter as they progress away from the object. Make studies of interior shadows, using the color media described in this book, to build your skills in illustrating interior shadows. Do not be discouraged at their apparent complexity. In your interior design illustrations, placing interior shadows, not too dark, in approximately the right locations, will in most cases be sufficient to "anchor" the shadowed objects to the page and help communicate your design ideas (3-45).

Surfaces in shade and shadow will appear transparent if they are of a value appropriate to the sunlit portion of the same surface. That is, shades and shadows on light-value surfaces will be lighter than those on dark surfaces (see also figure 1-7). In addition, the textures and patterns that appear on the sunlit parts of a surface should be continued into the shaded and shadowed portions of the surface. If the patterns and textures are not continued, these portions of the surface appear obscure and muddy, as if painted with black or gray paint (3-46).

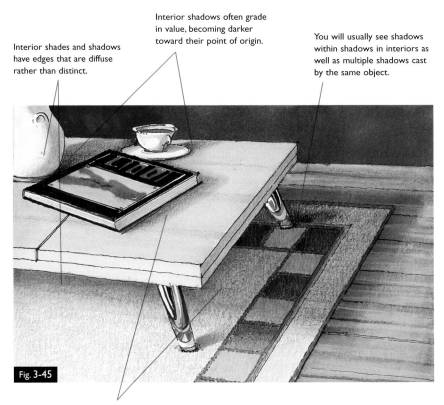

Interior shadows often grade in value, becoming darker toward their point of origin.

Interior shades and shadows have edges that are diffuse rather than distinct.

You will usually see shadows within shadows in interiors as well as multiple shadows cast by the same object.

Fig. 3-45

These shadows were made with warm grays #3 and #1: their colors were developed and their edges softened with color pencil. The gray markers are good for illustrating diffuse shadows because they can be made into any color and have predictable values.

Fig. 3-45 A typical interior shadow.

Fig. 3-46 The basics of exterior illumination and color are explained in terms of typical errors (a) and corresponding recommendations (b).

WHAT NOT TO DO:

SKY
Single marker color (*Sapphire Blue*) for sky is time-consuming, and gives cartoonlike appearance.

MODELING
No light-to-dark modeling on trees leads to flat appearance.

GRADATION
Lack of gradation of color leads to flat, "dead" illustrations.

MINGLING
Colors not "mingled" results in colors that are too bright, and to a lack of cohesiveness in the illustration.

MATERIALS
Material indication too detailed, time-consuming.

SHADOW TRANSPARENCY
Cool Grey #3 marker was simply applied over sunlit marker color, resulting in a hue mismatch. Lack of material indication gives shadow a "painted on" appearance.

REFLECTIONS
Windows with no indication of reflectivity appear "dead."

SHADOW VALUE
Same marker (*Cool Grey #3*) used for shadows, regardless of value of material, creating a mismatch between the sunlit and shadow values of each material.

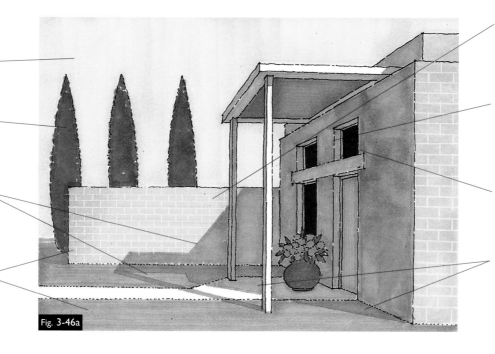

Fig. 3-46a

WHAT TO DO INSTEAD:

SKY
Sky indicated as gradation of hue with pencil (*Light Peach* to *Light Cerulean Blue*).

MODELING
Trees modeled with light and dark gives them a substantial look.

GRADATION
Values of color from light to dark; helps to "force" the shadows.

MINGLING
Colors mingled extensively help tie the illustration together while reducing chromas of the colors. For example, *Limepeel* and *Light Cerulean Blue* pencils were used over the brick; *Terra Cotta* pencil was used on the grass.

MATERIALS
Materials indicated as impressions instead of literally.

SHADOW TRANSPARENCY
Shadow color is a lower value, but same hue and chroma as sunlit colors. (Note the exception on the trees—used to create appearance of sunset light.) Material indications, grass and tree textures occur in shade and shadow as well as on sunlit surfaces. Note how mortar joint value is light in shadow to maintain visibility.

REFLECTIONS
Simple reflections in windows allow them to appear more alive.

SHADOW VALUE
The values of various materials correspond to one another in sunlight and shadow. Dark materials have dark shadows; light materials have lighter shadows.

Fig. 3-46b

Lighting Situations

There are a variety of lighting situations that can be created easily with the media and papers shown in this book, including exterior daylight (3-47), interior light (3-48), dusk—or dawn—light (3-49), and nighttime light (3-50). The approaches to illustrating these kinds of lighting situation are explained in detail in Chapters 4 and 7.

Fig. 3-47

Fig. 3-47 This illustration was used to show a new highway alignment and its planting program, as well as a water-retention study (foreground), in their context within the host district of a city.

The distinct shadow edges, the agreement of the shadows' directions, and the length of the shadows all provide clues to the direction of light and time of day. To focus the viewer's eye on the foreground—where the proposed design changes occur—that is where the contrast of the shadows is strongest and the light color the warmest. The shadows of the tops of the buildings on the ground are less apparent, as they are broken up by ground clutter and are more diffuse because they are farther away from the casting edges and washed out by ambient sky light.

The illustration was made by making a line drawing on tracing paper placed over a printout of an aerial photograph, using a *Black* pencil and a .5 mm pencil with 2H lead. The proposed design changes were drawn in the foreground; the farther into the distance the drawing receded, the less linework was added. The drawing was scanned and added as a Photoshop layer over a desaturated image of the aerial photograph (Image > Adjustments > Desaturate). The blending mode of the line drawing layer was set to "Multiply." Another layer was created, also set to "Multiply," and transparent shadows were added at the major buildings. A transparent warm-cool color gradient was added to the entire image on a final layer.

The image was plotted at about 16" x 16", and more detailed color (individual buildings, water, trees) was added with color pencil. The image was then rescanned and the highlights-lights, water spray and rings, and car colors-were added using an accent layer.

Fig. 3-48

Fig. 3-48 Both the diffuse shadows and the illuminated surfaces in this interior study grade in value. In fact, nearly every surface in an interior grades in value, usually in response to multiple sources of illumination. Note how the figures and storefront mullions have been made slightly darker, so the store interiors appear more luminous by contrast.

This drawing was created using a Pigma Micron 005 felt-tipped pen on tracing paper. Color was added on the reverse side of the tracing paper with some marker, but mostly with color pencil (see "The Retrocolor Technique," page 91). White accents were added to the front of the drawing with touches of white gouache applied with a small, fine brush. Kraft paper was placed behind the drawing before it was scanned to give it its warm tone.

Fig. 3-49

Fig. 3-49 The advantage of the view of a building exterior at dusk is that while it is dark enough to see the building's luminous interior and experience the dramatic effects of its lighting, there is still enough ambient sky light remaining to see the building's exterior forms and materials.

The line drawing for this university technical education building was made with *Black* pencil and a .5 mm pencil with 2H lead on tracing paper. Most of the building's lines were drawn with a straightedge so they would remain delicate and true. Color was applied to the back of the tracing paper with color pencil. The finished drawing was scanned with kraft paper behind it. The scanned image was opened in Photoshop, and the color was adjusted and lighting effects added, including street lights, up-down lights, and the uplighting of the glass tower top. 11" x 17".

Fig. 3-50 This lighting study for the upper level of a row of buildings with ground-level retail began as a typical daytime digital photograph.

It was opened in Photoshop and, using the *Hue/Saturation* adjustment (Image > Adjustments > Hue/Saturation), the *Colorize* box was clicked. The *Lightness* slider was used to darken the value of the whole image, while the *Hue* slider was adjusted to create its predominant purple-blue monochromatic hue.

The image was printed and *White* pencil was used to create the graded wash of light on the upper levels. *Deco Orange* pencil was used to add the ambient glow to the ground-level store interiors, and touches of other color pencils were used to add accents of color. White gouache was applied with a small, fine brush to enhance and intensify the light sources and lighting effects.

Fig. 3-50

Technique Strategies

The color drawing techniques that follow have a few things in common. They can all be used to illustrate design ideas relatively quickly, depending on how much information and character detail is required. Most of these approaches are covered in step-by-step detail in Chapter 7.

Color On Black-and-White Photocopy/Laser Print

One of the simplest and most straightforward color drawing techniques is the application of color media on a black-and-white photocopy or laser print of a line drawing. Its advantages are many: It is direct, has few steps, and you do not risk your original line drawing. It is an ideal technique for quick, loose concept sketches (2-13 and 2-16), but it can be used for more finished drawings as well (7-8 through 7-14).

You can also photocopy and print onto toned paper, such as Canson paper (3-51). This technique can be a time-saver if you color only a relatively small, specific area of the drawing, which will then become its focal point. This kind of drawing is called a *vignette* and, at its edges, the color usually grades to the background color of the paper.

Vignettes on toned paper work best if the paper is in the upper-middle value range, such as Canson's #343 "Pearl," #340 "Oyster," #490 "Light Blue," and #354 "Sky Blue." You will notice that lighter value color pencils appear luminous on the toned backgrounds.

Fig. 3-51 This line drawing study was photocopied onto Canson paper (#343, "Pearl"). While color pencil was applied directly to the photocopy, care was taken to not cover the lines excessively with the pencil in order to avoid obscuring them. In fact, very *little* color pencil was actually used on the subject of the drawing itself; it was utilized mainly for the suggested revisions to the existing stair area, in order to enhance the viewer's focus and interest.

If you find that the photocopy toner smears after photocopying onto Canson paper, spray it lightly with Krylon Crystal Clear. This will fix the toner to the paper. The light-value pencil is *White* Prismacolor; the shadow color pencil is Derwent *Blue Violet Lake* #27. 10" x 12".

Fig. 3-51

The Retrocolor Technique

The retrocolor technique is a fast and highly effective color illustration technique we use frequently at CommArts because it works best on common white roll tracing paper and mylar. It permits color design illustrations to be created quickly, lends itself to a wide variety of lighting situations, allows easy alteration, and scans and reproduces beautifully (3-52).

Retrocolor is the most *progressive* of color drawing techniques; it can be interrupted at almost any point and still result in a useful design communication tool. It is therefore ideally suited for design-intensive firms at which you may be called on at any time to "show what you've got" to a client who wants to see your progress. Or perhaps you have just run out of time: The retrocolor technique allows you to always have *something* useful available, whether it is solely a line drawing, a line drawing with only shade and shadows added, a line drawing with shadows and a touch of color, or the fully finished study with all the color.

Fig. 3-52

Fig. 3-52 This study was used to illustrate how the potential future build out for an urban district can be attractive and still include surface parking. The line drawing, along with shade and shadow, was done on the front side of a sheet of ordinary roll tracing paper with *Black* pencil. Color pencil was applied quickly to the back side of the sheet. The translucency of the paper not only allows the color to show through to the front, but also causes the quick, rough color pencil strokes to appear more smooth and even. The final step in this drawing was to add accents, using a small brush and white gouache, to the front of the drawing. 11" x 17".

Retrocolor On Tracing Paper

These illustrations are easy to make on tracing paper. The linework is drawn on the tracing paper as usual (3-53). Shade and shadow are applied to the same side of the paper as the linework (3-54). However, the color media is applied to the other side of the paper, where it cannot dim, obliterate, or smear the linework or shade and shadow application (3-55). This technique affords new opportunities for combining media. For example, *Black* Prismacolor—easily erasable and capable of producing smooth shade and shadow beautifully—can be used with xylene- or alcohol-based marker on the back side, before color

pencil is applied. The drawing's linework stays crisp and dark, no longer dimmed by color pencil. Color media of all types can be applied much more quickly and loosely, and when the drawing is turned right-side-over, the linework continues to organize the image into a coherent illustration (3-56). The color also appears smoother and more even. In addition, both the color and the linework can be easily edited without interfering with the other. Finally, design drawings done in the retrocolor technique lend themselves to a variety of dramatic lighting effects with little or no additional effort, as shown in figures 3-57 and 3-58.

Fig. 3-53 Line drawing on white tracing paper made with *Black* Prismacolor pencil and straightedge. A straightedge can help a designer "aim" her lines more easily toward the vanishing points, keep the lines thin, and apply them more quickly.

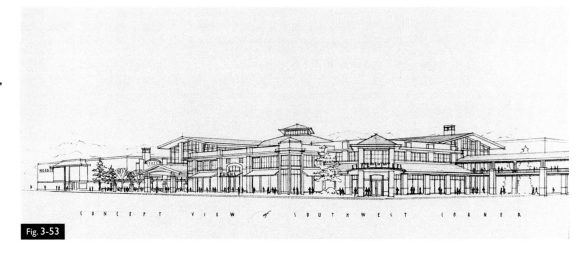

Fig. 3-53

Fig. 3-54 Shade and shadow have been applied, also with *Black* Prismacolor pencil, to the same side of the paper as the linework.

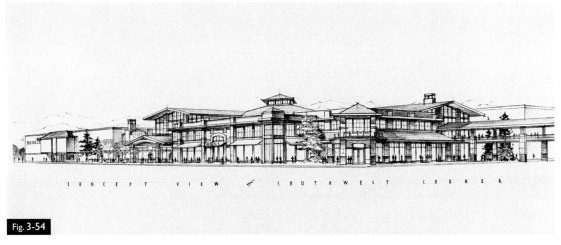

Fig. 3-54

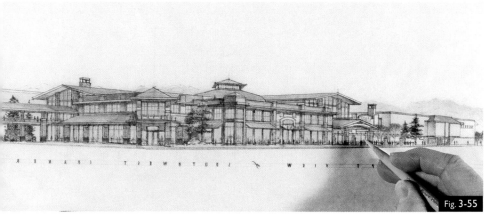

Fig. 3-55 Color is applied to the *back* of the drawing with color pencil. This step should be done while working on a toned surface, such as kraft paper, because the drawing is repeatedly turned over to evaluate progress. The color for this illustration took about an hour to apply.

Fig. 3-56 The finished drawing. Notice how the linework, unaffected by the color application, neatly organizes the rapidly applied color. Lighter colors have been used in the windows, as the drawing is transformed into an evening scene in subsequent steps. 4" x 17".

Fig. 3-56

Fig. 3-57 The illustration shown in figure 3-56 with kraft paper placed behind it. Note how the windows now appear illuminated.

Fig. 3-57

Fig. 3-58 The illustration shown in figure 3-56 with Pantone paper (#18-4051, "Strong Blue") placed behind it to the ground line of the building. This darker paper intensifies the lighter pencil colors even more than the kraft paper, instantly creating an evening scene. By adding a graded value to the lower part of the remaining kraft paper with *Black Prismacolor* pencil, a slight "glow" from the building was easily effected.

Fig. 3-58

Retrocolor On Mylar

The retrocolor technique can also be used on 3 mil or 4 mil, two-sided mylar (3-59). While the mylar is used in the same way as the tracing paper mentioned previously, it has the added advantage of being printable by a photocopier or laser printer without wrinkling and without jamming the machine. This allows the designer to print computer images onto a translucent surface, ready for additional linework, shade and shadow, and the retrocolor techniques described for tracing paper.

While drawing on mylar has a slightly different "feel" than drawing on tracing paper, its printability can be a significant time-saving advantage, since many kinds of images begin as computer-generated drawings. Mylar takes pencil, felt-tipped pen, marker, and color pencil just as well as tracing paper does.

There are a few differences to be aware of when working on printed mylar. First, an advantage: Since its surface is only minimally absorbent, linework, color media, and printed imagery can be completely erased from mylar using an electric eraser with a soft white erasing strip. Remember, however, that pressing too hard, too long, or using a more abrasive eraser can ruin the mylar's drawing surface. Second, if you draw with felt-tipped pen on the front (printed) side of mylar, you should let it dry before attempting to draw over it with color pencil, or the lines may smear. You can accelerate the drying time by placing the drawing under a desk lamp for a few minutes. Third, both xylene-based and alcohol-based markers can be used on the back of the drawing, but only alcohol-based markers can be used on the front, as the toner that comprises the printed image is soluble in xylene, and will smear.

Fig. 3-59 This is a concept view of the main street of a proposed town center. It began as a SketchUp model view that was printed on an 8½" x 11" sheet of two-sided, 3 mil drawing mylar, using a black-and-white laser jet office printer.

A Pigma Micron 005 felt-tipped pen and some pencil was used to add detail to the mylar print. Alcohol-based marker was used to add shade and shadow to the cars and the building on the left. Color pencil was used on the back of the drawing, as well as to the front of the drawing in certain places (such as the banners) to intensify the color. White gouache accents were also added on the front of the drawing with a small brush.

The drawing was then scanned and opened in Photoshop. Photographic elements, such as those seen through the retail windows on the left, were added, as were the clouds. The sign was made with the *Type Tool*. A final adjustment was made to the colors through adjustment layers before the image was printed. 8½" x 11".

Main Street, looking south

Sketch/Photo Combo

The sketch/photo combo drawing is a quick and effective way to present conceptual ideas when designing within an existing context. Its advantage is that only the proposed ideas need to be drawn, not the existing contextual elements. This can save the designer an enormous amount of time.

After a site visit, digital photographs are printed and used as an underlay, over which loose, conceptual ideas are drawn on tracing paper. Color is added later, using Photoshop.

Once the sketch overlay is completed, it is scanned and opened in Photoshop, then added as a layer over the digital photograph. The layer's blending mode is set to "Multiply." A final layer is added, using "Normal" blending mode, to introduce color and accents over the drawing area. In figure 3-60, the color was added as a new, third layer using Photoshop's color tools. By using three layers, the photograph, the line drawing, and the color can be adjusted independently.

Fig. 3-60

Fig. 3-60 This is one of a series of conceptual design studies for an existing town center. An idea for a seating area was sketched on tracing paper placed over a print of a digital photograph. After the line drawing was completed, it was scanned and added as a layer, in Photoshop, over the digital photograph. The drawing layer's blending mode was set to "Multiply."

Another layer was then created, with its blending mode set to "Normal." Color was added to the drawing on this layer using the *Elliptical Marquee Tool* and *Polygonal Lasso Selection Tool*, in combination with the *Brush Tool* and its airbrush capability. Texture was added to the plants using the *Noise* filter (Filter > Noise). (Photo and drawing: Carl Okazaki)

Hand Drawing/Digital Color

Many designers' digital color drawing techniques have evolved to such a point that their illustrations are almost indistinguishable from drawings they create entirely by hand (3-61). The clear advantage of this approach is that these color design drawings maintain a casual character that communicates to the viewer that the design is still in progress—that the process is not yet closed. The viewer feels invited to participate in that process.

These drawings communicate that character in two basic ways. First, the line quality is sketchlike. The lines frequently appear shaky and/or grainy, have extensions, and display a variation in weight across the drawing. The lines clearly appear to be drawn by hand. Usually, such hand drawings are made on tracing paper over a computer-generated wireframe, a photograph, or a combination, using felt-tipped pen or pencil. They are then scanned and opened in Photoshop, ready for additional layers of color application.

Second, the color is applied in what appears to be a casual, loose manner, using broad strokes, masks, and dabs of color in lieu of a precise, within-the-lines approach. This gives the drawings a very textural quality. The color is usually applied on a layer or layers whose blending mode is set to "Multiply," so the line character continues to show through the color application.

Fig. 3-61 This drawing of an airport waiting area was created with a felt-tipped pen on tracing paper over a computer-generated wireframe. Color was applied using the *Brush Tool*'s airbrush capability on separate layers whose blending modes were set to "Multiply." A variety of selection tools were used to isolate selected areas in order to introduce pattern on the floor and ceiling. The *Eraser Tool* was used to clean up "overspray." The *Noise* filter was used to subtly soften most parts of the image (Filter > Noise > Add Noise...).

The *Type Tool* was used for some, but not all, of the store signage. The type along the fascia of the circular ceiling recess was curved by selecting and placing individual words along the fascia, then using the *Transform* command (Edit > Transform) to conform them to the surface in the required perspective. Digital photo imagery was used to create some of the store interiors along the rear wall. (Illustration: Bryan Gough)

Fig. 3-61

Hybrid Color Drawing

Hybrid color drawings take advantage of the best of both digital and hand color techniques (3-62). It combines digital techniques—for large washes of color—with the speed of hand color application for small areas, detail, texture, and pattern. It is a very effective approach for color drawings requiring more detail and finish.

Once a line drawing is made—usually by hand—the drawing is scanned and opened in Photoshop. The first large washes of color and the arrangement of the major values are created digitally, much in the same way as early watercolor illustrations. (This step can actually be more time consuming when attempted by hand. Additionally, hand color media can create more texture than desired when creating background washes.) By using the *Paint Bucket Tool,* the *Gradient Tool,* and the *Brush Tool*—including its airbrush capability—you can easily set and adjust the major color and value arrangements that form the underpinnings for the visual impact of the drawing. Remember to create a value study of your drawing (see Chapter 7) to use as a guide for this step. These washes can be applied quickly, using different layers for different areas of the drawing, because they can be adjusted for maximum impact of hue, value, and chroma before proceeding with the hand color. The more precise hand color can be used to "clean up" edges later.

Once completed and adjusted, the drawing is plotted on a quality paper. The detail can be applied to the drawing using the traditional color media shown in this book. These media can usually be applied more quickly and deftly than digital media, since the use of hand media does not require you to repeatedly enlarge the selection to which you are applying the color. They also give the illustration its hand-drawn character.

After the detail is added, the finished drawing is scanned and reopened in Photoshop. Accents are added and final adjustments are made. The drawing is then printed or plotted for presentation.

Fig. 3-62 This hybrid color drawing was created to illustrate an urban street intersection reconstruction project that included a small new park (in the far corner).

The line drawing was made with *Black* pencil and a .5 mm pencil using 2H lead on tracing paper. It drawing was scanned and opened in Photoshop. After a value study was made, the *Gradient Tool* was used to create the large washes of color—on separate layers—for the roadway, trees and grass, distant buildings, and sky. These large washes set the color and value composition direction for the drawing. Once adjusted, the image was plotted on high-quality heavyweight paper.

Marker and color pencil were used to add detail as well as the texture and color of the trees, buildings, and cars. Accents were added with a small brush using white gouache. The completed image was rescanned and the colors adjusted. Final touches were added in Photoshop—traffic light colors, flower colors, and street names.

CHAPTER 99

ELEMENTS, MATERIALS, AND FINISHES

This chapter presents an encyclopedia of techniques you can use to illustrate a wide variety of typical elements, materials, and finishes used to create places for people. These techniques illustrate the most difficult—and most widely used—middle-ground views of these elements, materials, and finishes; distant views of design ideas have little or no detail, and close-up views are rarely drawn or, if they are, are frequently shown in silhouette.

The approaches to these techniques follow a similar pattern. First, the paper type is selected that will create the most effective background for the illustration. White paper is used for many of the techniques where ordinary lighting effects are required. Bristol paper is used in this chapter for the white paper, as it presents the techniques most clearly. However, these techniques can be effectively employed on the bond, trace, and diazo papers you typically use in practice. You will notice that toned papers, such as Canson paper, are used for techniques that depict various effects of light.

Second, once the linework is on the paper, the shade and shadow are added. In the examples shown, shade and shadow are often applied with gray marker, because the values can be chosen readily. An exception is the retrocolor technique, where—owing to the paper type (white trace) and small size of the illustration—the shade and shadow are more effectively applied with *Black* Prismacolor pencil.

Once the shadows are drawn, the marker base is applied, over which the pastel and/or color pencil follows. Fine-line felt-tipped pen (often Pilot Razor Point) is used to add the final delineation and augment the patterns and textures. Typically, digital techniques, accents, and color adjustments are added last, after the hand drawing is completed. Gold or silver marker accents, if needed, are added to the final *print* or *plot* of the illustration, since they cannot be read by a scanner.

This chapter illustrates only one material, finish, or element at a time. When you approach an entire drawing, however, all these parts will evolve *together,* as Chapters 6 and 7 will show. Your drawings may often not look like much after the first few steps, but don't be discouraged; a drawing usually does not "come alive" until the latter steps or even until you apply the accents.

You will find it very useful to have a wide variety of visual references available while creating design illustrations. One of the easiest ways to create such a resource is by organizing digital imagery on your computer, using scans from books and magazines, as well as images from search engine image banks and websites. Your source file may include such referents as people (sitting, standing, walking, leaning), architectural materials, landscape elements (trees, shrubs, ground covers, distant landscapes, and cityscapes), vehicles (including bicycles), lighting conditions of all kinds (both indoors and out), reflective materials (moving and still water, glass, windows, and metals), interior materials and finishes, furnishings, and a miscellany of whatever you may need if your project is specialized, such as animals, boats, or airplanes.

This chapter is organized around the space-defining planes for both interiors and exteriors as well as the elements that typically accompany each. An approach to illustrating people and automobiles is discussed separately in Chapter 5.

Your design illustrations need not be photographic, but instead should convey a coherent impression of the myriad ideas you have in response to the programs that guide the development of your projects. The detail in the illustrations that follow need not be included in your own color design drawings if it is not necessary. Remember, the point of design drawing, from conceptual through schematic, is to focus on overall ideas. Add only as much detail as necessary to communicate the character of those ideas. Let photographs of specific elements, such as furniture, and the sample boards that accompany your drawings provide the detail during these early stages of the design process.

The marker colors listed in this book name the xylene-based AD markers first, followed by the corresponding alcohol-based Prismacolor markers in parentheses. Where only an AD marker or only a Prismacolor marker is recommended, the marker is listed by itself. The color pencils listed are Prismacolor.

I N T E R I O R   M A T E R I A L S

Space-Defining Planes

Each of the three planes that make up all interior spaces—floor plane, wall plane, and ceiling plane—have typical elements, materials, finishes, textures, and ways of carrying light that give these planes, and thereby the interior itself, their character.

In one sense, the step-by-step techniques that follow are intended to provide you with a ready reference for at least one approach to illustrating the various elements that constitute these planes. In another sense, however, this approach is intended to facilitate the development of your own approach to design illustration. You can easily extrapolate from these techniques when you undertake to illustrate the myriad other elements you will encounter in your interior design work.

FLOOR FINISHES

The general issues you will confront when illustrating floor finishes are layout of the pattern, color, play of light (shadows and gradations), texture (smoothness, nappiness, etc.), reflections, and clarification of the pattern—in approximately that order. Most floor finishes can be illustrated by using the general approach shown here.

Wood (4-1, 4-2)

1 **Apply marker base.** *Sand (Sand)*, *Kraft Brown (Light Tan)*, and occasional strokes of *Redwood (Sienna Brown)* markers are used as the base colors, following the penciled help lines.

Fig. 4-1

2 **Develop wood colors with pencil.** *Jasmine* and *Cream* pencils were applied randomly in horizontal streaks, following the help lines. A light *Peach* pencil wash was then evenly applied over the entire wood floor surface.

3 **Add diffuse shadows and reflections.** A *Dark Umber* pencil was used to add the diffuse shadows at the base of the center wall and at the base of the hallway mullions. A light, graded wash of *Black* pencil was used to add the vertical reflections of the black elements in the floor, while a *Poppy Red* pencil was used similarly to add the vertical reflections of the red walls in the floor. A *White* pencil was used to create the floor reflections of the lightest parts of the spaces beyond. Note how both the reflections and diffuse shadows are gradients, most apparent nearest their sources.

Fig. 4-2

Floor Reflections using Photoshop (4-3 through 4-6)

1 **Evaluate the floor.** The drawing was evaluated to determine where the reflection should go and what would be reflected. Generally, the vertical elements are most obvious in reflections. Here, the side of the booth, the column at the wall, and the windows are most apparent (4-3).

2 **Copy and flip the part of the image to be reflected.** A reflection is an image of what occurs on one side of a reflective surface mirrored the same distance—in perspective—into the surface. Starting at the base of the booth, enough of the image is selected to "supply" the visible floor area with a reflection (4-4). This selected area is then copied and pasted in place. By doing so, the copied part of the image becomes its own layer. The blending mode of this new layer was set to "Multiply."

Fig. 4-3

Fig. 4-4

The *Transform* command (see page 208) was used to flip the copied image vertically (Edit > Transform > Flip Vertical) (4-5). The *Move Tool* was used to align the base of the reflection with the base of the reflected image. The Transform commands *Skew* and *Scale* were then used not only to align the reflection vertically with the reflected image, but also to align horizontals with the far vanishing point on the right.

3 **Reduce opacity, trim, and partially erase.** The *Opacity* slider for the reflection layer was used to reduce its opacity, thereby diminishing its intensity. The reflection was trimmed from all nonreflective surfaces, such as the rug and fireplace, using the *Polygonal Lasso Selection Tool* and the Delete key. The *Eraser Tool* and a small brush were used to erase the reflection from the foreground plant. In a final step, the *Eraser Tool*'s *Flow* (in the options bar) was set to 10% and a large, 200-pixel brush was used to slightly erase the "bottom" of the reflection, giving it the appearance of fading as it went further "into" the floor (4-6).

This technique will yield only the suggestion of a surface's reflection, but that is often sufficient to reveal its reflective character. It works best on semireflective surfaces such as wood and stone. It does not work as well on truly reflective surfaces, such as mirrors or very still water, since using this technique may make perspective issues more obvious. (Illustration: Grady Huff)

Fig. 4-5

Fig. 4-6

Rugs and Carpets (4-7, 4-8)

Impressions of patterns can easily be created to effectively illustrate those rugs and carpets intended for a room. Their textures should remain subtle.

1 **Draw the outline of the rug pattern with pencil.**

2 **Apply base color with marker.** Approximate the rug pattern *(left)* using the marker tip. *Sapphire Blue (Light Cerulean Blue)* and *Deep Salmon (Carmine Red)* markers were used for the pattern. *Buff (Brick Beige)* marker was applied to the interior, stroking toward the vanishing point.

The carpet *(right)* was also colored with *Buff (Brick Beige)* marker, and its border was colored with *Light Ivy (Putty + Cream)* marker. Shadows were added to both with *French Grey 30%* and *French Grey 50%* markers.

3 **Refine color with pencil.** Yellow accents were added to the rug with *Yellow Ochre* pencil. This pencil was also used to add a wash of color to the interior of the rug with the side of its point. This helped to bring up the texture of the paper, thus giving nap to the rug. The graded wash was continued on the rug toward the right with *Terra Cotta* and *Olive Green* pencils. The red and blue borders and patterns were washed with *Terra Cotta* pencil. The red only was muted with *Olive Green* pencil.

The carpet *(right)* was washed with *Bronze, Peach,* and *Burnt Umber* pencils. The subtle border pattern was added with *White* pencil, then flavored with *Bronze* pencil.

Fig. 4-7

Fig. 4-8

Add A Rug with Photoshop (4-9 through 4-13)

The *Transform* command allows you to easily add a rich, detailed, one-of-a-kind rug to an interior color drawing.

1 **The rug can be added last.** While decisions about room color can be predicated on the colors in a rug, it can also help to see an almost-finished color design drawing of a room—its materials, finishes, colors, and furniture—before making a final rug selection. (Drawing setup: Jirapong Chaijumroonpun)

2 **Determine the rug location.** In this scanned image of the drawing, another layer was created on which the rug was outlined using the *Line Tool* (4-10).

Fig. 4-9

Fig. 4-10

3 **Introduce digital rug image into drawing.** Many rug display and sales images show the rug "face on," or flat (4-11). Here, a rug is copied and pasted as a new layer into the drawing. (Courtesy: The Rug Source, www.rugsourcedenver.com)

4 **Conform rug to outline.** Once pasted into the drawing, the *Transform* command's *Distort* function was selected (Edit > Transform > Distort). The corner handles of the transform frame were selected and dragged to the corners of the rug's outline. The handle was also dragged toward the missing corner until the lower and right edges of the rug aligned with the outlines (4-12).

Fig. 4-11

Fig. 4-12

5 **Add final touches.** Once the rug was in place, the rug outlines were turned off. The opacity of the rug was reduced to about 50%, and the parts of the rug covering the foreground figure were deleted using the *Lasso Selection Tool* and the Delete key.

A shadow for the foreground figure was added on a new layer whose blending mode was set to "Multiply," making the shadow transparent. The shadow was applied with the *Brush Tool*, whose *Flow* was set very low, at 5%. The *Hue/Saturation* and *Brightness/Contrast* adjustments were used to give the shadow the appropriate hue and value.

Since the rug is highly detailed, the *Dry Brush* filter was used the give it a more drawinglike character (Filter > Artistic > Dry Brush; Brush Size = 2, Brush Detail = 10, Texture =1).

Finally, the *Brightness/Contrast* adjustment was used to darken and increase the contrast of the foreground figure a bit, lighten the rug, and darken the rest of the drawing very slightly. This increased the rug's central visual role in the composition (4-13).

Fig. 4-13

Terrazzo (4-14, 4-15)

Terrazzo has a number of distinguishing characteristics. It can be made in just about any color, its patterns can be large and complex, and many—although not all—of the colors have a unique grainy texture owing to the combinations of stone chips and matrix used to create the material. It is usually somewhat reflective, because it is polished during the final stages of installation.

1   **Draw the outline of the pattern** in pencil, so that the lines remain subtle. A .5 mm mechanical pencil with a 6H lead was used here.

2   **Apply marker colors** to the terrazzo pattern. Cool Grey #1 (Cool Grey 10%), Cool Grey #3 (Cool Grey 30%), Brick Red (Cherry), Pale Cherry (Mineral Orange), Flesh (Salmon Pink), Buff (Brick Beige), and Warm Grey #1 (French Grey 10%) markers were used for these particular colors.

3   **Apply graded washes with pencil.** The right side was washed with a mix of Light Peach and Jasmine pencils, and the left side was washed with French Grey 90% pencil. The two sides were graded into each other. Note how the wash on the left brings up the grain of the paper and imparts a texture similar to terrazzo.

4   **Stipple the areas of terrazzo** that have a highly visible stone chip content (this happens when the color of the stone chips differs significantly from that of the matrix). The central and outermost gray areas were stippled with White pencil that had a sharp point. The pencil was quickly rotated as its tip was lightly touched to the surface so that it would make an adequate mark. The pinkish areas were stippled in the same way with a Terra Cotta pencil.

5   **Add reflections** using white gouache, very slightly diluted, with the side of a long-tipped brush (see figure 2-10).

6   **Clarify the pattern.** The part of the pattern closest to the viewer was "enhanced" (re-outlined) with a Micron 005 felt-tipped pen.

Fig. 4-14

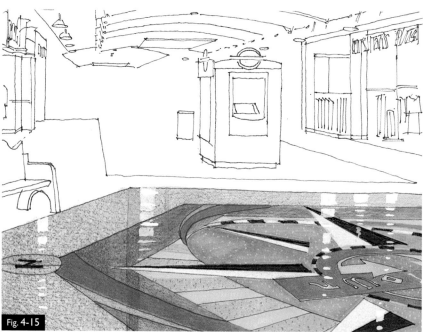

Fig. 4-15

Stone, Honed, and Polished (4-16, 4-17)

It is usually a good idea to illustrate floor surfaces last in an illustration, particularly those that have reflective qualities. By doing so, you will know which colors you will have to reflect in these surfaces.

1 **Apply color to stone.** *Cool Grey #1 (Cool Grey 10%)* marker was used to color the banding, and *Raw Sienna 234.9* pastel was applied to the remaining floor areas. The pastel that crept beyond the yellow portions of the floor area was removed with an electric eraser.

2 **Add reflections and shadows.** Reflections in the honed stone floor *(left)* are softer and less distinct than those for a polished floor. Nor do they go as far "into" the floor. The light-value reflections were added with *White* pastel, and the dark reflections and indistinct shadows were applied with pencil. *Cool Grey 50%* pencil was used to add reflections and shadows to the cool-colored stone banding; *French Grey 30%* pencil was used to apply the reflections and shadows to the warm-colored stone.

The reflections in the polished floor *(right)* have more distinct edges, *but should not have a visible outline.* They were delineated extremely lightly with a hard pencil. Colors are also reflected in polished surfaces but are more muted than the objects themselves. Here, the same color pencils were used for both the objects and their reflections, although the reflections were colored using a *much* lighter touch with the pencils. The white reflections were created simply by using an electric eraser, with an erasing template, to remove the yellow pastel.

Fig. 4-16

3 **Add stone texture, coloration, and joints.** Subtle coloration and veining were added to the stone with *Burnt Ochre* and *French Grey 30%* pencils. Some foreground stippling was added with a Micron 005 felt-tipped pen. A final and very important step was the addition of the stone joints, which were added with a .5 mm mechanical pencil with a 6H lead. These joints were drawn over everything—reflections, shadows, and highlights.

Fig. 4-17

Tile (4-18, 4-19)

Tile can be found in a wide variety of materials, colors, and finishes—from vinyl to ceramic, from matte to polished. Apply the techniques shown for the various floor materials to the tile type you happen to be illustrating. For example, if you are illustrating a ceramic tile with a high sheen (but not polished), you can add highlights similar to those shown in the illustration of the terrazzo.

The tile shown here is intended to be a simple vinyl tile with matte finish. However, most hard floor finishes will have *some* degree of reflectivity, as they are often buffed during maintenance.

1 Lay out tile lightly with pencil. The tile layout should be in correct perspective, because an error in its perspective can make the floor appear warped or tilted. Tile layouts, particularly those with a pattern that uses vanishing points that differ from those used for the rest of the picture, as shown here, can most easily and quickly be accomplished using a computer.

2 Apply marker color. Wash the entire floor with the *lighter* marker first. *Naples Yellow (Eggshell)* marker was used here for the wash, then *Light Ivy (Putty + Cream)* marker was used to touch color to the alternating tiles. The shadows were added beneath the tables with *French Grey 10%* and *French Grey 30%* markers.

3 Apply pencil washes to the floor. A *Light Peach* pencil wash was graded into a *Burnt Ochre* pencil wash on the right.

4 Add highlights. Because the tile has a matte finish, diffuse highlights were added with *White* pencil.

5 Trim edges of foreground tile. In this example, a .5 mm pencil was used to delineate or "trim" the foreground tiles. These rough edges can be trimmed with color pencil, which appears as a grout joint, in illustrating ceramic tile. In that situation, light-colored pencils should be used on dark ceramic tile and vice versa.

Fig. 4-18

Fig. 4-19

Interior Floor Plans (4-20, 4-21, 4-22)

A plan view is an abstract device used for organizing circulation, architectural, and interior elements in a place. When color is added to a plan—even diagrammatic color—the viewer can understand its information much more quickly and easily.

When the color and pattern of a plan are coordinated to the perspective views of the project, the viewer is yet more easily oriented. Impressions of floor materials and patterns not only make the plan seem more real and more attainable, but also pull the viewer's eye all the way to the floor plane. Quickly applied diffuse shadows help to visually "anchor" the various plan elements.

Select only quick and easy techniques for applying plan color, inasmuch as you are only creating an impression in an attempt to clarify your plan view.

1 **Draw the plan;** *poché* the wall cuts. The plan was drawn with a Micron 005 felt-tipped pen. The walls were pochéd with a *French Grey 70%* marker (4-20).

2 **Add marker color.** Marker colors were added to the materials on the floor plane (4-21). The rug patterns were dotted in with the tips of the markers. Remember that the rug patterns need only be approximate; a color photocopy or a strike-off (sample) of the real rug can be included on your accompanying materials board to provide the details. Diffuse shadows were added with *French Grey 10%, 30%,* and *50%* markers. Note how they contribute to the three-dimensional quality of the plan and help anchor the elements to the floor.

3 **Add color pencil detailing.** The marker colors of the outdoor patio pavers and the living room rug were both muted with a wash of *French Grey 30%* pencil, and the *Buff (Brick Beige)* marker on the bleached oak floor was simultaneously textured and muted by lines applied with a *Blue Slate* pencil and a straightedge. Other subtle washes of pencil color were added to adjust the colors of the furniture and tiles on the kitchen floor. *Deco Aqua* pencil was added to the glass line to help emphasize the location of the glazing.

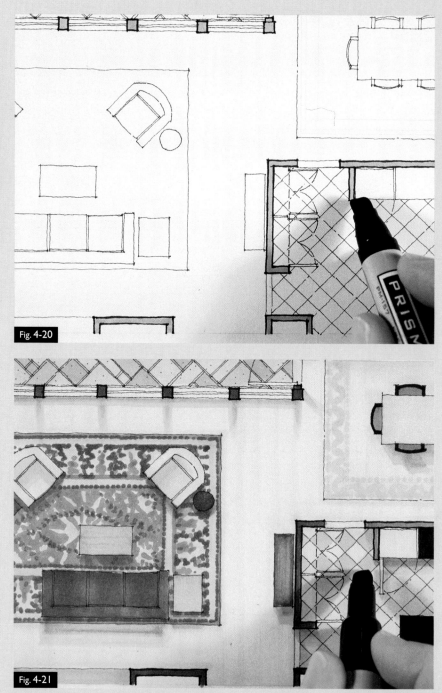

Fig. 4-20

Fig. 4-21

Fig. 4-22

WALL PLANE ELEMENTS

Wall Finishes

Consider two important issues. First, keep your rendition of these surfaces subtle and muted, because wall surfaces are the *backdrops* to the room. As in reality, wall surfaces that appear too intense and contrasting tend to overpower both the room and its occupants. It is much easier to make a wall surface more intense (if it appears too muted) than to mute one that is too intense.

Second, because wall surfaces are often smooth, take care to avoid graininess in your pencil washes. Graininess can occur when the pencil reveals the grain of the paper and the pencil's value contrasts too greatly with the value you have chosen for the wall surface. If you are applying graded pencil washes to a light wall, stick to light-colored pencils; on a dark wall, use darker pencils.

Painted Wall (4-23, 4-24)

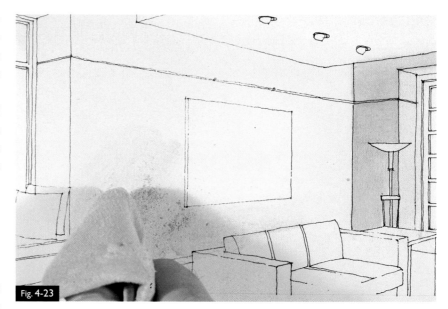

Fig. 4-23

1 **Apply pastel base.** In this example (4-23), the darker-colored end wall was first lowered in value with a *French Grey 10%* marker. However, unless you are faced with a special condition like this, use pastels to create a smooth wall color base. *Raw Sienna 234.9* stick pastel was scraped with a knife onto the wall area of the drawing, rubbed in with a facial tissue, then smoothed with a chamois. On the darker end wall, *Gold Ochre 231.7* stick pastel was applied in the same way.

2 **Trim; apply gradations.** The overapplication of pastel on areas where it doesn't belong was cleaned off or "trimmed" with an electric eraser using a soft, white erasing strip.

Graded washes were applied (4-24) to bring up the subtle, diffuse shadows and gradations of light with a *French Grey 20%* pencil. These gradations were then flavored with *Jasmine* and *Mineral Orange* pencils.

The darker end wall was treated in a similar way with *French Grey 30%* and *Mineral Orange* pencils. Some touches of even darker value were applied with *Terra Cotta* pencil.

Fig. 4-24

Decorative Paint Finish (4-25, 4-26)

There are many kinds of decorative paint finish that can add interest and richness to wall surfaces, such as sponging, cloth distressing, stippling, color washing, and dragging. The example shown in these drawings simulates a color wash finish called "brush wash" in multiple colors.

An excellent reference to follow when attempting to illustrate decorative paint finishes is *Recipes for Surfaces* by Drucker and Finkelstein (New York: Fireside, 1990). Experiment first with combinations of pastel and color pencil to find appropriate color combinations before you attempt an illustration.

1 **Apply pastel; distress with electric eraser.** A knife was used to scrape a *Cobalt Blue 512.5* stick pastel onto the drawing. It was spread with a facial tissue and smoothed with a chamois. Note that less pastel was applied to the more illuminated parts of the surfaces. An electric eraser with a soft white erasing strip was used (4-25) to "distress" the even blue finish. Slightly more pastel was removed from the illuminated areas. An erasing template was used to edge the shadows.

2 **Apply additional pastel colors; trim; apply gradations.** *Permanent Green Deep 619.9* stick pastel was scraped with a knife onto the wall surface, dabbed into the blue with a facial tissue, and wiped lightly with a chamois. *Light Oxide Red 339.9* stick pastel followed in the same way. These colors not only shift and mute the blue, but also soften the eraser marks.

The gradations were emphasized by lightly applying a *Cool Grey 30%* pencil with the side of its tip, then flavored with a *Blue Slate* pencil. Some touches of *Peach* and *Light Peach* pencils were added, using the sides of the pencils' tips, to bring up the warm color slightly (4-26).

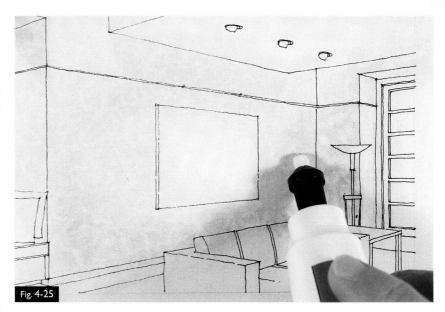

Fig. 4-25

Fig. 4-26

Patterned Finishes (4-27, 4-28)

A patterned wall finish is usually created by the use of wallpaper or stencils. The techniques shown here can suffice for either.

The patterns illustrated follow those produced by Bradbury and Bradbury Art Wallpapers for their Arts & Crafts collection. "Springfield Stripe" is used for the body of the wall, with a "Vienna Check Border" top and bottom. A "Thornberry Border" is used at the top of the wall as a frieze.

1 **Draw patterns in pencil; apply light markers for base.** First, the patterns were drawn lightly using a .5 mm pencil with a 6H lead. Light-colored markers were applied to the pattern so that the pattern would stay sufficiently in the background (4-27). *Naples Yellow (Eggshell)* marker was used for every other stripe as well as the sinuous stem in the frieze at the top. *Light Ivy (Putty + Cream)* marker was used for the leaves in the frieze and the tiny squares on the checkerboard borders. *French Grey 10%* marker was used for the edges of both the borders and the frieze.

Note that felt-tipped pens were *not* used to draw the patterns, so the edges would remain soft and unassertive.

2 **Apply pastel wash.** After the marker was applied, *Raw Sienna 234.9* stick pastel was scraped with a knife onto the wallpaper, rubbed in with a bare finger, then smoothed with a chamois. This both provided a background wall color and muted, softened, and unified the marker colors.

The pastel was erased from the berry locations on the frieze, and *Pale Indigo (Cloud Blue)* marker was applied as a final touch (4-28).

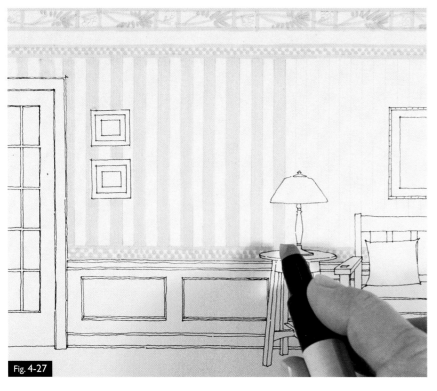

Fig. 4-27

Fig. 4-28

Wood Wainscot (4-29, 4-30)

The oak wainscot shown here is typical of the kind used with the wallpapers shown in figure 4-28. Wood wainscot can have more or less detail and, often, less apparent grain than that shown here.

1 **Apply marker base.** *Kraft Brown (Light Tan)* and *Pale Cherry (Mineral Orange)* markers were applied to the wainscot and door (4-29).

2 **Add pencil grain.** Swipes of *Terra Cotta, Mineral Orange,* and *Jasmine* pencils were applied, stroking along the direction of the wood grain, using the *sides* of the pencils' tips. Thin graphite pencil lines were applied for additional wood grain, using a .5 mm pencil with a 2H lead.

3 **Apply highlights and lowlights.** Highlights were added to those edges that roll toward a probable light source, with a *White* pencil. White gouache was applied to the same locations. Note that the gouache highlights are long, smooth, and lens-shaped. They were dimmed slightly by coloring them with a *Jasmine* pencil. Lowlights and shadow were added with a *Dark Umber* pencil and a straightedge (4-30).

Fig. 4-29

Fig. 4-30

Windows

Because windows are important elements in the design of an interior, they should neither remain blank nor attract too much attention. Detailed views through windows, unless presented for the purpose of illustrating specific relationships between indoors and outdoors, should be avoided. Instead, just enough visual information should be given to allude to something beyond, so that the viewer's attention remains in the room.

When you look at a professional photograph of an interior, the lighting of the space appears normal, but the view through the window is often indistinct and overexposed. The illustrated image works much the same way. The window wall should be darker—even if only slightly—than the exterior. If your interior view includes windows and you want to illustrate a very light interior view, you may want to consider a nighttime view through the windows.

Daytime View, White Paper (4-31, 4-32)

1 Color window wall. Light-value—even white—walls will appear darker than the windows. In this illustration, *Warm Grey #1 (French Grey 10%)* marker was applied vertically, followed by *Sunset Pink (Deco Pink)* marker, stroked horizontally to diminish streakiness. *Raw Sienna 234.9* stick pastel was applied by finger, smoothed with a chamois, and trimmed with an electric eraser (4-31).

2 Add color to exterior view. Because the wall now has a value, you will know how much color you can add to the exterior view without making it too dark. An effective combination of pencils starts with *Cool Grey 20%* applied first and lightly, with the side of the point, in abstract and rather random motions. This is followed by *Yellow Chartreuse* pencil, also applied with the side of the point and very lightly. *Cloud Blue* pencil is then applied over the gray pencil and in any remaining white spaces in the same manner. You may wish to blend the colors with a *White* pencil, if necessary. All three colors here were applied very quickly and right over the windows' muntins. Remember that the result should remain lighter than the interior wall.

3 Add color to window muntins, frames, and trim. In this illustration, the window trim, frames, and muntins were colored with *Cool Grey #1 (Cool Grey 10%)* and *Pale Indigo (Cloud Blue)* markers, one over the other. Because the trim was intended to be lighter than the walls, it was further colored with *Cool Grey 20%* pencil and flavored with a *Blue Slate* pencil. The frames and muntins were made darker, because they were silhouetted by the bright exterior, by using a *Cool Grey 50%* pencil and flavored with the same *Blue Slate* pencil.

At this point, the exterior appeared too dark in value, so an electric eraser was used to quickly lift off some of the exterior color without touching the muntins (4-32).

Fig. 4-31

Fig. 4-32

Daytime View, Toned Paper (4-33, 4-34)

1 **Apply color to exterior "view."** When using toned paper (Canson "Pearl" is used here), both the light and dark colors can be applied, giving the designer more control. *Yellow Chartreuse* and *Cloud Blue* pencils were applied first with fairly light hand pressure. *French Grey 10%* marker was used for the tree trunks. *White* pencil was then applied overall, with firm hand pressure, to create the sense of the illuminated exterior (the tree trunks received less pressure) as shown in the window on the right (4-33).

2 **Apply color to window frames and muntins.** *Pale Indigo (Cloud Blue)* marker was applied to window frames and muntins. *Blue Slate* pencil was then used to flavor the marker color. A *White* pencil was applied with a straightedge to add a highlight just inside the line of the window trim.

3 **Apply color to wall.** You now know how light you can make the wall color without diminishing the effect of the brighter exterior (that is, if you make the wall *too* light, the exterior will no longer appear illuminated). In this illustration, the wall was partially washed with *Peach* and *Mineral Orange* pencils (4-34).

Note: Pastel was not used on the wall in this illustration, because photocopy toner does not fuse particularly well to heavily grained and textured papers. When the overapplication of pastel is erased from paper of this type, the lines are erased as well.

Fig. 4-33

Fig. 4-34

Nighttime View (4-35, 4-36)

1 **Apply very dark marker.** A *Black* or very dark blue (such as a *Prussian Blue* AD marker or a *Navy Blue* Prismacolor marker) can be applied over the windows, including the muntins, to begin a simple night view. In figure 4-35, a *Black* marker was used to begin a slightly more complex night view, drawing in the foreground trees and shrubs. *Cool Grey #7* and *#9 (Cool Grey 70%* and *90%)* markers were used to add distant landforms. *Mauve (Greyed Lavender)* marker was used to color the sky.

2 **Draw window muntins with very light pencil.** The window muntins were drawn back in with a *White* pencil and a straightedge. These muntins can be flavored with other light pencil colors if necessary.

3 **Add highlights if desired.** Distant city lights were added with white gouache (4-36). The interior can be completed in the usual manner.

Fig. 4-35

Fig. 4-36

Drapes (4-37, 4-38)

1 **Draw folds, shadows, and major pattern elements with marker.** The recesses of the folds were drawn with a *French Grey 30%* marker, as shown in the drapes on the right (4-37). The major pattern elements were dotted in an even distribution with a *Pale Cherry (Mineral Orange)* marker. The shadows were added to the wall with a *Cool Grey #1 (Cool Grey 10%)* marker.

2 **Apply color wash.** The drapes were washed with *Lemon Yellow 205.3* and *Yellow Ochre 227.5* stick pastels and smoothed with a chamois. This wash could also have been applied with color pencil, creating a slightly more textured effect. After the color wash, the drapes will appear like those on the upper right (4-38). The pastel overcolor was trimmed with an electric eraser, removing some color from the inside of the drape next to the window. This easily creates the effect of the edges of the drapes being illuminated by the daylight.

3 **Apply secondary pattern.** A secondary "squiggly" pattern suggests finer print detail or embroidery. It was applied with a *Bronze* pencil, as shown in the lower right of figure 4-38.

4 **Accentuate recesses in folds.** The recesses in the folds, originally drawn with marker, were emphasized with *Bronze* pencil followed by a thin line of *Dark Umber* pencil, as the completed drapes illustrate. *Dark Umber* pencil was also used to create the pinch pleats at the top.

Fig. 4-37

Fig. 4-38

Sheer Curtains (4-39, 4-40)

The illustration of sheer (translucent) curtains can be somewhat tricky, in that they can quickly become too heavy looking. The following steps can reduce the risk of that happening.

1 **Draw curtains' surroundings.** The wall, window trim, and exterior view are all drawn first (4-39). Note that the curtains are outlined only in very light pencil, instead of felt-tipped pen, so they maintain a light appearance.

2 **Draw folds with marker.** The curtains on the left show the folds being drawn with a *Cool Grey #1 (Cool Grey 10%)* marker. Avoid drawing too many folds, especially over the glazing, so the curtain does not become too dark. This marker was also used to dot in the window frame and muntins behind the curtains. The pencil guidelines were erased after the marker was applied.

　　If your folds appear too dark or severe, they can be softened by an application of *White* pencil or pastel.

3 **Lightly tone window frame and muntins with pencil.** In figure 4-40, on the left, a *French Grey 20%* pencil was used to very lightly tone the frame behind the curtain, so that the glazed areas would appear brighter by contrast.

4 **Add subtle coloration.** You may wish to subtly flavor the color of the curtain. In the finished curtain on the left, *Cloud Blue* pencil was used to flavor the recesses of the folds and *Light Peach* and *White* pencils were used on the ridges.

Fig. 4-39

Fig. 4-40

Shades (4-41, 4-42)

1 **Draw the shades' surroundings first.** The shades should be drawn last so they can remain appropriately light.

2 **Add base color to shades.** A wash of *Ultramarine Deep 506.9* stick pastel was applied here (4-41), but any light pastel can be used.

3 **Create silhouette of window frame and muntins.** *Cloud Blue* pencil was applied over the pastel base with a straightedge, then darkened slightly with a *Cool Grey 30%* pencil.

4 **Add horizontal pleats.** A straightedge was used with a *Blue Slate* pencil to lightly apply the horizontal pleat lines (4-42).

Fig. 4-41

Fig. 4-42

Shutters (4-43, 4-44)

1 **Draw shutter elements with marker.** The shutters were drawn with a *Willow Green (Lime Green)* marker over light pencil layout lines. Felt-tipped pen lines can make the shutters appear too busy and diminish their softness. Note that the horizontal lines were drawn all the way across the shutter pair (4-43), with the frame elements added afterward. Use a marker sufficiently dark so the spaces between the louvers appear adequately bright.

2 **Trim edges of louvers and darken if necessary.** The top and bottom of each line of louvers were trimmed with a sharp *Blue Slate* pencil drawn along a straightedge. These trim lines were drawn right across the middle frame line and later erased.

   The *Blue Slate* pencil was then used to slightly darken the louvers—a step you can skip if your louvers are sufficiently dark.

3 **Lighten and edge.** If you accidentally draw your horizontal marker lines for the louvers too close together, use white gouache and a thin brush to reintroduce the white spaces.

   The frames of the shutters, as well as the center adjustment bar, were delineated using a .5 mm pencil with a 2H lead (4-44).

Fig. 4-43

Fig. 4-44

CEILINGS

Ceilings often exhibit subtle gradations of value as a result of their being illuminated from below by direct and reflected light. These gradations are often easiest to accomplish with pastel, combined with marker when necessary. Use photographs in books and magazines to help guide you when illustrating specific ceiling types.

Lay-In Ceiling, Tegular (4-45, 4-46)

1. **Lay out ceiling in pencil.** A .5 mm pencil with a 6H lead was used to lay out the ceiling illustrated here.

2. **Add graded color with pastel.** This ceiling was washed with *Raw Sienna 234.9* stick pastel, with *Gold Ochre 231.7* stick pastel used in the corners. Both colors were blended and smoothed with a chamois. Care was taken to allow the areas illuminated with reflected ground light to remain the white of the paper. *Ultramarine Deep 506.9* stick pastel was then used to lightly tint the back part of the white ground light reflection. It too was smoothed with a chamois (4-45).

3. **Erase layout lines.** When the layout lines are erased with an electric eraser and erasing template, a white T-bar grid is created. Because the ceiling is tegular, the shadow side of the recess is drawn in with the .5 mm, 6H pencil. This technique creates a grid pattern that is appropriately subtle (4-46).

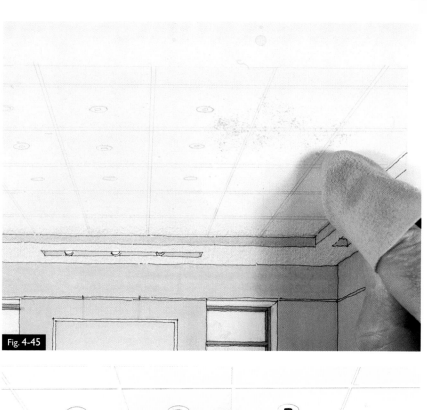

Fig. 4-45

Fig. 4-46

Beam Ceiling (4-47, 4-48)

1 **Apply shade and shadow with marker.** *French Grey 10%, French Grey 30%,* and *Clear Blender* markers were used to create shade and shadow that respond to uplight from the windows (4-47). Use a photograph of a similar condition for guidance if necessary.

2 **Apply ceiling colors.** *Indian Red 347.9* and *Raw Sienna 234.9* stick pastels were applied to the beams/joists and decking, respectively, including shade and shadow. Highlights were erased out with an electric eraser.

3 **Add detail.** The decking joints were added with a .5 mm pencil with a 6H lead and a straightedge (4-48). Shadows were touched up using a *Yellow Ochre* pencil on the decking and a mix of *French Grey 30%* and *Rosy Beige* pencils for the beams and joists.

Fig. 4-47

Fig. 4-48

Furnishings and Fixtures

Each kind of furnishing and fixture displays its own particular combination of telltale characteristics. These characteristics provide the visual clues that tell the viewer what he is looking at in a design illustration. Wicker, for example, is quite different from stainless steel in appearance. Why? Because wicker furniture is a combination of shapes, colors, textures, patterns, and kinds and degrees of reflectivity that differ sharply from the characteristics of stainless-steel furnishings and fixtures. The more often you attempt to draw those elements relevant to your profession, the more you will understand how to identify the clues necessary to communicate their most visually relevant qualities. This section will help you begin that understanding.

Those new (and many not so new) to the design profession often ask how to locate and draw furnishings in perspective design studies, both individual pieces and groupings. The gray "sidebar" pages that follow offer some suggestions.

Delineation and Location of Furniture (4-49 through 4-52)

You will frequently have to delineate and locate furnishings in design illustrations of places you are designing. Because your job is to create the places where the furniture belongs rather than the design of the furniture itself, it is best to delineate existing furniture designs appropriate to the place rather than attempt to invent furniture or draw it from memory. Unless you are an excellent furniture designer, invented furnishings can often look clumsy and seriously detract from an otherwise good design.

Figure 4-49 shows a "cut sheet" of a club chair and ottoman intended for the space in figures 4-50 through 4-52. (Courtesy Donghia Furniture and Textiles, 485 Broadway, New York, NY 10013)

Fig. 4-49

© Jeff Goldberg/Esto

Fig. 4-50

Fig. 4-51

Fig. 4-52

1 **Draw a standing figure in the desired location of the piece; rough-in the piece.** Figure 4-50 shows a roughly drawn standing scale figure, its head on the horizon line of the room perspective and its feet located at a corner of the furniture piece. This gives you a familiar reference with which to estimate the scale and proportions of the piece.

The pieces were roughed in, using the cut sheet as a reference, focusing on position and approximate shape. Accuracy of perspective is not important at this step.

2 **Refine perspective, scale, and proportions.** Once you have something on paper, you have something to manipulate. In figure 4-51, a new piece of trace was placed over the rough drawing. The most obvious straight lines of the piece, those that are perpendicular to one another, were extended to the *same* horizon line used for the room's perspective.

Vanishing points were established where these lines intersect the horizon. Of course, these points are different from those used to draw the elements of the room itself, although the horizon line is the same. From these new vanishing points, the chair and ottoman can be drawn so that, although rotated, they appear to be resting on the floor rather than awkwardly tilted.

The chair and ottoman were lightly redrawn using these vanishing points. Heights, widths, and depths of the parts were more accurately established, using both the standing figure for scale and a comparative visual estimation of proportion of one part to another. In other words, they were "eyeballed" as accurately as possible.

When the chair and ottoman were lightly blocked out, a *Black* Prismacolor pencil was used to refine the shapes in accordance with the cut sheet.

3 **Make final tracing.** The refined version of the chair and ottoman, shown in figure 4-51, was traced onto the final sheet using a Micron 005 felt-tipped pen. This step afforded yet one more opportunity to subtly refine the line illustration. Figure 4-52 shows the finished line drawing, ready for color.

Note that in the process of illustrating a selected piece of furniture, you become far more intimate with its nuances and subtleties. This is an invaluable dividend paid to those designers who create illustrations by hand.

Grouping of Tables and Chairs, with People (4-53, 4-54, 4-55)

You have probably had to draw a room or restaurant filled with tables, chairs, and people. These situations need not require the detailed, time-consuming effort you may imagine.

1 **Draw a foreground scale figure and table.** Begin by drawing the horizon line of the illustration's perspective, as shown in figure 4-53. Draw a rough figure in the foreground, where you intend to draw your first table, making sure its head is on the horizon. You will be able to estimate the sizes of furniture far more easily in the proximity of something as familiar in size as the human figure.

Draw in the approximate size of the tabletop (relative to your figure) at about midthigh. If the table is square or rectilinear, make sure its edges vanish to points on the horizon so it appears flat and not tilted. If the table is circular, draw an appropriately flat ellipse (freehand), or draw what appears to be a horizontal square in perspective, as shown here, and inscribe the ellipse within. Draw a vertical line from the center of the table shape down to align with the feet of your figure. This is where the base or legs of the table will be located.

Draw additional figures in the area where you intend to locate tables, always placing their heads on the horizon. This will help you estimate the size of additional tables within your seating area. Although the first ellipse was carefully drawn, enough of its shape is known so that the subsequent ellipses in the distance can be eyeballed, taking care only to relate their size to the nearest figure and make them progressively flatter as they near the horizon.

In this illustration, the surroundings for the tables and chairs were previously drawn on an underlying sheet. The layout step you see here was drawn with *Black* Prismacolor pencil, the perspective layout lines with a .5 mm pencil.

Fig. 4-53

2 **Rough-in figures and chairs.** In figure 4-54, seated figures were added to the tables, again using a *Black* Prismacolor pencil. The scattered standing figures were used as scale referents. This stage is often the most difficult to those new to design illustration. However, it becomes easier the more you do it. Collect and use photographs of similar situations to help you with the gestures and postures of the seated figures. Note that the detail should diminish as you progress into the background until you are drawing little more than heads and shoulders.

3 **Create final tracing.** A fresh piece of tracing paper was laid over the rough to make the final tracing in figure 4-55. The people, the furnishings, and the surroundings were drawn simultaneously. This ties everything together and gives the line drawing a unified look. A Micron 005 felt-tipped pen was used, so the linework remains thin and the final color drawing does not take on a "cartoonish" look.

With your rough as your guide, you can focus on editing and refining the drawing during this step. Note how the detail has been simplified as this part of the drawing progresses into the distance. This part of the information is kept fairly *simple,* because creating highly detailed people occupies too much time relative to their purpose in the illustration. Further detail can be added to the furnishings through the application of the color.

Fig. 4-54

Fig. 4-55

Leather (4-56, 4-57)

Leather and leatherlike materials can be found in most any color. Here, two classic colors are represented on a matching sofa and club chair.

1 **Apply marker base; consider direction of light.** In figure 4-56, *Delta Brown (Black)* marker was applied to the darker surfaces of the sofa, and *Burnt Umber (Dark Umber)* marker was used on the lighter, upward-facing surfaces. Note that although *Delta Brown (Black)* marker was used on the lower front of the sofa, the slightly lighter *Burnt Umber (Dark Umber)* marker was used behind the glass table. This is because colors appear slightly lighter behind glass as a result of veiling reflections.

Redwood *(Sienna Brown)* marker was applied to the shaded parts of the club chair, and *Pale Cherry (Mineral Orange)* marker was used on the more brightly illuminated faces. In both cases the lighter markers were used as blenders.

Note that wrinkles in the leather are indicated in this step with the darker markers.

2 **Add highlights.** The highlights on leather are often quite bright but most always have diffuse edges. In figure 4-57, a *White* pencil was used to add graded highlights on those surfaces that bend toward the light source, in this case the large window. Once the highlights were created with pencil, white gouache lines were added to the middle of the highlights to enhance their effect.

Note that *Mineral Orange* pencil was used on the brown sofa to indicate reflected light from the club chair, and *Blue Slate* was used on the other end to simulate a cooler light—such as daylight—from an "off-picture" light source.

Fig. 4-56

Fig. 4-57

Fabric, with Pattern (4-58, 4-59)

1 **Apply marker base.** In figure 4-58, darker-value markers were applied to the shaded surfaces, and lighter markers were applied to the illuminated surfaces. *Cool Grey #1 (Cool Grey 10%)* marker was applied to the upward-facing surfaces of the sofa; *Cool Grey #3 (Cool Grey 30%)* marker was applied to the surfaces that face away from the window. The stripes were added to those surfaces with *French Grey 10%* and *French Grey 30%* markers, respectively.

The pillow on the left has a *Naples Yellow (Eggshell)* marker base with *Light Ivy (Putty + Cream)* marker stripes and *Pale Cherry (Mineral Orange)* marker spots. The shadows were added with *French Grey 30%* marker. The plain pillow on the right has a *Buff (Brick Beige)* marker base with *French Grey 10%* and *30%* marker shadows.

The club chair has a *Naples Yellow (Eggshell)* marker base. The shaded faces were darkened with *French Grey 30%* marker.

Fig. 4-58

2 **Apply highlights, shading, and detail.** The sofa's illuminated surfaces were washed with *White* pencil, and the shaded faces were lightly washed with Derwent *Blue Violet Lake #27* pencil (4-59). The stripes and surfaces near the pillows were lightly washed with *Deco Orange* pencil.

Highlights were added to the pillows with *White* pencil, and *Deco Orange* pencil was applied to the shadowed parts of the folds. A *Bronze* pencil was used to add horizontal stripes to the left pillow, and detail was added to the pillow's orange spots with dilute white gouache.

The club chair's shaded faces were washed lightly with *Deco Orange* pencil, and graded washes of *White* pencil were applied to its illuminated surfaces. The pattern was added with a *Rosy Beige* pencil on the illuminated surfaces and lightly touched with *Henna* pencil on the shaded surfaces.

The glass table received a light wash of *Deco Aqua* pencil. Its foremost edge was lined with *Celadon Green*.

Fig. 4-59

Wicker, Rattan, and Cane (4-60, 4-61)

1 **Begin by applying the marker base.** The illuminated surfaces of the natural wicker and rattan chair and side table, as well as the wicker basket, were colored with a *Sand (Sand)* marker, and a *Kraft Brown (Light Tan)* marker was used on the shaded surfaces (4-60).

The same marker colors were used on the cane seat and back of the foreground chair. The white-painted wicker rocker required its immediate surroundings and background to be colored so that the white wicker would be visible in forthcoming steps.

2 **Apply pencil detail.** In figure 4-61, the natural wicker chair and side table were washed lightly with a *Yellow Ochre* pencil, after which vertical lines were added with a *Burnt Ochre* pencil. Horizontal lines were applied with a *Dark Umber* pencil. This quickly imparted a wickerlike texture. The shaded areas were darkened with a *Dark Umber* pencil.

The basket required the addition of a *French Grey 30%* marker, stroked horizontally along its contour, before a *Dark Umber* pencil was used to apply evenly spaced dashed lines in the same direction. Evenly spaced vertical lines were added along the basket's contour with a *Burnt Ochre* pencil.

The cane seat and back of the foreground chair received a wash of *Yellow Ochre* pencil, after which rows of black dots (to simulate openings) were applied with a Pilot Razor Point. Fine lines of diagonal cross-hatching were added with a *Dark Umber* pencil.

The fine strips of wicker were added to the white wicker rocker with a *White* pencil. To *one side* of the white pencil lines, *Cool Grey 70%* pencil lines were added so that certain portions of the wicker strips would be visible against insufficiently dark parts of the background. The sunlit surfaces of the white rocker were lightly washed with *Cream* pencil, and *Blue Slate* pencil was used to flavor the shaded surfaces.

Fig. 4-60

Fig. 4-61

Wood (4-62, 4-63)

The marker colors you choose as a base will largely depend on the kind of wood you intend to communicate in your design illustrations. In the illustration sequence shown here, the kitchen cabinets are intended to be a clear-grained wood, such as maple or fir, with a light stain and a matte finish. The table is a dark wood with reddish highlights, such as rosewood or Brazilian walnut, with a high finish. The freestanding pantry is intended to be an antique pine piece.

1 **Apply marker base.** *Sand (Sand)* and *Sunset Pink (Deco Pink)* were applied in sequence on the upper cabinets in figure 4-62, and *Kraft Brown (Light Tan)* and *Sunset Pink (Deco Pink)* markers were used on the lower cabinets. The lower cabinets were made slightly darker because they receive slightly less ambient light.

Burnt Umber (Dark Umber) and *Burnt Sienna (Terra Cotta)* markers were applied to the table. *Sand (Sand)* marker was added over the *Burnt Sienna (Terra Cotta)* marker to mute it slightly.

Pale Sepia (Goldenrod) was applied to the lighter face of the pantry, followed by *Sunset Pink (Deco Pink)* marker. The shaded and shadowed parts of the pantry were colored with *Kraft Brown (Light Tan)* marker, followed by *Sunset Pink (Deco Pink)* marker.

2 **Add detail.** Figure 4-63 shows both upper and lower cabinets subtly streaked with *Jasmine, Peach, Mineral Orange,* and *Cream* pencils.

Reflections were added to the table with a *White* pencil. In a typical full-color design illustration, the reflections in a horizontal surface are aligned with the lightest values and brightest sources of light that are located above and beyond that surface. In this case the window is the source of the strongest reflection. Because the objects and surfaces beyond are not all colored, a few light reflections have been "dropped into" the table surface to show how reflections work on a polished wood surface. Note that the reflections are strongest at the far edge, then fade away as they drop into the table.

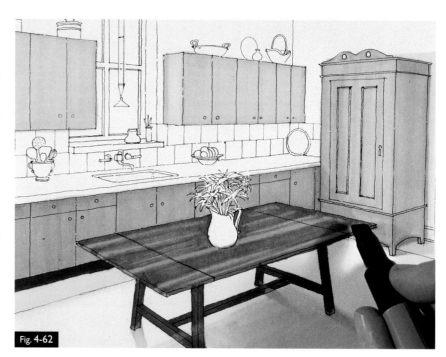

Fig. 4-62

Fig. 4-63

Local reflections, such as the pitcher of flowers, are created by making a reverse image in the table with the same pencils used to color the actual image. No pen outlines are used to delineate reflections, and less hand pressure is used with the pencils so that the reflection appears dimmer than the actual object. The lines formed by the table leaves were redelineated with a Pilot Razor Point.

French Grey 50% marker was used to add knots to the pine pantry. Streaks of *Mineral Orange, Cream, Jasmine,* and *Burnt Ochre* pencils were applied with the sides of the points. A straightedge was used with *Cream* and *Burnt Ochre* pencils to apply highlights and shadows to the moldings. Hints of wood grain and cracking were added with a .5 mm pencil with a 2H lead.

Stone (4-64, 4-65)

The colors of the markers you choose as a base are largely determined by the type of stone you wish to indicate. In the illustration here, a rose granite is indicated for the counter, and the backsplash is intended to be Chinese slate.

1 **Apply marker base.** In figure 4-64, *French Grey 10%* marker was applied to the granite counter, and *Cool Grey #2 (Cool Grey 20%), Cool Grey #3 (Cool Grey 30%),* and *Buff (Brick Beige)* markers were scribbled on the backsplash area.

Fig. 4-64

2 **Add detailing.** Shadows were added beneath the bowls and vase on the counter with a *French Grey 30%* marker in figure 4-65. The countertop was washed lightly with a *Light Peach* pencil, and a *White* pencil was used to add reflections of the uncolored objects. The counter was then stippled with *White, Black,* and *Peach* pencils. You will find that a sharp point and a slight twist to the pencil as it strikes the surface will make the stippling more delicate and effective.

Mineral Orange, Terra Cotta, and Burnt Ochre pencils were very lightly applied, using the sides of the points, to individual stones of the backsplash. A *French Grey 50%* pencil was used to darken the backsplash where it meets the counter, grading lighter as it moved up. A *White* pencil was likewise used to wash the wall beneath the cabinets, fading away as it moved downward. This creates the effect of under-cabinet lighting.

Fig. 4-65

Glass (4-66, 4-67, 4-68)

1 **Draw table's surroundings first.** Figure 4-66 shows the glass table saved until last in the illustration, so that the designer will know what colors are reflected.

2 **Color objects on the table and the surfaces beneath.** In figure 4-67, color was added to the objects on the table in the usual fashion. However, only marker was used to color those surfaces seen through the tabletop.

Fig. 4-66

When the reflections are drawn in the tabletop, they will remain crisp instead of becoming muddied by mixing with other pencil colors. *Willow Green (Lime Green)* marker was applied to the tabletop after marker was applied to those surfaces seen beneath.

3 **Draw reflections with pencil; add finishing touches.** Figure 4-68 shows the reflections, drawn with the same color pencils used to draw the objects reflected. Note that few outlines were used in the reflections—and those were drawn only faintly, in .5 mm pencil. To avoid confusion, the reflections

of the objects resting on the table were drawn and colored first, since they will partially block reflections of objects in the room beyond. The colors of reflected objects were added with color pencil.

The intense highlights in the reflections were added with diluted white gouache. White gouache and a small thin brush were also used to create the linear highlights at the table's edges. These highlights, once dry, were edged with a *Black* pencil and a french curve. Touches (dots) of white gouache were also added to the corners of the table, glasses, and the case of the wireless menu/order device.

Fig. 4-67

Fig. 4-68

Metals (4-69 through 4-72)

The following series of steps illustrates types of metal typically encountered by interior designers: brushed stainless steel, polished stainless steel, chrome, and polished copper.

Metals usually reflect the colors that surround them. The more polished a metal, the more distinct from one another are its darks, lights, and reflections; the less polished and more brushed the finish, the less distinct and more diffuse the reflections.

The shape of the metal determines the shape of the reflections. Flat pieces reflect like a mirror; if a flat surface is slightly warped, the reflection is likewise distorted. Cylindrical and tubular surfaces elongate reflections, stretching them into lines. Half-round objects curve reflections, and a truly spherical reflective object (particularly a polished sphere) gathers curving reflections into an intensely contrasting horizon along its middle.

1 **Illustrate everything that surrounds the metals.** In order to know what colors to reflect into the metals, they should be drawn last in an illustration (4-69).

2 **Add marker base.** The value of stainless steel can range from very dark to very light, depending on how it reflects the light. You can therefore successfully illustrate stainless steel at any value, depending on the lightness or darkness of the markers you choose to begin the illustration.

In figure 4-70, a *Cool Grey #2 (Cool Grey 20%)* marker was applied to the left side of the brushed stainless-steel cabinets, and *Warm Grey #3 (Warm Grey 30%)* marker was applied to the right side. *Warm Grey #1 (Warm Grey 10%)* marker was used as a blender between the warm and cool grays. The use of subtly different colors of gray indicates subtle differences in the hues of the light reflected from the cabinets. *French Grey 20%* marker was applied to the part of the stainless-steel countertop that reflects the red tile backsplash.

Note the wavy white spaces left in the cabinet faces. These will be turned into diffuse reflections in later steps. These reflections are wavy because the stainless steel used in applications of this kind is rarely perfectly flat, but instead has some degree of "oil canning." The vertical orientation of the reflections indicates that the reflected light sources are vertical.

The espresso machine and teapot were touched with *Redwood (Sienna Brown), Cool Grey #4 (Cool Grey 40%), Warm Grey #3 (Warm Grey 30%),* and *Warm Grey #1 (Warm Grey 10%)* markers.

The copper pot was colored with Burnt Sienna (Terra Cotta) and Pale Sepia (Goldenrod) markers.

3 **Add diffuse highlights and color washes to brushed metal; add sharp-edged lowlights to polished metals.** The edges of the white spaces left by the marker on the brushed stainless steel were softened and "diffused" by applying *White* pencil to their edges—exerting most hand pressure at the

Fig. 4-69

edge, then grading outward by using increasingly lighter hand pressure on the pencil (4-71).

Slate Blue and *Cloud Blue* pencils were used to wash the left side of the cabinets; *Peach, Light Peach, Jasmine,* and *Cream* pencils were used to wash the right side and the cabinet faces near the floor. These colors were applied because stainless steel reflects the colors of its surroundings, even though these reflections are quite diffuse rather than crisp-edged.

Burnt Ochre and *White* pencils were used to reflect the color and grout lines from the backsplash into the countertop. *French Grey 50%* pencil was then applied to mute these colors somewhat.

You will notice that the closer an object is to a brushed stainless-steel surface, the more clearly it reflects in that surface. Hence, the bottom of the blue bowl, the espresso maker, and the vertical tile grout lines of the backsplash are the most distinct reflections, whereas parts (such as the fruit) and elements farther away are more diffuse or (like the stool) do not reflect at all.

Very dark reflections with sharp edges have been added to the stool legs, the espresso maker, the teapot, and the copper pot. Because these objects are highly polished, they have very distinct-edged reflections. These dark reflections were added with a Pilot Razor Point.

4 **Add final touches.** In figure 4-72, small touches of reflected colors were added to the espresso maker, teapot, copper pot, and stool legs, using *Peach, Slate Blue, Orange, Poppy Red, Yellow Chartreuse,* and *Jasmine* pencils.

Highlights were added with white gouache to these elements and to the nosing of the stainless-steel countertop.

Fig. 4-70

Fig. 4-71

Fig. 4-72

Bathroom Fixtures (4-73, 4-74, 4-75)

These illustrations were colored on a blackline diazo print that was run through the machine at a faster-than-usual speed.

1 **Apply color to the fixtures' surroundings.** This makes it easier to determine how dark or light to make the fixtures and fittings.

In figure 4-73, the mirrors' images were drawn in pencil and colored with pencil. Then a wash of *Deco Aqua* pencil was applied to the mirrors to give them the slightly greenish characteristic tinge of mirrors and glass.

The marble counter, tub surround, and shower wall were easily created by first applying shading to their darker edges and surfaces with a *Cool Grey #5 (Cool Grey 50%)* marker and then washing all the marble surfaces with *White* pencil. Firm pencil pressure was applied to the upward-facing surfaces to make them the brightest. The surfaces in shade or illuminated by daylight were flavored with *Blue Slate,* and those surfaces illuminated by incandescent light were flavored with *Light Peach.* The shower wall grades from *Light Peach* at the upper left to *Blue Slate* on the lower right. The marbling was then applied with both the side of the tip and the point of the tip of a *Cool Grey 70%* pencil.

Fig. 4-73

2 **Apply darks and lights.** In figure 4-74, *Cool Grey #5 (Cool Grey 50%)* marker was applied to the chromed waste pipes beneath the lavatories, the deepest visible part of the tub, and the shaded sides of the water closet and bidet. *Cool Grey #3 (Cool Grey 30%)* marker was used to diffuse the edges of the darker marker.

Micron 01 and Pilot Razor Point pens were used to apply blacks to the chromed fittings, including the waste pipes, faucets, towel bars, and showerhead. A straightedge was used to keep the lines straight and crisp. *White* pencil was then applied to those parts of the fittings that appear to bend in such a way that they may reflect light toward the viewer of the illustration.

Deco Aqua pencil was used to color the glass lavatory bowls, including the glowing translucent bottoms that are visible beneath the counter. *Celadon Green* pencil was applied to their rims.

White pencil was applied to the tub, water closet, and bidet, with more hand pressure on the pencil where the surfaces face probable sources of light.

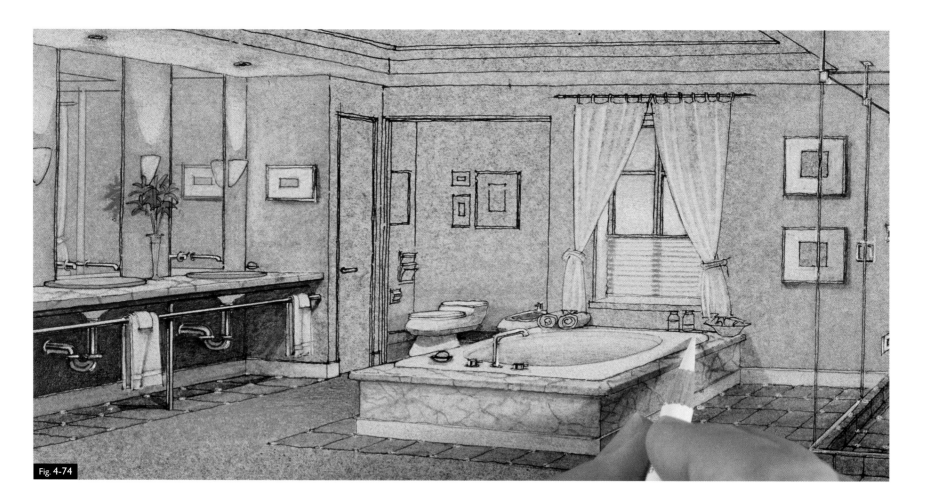

Fig. 4-74

3 **Apply flavorings and highlights.** Figure 4-75 shows the result of the addition of the final touches to the illustration. *Blue Slate* pencil was used to flavor the side of the tub that "sees" the bluish daylight from the window. The same pencil, along with *Celadon Green* pencil, was used to shade the side of the white water closet. *Light Peach* pencil was used to flavor the illuminated sides of the tub, water closet, and bidet. This is an important step, inasmuch as white bathroom fixtures reflect the colors—and colors of the light—in their surroundings.

Celadon Green pencil was applied, using a straightedge, to the edges of the glass walls of the shower, and *Deco Aqua* pencil was used to flavor the face of the glass.

White gouache highlights were applied, as the final touch, to the chrome, porcelain, glass lavatory bowls, and light fixtures.

Fig. 4-75

Lighting

Nothing so completes the effort spent in the creation of the mood or feel of a place as masterful lighting. Lighting effects are easy and fun to create. You will encounter basic lighting illustration techniques in this section, and you can see them deployed throughout this book.

In illustration, the successful creation of lighting effects depends fundamentally on making light sources and illuminated surfaces adequately luminous. As you have seen in Chapter 1, this means that the stronger the contrast between two adjacent values, the brighter and more luminous the lighter portion appears. The following illustrations will show that, on white paper, luminosity is created by surrounding light surfaces with values that are sufficiently dark. However, if you are creating design illustrations that are intended to show extensive lighting effects—whether sunlight or artificial light—you may find it easier to work on toned papers or white roll tracing paper. The reason is that on these papers, both dark and light value pencil colors are easily visible.

You will find lighting effects easier to create after you have mastered the easily attainable skill of making graded washes, in both marker and pencil, because you will discover that color, light, and shading must be constantly graded one into the others. Your chances of successfully creating the effects of lighting, particularly indoor lighting, will also be greatly increased if you first make a quick, rough value study of a proposed illustration. Once your study is complete, you can use it as a strategic reference for value arrangement, allowing you to concentrate on the tactics of technique as you create your illustration. You can find such a study in figure 4-79.

Ceiling-Mounted Lighting (4-76, 4-77, 4-78)

If ceiling-mounted light sources are to appear illuminated, the ceiling must be sufficiently darker than those sources. In most cases this is not a problem, because unless a ceiling is directly illuminated by uplighting, it usually appears slightly darker than the lower parts of a room.

Ceiling-mounted recessed "cans," adjustable "eyeball" spotlights, and track lighting often create parabola-shaped patterns on walls or artwork. When necessary, use an ellipse template to help create these shapes.

This illustration is shown on "Pearl" Canson paper.

1 **Create a quick lighting study.** See figure 4-79 as an example.

2 **Create the appropriate graded values on the ceiling;** outline illumination patterns on walls. *Cool Grey #5 (Cool Grey 50%), Cool Grey #3 (Cool Grey 30%),* and *Cool Grey #1 (Cool Grey 10%)* markers were used in figure 4-76 to create the ceiling gradations. Note that although the pendant light fixture is surrounded by some of the darkest marker values to make it appear sufficiently bright, the part of the ceiling it uplights is quite light. This inverted pool of light becomes progressively darker at its edges.

French Grey 30%, 10%, and *Clear Blender* markers were used on the suspended portion of the ceiling. Note that the marker was applied directly over the recessed can lights so that the gradation of values could be made more easily.

A *White* pencil was used with an ellipse template to make the parabolic shapes of light on the wall.

3 **Develop light effects with pencil.** *Deco Orange* and *White* pencils were used with firm hand pressure to color the pendant fixture in figure 4-77. Derwent *Blue Violet Lake #27, Blue Slate, Cloud Blue,* and *White* pencils were used to color the cool-colored portion of the ceiling, the pencil values corresponding to the ceiling values already in place.

White, Light Peach, Deco Orange, Mineral Orange, and *Burnt Ochre* pencils (named here in order of descending value) were used to create gradations on the ceiling shapes, walls, and floor. Note that the parabolic washes of light on the wall are most intense at the upper crown of the shape. It is in the same location that the wall value is graded to its darkest. The wall value is also graded darker against the merchandise, beginning a higher-contrast relationship that will help the merchandise to appear illuminated in the next step. Subtle shadows were added beneath the merchandise and the wall-mounted letters with a *French Grey 30%* marker, subsequently flavored with a Derwent *Blue Violet Lake #27* pencil. Avoid creating value contrasts between light and shadow that are *too* strong in interior design illustrations, because such value relationships will make the lighting appear too harsh.

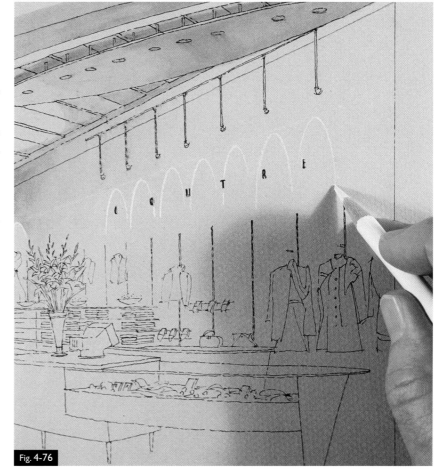

Fig. 4-76

The track lights on the pendant stems were darkened with *Black* marker and Pilot Razor Point in order to silhouette them against the wall. This helps the wall to appear more brightly illuminated by contrast.

Upward-facing surfaces—countertops, floor, and so forth—are more brightly illuminated as a result of the recessed ceiling-mounted downlights.

4 **Add final touches and highlights.** In figure 4-78, a variety of color pencils were used to add color to the items displayed, with *White* pencil added to the tops of the items and graded into their local colors farther away from the light sources.

The viewer's attention is kept on the illuminated wall and ceiling by the foreground elements being darkened with *French Grey 90%, 70%, 50%, 30%,* and *10%* markers. Color pencil was then lightly added to give them some hue. Silhouetting is a useful technique for both creating the sense of illumination and guiding the viewer's attention *if it works with your design intent.* Do not darken elements of your illustration if they play a critical part in the overall design idea you are trying to communicate. Silhouetting works here, because the purpose of the illustration is to feature the wall and ceiling.

White gouache was added as a final touch to the lights and the wall-mounted letters.

Fig. 4-77

Fig. 4-78

Lighting at the Wall Plane

Wall sconce, table lamp, and floor lamp (4-79 through 4-84)

1   **Create a quick lighting study.** A *Black* Prismacolor pencil and an electric eraser were used to make a quick lighting study (4-79) on a black-and-white photocopy of the line drawing. This 20-minute exploration will be used, during the creation of the more finished version of the illustration, as a guide in making its value arrangements and gradations of colors.

When creating lighting effects on white paper, such as Bristol (4-80, 4-81), use the following steps:

2   **Apply marker base.** In figure 4-80, marker base colors have been applied to the furniture, pictures, and floor. The walls have been left white, as they will be high in value. The shapes of the light patterns have been drawn and partially colored with *Cream* pencil.

Fig. 4-79

Fig. 4-80

3 **Add pencil.** Figure 4-81 shows graded washes applied to the walls with *French Grey 90%, 70%, 50%, 30%, 20%,* and *10%* pencils. The upper left wall, for example, was graded from gray to white with *French Grey 30%, 20%, 10%,* and *Cream* pencils. The *Cream* pencil grades into the white of the paper just above the lamp shade of the floor lamp. *Cool Grey 70%, 50%, 30%, 20%, 10%, Blue Slate,* and *Cloud Blue* pencils were used to create the gradations on the right side to suggest an off-picture incursion of daylight.

Note how the *French Grey* pencil series, with the addition of some *Black* pencil, was used to surround the table lamp shade with values dark enough to make it appear illuminated. The shade itself was colored with a light wash of *Deco Orange* pencil, followed by a heavy application of *Cream* pencil.

A combination of *Dark Umber* and *Burnt Ochre* pencils was used to grade the rug and soften its shadows. *Olive Green* pencil was used to darken the patterns in the shadow.

The white mats around the pictures were lightly flavored, grading from *Cream* to *Blue Slate* pencil, indicating reflection of both incandescent light and daylight.

Touches of white gouache were applied to the wall sconce, the table lamp base, and the ashtray.

Fig. 4-81

When creating lighting effects on white roll tracing paper (4-82, 4-83) with the retrocolor technique, use the following steps:

2 **Apply shade and shadow with** *Black* **Prismacolor pencil.** Graded washes of *Black* Prismacolor pencil are lightly applied to the line drawing to create the shade and shadow. One advantage of this technique is that the illustration is usable, if necessary, as soon as the shade and shadow are applied. A portion of the drawing is shown in figure 4-82.

3 **Apply color pencil to the** *back* **of the drawing.** In figure 4-83, *White, Cream,* and *Light Peach* pencils were applied most heavily, in the order named, to the crown of the parabolic shapes of light on the wall, then graded into the natural color of the paper. This was done on the back of the tracing paper, with a piece of brown kraft paper beneath as a work surface. The shadow area behind the lamp shade was washed with *Light Peach* pencil, again with color applied to the back of the drawing.

The creation of this illustration was significantly faster than that done on white paper, inasmuch as the light could be applied as well as the shadow. The color could also be applied more quickly and less carefully, because the translucent quality of the paper tends to smooth the look of the result when turned right-side-over. If color went past the lines, it could be quickly erased without harming the linework.

Fig. 4-82

Fig. 4-83

Specialty Lighting

Neon and pin lights (4-84, 4-85, 4-86)

Common specialty lighting is grouped in two categories: linear display and point display. Linear display lighting, such as neon, "light pipe," and linear fiber-optic lighting, are best illustrated in surroundings shown as very dark—at least those in the vicinity of the lights themselves. Point display lighting, including the many varieties of tiny incandescent "pin" lights or fiber-optic ends, are also best illustrated against dark surroundings. Both kinds are easy to draw.

The drawing series that follows was created on an ink-jet plot of an *inverted* line drawing. The line drawing was first drawn using a felt-tipped pen, then scanned and opened in Photoshop. It was inverted by using the like-named command (Image > Adjustments > Invert). This yielded a drawing with white lines on a black background that shows a neon sign, clear incandescent lamps, and pin lights on the surrounding plant materials.

1 **Mute white lines on all except neon tubes.** To allow the lighting to have the strongest value contrast with its surroundings, the remaining white lines are muted with marker. Any dark gray—even black—marker will do, as long as the line images can still be seen. In figure 4-84, a *Cool Grey #9 (Cool Grey 90%)* marker is used to mute the structure supporting the sign and the plant materials, and a warmer *French Grey 70%* marker is used to mute all sign elements except the neon tubes themselves.

2 **Add strong-chroma pencil colors to neon tubes and their backgrounds.** White neon tubes can be colored with a variety of strong-chroma, light-value pencils. The "neon" pencil series by Prismacolor—*Neon Red, Neon Orange,* and so on—is especially good for this purpose. Color pencil should also be applied to the letters and miscellaneous metals on the sign during this step. Of course, these metals will not be as bright as the neon, because only the neon has a white background.

In figure 4-85, the neon letters in the word "Eat" were colored with *Deco Orange* pencil, and the surrounding pan channel letters were colored with *Carmine Red* and *Poppy Red* pencils. *Tuscan Red* pencil was used on the sides, or "returns," of the letters.

Fig. 4-84

Fig. 4-85

Fig. 4-86

The neon lettuce in the hamburger and the pointing fingers are *Yellow Chartreuse* pencil, and *Jasmine* pencil was applied to the large arrow behind the word "Eat." Note how much dimmer the pencil colors are when applied to the black part of the print.

Olive Green and *Jasmine* pencils were applied quickly and roughly to the plant materials, using the sides of the points, to give them both color and texture.

3 **Apply light "halos" and washes; add pin lights.** Neon light is usually intense enough to cast a glow of light in its immediate vicinity. In figure 4-86, graded washes of *Yellow Chartreuse, Deco Orange,* and *White* pencils were added to the vicinity of similarly colored neon. These pencils, with the addition of *Pink* pencil, were also lightly applied to the pavement and figure beneath the sign.

White gouache was used to create the impression of clear incandescent lamps on both the large arrow behind the word "Eat" and the pin lights in the plant materials.

Note that after Step 2, the drawing can also be scanned and opened in Photoshop to provide an alternative way of finishing it. The light "halos" can be added using the airbrush capability of the *Brush Tool*, but be sure to begin by setting the *Flow* at quite a low percentage—about 10% or so. The *Brush* or *Pencil Tool* can be used to add the white accents and pin lights.

Neon Using Photoshop (4-87 through 4-93)

You can easily and quickly create discrete lines, shapes, or words in neon using Photoshop.

1 **Scan drawing and make new layer; create shapes or words.** Be sure to select a drawing or an area of a drawing that is fairly dark so that the neon will appear appropriately bright by contrast. Make the shape you ultimately want to appear in neon using the *Brush Tool*, *Pencil Tool*, or *Line Tool*, using a light color at a strong chroma (i.e., its most saturated). If you are creating a sign, use the *Type Tool*. The font used in this example is Bermuda LP (4-87).

2 **Open *Layer Style*. Select stroke color.** The layer destined to become neon (in this example, the type layer) was kept active and the *f* button at the bottom left of the *Layers Palette* was selected (4-88). This displayed a small drop-down menu with the choices for layer style. *Stroke* was selected from the bottom of this menu, which opened the *Stroke Layer Style* dialog box, right. The color swatch was double-clicked, the *Color Picker* opened, and the neon color selected. The size was set to 7 pixels in this example, but it may need to be different for your own drawing. The position was set to "Outside" (which allows the original colored line to remain showing, but note how the stroke shifted its hue), the blending mode was set to "Normal," and the opacity to 100%. The result is seen in figure 4-89.

Fig. 4-87

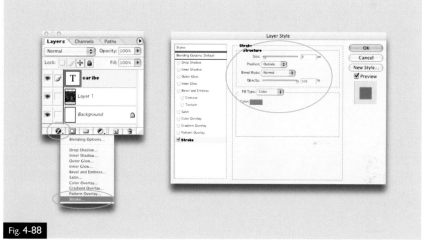

Fig. 4-88

Fig. 4-89

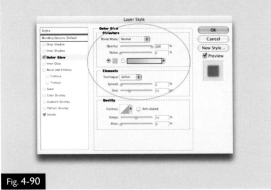

Fig. 4-90

3 **Create outer glow.** Next, *Outer Glow* was selected from the list on the left side of the open *Layer Style* dialog box (4-90). The color box was double-clicked and a second strong-chroma color (a neighbor of the stroke color on the color wheel) was chosen from the *Color Picker*. This glow color introduces a second color of neon into the sign.

The blending mode was set to "Normal" and the opacity to 100%. In the *Elements* box, the technique was set to "Softer." The spread and size were experimented with to create a glow appropriate to a wall-mounted neon sign (4-91). The drawing could be stopped at this point, as sufficient "neon" effect has been created. Or you can add a drop shadow (4-92, 4-93) to create additional glow and color.

Fig. 4-91

4 **Create drop shadow.** To introduce additional color and depth to the neon sign, the "Drop Shadow" option on the left side of the *Layer Style* dialog box was selected (4-92). Not an absolutely necessary step for creating the neon effect, it can add additional color and help the neon stand away from a surface. As with the outer glow, the drop shadow need not be the exact color of the stroke.

Figure 4-92 shows, circled in red, the adjustments used to create the drop shadow in figure 4-93. The *Distance, Spread,* and *Size* sliders were experimented with to create an additional colored glow of an appropriate size and distance from the sign. This glow, however, can be positioned below, above, or to the side of the sign by clicking and dragging the *Angle* adjustment line. In this case, the angle "90" indicates that the drop shadow is located directly below the sign.

Note that on the right in figure 4-92, each of the layer styles shows up as a sublayer within the effects layer. You can double-click on each of the *f* icons to reopen the *Layer Style* dialog box and make further adjustments to the layer styles. Likewise, you can eliminate any of the effects (layer styles) by dragging them to the trash can at the lower right of the *Layers Palette.*

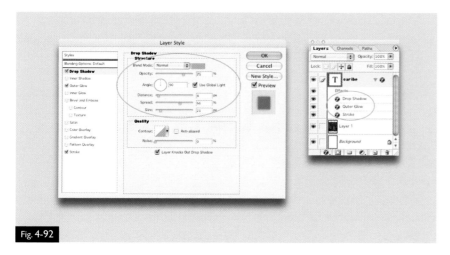

Fig. 4-92

Fig. 4-93

Accessories

Accessories have a surprising effect on interior places, as well as on the design illustrations of such places. Artwork, books, flowers, pottery and vases, bowls of fruit, plants, sculpture and candles, even lamps and fireplaces, all provide an opportunity for focal points and accents of color. They contribute a finer level of scale to a room and can make a place seem rich and interesting.

Paintings, Prints, and Photographs (4-94, 4-95)

Graphic art in real places provides points of interest. Part of what gives a picture its ability to focus attention within a place is often its wealth of detail. However, its purpose in a design illustration is somewhat different. Because it is usually the designer's job to orchestrate the development of a place in its entirety, graphic images in design illustrations are simplified so that they take their place as part of the larger idea.

1 **Apply marker base to frames and picture images.** These images can be imitated or invented and are drawn using the marker tip only (no lines). As figure 4-94 shows, this also allows the designer to create the images quickly and keep them appropriately indistinct. *Pale Sepia (Goldenrod)* marker was applied as a base for the gilded frame.

Fig. 4-94

2 **Add details.** In figure 4-95, a *White* pencil line was applied with an ellipse template to the painting over the fireplace. A graded wash of *White* pencil was then applied below to create a parabolic wash of light from the ceiling-mounted eyeball spotlight. The colors in the picture were then enhanced slightly with color pencil to prevent them from appearing too washed out by the white, with care taken to keep the colors within the parabolic shape *lighter* in value than those outside its shape.

The mat surrounding the picture was colored with a *Sand (Sand)* marker, then darkened at the top with a *French Grey 70%* marker. *Jasmine* and *Yellow Ochre* pencils were used to add color to the gold frame, which was then highlighted with white gouache.

The white mats around the pictures to the right were flavored with *Cream* and *Cloud Blue* pencils.

French Grey 30% and *10%* markers were used to create the diffuse shadows behind and beneath the pictures.

Fig. 4-95

General Accessories (4-96, 4-97, 4-98)

Books, flowers, plants, bowls of fruit, and various kinds of pottery are common accessories in interiors. They take additional time to illustrate, but are important to include in design illustrations to impart a degree of animation and realism to your ideas that help them appear probable.

1 **Make accessories legible by darkening backgrounds as necessary.** In most cases, diffuse shadows will add presence to your accessories. In figure 4-96, *French Grey 90%, 50%, 30%,* and *10%* markers were used to create the diffuse shadows. Other marker colors can, of course, be used for this step, depending on the local colors of the surfaces on which the shadows occur.

Sometimes the backgrounds of accessories must be darkened to give the accessories emphasis. Note, for example, how the cabinet doors behind the tulips on the coffee table are progressively darkened. This was done so that the tulips would be a bit more vivid in the finished illustration.

2 **Apply base colors with marker.** Marker base colors are applied in figure 4-97. *Sand (Sand), Naples Yellow (Eggshell), Sunset Pink (Deco Pink), Kraft Brown (Light Tan),* and *Burnt Sienna (Terra Cotta)* markers were used on the stone fireplace, and *Willow Green (Lime Green)* marker was applied to the bookshelves and cabinets. The blue marker used in the illustration is *Pale Indigo (Cloud Blue)*. The large foreground vase has a *Pale Sepia (Goldenrod)* marker base, and the smaller vase is a combination of *Willow Green (Lime Green)* and *Pale Indigo (Cloud Blue)* markers. These colors were used randomly for the base colors of the books as well.

3 **Add pencil detailing; apply highlights.** At this stage, color pencil can be applied to add smaller touches of color, more brilliant color, and to shift base colors. In figure 4-98, *Cool Grey 50%* and *30%* pencils were used to mute the green of the bookcases. *Black* pencil was added to the darkest recesses between and behind the books. *Carmine Red* and *Jasmine* pencils were applied to the flowers; *Yellow Chartreuse* and *Limepeel* pencils were added to the leaves of the tulips. Touches of *Celadon Green* and *Blue Slate*

Fig. 4-96

Fig. 4-97

pencils were used to flavor some of the stones in the fireplace. *Olive Green* and *Limepeel* pencils were used to color the plant on the right; *Poppy Red, Jasmine,* and *Black* pencils were added to the books. The apples were colored with *Poppy Red* and *Tuscan Red,* and *Limepeel* and *Jasmine* pencils were used for the pears. *White* and *Jasmine* pencils were applied to both large vases in the foreground. *Deco Aqua* was added to the tulip vase on the coffee table and to the bottles on the counter.

White gouache was used to add highlights to the fruit, vases, and small lamp to the left of the fireplace, as well as to the flowers on the mantle and the plant on the right.

Fig. 4-98

Fire in a Fireplace (4-99, 4-100)

1 **Outline flames; blacken surroundings.** In figure 4-99, the flames were lightly outlined in pencil. Black marker and Pilot Razor Point were used to darken the soot-blackened surroundings—the back of the firebox, foreground logs, and andirons. *French Grey 50%* marker was used to darken the sides of the firebox.

These very dark surroundings will, of course, help make the fire appear more luminous. Note the bits of flame separated from the main body of the fire.

2 **Apply color pencil to flames, firebox, and hearth.** *Neon Orange* pencil was applied to the outside edges of the flames in figure 4-100. A light wash of the same color was added to the side of the firebox and the hearth. *Canary Yellow* pencil was graded from the *Neon Orange* to the centers of the flames, which were allowed to remain white. *Yellowed Orange* pencil was used to lightly wash the boundary between the edge of the flames and their black background, giving the fire a subtle glow.

Fig. 4-99

Fig. 4-100

EXTERIOR MATERIALS

You will notice that the discussion and illustration of materials for exterior views is not separated into those for "architecture" and those for "landscape architecture." Rather, they are integrated into groups similar to those used for interior materials: ground plane materials, wall plane materials (and windows), and roofs/skies.

There are two reasons for this grouping. First, architectural and landscape materials exist together. That is, landscape materials are just as important as architectural surfaces in composing effective exterior spaces and forms. The best design teams are facile in utilizing both to create exemplary exterior surroundings. Second, because the fields of architecture and landscape architecture are typically categorized as separate disciplines, teachers, practitioners, and, particularly, the print media sometimes tend to emphasize one at the expense of the other. One is exalted while the other is ignored. In fact, this separation is unfounded. Both fields are mere categories in the larger and more important endeavor facing the designer in making good places for people. The approach to the organization of the material that follows is but a small attempt to acknowledge this fact.

Ground Plane Materials

Ground plane materials, like those of wall and roof planes, need be distinguished only close at hand. Detail should be applied to these materials only in the foreground of the view, allowing them to simplify as they proceed into the distance.

PAVING

Brick (4-101, 4-102)

This illustration shows brick paving in a typical herringbone pattern. Note how the pattern becomes simplified as it recedes into the distance.

1 **Apply marker base.** *Redwood (Sienna Brown)* marker was applied, stroked toward the 45° vanishing points on the horizon.

To find the 45° vanishing points, draw a simple square shape on the walkway surface, estimating a square as best you can. This square should be drawn using the vanishing point(s) for the picture. In this picture, the vanishing point is in the center and the "H" denotes the horizon line. Draw diagonals through opposite corners of your square and extend them until they come to the horizon line. In this illustration, you will notice arrows to either side of the walkway, inasmuch as the 45° vanishing points are outside the edges of the picture.

Stroking the marker toward these vanishing points (first one, then the other) has established a subtle diagonal gridded texture on the walkway surface. Touches of *Willow Green (Lime Green)* and *Pale Indigo (Cloud Blue)* markers were also added, in the same way, to weaken the chroma of the base marker (4-101). Note how the marker application begins to appear like brick.

2 **Add shadow with marker.** *Burnt Umber (Dark Umber)* marker was used to add the shadow.

3 **Apply joint pattern.** Figure 4-102 shows the finished material. The actual herringbone pattern was drawn in the foreground with a .5 mm pencil using a 2H lead. This pattern is time consuming, so if you do not have to communicate the pattern in detail, it is best to avoid its exact replication. Instead, use the diagonal dashed-line pattern shown just behind, drawing the dashed lines toward the same 45° vanishing points mentioned earlier. Note that in the shadow a *French Grey 30%* pencil was used to continue the pattern.

Fig. 4-101

Fig. 4-102

Flagstone Pavers (4-103, 4-104)

Flagstone pavers are available in many materials, colors, and patterns. Sandstone and bluestone pavers are illustrated here as examples. Select your marker and pencil colors according to the materials you want to illustrate.

1 **Apply marker base, including shadows.** Figure 4-103 shows *Buff (Brick Beige)* marker used as the predominant color for the sandstone (foreground), with touches of *Sunset Pink (Deco Pink), Sand (Sand),* and *Pale Cherry (Mineral Orange)* markers added for color variation. *Kraft Brown (Light Tan)* marker was used to make the shadow.

The bluestone was created with *Cool Grey #1 (Cool Grey 10%)* marker and touches of *Buff (Brick Beige)* and *Sunset Pink (Deco Pink)* markers. Its shadow was created with a *Cool Grey #3 (Cool Grey 30%)* and *Sunset Pink (Deco Pink)* markers.

2 **Mute color** (if necessary). If the chroma of the paver colors seems too strong, you can mute them with complementary markers, pencils, or pastels.

In this example, the marker colors of the bluestone were muted with a light application of *Light Oxide Red 339.9* stick pastel that was rubbed with a chamois. The sandstone was similarly muted with *Ultramarine Deep 506.9* stick pastel.

3 **Add final touches.** Figure 4-104 shows the finished flagstone. A *Black* pencil was applied with varying pressure to create joints between the sandstone pavers. *Olive Green* pencil was added to suggest plant materials growing between the pavers (moss, thyme, grass, etc.). The same *Black* pencil was very lightly applied, with a more consistent hand pressure, to create the tighter joints between the bluestone pavers.

Fig. 4-103

Fig. 4-104

Concrete, Plain and Decorative (4-105, 4-106)

1 **Apply marker base.** In figure 4-105, a *French Grey 10%* marker was applied to the sunlit surfaces of the plain concrete planter and seat. The shaded sides of these elements were darkened with *French Grey 20%* and *30%* markers.

Buff *(Brick Beige)* marker was used for the lighter portions of the pattern on the walking surface, and *Sand (Sand)* marker was applied to the slightly darker segments. A *Pale Lime (Jade Green)* marker was used for the small triangular accents.

French Grey 30% marker was used to apply the shadow of the tree canopy on both the plain and decorative concrete. *French Grey 40%* marker was used to darken these shadows only in the portions colored with the *Sand (Sand)* marker.

2 **Add details.** A Schwan Stabilo pencil pastel *#675* was applied lightly over those decorative concrete areas colored with the *Sand (Sand)* marker in figure 4-106. It was rubbed in lightly by finger, then wiped lightly with a chamois. The shadows on these areas were darkened with a *Burnt Ochre* pencil. The shadows on the lighter areas were flavored with a *Peach* pencil.

The foreground decorative concrete was textured in a random pattern with a .5 mm pencil using a 2H lead. It was also stippled with the same pencil and a Pilot Razor Point.

The plain concrete in sunlight was flavored with a *Light Peach* pencil, and the shaded surfaces were flavored with a *Light Cerulean Blue* pencil.

Fig. 4-105

Fig. 4-106

GRASS AND GROUND COVERS

Lawn Grass (4-107, 4-108)

1 **Apply marker base.** In figure 4-107 *Light Olive (Leaf Green)* and *Sand (Sand)* markers were applied to the grass areas in sunlight; *Dark Olive (French Grey 80%)* marker was used to create the shadows. Note that the markers were applied parallel to the help lines, which were added to indicate the contour of the ground. Leaf litter, created with small dashes of *Kraft Brown (Light Tan)* and *Burnt Umber (Dark Umber)* markers, has collected most densely in the nooks and crannies of the rocks.

2 **Apply texture and highlights.** A Pilot Razor Point was applied to the shadow areas, with an up-and-down vertical stroke and moving parallel to the help lines, as shown in figure 4-108. After a *Canary Yellow* pencil flavoring was added to the sunlit areas, *Cream* pencil was applied to the foreground sunlit areas, again with the use of an up-and-down stroke and following the help lines. This textural stroke was faded out toward the background and gradually replaced with a sweeping stroke of the *Cream* pencil, following the help lines. *Lilac* pencil was used to flavor the background grass, fading it into the distance. *Olive Green* pencil was used to flavor both sunlit and shadow areas, with the use of large up-and-down strokes. The dead leaves were accented with *Burnt Ochre* and *Jasmine* pencils, and a tiny shadow was placed under each leaf with a Pilot Razor Point.

Fig. 4-107

Fig. 4-108

Berms and Banks (4-109, 4-110, 4-111)

1 **Make line drawing.** As figure 4-109 shows, the ridge lines should be drawn first, using a gradually sloping contoured line. These lines should be drawn light enough that they do not show in the final drawing.

2 **Add help lines and apply marker base.** Thin help lines run approximately perpendicular to the axes of the berms, curving smoothly and gently. Because the forms are grass covered, *Light Olive (Leaf Green)* and *Sand (Sand)* markers were applied, following the help lines as indicated in figure 4-110. *Dark Olive (French Grey 80%)* marker is used to indicate tree shadows, which originate to the right of the drawing. Note how the shadows conform to the terrain.

3 **Add highlights, shading, and texture.** In figure 4-111, the same techniques were used to finish the drawing as those used for lawn grass in figure 4-108. *Olive Green* pencil was used to darken the hollow in the distance, and *Cream* pencil was used on the hillside. The resulting graded value gives a sense of volume to the landforms and distinguishes between them.

Fig. 4-110

Fig. 4-109

Fig. 4-111

Ground Covers (4-112, 4-113)

1   **Apply marker base.** In figure 4-112, *Olive (Olive Green)* marker was applied to the foreground ground cover, with a horizontal, curving stroke used to approximate pachysandra. The white spaces between the *Olive (Olive Green)* marker strokes were colored with *Yellow Green (Limepeel)* marker. To the right of the pachysandra, iris leaves were created with *Yellow Green (Limepeel)* marker, followed by *Pale Indigo (Cloud Blue)* marker. Just beyond, among the rocks (as well as among the more distant rocks by the gazebo), a *Willow Green (Lime Green)* marker was applied to the low, mounded grasses.

The water grasses were colored with a quick upward stroke of *Yellow Green (Limepeel)* marker, and *Olive (Olive Green)* marker was used to add darker color to their base.

Beyond the water grasses on the left, the tip of an *Olive (Olive Green)* marker was used to dot in a ground cover that recalls vinca. Note the white areas that remain between the dots of green.

The lawn in both foreground and background is intended to approximate a bluegrass, illustrating a quicker grass technique than those illustrated in figures 4-107 through 4-111. *Yellow Green (Limepeel)* was applied in long horizontal strokes, followed by *Pale Indigo (Cloud Blue)* marker applied similarly. The shadows on the grass were made with *Olive (Olive Green)* marker.

Fig. 4-112

The short vertical strokes in the distance are stems of a flower mass. These were made with an *Olive (Olive Green)* marker followed by a *Pale Indigo (Cloud Blue)* marker.

2 **Add details.** In figure 4-113, *Black* marker was added to the foreground pachysandra-like ground cover to give it depth. *French Grey 50%* and *Black* markers were applied between the iris leaves to the right.

French Grey 50%, 30%, and *10%* markers were used to create the rocks. *Black* marker was used to emphasize the horizontal fissures.

Yellow Ochre and *Jasmine* pencils were used to bring out the colors of the yellow flowers in the center and to the left of the rock mass, respectively. *Pink* pencil filled in the white spaces as flowers on the shrub just above.

Black marker was added to the water grasses with a quick upward stroke of the marker tip. This stroke was used to create the grasses in shadow and silhouette.

Blue Slate pencil "flowers" were added to the white spaces between the vinca leaves, beyond the water grasses on the left.

Poppy Red pencil was applied to the top of the distant flower mass to approximate tulips.

Fig. 4-113

SHRUBS

Deciduous Shrubs (4-114, 4-115)

The shrubs shown here are generalized indications and not intended to represent specific plant types. Specific shrubs can be drawn with these techniques, however, by approximating their habit, size, and coloration.

1 **Apply marker base.** Shrubs of various colors are shown in figure 4-114, each with a marker base applied using the point of the marker tip, stipple fashion:

(1) *Light Olive (Leaf Green)* and *Olive (Olive Green)* markers
(2) *Slate Green (Teal Blue)* and *Cool Grey #7 (Cool Grey 70%)* markers
(3) *Yellow Green (Limepeel)* and *Olive (Olive Green)* markers

Cool Grey #9 (Cool Grey 90%) was stippled on all the shrubs to create the darkest areas. *Dark Olive (French Grey 80%)* marker was used to indicate shadows on the grass.

Fig. 4-114

2 **Create highlights, shadows, and contrasts.** Figure 4-115 shows the finished illustration. *Apple Green* pencil was added to the sunlit parts of shrub (1), with *Cream* pencil applied over it. *Pink* pencil was used to make the flowers. A graded pencil wash was applied to the fence behind, allowing the shrub to stand out by contrast.

The sunlit leaves on shrub (2) were washed with *Olive Green* pencil and again lightened with *Cream* pencil. *Indigo Blue* pencil was applied to the shaded parts. *French Grey 20%* pencil was used to draw the branching beneath.

Shrub (3) was colored with a *Jasmine* pencil on its lightest foliage, then lightened with *Cream* pencil. *White* pencil was used for the blossoms. A Pilot Razor Point was used to add vertical strokes to texture the shrub shadows on the grass.

3 **Stipple for texture.** A Pilot Razor Point was used to stipple the shrubs for additional texture.

Fig. 4-115

Evergreen Shrubs (4-116, 4-117)

Juniper and pine shrubs, two typical evergreen shrub types, are illustrated in the following steps.

1 **Apply marker base.** *Slate Green (Teal Blue)* marker was applied to the junipers with the point of the marker tip flicked in a series of fanlike

patterns, as shown in figure 4-116. The pines on the right were drawn with the broad side of the tip of an *Olive (Olive Green)* marker. Again, the tip was flicked upward from the center of the shrub.

2 **Add highlights, texture, and shading.** In figure 4-117, the junipers to the side and rear of the fountain are shown in their summer foliage color. *Cream* pencil with *White* pencil over it was applied to the sunlit sides of each shrub, with the pencil flicked upward to maintain the spiky habit of the

Fig. 4-116

foliage masses. On the shaded sides *Terra Cotta* pencil was added to dull the somewhat intense marker color (and to repeat the brick color). Pilot Razor Point was used to create dark areas in each shrub, again flicked upward with the stroke, and to stipple the shrubs for additional texture. The junipers in front of the fountain at the bottom middle of the drawing are shown in their winter foliage color, similar to that of an andorra juniper *(Juniperus horizontalis plumosa)*. They were drawn by washing each shrub

with *Terra Cotta* and *Greyed Lavender* pencils, with *White* pencil flicked upward on the sunlit sides. Pilot Razor Point was used to create the darkest texture and for stippling. The pine shrubs on the right are similar to the mugo pine *(Pinus mugo mughis)*. The sunlit needles were highlighted by flicking *Jasmine* and *White* pencils outward from the curved vertical branches (drawn with Pilot Razor Point), and the dark, shaded needles were drawn with Pilot Razor Point, using the same stroke.

Fig. 4-117

WATER

Still Water, Foreground (4-118 through 4-121)

This illustration was drawn on brownline diazo paper with a toned background.

1   **Apply color to the water last.** Only the foreground vegetation is excluded, because it must be drawn over the completed water (4-118).

Fig. 4-118

2 **Draw in base color for water; outline reflections.** In figure 4-119, *Olive (Olive Green)* marker was used to apply the marker base to the water, stroking horizontally. A medium-value marker color should be used for the marker base so that both dark and light reflections will show, although the hue of the marker color may range from a blue, green, or brown to a gray. *White* pencil was used to draw the outlines of the reflections. After they were initially drawn with straight lines to ensure accuracy, they were then altered to indicate the slight movement of the water.

Fig. 4-119

3 **Draw reflections with color pencil.** Figure 4-120 shows the reflections being drawn with the same color pencils that were used to draw the objects themselves. Use light to medium hand pressure on the pencils; the colors of the reflections should have a slightly lower value and weaker chroma than those of the objects themselves. This happens automatically, because they are drawn over the *Olive (Olive Green)* marker base color. The reflections were flavored with an *Olive Green* pencil to add the effect of the greenish water.

Fig. 4-120

4 **Add sky reflection.** *White* pencil was used to apply the reflected sky color to the water in figure 4-121. It was applied as a slightly wavy line. Note that the reflection becomes brighter toward the horizon, as the angle of the view becomes more oblique. *Greyed Lavender* and *Blue Slate* pencils were used to flavor the reflected sky color.

Fig. 4-121

Still Water, Middle Ground (4-122, 4-123, 4-124)

1   **Apply color to the water's surroundings first.** Figure 4-122 shows the surroundings completely colored.

2   **Draw reflected elements in the water.** The elements touching the water's surface are drawn (in reverse) in the water first (4-123). Note that their reflected image is slightly darker than the elements themselves. In this illustration, the reflections of the stone curb and the stepping stones were drawn with *French Grey 20%, Cool Grey #2 (Cool Grey 20%),* and *Buff (Brick Beige)* markers. The water grasses will be drawn last, as they will be drawn with color pencil; the lilies have no reflection because they lie flat on the water's surface.

    The plant materials beyond the water are drawn in next, using a *Dark Olive (French Grey 80%)* marker. The determination of which elements will reflect in the water is established by reversing the image at the point where its base is intersected by an imaginary extension of the plane of the water. For example, the small leaf mass interrupting the triple tree trunks in the center of the illustration is shown reflected in the water. This was established by trial and error, using a pair of dividers with one end located at the approximate intersection of the base of the trunks and the plane of the water while the other end touched the leaf mass. The end of the dividers touching the leaf mass was swung around to see whether it reached the water, while the other end was held stationary. Because it did reach the water, the reverse shape of the leaf mass was drawn in the water with the aforementioned marker. With the use of this quick technique, reflections can easily be established.

3   **Add final touches.** In figure 4-124, *Cool Grey #2 (Cool Grey 20%)* marker was applied to the water, darkening the curb reflection and the formerly white areas. *Cool Grey #3 (Cool Grey 30%)* was used to make the curb reflection adequately dark as compared with the water.

    Cloud Blue pencil was used to shift the color of the sky reflection. *Black, Limepeel,* and *Yellow Chartreuse* pencils were used to create the reflections of the water grasses. *Cool Grey 10%* pencil was added to make the ripples around the grasses.

Fig. 4-122

Fig. 4-123

Fig. 4-124

Moving Water (4-125 through 4-128)

Moving water is most easily drawn on a toned paper, whether diazo, trace, or Canson paper. This is because the water can be drawn as added shapes with light-value pencils. You will find the use of photographs of moving water most helpful as references.

This illustration was drawn on brownline diazo paper with a toned background.

1 **Draw surroundings first.** In figure 4-125, space was left for both the water jet and the waterfall.

Fig. 4-125

2 **Draw water jet and waterfall.** *White* pencil was used to draw the water forms (4-126), and *Warm Grey 30%* pencil was added to the shaded sides of the water forms. *Blue Slate* pencil (one of the pencils used to draw the sky) was then used to flavor the water forms, indicating reflected sky.

Fig. 4-126

3 **Draw pool surface and splashing water.** *Slate Green* marker was used as a base for the water color in the pool, drawn in carefully around the falling "strings" of water. *Copenhagen Blue* and *Peacock Green* pencils, utilized in the sky, stone, and plant materials as well, were used to flavor the marker color.

White pencil was used to create the effect of the splashing water, with the pencil flicked in short, upward strokes (4-127). *Blue Slate* pencil was then used to flavor the splashing water.

Reflections were added to the less disturbed parts of the water's surface with *Light Peach* and *Dark Umber* pencils. *White* pencil was again used to add ripples to the less disturbed portions of the water's surface.

Fig. 4-127

4   **Add highlights.** Figure 4-128 shows the finished water. Straight lines of white gouache were applied to the straight-moving water forms, and wavy lines were added to the less disturbed areas of the pool. Dots of white gouache were stippled into the areas of the more disturbed water, such as the crown of the water jet and the splashes in the pool.

Fig. 4-128

Rocks (4-129, 4-130, 4-131)

1 **Draw rocks' surroundings.** Rocks usually lie nested in other materials, whether soil, plant materials, or other rocks (4-129), so their bases usually appear flat and/or interrupted by these materials.

Fig. 4-129

2 **Apply base color.** In figure 4-130, these sandstone rock colors were made from a mixture of *Sunset Pink (Deco Pink)* and *Buff (Brick Beige)* markers. Of course, rocks can be a wide variety of colors, so the base colors of the rocks you illustrate should reflect the geologic region of your project.

Fig. 4-130

3 **Add shading, fissures, clefts, and texture.** Figure 4-131 shows the finished rocks. Swipes of *Kraft Brown (Light Tan)* and *French Grey 40%* markers were quickly applied, using the broad edge of the tip, to add shading, clefts, and fissures. A *French Grey 70%* marker was used for the darkest parts of the shading.

A blend of *Willow Green (Lime Green)* and *French Grey 20%* markers was used to dot in lichens on the foreground rocks. A light wash of *Burnt Ochre* pencil on the sunlit faces of the rocks and *French Grey 70%* pencil on the shaded sides give the rocks texture. Stippling was added in the foreground with a Pilot Razor Point.

Fig. 4-131

Landscape Plan Views (4-132 through 4-135)

A plan is an intellectual construct, presenting a view of a place rarely, if ever, seen by most users. It is a tool for communicating conceptual information about that place: information about use areas, their shapes and sizes, and their relationships to each other and to the larger landscape. It can illustrate ideas about circulation, about the relationship between structures and the landscape, and about what materials—both plant and architectural—have a relationship to the ground plane. It can even delineate the distribution of lighting.

Although a plan is not a "real" view of a place, it can still provide some information about its feel and character through the use of color, shade and shadow, pattern and texture. These additional layers of information can expand the plan of an idea from a purely intellectual construct to include some of its experiential qualities as well.

Color not only adds legibility to the functional distinctions of a plan, but can also be used to illustrate the types, patterns, and textures of paving materials, ground covers, shrubs, trees, and vehicles. The addition of shade and shadow to these elements of a plan brings the suggestion of the third dimension. The plan becomes a tool to communicate information *and* experience.

Perhaps most important, however, is that by making the plan more legible through the use of color, pattern, texture, shade, and shadow, the designer invites a wider understanding and participation in the design of the place by fellow designers and nondesigners as well.

There is no one correct approach to color for plans. Almost any combination of colors can be used, provided adequate differentiation between elements and materials can happen when required by the designer. The scheme illustrated here tends toward the medium-to-high-value colors so the lines remain easily visible. Note, too, that through the use of fewer colors in a variety of combinations, the resultant color scheme tends to hold together.

1 **Apply marker base.** In figure 4-132, *Willow Green (Lime Green)* and *Naples Yellow (Eggshell)* markers were applied to the grass areas, and *Olive (Olive Green)* marker was added to the ground cover next to the building. Note that a dark color like olive can be applied to areas where there is no need to see graphic information beneath it.

The marker colors for the wide variety of paving materials were applied next (4-133). The marker base for an area of existing brick paving, located in the lower half of the drawing, was applied with *Redwood (Sienna Brown)* marker. *French Grey 10%* marker was used to represent the existing concrete paving at the upper right and left sides. A blend of *Sunset Pink (Deco Pink)* and *Naples Yellow (Eggshell)* markers was used for the native sandstone transitional pavers and as a base material around the center fountain and the monuments. The walkways in the central part of the project were colored with a *Buff (Brick Beige)* marker, representing a proposed colored concrete.

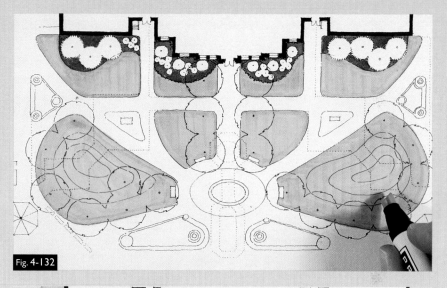

Fig. 4-132

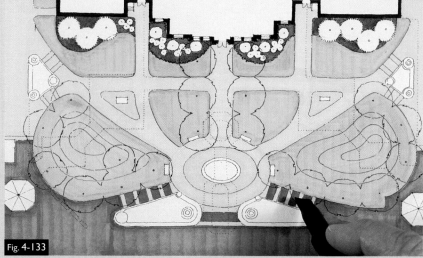

Fig. 4-133

If you are illustrating a plan with a uniform paving material, its color can remain the color of the paper to save time.

In figure 4-134, color was applied to the remaining elements. A combination of *Willow Green (Lime Green)* and *Pale Indigo (Cloud Blue)* markers was applied to the conifer trees on the upper left and upper right; *Pale Indigo (Cloud Blue)* and *Sunset Pink (Deco Pink)* markers were combined on the smallest shrubs, and *Sand (Sand)* and *Flesh (Salmon Pink)* markers were used together for the larger shrubs.

The bluish flowers were made by mixing Derwent *Blue Violet Lake #27* and *Blue Slate* pencils; *Poppy Red* and *Spanish Orange* pencils were used for the remaining flowers.

The trees were colored with *Yellow Green (Limepeel)* marker. Note that transparency is maintained. The base color of the water in the center fountain was made with a combination of *Willow Green (Lime Green)* and *Pale Indigo (Cloud Blue)* markers.

2 **Mute color, add shadows, details, and notes.** You will often find that as a composition of color, your plan must be adjusted once the marker base colors are in place. In figure 4-134, the brick appears too dark and too strong in chroma. Likewise, the trees are also too strong in chroma.

In figure 4-135, greater agreement is established between the values and chromas of the colors. The sunlit brick was muted with a *French Grey 20%* pencil. This weakened the chroma of the base marker color, lightened its value, and created a texture. The shadow on the brick was applied with a *Burnt Umber (Dark Umber)* marker, then flavored with a Derwent *Blue Violet Lake #27* pencil.

The shadows elsewhere on the drawing were first applied with *Pale Indigo (Cloud Blue)* marker, then modified with a variety of color pencils, depending on which surface they fell.

The colored concrete walkway was washed lightly with *Peach* pencil, and the sandstone surfaces with *Peach* and *Burnt Ochre* pencils.

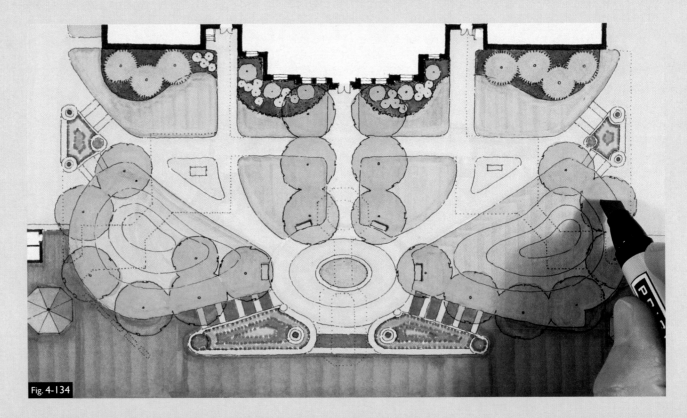

Fig. 4-134

The marker shadows on the colored concrete walks were washed lightly with *Burnt Ochre* pencil, so that the marker still showed through.

The sunlit sides of the large trees were washed with *Light Peach* pencil to both mute and lighten the color of the marker base; the shaded sides were washed with *Olive Green* pencil. The trees were then entirely washed with *Burnt Ochre* pencil.

The grass was washed with *Jasmine* pencil, slightly more heavily where the sides of the berms face the sun. The shaded sides of the berms, as well as the shadows on the grass, were washed with *Olive Green* pencil.

The remaining surfaces and elements, other than the grass, were also washed lightly with *Jasmine* pencil to quickly tie the colors of the plan together and effect a sense of warm light.

The water in the center fountain was made with *Deco Aqua* and *White* pencil in the sunlight, and its shadow was made with Derwent *Blue Violet Lake #27* pencil. The highlights were applied with white gouache.

The notes were added last. Those in capitals were made with a Pilot Razor Point; those in script were written with a Micron 005 pen.

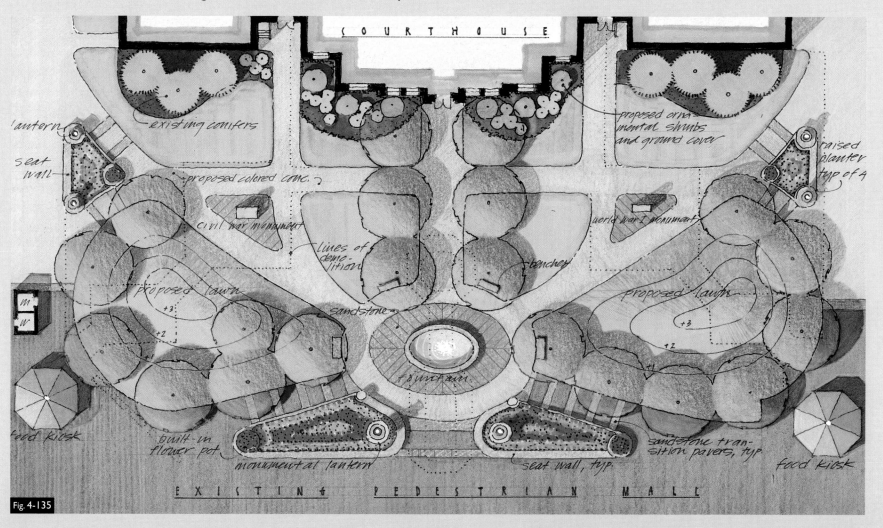

Fig. 4-135

Wall Plane Materials and Windows

WOOD

Wood wall surfaces are usually finished with paint or stain. Paint finishes, of course, are available in any color. Stains also come in a variety of colors and types and usually, but not always, allow at least some of the natural wood grain to show through. Some stains can make wood appear "weathered" by turning it a silver gray.

The coloration techniques shown for a particular material need not be reserved for that material. For example, the color approach shown here for vertical wood siding can be used for, say, wood shingles to give them a more weathered appearance.

Wood Shingles (4-136, 4-137)

The shingles illustrated here are intended to appear with a semiweathered stain, where a warm gray overtone mutes the new wood. The shingle texture should be subtle so that it does not overwhelm the building details.

1 **Apply marker base.** In figure 4-136, *French Grey 30%* marker was used for the shaded and shadowed areas, followed by *Sand (Sand)* marker. *French Grey 10%* marker was applied to the sunlit surfaces, followed by *Buff (Brick Beige)* marker. The markers were stroked horizontally to apply the color.

2 **Add pencil details.** Figure 4-137 shows the finished shingles. *French Grey 70%* pencil was used to create the continuous horizontal shadows made by the butt ends of the shingles. This line is kept quite thin.

Peach and *French Grey 30%* pencils were used to quickly add the spots of color between the horizontal lines. A .5 mm pencil with a 2H lead was used to add the random vertical marks between the horizontal lines.

Fig. 4-136

Fig. 4-137

Vertical Wood Siding (4-138, 4-139)

The base color of this siding was created similarly to that of the shingles. However, different pencils were added in the final steps to give it a more weathered look.

1   **Apply marker base.** Figure 4-138 shows *French Grey 30%* and *Sand (Sand)* markers applied to the shaded areas as well as the shadows that diagonally cross the sunlit surface. The sunlit surface received an application of *French Grey 10%* marker, followed by *Buff (Brick Beige)* marker. These markers were applied with vertical strokes.

2   **Add pencil detail.** Because certain boards are slightly darker or lighter than others, streaks of *French Grey 50%, 30%,* and *10%* pencils were applied with a straightedge (4-139).

The entire surface, in both sunlight and shade, was washed lightly with *Celadon Green* pencil. The surfaces in shade, as well as the shadows, were lightly washed with Derwent *Blue Violet Lake #27* pencil.

A straightedge was used to add light vertical lines, drawn with a .5 mm pencil with a 2H lead. Note that these lines need not be added to every board. The same pencil was used to apply some stipple texture to the wood.

Fig. 4-138

Fig. 4-139

Board and Batten and Lap Siding, Painted (4-140, 4-141)

1 **Apply marker base.** Figure 4-140 shows *Sand (Sand)* marker applied to the sunlit surfaces of the board and batten building in the background. *Mocha (Light Umber)* marker was added to its shadow and shaded surfaces.

The sunlit surface of the foreground lap-sided building was colored with *Buff (Brick Beige)* marker, followed by *Light Ivy (Putty + Cream)* marker. *Kraft Brown (Light Tan)* marker, followed by *Willow Green (Lime Green)* marker, was used for the shadow.

Note that the light "help lines" for the battens and lap siding are used to guide the marker strokes and subsequent detailing.

2 **Add pencil detailing.** In figure 4-141, a *Yellow Ochre* pencil wash was applied over the sunlit, shaded, and shadowed surfaces of the board and batten siding. A *Cream* pencil was used to "force" the shadow at the top of the sunlit surface. The painted battens were added with *Terra Cotta* pencil and a straightedge. The battens are sufficiently dark that no shadow is necessary. However, if the battens were painted the same color as the boards, a shadow line with a *Sepia* pencil, added to the right of each batten, would help make them visible.

The lap siding was washed with a *Celadon Green* pencil, and its shadow too was forced with a *Cream* pencil. *Yellow Ochre* pencil was then used to flavor the surface, providing a degree of color "agreement" with the board and batten color.

Horizontal shadow lines, beneath the heel of each piece of lap siding, were applied with a *Cool Grey 70%* pencil.

Derwent *Blue Violet Lake #27* pencil was used to flavor the shade and shadow on all surfaces.

Note that the telltale profile edge of the lap siding was added at the lower outside corner and where it abuts the window trim. This edge was added with a Micron 005 pen.

Fig. 4-140

Fig. 4-141

MASONRY

Stucco and Concrete Block (4-142, 4-143)

Stucco can be natural—made of portland cement, lime, and sand—or synthetic, often referred to as "EFIS" (Exterior Finish Insulating System). Natural stucco is available in many textures and colors, but the colors are typically muted and can appear mottled when dry. Synthetic stucco usually appears more uniform (no mottling) and is available in almost any color—some quite strong—as well as textures similar to those of natural stucco.

Concrete block is also available in a variety of colors—again, usually weak in chroma, depending on the colors of the aggregate and portland cement used to make it. It too comes in a wide choice of textures, such as the usual plain-face, split-face, and ground-face finishes.

In the masonry finishes illustrated here, the concrete block is a warm color with a plain-face finish. The foremost building forms behind are intended to be natural stucco, and the green-yellow and yellow-red forms are colors more likely achieved with synthetic stucco.

1 **Apply marker base.** Figure 4-142 shows *French Grey 10%* marker applied to the sunlit faces of the portal and *French Grey 50%* marker used for the shaded faces. The capitals of the columns and the staircase were colored with *Pale Sepia (Goldenrod)* marker.

Warm Grey 50% and *10%* markers were used on the shaded and sunlit faces, respectively, of the purplish building form. The green-yellow form was colored with *Dark Olive (French Grey 80%)* marker on the shaded surface and *Olive (Olive Green)* marker on the sunlit surface. On the most distant building form, *Redwood (Sienna Brown)* and *Pale Cherry (Mineral Orange)* markers were used to color its shaded and sunlit sides, respectively.

2 **Add modifying colors and details.** In figure 4-143, the sunlit surface of the foreground building form was rubbed with *Indian Red 347.9* stick pastel. Then both its sunlit and shaded surfaces were dabbed with an electric eraser to remove some of their color to give them a mottled appearance.

The sunlit surface was then spotted with the side of a *Yellow Ochre* pencil, and the same was done to the shaded side with a *French Grey 30%* pencil, increasing the mottled effect.

The remaining left-facing surfaces (in shade) in the illustration were washed lightly with Derwent *Blue Violet Lake #27* pencil, suggesting the reflection of north light. The right-facing, illuminated surfaces were washed with *Yellow Ochre* and *Jasmine* pencil, simulating the effect of low sun.

Horizontal mortar joints were added to the sunlit surfaces of the concrete block with a .5 mm pencil using a 2H lead. The mortar joints on the surfaces in shade were supplied with a *French Grey 10%* pencil. Note how the vertical mortar joints gradually disappear as the portal recedes into the distance.

Note how both the foreground concrete block and foreground stucco are stippled for additional texture. The sunlit surfaces are stippled with the .5 mm pencil mentioned earlier, and the shaded surfaces are stippled with both a *French Grey 10%* pencil and a Micron 005 pen.

Fig. 4-142

Fig. 4-143

Brick, Middle Range (4-144, 4-145)

1 **Apply marker base.** *Kraft Brown (Light Tan)* marker was applied to the entire brick surface in figure 4-144. *Burnt Umber (Dark Umber)* marker was used to draw the shadows and darken the shaded surfaces.

A *Light Peach* pencil wash was applied over the sunlit surface at medium hand pressure. Less pressure was used to apply a *Peach* pencil over the shadows and shaded surfaces.

2 **Add mortar joints.** In figure 4-145, a *French Grey 10%* pencil was applied with a straightedge to draw thin, evenly spaced lines toward the same vanishing point used to draw the building.

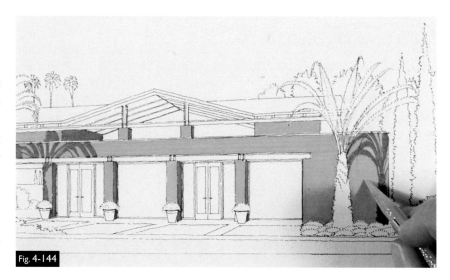

Fig. 4-144

Fig. 4-145

Stone, Uncoursed and Roughly Squared (4-146, 4-147, 4-148)

Stone is available in a wide variety of types and "earth" colors, ranging from grays and blues to yellows and reds. Your choices of types and colors will depend on the budget for and location of your project. The stone can be jointed in many different ways, from completely random to coursed and bonded. The stone shown here, like most stone finishes, is used as a facing over a substrate.

The "roughly squared" stone illustrated here, although not laid up in contiguous rows, is still arranged as approximately level.

1 **Apply marker base.** In this particular illustration (4-146), *Sand (Sand)* marker was applied as a base color for the stone in shade and shadow, and *Buff (Brick Beige)* marker was used for the base color in sunlight.

Note the horizontal help lines, added with pencil. Although the stone is rough, these help lines assist in keeping the stones in perspective when the marker colors are applied and the joints drawn in subsequent steps.

2 **Add stone coloration.** In figure 4-147, touches of *French Grey 20%* and *Light Ivy (Putty + Cream)* markers were used to add stone colors to the wall in the sunlit areas. *French Grey 50%* marker was used to add darker stone colors in the shade and shadow. Note how some of the marker strokes turn the corners in the same way as credible stone masonry.

Raw Sienna 234.9 stick pastel was rubbed randomly onto the sunlit parts of the stone, and *White* stick pastel was applied to the sunlit surface where it meets the shadow, "forcing" the shadow.

Smudges of Schwan Stabilo *#620* and *#600* pencil pastels were randomly applied to both sunlit and shaded surfaces. A light wash of Derwent *Blue Violet Lake #27* pencil was applied to those shaded surfaces that "see" the sky.

Fig. 4-146

2 Add joints. Figure 4-148 shows the finished illustration after the joints have been added. In the surfaces in shade and shadow closest to the viewer, *Black* pencil was used to make the joints, with light but varying hand pressure. This makes the joint lines slightly lighter in some places and darker in others, quickly simulating joints of varying widths. On the sunlit surfaces, as well as the more distant stones in both sun and shadow, a .5 mm pencil with a 2H lead was used the same way for the same purpose.

The stone pattern can be invented as it is drawn. The pencil is rarely lifted from the page. Note, too, that every single stone need not be drawn. Rather, only enough must be drawn to ensure the impression of the stone units.

Some stippling was added to the foreground stones with a Pilot Razor Point.

Fig. 4-148

Fig. 4-147

Stone, Dimensioned in a Running Bond (4-149, 4-150)

1 **Apply marker base.** The use of a series of gray markers *(Warm, Cool, French)* can create the impression of stone quite easily, as many kinds of stone have subtle (very weak-chroma) color and the values can be easily controlled.

In figure 4-149, *French Grey 10%* marker was applied to the sunlit surfaces, and *French Grey 50%* marker was used on the surfaces in shade and shadow. The surfaces angled 45° toward the sun were left white, and those angled away from the sun were colored with a *French Grey 20%* marker.

The header stones and base course are intended to be slightly darker in value than the rest of the stone. Thus, the marker sequence applied to them was likewise slightly darker. *French Grey 20%* was used on the sunlit surfaces, and *French Grey 10%* marker was applied to those surfaces angled toward the sun. *French Grey 30%* marker was used on the surfaces angled away from the sun.

Additional strokes with the broad edge of the *French Grey 10%* marker were applied to the sunlit surfaces to create the impression of stone units slightly darker than the others.

2 **Add color and detail.** The subtle coloration of the stone will depend on the kind of stone you intend to imitate. In figure 4-150, *Indian Red 347.9* stick pastel was applied randomly and rubbed lightly by finger over the marker base. Schwan Stabilo *#692* and *#620* pencil pastels were also applied the same way, then lightly wiped with a chamois.

The surfaces in shade and shadow were flavored with a Derwent *Blue Violet Lake #27* pencil.

The joints were added by lightly applying a .5 mm pencil, using a 2H lead, with a straightedge. The joints in shadow were applied with a *French Grey 10%* pencil.

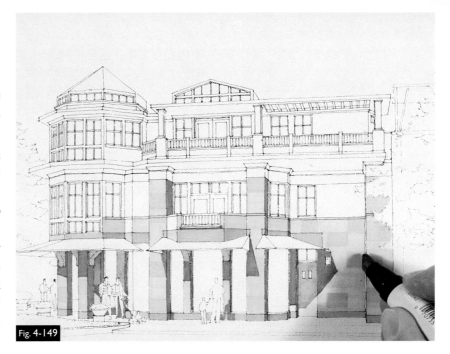
Fig. 4-149

Fig. 4-150

Precast Concrete (4-151, 4-152)

Precast concrete is an architectural finish material that can be cast in virtually any shape with a wide variety of textures and can be colored with a variety of concrete colorants. It can be cast in sizes up to certain economical maximums, so the precast concrete finish of a project is characterized by its precise shapes and the joints between them.

The precast concrete illustrated here has two colors and two textures.

1 **Apply marker base.** *Buff (Brick Beige)* and *French Grey 20%* markers were applied in alternating stripes on the piers and retaining walls of the bridge (4-151); *Buff (Brick Beige)* marker alone was used for the precast of the arch. *French Grey 30%* marker was used for the shade and shadow on the gray color, and *Sand (Sand)* marker was used to make the shade and shadow on the buff color.

Fig. 4-152

Fig. 4-151

2 **Add detail and finishing touches.** In figure 4-152, a Schwan Stabilo *#680* pastel pencil was used to enhance the color of the *French Grey* stripes. The close-range portion of this darker precast concrete was also stippled with the fine-point end of a *Light Tan* Prismacolor marker to impart a subtle texture effect. The lighter color was given a much finer stipple texture with a .5 mm pencil using a 2H lead.

The surfaces of the darker color that are in shade and shadow were lightly washed with a *Burnt Ochre* pencil. The colors of the corresponding surfaces on the lighter precast concrete were enhanced with flavorings of *Yellow Ochre* and *Peach* pencils. The recessed joints between the panels of the foreground precast concrete were first darkened with a *Burnt Ochre* pencil, then edged with a .5 mm pencil using a 2H lead.

METAL

Corrugated Metal Siding (4-153, 4-154)

Corrugated metal siding is seen most often with its typical galvanized finish. As such, it is semireflective and tends to display faint but noticeable diffuse reflections of the colors that surround it. It can also display white highlights which, close up, have diffuse edges.

Any combination of gray markers can be used to successfully illustrate galvanized metal. The combination you select will depend on your intentions for the overall scheme of colors you have for your design illustration.

1 **Apply marker base.** In figure 4-153, *Cool Grey #5 (Cool Grey 50%)* marker was used for the shadows on the foreground building, and *Cool Grey #3 (Cool Grey 30%)* marker was applied for the shadow on the background building.

The foreground building's sunlit surface grades horizontally from *Warm Grey #3 (Warm Grey 30%)* marker at the doors to *Warm Grey #2 (Warm Grey 20%)* through *Warm Grey #1 (Warm Grey 10%)* markers behind the red chair. The sunlit wall on the background building was colored with *Cool Grey #1 (Cool Grey 10%)* marker.

Color was added to the chairs to show the reflectivity of the siding. An easy way to introduce reflected color to the siding is by rubbing it lightly with pastel colors that are related to colors close by. In this example, part of the background siding was rubbed with Schwan Stabilo *#692* pencil pastel (the color reflected is not shown). The wall behind the red and blue chairs was rubbed with *#310* and *#430* pencil pastels respectively.

2 **Add detail.** *White* pencil and a straightedge were used to apply the horizontal highlights on the foreground building (4-154).

In the shadows on both buildings, *Cool Grey 70%* pencil was applied in the same fashion to add shading in the recesses of the corrugations. *Cool Grey 50%* pencil was applied in the same way to add texture to sunlit surface of the background building.

The shadows on both surfaces were flavored with *Copenhagen Blue* pencil.

Fig. 4-153

Fig. 4-154

Architectural Metal Panels (4-155, 4-156)

Architectural metal panels are available in virtually any color and many types of finish, ranging from gloss to matte and smooth to textured. They are usually custom fabricated in modular form for a project and therefore have joints of varying widths. These joints can appear very light to very dark, depending on the angle of light.

A typical medium-finish panel, illustrated here, often displays gradations of light and color as well as diffuse highlights.

1 **Apply marker base.** In figure 4-155, *Pale Cherry (Mineral Orange)* marker was applied to the entire column, and *Kraft Brown (Light Tan)* marker was used for its shadow. The shadow was pronounced near its top with a *Redwood (Sienna Brown)* marker. The chroma of the sunlit portion of the column was reduced slightly with a *French Grey 10%* marker.

Cool Grey #5 (Cool Grey 50%) marker was applied as a shadow on the building panels, and a gradation of *Cool Grey #1* and *#2 (Cool Grey 10%* and *20%)* markers was applied from the bottom upward toward the shadow. The entire wall was then washed with a *Celadon Green* Prismacolor marker.

2 **Add pastel and detail.** Figure 4-156 shows that pastel was applied to modify the panel colors. Pastel was used because it appears smooth and does not pick up the grain of the paper.

White stick pastel was added to the upper portion of the sunlit face of the column, as well as the wall, to force the shadow. Schwan Stabilo *#430* pencil pastel was applied to the shadow on the wall.

Reflections and highlights were applied with color pencil. A *White* pencil was used to add diffuse highlights to both the front and back of the column, with the stronger highlight on the front. Note that these highlights were drawn over the joints so that they remain smooth and consistent. Highlights were also applied to the edges of the panels with a straightedge, again using a *White* pencil. Diffuse reflections from the ceiling and guardrail were added by light application of *White* and *Burnt Ochre* pencils to the wall panels.

A final touch of *Cool Grey 70%* pencil was added to darken the joints and to interrupt the highlights and reflections drawn in the previous steps.

Fig. 4-155

Fig. 4-156

THE TRANSFORM COMMAND

Photoshop's *Transform* command (Edit > Free Transform) is an extremely useful tool for color drawing. It allows you to conform an image to just about any planar shape. You can scale, rotate, skew, distort, or change the perspective of that image (which, when selected, copied, and pasted becomes its own layer), so you can introduce elements to a scanned drawing and match them to the perspective of that drawing. In figures 4-157 through 4-163, one of a number of color studies for the renovation of a curtain wall system is "tried on" the perspective view of the building so that it may be evaluated along with a proposed canopy.

The *Transform* command can also be used to flip an image, either horizontally, vertically, or both. If you are not familiar with the various Transform commands, experiment with each of them to familiarize yourself with their capabilities and limitations. The *Transform* command works better with planar images than with images that have deep, three-dimensional characteristics.

When you access the *Transform* command (Edit > Transform), another drop-down menu displays all the choices available for the command (4-160). However, the keyboard shortcuts for this tool are worth learning, as you will frequently want to quickly shift from one to another. You can enable *Free Transform,* which allows you faster access to all the basic Transform commands, by pressing Command-T (on a Mac) or Control-T (in Windows). You will see the transform frame appear around your layer, enabling the *Scale* command. However, by moving your cursor *inside* the transform frame, holding down the Control key and either clicking the mouse (Mac) or right-clicking the mouse (Windows), the drop-down menu for all the Transform commands appears. These shortcuts allow you to switch rapidly from one command to another.

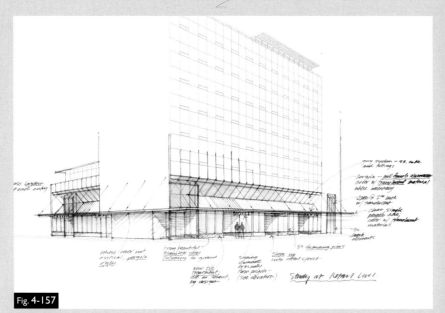

Fig. 4-157

Fig. 4-157 A sketch study for a proposed glass canopy, drawn over a computer-generated perspective view.

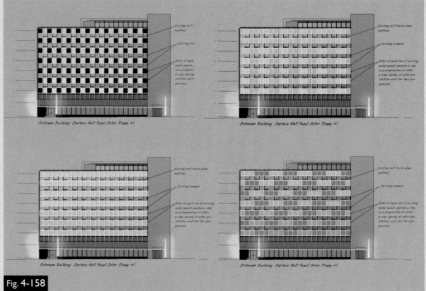

Fig. 4-158

Fig. 4-158 A few of a number of color studies created for the renovation of the building's façades. These studies were quickly generated in Photoshop over a computer-generated line drawing.

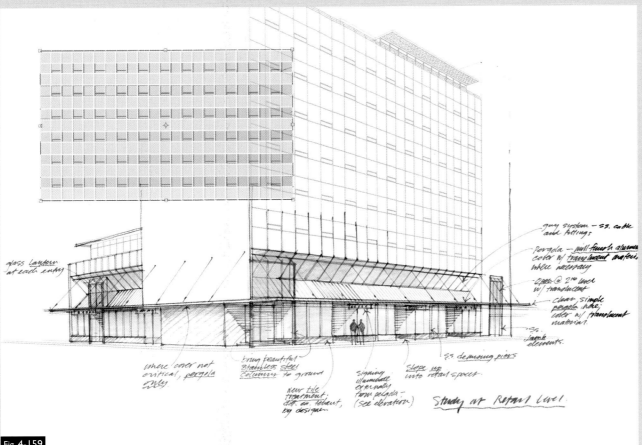

Fig. 4-159

Fig. 4-160

Fig. 4-159 In order to evaluate what one of the color studies might look like when combined with the proposed canopy, it was selected, copied, and pasted into the scanned perspective study using Photoshop. The opacity of this layer was then decreased to about 50% using the *Opacity* slider, so the layer became transparent enough to see through. The *Free Transform* command was then applied to this layer.

Fig. 4-160 The layer was then moved so its lower left coincided with the lower left of the curtain wall in the perspective view. The right side of the layer was scaled so that it aligned with the right side of the perspective view of the curtain wall.

The cursor was then moved within the transform frame, the Control key was pressed, and the mouse was clicked (Mac) or right-clicked (Windows). This brought up all the Transform commands, as shown, and the transform frame was changed from the *Scale* to the *Skew* command.

Fig. 4-161 Using the *Skew* command, the corners of the color study layer were dragged to the corners of the perspective view of the curtain wall.

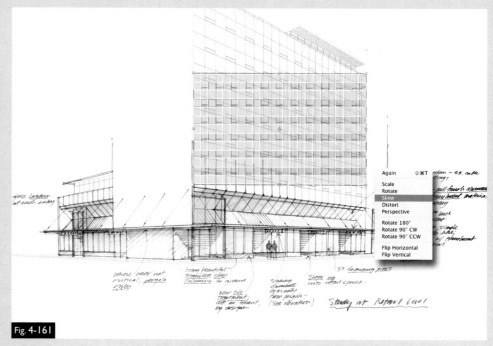

Fig. 4-161

Fig. 4-162 The Return key was pressed, completing the transformation. The *Opacity* slider was restored to 100%.

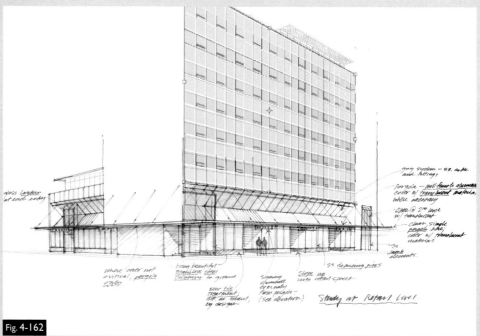

Fig. 4-162

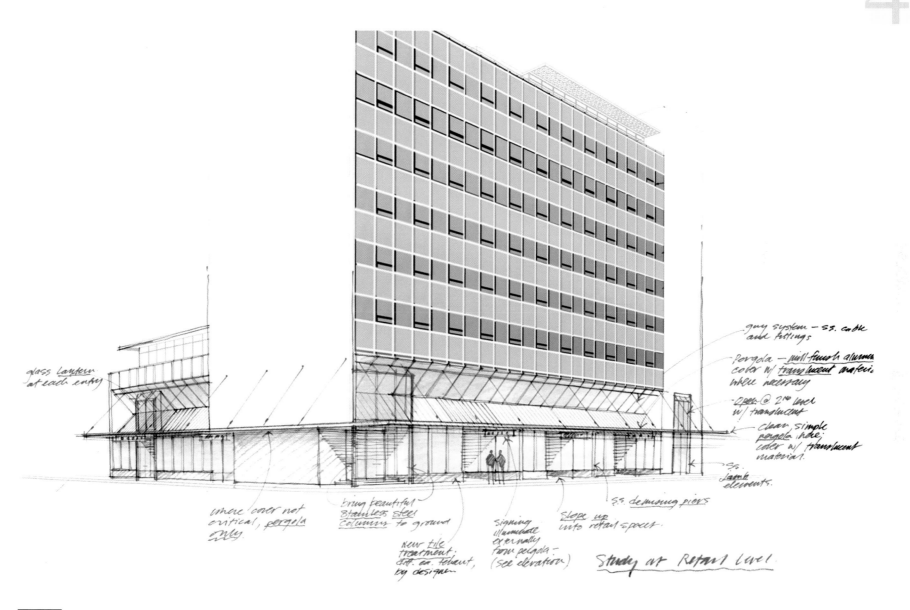

glass lantern
at each entry

guy system — s.s. cable
and fittings

pergola — mill finish alumen
color w/ translucent materi.
where necessary

open @ 2nd level
w/ translucent

clean, simple
pergola here;
color w/ translucent
material.

s.s.
jamb
elements.

where cover not
critical, pergola
only.

bring beautiful
stainless steel
columns to ground

s.s. demising piers

slope up
into retail space.

New tile
treatment;
diff. ea. tenant,
by designer

signing
illuminated
externally
from pergola —
(see elevation)

Study at Retail Level

Fig. 4-163

WINDOWS

Windows have been called the "eyes" of a building and play an important role in its animation.

1 **Add color to the window's surroundings first.** In figure 4-164, color was added to everything except the window surface and the objects seen through it. The trees will be completed, along with the shrubs, after the reflections are drawn, inasmuch as these plant materials will interrupt the view of the reflections.

Fig. 4-164

2 **Apply marker to everything seen through the window.** Marker *only* is applied at this stage (4-165), with the use of colors appropriate to the objects. *Cool Grey #9 (Cool Grey 90%)* was used to darken the interior beyond.

Fig. 4-165

3 **Add reflections with color pencil.** Figure 4-166 shows that *White* pencil was used to lightly lay out the reflections, drawn directly over the objects seen through the window. Color pencil was used to add color to the reflections, the designer making sure that the reflections were slightly darker and slightly weaker in chroma than the colors of the reflected objects themselves. Care was taken to apply these colors *lightly* and smoothly, so that the objects *in* the window could still be seen after the reflection was completed.

To avoid confusion, the reflections of objects closest to the window surface were drawn first, then the objects progressively farther away from the window were drawn. Thus, the undersides of the awnings were drawn first, then the stone forming the left window jamb, the figures, the green car on the left, the streetlight, the brown car on the right, and so forth.

Fig. 4-166

4 **Add reflected background if necessary.** Once the reflections of the objects seen in the picture in front of the window were drawn, a simple background reflection was added, as shown in figure 4-167. Because the environment appears to be urban, building reflections were added with *Terra Cotta, Burnt Ochre,* and *Dark Umber* pencils. *White* pencil was applied over *Light Cerulean Blue* pencil to create the reflection of the sky.

5 **Add trees and shrubs, their reflections, and finishing touches.** The tree reflections were drawn over the other reflections, using a *Cool Grey 70%* pencil with touches of *White* pencil on the sunlit edges. The shrub reflections were added, followed by the trees and shrubs themselves. The items in the windows, such as the manikins, were reoutlined with a Pilot Razor Point so that they would appear more solid than the reflections.

Fig. 4-167

Daytime Windows, Middle Ground (4-168, 4-169, 4-170)

Rather than simply making the openings black, a designer can make daytime windows more lifelike and animated. They typically have three components: street-level window detail (those elements seen *through* the windows), the upper-level reflection mass, and the reflection of the sky.

1 **Draw those elements seen through street-level windows; add upper-level reflection mass.** The street-level elements in figure 4-168 are manikins in the window of a retail store. Directly behind the manikins, the low wall and other subordinate details are colored with markers of medium value. In this case, a *Cool Grey #6 (Cool Grey 60%)* marker was used.

The far background at the first level, as well as the upper-level reflection mass, should be colored with a marker that is quite dark in value—a low-value gray to black. In this example, a *Cool Grey #9 (Cool Grey 90%)* marker was used. The term "reflection mass" indicates that the buildings and trees reflected into the (usually tinted) upper-level glass are so dark that they appear as a single mass whose only clear distinctions are the spaces between them and the silhouette of their top edge.

Note that this dark marker is applied directly over the window muntins. This is faster than attempting to avoid each muntin with the marker, and the muntins can be redrawn with pencil in a later step.

2 **Add pencil detail.** In figure 4-169, the manikins have been toned down with a *Cool Grey #3 (Cool Grey 30%)* marker. They were then lightly washed, just enough to give them some hue, with pencil. In this case *Celadon Green, Jasmine,* and *Blush Pink* pencils were used. The sky reflection was lightly washed with *Light Cerulean Blue* pencil.

Fig. 4-168

Fig. 4-169

3 **Add details and muntins.** The fluorescent ceiling lights of most commercial buildings are visible from the outside even during the day. In figure 4-170, these lines of lights are drawn with a *White* pencil and a straightedge aimed toward a vanishing point. It usually does not matter toward which vanishing point, in a typical two-point perspective, the rows of lights are aligned. The display lights in the retail windows on the first level are dotted in with white gouache.

The muntins and frames of the windows should be trimmed to consistently "read" against the glass and its reflections. They can be darker or lighter than the glass and its reflections, or they can be both, so that they read against all combinations of value. In figure 4-170, a *White* pencil was first applied to the frames and muntins of the windows with a straightedge. Then, where necessary, the shaded sides of those frames and muntins were edged with a *French Grey 90%* pencil in the same way.

Fig. 4-170

Dusk Windows (4-171 through 4-175)

Windows at dusk are very easy to illustrate. The advantage of showing a building at dusk is that although the exterior of the building (with its materials and finishes) is still visible, additional information about the interior of the building—its uses, spaces and the character of its lighting—can also be revealed.

Dusk windows are most easily illustrated on white roll tracing paper, using the retrocolor technique (see figures 7-51 through 7-54).

1 **Apply color to those elements seen through the street-level windows.** Your entire building will have more appeal if the street-level windows display goods and appropriate activity instead of remaining blank. Draw those elements—whether retail, restaurant, office, or other types—one might see through such windows. In this example, pencil was used so as to keep the outlines of the elements from being too visually assertive. Note that they are drawn simply and detail is kept to a minimum.

The color is applied to the back of the drawing with a variety of color pencils. Figure 4-171 shows the drawing on white tracing paper with brown kraft paper placed behind it.

2 **Add window illumination.** Figure 4-172 shows the back side of the illustration after color pencil was applied to the windows. *Jasmine* pencil was applied first, with medium hand pressure, followed by *White* pencil at heavy hand pressure. These two pencils were applied quickly and loosely. Although some of the pencil spilled outside the lines, the mistakes are not noticeable, because when the illustration is turned right-side-up, the lines are not occluded by the pencil. This effect applies to the window muntins as well, also colored over on the back side but perfectly visible from the front of the drawing.

The figures standing in front of the window were darkened with *French Grey 90%* marker. Because the foreground elements were made to appear in silhouette, the windows appear brighter owing to the value contrast.

Note that glowing windows also throw light on soffits, column edges, sidewalks, and so on, not only helping to reveal further information about the building, but adding drama and interest to the illustration as well.

Fig. 4-171

Fig. 4-172

3 **Add final touches.** Figure 4-173 shows touches of white gouache added for lights and sparkle in the street-level windows. Color has also been added to the foreground figures which, although they remain in silhouette, gives them a touch more character.

Fig. 4-173

4 **Adjust after scanning.** Once the drawing is scanned (with the brown kraft paper still behind the drawing), the contrast can be enhanced in Photoshop (4-174), if necessary. A dusk scene can be turned into a night scene (4-175) simply by substituting a very dark blue paper (Crescent, Canson, or Pantone) before scanning—or the background color can be replaced in Photoshop (Image > Adjustments > Replace Color . . .).

Fig. 4-174

Fig. 4-175

Night Windows (4-176, 4-177, 4-178)

1 **Photocopy or plot line drawing on dark paper.** The line drawing was photocopied onto dark blue Canson paper. You can also plot your line drawing on a heavyweight bond paper with an ink-jet plotter, once you add a dark background in Photoshop. As you can see in figure 4-176, the background is quite dark, but the drawing's linework is still visible.

2 **Draw street-level window elements.** A line drawing of the elements in the street-level windows was made with a Micron 005 pen. In figure 4-176, the manikins are colored with pencil as brightly as possible. The lower part of the window display area is colored with *White* pencil to simulate the high illumination of the horizontal surfaces from the display lighting above.

The background ambient glow was added, as shown on the left, with a *Deco Orange* pencil, blending into the area colored with the *White* pencil in the lower part of the window.

Although the manikins are recognizable as such, note that the juxtapositions of colors and forms can make the overall effect somewhat abstract. Care was taken not to spend too much time making the window display unduly realistic or detailed, as its role in the illustration is secondary. Note, too, that as the street-level window images were colored, the silhouetted figures in front of the windows were carefully outlined by the colors and remain the tone of the paper.

3 **Add window illumination.** *Jasmine, Deco Orange,* and *White* pencils were used to fill in the upper window apertures with light. In figure 4-177, these pencils were used to create subtle shifts in color temperature, suggesting various locations of the sources of light. The fact that the entire interior of the building is also unevenly illuminated helps to create a more realistic lighting scenario.

In this step it was much easier to apply the color right over the window muntins. They were quickly drawn back in the subsequent step.

Fig. 4-176

Fig. 4-177

4 **Add details.** Figure 4-178 shows "spill light" added to the surrounding surfaces. The light on the soffits, sides of columns, and various edges was applied with a *Deco Orange* pencil. The light on the sidewalk was added with a *White* pencil.

The window frames, muntins, and balcony railings were redrawn with a *Black* pencil. Lights and highlights were dotted in with touches of white gouache.

Fig. 4-178

Daytime Windows, Large Buildings (4-179, 4-180, 4-181)

The daytime windows in large buildings have many of the same components as those in smaller buildings. There are a reflection mass and a sky reflection. You can even see the ceiling-mounted fluorescent lights. Usually, however, the viewer is far enough away from the drawing so that details to street-level windows are unnecessary.

In many tall buildings, you will notice that the sky reflection often grades to a brighter value as the building goes higher. This is because, relative to the viewer's sight line, the angle of the building's surface relative to the sky reflection becomes progressively more oblique. In addition, the values of the reflections in the windows can become much darker or lighter as the building surfaces change direction, such as in turning a corner. As the orientation of a surface changes, what that surface is reflecting suddenly changes as well. The reflections in the windows of a building often have a *darker average value on its sunlit faces and appear to have a lighter average value on the faces in shade.*

Fig. 4-179

Fig. 4-180

1 **Estimate and draw size and shape of reflection masses.** The reflections of objects (trees, other buildings) were quickly estimated and drawn on the faces of the buildings shown in figure 4-179. These rough, approximate reflections even included buildings not shown in the picture.

The reflection masses are typically drawn with a black marker or a very dark cool gray marker. Distant reflection masses, including those appearing where the building faces change direction, can be drawn in a slightly lighter gray. In this example they are drawn with a *Cool Grey #8 (Cool Grey 80%)* marker.

2 **Add marker base for sky reflection.** In figure 4-180, the sky reflections were filled in with a variety of cool gray markers. In the case of the low building with the parabolic roof, as well as the large building just behind it, the remaining windows facing to the right were filled in with *Cool Grey #7 (Cool Grey 70%)* marker.

The bays and windows facing other directions were filled in with *Cool Grey #5, #3,* and *#2 (Cool Grey 50%, 30%,* and *20%)* markers. Note that the see-through corners were made slightly lighter than the gray on the adjacent ceilings.

3 **Apply color washes, clouds, mullions, and lights.** Figure 4-181 shows that the sky reflections *only* were washed with *Blue Slate* pencil. Progressively more *White* pencil was added over the *Blue Slate* pencil as the buildings increase in height. A mixture of *Celadon Green* and *Deco Aqua* pencils were applied in a light wash over the windows at the see-through corners.

Some streaks of *White* pencil were added for clouds in the upper windows of the building on the left.

Ceiling-mounted fluorescent lights were added, using a *White* pencil and a straightedge aimed toward the vanishing points. Note that these white dashes were applied over the darker reflection masses and the lighter sky reflections alike.

The window mullions were added last. *Black* pencil was used with a straightedge to apply the mullions to the lighter areas of the windows, and *White* pencil was applied over the darker areas.

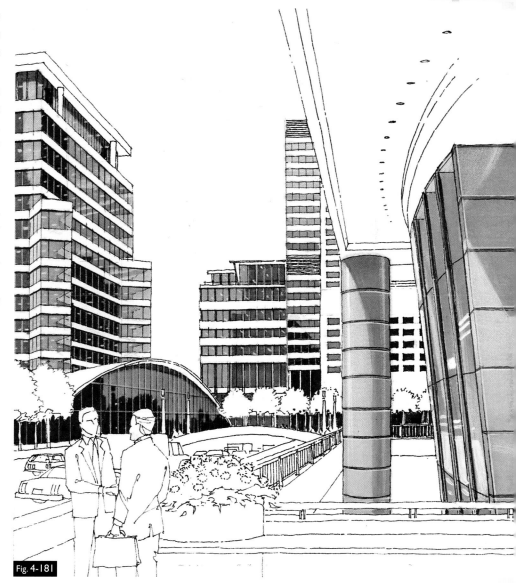

Fig. 4-181

Photographic Window Reflections (4-182 through 4-187)

Photoshop can also be used to demonstrate the reflective character of windows. These will not be true reflections, because the windows will not mirror what they "see." However, these kinds of reflections can impart a sufficient sense of building-front glass to a drawing, and they are appealing because they can be accomplished quickly and efficiently. When introducing photographic elements into drawings, make them sufficiently muted so they neither distract from the intended focus of the drawing nor detract from its hand-drawn character.

1 **Do windows last.** Everything in the drawing was illustrated except for the windows (4-182). During the last stages of creating the reflection, this helped to keep the reflection at an appropriate level of assertiveness. The mullion system was drawn to act as a guide in later steps. The drawing was then scanned and opened in Photoshop.

2 **Copy and paste windows.** A portion of the windows from an unrelated digital photograph (4-183) was copied and pasted into the scanned drawing (4-184). Almost any window image will do.

Fig. 4-182

Fig. 4-183

Fig. 4-184

3 **Cover window area with photo image.** In the *Layers Palette,* the new photo layer was selected and its opacity was reduced to about 50%. This allowed the photo image to be manipulated while the drawing behind it remained visible.

The *Transform* command was used to stretch the photo image over the window area of the drawing (4-185). The fact that the image became somewhat distorted did not matter in the final result. However, care was taken to keep the vertical elements in the photo image—pilasters, mullions, etc.—parallel with the mullions in the drawing.

4 **Apply transformation; trim photo image.** Once the photo image was positioned, the transformation was applied. The image was then trimmed to fit the window area using the *Polygonal Lasso Selection Tool.* The *Rectangular Marquee Selection Tool*, the *Lasso Selection Tool*, and the *Eraser Tool* were all used to delete photo imagery that covered those parts of the drawing in front of the windows (4-186).

Fig. 4-185

Fig. 4-186

5 **Add mullions, secondary reflections, and detail; adjust.** On a new layer, mullions were drawn with the *Line Tool* (4-187). The underlying mullions on the drawing were used as a guide. Another new layer gives a darker shadow edge to the mullions and the return at the window head. This adds a sense of dimension to the mullions and window system. Since the darker lines are on their own layer, they can be easily erased if necessary without disturbing the lighter gray mullion faces.

The *Dry Brush* filter was used to make the photo image appear more subtly like a drawing (Filter > Artistic > Dry Brush; Brush Size = 2, Brush Detail = 8, Texture = 1). Additionally, the *Brightness/Contrast* adjustment was used to darken the photo image and increase its contrast (Image > Adjustments > Brightness/Contrast).

"Secondary" reflections were added to the photo image reflection. This gives the reflection some association with its context. The red flowers were copied, pasted, and moved to the left. The same was done with the portion of the hedge that is perpendicular to the window plane. Once placed, the opacity of these elements was reduced to about 50%. The hedge reflection also conveniently obscures an inappropriate image of a distorted car, lower left.

Frequently, lights in buildings are of sufficient intensity—even in daytime—to be seen through glass and its reflections. Here, another layer was created and a simple hanging light was created (in Photoshop). It was duplicated repeatedly, distributed along the window, and reduced in size, using the *Transform* command. Once in place, the lights were merged into a single layer. When the opacity of the layer was reduced to about 80%, the lights appeared to be behind the glass.

Fig. 4-187

TREES

Trees help to shape, animate, and soften the wall planes of outdoor places. The architecture of tree forms is as critical to the successful creation of the character of these places as is the architecture of their built forms. Thus, the designer's attention to the size, proportion, and massing of trees in design illustrations is as important as that given to the building elements.

The rules of light, shade, and shadow apply to the development of tree forms every bit as much as they do to architectural forms. The canopies of trees in foliage have an illuminated side, a shaded side, and usually a bottom or underside that is also in shade. Their shadows can be seen on the ground, usually punctuated with oblong penetrations of sunlight.

The branches of bare trees, as well as those seen in leafy tree canopies, can contrast with their backgrounds in order to maintain legibility. If part of a background is dark, the branches can be made lighter; if the background is light, the branches can be darker—all on the same trees. Details can often help to make a tree sufficiently convincing. For example, a tree can easily be made to appear more "leafy," less heavy and opaque, by allowing more sky to be visible through its canopy. Likewise, bare trees often appear with the shadows of their branches on other branches and spiraling down their trunks.

Bare Deciduous Trees, Foreground (4-188, 4-189, 4-190)

In most illustrations a foreground tree is only partially visible. The tree, as well as its shadow, is usually used as a way to "frame" the middle-ground view.

1 **Draw trunk and main branches.** As figure 4-188 shows, only the trunk, main branches, and a light outline of the canopy edge were used to begin the drawing. The rest of the branching will be added in a later step. If necessary, use a photograph of a tree as a reference when drawing this significant component of a design illustration.

The background and surroundings of the tree were added next. The sky was applied with pastel, and the sidewalk and grass were added with marker.

Marker was then added to the trunk and main branches. *French Grey 70%* marker was applied to the shaded sides of the trunk; *French Grey 50%* marker was added to the sunlit side.

Fig. 4-188

2 **Add fine branching, shadows, and texture.** Once the larger branches and trunk were drawn with marker, the smaller branches were extended to the predetermined outline edge with a *French Grey 70%* pencil. In figure 4-189, these branches were drawn by applying more pressure to the pencil at each branch's point of origin, then easing pressure on the pencil to make the branches thinner near the edge of the canopy. Note that the fine branches at the edge of the canopy were lightly washed with the side of the *French Grey 70%* pencil to quickly replicate the density created by the mass of even smaller branches.

When the small branches were completed, shadows were applied to the large branches and trunk with a *French Grey 70%* marker. A *French Grey 10%* pencil was used to wash the sunlit portion of the trunk. Thin, wavy lines of *Black* and *French Grey 10%* pencil were drawn along the main branches and trunk to create a bark texture. The trunk and fine branch masses were stippled with a Pilot Razor Point.

Fig. 4-189

3 **Add ground shadow.** A bare tree is accompanied by a shadow that has two separate components. The trunk and main branches cast darker, more distinct shadow, and the finer branches create areas of lighter, diffuse shadow.

In figure 4-190, *Yellow Green (Limepeel)* marker was used as a base color for the grass, and *Olive (Olive Green)* marker was used as a base color for the shadows of the trunk and main branches. *French Grey 40%* marker was used to continue these shadows onto the concrete sidewalk.

Sunset Pink (Deco Pink) marker was added to the grass to mute the green slightly. *Celadon Green* pencil was applied to portions of the grass to make it more bluish green.

Copenhagen Blue pencil was applied lightly over the shadow on the grass to add the lighter, diffuse shadow. *Blue Slate* pencil was used for the same purpose on the sidewalk.

Fig. 4-190

Bare Deciduous Trees, Middle Ground and Background

(4-191, 4-192, 4-193)

The preliminary line drawings for bare trees in the middle ground or background of a design illustration are prepared similarly to those for bare foreground trees. The trunks, main branches, and penciled canopy outlines are drawn first.

1   **Apply color to the background.** In figure 4-191, color was first applied to those elements seen *through* the closer trees. *French Grey 30%* marker was applied to the canopies of the line of trees in the middle of the drawing. *French Grey 10%* marker was added to the next more distant layer of trees. *Cool Grey #1 (Cool Grey 10%)* marker was applied over the *French Grey 10%* marker as well as to the most distant tree/hill forms.

The sky is a blend of Schwan Stabilo *#430* pencil pastel (top) and *Light Oxide Red 339.9* (middle) and *Ultramarine Deep 506.9* (lower) stick pastels. The sky near the horizon was left white.

Color was added to the building, with care taken to keep its value relatively light and the contrast minimal between its sunlit and shaded surfaces.

2   **Add the trunks, main branches, and shadows beneath the trees.** The shadows beneath the middle row of trees, as well as the trunks and main branches visible against the lighter backgrounds, were added with *French Grey 70%* and *50%* markers (4-192). The trunks visible against the darker backgrounds were left white, then toned with a *French Grey 10%* marker.

The shadows of the middle-ground trees on the right were first applied with *French Grey 50%* marker—for the trunks and main branches—followed by a wash of *French Grey 10%* marker for the diffuse shadows of the smaller branch masses.

Touches of *Olive (Olive Green)* marker were added for evergreen shrubs beneath the middle row of trees; the embankment beyond the distant fence was washed with a blend of *Willow Green (Lime Green)* and *Buff (Brick Beige)* markers.

Fig. 4-191

Fig. 4-192

3 **Add fine branching.** In figure 4-193, the finer branches were added with a *French Grey 70%* pencil. The finest branching, of course, is located at the outer edge of the tree canopies. These branch masses were added with the side of *Burnt Ochre* and *French Grey 50%* pencils.

The trunks of the middle row of trees were lightened and darkened with very light touches of *French Grey 10%* and *90%* pencils, respectively. *Jasmine* pencil was used to brighten the sunlit sides of the trunks. Pilot Razor Point was used to stipple the closest tree canopies.

Fig. 4-193

Bare Deciduous Trees, in Front of Graded Background

(4-194)

Use a light-value color pencil when drawing bare trees or shrubs in front of dark values such as shadows, windows, or darkened skies. In figure 4-194, *Cream* pencil was used to draw the part of the shrub that is in front of the part of the wall in shade. *Warm Grey 20%* pencil was used to draw the tree in front of the darkened sky on the right, and *Warm Grey 50%* pencil was used to draw the bare tree on the left. This technique works best when there is little or no color pencil on the surface over which you intend to draw these plant materials.

Fig. 4-194

Deciduous Trees in Foliage, Foreground (4-195, 4-196, 4-197)

This illustration was drawn on toned paper.

A foreground deciduous tree in foliage, like its bare counterpart in figure 4-190, is rarely shown in its entirety. Note that the larger branches are drawn first, but darkened in later steps.

1 Draw foliage with marker. The outline of the tree canopy was delineated with a thin pencil line to serve as a guide for the marker application. In figure 4-195, *Yellow Green (Limepeel)* and *Olive (Olive Green)* markers were used to begin the foliage, stroked diagonally with the broad side of the marker tip. Autumn foliage can also be drawn as easily, beginning with such markers as *Brick Red (Cherry), Pale Cherry (Mineral Orange),* and *Pale Sepia (Goldenrod).*

2 Complete foliage, draw branches, begin shadows with marker. As figure 4-196 shows, *Dark Olive (French Grey 80%)* and *Cool Grey #9 (Cool Grey 90%)* markers were added to complete the foliage.

A pointed-nib Design Marker was used to darken the smaller branches. This resulted in a series of broken, rather than continuous, lines, because the view of the branches is interrupted by the leaf clusters.

After the marker base colors for the grass were applied, *Dark Olive (French Grey 80%)* marker was applied in a series of close *horizontal* strokes. The same type of stroke was used to apply *Cool Grey #5 (Cool Grey 50%)* marker for the sidewalk shadows. *Burnt Umber (Dark Umber)* marker was applied with a *diagonal* stroke to the brick wall.

3 Add highlights, detail, and finishing touches. In figure 4-197, *Cream* pencil was applied over the foliage drawn with the *Yellow Green (Limepeel)* marker. *Light Cerulean Blue* pencil, with *White* pencil applied over it, was used to add the bits of sky visible through the canopy of the tree.

Cool Grey #5 (Cool Grey 50%) marker was used to draw the shadows on the trunk. *Cream* and *White* pencils were used to wash the sunlit areas between the shadows. A light wash of *Burnt Ochre* pencil was then applied

Fig. 4-195

Fig. 4-196

over the entire trunk. Further trunk texture was applied with a Pilot Razor Point, by stippling and adding diagonal strokes to the shadow areas.

A wash of *Olive Green* pencil was applied over the marker shadows on the grass, followed by a vertical texture added with a Pilot Razor Point. *Cream* pencil was used for adding a similar texture to the sunlit portions of the grass.

Peach pencil was used to flavor the marker shadows on the brick wall, and a wash of *Peach* and *White* pencil was added to the sunlit portion. The mortar joints were added with a *White* pencil and a straightedge to give the shadow a transparent quality.

Copenhagen Blue pencil was used to flavor the shadows on the sidewalk; *White* pencil, flavored with *Peach* pencil, was used to enhance the sunlit areas.

Fig. 4-197

Deciduous Trees in Foliage, Middle Ground (4-198, 4-199, 4-200)

This illustration was drawn on toned print paper.

1. **Apply marker base.** In figure 4-198, *Yellow Green (Limepeel)* marker was used for sunlit foliage, *Olive (Olive Green)* marker for foliage in middle light, and *Dark Olive (French Grey 80%)* marker for foliage in shade and shadow. Note that the lines of the buildings still show through the foliage in places and act as a guide for applying color to those surfaces behind the trees.

2. **Create shadows with marker.** A variety of markers were used in figure 4-199 to create the shadows cast by the trees—darker values on dark surfaces, lighter values on light surfaces. *Horizontal* strokes were used for shadows on the ground, and *diagonal* strokes were used to make the shadows on the vertical surfaces parallel to the direction of the sunlight.

3. **Add color to surfaces seen through the trees.** The appropriate colors were applied to those surfaces not touched by the markers used to create the foliage. These colors were applied with color pencil to the building surfaces and the sky.

4. **Apply highlights, details, and finishing touches.** In figure 4-200, a mixture of *Jasmine* and *Cream* pencils was applied over the sunlit side of the trees. Branches were added with a pointed-nib Design Marker and a Pilot Razor Point, with the use of intermittent strokes. *Cool Grey #9 (Cool Grey 90%)* marker was used to stipple some even darker areas of the leaf masses. Details, highlights, and flavorings were added to the surrounding sunlit and shadowed surfaces.

Fig. 4-198

Fig. 4-199

Fig. 4-200

Deciduous Trees in Foliage (Abbreviated Technique)

(4-201, 4-202, 4-203)

1 **Apply sky, distant objects, and marker base.** In figure 4-201, color was applied to the sky and the building in the distance, similarly to the way it was done in figure 4-191. However, in this example there is no need to extend the color of the background building very far below the outline of the tree canopies, inasmuch as it will be blocked by the dense foliage.

Yellow Green (Limepeel) marker was applied to the upper sunlit sides of the trees with the broad *edge* of the tip. Note how the strokes were oriented outward from the center of the trees. *Olive (Olive Green)* marker was carefully applied between these lighter strokes on the *shaded* side of each tree. You can see how the trees within the mass repeat the light-dark pattern, one against the other, individuating trees within the mass. The darker marker was also applied to the *bottom* of each canopy, forming a rough, continuous line of dark value between the canopies and trunks.

2 **Develop tree forms, colors, and shadows.** *Black* marker was applied to the darkest areas beneath the trees in figure 4-202. As it was worked upward into the tree canopies, the *Black* was dotted in with the marker tip.

Black marker was also used on the left side of the middle-ground tree to the right. *Olive (Olive Green)* marker was used to pick up where the black left off as the color progressed toward the sunlit side.

Olive (Olive Green) marker was also used to apply the shadow of the tree on the ground as well as the long shadows in the field beyond. *Yellow Green (Limepeel)* marker was used on the sunlit portions of the field.

The sunlit sides of the trees and fields were muted with *Sunset Pink (Deco Pink)* marker, and *Willow Green (Lime Green)* marker was used as a transition color between the sunlit and shaded sides of the tree canopies.

The most distant hills, near the horizon, were colored with *Cool Grey #1 (Cool Grey 10%)* marker; *Cool Grey #3 (Cool Grey 30%)* marker was used on the next closest "layer" of trees. The layer of trees just in front of these were drawn with *Cool Grey #1 and #3 (Cool Grey 10% and 30%)* markers, then washed with *Willow Green (Lime Green)* and *Naples Yellow (Eggshell)* markers.

Fig. 4-201

Fig. 4-202

3 **Add details.** You may frequently find that when you have applied the marker base to a tree canopy in foliage that is seen against the sky, you have not left adequate "white spaces" showing. As a result, the canopy can appear too opaque and heavy. This was the case with the closest trees in figure 4-203. To remedy the situation, *White* pencil was added to the upper parts of the canopies of the trees on the left and right to "open them up."

Peach pencil was used to flavor the sunlit sides of the tree canopies and their trunks, helping to create the effect of morning or late afternoon sun. If you want the light to appear as if it is occurring later in the day, use *Jasmine* pencil or no pencil flavoring at all.

Fig. 4-203

Evergreen Trees, Foreground (4-204, 4-205, 4-206)

The evergreen trees illustrated in this sequence of steps are typical of the many kinds of evergreen found throughout the world. Tree (1) is a sprucelike tree. By using the stroke shown in the inset you can, by varying the form, draw trees similar in form to that of the spruce (genus *Picea*), such as the hemlock *(Tsuga),* fir *(Psuedotsuga* and *Abies),* larch *(Larix),* and cedar *(cedrus).* Tree (2) is a pinelike tree, and the stroke *(inset)* can be used for drawing the many types of pines *(Pinus).* Tree (3) is a cypresslike tree *(Chamaecyparis),* and the stroke used to draw it may be applied to similar tree forms, such as the juniper *(Juniperus)* and the yew *(Taxus).*

1 **Apply marker base to foliage.** In figure 4-204, *Slate Green (Teal Blue)* marker was applied to the sprucelike tree, using the stroke shown in the inset. In this particular example, a Colorado blue spruce *(Picea pungens glauca)* tree form was created.

A *Cool Grey #7 (Cool Grey 70%)* marker was used for the pinelike tree, following the stroke technique shown in the inset. For best results, use a marker that is slightly dry to create the feathered edge at the end of the stroke. The tree form in this example is a ponderosa pine *(Pinus ponderosa).*

A *Slate Green (Teal Blue)* marker was also used, following the stroke shown in the inset, to begin the cypresslike tree.

1   **2**   **3**

Fig. 4-204

2 **Develop color, shading, and trunks with marker.** In figure 4-205, *Cool Grey #9 (Cool Grey 90%)* marker was stippled on the underside of the foliage masses of the sprucelike tree. It was also used to darken the tips of the masses on the shaded side of the tree.

Olive *(Olive Green)* marker was applied over the *Cool Grey #7 (Cool Grey 70%)* marker base of the pinelike tree. *Cool Grey #9 (Cool Grey 90%)* marker was used on the underside of the foliage masses to develop their

shading. The trunks were drawn with *Redwood (Sienna Brown)* marker, with *Cool Grey #9 (Cool Grey 90%)* marker used on the shaded sides.

Olive *(Olive Green)* marker was applied over the *Slate Green (Teal Blue)* marker base of the cypresslike trees, with the same stroke as that shown for that tree in the inset in figure 4-204. *Cool Grey #9 (Cool Grey 90%)* marker is stippled on the shaded sides of the trees, in gradually diminished amounts as it progresses toward the sunlit side.

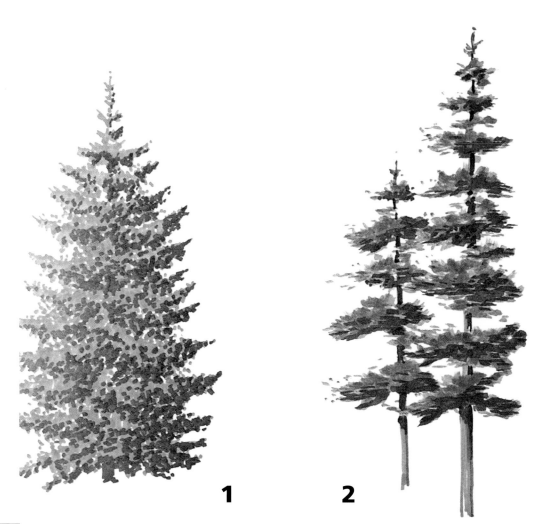

1

2

3

Fig. 4-205

3 **Add highlights and final touches.** Figure 4-206 shows that *Olive Green* pencil was used to wash the entire sprucelike tree and *White* pencil was applied to the sunlit foliage masses with an upward stroke. Touches of *Burnt Ochre* pencil were added to indicate dead foliage.

Jasmine pencil was used to highlight the sunlit tops of the foliage masses of the pinelike tree. *Olive Green* pencil was added to its shaded areas to bring out their color. Pilot Razor Point was used to add a needlelike texture to the shaded sides of the foliage masses. Again, touches of *Burnt Ochre* pencil were used to add dead foliage. *Cream* and *White* pencils were applied to the sunlit parts of the trunks for highlights, and *Dark Umber* and Derwent *Blue Violet Lake #27* pencils were added to the shaded areas.

Jasmine and Cream pencils were applied to highlight the sunlit areas of the cypresslike tree. Note the small fan-shaped texture patterns created with these pencils.

Fig. 4-206

Evergreen Trees, Middle Ground and Background

(4-207, 4-208)

1 **Draw middle-ground trees first.** A pointed-nib Design Marker can be used to draw the middle-ground trees, with a simple slanted stroke over a vertical trunk line. The example in figure 4-207 shows a Sanford Sharpie—a felt-tipped pen with a similar tip—is being used for this step. As the inset shows, the stroke is slanted in opposite directions on opposite sides of the trunk.

The closer trees, drawn on the extreme left and right, were created by stippling a *Cool Grey #9 (Cool Grey 90%)* marker over a vertical trunk line. These trees will remain dark, because they are silhouetted by the lighter trees in the background.

2 **Add trunks.** *Warm Grey 20%* pencil was used to draw the trunks of the trees with intermittent lines.

Fig. 4-207

3 **Draw distant trees.** Once the middle-ground trees were drawn, the point of an *Olive (Olive Green)* marker was used to add the distant trees—the marker was repeatedly flicked upward, quickly producing a simple evergreen-like shape with a wider bottom and narrower top (4-208).

The same stroke was used in applying a Pilot Razor Point to suggest both tree-mass texture and shading. These lines were drawn more densely at the crest of the hill so that it would contrast more strongly with the mountain beyond.

Jasmine pencil was applied, with the same stroke, to create a low-sun effect on the trees.

Note that *Blue Slate* pencil was used just behind the middle-ground trees to create greater contrast with the distant tree mass.

Fig. 4-208

Palm Trees (4-209, 4-210)

An important element in the illustration of palm trees is the accuracy with which the shape and proportion of the trees are created.

1 **Color the sky; apply marker base to the tree canopies.** In figure 4-209, *Yellow Green (Limepeel)* marker was applied to the sunlit portion of the tree canopies, and *Olive (Olive Green)* marker was applied to the shaded side. The markers were applied with the tip of the point, flicking outward from the center of the canopy. This gives a pointed end to the marker strokes. *Willow Green (Lime Green)* marker was used as a wash over both base colors to shift their colors.

2 **Apply color to trunks; add details.** *Kraft Brown (Light Tan)* marker was added to color the trunks, dead fronds just beneath the tree canopies, and dying fronds within the canopies themselves (4-210).

French Grey 70% marker was used to darken the shadows on the trunks. Light washes of *Cool Grey 30%* pencil were applied to the tree canopies, becoming slightly heavier washes as the trees progressed into the distance. This both lightened the value and weakened the chroma of the canopy colors, creating a sense of atmospheric perspective.

Burnt Ochre and *French Grey 70%* pencils were crosshatched to create a texture on the trees closest to the viewer.

Fig. 4-209

Fig. 4-210

Multiple Street Trees (4-211 through 4-217)

If you are creating an illustration that requires multiple versions of a relatively uniform element, you may save time by creating the elements in Photoshop. In this example, an illustration of an urban streetscape design required multiple palm trees.

1 **Create streetscape, add color;** allow tree layout lines to remain visible. Color was added to the streetscape line drawing, but enough of the palm tree layout linework (circles on lines) was left showing to guide the placement of the tree images (4-211).

2 **Locate digital tree image, isolate, and create shadow.** An appropriate digital image of a palm tree was located (courtesy: www.desert-tropicals.com) (4-212). The image is appropriate because the direction of light on the tree is the same as that in the drawing, and because it works with the project's climate as well.

The tree image was selected with the *Lasso Selection Tool*, copied, and pasted into its own document (4-213). A portion of the trunk was copied and pasted to increase the height of the tree (perhaps wishful thinking) and some additional texture added with the *Pencil Tool*. A shadow was created with the *Brush Tool* on a separate layer (4-214).

Fig. 4-211

Fig. 4-212

Fig. 4-213

Fig. 4-214

3 **Copy and paste tree into drawing.** The tree was copied and pasted into the streetscape. The *Transform* command was used to size the tree according to the tree layout lines (4-215).

4 **Replicate tree.** Once resized, the tree was duplicated all the way up the street (4-216). The *Move Tool* was positioned over the tree; the Option key (Mac) or Alt key (Windows) was held down, and the duplicate tree moved to the next position. The closest trees were placed first, then the foreground row was replicated; the same process was repeated for the background row. In this way, the trees were made to overlap according to the rules of perspective. As the trees were positioned into the distance, the *Transform* command was used to diminish their sizes as necessary. Once positioned, the trees were merged into a single layer. Parts of their trunks were erased where they were occluded by foreground elements.

5 **Copy, paste, and replicate tree shadows.** As a final step, the tree shadow was copied and pasted into the streetscape drawing. Its blending mode was set to "Multiply" (4-217).

The shadow was replicated in the same way as the trees and, once placed, the multiple shadows were merged into a single layer, distinct from that of the trees. Parts of the shadows were erased where they covered

inappropriate places. The shadows were established as a separate layer so they could have a different blending mode than the trees and be adjusted separately from them.

Fig. 4-216

Fig. 4-217

Fig. 4-215

Climbing Vines (4-218, 4-219)

1 **Apply color and shadows to climbing surface.** Color was first added to the stone bridge, including those parts seen through the openings in the plant material. Shadows cast by the vine mass were added below and to the left of each part of the mass.

2 **Apply marker base to vine mass.** *Willow Green (Lime Green)* and *Yellow Green (Limepeel)* markers were applied to the vine mass. Figure 4-218 shows *Olive (Olive Green)* marker being applied to the recesses and parts of the vine mass in shade.

3 **Add pencil wash.** In figure 4-219, a *Dark Green* pencil was applied as a light wash, using the side of the point. This not only shifts the color of the vine mass, but quickly adds an appropriate texture as well.

Fig. 4-218

Fig. 4-219

BACKGROUNDS

Urban Backgrounds (4-220, 4-221)

There are some distinct guidelines that will help you to easily create urban backgrounds: As the distance increases in an urban background, increase the value of the colors and decrease the value contrast *between* colors. The chroma of the colors should become weaker, and the hues should tend more toward the bluish range. Less detail should be shown on the buildings.

1 **Apply marker base.** Because colors in the outdoor urban landscape are predominantly weak in chroma, gray markers were used as the base (4-220). *Cool Grey #7 (Cool Grey 70%)* was the dominant marker used in the foreground, along with touches of *Cool Grey #9 (Cool Grey 90%)* and *Black* markers. Successively lighter cool gray markers were applied to the buildings as the distance increased.

2 **Flavor walls of buildings with pencil.** In figure 4-221, the walls of the closest buildings were flavored with warm-hued pencils, including *Terra Cotta, Peach, Jasmine, Mineral Orange, Burnt Ochre, Dark Umber,* and *Light Peach. White* pencil was used for highlights.

Fig. 4-220

The buildings in the middle-to-far distance were flavored with *Light Peach* pencil on their sunlit sides and *Light Cerulean Blue* pencil on their shaded sides. *White* pencil was also added to the most distant building surfaces to increase the value and decrease the chroma of the pencil flavorings. The entire distant part of the drawing, including buildings, was flavored with *Jasmine* and *Cream* pencils to create the effect of haze.

3 **Add window treatments.** A Pilot Razor Point was used to darken the windows on the sunlit sides of the closest buildings. A *Cool Grey 70%* pencil was added to windows on buildings farther in the distance. A mixture of *Light Cerulean Blue* and *White* pencils was used to create the effects of reflected skylight on the windows of the shaded sides of the closest buildings. A Pilot Razor Point was used to draw the muntins, frames, and shaded recesses.

Fig. 4-221

Rural Backgrounds (4-222, 4-223, 4-224)

The color phenomena exhibited in urban backgrounds are similar in rural backgrounds. The chroma of the colors becomes weaker, their values increase, and the apparent textures diminish as the distance increases. However, the hues seen in rural backgrounds generally form a clockwise progression around the color wheel, from green yellows in the foreground to purple blue or purple in the far distance.

1 **Apply marker base to the foreground.** In figure 4-222, *Cool Grey #9, #7, and #5 (Cool Grey 90%, 70%, and 50%)* markers were used to create a dark foreground mass of trees, producing a more dramatic effect of distance through value contrast. *Burnt Umber (Dark Umber)* marker was used for the roof and deck of the building.

2 **Add help lines; create distant trees and fields with marker.** In figure 4-223, rolling help lines were introduced to help guide the addition of distant fields, roads, and land contours. *Cool Grey #5 (Cool Grey 50%)* marker was used to stipple in the trees on the first ridge, in the middle of the drawing. Shade and shadows were added with a *Cool Grey #7 (Cool Grey 70%)* marker.

Light Ivy (Putty + Cream) and *Buff (Brick Beige)* markers were added to the fields, along with touches of *Yellow Green (Limepeel)* marker.

The trees on the hill beyond the first ridge were stippled in with a *Cool Grey #3 (Cool Grey 30%)* marker. *Cool Grey #1 (Cool Grey 10%)* marker was applied to the farthest hillside.

Fig. 4-222

Fig. 4-223

3 **Apply pencil.** In figure 4-224, *Olive Green* pencil was used to wash the foreground trees as well as the trees on the first ridge. The foreground trees were then stippled with a Pilot Razor Point.

Olive Green and *Peacock Green* pencils were used to flavor the trees on the next ridge. *Peacock Green* pencil only was used to flavor the next ridge beyond.

Peacock Green and *Blue Slate* pencils were used on the ridge beyond that, and *Blue Slate* and *Greyed Lavender* pencils were used to flavor the last ridge before the mountain. A mixture of *Greyed Lavender* and *White* pencils was lightly applied to the mountain.

Fig. 4-224

Photo Contexts (4-225, 4-226, 4-227)

Design drawings can easily be incorporated into photographic contexts and backgrounds. Backgrounds that have few indications of perspective directionality—such as obvious vanishing points or lines—are the easiest to incorporate into a design drawing.

One exception is photographs used as underlays for design drawings, as when the drawing is an addition or revision to something within the photograph, such as a building or part of a landscape. In those situations, of course, the drawings will match the perspective of their contexts. Examples of these kinds of photo contexts can be seen in the urban environments in figures 3-14 to 3-16 and 3-47.

1 **Create color drawing.** The color drawing of the subject is created and scanned (4-225).

2 **Determine context image.** The context image shown here (4-226) is a digital photograph of the actual site for the duplex residence illustrated in figure 4-225. Note that it has no obvious perspective lines or vanishing points.

3 **Copy and paste the context image into the drawing.** The site photograph was copied and pasted into figure 4-225. Its opacity was reduced to about 50% so that the building and its landscaping could be seen through it. Using the *Polygonal Lasso Selection Tool* with the Delete key and the *Eraser Tool*, the context image was removed and no longer blocked the building and its landscaping.

Fig. 4-225

Fig. 4-226

4 **Obscure or filter the context image.** In most cases, it is a good idea to obscure or filter the photographic context image to reduce the visual dissonance between the drawing and the photograph. Here the context image was lightened and reduced in contrast using the *Brightness/Contrast* adjustment (4-227). It was also colorized to a sepia tone with the *Hue/Saturation* adjustment. Additionally, its opacity was reduced. The result is that the photograph provides an appropriate context for the drawing without being unduly obvious.

Using filters on photographic context images may also help you to reduce the potential for dissonance. The *Dry Brush* filter (Filter > Artistic > Dry Brush) can make the photograph look more like it was rendered with markers or watercolor. The *Spatter* filter (Filter > Brush Strokes > Spatter) can help make images with many lines look more like the lines were drawn by hand. Remember that not all filters will be available to you if your file is in CMYK mode. You can easily change the mode of your file through the *Image* command (Image > Mode > RGB Color).

Fig. 4-227

SLOPING ROOFS

The Overhead Plane: Roofs and Skies

Sloping roofs and skies work together in a design drawing. Roof materials can be represented with a variety of media. They should be appropriately subtle and follow the rules of perspective. Skies can add a level of finish and even be a source of drama in a design drawing.

Shingle Roof (4-228, 4-229)

The shingle techniques shown in these illustrations can, depending on your color selections, be used for asphalt, wood, slate, or concrete shingles. The shingles illustrated in this example are wood shingles.

1 **Apply marker base.** First, an assumption was made that the light was coming from the left, determining which parts of the roof would be in shade and shadow. In figure 4-228, *French Grey 10%* marker was applied to the more directly illuminated surface, and *French Grey 30%* marker was used on the right-facing roof surface.

Note the light pencil help lines drawn on the roof. These lines radiate from the vanishing points and help guide the marker strokes. Streaks of *Buff (Brick Beige)* were added to the roof, stroked along these lines.

The dappled tree shadow to the left was made with *French Grey 70%, 50%,* and *30%* markers.

Fig. 4-228

2 **Add pencil texture.** As figure 4-229 shows, a .5 mm pencil with a 2H lead was used to draw the shadows of the butt ends of the shingles on the lighter slope of the roof. These lines were guided by the aforementioned help lines and were drawn with a short, choppy, back-and-forth motion along a straightedge. This motion imparts an uneven density to the line. Because this pencil does not show in the shadow on the left, a *Light Peach* pencil was used to continue the same line into the shadow. Note that a few individual shingle lines were added *along* the roof slope as well, with the use of both pencils.

A Micron 005 pen was used with the same kind of back-and-forth stroke to make the lines on the darker roof slope.

Fig. 4-229

Metal Roof, Standing Seam (4-230, 4-231)

1 **Apply marker base.** Metal roofs can be any color, but are typically muted. In figure 4-230, *Cool Grey #3 (Cool Grey 30%)* marker was applied to the more directly illuminated roof surfaces, and *Cool Grey #5 (Cool Grey 50%)* marker was used on the surfaces receiving less light. *Willow Green (Lime Green)* marker was then used to wash all roof surfaces.

To shift the color slightly, *Sand (Sand)* marker was added to the darker parts of the roof, and *Buff (Brick Beige)* marker was applied to the lighter surfaces.

Note the pencil help lines, once again added to keep the marker strokes—and subsequent pencil strokes—aligned toward the vanishing points for the sloping roofs.

Fig. 4-230

2 **Add pencil detail.** Figure 4-231 shows the completed roof. *French Grey 70%* pencil was applied with a straightedge to create the standing seams on the lighter roof surfaces, and side-by-side lines of *French Grey 10%* and *French Grey 70%* pencil were added to the darker roofs.

Notice that the standing seam lines are evenly spaced and each aims toward the respective vanishing points for the sloping roofs.

Tile Roof (4-232, 4-233)

1 **Apply marker base; modify color with pastel.** *Kraft Brown (Light Tan)* marker was applied to the sunlit portion of the roof, and *Burnt Umber (Dark Umber)* marker was used for the shadow.

A random application of Schwan Stabilo *#620*, *#675*, and *#690* pencil pastels was blended by finger on the sunlit portions of the roof. The excess was brushed away with a drafting brush.

2 **Add pencil detail.** In figure 4-232, *Black* pencil was added to the dark spaces between the rows of tiles. Note that each of these lines radiates from the roof's vanishing point, shown lightly in pencil above the roof.

Fig. 4-231

Fig. 4-232

3 **Apply finishing touches.** Figure 4-233 shows the rest of the black lines added to the roof. Note that not every line need be applied. *French Grey 30%* pencil lines were lightly added to the shadowed parts of the roof.

Dashes of *Terra Cotta* and *Light Peach* pencil were applied to give additional texture. A pointed-nib Design Marker was used to dot in the dark tile ends at the eaves.

Fig. 4-233

SKIES

Daytime Sky (4-234, 4-235, 4-236)

A daytime sky often appears as a gradation of color and, under normal, clear weather conditions, is usually lighter at the horizon and grades to a darker blue toward the zenith. Daytime skies—even those on large drawings—can be created very quickly and easily with pastel.

1 **Apply pastel.** You will find it easier, when planning a design illustration, to apply the sky first, before color is added to the roofs and treetops. When sky color spills onto these adjacent surfaces, it can be erased without disturbing their color.

In figure 4-234, *Ultramarine Deep 506.9* stick pastel was applied quickly and roughly in the area closest to the horizon, with care taken to leave the white of the paper just above the horizon. Higher in the sky, a Schwan Stabilo

Fig. 4-234

#430 pencil pastel was also quickly applied as a transitional color to the darker *Cobalt Blue 512.5* stick pastel, added to the top part of the sky.

2 **Mix pastel with fingers or facial tissue.** Figure 4-235 shows the three pastels being mixed with a facial tissue to form a graded blue sky. If the gradation is not consistent when the excess is brushed away, additional pastel or color pencil can be applied to create consistency.

3 **Apply finishing touches.** The finished sky is shown in figure 4-236. To keep the sky gradation consistent, it was wiped with a chamois only at the bottom, near the horizon. The rest was simply brushed with a drafting brush. Pastel that found its way into the trees was erased away with an electric eraser using a soft white erasing strip.

Protect the original illustration with a layer of tracing paper, because it can smear easily. Use a color photocopy or a color bubble-jet copy of the illustration for review and presentation purposes. Use a spray fixative only if you must, because fixative tends to mute the colors of the pastel.

Fig. 4-235

Fig. 4-236

Dusk (or Dawn) Skies (4-237 through 4-240)

There are two easy ways to make dusk or dawn skies. Both use toned paper techniques and work well in illustrations in which the windows will be illuminated.

A. On white tracing paper (4-237, 4-238, 4-239)

1 **Apply sky colors to the back of the tracing paper.** In figure 4-237, *Pink, Blush Pink,* and *Deco Orange* pencils were applied near the horizon and faded into the color of the paper. *Cobalt Blue 512.5* stick pastel was applied to the part of the sky farthest from the setting (rising) sun and will also be faded onto the paper color from the opposite direction.

Note that the illustration is created with brown kraft paper placed beneath the tracing paper so that the effect of the light colors is more obvious.

2 **Blend colors.** The pastel was rubbed into the paper and smoothed with the fingers. *Blush Pink* and *Deco Orange* pencils were also added to the *front* of the paper for the purpose of adding streaks of pink and orange *over* the blue sky color.

3 **Add finishing touches.** Figure 4-238 shows that the pastel was erased from the trees. A few stars were added, with white gouache, to the front of the illustration. Elements that abut the sky, in this case deciduous and evergreen trees, can be silhouetted against the sky by filling in their forms with a *Black* marker on the front side of the illustration. This makes the sky appear still more luminous by contrast. Figure 4-239 shows the intended final form of the illustration—as a color photocopy.

Fig. 4-237

Fig. 4-238

Fig. 4-239

B. On dark paper (4-240)

A dusk or dawn sky is very easy to create on dark paper, because the effect requires that the sky be only partially colored.

1 **Photocopy or plot your line drawing on dark paper.** The line drawing was scanned and opened in Photoshop. It was given a dark blue background applied as a gradient that is slightly darker at the top and lighter at the bottom, then plotted on an ink-jet plotter (4-240). You can also photocopy your line drawing on a dark Canson paper.

2 **Apply color pencil in a progression of graded washes.** *Deco Orange, Blush Pink, Pink, Light Cerulean Blue,* and *Copenhagen Blue* pencils were applied, in the order listed, from the horizon up. Each pencil color was graded one into the other; the sides of the pencil points were used, which yielded a wider and smoother stroke. Horizontal clouds, appearing as streaks of color, were added with *Pink* and *Deco Orange* pencils.

Note that the colors used form a progression around the color wheel, from yellow red at the horizon to purple blue. The purple blue in this example, *Copenhagen Blue* pencil, was, in turn, faded into the paper color.

Pastel was not used in this example because when erased it can lift the dark coating from the paper, resulting in unwanted streaking.

3 **Add touches of white gouache for stars.**

Fig. 4-240

Daytime Skies with Clouds (4-241, 4-242)

Clouds are easy and fun to create. For this reason, however, they can easily be overdone, becoming portentous, fussy, and a distraction from the original purpose of the illustration. Clouds should remain as background, helping to create the context for your design ideas.

1 **Make a daytime sky.** Use the same materials and techniques for creating a daytime sky as those illustrated in figures 4-234 through 4-236.

2 **Erase away sky to create clouds.** An electric eraser with a soft white erasing strip is used in figure 4-241 to create the cloud forms by erasing away the pastel base used to make the sky. These forms can be virtually any shape and oriented in any direction, depending on the sky effect you want. Use photographs of cloud forms to guide your efforts.

3 **Add final touches.** You can simply stop after step 2 and have very satisfactory clouds for the purposes of most design illustrations. If you wish, you can add some color to the clouds, inasmuch as they are often tinted by the color of the sky—as during sunsets, for example.

In this instance (4-242), *Light Oxide Red 339.9* stick pastel was mixed with *White* stick pastel on the sunlit sides of the cloud forms, then rubbed with a facial tissue and brushed with a drafting brush. Other very light pastel colors can also be used for tinting clouds.

Fig. 4-241

Fig. 4-242

Sky with Clouds, Using Photoshop (4-243 through 4-248)

Skies can also be easily added to a color design drawing using Photoshop. In the example shown in figure 4-243, a sky had been established using the *Gradient Tool*. However, it was determined that more texture in the sky would add to the interest and richness of the drawing.

1 **Copy and paste appropriate sky image.** The *Rectangular Marquee Selection Tool* was used to copy the sky from the digital photograph in figure 4-244, then paste it into the drawing (4-245). Note that the treetops were removed using the *Clone Stamp Tool*.

Fig. 4-243

Fig. 4-244

2 **Cover drawing's sky area with image.** Since the sky image was pasted into the scanned drawing as a separate layer, the opacity of the layer was reduced to about 50%. The *Transform* command was used to enlarge the sky image so it covered the entire sky area of the drawing. The *Lasso* *Selection Tool* and the *Polygonal Lasso Selection Tool* were used to select the sky area (4-246). This selection was saved so that, once the layers were flattened, it would still be possible to adjust the sky if necessary (Select > Save Selection . . . > *name the selection*).

Fig. 4-245

Fig. 4-246

3 **Delete sky image from all but the sky area of drawing.** Once the sky selection was saved, the selection was inverted (Select > Inverse) and the Delete key was pressed. This removed the sky image from all but the sky area of the drawing (4-247).

Fig. 4-247

4   **Adjust and save.** When composing a view for a design drawing, it is very important *not to let support elements in the drawing overwhelm its subject.* Given its large size, the contrast of the sky in figure 4-247 threatened to take "center stage" away from the drawing's subject—the composition of plant materials forming a gateway into an urban district at one of its major intersections.

The blending mode of the sky image layer was changed from "Normal" to "Multiply" (4-248). This also allowed the color gradation of the original sky to show through. The *Brightness/Contrast* adjustment was used to lighten the sky and reduce its contrast a bit, making its impact slightly more subtle.

Fig. 4-248

CHAPTER 271

SCALE ELEMENTS: FIGURES AND AUTOMOBILES

The inclusion of human figures and automobiles in your color design drawings gives the viewer of those drawings a comparative reference by which the sizes of all parts of the ideas expressed can be quickly judged. They also add a welcome and necessary level of human activity to the illustrations of the places you design.

However, there is an irony in introducing these scale elements into your drawings. On one hand, these "hard-to-draw" elements seem to be a time-consuming bother as compared with the "real work" of illustrating the ideas themselves. On the other hand, they are precisely the point. By introducing these elements—people and, where appropriate, the cars they drive—into all design drawings, from conceptual sketches to presentation drawings, you keep those for whom these places are created in the forefront of your attention.

Nevertheless, it is important to not belabor these elements by spending too much time in their creation or by allowing them to attract undue attention. Although designers are in many ways inventors, remember that your task does not include the design of people and cars. Trace, copy, or digitally import these elements whenever it is opportune to do so. Keep them simple and use a level of detail appropriate to the drawing.

DRAWING FIGURES IN COLOR

Your lifelong experience with your fellow humans allows you to estimate the relative sizes of the forms, spaces, and elements that surround them. Their presence in a place helps you to judge how big or small something is. Likewise, the addition of human figures to design drawings adds a critical element of *scale*, as well as animation and vitality, to your design ideas (5-1). However, because of this very familiarity, the figures in a design drawing can sometimes attract the viewer's attention unnecessarily. Poorly drawn or visually demanding figures can distract the viewer from the purpose of the drawing and, worse, can detract from otherwise good design ideas. Human figures should blend into the design drawing and act as a subtle reference for the viewer.

Fig. 5-1

Fig. 5-1 Although only a few figures would have sufficed for scale, the multitude of figures here adds vitality to this redesigned entertainment complex. Note how simply the figures are drawn because they are relatively distant in the illustration. See the enlargement in figure 5-7.

Trace and Digital Files

Because your task as a designer is to design our surroundings but not the people who occupy them, you may wish to trace figures from photographs or one of the many "entourage" books available, or import them digitally. This is always best when the opportunity arises—just the right figure or an automobile at precisely the angle you need. But relying on tracing or importing can be more time consuming than it may seem. First, the right figures must be located—that is, appropriate in dress and activity for the project type and location. Second, figures are more effective if you can engage them in the place you are making: sitting on the bench, facing a particular way, relaxing in a seating area, or window shopping at a certain storefront. These requirements can narrow the field of suitable candidates for traced or imported figures considerably. When appropriate trace figures *are* located, they must then be enlarged or reduced on a photocopier, usually a number of times, to achieve the right scale. Even when

the drawing is complete, the figures can have an awkward look (facing or walking in odd directions, too much clothing detail, etc.) that often accompanies those imported from a different context.

Simple, Believable Figures

You may find it easier and faster to learn to draw simple, believably proportioned figures to use where and when necessary (5-2, 5-3). By learning to draw acceptable figures that are standing, sitting, and walking, you will have most all the positions of the human figure you need for your design work. You will also find the design drawing process more fluid if you do not have to stop to search for figures from photo references, digital files, or websites. Instead, use photographs, entourage books, and websites more for visual references for things like clothing types, postures, and accessories as you position and draw your own figures.

Fig. 5-2 These simple standing and walking figures add scale to a street section drawn at 1" = 10'.

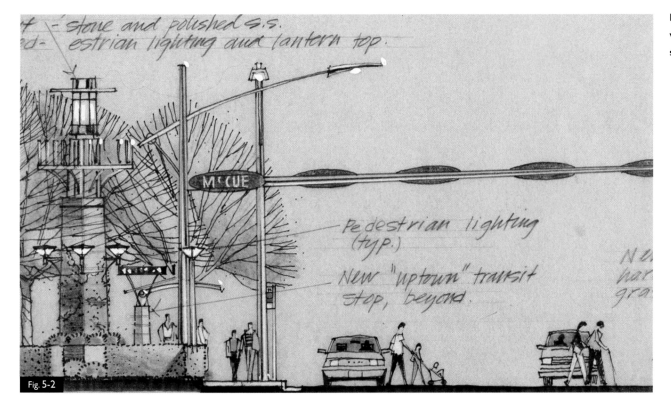

Fig. 5-2

Fig. 5-3   These seated figures do not have to be highly detailed to animate this semi-enclosed restaurant.

What constitutes a well-drawn scale figure? The most important quality of a scale figure is the naturalness of its proportions. That is, the relationships of the parts of the figure to one another should look about right (5-4). Well-proportioned figures, even as outline shapes in a drawing, are very useful not only for the viewer of a design illustration, but for the designer as well. You use figures as an instant comparative scale, during the drawing process, for making the parts of the design an appropriate size. Once you have a feel for drawing outline figures that are believably proportioned, attempt simple clothing and accessories on an overlay of tracing paper (5-5). These elements need not be elaborate or highly detailed, but the clothing you draw on your figures should be appropriate for the type of place you are creating and its climate (5-6). Remember, too, that the more distant a figure is in a drawing, *the simpler its clothing and level of detail should be* (5-7). The colors and details of the clothing on your figures can be any that appear believable (5-8). One of the best ways to choose colors for the clothing of your figures is to recombine colors already in use elsewhere in the drawing. Figures are good agents of repetition and can help create a color rhythm by distributing selected colors throughout the illustration.

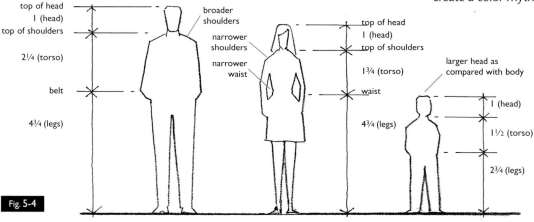

Fig. 5-4

Fig. 5-4 The proportions of these three typical figures are expressed in "heads." The torso of the middle figure, for example, is 1¾ times as high as her head. The width of each figure is roughly 3 times its head width. Some additional distinguishing characteristics are also noted.

Fig. 5-5 Figures with clothing and detail added. Note that figures in design illustrations rarely get more detailed than this.

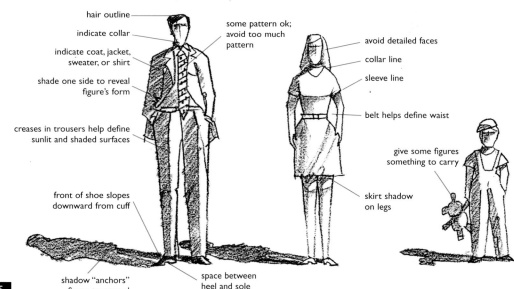

Fig. 5-5

Fig. 5-6 The walking figure is appropriately dressed for the New York location of this store.

Fig. 5-7 A detail of the illustration shown in figure 5-1. All of the figures in 5-1 appear quite distant because of the scope of this multiple-vanishing-point view. The standing figures vary in size according to their location in the illustration, but are about ¼" high in the original 11" x 12" illustration.

Fig. 5-8 The full colored figures shown in figure 5-5. The shade and shadow were applied to the front of the white tracing paper, and the pencil colors indicated were applied to the back.

Fig. 5-6

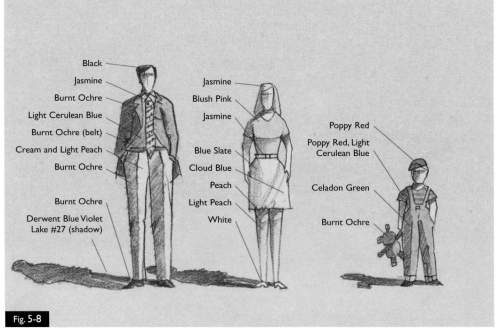

Fig. 5-8

Fig. 5-7

Introducing Figures into the Design Drawing Process

Once you are comfortable drawing a well-proportioned generic figure, practice drawing figures in the early stages of your design drawings, in both elevation and perspective. In a typical eye-level perspective, the heads of all standing figures will be on or near the horizon line. Larger figures will appear closer to the viewer, and smaller figures appear farther away (5-9).

A typical design drawing process is shown in figures 5-10 through 5-16. Note how figures are used during the inception of the design drawing to estimate the dimensions of its forms and spaces. These figures are not necessarily those used in the later stages of the drawing to provide scale and animation. Once a rough perspective view of the place is developed (5-10, 5-11), quickly drawn figures are introduced on a subsequent layer of tracing paper for location and action (5-12), then refined (5-13) by being given better proportions, clothing, and detail. After this stage, the *entire* line drawing is again edited as it is refined. It is then ready to receive shade, shadow, and color (5-14). Note that color is first applied to everything *but* the figures (5-15). Once the colors for the design are determined and applied, the same palette is then used on the figures in various recombinations (5-16).

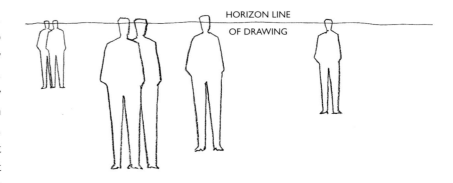

HORIZON LINE
OF DRAWING

Fig. 5-9

FIG. 5-9 Outline figures at various distances from the viewer. To begin drawing one of these figures, determine where you want its feet to be. Then use the proportions shown in figure 5-4 to help you draw a well-proportioned figure between the horizon line and the desired location of its feet. After some practice, you will be able to draw these figures quickly.

FIG. 5-10 The beginning of a design study in perspective. The figures are used to quickly determine comparative sizes of nearby forms and spaces.

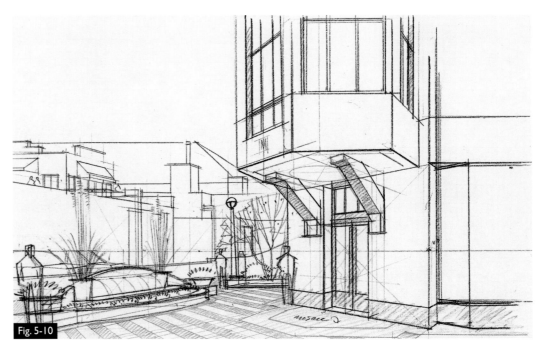

Fig. 5-10

Fig. 5-11

Fig. 5-11 An additional layer of design exploration. The figure was used to help approximate the correct size of the decorative pots.

Fig. 5-12

Fig. 5-12 Gestural figures are located and manipulated to determine how they may best interact with the surroundings.

Fig. 5-13

Fig. 5-14

Fig. 5-13 The figures are refined in proportion, gesture, clothing elements, and detail on a subsequent layer of tracing paper.

Fig. 5-14 The layer of tracing paper with the rough gestural figures was removed, and the combination was traced a final time with a Micron 005 pen. The image was refined and edited in the process, with all the information on one sheet of white tracing paper.

Fig. 5-15 Shade and shadow were applied to the front of the final line drawing, and pastel and color pencil were first applied to the designed elements on the back of the sheet.

Fig. 5-16 The completed drawing. The palette of colors used for the designed elements was also used for the figures.

Fig. 5-15

Fig. 5-16

Digital Figures

There may be situations in which it makes sense to use digital images of figures in color drawings. However, photographic images of figures are usually too detailed and too overt (that is, their contrast is too extreme) to fit comfortably, visually speaking, into a drawing. Often, in an attempt to reduce these problems, the opacity of directly imported photographic figures is reduced, resulting in figures that have a see-through, ghostlike quality.

The sequence shown in figures 5-17 through 5-20 demonstrates a way to reduce this problem. After being traced, the figures here could certainly have been colored by hand as well.

Fig. 5-17 In this scanned drawing, photographic figures were added digitally on their own Photoshop layer. Notice the lack of visual agreement between the drawing and the photographic figures. The image was printed, then used as an underlay to create a line drawing of the figures on tracing paper. Note that the heads of the figures are all on roughly the same horizontal line. (Setup by Jirapong Chaijumroonpun)

Fig. 5-18 The line drawing was scanned, opened in Photoshop, then copied and pasted into the drawing *beneath* the layer with the photo images on it. Its blending mode was set to "Multiply." Lines seen through the figures were covered. Here, the layer with the photo images of the figures is temporarily turned off in order to display only the line drawing.

Fig. 5-17

Fig. 5-18

Fig. 5-19

Fig. 5-20

Fig. 5-19 In this view, the line drawing of the figures has been turned off. The *Dry Brush* filter was used on the photo images of the figures, making them look more like they were drawn with a marker (Filter > Artistic > Dry Brush . . . ; Brush Size = 10, Brush Detail = 0, Brush Texture = 1).

Fig. 5-20 The *Opacity* slider was used to reduce the opacity of the figures layer to 48%. This not only allowed the layer with the traced lines of the figures to show through, but also reduced the overt photographic character of the photo figures. The figures now fit better visually into the drawing.

AUTOMOBILES

Architects and landscape architects frequently find themselves in the position of having to draw automobiles. Being able to do so is an indispensable skill when design ideas must be illustrated within realistic outdoor contexts.

Cars are not difficult to draw. Begin by taking care of first things first. An automobile traced from a photograph or imported digitally into a drawing frequently does not look "quite right" because the car does not conform to the perspective of the drawing it is traced into. When drawing an automobile from scratch, draw a scale person or persons directly beside or in front of the place where you intend to locate an automobile. Then, when you draw simple box shapes that are the approximate sizes of the lower and upper parts of the automobile, you can both judge (by referencing the figure) how large the automobile should be *and* make sure that it conforms to the perspective of the drawing (5-21). You can do this by drawing the boxes using vanishing points that are located on the drawing's horizon line. The scale figure(s) also allows you to estimate the proportions of the automobile—width to length to height—as well as approximate the distance between the front and back wheels.

Once the basic box shapes are in place, draw an automobile shape that stays within the confines of the boxes (5-22). You will find it much easier to draw using photographic references to help you with the proportions of the basic shapes, rather than attempting to rely on memory. Many automobile manufacturers' websites have a "360° view" capability that allows you to spin a selected model and view it from any eye-level angle. If your drawings of automobiles are large enough, you can create their final version freehand. However, if the drawings are small, a french curve and ellipse templates can be helpful when drawing them in their final version (5-23), as lines that are too shaky can make the cars appear wrinkled and dented. Remember to use a minimum of detail on the cars, so the attention of the viewer remains on the designed elements within the drawing.

An illustrated step-by-step process for drawing automobiles in the middle ground is shown in figures 5-21 through 5-25. The steps used to draw more distant automobiles are shown in figures 5-26 through 5-28.

Fig. 5-21

Fig. 5-22

Fig. 5-21 To begin, the automobiles were laid out along with the layout of the design ideas. Human figures were placed at the proposed locations of the automobiles, so a comparative element could be used to quickly size them. The upper and lower forms of the automobiles were initially drawn as simple stacked boxes. The vanishing points for the vehicles were located on the same horizon line used for the rest of the drawing. In fact, in this illustration the vanishing points for the automobiles are the same as those used to draw the building.

Fig. 5-22 The automobiles were quickly shaped from the box-shaped guides. Photographs were used-not traced, but for information-to guide the creation of the shapes.

Fig. 5-23

Fig. 5-23 On a fresh sheet of white tracing paper, the final line drawing was made. In this illustration, the trees, building, and plant materials were drawn freehand with a Micron 005 pen. However, the cars were traced using a french curve and a straightedge. This makes the subtle curved lines of a car much easier to draw and gives it a smoother, more machinelike look. As few lines as possible were used. The wheels were drawn with a small-ellipse template (Pickett, No. 12631), because credible wheels are difficult to draw freehand.

Fig. 5-24

Fig. 5-24 The final line drawing was photocopied onto Bristol paper. *Cool Grey #3 (Cool Grey 30%)* marker was used for the windshields, and *Black* marker was used for silhouetted seats, headrests, and the heavily tinted back windows of the foremost vehicle. Marker base colors were then applied to the car bodies. Any believeable color will do. Often, the body colors of automobiles are the same as those used elsewhere in the illustration so that the cars appear to "belong" to the color scheme when the illustration is complete.

Fig. 5-25

Fig. 5-25 *Black* marker was applied to the lower parts of the plastic bumpers, the wheel wells, and the far tires (seen in silhouette) of the closest vehicle. *Cool Grey #7 (Cool Grey 70%)* marker was applied to the closer tires.

Cool Greys #9, #5, #3, and *#1 (Cool Greys 90%, 50%, 30%,* and *10%)* markers were used to create the diffuse shadows beneath the vehicles. A *Cool Grey #1 (Cool Grey 10%)* marker was also applied to the asphalt parking lot surface, then flavored with a *Cloud Blue* pencil.

The concrete curb in the background and the foreground walkway were colored with *French Grey 10%* marker and flavored with a *Light Peach* pencil.

Swipes of *White* pencil were applied to the upward-facing surfaces of the cars-hoods, roofs, and windshields.

A *Deco Aqua* pencil was then used to lightly wash the windshields, followed by the *White* pencil for highlights.

Fig. 5-26

Fig. 5-26 Once the surroundings were drawn for these distant automobiles, figures were positioned where automobiles were to be located. The figures and the automobiles use the same horizon line (and, again in this case, the same vanishing points) as used for the buildings. This ensured that the automobiles would appear "level" and in visual agreement with the building. The figures were used for comparative scale in drawing the first forms of the cars. Note that the foremost cars (light red) were fully drawn, from roof to wheels. The cars beyond, however, were only partially drawn-mostly as roofs and windows. Photographs were used for reference as necessary.

Fig. 5-27

Fig. 5-27 The roughly drawn automobiles were traced onto the overlay, edited for perspective, and simplified. Because these cars are more numerous and more distant than the middle-ground cars, they were drawn freehand with a Micron 005 pen. As few lines as possible were used, and the strokes were made quickly to keep the lines smooth.

The finished illustration was photocopied onto Bristol paper. *Cool Grey #3 (Cool Grey 30%)* marker was used for the windshields, and various marker base colors were applied to the bodies. Note that the colors were kept somewhat muted so the viewer's attention would be drawn to the designed elements.

Fig. 5-28

Fig. 5-28 *Cool Grey #7 (Cool Grey 70%)* marker was applied to the illuminated tires, and *Black* marker was added to the wheel wells, seats, headrests, and those tires that appear in silhouette. *Cool Grey #9 and #5 (Cool Grey 90% and 50%)* markers were used to add diffuse shadows beneath the cars. Note how this shadow "anchors" the cars to the ground.

Streaks of *White* pencil were applied to upward-facing surfaces and windshields. *Poppy Red* pencil was added to the taillights. *Celadon Green* pencil was used to flavor the color of the window glass. The widespread use of this color helps to tie the cars together visually, as a mass.

Pale Indigo (Cloud Blue) marker was added to the hubcaps, and a blend of *French Grey 10%* and *Cool Grey #1 (Cool Grey 10%)* markers was used to create the mottled color of the asphalt parking lot.

PRESENTATION

II

"**H**ere is the golden rule . . . With color you accentuate, you classify, you disentangle. With black you get stuck in the mud and you are lost. Always say to yourself: Drawings must be easy to read. Color will come to your rescue."

| *Le Corbusier*

CHAPTER 291

COLOR AND COMPOSITION IN ILLUSTRATION

When you begin to think about how to use color as part of the *composition* of an illustration, it should be considered in two ways. First, consider how the colors can be related to one another. Then consider what role color plays in the composition as a whole. As you will see in this chapter, these two ways of thinking about color are both important when you attempt a color presentation drawing.

You may also notice that there are no extended discussions of color "schemes" in this chapter. Such schemes of color as "complementary," "analogous," "triadic," and so on are actually predicated on arrangements of hues only. It is rare that the designer has the luxury of selecting the hues for a project—or its illustration—without constraint. In most situations, at least some of the hues you must work with on a project are usually pre-selected, owing to the range of color found in the natural materials destined for the project, the preferences of the client, or perhaps because certain colors already exist in the project, as often happens with remodel work.

This chapter introduces you to the idea that *any* arrangement of hues can be made to "go together" and that successful color design drawing for presentation depends on the designer's skill at orchestrating all three dimensions of color within the illustration as a whole. The discussion that follows is an overview of the approach to color and drawing composition we frequently use at CommArts when developing color design illustrations and working with illustrators. You may find it helpful to think of this overview as a checklist to use when you develop your own color design drawings for presentation.

There are a number of illustrations in this chapter that have been created by professional illustrators. Although the media they use differ somewhat from those used in the rest of the book, it matters little, because the principles of color and pictorial composition these illustrations so exquisitely manifest can be created in many kinds of color media.

How Colors Relate to One Another: The Contrast of Colors

The relationships between colors are established by the similarities and differences that are created in their dimensions of hue, value, and chroma. These relationships can be described as degrees of *contrast*. As you know, when you experience contrast, you perceive differences in a quality of a thing. These differences can range from subtle variation to the maximum of opposites. For example, the temperature of an object may be hot in one area, cool in another. Its texture may be smooth, rough, or of several possible variations between the two extremes.

The same holds true for color. In Chapter 1, you saw that *each* of the three dimensions of color also had a range of possible expression. The chroma of an object's color can range from weak to strong; its value may be anything from very dark to very light—or its surface may gradate from one value to another. It may be of a single hue or made up of several hues that are similar—or are, perhaps, very different from one another.

The first systematic exploration of the differences in the qualities and dimensions of color expressed as contrast is credited to Johannes Itten. He was a master at the Bauhaus, where he conducted courses in color from 1919 to 1938. Itten formulated an approach to color study that expressed its qualities as seven kinds of color contrast: contrast of hue, light-dark contrast, cold-warm contrast, complementary contrast, simultaneous contrast, contrast of saturation, and contrast of extension (Itten 1973). Itten's book, *The Art of Color,* remains a classic in color instruction to this day.

The designers at CommArts also work with color in terms of its contrasts, but primarily as an expression of contrasts that occur within its three dimensions—contrast of hue, contrast of value, and contrast of chroma. *It is how these*

Fig. 6-1 This watercolor rendering of the San Diego Exposition was made for architect Bertram Goodhue by Birch Burdette Long sometime before 1915. It is an exquisite example of the classic approach to rendering exterior views of buildings. Long used a wide variety of hues, as well as a full range of values, for the colors in the illustration. The chromas of the colors, however, are limited to the very weak end of the chroma scale. (Illustration: Birch Burdette Long)

Fig. 6-1

contrasts are orchestrated that determine the expressive direction of not only the colors used for a project, but also the color illustrations used to communicate the project's various aspects.

Although these three color contrasts are discussed separately in the paragraphs that follow for the sake of clarity, you will generally experience these contrasts all at the same time when you look at a composition of colors. When a designer selects the colors for an interior color scheme, for example, he limits the range of contrasts of certain dimensions of the colors while allowing other dimensions a greater range of contrast. By judiciously selecting *which* dimensions are limited in contrast and to *where* in the range of possibility they are limited, he will determine the expressive direction of the color scheme. Further, it is the imposition of these limitations on the possible ranges of hue, value, and chroma contrast in a color scheme that helps to unify it by introducing a level of order. For example, an illustration of a building's exterior, including its site and context, may have a wide range of hue owing to the variety of building materials, plant materials, and sky. Its colors may range from very dark to very light in value, as certain parts are in shade while others are in sun. To introduce a level of visual order to the scheme of colors, the designer may choose to limit the contrast in chroma of the colors to within a narrow, relatively weak range. This allows the illustration to have interest and *punch,* but also imposes a degree of order resulting from the common level of chroma shared by the colors (6-1).

Hue Contrast

The contrast between hues can range from subtle to dramatic. Look at the color wheel in figure 6-2. You will notice a relationship between any hue you happen to select and the hues on either side of it. If you choose purple blue, for example, you see that it is related to both its neighbors, purple and blue. Green yellow and yellow red both contain a measure of yellow. Side-by-side hues on the color wheel contrast little with each other and are called *analogous hues* (6-3). The farther away hues are from each other on the color wheel, the more they contrast. The strongest contrast in hue, of course, occurs when hues are diametrically opposed on the color wheel—red and blue green, for example. Hues that occur opposite each other are called *complementary hues.*

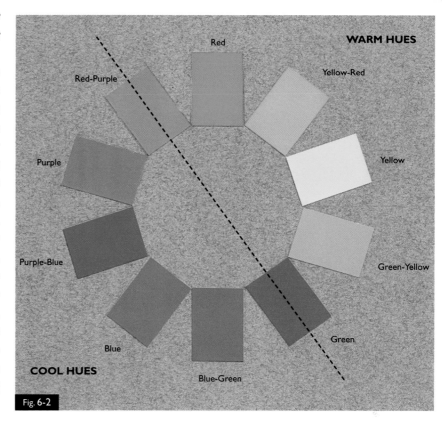

Fig. 6-2

Fig. 6-2 The color wheel. Every color wheel has a warm side and a cool side. On this particular wheel, the hues green and red purple form the dividing line between the warm and cool hues and can themselves be made either warm or cool.

Fig. 6-3

Fig. 6-3 Analogous hues red, yellow red, yellow, and green yellow are predominant in this illustration. Note that in the analogous color scheme for the building, the grays are actually very weak-chroma yellow. The hue yellow has been mixed, in varying amounts, into most of the colors used in the drawing.

Fig. 6-4 This simple cut-paper exercise shows what happens when a color composition has a wide range of hue contrast and the values and chromas of the colors are held consistent. In this example, the values of the colors are limited to the very high range, and their chromas are limited to a weak range. The color in the center is a neutral gray.

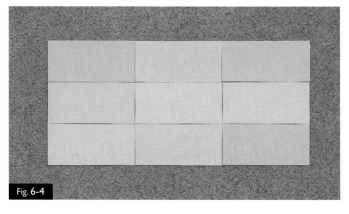

Fig. 6-4

Simultaneous Contrast

Complementary hues are so named because they enhance or "complement" each other. Red makes blue green look its "blue greenest," and vice versa. Green yellow most enhances the hue purple. In fact, the *Munsell System* hue arrangements are based on this phenomenon. Each hue is placed opposite its *visual* complement on the Munsell color wheel. When you see a color, your built-in perceptual faculties conjure up its complement. To experience this in its most obvious form, gaze at an intense color under good lighting for about a minute, then shift your gaze to a neutral surface of white or gray. You will experience an *afterimage* of the colored shape in its *complementary* color (6-5). For the same reason, if you look at a color and a neutral gray together, the gray will be tinged with the complement of the color with which it is seen (6-6). This effect is called *simultaneous contrast*. Likewise, when *any* two colors are placed together, each subtly influences the other by its presence. You can imagine, then, the variety of subtle color interactions that might occur when a viewer looks at an entire painting, illustration, or built composition. *Every arrangement of colors creates unique affiliations and tensions, depending on the amounts, qualities, and proximities of the colors in the arrangement.* This phenomenon has special meaning for designers of places, in that each intended arrangement of colors should be studied, first inexpensively on paper, then eventually mocked-up in its finished location as construction nears an end.

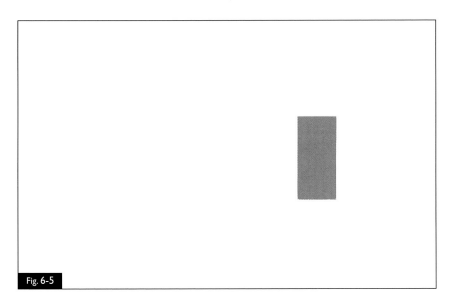

Fig. 6-5

Fig. 6-6

Fig. 6-5 Look at the red rectangle from about six inches away, under a fairly bright light, for about 30 seconds. As your eyes become accustomed to the red, they will begin to generate its complementary color, blue green. As you continue to look, the rectangle's edges will seem to fluoresce with an "aura" of blue green as your eyes make small movements. If you move your gaze about an inch to the side, you will see how the afterimage, still partially covering the red, begins to dull the red!

After about a minute, shift your gaze completely away from the red to the blank white area to the left. In a second or two, the afterimage, roughly in the rectangular shape, will fluoresce blue green for five to ten seconds before it fades away.

Fig. 6-6 The gray rectangles in the centers of the colored squares are exactly the same. Use a fairly bright light as you look from one square to the other from about six inches away for about a half minute. Each gray rectangle will become tinged with the complementary color of the square it is within.

Warm-Cool Contrast

A color wheel can be divided into halves, with warm colors on one side and cool colors on the other. On the Munsell color wheel, this division happens along a line formed between the complementary hues green and red purple (6-2). These two hues can be adjusted to become either warm or cool (6-7). *Warm colors* are so named because they are associated with the colors emitted from archetypal heat sources like fire or incandescent lamp filaments. They can also raise the perceived temperature of a place, subtly stimulate appetite, and increase a person's predisposition to outgoing behavior. *Cool colors* are associated with things cool, such as the color of north sky light seen on objects in the shade. Cool colors can lower the perceived temperature of a place and have a quieting effect as they subtly influence the occupants of a place to become more introverted. Warm-colored objects seem to advance toward the viewer and appear more figural in a composition (6-8), whereas cool colors are more passive and seem to recede. These principles are particularly important tools in the creation of spatial effects in an illustration (see figure 1-11).

Fig. 6-7 The hues red purple *(above)* and green *(below)* occur on the dividing line between warm and cool hues on the color wheel. The cool (slightly bluish) versions of both hues appear on the left, and the warm (slightly yellow-reddish) versions appear on the right.

Fig. 6-8 Note how the straightforward arrangement of the warm and cool hues in this illustration create not only a startling image of the building, but one with a very clear center of interest. The strength of this view is assisted by the arrangement of the major value groupings, whereby the subject building and the sky immediately beyond are the lightest values in the composition and everything else grades darker from there. In addition, the hue and value arrangements are believable in that they could be those encountered in an early morning sunrise. (Illustration: Douglas E. Jamieson)

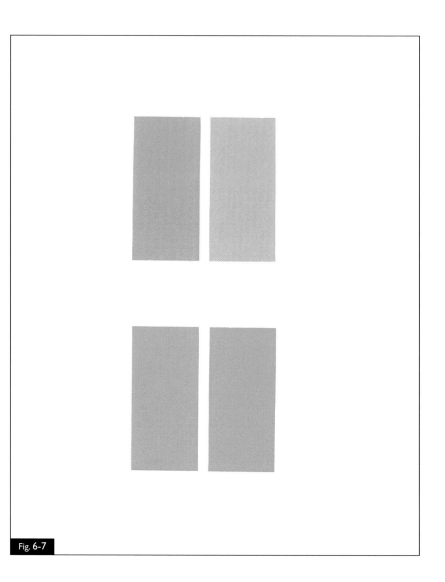

Fig. 6-7

Fig. 6-8

Value Contrast

Contrasting the values of colors is one of the most powerful ways to establish the impact of a color composition. Like the other dimensions of color, the values of the colors of a composition can range widely or can be limited to a particular location on the scale of light to dark. If the range of values of the colors is limited to light values, the composition is said to be done in a *high key* (6-9). Likewise, if the colors of a composition are mostly in the low range of values, it is a *low-key* composition.

The contrast of value is also the most powerful ally you have in making the idea in a design illustration easily legible. The skillful handling of this kind of contrast can make the illustration more compelling at first glance, as well as more easily readable from a distance. A typical color design drawing created for presentation purposes should be *built primarily on value contrast* for its legibility and dramatic impact. The color dimensions of hue and chroma are used to further enhance legibility while adding character and richness. There are, of course, exceptions to this principle, especially when you attempt to create a particular quality in an illustration that calls for less value contrast, such as in the high-key illustration shown in figure 6-9. However, you will notice that in their strongest, most dramatic design illustrations, professional illustrators in most cases not only use a *full range of values,* from very dark to very light, they also arrange these values in a way that most advantageously and legibly guides the eye to the focal point of the design idea. At the same time, they use these arrangements to create the illusion of spatial depth in the illustration (6-10)! You will be introduced to an approach to creating these value arrangements in

Fig. 6-9 This illustration gives an example of restraint in the value and chroma dimensions of the colors used. Although the hues are analogous-red, yellow red, yellow, and green yellow-with complementary accents of purple blue in the shade and shadow, note how an overtone of the hue yellow informs all the other colors.

The values of the colors are limited to a very high range, and the chromas are restrained to the weak end of the scale.

Through the careful arrangement of its colors, the illustrator creates a powerful composition that allows the viewer to almost feel the bright sun, heat, and dust of Cairo, Egypt. (Illustration: Frank M. Costantino.)

Fig. 6-9

Chapter 7. A dramatic and thoughtful value arrangement not only gives a design illustration "punch," it provides for a more successful reproduction of the illustration in printed media, especially media with limited color or with only black-and-white reproductions, such as a newspaper.

Yet it is this very reason that certain kinds of computer-generated design illustration seem overbusy, to the point of appearing frenetic. When these illustrations are created by importing imagery from other sources, such as signing, figures, automobiles, skies, and backgrounds, they exhibit a wide variety of hues, values, and chromas. Such illustrations have a collagelike quality because that is the way they are composed.

Fig. 6-10

Fig. 6-10 **This illustration embodies many, if not most, of the color and composition ideas presented in this chapter. The vertical format, the repeated vertical forms, the location of the horizon line, and the use of color all work together to create a composition that is stunning in its impact.**

The values of the colors range from almost black to touches of pure white. However, you need only to squint slightly to realize that the various areas of the illustration are carefully assigned groups of similar values, which not only help to frame the illustration, but also create a strong focus and sense of spatial depth within. To be sure, other contrasts of

value occur within the illustration, but the illustrator took care to see that none of the minor contrasts were so strong or demanding that they compete with the impact of the major value groupings.

The hues used in the illustration come from all parts of the color wheel, and although the warm hues predominate, they are intermixed with each other *and* with the cool hues to produce many subtle and sophisticated colors.

The chromas of the colors are held to a relatively weak range throughout and act as a unifying agent for the composition. (Illustration: Thomas W. Schaller)

Chroma Contrast

The chromas of the colors in a composition can range from very weak—almost pure gray—to very strong and vibrant (6-11). The way chroma is orchestrated, as with hue and value, can help determine the emotional impact of the composition. Strong-chroma colors are stimulating to most people, connoting excitement and activity. In our culture, we often see a higher proportion of strong-chroma colors associated with places for children, retail establishments, and entertainment (6-12). Medium-to-weak-chroma colors are more frequently associated with places in which people spend longer periods of time, such as residences and offices. These kinds of color are also generally perceived as more relaxed, calm, serene, upscale, and sophisticated.

You will find that the colors of most exterior design drawings and illustrations are in the middle- to weak-chroma range, inasmuch as this is the chroma range of most natural materials. You have seen what happens to man-made materials left outdoors, as sun and weather conspire to bleach colors to their most grayed versions. Consequently, building designers often choose colors for the man-made materials and finishes on building exteriors that are sympathetic to these natural colors. Color drawings of many kinds of interior places are also in the middle- to weak-chroma range, particularly given our culture's propensities for colors in this range of chroma. However, accents of strong-chroma color are often found in illustrations of both interior and exterior views, not only because these accents tend to balance large areas of weaker-chroma colors, but because we enjoy strong-chroma colors in small doses (6-13). Such doses usually appear in our drawings in small, subordinate areas. They also often appear in our lives within small segments of time—in those things that are relatively short-lived, such as flower masses, clothing, walls, or pieces of furniture, whose colors can be easily changed as we tire of them.

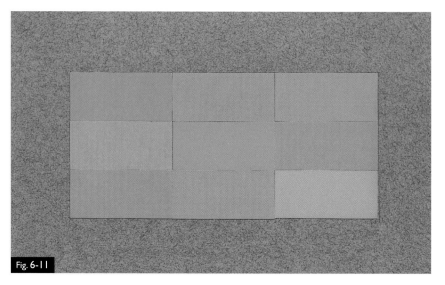

Fig. 6-11

Fig. 6-11 This cut-paper exercise illustrates a color scheme with a limited range of hues (yellow through red-purple) and strictly limited values, but the chromas of the colors are unrestricted and range from very weak to very strong.

Compare the impact of this color composition to that in figure 6-4.

Fig. 6-12

Fig. 6-12 This drawing of an entertainment and retail plaza has many areas of strong-chroma color. Note how these colors are enhanced by setting them within dark, weak-chroma surroundings.

Once the line drawing was made by hand, color and imagery were added using Photoshop. (Photographs: Devin Doyle, www.devindoyle.com; color: Grady Huff)

Fig. 6-13

Fig. 6-13 The colors of the roof and stucco on the third-level walls, column bases, and curb have a similar "weathered" look that is sympathetic, albeit in different hues, to that of the stone on the lower part of the building.

The warm gray stucco and gray-green roof were held to a similar value to that of the stone, and the chromas of the colors of the stucco and roof are even somewhat weaker than those of the stone, helping to feature it slightly.

Note the balancing effect the smaller accents of strong-chroma colors of the potted flowers, the figures' clothing, and the tiled fountain wall have on the overall composition.

COLOR CONTRAST AND IMAGE COMPOSITION

All illustrations that attempt to manifest a three-dimensional view on a two-dimensional surface—whether that surface is paper or a computer screen—are created with four basic visual elements. Line, shape, color, and texture must be arranged in the most effective way to create images of form, space, light, and materials.

Most color design drawings are created as vehicles to communicate design ideas. The viewer of a design drawing typically looks "into" the drawing to find the design information, whether it is a plan, elevation, axonometric, or perspective view. This information is usually made up of smaller, individuated ideas that have been assembled to form the illustration. A perspective view, for example, shows the designer's ideas about the floor plane—its variations in level, its finishes, the furnishings that might rest on it; the wall plane—its penetrations, its materials and finishes, shelving and cabinetry; and the ceiling plane—its fixtures, its penetrations, its variations in height, its colors and finishes, and so on. This view assembles these many ideas into a single drawing, often giving the designer her first view of how a multitude of ideas and decisions appear in concert. It also allows viewers to participate in the assessment of these ideas.

You will find, however, that during your career as a designer there will be many times when you want to create illustrations of your ideas that go beyond the simple delivery of design information. You will want to present this design information in the most effective way. This means you must shift your perception and begin to look "at" your drawings as graphic compositions, not only "into" them for the information they contain.

When you prepare a color drawing to present design information in this way, you must take into account the perceptual habits and needs of the viewer and understand the way in which he responds to various kinds of visual organization (Feldman 1987). However, each illustration is unique, so an approach that creates the most effective presentation in one situation may not be appropriate for another. Instead, it is more effective to begin each new presentation-level illustration by evaluating the opportunities and constraints that the subject matter presents to the designer. This part of the present chapter, as well as the first part of Chapter 7, introduces you to design principles that, when realized, can help you create more effective, dramatic, and satisfying design presentation drawings in color. These principles—unity, balance, proportion, and rhythm—reflect our innate perceptual needs and are common to all the representative graphic arts. Use them to evaluate your approach to color in your illustrations as you proceed. It is worth noting the degree to which these principles interrelate as each contributes to the visual order of the image.

A Unified Image

Unity is the design principle that is concerned with how an image will be seen *as a whole*. It is considered by some designers to be the only principle of pictorial composition, toward which all others work in support.

Effective color drawing for the purposes of presentation really begins upstream from the application of color. It starts with the initial compositional decisions the designer makes in regard to the underlying skeleton of the illustration, the line drawing. Many of these decisions are simple and easy, but only if the designer addresses them at the outset.

It is worth deciding, before you invest the time (and fee), whether a presentation drawing is needed or a quick sketch can serve the purpose. If a presentation drawing *is* justified, make sure you are clear about the purpose of the illustration and what exactly it must communicate. The line drawing that is generated initially is really the armature that shapes the image and determines its degree of impact. The time spent developing a well-composed line drawing will prove to have been worthwhile when you are ready to arrange its values, color, and effects of light.

For example, a simple and often overlooked consideration is the drawing format. Format is the orientation of the page: vertical, oblong, or square. A horizontal, or oblong, format can help a picture with a horizontal emphasis to appear more at home on the page. A vertical format can do the same for a vertically oriented subject, such as a high-rise building. Note the contribution of the picture's format to its impact in figures 6-8 and 6-18.

Another consideration is the location of the picture's horizon. The horizon is usually placed above or below the center of the picture, inasmuch as bisecting the picture with the horizon may give the composition a static quality. If you place the horizon high in the picture, more ground plane will show. This approach is particularly good if you have a large amount of information to communicate about the ground or floor plane, such as that found in an aerial or "bird's-eye" perspective view (6-14). However, a high horizon may burden the

Fig. 6-14 In this illustration the horizon line is above the picture and off the page by a significant distance, resulting in the aerial perspective, or "bird's-eye" view, shown. Views of this kind are particularly good for communicating forms, spaces, and plan relationships (such as circulation) simultaneously, especially to viewers unfamiliar with the conventions of plan views.

As a general rule of graphic design, diagonal lines introduced into a picture are more dynamic than those that run orthogonally. Note the degree to which this effect influences the view shown here.

It is also worth noting how the color is arranged in this illustration. The yellow-red roofs immediately dominate your attention. The larger roof in the upper center is balanced by the smaller roof in the lower left. Note, too, that although the cooler hues of green, blue green, blue, purple-blue, and purple are dominant in terms of area, yellow has been repeatedly mingled with green to create many areas of green-yellow. Moreover, the yellow-red used on the roofs has been mingled into many of the other areas of the illustration, including the tree canopies. Likewise, the purple and purple-blue of the shadows have also been mingled into many areas. As you can see in this and other illustrations in this chapter, mingling is another way to unify an illustration and create balance between the warm and cool hues.

Fig. 6-14

The picture gets darker toward its edges, particularly its bottom edge. This helps to keep the viewer's attention focused on the center of interest within the illustration. (Illustration: Douglas E. Jamieson)

unsuspecting illustrator of a single building exterior, for example, with having to illustrate more ground plane elements than she planned. A low horizon creates the opposite condition, with less ground plane and more sky or ceiling showing. It also provides the conditions for more dramatic perspective in drawing tall structures, such as those shown in figures 6-16 and 6-18.

Most designers and illustrators unify their drawings simply by making one feature dominate the viewer's attention, while other features are subordinate to the *dominant* feature. This is usually done by establishing a focus or center of interest in the picture—a dominant idea, form or group of forms, or space. This is the reason it is important to be very clear initially as to the purpose of the illustration, because without clarity of purpose, it is difficult to decide on its focus. The features of secondary or *subordinate* interest are arranged in visual support of the center of interest. For example, a view may be so arranged that the perspective lines of secondary elements lead the viewer's eye, usually gradually or indirectly, toward the center of interest.

Your arrangement of color contrasts can play a significant role in unifying the image. It may be that certain of the most vivid contrasts of the colors—for example,

value contrast—occur within the center of interest and thereby help to hold the viewer's attention there (6-16). Ironically, the slight diminution of the contrasts of the colors throughout a composition can also help to unify a color design drawing. You can see this effect, called "mingling" of colors, in many works of fine art— particularly impressionist paintings—as well as in professional design illustrations (6-15). Stated simply, all colors used in the illustration are used in almost all parts of the illustration, but in differing amounts. For example, color pencil used in one part of a drawing may be used to flavor the colors of several other parts of the drawing. If this idea is repeated with many of the pencils used to color the drawing, the drawing begins to take on a more complex and interesting, as well as somewhat more muted, coloration. You can notice the unifying effects of this approach to color in many of the illustrations in this chapter and throughout the book.

The overall value arrangement plays a critical role in unifying the picture image of a presentation drawing. Many small, disparate patches of dark and light in a drawing or computer illustration can fragment its overall impression, unnecessarily distracting the viewer from seeing the ideas within as adding up to a whole or sum that is greater than its parts. Illustrations that have a

Fig. 6-15

Fig. 6-15 This illustration is an excellent example of the intermixture or "mingling" of warm and cool colors to unify the illustration and produce subtle but lively colors as a result. The hues, taken from the yellow-red, green, and purple-blue regions of the color wheel, form an approximate *triad* that, when mixed with one another, create subtle, more neutral colors. However, the colors created by these mixtures are far more interesting and lively than any single colors that may have been used. (Illustration: Ronald J. Love)

purposeful, overall arrangement of its *major* value groups are easier to understand and deliver a unified impression to the viewer (6-16). Developing your skill in arranging the major value groups of a presentation drawing is a critical part of successful presentation drawing; this subject is covered further in Chapter 7.

Although there are different kinds of color contrast in an illustration, some of the most vivid occurring within or on behalf of steering the viewer's attention to the center of interest, remember that these contrasts can occur only if they have a foil or background that allows them to be seen. Often, a consistent level in the chroma of the colors (usually on the weaker end of the scale of possibility) in an illustration not only helps to provide a foil against which accents of stronger chroma color can be perceived, but this consistent dimension is yet another means of unifying the illustration (6-17).

Fig. 6-16 The illustrator of this image has marshaled a full range of values, from black to white, to create a very powerful image. The darkest range of values is utilized in the foreground, and a medium range is used for the background; the very lightest values are saved for the center of interest. Note, too, that the strongest value *contrasts* also occur here, between the focal point and its surroundings.

Even though, when squinting at this illustration, you see the values arranged in major groupings, there is still sufficient contrast within each grouping that its features and figures remain discernible.

Once again, as in many of the other illustrations in this chapter, the minglings and gradations of the colors help to unify the composition. (Illustration: Thomas W. Schaller)

Fig. 6-16

stainless steel tenant signing on polished stainless steel bar - uplit from lights mounted above curved "brow"

"brow" and pop- windows for mine on the sheet

5th sheet view of

GAS COMPANY TOWER

Beautiful polished metal identity plaque for tenants; top is internally illuminated

Fig. 6-17

Fig. 6-17 Although this study is composed mostly of weak-chroma colors, the strong-chroma accents are more noticeable because of them. This chroma contrast helps to keep the viewer's attention on the proposed display windows—the purpose of the illustration.

This drawing was created by applying marker and color pencil to a photocopy of a line drawing on Canson paper.

Introducing Balance

Each picture we see we perceive, whether consciously or not, on a visual scale somewhere between balanced and unbalanced. "Size, shape, color, 'temperature' and texture are experienced as if they are heavy or light, solid or transparent, floating or sinking. Also, there is no doubt that colors and textures can tip the optical scales we carry inside our heads. An artist who doesn't know about those scales is trying to walk with one leg" (Feldman 1987, 241).

Balance in pictures can be easily accomplished by using the device of *symmetry,* whereby the handling of the visual elements on one side of the picture is matched by that on the other side, whether horizontal or vertical. Symmetrical compositions lend an air of precision and order to an illustration and are useful for views of formal gardens, rooms, or building entries. Yet they can make a picture appear static if your intent is a greater degree of dynamism. For that reason, the majority of illustration compositions are *asymmetrical* and achieve balance through less obvious means. Asymmetrical balance is often approached through "leverage," whereby a substantial visual weight is counteracted by something much smaller, usually at some distance from the greater weight (6-18). The distance between the two acts as a "lever arm," balancing the weights much as objects are balanced in physics. "Although gravity does not actually operate on the objects in paintings, we perceive them *as if* it does" (Feldman 1987, 241).

Fig. 6-18 The illustrator says, "This particular image was designed expressly as a piece where pure color, rather than tonal value or representation of shape, was intended as the primary compositional device. Tangible elements of earth and man-made objects are expressed in warm tones of red and gold while atmospheric elements—sky and water—are treated in cooler shades of green and blue." Note how he has arranged the image so that the warm and cool colors are distributed in a way that balances the illustration.

You will also find that the value composition of the illustration is, nevertheless, in balance. The foreground cliff and the darkened water at the bottom of the illustration visually balance the larger mass of the structure sweeping to the upper left, grading darker as it does so. (Illustration: Thomas W. Schaller)

Fig. 6-18

Balance can be created by the way the artist stimulates and guides the interest of the viewer. Smaller areas that pique our curiosity can balance the larger areas in a composition. Color is often used to this end. Large areas of one color or a group of related colors are often balanced with a small, vivid "accent" of a similar color or one from the opposite side of the color wheel (6-19). For example, a composition made up of grayed blues and blue greens may be balanced by a touch of intense red in just the right location.

A Sense of Proportion

Proportion is the relationship of the *sizes* of the parts of a composition to one another and to the whole. Because there are no rules governing these relationships, they are largely dependent on the judgment of the artist or illustrator.

When you consider proportion, you are also considering the issue of balance. When the parts of an image seem to be in the right proportion to one

Fig. 6-19

Fig. 6-19 The small (in area) but vivid yellow-red of the campfire helps to balance the weaker-chroma gray-green and green-yellow hues of the paper and applied color, respectively.

This study was made with color pencil and pastel (for the fire and smoke) applied to a photocopy of a line drawing on Canson paper.

another, you have a sense of balance. Symmetry, as mentioned in the discussion of balance, is based on equal proportions. When the subject of horizon line location was discussed, a composition having equal amounts of sky and ground was described as static. Better *proportions* of the picture might appear, for example, as one-third ground, two-thirds sky. When considering a vertical or horizontal format for an illustration, you must decide on the proportion of length to width of the picture. The Greeks derived what they considered the ideal proportions, called the *Golden Mean*, whereby the relationship of the smaller part to the larger part was the same as the larger part's relationship to the whole, or roughly 1:1.6. In whole numbers, this is 5:8. Throughout history, architects have used the Golden Mean to create height-to-width proportions for doorways, windows, and entire building façades. Artists have even used this proportion to format their pictures.

Proportion also applies to color. When is there too much of a certain color, not enough of another? What proportions seem balanced? Does the way the illustrator proportioned the colors in figure 6-14 give a sense of balance? When the issue of color is addressed in terms of proportion, you can think of it in terms of amount or *area*. In the previous discussion of unity, the terms *dominant* and *subordinate* were used to describe the degree to which parts of the illustration are intended to attract the viewer's attention. Here, these terms are used to describe the amount of area a particular color quality occupies in the composition. When a limited range of color dimensions are dominant (in terms of area) in a composition, it helps the picture to appear more coherent. For example, the preponderance (in area) of a particular hue in a picture—for instance, red, including the light reds and dark reds, the vivid reds and the grayed reds—will go a long way toward creating an image that appears unified (6-20). Likewise, the preponderance of other colors in the illustration whose dimensions are closely related will further help to unify the image. If most of the area of an illustration has colors that are mostly grayed, for example, a further level of unity is created. The same goes for the lightness/darkness of the colors in the illustration. Of course, the colors in this picture should contain areas of contrast in hue, lightness/darkness, and grayness/intensity as well (6-21). "When . . . similarities overpower contrasts, the result is boredom. When contrasts overpower similarities, the result is chaos. A successful design must avoid both these extremes" (Goldstein 1977, 216).

Fig. 6-20 This marker and color pencil drawing on a blackline print shows a preponderance of a yellow-red hue in the composition. Although the dominance of a particular hue helps to unify the image, closer inspection shows that the yellow-red is more red in some places and more yellow in others. Such variation adds interest to the drawing and does not detract from the ability of this hue—or, more accurately, this close-knit group of hues—to unify the composition. Other hues, the green in particular, play a subordinate, balancing role. (Drawing: Henry Beer)

Fig. 6-20

Fig. 6-21

Fig. 6-21 Another way to unify an illustration with hue is to give it a certain hue "cast." This watercolor illustration uses a variety of hues—yellow-red, green, purple-blue, and purple. However, all colors have been infused with a yellow-reddish cast—even the green trees and the purple-blue sky. The effect not only gives this illustration the glow of a sunrise (or sunset), it also implies the relaxed and magical atmosphere of an oceanside retreat.

A similar effect can be created in illustrations that use the media covered in this book, by flavoring each color with pencils appropriate to the hue you wish to cast. (Illustration: Curtis James Woodhouse)

These are all questions of judgment not answered by a simple rule. Rather, the answers come from a consideration of the purpose of your illustration and your artistic and design intent. A landscape scene at dusk will, for example, be more likely to have a predominance of blue and blue-green hues than an illustration of an interior finished with natural wood (6-22).

Proportion is often confused with *scale*. Whereas proportion is concerned with the relationship of the sizes of things to one another, scale is the relationship of the sizes of things to *people*. Compositions meant to communicate ideas about places for people should include illustrated people, or at least human-scaled elements such as cars or furniture, so that the viewer can evaluate the ideas about a place, focused on those who must use it and live with it.

Fig. 6-22 This rendering from the 1920s shows a winter dusk scene created for the purpose of illustrating a residence. The predominant hue is purple-blue— even the seemingly white snow is actually a very high-value, weak-chroma purple-blue for the most part.

Notice how color has been used by the illustrator to push beyond mere illustration of a house. By arranging the house as a winter dusk scene, with cool and weak-chroma colors on the exterior and touches of warm, strong-chroma colors to imply the interior glow, the illustrator communicates the very essence of shelter—warm, protected, and secure against the elements. (Illustration: Edward Dixon McDonald)

Fig. 6-22

The Beat of the Rhythm

Rhythm helps to unify a pictorial composition by introducing flow and various kinds of repetition, whether of line, shapes, colors, or textures. Such repetition can be regular, irregular, or progressively changing. The gradations of value and color shown throughout this book, for example, introduce rhythm into the compositions by consistently repeating change of color or value—or both—across a surface.

Discrete areas of color can be used to introduce rhythm in a composition by positioning them in various parts of the picture repeatedly (6-23). Or a color can be woven more subtly through the composition by mingling it with the other colors, as mentioned earlier and illustrated in such examples as figures 6-15 and 6-21.

Repetition of limited ranges of the dimensions of the colors in an illustration, so that these limited ranges occupy a dominant portion of the illustration area, is another way of introducing rhythm. This is implicit in various other parts of this chapter, such as in the discussion of high-key and low-key illustrations. In figure 6-9, for example, the repeated quality of the various colors is their lightness of value. Note, too, the other qualities of the colors in this illustration that have been repeated. A yellow hue, for example, has been used in almost every area of the illustration, along with the other hues employed. Through the repeated use of certain color qualities, the illustration is quite successful in creating a clear and unified image.

If you are new to the idea of color and pictorial composition, the contents of this chapter may seem a bit overwhelming. If you have had previous experience with these ideas, you may find this chapter a good refresher. Whatever your level of experience in composition, one thing is certain: The more you work with these ideas when composing your own presentation drawings, the more familiar they will become. Before long, you will find that they are an integral part of your abilities as a designer and are applicable not only to design illustration, but to a wide range of design circumstances.

Fig. 6-23 The same colors—yellow red, yellow, green-yellow, and purple-blue—occur repeatedly throughout this study drawing. By limiting your palette of colors, the rhythms created by repeated colors become unavoidable.

Fig. 6-23

CHAPTER 315

APPROACHES TO CREATING COLOR DESIGN DRAWINGS

Many designers become so absorbed in a project that they forget there are many smart ways to save time and effort during the design communication stages of the process. Too often, they spend time doing renderings when a simple line sketch would suffice. It is wise to spend a little time thinking about a strategy for producing your drawings before proceeding. By answering a few questions about your objectives before an upcoming presentation effort, you can save yourself significant time, effort, and fees.

First, ask yourself, What is the purpose of these drawings? Are you creating a quick impression of massing, proportions, relative scale, and major elements? Or must you communicate a finer grain of character information that includes, say, window mullion layout and more articulated shadows? Decide what level of information you *must* communicate for the presentation at hand.

Second, who is your audience? Do you simply want to relate an idea to peers—members of your design team, perhaps? Are you communicating to a client who is comfortable with and able to "read" fairly rough, quick drawings showing the refinement of a concept? Or are you presenting to a lay group who may misinterpret the character of a quick study? Do your drawings need to persuade and, if so, to what extent?

Finally, in light of the first two questions, ask yourself how much of your time the drawings are worth. Corollary to this is, of course, how much time you *have*. What is at stake? Stopping what you are doing to take the time to tailor your approach to your design communication task will be time well spent.

This chapter discusses and illustrates a step-by-step process for creating various types of color design drawings. Some of the examples are simple illustrations of design ideas and were made quickly, and others were somewhat more carefully prepared for presentation purposes.

First, you will review some of the basic considerations useful for beginning a drawing, including how to prepare a line drawing, the creation of a value strategy, and what to consider when making a scan of your line drawing for your final color illustration. The rest of the chapter shows the approaches we use most frequently at CommArts for creating color design drawings, which include the variety of useful papers first introduced in Chapter 2. The remainder of the chapter shows how to include written information with your drawings, and some useful approaches to creating single and multiple presentation sheets.

THE FIRST CONSIDERATION: MAKE THE LINE DRAWING

Line is the most basic graphic convention used for creating images in the design professions. Whether a designer works by hand or on a computer, he is responsible for apprehending three-dimensional ideas on a two-dimensional surface, whether a sheet of paper or a computer screen. Line drawings also form the basis for the approach to color design drawing covered in this book.

At CommArts, we use the drawing approach that most effectively and efficiently communicates the idea at hand. This may be a hand-drawn perspective sketch, a digital illustration, or a hybrid drawing—a hand drawing with digital enhancement. A quick, hand-drawn perspective sketch is often sufficient to communicate an early idea to a client and is frequently the most cost-effective approach in terms of fee. Convincing scale elements—figures, furniture, and accessories—are usually most easily added by hand. Quite often a perspective view of a design idea is also the most effective communication tool, as it is one of the few devices that can instantly show the *relationships* between the boundary planes of the space and its contents. An interior perspective study sketch, for example, may include walls, ceiling, floor, furnishings, and a first attempt at choosing materials and colors.

If an existing building or space is being remodeled, it is usually most effective to simply trace a digital photograph of the desired view. While tracing the photograph, the designer can add the design changes by hand, using the vanishing points and horizon line established by the photograph.

Sometimes it is most efficient to build a quick and simple scale study model of a particularly difficult view, either digitally or by hand. SketchUp is an excellent application for quickly and easily creating digital models. If the model is created by hand, remember to keep it simple, building only the necessary elements. A digital picture can be taken of the model and traced to make a line drawing that includes the necessary additional detail.

Keep your line drawings small. Since the advent of high-quality color reproduction techniques, it is no longer necessary to create design drawings the size of a bed sheet. We typically create line drawings ranging from 8½" x 11"

(letter size) to 11" x 17" (ledger size) and enlarge them during the photocopying process. Working at this size, the designer can create design drawings much faster and remain at a greater "distance" from the image, allowing her to keep an eye on the "big picture" and not get lost in the details. When line drawings are conceived at a small scale, it is important to keep your linework correspondingly *thin,* because photocopy enlargements enlarge *everything,* including line thickness. It is not necessary to use a hierarchy of line weights when making line drawings destined for color, inasmuch as the color—especially the value arrangements—will make the finished image legible.

We typically use a Micron 005 pen or a 4x0 technical pen for very small line drawings (7-9). The Micron works best on tracing paper, and the technical pen works best on drawing *vellum*. A *Black* Prismacolor pencil is another excellent line medium for these drawings; its line can be kept quite thin if the pencil is applied with the use of a straightedge (see figure 7-44). Although a *Black* Prismacolor can generate a rich, dark line similar to that of a felt-tipped pen, it has the advantage of being easily erasable. Use an electric eraser with the soft, white erasing strip intended for use on mylar. These line media can, of course, be mixed in a single drawing as necessary. Their common advantage is that they all reproduce well when photocopied or scanned. Graphite pencil can also be used when necessary and can be combined with other line media. However, graphite pencil does not photocopy or scan as well as the line media mentioned earlier, unless it is soft or is applied with sufficiently firm hand pressure.

Color Sketch or Presentation Drawing?

Most situations in the earlier parts of the design process do not require the designer to plan the perspective views he uses to communicate his design ideas, beyond making sure that the image includes the information he intends to convey. The edges of this view may simply fade away or may be delineated by a rectangular boundary that defines the edges of the picture more uniformly.

However, you have found that there are occasions during the design process—most frequently in the latter parts of concept development through the design development phase of a project—when you want your illustration, whether created by hand or computer, to convey your ideas with more visual impact.

When you intend to create greater impact with your color design drawings, it does not necessarily mean you have to spend significantly more time making the drawing in an attempt to attain the perfection of a rendering.

Instead, you must look at your drawing in a different way. Rather than only looking *into* the drawing for design information, you must also begin to look *at* the drawing as a graphic composition in its own right.

The ideas introduced in Chapter 6—unity, balance, proportion, and rhythm—can be brought to bear as you create your line drawing, in deciding on issues such as format, horizon location, symmetry, and scale. These ideas will continue to inform your drawing in various other ways as you apply the color media, as illustrated by the examples in Chapter 6 and later in this chapter. However, there is another important compositional issue worth considering when creating a line drawing for presentation purposes.

Layers of Space

When you look at the work of professional design illustrators, you may notice that there are objects and elements that appear quite close to the viewer and, depending on whether the view is an interior or exterior, objects and elements in the distance as well. The focus of the illustration is usually found between these close and distant components. In other words, the illustration has a foreground, a middle ground, and a background. This layering of space creates, in the words of William Kirby Lockard, FAIA, considerably more "spatial interest," because the various objects and elements between the foreground and distance successively and partially obscure one another.

This spatial situation differs from typical design drawings that have little or nothing behind or in front of the subject of the drawing. To be sure, there is nothing wrong with the typical design drawing, as it can be created quickly and efficiently communicates the essentials of the design idea. Drawings with foreground and background take slightly longer to create, but tend to have more impact inasmuch as that is how we see the world, more contextual information is communicated, and more opportunities are provided for a strategic arrangement of the major value groups of the drawing.

The first step in creating layers of space in an illustration is to select your view. Walk your plan in your imagination, as a photographer might, mentally composing views of the part or parts you intend to illustrate. You can turn from side to side, zoom in or pull back for a wider, more inclusive shot. Usually, by including some foreground feature or element in your view, you may ensure more opportunities for creating visual impact when you begin the value studies (7-1, 7-2). The feature or element may be an architectural element, furnishings, plant materials, or figures—or a combination. Except for figures, the elements shown in the illustration should either exist or be proposed, because to add gratuitous elements to a design drawing solely for the purposes of picture composition can be misleading.

Fig. 7-1a

Fig. 7-1b

Fig. 7-1 Line drawings of a conceptual view for a restaurant. Figure 7-1(a) shows how the view may have looked had the issue of spatial interest not been considered. The foreground, in particular, is even and uneventful. The view shown in figure 7-1(b) resulted after the plan was consulted and the view broadened to include the proposed stands of bamboo and the potted bonsai tree. Standing figures were also introduced to help punctuate the rather even field of seated figures.

Fig. 7-2a

Fig. 7-2b

Fig. 7-2 These line drawings show the exterior view of a proposed building for office and retail uses. In figure 7-2(a), the building is shown as an isolated entity, mostly devoid of context. Figure 7-2(b) shows the building viewed from across the intersection, on the entry patio of a neighboring building. The architectural elements, plant materials, and figures introduce a foreground to the drawing.

THE SECOND CONSIDERATION: CREATE A VALUE STRATEGY

Once the line drawing has been created and its major parts have been arranged in a spatial hierarchy, it is important to consider the arrangement of its *major groups* of value, particularly if your intent is to use your drawing for presentation purposes. Value is particularly important and the most influential of the three dimensions of color in a design drawing, not only because it is the most pivotal in creating the effects of light, but because it is the only one of the three dimensions of color that produces a visual impact on its own, independent of the remaining dimensions.

Rather than allowing unlimited variations in the arrangement of the major values, as fine art and graphic design illustrations may, most color design drawings lend themselves to a more limited number of possible value arrangements. This is because those values will be influenced by the general level of the values of the colors selected for the project *and* by the lighting possibilities for the project, both natural and artificial.

When you look at an illustration whose *major values* are arranged in a way that give it impact, you will notice that the areas of dark, medium, and light values tend to be contiguous—that is, linked together in zones of like value—rather than scattered in many independent spots of lights, mediums, and darks. You can see these major value groups, either in an illustration or in a real-life view, by simply squinting your eyes almost closed as you look at the composition. What at first appears to be a wide range of values now migrates toward the lighter, medium, and darker parts of the value spectrum, making it easier for you to distinguish the larger arrangements of these value groupings. It is these major value groupings that, if arranged for maximum visual impact *before* the color application is begun, will make a dramatic color design drawing far more probable.

Creative arrangement of the major value groups will give your color design drawings more impact—but why? First, they help to hold the illustration together and focus the viewer's eye in the direction of the center of interest. If the illustration has no major groupings of value, it will appear unnecessarily fragmented or "busy." Second, the contrasts of major value groupings can give the view an appearance of depth or distance. Stronger contrasts are a general characteristic of the value relationships between things that are closer to a viewer. As distance increases, this contrast lessens. When this phenomenon is used in a drawing, the appearance of depth is increased dramatically.

Perhaps the most graphic benefit of the effective arrangement of major value groups, however, is how these arrangements can create a luminous drawing. When you see a lighter area against or through a darker area, the lighter area appears even lighter. The darker the surrounding dark area, the brighter the lighter area appears. This phenomenon is particularly effective in creating dramatic illumination in a drawing.

The Value Study

A *value study* may appear to be of little consequence, even somewhat of a bother, as compared with the power of a dramatic color drawing. However, the value study is your ticket to that compelling color illustration. Once you have completed your line drawing, but before you attempt to apply color, you will need a road map that tells you, in general terms, how dark or light to make your colors as you apply them to the drawing. By arriving at a satisfying and dramatic arrangement of values before you begin color application, you complete a critical series of decisions which then allows you to focus on color application techniques.

Value studies are quick and easy to make. Begin by using a black-and-white photocopier to reduce your line drawing to a small size, about 5" x 7". Make a few copies, as you may do more than one study. The smallness of the paper allows you to keep your illustration at "arm's length" for this important step and to stay focused on the major groups of value instead of getting caught

up in the details of the drawing (7-3). Alternatively, you may prefer to scan your line drawing (since it should be scanned eventually anyway) and print a small black-and-white version of your drawing for use as a value study.

Restrict yourself to the use of black-and-white media, so you can focus on value *only*. Black and gray markers (your choice of warm, cool, or French gray makes little difference), *Black* Prismacolor pencil, and white gouache or correction fluid can all be useful in making these studies. You can work directly on the photocopies on bond paper, or you can place white roll tracing paper over the small images and quickly scroll through a series of possible value arrangements (7-4).

Fig. 7-3a Fig. 7-3b Fig. 7-3c

Fig. 7-3 These quick, rough studies—4" x 5" each—were created to explore some of the possible major value arrangements for the interior shown in figure 7-1(b). In figure 7-3(a), *Black Prismacolor* pencil was used to create the light conditions for an overcast day, when no direct sunlight enters the space. Parts of the soffits and spandrel panels were darkened with graded values so that the exterior appears sufficiently bright. Note also how the foreground was made very dark, allowing the lower

central part of the drawing to appear quite bright by contrast.

In figure 7-3(b), the value study was drawn on white tracing paper placed over the small line drawing. Direct sunlight is coming from the right, creating a dark mass on the right side of the drawing. However, this mass would not be uniformly dark in the finished drawing, but would be a series of contrasts within this dark mass. Notice how the darks on the left side of the drawing help to balance the dark mass on the right.

Figure 7-3(c) shows a value study as a night scene, where gray markers were used to quickly add dark, even values to the sky and building beyond the glass plane. Because of the dark exterior, as well as the darkened foreground, the main part of the interior appears quite bright by contrast.

Each of these studies holds the kernel of a value arrangement idea for the finished drawing. Figure 7-3(a) was selected to guide the value arrangement for the drawing shown in figure 7-41.

Fig. 7-4 Three different lighting conditions were studied for the line drawing shown in figure 7-2(b). In figure 7-4(a), the light comes from behind the viewer and toward the building. This creates a situation in which the foreground is quite dark, the building is generally a medium value (owing to the values created by local tone as well as shade and shadow), and the background is light in value.

In figure 7-4(b), a dusk scene was created in which, although the sky is brighter toward the left side, the brightest area remains at the center of interest—the main corner of the building. This area is brightest because the highest value contrasts were deliberately created there. The sky was darkened with a series of *Cool Grey* markers ranging from 20% on the left to 70% on the right. The foreground was also created with *Black* marker, keeping it in silhouette to help the building and sky appear brighter. The values of the building walls and street surface were created with *Black* Prismacolor pencil, and the windows remain the white of the paper.

Figure 7-4(c) shows the building illuminated by morning sun. In this situation the entire left side of the building is in shade. In response, the sky and building against the brighter facade were darkened. This not only forces the sunlit facade to appear brighter, but helps to balance the distribution of values in the drawing. Note how these two dark masses are also balanced by a third set of dark values at the ceiling, column, and planter wall on the left side of the drawing. White gouache was applied to the upper windows on the shaded side of the building to create reflections of brighter sky, adding interest and "sparkle" to the darker face of the building, but not in such amounts as to fragment the dark mass.

Figure 7-4(a) was the study used as a value guide for the completed drawing shown in figure 7-48.

Fig. 7-4a

Fig. 7-4b

Fig. 7-4c

These studies should be accomplished fairly quickly. It will probably take between 20 and 40 minutes to make each study. You may have some initial difficulty in arriving at a satisfactory value arrangement, in part, perhaps, because of the novelty of planning a drawing in this fashion. You may create two or three studies before you arrive at an arrangement of values that is most appropriate for the view you have selected for your design ideas. The hardest part is settling on an arrangement of large value patterns that feels right for the drawing. Once you hit this "aha!" point in your exploration, finishing the study becomes easy.

You may find it helpful to somewhat exaggerate the values in your studies so you can easily perceive their impact. In the finished color drawing there will, of course, be smaller areas of value contrast within the major areas of value you have established, but these contrasts should not be so large or emphatic that they overwhelm or fragment the major value groups within which they lie.

It is a good idea, after you create a value study, to do something else for a while and then come back to it. This allows you to look at the study with a fresh eye and usually results in the addition of refinements to the study or ideas for a better value arrangement in a new study. Once you arrive at a value arrangement that suits your goals for the drawing, keep it in view and use it as a frequent reference as you apply color to the finished drawing. It will prove to be an invaluable guide as you create a strong and dramatic color design drawing, regardless of the hues you use.

Your ability to arrange the major values of color design drawings will become stronger as you increasingly take notice of the most interesting and dramatic major value groupings in your surroundings, as you think more frequently in strategic terms about the value arrangements of your drawings, and as you generate more of these studies.

THE THIRD CONSIDERATION: THE SCAN

Once your drawing is completed, it should be scanned and turned into a digital image. That way, regardless of how you decide to proceed with color application, you will have safely duplicated and filed your line drawing electronically.

You can easily create a digital copy of your line drawing using a flatbed scanner. These scanners are relatively inexpensive and capable of creating both black-and-white and color scans of drawings that are of a quality and resolution more than sufficient for use in the approaches to color drawing discussed throughout this book. Note, however, that most inexpensive scanners of this type will handle sheet sizes only up to letter size (8½" x 11"). Scanners that accommodate larger paper sizes—ledger size (11" x 17") and greater—are far more expensive and, while convenient, are not critical for most color drawing tasks. Ledger-sized original drawings can always be scanned in two halves and combined using Photoshop.

All scanners come with utility software that allows you to control the quality of your scans and select the destination file of the resulting digital image. The software will guide you through the scanning process and will have both basic and advanced settings.

Most flatbed scanners are capable of scanning to at least 1,200 dpi, and many scan to higher resolutions—up to 4,800 dpi. For your color drawings, presentation prints, and large-scale presentation plots of those drawings, do not scan at that image resolution, since the higher the scan resolution of your drawing, the larger its file size. File size is important. As you work in Photoshop, you will add layers—sometimes many layers. With each layer, the file size of your illustration increases and the layered files can become quite large. The result can be sluggish computer performance leading to delays in your workflow.

Use the following rules of thumb when scanning original drawings that are between letter and ledger size:

If your final presentation sheet size will be ledger size, scan your original at about 150 dpi.

If your final presentation sheet size will be between 18" x 24" and 24" x 36", scan your original at about 220 dpi.

If your final presentation sheet size will be 36" x 42" or larger—or if you intend to use your images in documents that will be reproduced by offset printing—scan your images at no less than 300 dpi.

Remember, these are only rules of thumb. Even if a large presentation plot of a drawing is slightly pixelated as a result of an image resolution that is too low, it will most likely still be useful for presentation if the audience is at least a few feet away from the "softened" image.

THE FOURTH CONSIDERATION: APPROACHES TO COLOR MEDIA

Your scanned line drawing can, as a digital image, be printed by laser printer, plotter, or photocopier—onto bond, Bristol, and ink-jet papers, toned Canson paper, and even mylar. You may also choose to apply your color—or some of it, anyway—digitally, using Photoshop.

Your selection of specific colors for your design drawings will depend on a number of factors: the scheme of colors you have chosen for the place you are designing, the colors of the natural materials you intend to include in your project—stone, brick, wood—as well as the colors that are available in the natural and man-made materials that you *have* chosen.

However, there are some general color ideas you may wish to keep in mind as you develop your color design drawings. First, when the expression of your color scheme is an important part of your purpose in creating a drawing, accompany the drawing with a color and materials board that shows actual paint samples, material swatches, and pieces of the natural and man-made materials you intend to use. By doing so, you can minimize misunderstandings about color that result from the effects of illumination or mismatches that occur within your drawing.

Second, you will notice that the color media used for the illustrations in this chapter tend to fall into four groups: warm colors—reds, yellow-reds, and yellows; cool colors—purples, purple-blues, and blues; transitional colors—greens or red-purples (usually greens in these drawings) that can be made either warm or cool (see figure 6-7); and the neutrals and near-neutrals, including white, black, cool gray, warm gray, and French gray markers and pencils.

Third, almost *any* combination of colors can be made to work together to create a design drawing that appears unified. This can be done by intermixing the various color media used to create the drawing, much the way artists—particularly painters—work with color, as discussed in Chapter 6. Even though an object in the drawing may be predominantly of one hue, other color media used elsewhere in the drawing can be used to flavor that hue. In figure 6-23, for example, the *Peach* pencil used on the building to the left was also used on the sunlit parts of the trees and sidewalk; in figure 3-62, *Jasmine* pencil was used to wash the grass, trees, buildings, and roadway. This intermixture of colors is a key to rich and interesting color design drawings.

White-Paper Drawings

Color media appear at their lightest value and strongest chroma when applied to white paper. For this reason, white paper is excellent for illustrating design ideas that have "high-key" (light-value) or strong-chroma color schemes. White papers useful for color design drawing range from the lower-quality bond paper to the high-quality Bristol paper.

Bond Paper

Bond paper, the type found in most photocopiers and laser printers, lends itself to quick sketches in which color quality is not paramount but some color is desirable. Duplication is rapid, the original is preserved, and there is no need to seek out special paper. Color design drawings on bond paper are adequate for many kinds of design illustration tasks (7-7). You may want to stock your photocopier with 24 lb. or heavier paper, which will give your drawing surface a more substantive feel.

Bond paper is also a good surface for generating conceptual design ideas over enlarged photographs of existing conditions (7-5, 7-6). Images (both line and tone) printed on bond paper by laser jet printers make excellent base drawings over which color media may be used to quickly develop and enhance design ideas expressed as rudimentary computer images (1-6, top).

Bristol Paper

The development of a color design drawing on Bristol paper is shown in figures 7-8 through 7-14. Bristol paper was chosen for this drawing because its approximately triadic hue scheme—yellow/blue-green/purple-blue—is mostly light in value. Note that in the value arrangement for the drawing (7-10), a darker-value foreground also forces the main part of the drawing to appear lighter. Another level of luminosity is established by placing the row of dark-value figures in front of the brightly illuminated food-service tenants in the distance.

Once the gray marker was applied to create the basic value arrangement, pastel was applied to the major expanses of color in the illustration (7-12). The pastel not only smooths the appearance of the marker strokes and has a luminous quality in its own right, but it is a color application over which further refinements of color can be added with color pencil.

It is informative to look closely at the line illustration shown in figure 7-9, in that it is a hybrid of computer and hand drawing. However, it is hardly

Fig. 7-5 A photograph of an existing
condition, desaturated in Photoshop
(Image > Adjustments > Desaturate)
and printed on bond paper via laser
printer.

Fig. 7-6 A sketch study in color, using
Pilot Razor Point, alcohol-based marker,
and color pencil, drawn directly on the
bond paper print shown in figure 7-5.

Fig. 7-7

Fig. 7-7 This study was drawn on an 8½" x 11" sheet, using alcohol-based marker, pastel, and color pencil over a tonal image produced by a laser jet printer on bond paper. The tonal image was generated by computer using Form•Z. (Drawing: Jim Babinchak)

recognizable as such, as it appears hand drawn in its entirety. You may find that in many drawing situations, a computer can quickly and conveniently supply the basics of the larger architectural forms and spaces, as shown here, whereas hand drawing is often faster and more appealing in illustrating figures, furnishings, accessories, and detail. To unify the look of the hand-detailed computer drawing *and* avoid retracing the computer portion of drawing, the computer-generated portion was first "filtered" on the computer to make its lines appear hand drawn (7-8). This resulted in a line illustration in which the hand-drawn and computer-generated portions are indistinguishable.

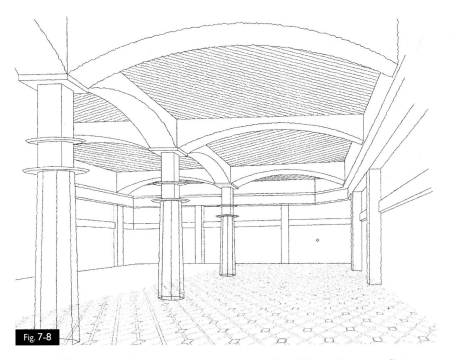

Fig. 7-8

Fig. 7-9

Fig. 7-8 This computer image began as a typical straight-line wire-frame with the hidden lines removed. It was imported into Adobe Illustrator, all the lines were selected, and the *Roughen* filter was applied so that the drawing appeared more hand-drawn. The "size" setting was .20, and the frequency was 20/inch.

The illustration was then imported into Adobe Photoshop to add the floor pattern. Diagonally oriented floor patterns can be more quickly and successfully added to a drawing by computer than by hand. The pattern was first developed as an orthographic image, then made to conform to the perspective view by using the "perspective" command within the "transform" menu.

Once the floor pattern was added, the image was photocopied onto a sheet of 11" x 17" translucent drawing *vellum* (Clearprint 1000H). Note that drawing vellum does *not* need a special carrier when introduced into the photocopier's side feed. (Computer illustration: Nat Poomviset)

Fig. 7-9 A sheet of ordinary roll tracing paper was placed over the vellum image shown in figure 7-8, and the additional elements of the view—furniture, people, accessories, and details—were roughed out. This rough was then placed *behind* the vellum image, and the rest of the view was traced onto the vellum with a Micron 005 and a 4x0 technical pen. Newly hidden or unwanted lines were easily erased, using a pink erasing strip in an electric eraser. Correction fluid can also be used, because the finished line drawing will be photocopied onto the Bristol.

Fig. 7-10

Fig. 7-10 The value study shown at the top is a 5" x 6" photocopy reduction of the line drawing. Note how the main part of the view appears brighter because of the darkened foreground.

The color media used for this approximately triadic hue scheme are as follows. In this example, the near-neutrals happen to be all markers: (1) *French Grey 10%*, (2) *French Grey 20%*, (3) *French Grey 30%*, (4) *French Grey 50%*, (5) *Cool Grey 10%*, (6) *Cool Grey 20%*, (7) *Cool Grey 30%*, (8) *Cool Grey 40%*. The greens are (9) *Permanent Green Deep* *619.9* stick pastel, (10) *Deco Aqua* pencil, (11) *Celadon Green* pencil. The purple blues and purple are (12) *Ultramarine Deep 506.9* stick pastel, (13) *Blue Slate* pencil, (14) Derwent *Blue Violet Lake #27* pencil. The reds are (15) *Light Oxide Red 339.9* stick pastel, (16) *Poppy Red,* (17) *Tuscan Red* pencils, (18) *310* pencil pastel. The yellows and yellow-reds are (19) *Raw Sienna 234.9* stick pastel, (20) *Gold Ochre 231.8* stick pastel, (21) *#690* pencil pastel, (22) *Cream,* (23) *Light Peach,* (24) *Jasmine,* (25) *Burnt Ochre,* (26) *Raw Umber,* (27) *Dark Umber* pencils.

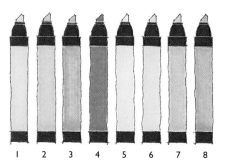
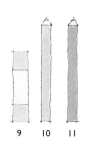
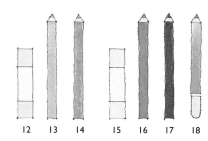
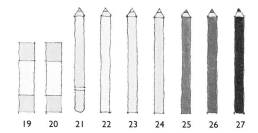

1   2   3   4   5   6   7   8   9   10   11   12   13   14   15   16   17   18   19   20   21   22   23   24   25   26   27

Fig. 7-11

Fig. 7-12

Fig. 7-11 Once the line drawing was photocopied onto Bristol paper, the major values were applied with gray markers, with the value study used as a guide. The use of gray marker is an easy way to establish the value arrangement while still allowing subsequent layers of pastel and pencil. The cool grays make a good base for cool colors, and the French grays and warm grays make a good base for warm colors.

All the French gray markers (*10%, 20%, 30%,* and *50%*) shown in figure 7-10 were used to establish the value gradations in the lower part of the foreground; all the cool gray markers shown were used on the upper part. However, the contrast was intentionally diminished as the drawing recedes, and only the *10%* and *20%* grays were used in the distance.

Fig. 7-12 To keep the drawing light, pastel was used to tint its major elements and surfaces. On the smaller of these surfaces, the pastel was drawn directly on the surface; on the larger surfaces, the pastel was scraped onto the drawing surface from the pastel stick with an X-acto knife. This avoided the possibility of the pastel application showing streaks. Once the pastel was applied, it was smoothed with a finger, then by a facial tissue.

Raw Sienna 234.9 stick pastel was applied to both the floor and ceiling. *Gold Ochre 231.8* stick pastel was used on the foreground floor and blended into the lighter pastel in the distance.

The illuminated undersides of the arches near the columns were colored with a blend of *Raw Sienna 234.9* and *Light Oxide Red 339.9* stick pastels to express the color of the incandescent uplighting.

The columns, as well as the sign panels in the distance, were colored with a blend of *Permanent Green Deep 619.9* and *Ultramarine Deep 506.9* stick pastels. Note the gradation of the column color, created by adding *Raw Sienna 234.9* stick pastel to the lower parts of the columns.

Once the pastel was applied, unwanted coverage was easily erased with an electric eraser with a soft white erasing strip and an erasing shield.

Fig. 7-13 Color pencil and pastel were used to bring up the color of the details of all parts of the drawing except for the figures. *Raw Umber* pencil and a flavoring of *Burnt Ochre* pencil were applied to the corners of the ceiling where the illumination drops off. *Blue Slate* and Derwent *Blue Violet Lake #27* pencils were used to darken the corners where the arches meet.

Cream and *Light Peach* pencils were combined to color the banding on the sign panels and the banquette seating. *Jasmine* and *Dark Umber* pencils were used to create a cross-hatch pattern over a light wash of *Burnt Ochre* pencil on the foreground banquette seat back to simulate the pattern created by cane backing. The corresponding seat backs in the distance received only a light wash of *Burnt Ochre* pencil.

Celadon Green and Derwent *Blue Violet Lake #27* pencils were used to color the tabletops, chair backs, and legs. The table edges and chair seats were colored with a mix of *Burnt Ochre* and *Jasmine* pencils.

Tuscan Red pencil was applied to the dried flowers on the tables, the dried wreaths, and the wine bottles. The bluish floor tiles were colored with *Blue Slate* and Derwent *Blue Violet Lake #27* pencils, and the dark tiles were colored with a *Dark Umber* pencil.

A mixture of *Gold Ochre 231.8* stick pastel and *#692* pencil pastel was applied lightly across most of the food-service tenant openings, figures included, to approximate the glow of colored light.

Fig. 7-13

Fig. 7-14

Fig. 7-14 The only exception to the use of lighter markers in the more distant parts of the drawing is the application of *French Grey 50%* marker to the line of figures in front of the food-service tenants. This play of value was used to allow the food-service tenants to appear more luminous.

Once color was applied to the various parts of this design idea, the same color pencils were recombined and applied to the figures. First, *French Grey 30%* and *50%* markers and *Cool Grey 30%* and *40%* markers were applied randomly to the hair and clothing, followed by the pencils. One exception is some discreet touches of *Poppy Red* pencil.

White gouache was mixed with yellow opaque watercolor to create an opaque color to apply to the letters of the food-service tenant signs with a very thin brush. This color was intended to approximate a gold leaf finish on the letters. Note that these letters were applied slightly above and to the right of the existing letters, resulting in what appears to be a drop shadow beneath each letter. Touches of white gouache were also applied to the recessed light in the ceiling.

Toned-Paper Drawings

When you make a white-paper drawing, the illusion of illumination must be created by surrounding lighter values with darker values. Toned papers provide an opportunity to easily and quickly create dramatic color design drawings, because the designer can apply both dark *and* light values to the drawing.

One of the major advantages in working on a toned drawing surface is that partial color application on a line drawing not only can have a dramatic impact by itself, but often precludes having to add color to the rest of the drawing. This makes toned-paper drawings both effective and efficient as design communication devices.

Design drawings on toned paper are particularly effective in communicating lighting concepts. Interior illumination, dusk scenes, and night views are easy to create with the use of toned papers.

Canson Paper

Canson paper comes in a wide variety of subtle light-, middle-, and dark-value colors. It has a distinct texture that imparts a pleasing, diffuse quality to applications of color pencil. This not only adds a consistency to a drawing, but also helps to mask streaky applications of pencil.

Figures 7-15 through 7-21 show the development of a color design drawing of an interior seating area on Canson paper. The paper color was selected because it was sympathetic to the preponderance of warm analogous colors in the scheme. These colors were emphasized by the addition of purple-blue complementary accents.

The foreground was darkened to emphasize the skylight illumination of the more distant part of the drawing. Note, too, that color media were applied to only about two-thirds of the drawing, helping to define its center of interest.

Fig. 7-15

Fig. 7-16

Fig. 7-15 This line drawing was drawn on tracing paper with a Micron 005 pen.

Fig. 7-16 The line drawing was photocopied onto "Sand" Canson paper and sprayed with Krylon Crystal Clear acrylic coating.

Fig. 7-17

Fig. 7-17 A small value study was done first with *Black* Prismacolor pencil on a photocopy reduction of the original line drawing. The foreground was darkened, because it was under the curved balcony and because such treatment would emphasize the skylighted fireplace area beyond. The darkened foreground also provides a good "frame" through which to view the seating area.

The color media used in this analogous-with-complementary-accent scheme are the neutrals and near-neutrals of (1) *White,* (2) *Black* pencils; (3) *French Grey 30%,* (4) *French Grey 50%,* (5) *French Grey 70%,* (6) *French Grey 90%,* (7) *Black* markers; the reds, yellow-reds, and yellows of (8) *Terra Cotta,* (9) *Light Peach,* (10) *Peach,* (11) *Mineral Orange,* (12) *Burnt Ochre,* (13) *Spanish Orange,* (14) *Yellow Ochre,* (15) *Jasmine* pencils; (16) *310,* (17) *680,* (18) *685* pencil pastels; (19) *Eggshell,* (20) *Blush Pink,* (21) *Sienna Brown* markers; the green yellows of (22) *Olive Green,* (23) *Dark Green* pencils; (24) *Olive Green* marker; the purple-blue complementary accents of (25) *Blue Slate,* (26) *Light Cerulean Blue,* (27) *Indigo Blue* pencils; (28) *Peacock Blue* marker.

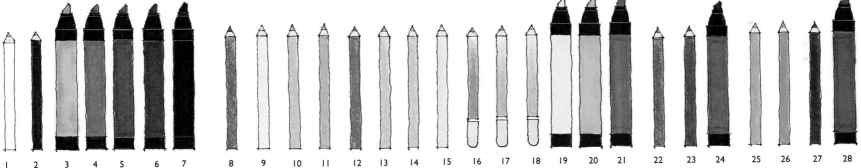

| 1 | 2 | 3 | 4 | 5 | 6 | 7 | 8 | 9 | 10 | 11 | 12 | 13 | 14 | 15 | 16 | 17 | 18 | 19 | 20 | 21 | 22 | 23 | 24 | 25 | 26 | 27 | 28 |

Fig. 7-18

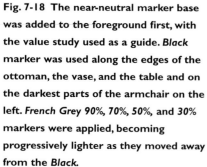

Fig. 7-19

Fig. 7-18 The near-neutral marker base was added to the foreground first, with the value study used as a guide. *Black* marker was used along the edges of the ottoman, the vase, and the table and on the darkest parts of the armchair on the left. *French Grey 90%, 70%, 50%,* and *30%* markers were applied, becoming progressively lighter as they moved away from the *Black.*

Fig. 7-19 The marker base colors were applied to the remaining elements in the center of interest of the drawing. *Olive Green* marker was added to the chair on the right and the rug. *Peacock Blue* marker was applied to the upholstery of the sofa on the left; *Sienna Brown* marker was used to color all the woodwork as well as some of the carpet pattern.

The ceiling that forms the underside of the curved balcony was darkened in places with gradations of *French Grey 50%, 30%,* and *10%* markers to effect a contrast with the more brightly illuminated space beyond *and* between the pendant light fixture and the ceiling itself.

The areas directly beneath the fireplace mantle, the hearth, and the upper cornice (above the painting) were treated with gradations of *French Grey 50%, 30%,* and *10%* markers. The sandstone was colored with *Blush Pink*

and *Eggshell* markers. Note how the toned paper mutes the marker colors. Gradations of *French Grey 90%, 70%,* and *50%* markers were applied to the interior of the fireplace to provide adequate contrast and make the flames appear more luminous.

The value contrasts in the distance were deliberately made weaker than those in the foreground of the drawing.

Fig. 7-20

Fig. 7-20 Detail was added to the foreground elements with color pencil. A zigzag pattern was applied to the green armchair with *Dark Green* pencil, followed by *Terra Cotta* pencil for the reddish dots within the pattern. A wash of *Peach* pencil was applied to the illuminated surfaces of the chair, slightly more heavily closer to the table lamp. Note how the *Peach* pencil not only adds highlights but also mutes the green hue. *Indigo Blue* pencil was used on the surfaces in shade. *Blue Slate* pencil was added as a natural-light highlight on the edges of the chair that face the skylight above.

The sofa on the left was first washed lightly with *Olive Green* pencil. *Blue Slate* pencil highlights were added, followed by *Indigo Blue* pencil for shading. The highlights on the cushions of the armchair to the left were applied with *Mineral Orange, Yellow Ochre,* and *Jasmine* pencils. The rug was detailed with *Burnt Ochre, Yellow Ochre,* and *Indigo Blue* pencils. A graded wash of *Peach* and *Spanish Orange* pencil was applied lightly to the rug to create the effect of illumination from the table lamp.

Because the table lamp was intended to be a replica of a Dirk Van Erp lamp, it was colored with *Mineral Orange, Spanish Orange,* and *Jasmine* pencils. *Mineral Orange* and *Jasmine* pencils were also used to wash the top of the end table. The ottoman in the right foreground was very lightly washed with *Terra Cotta* pencil. A highlight from the table lamp was added to the seat cushion with a blend of *Mineral Orange, Spanish Orange,* and *Jasmine* pencils.

The foreground ceiling was quickly colored with *#680* pencil pastel, followed by *Yellow Ochre* and *Jasmine* pencils. The pendant light fixture shade was colored with *Light Peach* pencil, grading into *Blush Pink* pencil near the top. Once the shades were colored with the light pencils, the silhouetted cutout patterns were darkened with a Pilot Razor Point. The ceiling highlights were also added with *Light Peach* pencil.

The vase with the flowers was colored with a *Blue Slate* pencil; the leaves were colored with *Celadon Green* and *Olive Green* pencils. The flowers were colored with *#310* and *#680* pencil pastels to give them added brilliance.

Fig. 7-21

Fig. 7-21 Once the foreground seating area was completed, it was easier to determine how light the surface of the fireplace should appear. First, the fire was drawn in the fireplace according to the illustrated steps in figures 4-99 and 4-100. After the fire was drawn, the wrought-iron screen was drawn directly over it with a *Black* pencil.

Because a skylight was destined to go directly above the fireplace, beyond the top edge of the drawing, a wash of *Light Peach* pencil was applied to the tops of the stone ledges, the mantle, and the floor. The same pencil was used to apply a light wash across the face of the fireplace, with care taken not to extend this wash up into the marker shadows cast by the stone ledges. As these washes were worked progressively higher, toward the source of light, more pressure was applied to the pencil. The upper ledge and the stones above it were also washed with *White* pencil to make them even brighter. These washes were applied directly over the details of the fireplace, such as the candles on the mantle and the hanging utensils, which

allowed these washes to remain smooth and consistent. Highlights were also added with *Light Peach* pencil to the tops of some of the stones on the face of the fireplace. Note, too, the addition of a flavoring of *Light Cerulean Blue* pencil to the shaded wall on the upper right side.

After the stone colors and highlights had been applied, the candles were colored with *Cream* and *White* pencils. The wrought-iron candlesticks and fireplace utensils were retraced with a *Black* pencil. The remaining ceiling pendant lights were colored in the same way as the foreground fixture; the ceiling directly above them was highlighted with *Jasmine* and *Mineral Orange* pencils.

Final touches were added. The column beside the fireplace was tinted with *#680* and *#685* pencil pastels. White gouache highlights were added to the candle flames and light fixtures. The foreground vase at the top of the ottoman was highlighted with *Light Cerulean Blue* pencil to introduce a balancing touch of blue to the composition.

Ink-Jet Paper

You can use an ink-jet plotter to create your own custom-toned drawing papers, making the exact color background you require. The background can even vary in color across its surface in any way you wish, similar to the background "washes" watercolorists frequently make at the beginning of an illustration. If you want a background of a single color, simply open your scanned line drawing in Photoshop. Make a new layer and set the layer's blending mode to "Multiply." Open the *Color Picker* and make the exact color you want. Click on the *Paint Bucket Tool*, then use it to click on your drawing image. The color of your drawing's background will change to your chosen color, but the lines of your drawing will still show. Use the Adjustment commands (Image > Adjustments) to "tune" your background color as necessary. You are now ready to begin drawing, using hand or digital media.

If you are intending to use hand media, first plot your image at the required size on a paper appropriate for hand media. The drawings created on ink-jet paper in this book were plotted on a Hewlett Packard 800 PS plotter using HP's Heavyweight Coated Paper C6569C (see Chapter 2).

You can also create a background whose color varies (7-23). Follow the same steps as you would for creating a background of a single color except when using the *Color Picker*, select both a foreground and a background color. Then, instead of using the *Paint Bucket Tool*, use the *Gradient Tool* to make a drawing background that is an even gradient of two colors (or more if you wish—see figures 3-14 through 3-17). Remember to click on the gradient bar in the options bar near the top of the Photoshop window. This will open the *Gradient Editor;* in the *Presets* box, select the "Foreground to Background" gradient type.

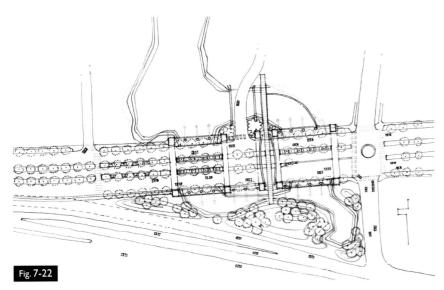

Fig. 7-22

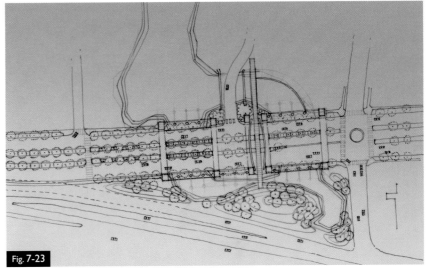

Fig. 7-23

Fig. 7-22 This plan drawing was made on white tracing paper with a Micron 005 felt-tipped pen.

Fig. 7-23 After the line drawing was scanned, it was opened in Photoshop. A new layer was created and named; its blending mode was set to "Multiply."

The *Color Picker*'s *Foreground* color box was clicked and a weak-chroma yellow red—a kraft brown—was selected. The *Background* color box was clicked and a weak-chroma purple-blue—a grayed violet—was chosen.

The *Gradient Tool* was then selected. The downward-pointing button beside the *Gradient* swatch in the options bar was clicked and the "Foreground to Background" gradient preset was chosen. Additionally, from the row of gradient geometry icons just to the right of the *Gradient* swatch, the *Linear Gradient* box was clicked.

The cursor was placed in the lower left of the drawing, clicked and dragged to the upper right, and released. The resulting gradient formed the base on which the remainder of the drawing was competed.

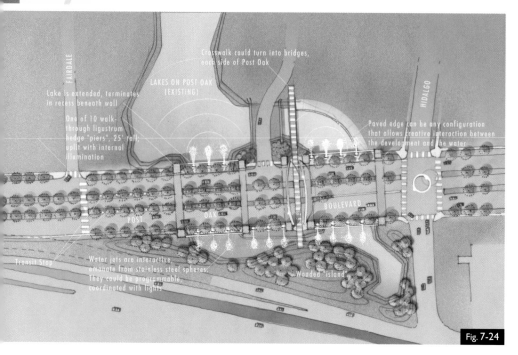

Fig. 7-24

Fig. 7-24 Although the color for this plan was applied digitally, the line drawing, with its graded wash background, could have been plotted and colored using hand media.

Hybrid Color Drawing

The distinction between hand drawing and digital drawing is becoming increasingly blurred. This is because the computer is becoming more useful as a color drawing tool, saving time, effort, and fees when incorporated into the color drawing process wisely. Hybrid color drawing incorporates both hand and digital drawing techniques in an illustration (7-25 through 7-28, and 7-29 through 7-34).

This approach to color drawing relies on digital tactics for certain time-saving drawing techniques while using hand drawing tactics for others. Generally, the computer is used for applying background color to broad areas of the drawing, layering transparent washes, importing surrounding support elements (those that lie outside the design effort), creating accents, and making adjustments. Hand drawing is used to quickly add detail, texture, and richness, imparting its unmistakable (and often endearing) character.

This approach can also free up the designer to concentrate on the *designed* parts of the drawing. As you know, a design is always evolving, especially (and sometimes irresistibly) during the process of its illustration. It is on this process that we, as designers, often need to remain focused, subtly revising and refining the design as we go.

The first step in the creation of a hybrid color drawing is the same as in other kinds of color drawings: Start with a line drawing, which can range in character from a quick, loose sketch to one that is highly detailed. The advantage of using a drawing with hand-generated character is that this character will show through in the final illustration. When completed, the line drawing is scanned and opened in Photoshop.

With the line drawing complete, take some time to plan your drawing with a value study, especially if you intend to use it for presentation purposes. A few small (approximately 3" x 5") black-and-white prints of the line drawing should be generated, and major value arrangements explored with a *Black* pencil (7-26). You will find the study you decide to use extremely helpful in guiding your color decisions when making your finished drawing. Using it as a guide, apply the broad background washes of color to the line drawing with confidence.

In most cases, a new layer is created for each area of digital color—foreground on one layer, sky on another, large areas of trees or building tones on another, shadows on still another, and so on. The blending mode for these layers is usually set to "Multiply," making them transparent and allowing the linework to show through. The color is frequently applied to these layers with the *Gradient Tool* set on "Foreground to Background" or using the *Brush Tool*'s airbrush capability. That way, the large color areas can be dynamic blends of colors rather than uniform applications of a single color (7-27).

Fig. 7-26

Fig. 7-25

Fig. 7-25 This drawing is intended to illustrate the character of a "gateway" into an urban district created by a redesigned and rebuilt Interstate highway bridge, including the treatment of the concrete finishes and lighting, and the addition of salutatory pylons.

Fig. 7-26 A few small (3" x 5") black-and-white prints were made of the line drawing on bond paper and used for value studies. The studies, made with a *Black* pencil, explored ways to make the underside of the bridge and its elements the focus of the drawing. The study shown here begins to arrange the values of large parts of the drawing—the foreground and the sky—in order to focus the viewer on the designer's area of interest: the underside of the bridge, its illumination, and its pylons.

Note, however, the departures from the value study in the final arrangement of the major values in figure 7-27, in which the right part of the sky is darker and the roadway under the bridge is lighter, focusing attention even more on the bridge area. A value study will help you set a direction for your illustration, but give you flexibility to make improvements as you proceed.

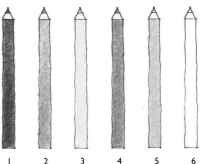

1 2 3 4 5 6

The color pencils used to enhance the illustration after it was plotted (7-27) are (1) *Burnt Umber*, (2) *Burnt Ochre*, (3) *Jasmine*, (4) *Olive*, (5) *Limepeel*, and (6) *White*.

Fig. 7-27

Fig. 7-27 Using the value study as a guide, graded washes were applied to the drawing in Photoshop.

A new layer was made for the sky and its Blending Mode set to "Multiply." Using the *Color Picker*, a yellow-red was selected for the foreground color and a dark brown for the background color. The sky area was selected with the *Polygonal Lasso Selection Tool*, avoiding the pylon forms. The *Gradient Tool* was used, with the "Foreground to Background" preset chosen, and a gradient was made from lower right to upper left on the selected sky area.

To darken the distant building tops, the buildings showing above the top of the bridge spandrel were selected. The dark brown color was switched to become the foreground color, and the *Gradient Tool's* preset changed to "Foreground to Transparent." A gradient was "snapped" (clicked and dragged) from the bottom of the buildings upward. As a final step, the building façades facing the brightest part of the sky were selected, the yellow-red substituted for the foreground color, and

a gradient was snapped from the top down, creating the impression that the building tops were illuminated by the glowing sky.

The foreground of the drawing was colored in a similar way. A new layer was made and its blending mode set to "Multiply." Light and dark weak-chroma yellows were selected for the foreground and background colors through the *Color Picker*. The area of the drawing from the top of the bridge spandrel downward was selected, excluding the pylon tops, which were left white.

Gradients were also used on smaller areas, such as the pylon bases, bridge columns, spandrel face, and underside of the bridge spans-all "Foreground to Transparent" gradients using the darker yellow.

The image was then plotted on a heavyweight paper. The resultant plot, about ledger size (11" x 17"), was ready to receive hand color media.

Fig. 7-28

Fig. 7-28 The hand-color stage of this drawing is made up mostly of final touches, tweaks, and the application of accents.

A wash of *Dark Umber* pencil was added to the bridge spandrel and foreground figures. *Olive Green* pencil was used for the foreground grass, as well as more distant shrubs and trees. *Limepeel* and *Burnt Ochre* pencils were also applied to plant materials. *Jasmine* pencil was added to alternate stripes of the concrete walls and columns; a graded wash of *Jasmine* pencil was applied to the top of the salutatory pylons. *White* pencil was applied to the crosswalk stripes, faint vertical reflections in the roadway, a bottom-up graded wash on the pylons, and the illuminated windows in the distant buildings.

White and scarlet-red gouache accents were added for lights, headlights, taillights, traffic lights, and flowers. The brightest parts of the pylons were also enhanced with white gouache.

The drawing was then rescanned. Subtle red and white "glows" were added to the headlights, traffic lights and taillights using the airbrush capability of Photoshop's *Brush Tool*, whose *Flow* (located in the options bar) was set to 5%. When completed, adjustment layers were used to tweak the overall color of a flattened copy of the image before and during printing.

Fig. 7-29 This line drawing is the first step in the illustration of a proposed design concept for a public open space in a major urban district. The proposal brings together two existing private open spaces bifurcated by the district's main boulevard.

The line drawing was created over a photo collage of the existing open space. Proposed buildings, conforming to the perspective of the photographs, were added to the drawing as it was made. The drawing was created on white tracing paper, using a *Black* pencil and a .5 mm pencil with 2H lead. 7" x 16".

Fig. 7-30 The line drawing was printed at about 2" x 6" on a black-and-white printer for value studies. The study shown here, made using *Black* pencil, is a value arrangement intended to focus attention on the major space by offsetting it through value contrast. Note how the surfaces of the drawing and its elements darken the farther away from the open space they get, making them appear to glow subtly. Notes were added as a series of reminders about the elements and drawing tactics to include as the drawing progressed.

The color pencils used to enhance the plotted illustration (7-33) are (1) *Pink*, (2) *Terra Cotta*, (3) *Peach*, (4) *Burnt Ochre*, (5) *French Grey 20%*, (6) *Jasmine*, (7) *Yellowed Orange*, (8) *Limepeel*, (9) *Olive*, (10) *Dark Green*, (11) *Blue Slate*, and (12) *White*.

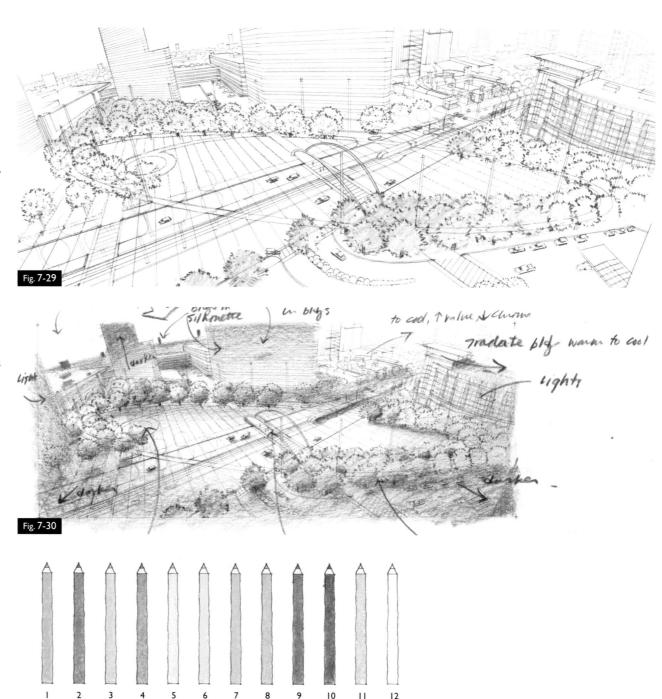

Fig. 7-29

Fig. 7-30

1   2   3   4   5   6   7   8   9   10   11   12

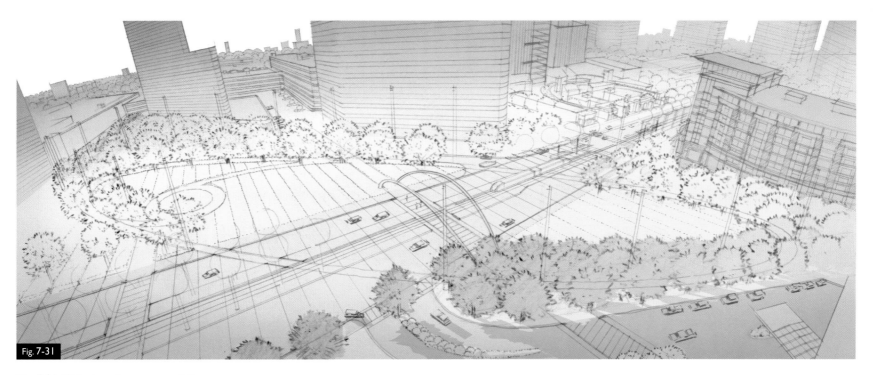

Fig. 7-31

Fig. 7-31 This step shows some of the first washes of color applied in Photoshop, using the value study as a guide.

Three large, light-to-dark color gradients, each on its own Photoshop layer (blending mode set to "Multiply"), are utilized in this step: the distant buildings, the central green space (including trees), and the reddish-yellow roadway. A darker gray, in another layer, was added to the foreground trees, including their shadows, as well as to the building on the right. This adds visual weight to the illustration, balancing the darker buildings at the upper left.

Fig. 7-32

Fig. 7-32 Photoshop was used to make time-saving additions to the illustration during this step.

The existing background buildings on the right were added as digital images, copied and pasted from the original photograph on which the line drawing was based. They were added on a new layer whose blending mode was set to "Normal." Note how the sides of these buildings were selected and colored, using the *Hue/Saturation* adjustment command (Image > Adjustments > Hue/Saturation) to create the impression these faces are being illuminated by the setting sun. Likewise, the rows of palm trees on the boulevard's median were begun on their own layer, with the blending mode set to "Normal." The trees were adjusted for scale and perspective using the Transform commands.

Color was added to the deciduous trees on another layer (blending mode set to "Multiply"), using the airbrush capability of the *Brush Tool*. A darker green was used on the shaded side of the trees, while a warmer green was used on the sunlit side. This helped to develop the dimensionality of the trees.

A shadow layer was also added, with the blending mode set to "Multiply" and the *Brush Tool* using a soft round brush and a very weak-chroma purple. The shadows were made with soft edges, since the glowing sky (seen in the next step) was intended as a more diffuse light source than usual.

Fig. 7-33

Fig. 7-33 The final elements were added digitally before plotting and hand drawing. The addition of palm trees was completed in its layer. A *"sky"* layer was created and its blending mode was set to "Normal." The sky area was selected and a "Foreground to Background" gradient was added with the *Gradient Tool* and snapped horizontally using a fairly strong-chroma yellow-red and purple.

Additional building façades were added to the proposed neighboring project on the right by digitally copying and pasting images from the project illustrations. As a final step, a copy of the entire illustration was flattened and plotted at about 7" x 17", ready for hand color media.

Fig. 7-34

Fig. 7-34 Once plotted, *Limepeel*, *Olive Green*, and *Jasmine* pencils were used to add color and texture to the two different types of turf creating the bands of color on the grass in the open space. Similarly, the roadway and sidewalks were colored with *White* and *French Grey 20%* pencils, extending the banding effect across these paved areas.

The residential building on the right was colored with *Burnt Ochre*, *Terra Cotta*, *White*, and *French Grey 20%* pencils. This building was hand colored since no illustrations were readily available for copying and pasting digitally onto the façade.

Other applications of color pencil were used to subtly add texture to the computer-generated washes made in previous steps. A light wash of *Dark Green* pencil was applied to the distant tree masses. *Peach* pencil was applied to the sunlit portions of the tree canopies that surround the open space, while *Blue Slate* was used to flavor the color of their shaded sides as well as the foreground shadows on the streets. *White* pencil was used on the crosswalk stripes, while *Pink* and *Yellowed Orange* pencils were used on the large beds of flowers to the left.

Accents of white gouache were used to add illumination to the buildings' windows, as well as to create the lights of the distant city. Yellow gouache (Windsor Newton's *Golden Yellow*) was used to accent the sunlit foreground trees, as well as certain building windows. The drawing was then scanned, and final accents were added in Photoshop. The fountain was added on its own layer, using the *Brush Tool*'s airbrush capability. Note the fine mist blowing to the right of the fountain, added by using a large, soft round brush and reducing the *Flow* of the airbrush to about 5%.

The polished stainless steel light pylons surrounding the open space were made on their own layer using the *Line Tool*, with the blending mode set to "Normal." At this distance, their reflective character was easily created by applying one or two white lines and a dark line to each pylon. On the sunlit pylons, a thin, bright red line was also added as a sky reflection. The lighted tips were also made with the *Line Tool*. The pylons' faint glow was added with the *Brush Tool*'s airbrush capability with its *Flow* set very low (5%).

You will notice that a new building has appeared in the upper left. This building was under construction at the time this illustration was being created and overlooked until the illustration was almost complete. It was added as a new layer, first by creating its outline and *help lines* (lines that are made with the *Line Tool* on a separate layer. These lines run to the vanishing points and are used as perspective guides. (They can be turned off by turning off the layer.) Once the help lines were in place, each of the two faces of the building were copied and pasted digitally into the illustration. The *Transform* command was then utilized to conform each building face image to the perspective arrangement dictated by the help lines.

While preparing this "color base" for certain kinds of presentation drawings, you may find it easier to continue to add certain elements using Photoshop before beginning the hand drawing stage. For example, large areas of shade and shadow can be added using a separate layer. By selecting a low-chroma color and setting the layer's blending mode to "Multiply," you can use a hard round brush from the *Brushes Palette* to make consistent, transparent shadows. Those surfaces that are simply shaded can be selected and lightened slightly, as necessary, since shaded surfaces often receive light reflected from other surfaces. You may also wish to add such contextual elements as façades of neighboring buildings, tree groupings, backgrounds, and skies as pieces of digital photographs, allowing you to focus more of your time and energy on the illustration of your design ideas.

Once completed, you can plot your "color base" and develop the drawing's detail using hand color media and the techniques shown in this book. (You can also print your drawing, as long as your color printer can produce matte prints—waxy or slick finishes are incompatible with hand color media.) This stage can be relatively fast and easy, since much of the "groundwork" is already complete.

The final step involves rescanning the completed drawing in order to make adjustments, adding accents and notes, as well as saving the drawing as a digital file and then printing and plotting it. Make sure your scan is of sufficiently high resolution so that your illustration can be plotted as large as necessary.

Tracing Paper and Mylar

Ordinary white roll tracing paper is perhaps the most versatile of all the papers used in the design profession. Its translucency facilitates the iterative process of design. It easily accepts the color media used in this book and is capable of allowing color to show through the paper, a distinct advantage. It can be used as a white paper or a toned paper of any color. It can be used for quick sketches or more finished design drawings, for interiors as well as exteriors, for daytime scenes or dusk views.

Its major advantage for color design drawing is the *quality* of its translucency. Color applied to the back of a drawing on white roll tracing paper shows through the paper more brilliantly and less muted or tinted than through either of its thicker cousins, drawing vellum and drawing mylar. In addition, color applications to the back of a drawing on this kind of tracing paper appear more *evenly* applied than they actually are. This means that a designer can apply color media to the back of a drawing more quickly and less carefully than when applying color in the usual fashion to the front of a drawing.

When a drawing of this kind is placed over a sheet of muted-color or gray paper, a more subtle version of that color also shows through the translucent tracing paper and forms a background color for the drawing. In addition, the backing paper can also subtly influence the colors and, especially, the values of the color media. If marker has been applied to the drawing, its colors will shift toward the backing paper color in both hue and value, because the marker is transparent. Darker-value color pencil on the drawing tends to appear slightly darker; lighter color pencils appear more luminous because of their semiopacity and their contrast with the darker-value backing paper. In other words, if a paper color other than white is placed behind a color design drawing on trace, it becomes a toned-paper drawing instantly (see figures 3-57, 3-58). When this kind of drawing, together with its background, is reproduced by color photocopier or bubble-jet copier, the result is a toned-paper image.

Retrocolor

The process of applying color to the back of a drawing on tracing paper or drawing mylar can be called *retrocolor,* a term passed along to this author by architect, teacher, and professional illustrator Paul Stevenson Oles, FAIA.

The complexities of color application can be separated into simpler, more discrete tasks by using the retrocolor technique. Figures 7-35 through 7-61 show the various steps involved in using retrocolor for four different kinds of illustrations. In all four, the value arrangements—including shade and shadow—were applied first, to the *front* of the line drawing. The color media, usually color pencil (although marker and pastel can also be used), are subsequently applied to the *back* of the tracing paper drawing or mylar. Of course, color can also be applied to the front of the drawing as well when the need arises.

The retrocolor approach to color design drawing has a number of advantages. The first concerns the value arrangements of the drawings. As mentioned before, value is one of the three dimensions of color and, where illustration is concerned, is the most important. In retrocolor, it is considered and applied separately, not only simplifying the color design drawing process, but also greatly increasing the chances that the drawing will have a stronger value composition.

Second, this approach can be more efficient than others. At any stage during the development of a retrocolor drawing, its useful life as a design communication tool can begin. In a professional design office, a designer must be prepared to present her ideas at any point during the design process, not only upon its completion. If necessary, a retrocolor drawing can be shown as a line drawing. It can also be shown as a tone drawing if it must be pressed into service before the application of color to the back or if the color and materials decisions are delayed.

A third advantage is a component of efficiency: speed. After the values are applied to the front of the drawing, the color can be added to the back very quickly. This is because a rough, quick application of color on the back will neither disturb nor diminish the crisp, dark quality of the linework on the front of the drawing. Moreover, loose applications of color on the back do not appear so from the front, because the undisturbed linework maintains the ordered look of the drawing.

Fourth, the retrocolor technique is forgiving. Colors can be quickly altered or erased and changed without disturbing the lines or value applications on the front of the drawing.

Fifth, color design drawings made with the use of the retrocolor technique lend themselves to dramatic, high-quality reproductions even before the color is applied. The line drawings by themselves can be reproduced by office photocopier or plotter. After the values are applied to the front of the drawing, but before color is added to the back, the drawing can be scanned and printed. In addition, excellent black-and-white copies can be made of the drawing by employing the black-and-white function of a *color* photocopier or by using a digital black-and-white photocopier. These copies possess a far greater range of grays than those made by an ordinary black-and-white office photocopier. Once the color *is* applied to the back of the drawing, you will find that the mood and dramatic qualities of your drawing can be altered simply by changing the color of the backing paper.

The four retrocolor drawings discussed in the following paragraphs are examples of types of color design drawing that are frequently used at CommArts.

The Pastel "Quickie"

Pastel can be a very useful color medium for designers. The extent of the color capability of pastel ranges from brilliant to subtle, and perhaps its most useful attribute is that it can be applied very quickly and easily, making it an ideal medium for use in concept studies (7-35 through 7-41).

Yet pastel is also, to some degree, uncontrollable. This is especially true of pastel as compared with color pencil in attempting to apply color to the edges of shapes. However, rather than trying to control the medium precisely, most designers tend to relax and apply pastel more loosely than other color media. The results can be less uncontrolled than the designer may fear at first, because the undisturbed network of lines on the front of the drawing orders the color application more concisely than it appears from the back.

This medium also blends beautifully and easily, particularly on tracing paper, often giving the colors of the finished drawing a mingled quality similar to that of watercolor.

Fig. 7-35 The basic forms for this line drawing were created by computer as a wire-frame drawing. It was used as an underlay, over which the furnishings, figures, and design details were added. The combination was traced onto an 11" x 17" sheet of drawing vellum with a Micron 005 pen and a 4x0 technical pen.

Fig. 7-36

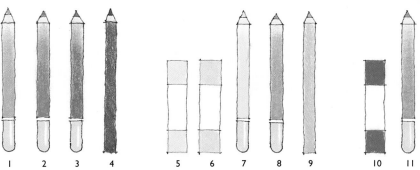

Fig. 7-37

Fig. 7-36 The line drawing was reduced to a small size, about 6" x 8", so that value studies could be made quickly. The study shown here took about 20 minutes to make and was drawn on bond paper with a *Black* Prismacolor pencil.

Because the illustration this study was prepared for was intended as a quick concept study, it was decided that the light should be diffuse rather than direct sunlight. This saves the time of illustrating extensive shade and shadow. Moreover, because this place is a story below grade, it was decided that the colors should be light in value. Ironically, to make this appear so, the foreground elements were darkened and linked together by the darkened floor. Thus, the rest of the space appears lighter by contrast. Note, too, that contrasts still occur within the major areas of value. Although the main part of the space is generally of much lighter value, contrasts still occur even though they are smaller and weaker than those between foreground and middle ground. It was still possible to take advantage of value-contrast opportunities to make things "read"—figures were darkened against lighter backgrounds, and window frames were both lightened and darkened against contrasting backgrounds.

Fig. 7-37 The pastels and pencils used for the illustration. The simple color arrangement of the finished illustration is a warm-cool relationship, a complementary scheme mostly between the hues of yellow and purple blue, with some secondary use of green yellow and yellow red. The green yellows are (1) *#599,* (2) *#600,* (3) *#575* pencil pastels and (4) *Olive Green* pencil. The warm hues used were (5) *Raw Sienna 234.9* stick pastel, (6) *Indian Red 347.9* stick pastel, (7) *#692,* (8) *#680* pencil pastels, and (9) *Peach* pencil. The cool purple blues used were (10) *Cobalt Blue 512.5* stick pastel and (11) *#430* pencil pastel.

Fig. 7-38

Fig. 7-39

Fig. 7-38 This quick color study took about 15 minutes. A sheet of white roll tracing paper was placed over the value study shown in figure 7-36. Pastels were loosely applied and blended in order to experiment with colors being considered for the final application.

Fig. 7-39 *Black* Prismacolor was applied to the front of the line drawing on tracing paper, with the value study being used as a guide. Notice the other, more subtle, contrasts established to help create the effects of light, such as the spandrels and soffits darkened against the window edges and diffuse shadows radiating from probable sources of light.

Even though the foreground is much darker than the middle ground of the illustration, it is worth noticing that value contrasts, weak as they are, still *do* occur within this darker part of the drawing. This is particularly noticeable on the paving, as it keeps the foreground from appearing two-dimensional and diorama-like.

Fig. 7-40

Fig. 7-40 Here the color media are being applied to the back of the tracing paper, which took about an hour. The pastels must be applied slightly more heavily on the back of the tracing paper to have them appear sufficiently dense on the front of the drawing.

The pastel was roughly scribbled on the back, staying approximately "within the lines." Once it was applied, it was lightly blended with a fingertip. The result as seen from the front of the drawing is similar to the minglings of color seen in watercolor illustrations. Of course, the heavier the black pencil application on the front of the drawing, the more heavily the pastel had to be applied to the back so that it would show through the pencil—hence the heavy application of *Cobalt Blue 512.5* stick pastel to the foreground area of the drawing. Errors in color application were quickly erased with an electric eraser with a soft, white erasing strip.

The color was generally applied from the top of the drawing, working downward, to avoid unnecessary smearing or lifting of the pastel. The only color pencil used was *Peach* for skin tones and *Olive Green* for the foreground bamboo plants. The *Olive Green* pencil was applied to the *front* of the drawing because the bamboo was sufficiently dark as to be opaque.

The pastel was *not* sprayed with fixative upon completion of the color application, inasmuch as fixative can deaden the color. Rather, the finished drawing was handled very carefully. The back of the illustration was protected with another layer of tracing paper and stored in an individual folder.

Fig. 7-41

Fig. 7-41 The finished illustration, shown with a white paper backing. White gouache highlights were added to the elements in the store window and to the water in the pool on the left. To minimize handling of this mostly pastel drawing, a color bubble-jet enlargement of the drawing was used for presentation purposes and smaller color photocopies were used for distribution.

An Exterior Daytime View

Figures 7-42 through 7-48 illustrate an approach to creating a more finished exterior view of a proposed building within its context, using the retrocolor technique. Discussions of how the line drawing was made, the shade and shadow approached, the color applied, and foreground drawn are included in the captions to the illustrations.

The line drawing of this building (7-42) was done on white roll tracing paper with a *Black* Prismacolor pencil and a straightedge. A straightedge was used for two reasons: First, the lines can be made finer (appropriate to the small size of the drawing and the detail involved). Second, such lines can be drawn more quickly with a straightedge, particularly when they must be aligned with distant vanishing points.

A value study was developed (7-43) that used the darker foreground and surrounding contextual elements as a darker frame that sets off the subject building. The middle ground (the building itself) is a medium value; the background is the lightest value, although it too darkens near the top, completing the effect of a darker "aperture" through which the subject building is viewed.

A rather unrestricted palette of colors was used for the drawing, with the lightest and warmest colors reserved for the subject building. Although the foreground also has warm colors, these colors have been both darkened and "cooled" by the application of blue pencil. Many of the colors in the composition were determined either by existing colors, such as those in the foreground, or by the range of colors available for local natural materials, such as the sandstone shown on the building.

Fig. 7-42

Fig. 7-42 Because the original drawing was used for the color application, a black-and-white photocopy of the drawing (shown here) was made both to keep as a record and in case the original was ruined and another line image had to be made. (Hand shown for scale.)

The original drawing is 12" x 17½".

Fig. 7-43

Fig. 7-43 The value study and color media used for the drawing are the neutrals and near-neutrals of (1) *White 100.5* stick pastel; (2) *White* pencil; (3) *French Grey 10%*, (4) *French Grey 30%*, (5) *Cool Grey 30%*, and (6) *Black* pencils; as well as (7) *French Grey 20%*, (8) *French Grey 30%*, (9) *French Grey 50%*, (10) *French Grey 70%*, (11) *French Grey 90%*, (12) *Cool Grey #3 (Cool Grey 30%)*, (13) *Cool Grey #5 (Cool Grey 50%)*, (14) *Cool Grey #7 (Cool Grey 70%)*, (15) *Cool Grey #9 (Cool Grey 90%)*, and (16) *Black* markers.

The cool colors are (17) *Ultramarine Deep 506.9* and (18) *Cobalt Blue 512.5* stick pastels; as well as (19) *Blue Slate*, (20) *Copenhagen Blue* and (21) Derwent *Blue Violet Lake #27* pencils. The warm colors—reds, yellow-reds and yellows—are (22) *Jasmine*, (23) *Light Peach*, (24) *Peach*, (25) *Yellow Ochre*, (26) *Terra Cotta*, (27) *Burnt Ochre*, and (28) *Tuscan Red* pencils; as well as (29) *Redwood (Sienna Brown)*, (30) *Burnt Umber (Dark Umber)*, and (31) *Delta Brown (Black)* markers.

The greens and green yellows are (32) *Yellow Chartreuse*, (33) *Limepeel*, (34) *Deco Aqua*, (35) *Celadon Green*, and (36) *Olive Green* pencils; as well as (37) *Olive (Olive Green)*, (38) *Dark Olive (French Grey 80%)*, (39) *Deep Evergreen (Peacock Blue + Dark Green)* markers.

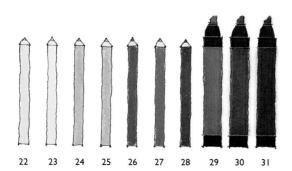

1 2 3 4 5 6 7 8 9 10 11 12 13 14 15 16

17 18 19 20 21

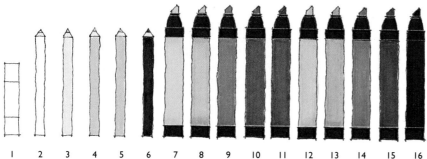

22 23 24 25 26 27 28 29 30 31

32 33 34 35 36 37 38 39

Fig. 7-44 Once the line drawing on tracing paper was made, the shade and shadow were applied to the *front* of the line drawing with *Black* Prismacolor pencil. The shade and shadow were first "roughed in" with red pencil on a photocopy of the original, then placed behind the tracing paper to use as a template for the drawing shown enlarged here. Thus, the primary focus could be on the quality of the pencil application instead of layout issues.

Note that the shadows are drawn more lightly on the glass. Although shadows do not actually fall *on* glass (unless it is dirty), but *through* it, the shadows in this drawing were lightly drawn on the glass to avoid confusion and to allow the forms of the building to be more completely revealed in this particular case. Note, too, that the shadows are graded darker toward their edges, "forcing" the sunlit surfaces to appear slightly brighter.

Fig. 7-44

Fig. 7-45 Once the shade and shadow application was completed on the front of the drawing, it was turned over to begin the color application on the back. The color was begun on the left (tentatively at first, to determine how much hand pressure was needed) and progressed toward the right.

The color application could have begun at any point on the building, but it is best not to have your hand resting on a finished color application as you work, because you can smear and lift the color, as well as buckle the paper with hand oils and moisture. If you must rest your hand on completed color, rest it on a folded piece of bond paper placed over the color.

The drawing was placed over a sheet of brown kraft paper as the color was applied and evaluated, as that was the paper intended for use as a backer sheet when the finished color photocopies were made.

French Grey 10% pencil was applied nearest the shadow edges on the upper part of the building, then graded to a *French Grey 30%* farther away, helping to force the shadow with a lighter value. The lighter parts of the shadows were flavored with *Peach* pencil, grading into the Derwent *Blue Violet Lake #27* pencil that covers the rest of the shadow. Notice how roughly (and, thus, quickly) the color can be applied and still achieve the subtle and refined results visible from the front of the drawing, seen in figure 7-46.

The lighter parts of the glass were colored with *Deco Aqua* pencil, which grades into the darker *Celadon Green*

Fig. 7-45

pencil. The parts of the glass in shadow were flavored with *Jasmine* pencil to imply an illuminated interior. The designer used this approach to the glazing color, instead of drawing reflections, to ensure that the finished illustration did not appear too busy.

The darker-value stone, as well as the stone in shadow, was colored with a blend of *Burnt Ochre* and *Terra Cotta* pencils. The lighter, sunlit stone was colored with a loose mixture of *Light Peach, Peach,* and *Yellow Ochre* pencils.

Note how the *Light Peach* pencil is used to force the shadow.

The designer took time to add touches of color to the elements displayed in the storefront windows. This ensures that the windows will appear both interesting and transparent; when there is nothing to see through an important window, it can appear unnecessarily opaque. A blend of *Celadon Green* and *Jasmine* pencils was used to color the awnings directly above the storefronts.

Fig. 7-46 This stage shows the completed color on the building and the sky.

Before color pencil was added to the roof, the sky was quickly applied, with pastel, to the back of the drawing. A blend of *White 100.5* and *Ultramarine Deep 506.9* stick pastels was applied to the lower part of the sky, just above the roof. This mixture was graded into *Cobalt Blue 512.5* stick pastel, applied to the upper part of the sky. A small amount of the *White 100.5* stick pastel was also applied to the *front* of the drawing to create the faint, streaked clouds.

Once the pastel colors were blended, the overcolor on the roof area on the back of the drawing was erased with an electric eraser using a soft, white erasing strip. The roof color was applied with a *Cool Grey 30%* pencil. *White* pencil was used over the roof color to highlight the center roof panel on the turret.

A blend of *Olive Green, Limepeel,* and *Yellow Chartreuse* pencils was applied to the planters. To ensure adequate brightness for the polychrome terra-cotta capitals at the top of each stone pilaster, white gouache was mixed with various opaque watercolors and applied to the capitals on the *front* of the drawing.

Fig. 7-46

Fig. 7-47 After the color was applied to the subject building in the middle ground, it became clear how dark the foreground must be to provide adequate value contrast. Owing to the size of the drawing, dark markers, instead of pencils, were first applied to create base foreground colors of appropriate value. Once the marker was applied, the designer used color pencil to "tune" the marker color by applying it both on the back and the front of the drawing.

Black marker was applied to the ceiling supported by the brick column; *Burnt Umber (Dark Umber)* marker was used on the lighter sides of the column and brick planters, and *Delta Brown (Black)* marker was added to their darker sides.

The low plant materials were darkened with a mixture of *Dark Olive (French Grey 80%)* and *Deep Evergreen (Peacock Blue + Dark Green)* markers. Note that the mixture of these markers, although looking rough and blotchy on the back side of the tracing paper, appears much smoother on the front and looks rather like watercolor. The concrete sidewalk and planter bases were colored with *French Grey 70%* and *90%* markers; the grass was colored with *Olive (Olive Green)* marker and graded into *Dark Olive (French Grey 80%)* marker. Color was added to the flowers with *Burnt Umber (Dark Umber)* and *Redwood (Sienna Brown)* markers.

The figures were colored with *Black* and *Burnt Umber (Dark Umber)* markers,

Fig. 7-47

and *Redwood (Sienna Brown)* marker was used to add color to the skin, sweater, and handbag. The shirt on the center figure, as well as the curb behind him, was toned with a *Cool Grey #5 (Cool Grey 50%)* marker.

The shadow in the street was colored with a series of cool gray markers to create a gradation. Beginning at the outer edge, *Cool Grey #9, #7, #5,* and *#3 (Cool Grey 90%, 70%, 50%,* and *30%)* markers were applied across the

shadow. The same markers were also used to create the strong contrast against both ends of the subject building by darkening the neighboring and background buildings. Note that the sunlit portion of the street is also progressively darkened toward the right with *French Grey 20%, 30%, 50%, 70%,* and *90%* markers.

Color pencil was used to flavor many of the dark foreground elements by applying it to the *front* of the drawing.

Copenhagen Blue pencil, used to imply reflected sky color, was lightly applied to the lower left of the foreground column, planter, and concrete, as well as to the building shadow in the street. *Olive Green* pencil was used to flavor the shrubs and grass. *Tuscan Red* pencil was added to bring up the colors of the flowers.

Fig. 7-48

Fig. 7-48 An image of a copy of the finished drawing. This copy was made with brown kraft paper placed behind the tracing paper original.

Before this copy was made, touches of white gouache were added to the potted flowers, as well as to upper parts of the storefront windows and some of the office windows, to imply the sparkle of light sources. *White* pencil was added to the sidewalks and crosswalks and was used to highlight bare tree branches in front of dark backgrounds.

A Dusk View

A dusk view of a project can convey the drama of its illumination while its exterior forms, materials, and colors remain visible. Dusk views are often more useful than night views from a design communication standpoint, in that they convey more design information.

Figures 7-49 through 7-54 show the development of a dusk view of the same building illustrated in the preceding daytime view. A dusk view of a project has some similarities to the way its daytime counterpart is developed, although the shade and shadow and the window treatment are handled differently.

Fig. 7-49

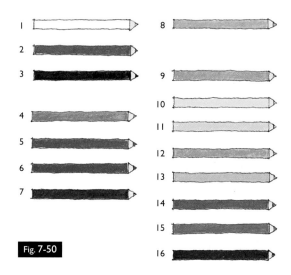

Fig. 7-50

Fig. 7-49 The line drawing used for the daytime view of this building was photocopied onto tracing paper.

This close-up shows shade and shadow being applied with a *Black Prismacolor* on the front of the drawing, in much the same way it was applied in the daytime view. You can see, however, that the shadows do not have distinct edges, because the only light sources—the windows and the ambient sky—are diffuse. The surfaces facing away from (or hidden from) the sky and the windows are the darkest, such as the soffits and the tops of the stone pilasters. Note that the values applied to the building are still light enough to allow color to show through them from the back of the drawing.

Fig. 7-50 The color pencil palette used to create the dusk scene. The neutrals and near-neutrals are (1) *White*, (2) *Cool Grey 70%*, (3) *Black*. The cool colors are (4) Derwent *Blue Violet Lake #27*, (5) *Violet*, (6) *Copenhagen Blue*, (7) *Indigo Blue*. The green pencil is (8) *Celadon Green*. The warm colors are (9) *Pink*, (10) *Jasmine*, (11) *Deco Orange*, (12) *Mineral Orange*, (13) *Peach*, (14) *Terra Cotta*, (15) *Burnt Ochre*, (16) *Dark Umber*.

Fig. 7-51 Once the values were applied to the front side of the drawing, the window illumination and its effects were added to the back side of the drawing. *Deco Orange, Jasmine,* and *White* pencils were applied as graded washes of color to the windows, right over the smallest mullions. These gradations span several windows at a time, resulting in some areas of the windows being lighter in value and others darker. This creates a less even lighting effect and imparts a less institutional, more intimate feel to the building.

The designer approached the retail windows at the first level by first coloring the items in the windows with small, intense touches, using a variety of color pencils. Because the downward-oriented halogen lighting is often used as retail display lighting, the remaining uncolored areas at the bottom of the window were colored with *White* pencil. This pencil was graded into *Jasmine* pencil farther up the window, which in turn was graded into *Deco Orange* pencil.

The surfaces perpendicular to the window plane that would logically receive spill light from the windows (soffits, sides of pilasters, sidewalks, etc.) were colored with *Deco Orange* and *Jasmine* pencils. Note how these surfaces were kept lighter in value when the the front of the drawing was shaded in the previous step.

This stage of the drawing is shown backed with a sheet of dark blue paper to make it more visible.

Fig. 7-51

Fig. 7-52 The pilasters and lower stone-clad portions of the building were the next areas to receive color. *Terra Cotta* pencil was used to add color to the foundation and header band that appears at the top of the first-story windows and the bottoms of the projecting balconies. The spandrels just above the header band were colored with *Burnt Ochre* pencil.

A gradation of *Mineral Orange, Burnt Ochre,* and *Dark Umber* pencils was applied to the pilasters. The illuminated edges of the columns were colored with *Peach* pencil.

Celadon Green pencil was added to the awnings and the metal roof. *Cool Grey 70%* pencil was applied over the green pencil on the roof to shift its color to a cooler hue and to increase its contrast with the sky beyond.

The near-neutral surfaces on the upper part of the building—columns, fascias, and stucco walls—were washed with a Derwent *Blue Violet Lake #27* pencil. This step shifted these neutral colors from a dull gray to a more probable color that implies a reflection of the sky.

This stage of the drawing is shown backed with white paper.

Fig. 7-52

Fig. 7-53 In this step, color pencil was used to make the sky, although pastel could have been used as well. *Indigo Blue, Copenhagen Blue, Violet, Pink,* and *Mineral Orange* pencils were rapidly applied and graded one into another, in that order, from left to right. The hand pressure on the pencils was gradually decreased as the sky became brighter in the lower right.

Fig. 7-53

Fig. 7-54

Fig. 7-54 Final touches were added to the *front* of the drawing. *Poppy Red, Yellow Chartreuse, Pink, Blue Slate,* and *White* pencils were added to enhance the colors in the store windows.

Touches of white gouache were added to the upper parts of the retail windows to imply display lighting. White gouache was also used to apply the sliver of moon and the stars.

The finished drawing was backed with brown kraft paper because of the warm color it imparts to the scene.

Retrocolor Hybrid Using Mylar

A retrocolor hybrid is a retrocolor drawing whose front-side images are created both by computer and by hand. These drawings capitalize on the advantages that both the computer and hand drawing bring to the design process.

A designer is often called upon, during the earlier stages of the design process, to provide a preview of what a project or its parts may look like upon completion. These preview drawings are partly design ideas that exist thus far in the process and partly wishful thinking—the design team's intention for the feel of the completed project, even before its specifics are designed. These drawings often provide a kind of visual goal as well—images that can guide the design team as it develops the project.

The brain/hand combination of the designer not only has a vast capability for imagining what a proposed place may look and feel like by relying on a lifetime of visual experience, it can also quickly produce useful impressions of these imaginings with few additional inputs and with the simplest of drawing materials. The slowest and most inefficient part of the brain/hand process is "setting up" the rudiments of the view—determining the best angle and blocking out the perspective of the basic forms. Fortunately, these setups can be quickly, easily, and accurately handled with such computer applications as SketchUp.

Two-sided translucent drawing mylar is as useful as white tracing paper when using the retrocolor technique. While its "feel" is different from that of tracing paper, you will find that line media, color pencils, and markers can be used on it just as effectively. It has the additional advantage of being compatible with copiers and laser printers. By replacing a sheet of your printer's paper with a similarly sized sheet of 4 mil drawing mylar, you can print images from your computer to a translucent drawing surface on which the retrocolor technique can be readily used. The same speed and efficiencies are available with this technique as with tracing paper, which is discussed on page 345. Line and color media are easily erased from mylar using an electric eraser and the white erasing strips intended for the medium.

The steps used to create the illustration are shown in figures 7-56 through 7-61, beginning with a view from a SketchUp model (7-55). In this sequence, an eye-level view from the model (7-56) is "exported" as a single .tif image. The

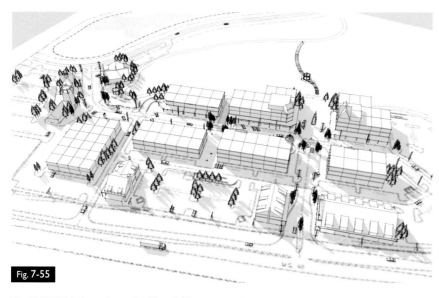

Fig. 7-55

Fig. 7-56

Fig. 7-55 This is a view of a SketchUp model of a proposed town center. The view in 7-56 was taken from this model, using a camera position set at the upper right, looking down the street toward the building with the tower, on the left.

Fig. 7-56 The eye-level view of the SketchUp model provides an accurate perspective "block-out" on which a loose color sketch study of the character potential of the street and its buildings can be made. It was first saved as a page in the model, then exported and saved as a .tif file.

image is opened in Photoshop and its lines roughened with the *Spatter* filter (Filter > Brush Strokes > Spatter). You can read more about this filter in Chapter 8. The image (shadows included) is then printed on mylar. Once printed, the additional information and detail is simply added to the front side of the printed image as a *continuation* of the "drawing" that originated as a SketchUp model view (7-57). *No retracing of the existing SketchUp lines is necessary,* saving time and effort. Note that since mylar is not absorbent like tracing paper, liquid color media—especially felt-tipped line media (Micron 005, Pilot Razor Point, etc.) will take longer to dry to avoid smearing. An easy way to speed drying is to place your completed line drawing under a flexible-arm drawing light, within a few inches of the lamp, for a couple of minutes.

After the linework and tones, including shade and shadow, were completed on the front of the mylar, color was quickly added to the *back* of the drawing with marker and color pencil (7-59). When the hand color application was completed, a piece of brown kraft paper was placed on top of it before the scanner lid was closed and the drawing was scanned, front down (7-60).

The scanned image was opened in Photoshop; the final touches were applied and the color adjustments completed (7-61).

Fig. 7-57 The view in 7-56 was opened in Photoshop and its linework "roughened" using the *Spatter* filter (Filter > Brush Strokes > Spatter . . . ; Spray Radius = 3, Smoothness = 7). The sign on the left was added with the *Type Tool.* The banners and poles were hand drawn and added as a layer; the image was then printed on an 8½" x 11" sheet of two-sided, 4 mil drawing mylar, using a black-and-white laser printer.

A Micron 005 felt-tipped pen was used on the *front* of the mylar printout to quickly and loosely add detail to the buildings, automobiles, and foreground plant materials. Additional figures were also added by hand. *French Grey 70*% and *French Grey 90*% markers were used to add shade and shadow to the buildings on the left as well as to deepen the shadows beneath the cars.

Main Street, looking south

Fig. 7-57

Fig. 7-58 On the *reverse* side of the mylar printout, color pencil was quickly added to the image. *Peach* and *Jasmine* pencils were applied to the upper levels of the buildings on the left side. *Terra Cotta* pencil was added to the facade of the foreground building on the left.

Jasmine pencil was applied to the sunlit portion of the corner dome on the left side, transitioning to *Yellow Ochre* pencil in the shade. A reflection of the sky was added on the shaded side using *Blue Slate* pencil. *Blue Slate* was also used to flavor the shade and shadow of the building on the left. *Celadon Green* pencil was applied to the windows of the building on the left, as well as to the upper body of the parked truck.

On the right side of the drawing, *Yellow Ochre* pencil was used on the upper story of the partially visible building, while a gradient of *Terra Cotta* to *Yellow Ochre* pencil was applied to the columns.

Celadon Green and *Burnt Ochre* pencils were used on the foreground shrubs; *Olive Green* and *Limepeel* pencils were used on the trees. Because the branching of the trees was so dense, these color pencils were applied to the *front* of the drawing in order to overcome the excessive amount of black on the printout.

Pink and *Jasmine* pencils were applied as a gradient on the banners. *Blue Slate* pencil accents were added to the front of the printout.

As finishing touches, a sky-color gradient was added with Derwent *Blue Violet Lake # 27*, *Blue Slate,* and *Cloud*

Main Street, looking south

Fig. 7-58

Blue pencils, from left to right. *White* pencil was applied to the cornice and window surrounds of the building on the left, as well as to the figures, parking striping, and the windows on the right. White gouache accents were added to show display and accent lights visible through the windows.

After the color was applied to the mylar printout, it was first scanned with white paper behind it, as shown here. Note the intensity of the color and the contrasts in the image. This is frequently the initial result upon scanning a color drawing. It is easily remedied by making adjustments in Photoshop.

Fig. 7-59 These markers and pencils were used to add hand color in 7-57 and 7-58. The markers used in 7-57 were (1) *French Grey 90%* and (2) *French Grey 70%*. The pencils used in 7-58 were (3) *Pink*, (4) *Terra Cotta*, (5) *Peach*, (6) *Yellow Ochre*, (7) *Jasmine*, (8) *Limepeel*, (9) *Olive*, (10) *Celadon*, (11) *Blue Slate*, (12) *Cloud Blue*, (13) Derwent *Blue Violet Lake #27*, and (14) *White*.

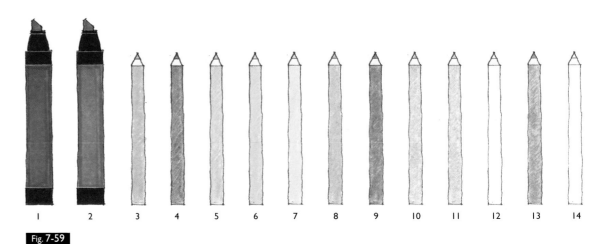

Fig. 7-59

Fig. 7-60 This image shows the same colored mylar printout, this time scanned with brown kraft paper behind it. Although the chroma of the colors still appears too strong, note how the brown tone helps to unify and warm the drawing.

Main Street, looking south

Fig. 7-60

Main Street, looking south

Fig. 7-61

Fig. 7-61 After the scan of the image in 7-60 was opened in Photoshop, a few adjustments were made.

The chroma of the entire image was weakened through the use of adjustment layers. A hue/saturation adjustment layer was added, and the *Saturation* slider moved to the left until the saturation (chroma) of the image appeared more realistic.

Then, the colors of both the sunlit and shadowed parts of the street (as well as the entire shaded right side of the drawing) were adjusted to make their color more interesting and alive, using the *Replace Color* command. The entire shade and shadow area was loosely selected with the *Lasso Tool*. The *Replace Color* command was activated (Image > Adjustments > Replace Color . . .) and the shadow area sampled with the eyedropper. The *Hue* slider was used to shift its hue slightly more toward purple; the *Saturation* slider was used to strengthen the chroma of this area just a touch. The process was repeated for the sunlit portion of the street, shifting the hue from its original pinkish color to a more yellowish one.

Digital images were added to the left foreground of the building to give them a sense of depth and vitality. Such images are usually introduced to the illustration as a layer; the opacity of this layer is frequently reduced, as in this example, so the images do not overwhelm the rest of the illustration.

A dark background was added to the sign, and its letters were retyped using an intense blue.

Since the sky appeared too streaky once the image was scanned, a digital photographic sky was added as a layer that covered the original sky (see 4-243 through 4-248). Both its color and opacity were adjusted to keep it from overwhelming the rest of the drawing. *When adding skies, especially those with clouds, be sure the light in the sky and on the clouds agrees with the sun direction used for the rest of the drawing.*

ADDITIONAL LAYERS OF INFORMATION

Color design drawings must do more than communicate a beautiful (it is hoped) image. They differ from strictly artistic drawings in that they must communicate information about design ideas, usually for places—buildings, interiors, landscapes, urban districts, and regions.

These drawings frequently act as the "working drawings" for the early stages of the design process and, just as in working drawings, their communicative power can be greatly magnified by additional layers of information, such as notes and photographs. Once scanned, drawings and photos can be combined in myriad ways and accompanied by notes to tell the story of the design ideas being communicated. The resulting compositions can then presented by digital projection, as printed sheets, or as enlarged, plotted sheets.

Notes

Notes work well with design drawings as long as they do not block critical graphic information. They usually work best by occupying a secondary, rather than dominant, role in the overall image. Notes can range from a more formal arrangement or the more casual annotations in figure 7-62. Generally, the more "finished" the drawing or presentation of the graphic material, the more formal the arrangement of the accompanying notes. Thoughtfully sized and placed notes can enhance a color design drawing just as words, beautifully designed and applied, can enhance the architecture of a building.

Notes can be as helpful to the designer as they are informative to the drawing's intended audience. Because design drawings are a synthesis of an often surprisingly large amount of disparate information, the detailed thought that goes into forming them is sometimes forgotten. Adding notes directly to the design drawing is a good and easy way to document such thinking.

Notes are also frequently added to design drawings as a way to ensure that specific points about the design are clearly evident. They can even help guide the designer through a presentation of the drawings, particularly if the notes are numbered. The audience will find notes helpful when they review copies of the drawings at a later time, especially once memory of the presentation has faded.

Hand Notations

Handwritten notes are quite adequate for design drawings. There is no need to use "architectural" lettering unless you prefer it. Script, or a hybrid of script and lettering, can often be faster and yet still attractive (7-62). There are also a variety of informal digital fonts, such as Adobe's Legault, shown in figures 7-63 and 7-64.

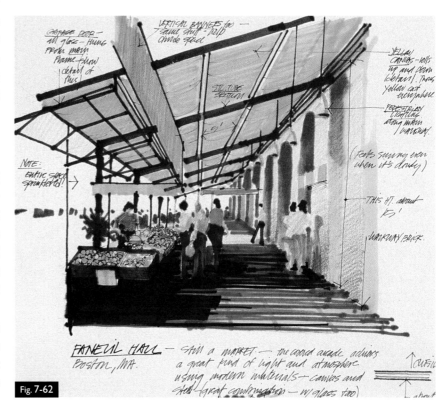

Fig. 7-62

Fig. 7-62 Handwritten notes accompany an on-site sketch. When each note is given a title, the information is easier to take in at a glance.

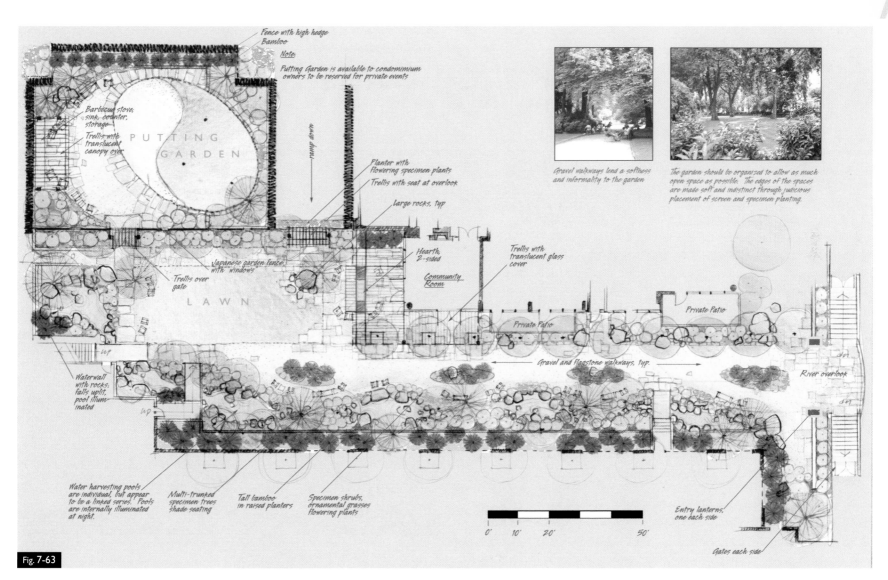

Fence with high hedge
Bamboo

Note:

Putting Garden is available to condominium
owners to be reserved for private events

Barbecue stove,
sink, counter,
storage

Trellis with
translucent
canopy over

PUTTING

GARDEN

ramp down

Planter with
flowering specimen plants
Trellis with seat at overlook

Large rocks, typ

Hearth,
2-sided

Community
Room

Trellis with
translucent glass
cover

Japanese garden fence
with "windows"

Trellis over
gate

LAWN

Private Patio

Private Patio

Gravel and flagstone walkways, typ.

River overlook

Waterwall
with rocks,
falls uplit,
pool illum-
inated

Water harvesting pools
are individual, but appear
to be a linked series. Pools
are internally illuminated
at night.

Multi-trunked
specimen trees
shade seating

Tall bamboo
in raised planters

Specimen shrubs,
ornamental grasses
flowering plants

Entry lanterns,
one each side

Gates each side

Gravel walkways lend a softness
and informality to the garden

The garden should be organized to allow as much
open space as possible. The edges of the spaces
are made soft and indistinct through judicious
placement of screen and specimen planting.

0'   10'   20'   50'

Fig. 7-63

Fig. 7-63 This presentation page was composed in Photoshop. It consists of a hand-drawn color plan (with accents made in Photoshop) and digital supporting photographs. The material was arranged in a "landscape" (horizontal) orientation whose proportions allow it to be printed at either 8½" x 11" or 11" x 17", or plotted at an "Arch D" (24" x 36") sheet size.

A low-chroma color gradient was added as a background to keep the visual emphasis on the images and not on the contrast between image and background. Gill Sans was used to label the larger areas ("Lawn," "Putting Garden"), but the gray color keeps its large size from distracting from the information within the drawing.

Adobe's Legault font, selected for its informal, handwritten character, was used for general notes. The leader arrows are organized in groups of diagonals having the same orientation. The diagonal direction of the leaders keeps them from being confused with the orthogonal lines of the architectural drawing.

The Digital Presentation Page

Pages of related drawings, photographs, and notes can be easily and effectively composed using a variety of applications, such as Photoshop or Adobe Illustrator (7-63). For more extensive, multipage presentations, especially those requiring larger amounts of running text, consider using Adobe's InDesign (7-64). This application facilitates the placement and sizing of drawings and photographs, allows text to automatically flow from page to page, and enables the designer to make font and page numbering changes that automatically carry through all pages of the document.

Fig. 7-64 This sheet from a multipage lighting study document for an urban district was created in Adobe InDesign. The images were produced and annotated before being imported into the document. Note the running text (upper left) and captions, which allow the document to be self-explanatory, like a magazine.

As in 7-63, the notes are kept clear of critical visual information in the images, and the arrow leaders are organized to reduce visual confusion.

in Figures 6 and 7, and can create the perception of a pedestrian safety issue. This condition can be turned into an opportunity: Introduce a luminaire that can uplight trees without having to be recessed into the ground (Fig.8) At the same time, enhance the ability of this luminaire to

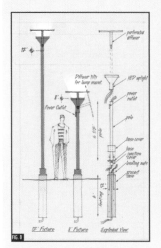

Fig.8 The "kit of parts" for the pedestrian/tree light consists of a precast base, simple steel or aluminum pole, uplight luminaire and a perforated diffuser that reflects part of the light downward while allowing the remainder to uplight the tree structure.

Fig.9 An illustration showing the pedestrian/tree light in place beneath established trees along Westheimer

Fig. 7-64

CHAPTER 371

DIGITAL COLOR DRAWING

Whatever media you use to accomplish your design communication tasks, it is most important that, as a designer, you convey your ideas effectively and efficiently. Your choice of media and technique should be appropriate to both the task at hand and the time you have available to make it happen. Before you begin any drawing task, take some time to think about your media options, the time you have available, and the purpose of your drawing effort. By planning your approach before you start a drawing, you can save a significant amount of time and effort later, after it is too late to start over. The media for and approaches to color design drawing presented in this chapter are the last of a wide variety of color drawing media and techniques discussed in this book and available for your consideration.

There are times when you may find it more appropriate to apply color to a drawing using digital techniques rather than hand media. This chapter discusses and illustrates a variety of those techniques and approaches—all using Photoshop—that are relatively simple and straightforward. In most cases, color is applied digitally to a line drawing that has been created by hand, then scanned—so technically, these kinds of drawings are still "hybrid" color drawings. In Photoshop, the color is applied in transparent layers so the original line drawing is always visible, maintaining its "hand-drawn" character. Minimal amounts of opaque color are also added for accents and special effects. Filters may also be applied to further enhance this character (see figures 8-63 through 8-74).

However, there are certain situations in which a color "drawing" may, in fact, use all photographic or digitally derived imagery to quickly and effectively communicate a design idea (8-42 to 8-58). While this may not be "drawing" per se, all the designer's skill in perspective, light, color, materials representation, and composition must still be brought to bear to make this kind of illustration effective. The media the designer uses to communicate ideas will continue to evolve, but the necessity for competence in these fundamental skills will always remain the same.

You will find digital color drawing has both advantages and disadvantages, depending on the skills and habits of the individual designer. Digital media is very forgiving: You can easily undo mistakes by simply "stepping backward," using Command-Z (Mac) or Control-Z (Windows) to undo a single step, or the *History Palette* to undo many steps. Your work is almost infinitely adjustable via the Adjustment commands. You can frequently generate your illustration in fewer steps, since no rescanning of hybrid drawings is required. You may also find that the resultant prints or plots of digital color drawings have an inherently richer, more vibrant color than those that are hand drawn and subsequently scanned.

Some find disadvantages in using digital rather than hand media for color design drawing. They experience the approach as too removed from the direct feel and touch of hand media. The drawings can be too smooth and uniform, resulting in illustrations with that archetypal, stiff "computer" look due to a lack of the textural character that is usually abundant in hand drawings. Digital illustrations also run the risk of appearing scattered and chaotic, usually because the thoughtful arrangement of large value groupings has been neglected, or a large number of digital images whose illumination character do not agree have been imported into the illustration—or both.

If you utilize digital color drawing in a way that leverages its strengths, you may realize increased speed in creating your illustrations, since large areas of color and gradients can be applied very quickly and easily. At CommArts, we have found that the key to working quickly and effectively with digital color drawing is to first *make sure there are adequate detail, interest, and accuracy in the line drawing* to which the digital color will be applied. Second, *once the line information is in place, apply the color more loosely,* even in a diagrammatic way,

when the need arises. The color, value arrangement, and materials indications achieved through color technique (see Chapter 4) all help to make the information already embedded in the line drawing more legible and create a focus to the drawing.

APPROACH

The general approach to digital color drawing is fairly simple. The color is applied to a line drawing—usually hand drawn, which gives it a more relaxed, sketchlike character—that has been scanned and opened in Photoshop. The color is applied with a digital pen and tablet (3-9), using a few of Photoshop's tools. The tools most frequently used include the *Gradient Tool*, *Brush Tool*, and the *Pencil Tool*. These, along with those less frequently used—such as the *Eraser Tool*, *Line Tool*, *Clone Stamp Tool*, and *Paint Bucket Tool*—are, of course, used in combination with the selection tools, *Move Tool*, and other tools in the Photoshop toolbox on an as-needed basis.

The colors are applied in layers, as necessary, so they can be adjusted in groups to optimize the major value groupings of the drawing. Areas are also often selected within the layers for further adjustment, as needed. The blending modes of the layers are usually set to "Multiply," making the colors transparent (not unlike markers or watercolor) and allowing the linework to show through. However, when intense or opaque colors are required, the blending mode of a layer is set to "Normal."

Since most of our design work at CommArts takes place in the conceptual and schematic phases of projects, we often show our clients large numbers of illustrations and studies that are drawn freehand. In order to maintain that continuity and character, and to create an open invitation for clients to participate in the design process, we generally avoid showing drawings that appear too "finished," since presentation materials that are too refined can send the subliminal message that the design process is closed to further intervention. To that end, we often use certain Photoshop filters on digital color drawings to make them appear sufficiently loose and informal. A filter used over an entire flattened drawing also serves to unify the image. More on the most effective filters used for digital color drawing can be found on page 407.

BASIC DRAWING TYPES

At CommArts, we repeatedly use a few basic types of digital color drawing that are easy to create and lend themselves equally well to quick sketches and more "finished" illustrations.

Sketch/Photo Combo

The sketch/photo combo is just that: an easy way to draw "over" a photograph in order to quickly illustrate proposed design ideas about and changes to an existing condition (8-1 through 8-5).

A digital photograph of the area to be redesigned is printed on letter- or ledger-size paper, depending on the content and detail required in the finished drawing. White tracing paper is placed over the image and the proposed changes loosely drawn. You can use whatever line media with which you are most comfortable, provided its lines are sufficiently dark to be legible upon scanning. The tracing paper drawing is then scanned and the scanned file opened in Photoshop, copied, and pasted into the digital photograph. The photograph will comprise one layer; the line drawing becomes a second. The color is applied digitally over the drawing area using a third layer. Since the color is added digitally, its opacity—and whether it obscures parts of the existing photographic image—can be controlled.

These kinds of drawings are frequently used at CommArts to initiate a dialog with clients about conceptual remodel ideas. Figure 3-60 shows another example of this approach.

Fig. 8-1

Fig. 8-2

Fig. 8-1 This digital photograph shows the "before" view of a courtyard in an existing retail center. (Photo: Taku Shimizu)

Fig. 8- 2 White tracing paper was placed over the photograph and an idea for a proposed glass-roofed "conservatory" café was quickly drawn and annotated using a Pentel Sign Pen. The drawing was scanned, then copied and pasted over the digital photograph in Photoshop. The blending mode of the line drawing layer was set to "Multiply." Note how the underlying photograph was brightened and its contrast reduced (Image > Adjustments > Brightness/Contrast), allowing the line drawing to become more legible. (Drawing: Taku Shimizu)

Fig. 8-3

Fig. 8-4

Fig. 8-3 A new layer was then added on *top* of the photograph layer but *underneath* the line drawing layer, its blending mode set to "Normal." This layer was used to add just enough color to give some opacity to the proposed building and supporting elements, such as shrubs, planters, signing, and figures. (Drawing: Taku Shimizu)

Fig. 8-4 Here, the line layer is turned off to better display the extent of the color added to the color layer. Most of the color was added using the airbrush capability of the *Brush Tool*. Note the use of the *Noise* filter (Filter > Noise > Add Noise . . .) on the shrubs in the cast stone planters. (Drawing: Taku Shimizu)

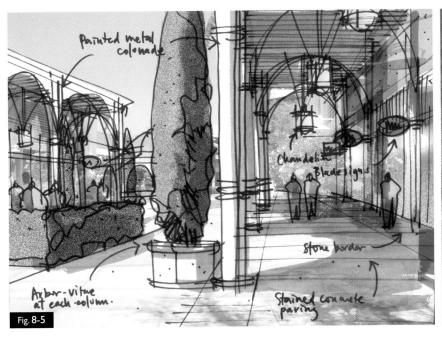

Fig. 8-5 These drawings are additional examples of the sketch/photo combo technique used in the same project presentation. (Drawings: Taku Shimizu)

Hand Line Drawing / Digital Color

This straightforward approach to digital color drawing is widely used at CommArts (8-7 through 8-20) as well as other professional design firms (8-25 through 8-41). The linework for the drawing is completed on tracing paper, often over a computer model "block-out" (such as those generated by SketchUp or Form•Z), with the design development and detail added during the creation of the line drawing itself. Once the line drawing is scanned, it is opened in Photoshop. Color is added to the elements in the image on various layers, usually with each layer accommodating similar families of elements. This makes it easier to adjust these families at or near the end of the drawing process, and to optimize their roles in the finished composition.

Photographic images of backgrounds, automobiles, figures, and contextual plant materials are frequently imported into these kinds of drawings to provide scale and context. While these elements lie outside of the designer's "design" responsibility, care must be taken to integrate their lighting and general character (line quality, color, texture, and contrast) with the rest of the image, so that a seamless, unified picture results. Filters (8-63 through 8-74) are often used to help create this sense of unity by introducing a common texture or character to all parts of the flattened image.

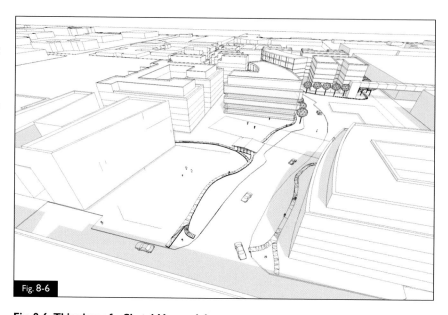

Fig. 8-6

Fig. 8-6 This view of a SketchUp model for a proposed mixed-use development was printed as an 11" x 17" image and shows the relationship of one of the major public open spaces to both the main thoroughfare and the surrounding residential buildings. (SketchUp model: Chris Blechar)

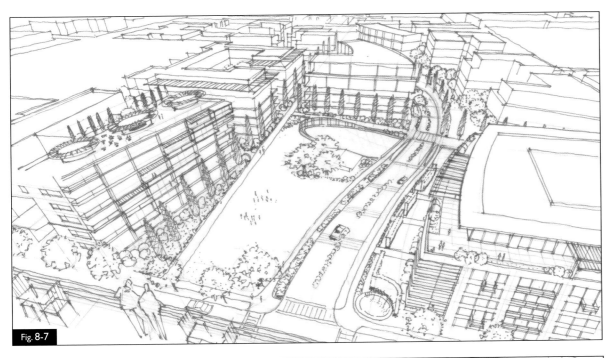

Fig. 8-7

Fig. 8-7 A sheet of white tracing paper was placed over the model view. A .5 mm pencil was used to lightly draw the conceptual character of the buildings, open space, roadways, and sidewalks. Incorporated into this drawing were ideas that were developed by the design team in preceding studies. A Micron 005 felt-tipped pen was used to draw the final linework directly over the light pencil lines.

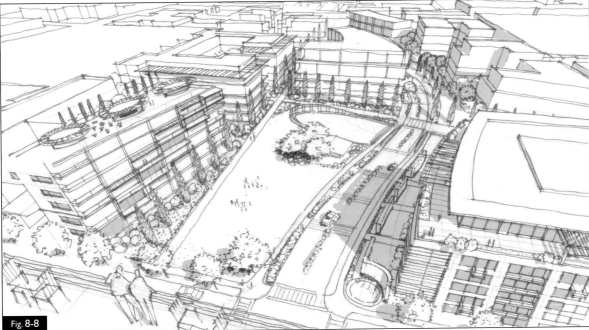

Fig. 8-8

Fig. 8-8 A new layer was created and its blending mode set to "Multiply." A low-chroma purple was selected with the *Color Picker* and, using the *Brush Tool* with a hard round brush, shade and shadows were applied to the image, using the shadows on the SketchUp model as a reference. Some windows in the drawing were also darkened for punctuation, using the same brush and color.

Fig. 8-9 Next, a new layer was established on which color was added to the glass areas of the façades facing the open space. The blending mode was once again set to "Multiply." On certain small areas of glass, the blue green was applied with the *Brush Tool* and a hard round brush. For larger areas of glass, the facade was selected and the *Gradient Tool* was used to apply a "Foreground to Background" linear gradient that ranged from pale blue-green to pale yellow. All color was applied directly over the shadows.

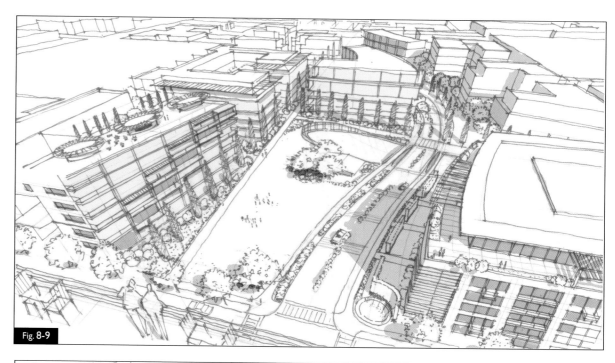

Fig. 8-9

Fig. 8-10 Once again, a new layer was established and its blending mode set to "Multiply." Color was added to the roadways and walks, using the hard round brush and the *Brush Tool*. The *Eraser Tool* was used to clean up where necessary—easy to do, since this color was on its own layer.

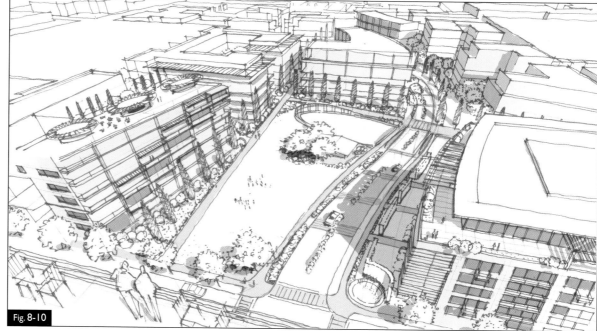

Fig. 8-10

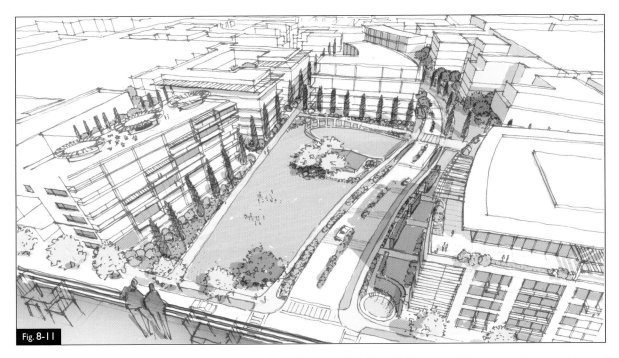

Fig. 8-11

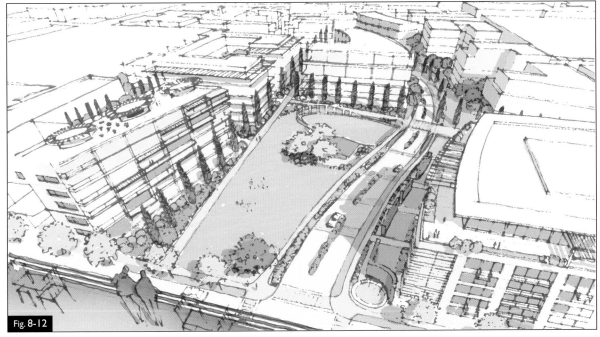

Fig. 8-12

Fig. 8-11 In the final steps, three more layers were established: one for the color of the ground plane and plant materials; another to add color to the foreground roof (figures, tables, chairs, and guardrail); and a third layer to add color accents to the masses of flowers. The blending mode for the first two layers was set to "Multiply"; the third layer's blending mode was set to "Normal," allowing the flowers' colors to remain opaque and thereby have more visual impact.

A hue/saturation adjustment layer was inserted immediately above the background line drawing—the lowest layer in the *Layers Palette.* This adjustment, used to give the lines of the line drawing a more sepia (or brownish) hue, was made by checking the *Colorize* box and manipulating the *Adjustment* sliders. As a result, the warmer line color gave a warmer tone to the entire drawing.

Once the drawing was substantially complete, the various layers were adjusted slightly in hue (*Hue*), value (*Lightness*), and chroma (*Saturation*) to create maximum legibility.

Fig. 8-12 The *Dry Brush* filter was used on the flattened image to give an even more exaggerated loose character to the drawing (Filter > Artistic > Dry Brush . . . ; Brush Size = 0, Brush Detail = 10, Texture = 1).

Fig. 8-13

Fig. 8-14

Fig. 8-13 This view of the SketchUp study model of a new town is the same model as that shown in figure 7-55. This view shows the relationship among the buildings, streets, sidewalks, covered walkways, and activities planned for the open space.

Fig. 8-14 A sheet of white tracing paper was placed directly over an 8½" x 11" printout of the model view.

Using a .5 mm pencil, the linework for the building fenestration and detail, additional cars, trees, figures, and banner poles was very lightly drawn. An ordinary 2H pencil was then used to quickly draw the scene directly over the light layout lines. A .5 mm pencil was used for the thinner lines, and a *Black* pencil for the conifer trees.

Once drawn, the tracing paper-based line drawing was scanned and introduced as a layer in Photoshop, over the model image from which it was derived. The line drawing's blending mode was set to "Multiply." This allowed the shadows of the model image to appear in the result,

shown here. (Additional shadows were added for elements newly introduced in the line drawing, on a new layer.) This approach also enabled the model image and the line drawing to be adjusted independently of one another in order to produce the strongest resultant image.

A partial photographic image of the distant tree line (8-15) that forms the background of the proposed project site was copied and pasted into the image, quickly and easily providing a realistic background. Once in place, it was desaturated (Image > Adjustments > Desaturate) to remove its color. Note that by using the *Brightness/Contrast* adjustment command (Image > Adjustments > Brightness/Contrast . . .), the tree line was significantly lightened and

its contrast reduced so its realism does not visually conflict with the hand-drawn quality of the foreground.

The open space in the center of the drawing was revised from a skating rink with a shelter at one end to a sledding hill with a pavilion and boardwalk on piers in the wetlands beyond. White tracing paper was placed over a printout of the drawing, and the sledding hill, pavilion, and supporting elements were drawn. This small drawing was scanned, copied, and pasted as a "patch" for the digital image over the previously drawn skating rink design. In order to facilitate future steps, the image was flattened before proceeding with snow and color.

Fig. 8-15 A digital photograph of the tree line seen beyond the proposed site. (Photo: Kirsten Laraby)

Fig. 8-15

Fig. 8-16

Fig. 8-16 The client reviewed the drawing shown in figure 8-14 and requested that it be turned into a snow scene, in color, to emphasize the site's winter appeal. After the snow had been added (see 8-21 through 8-24), the color was introduced as shown in figures 8-17 through 8-20.

Fig. 8-17

Fig. 8-18

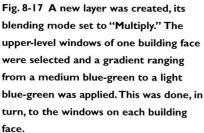

Fig. 8-17 A new layer was created, its blending mode set to "Multiply." The upper-level windows of one building face were selected and a gradient ranging from a medium blue-green to a light blue-green was applied. This was done, in turn, to the windows on each building face.

Another layer was made and its blending mode again set to "Multiply." A yellow-red brick color was selected from the *Color Picker* and applied to selected building façades. Slightly different colors were used to add color to spandrel bands and lintels. Note that the sunlit face of the building on the right was selected and its color adjusted (Image > Adjustments > Hue/Saturation . . .) to appear sunlit by increasing its value and chroma.

Fig. 8-18 A new layer was established for the yellow ochre color of the left building and foreground domed corner.

Once the color was applied to the dome and its flagpole base, each facet of the dome was selected and adjusted with the *Hue/Saturation* adjustment, making each respond to the light with a slightly different in color. This helped to give it a three-dimensional quality. The *Line Tool* was used to add horizontal lines, creating a pattern reminiscent of shingle shadows.

On another new layer (blending mode set to "Normal"), digital photographic imagery of lighted store interiors was added to the first floor of the buildings, just visible beneath the roofs of the covered walkways. Once added, the *Eraser Tool* was used to erase this imagery from everywhere it did not belong, such as the building columns and sidewalk. The *Line Tool* was used to add black window mullions *over* the image. Note how much life this small amount of imagery adds to the buildings.

Fig. 8-19

Fig. 8-20

Fig. 8-19 In this step, color was added to trees, cars, and figures on a new layer whose blending mode was once again set to "Multiply." Note that the snow remains free of these applied colors, both because it is kept at the topmost layer in the *Layers Palette* and because its blending mode is set to "Normal," making it opaque.

Fig. 8-20 A new layer was created for color accents. Because the colors had to be opaque, its blending mode was set to "Normal" and positioned at the very top of the *Layers Palette,* just above the snow layer.

On this layer, fire was added to the community fire pit, using the *Pencil Tool* with intense yellows and yellow-reds selected from the *Color Picker.* While the yellow-red was in the *Color Picker*'s *Foreground* color box, the *Brush Tool* was used with a soft round brush to add the glow of the spill light from the storefronts to the sidewalks. To keep from overdoing this effect, the *Flow* control in the options bar was set to 7%. A faint column of smoke from the fire was added by simply changing the color in the *Foreground* color box to a light, very low-chroma blue. (The brush and its *Flow* setting remained unchanged.)

Finally, pairs of banner shapes were selected, a yellow to yellow-red "Foreground to Background" color gradient applied, and blue accents added with the *Pencil Tool* and a hard round brush.

Upon completion of the drawing, a copy was flattened. A color balance adjustment layer was used to shift the entire drawing ever so slightly warmer. This was done by clicking on the *Adjustment Layer* icon at the bottom of the *Layers Palette,* selecting *Color Balance* from the drop-down menu, and then "Highlights" in the *Tone Balance* box. The top and bottom sliders were then moved toward Red and Yellow, respectively.

How to Make Snow

Creating a snow scene using Photoshop is surprisingly fast and easy. After a snowfall, all upward-facing surfaces turn white. These surfaces have the same responses to shade and shadow as all forms, except that shade and shadow on snow usually has a bluish cast, since it reflects the color of the sky.

The deeper the snow, the more the "blanket" becomes three-dimensional. Its depth is communicated through shading, and its edges are soft and indistinct (8-21 through 8-24).

Fig. 8-21

Fig. 8-22

Fig. 8-21 The illustration in figure 8-14 has been desaturated and given a bluish cast (Image > Adjustments > Desaturate) and colorized (Image > Adjustments > Hue/Saturation > "Colorize" > *use sliders*).

Fig. 8-22 A new layer was created (blending mode "Normal") and named *"snow."* All upward-facing horizontal surfaces were selected, and the *Paint Bucket Tool* was used to apply white to the selected areas.

Fig. 8-23

Fig. 8-24

Fig. 8-23 Another layer was created (blending mode "Multiply") called *"shadows."* The areas to receive major shadows were selected. In order to create a comparison, the *Polygonal Lasso Selection Tool* was used for the roof areas on the left side of the drawing, while the *Lasso Selection Tool* was used for those on the right.

A shadow color was selected by sampling the shaded wall area with the *Eyedropper Tool*, then the *Paint Bucket Tool* used to add the shadow color. Note how the shadows on the right, made with the *Lasso Selection Tool*, appear to be falling on a more uneven surface than those on the left.

Fig. 8-24 To give the snow the appearance of depth, the sides of the snow "blankets" were shaded on the *shadows* layer with the *Brush Tool*'s airbrush. Its *Flow* control (located in the options bar) was set to 5%, allowing repeated passes with a variety of sizes of soft round brushes, depending on the size of the surface being shaded. The brushes gave the shadows their indistinct edges.

The gradients on the gabled roof and the first floor arcade roof were created by first selecting those areas, then making repeated passes with larger soft round brushes. The amount of color applied was also controlled by the amount of hand pressure applied to the pressure-sensitive pen tablet.

Lockard Creative

One firm that makes exemplary use of digital color with hand line drawing in its work is Lockard Creative. It provides planning, design, conceptualization, and visualization services to design firms and developers in the retail, restaurant, hospitality, and entertainment industries.

Scott Lockard, the founder of Lockard Creative, wrote of his early education and experiences as a designer: "I learned to draw, perspective in particular, from my dad [William Kirby Lockard, FAIA], but he also taught me a lot of what I know about how to design [since] I certainly use 'drawing as a means to architecture.'" Lockard explained that the early development of his design drawing skills was his ". . . ticket to the design party." Indeed, in one of his first jobs, he was surprised to find himself in the position of ". . . a much-valued junior designer, regardless of my lack of project-related experience. It was my ability to be of *use* to a design team that gave me exposure, experience and, eventually, expertise in design."

Lockard describes his drawing process as a "natural evolution of the [William Kirby Lockard] methodology, i.e., using drawing as a design tool and prioritizing embellishments in relation to the deadline. I have added two tools: the construction of CAD models, using them as working design tools (as well as for easy view selection), and the use of Photoshop for color and general image management. . . . And in order to make the best of these new tools it is, of course, invaluable to understand the old ones—like perspective construction."

Lockard looked back over his ongoing career and observed that "a good measure of my success is also attributable to not having a design axe to grind, but rather welcoming a wide range of programmatic and stylistic challenges." His experience as a member of many design teams, on which he is often asked to create three-dimensional views of projects, has led Lockard to observe that he is subsequently the one who drives the formal, spatial, and character development of the project: "Whoever draws first, designs."

Figures 8-25 through 8-41 show, captioned in his words, his step-by-step approach to illustrations for two recent projects.

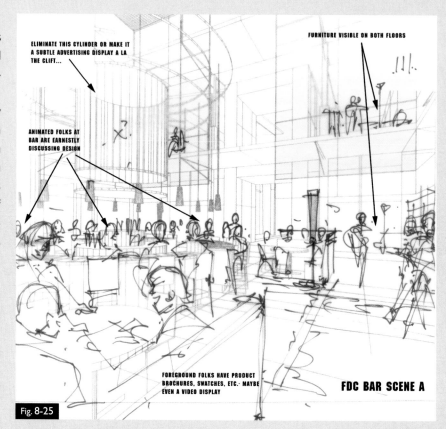

ELIMINATE THIS CYLINDER OR MAKE IT A SUBTLE ADVERTISING DISPLAY A LA THE CLIFT...

FURNITURE VISIBLE ON BOTH FLOORS

ANIMATED FOLKS AT BAR ARE EARNESTLY DISCUSSING DESIGN

FOREGROUND FOLKS HAVE PRODUCT BROCHURES, SWATCHES, ETC.- MAYBE EVEN A VIDEO DISPLAY

FDC BAR SCENE A

Fig. 8-25

Fig. 8-25 A rough sketch is done over various CAD views for angle selection. The CAD model in this case is simplistic, but has all the major spatial elements. Ideally, the model should be a working design tool that reflects and tests the current level of spatial resolution. Entourage is scribbled in to assist in understanding scale and forthcoming content.

Fig. 8-26

FDC BAR SCENE B

Fig. 8-26 An alternate (rejected) view angle. This angle is less successful in communicating the relationship of the center lounge area to the larger space and showrooms.

Fig. 8-27

FDC BAR SCENE A

Fig. 8-27 In the selected view angle, reference furniture and people are pasted into the "sketched over" **CAD** view. For a looser drawing or more distant viewpoint, this step can be skipped. The references are an aid in drawing the entourage and allow for easy experimentation in placement and composition. The collage is printed out, then drawn over directly, adding detail and working out unresolved conditions. This step can be accomplished in Photoshop, which will also be used later for all the color.

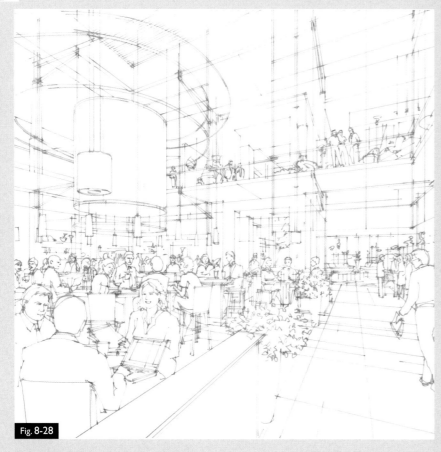

Fig. 8-28

Fig. 8-28 The entire layout is traced using a Razor Point on 11 lb. tracing paper; this puts the whole drawing in the same "hand." The entourage should be kept plain; it should support the space and not draw the eye by being too realistic or overwrought. Some of the CAD linework may be retained if it is helpful.

Fig. 8-29

Fig. 8-29 A reference image for a color palette. It is helpful to use a reference for colors—keep a collection of the ones you like. This will make it simpler to decide on colors later on, particularly under conditions where reflections, highlights, or shadows drastically change a basic color. Study the reference for unexpected complementary colors and accents. Good references can be found in design magazines and in travel or coffee-table books. (Fullerton Hotel Post Bar: Interior Designer HBA/Hirsch Bedner Associates; photograph: Peter Mealin)

Fig. 8-30

Fig. 8-31

Fig. 8-30 Scan the linework (at around 150 dpi) as a grayscale image. Open it in Photoshop, convert it to RGB, and adjust its density as needed with the *Brightness/Contrast* and/or *Levels* commands. Don't "burn out" the lines, but adjust them enough to get a nice white background. Create a second layer for color and set this layer's blending mode to "Multiply." Using your reference image, apply color in an analogous manner. With the *Brush Tool* at 100% opacity, paint quickly, concentrating on rough placement but also on applying the *full range* of colors from the reference, including accents and "unexpected" colors.

Fig. 8-31 Reduce the *Brush Tool*'s opacity to 60–70% after roughing in. This will allow the blending of colors. Holding the Alt key switches the paintbrush to an eyedropper, allowing you to pick existing colors from within the image to blend with others. By clicking and brushing here and there with progressively smaller brushes, the roughly colored image can be cleaned up and tightened.

Fig. 8-32

Fig. 8-33

Fig. 8-32 After the basic coloring is complete and "tight enough," create another layer above the color layer. Leave its blending mode set to "Normal." Create selection areas with the *Lasso Tool*. Then use the *Gradient Tool* and its "Foreground to Transparent" option (usually linear, less often radial) to add slight "reflections" to glass. Complex selections should be saved. When saved, selections become additional channels that can be recalled (or *loaded*). Using a small brush, add highlights to the appropriate edges of people, walls, and especially cables or other thin or shiny objects.

Fig. 8-33 Additional elements such as signs and spotlights should be kept on separate layers for easier editing. In general, minimizing the number of layers helps cut down on confusion and mistakes. Signs are made with the *Text Tool* and contoured to fit the appropriate figure. Spotlights are gradients applied to cone-shaped selections and feathered four to six pixels (feathering softens the edges of a selection by fading them. You can do this by entering a Feather value—the width of the softened edges in pixels—in the box in the options bar when the lasso or marquee tool is selected). The light source itself is done with the *Airbrush Tool*. Overdoing spotlights is a common temptation.

Fig. 8-34

Fig. 8-34 The layered Photoshop image is saved (and saved often during the process), and a separate flattened file is made. A Photoshop file can be saved as a .tif, .pict, .pcx or other file type. A .tif file retains all channel information, so if your .tif contains any saved selections, they can usually be deleted, as they increase file size dramatically.

The flattened file can undergo additional adjustments, but major changes should be done in the .psd file—the file format native to Photoshop. Typically it is a good idea to add some noise to the flattened image (usually 10–12%, normal, not monochromatic). Most files can also benefit from some *Levels* adjustments after flattening to increase density and saturation.

Fig. 8-35

Fig. 8-36

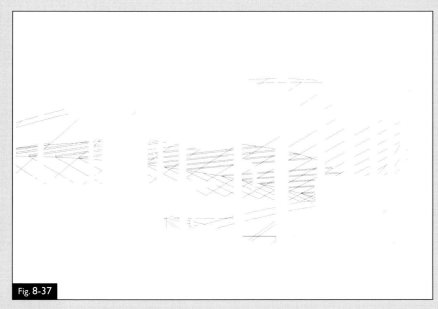

Fig. 8-37

Fig. 8-35 In this project, the **CAD** model serves as one "document" for the design and development of plans, elevations, and perspectives. The model is not "airtight," or appropriate for use as computer-renderable model, but for a design tool and shared database, it is fine. Various views are considered and a hidden-line plot is made.

Fig. 8-36 The hidden-line plot is traced (using Razor Point pen on 11 lb. tracing paper); detail and people are added.

Fig. 8-37 A small amount of the CAD model linework is retained, with the balance replaced by hand-drawn linework.

Fig. 8-38 The final linework composite.

Fig. 8-38

Fig. 8-39

Fig. 8-40

Fig. 8-41

Fig. 8-39 As with the design center interior, lines are scanned as the bottom layer in a Photoshop file. Color is applied via a pen tablet onto a "Multiply" layer above the linework layer.

Fig. 8-40 A view of the color layer only.

Fig. 8-41 Finally, a few highlights and a very light "atmosphere" (near the skylights, with the airbrush capability of the *Brush Tool*) is added on a "Normal" layer above the color. The layered Photoshop file is saved and a separate flattened file is made. Noise is added to this file and the density is adjusted slightly using the *Levels* command.

In general, it is wise to keep three files for an image: the original layered .psd file, the flattened file with noise and final density adjustments, and a compressed file (.jpg) made from the final flattened file. This smaller compressed file is useful for sending via e-mail or for indefinite computer storage. Most often, the larger .psd and uncompressed files will warrant being backed up and eventually removed from typical hard drives. Any later amendments should be made to the .psd or flattened file and not to the .jpg.

Digital Image Collage

There may be occasions when design communication requires little (if any) "drawing," because color is applied with a tool over an armature composed of lines on a two-dimensional surface. In these cases, a digital photograph is used as the "base view" to which additional digital imagery is added to create a complete image of a design concept. Opportunities to use this approach usually present themselves in the communication of urban and landscape design ideas, where *nondirectional* elements such as plant materials and figures comprise the major design additions to the base image. However, at CommArts, we find these kinds of illustrations to be the exception rather than the rule. Most of our illustrations remain hybrids of hand drawing and digital imagery.

The illustrations shown in 8-42 through 8-49 were made to show how a proposed revitalization of a major urban boulevard could both introduce a needed intermediate scale to the boulevard and provide a more hospitable environment for pedestrians and drivers alike. The proposal included expanded sidewalks with patterned paving, the addition of live oak shade trees along the new sidewalks, and the enhancement of the boulevard's medians with colorful annuals, perennials, and specimen shrubs. Date palms were proposed as an iconic tree form that could be dramatically illuminated at night.

The large, polished stainless steel arches are one of six pairs erected along the boulevard previously as part of an identity program for the district created by CommArts in collaboration with SWA Group.

An important part of the boulevard's proposed revitalization is its lighting. Figures 8-50 through 8-58 show how Photoshop can be used to turn a daytime view into a nighttime view by manipulating existing layers and adding new ones, in order to illustrate various lighting strategies.

Fig. 8-42 A view of the boulevard before the design elements were introduced. This view was made by splicing together four overlapping photographs.

Fig. 8-42

Fig. 8-43 A plan of the boulevard, with proposed revisions, was created by the project engineer. The project landscape architect estimated tree types, sizes, and spacing for the project.

A SketchUp model was made of this section of the boulevard, based on the engineer's plan. Trees were added to the model in accordance with the landscape architect's recommendations. Through trial and error, the finished model was oriented to conform as closely as possible to the view of the boulevard seen in 8-42. A .jpg image of the model was exported and opened as a layer placed on top of the photographic view. Its opacity was reduced in order to make the photographic image visible; the two images were aligned. The model

Fig. 8-43

view was then used as a template to accurately locate and size the trees for the illustration. As its own layer, it could be turned off and on as needed.

Another layer, shown here, was

created and named *"help lines."* The close vanishing point was located and vanishing lines were made as necessary to ensure that the elements introduced into the illustration (trees, figures, etc.)

conformed to its perspective. This layer was also turned on and off as needed.

Fig. 8-44 Images of two different, mature live oak trees were copied from digital photographs of other areas within the district. A new layer was created, and these images were pasted into position—on the far side of the street—using the SketchUp image beneath as a guide. Alternating two different trees kept the tree line from appearing too uniform. Note that the sun's position on the tree canopy—coming from the upper left—generally corresponds with the sun's position in the base photograph.

The trees were duplicated by using the *Move Tool* to click on and drag a tree image while holding down the Option key (for Mac) or the Alt key (for Windows). After duplication, the *Transform* command was used to scale

Fig. 8-44

down each tree; the SketchUp image and the help lines functioned as guides. Once positioned, the overlap positions of the trees were corrected by rearranging the positions of the tree layers in the

Layers Palette. When the tree arrangement was complete, the tree layers were linked and merged to create a single *"live oaks, left"* layer in order to keep the file size as small as possible.

Fig. 8-45 A digital image of a date palm was pasted and then repeated in the median, the same way the images of the live oaks were introduced and arranged in 8-44.

The flowers in the median were applied with the *Pattern Stamp Tool*, located by clicking and holding the *Clone Stamp Tool* in the toolbox. With this tool, you can "paint" a selected area with the contents of any image you choose. (Such an image is called a *pattern*.) In this example, the *Rectangular Marquee Tool* was used to copy a part of a digital image that was *exclusively* flowers. It was pasted into a new image (File > New . . .) and sized with the *Transform* command to fill the entire new image area. With this new image open, it was turned into a pattern (Edit > Define Pattern . . . > *name new pattern* > OK). To "paint" the flowers with the new pattern, the *Pattern Stamp Tool* was selected. In the options bar, the arrow button beside the *Pattern Sample* window was clicked. This opened a drop-down menu of all the patterns available to the tool. The new flowers pattern was located and selected.

In the illustration, the *Lasso Selection Tool* was used to delineate, on a new layer, where the flowers were to be "painted." An appropriately sized soft round brush was chosen from the options bar. By touching the pen to the digital tablet (or by holding down the

Fig. 8-45

mouse button), the flowers were "painted" on the illustration, but only within the selected area. The *Hue/Saturation* adjustment was then used to create the colors seen here.

The sidewalk on the right had been previously designed and illustrated in a separate plan view of the area. The *Rectangular Marquee Tool* was used to select and copy a straight portion of the walkway from that digital plan image and paste it into this illustration. Using the *Transform* command (see figures 4-157 through 4-163), this section of sidewalk was conformed to the perspective of the drawing. The *"help lines"* layer was turned on and used to guide the shape of the walkway.

A car was pasted at the location of what will appear as a driveway in future steps, to the right of the new sidewalk.

Fig. 8-46 The row of live oak trees on the right side of the illustration were easily added by copying them as a group from another digital photograph (taken in the same area, inset) and pasting them here. Once pasted, they were scaled and rotated with the *Transform* command. When in place, the foreground tree was again selected, copied, pasted, and scaled larger to create the foreground tree.

Sections of the foreground tree's leafy canopy were selected with the *Magic Wand Tool*, copied, and pasted to provide it with a denser canopy. Once arranged, these new layers were linked and merged in the *Layers Palette,* then darkened slightly with the *Brightness/Contrast* adjustment command.

Fig. 8-46

Fig. 8-47 In this step, a tree shadow was introduced to the foreground sidewalk, then copied and pasted repeatedly into the distance (see figures 8-59 through 8-62). Each time the shadow was copied and pasted, the *Transform* command was used to reduce its scale. The same process was used for shadows on the left side of the street.

The shadow used on the sidewalk was the same as that used for the car at right. A copy of the shadow was placed over the car, its blending mode set to "Multiply." Using the *Transform* command, the shadow was rotated so the shadow-light pattern was diagonal; it was then stretched with the command's *Scale* function. The outline of the car was selected with the *Polygonal Lasso*

Fig. 8-47

Selection Tool and all shadow, except that on the car, was deleted (Select > Inverse) with the Delete key.

The foreground date palm tree shadow was drawn on a new layer whose blending mode was also set to "Multiply." The *Brush Tool,* fitted with a hard round brush, was used to draw the shadow. The color was created by using the *Eyedropper Tool* to sample the other shadows that fell on the same surface. This shadow was also copied, pasted, and scaled down with the *Transform* command as it was repeated into the distance, using the help lines as a perspective guide.

Fig. 8-48

Fig. 8-48 In this step, cars and figures were added to the illustration, lending needed vitality to the scene.

The cars were selected and copied from a similar photograph taken of the same street, allowing them to conform to the scene once pasted in place. Note that the highlights and shadows of the cars agree with the light in the rest of the illustration.

Digital images of walking figures were also copied and pasted into the illustration, keeping all the heads of the figures on the horizon line, no matter what their size. The figures in the distance on the extreme left of the illustration were in the original photograph (8-42) and are at a slightly higher elevation. The figures in shade were darkened (Image > Adjustments > Brightness/Contrast). Tree shadows were added over the closest figures to quickly create the effect of dappled light. Excess shadow was eliminated by selecting the figures' outlines, inverting the selection (Select > Inverse), and pressing the Delete key.

Fig. 8-49 A copy of the illustration was made and flattened. The *Dry Brush* filter (Filter > Artistic > Dry Brush; Brush Size = 2, Brush Detail = 8, Texture = 1) was applied to the image. While this filter reduces some of the detail (none of it critical), it also softens and unifies the image. This is an especially useful filter for reducing the stiff quality that illustrations with a large amount of photographic imagery frequently take on.

Fig. 8-49

Fig. 8-50 Because the purpose of the nighttime view of the boulevard was to illustrate the lighting strategies proposed to enhance its safety and ambience and legibility, no value study was created before beginning this illustration. Instead, the illustration was based on the existing daytime illustration; its layers were manipulated, and new ones added. During the course of creating the nighttime view, these layers were constantly adjusted to ensure the lighting elements and effects remained the primary focus of the illustration.

Nighttime photographs of other parts of this district were used as references to guide the ambient night color of the large surfaces in the illustration—the sky, buildings, and pavement. These photos

Fig. 8-50

were invaluable, since a place's nighttime color often has unique characteristics.

As first steps, the shadow layers were turned off; the layers containing the figures were also temporarily turned off

to simplify the view. The layers containing the trees, cars, and median flowers were darkened by reducing their brightness (Image > Adjustments > Brightness/Contrast . . .).

Fig. 8-51 Adjustment layers were used to change the color character of the large surfaces in the illustration, since they could be easily readjusted—or even eliminated—should the need arise later in the illustration process.

The background buildings were selected and a hue/saturation adjustment layer was made to emulate the buildings in a nighttime ambient glow of sodium street light. The *Lightness* adjustment was reduced, the *Hue* slider was moved to make the buildings more reddish, and the *Saturation* adjustment was increased.

Fig. 8-51

Fig. 8-52 The sky and ground planes were selected and another hue/saturation adjustment layer was made. Again, the *Lightness* adjustment was reduced, the *Hue* slider moved to make the surfaces more reddish, and the *Saturation* adjustment increased. The ground plane selection outline was then deleted, leaving only the sky selected. The *Saturation* adjustment was then increased to give the sky a more intense "sodium glow," common in cities with high-pressure sodium street lighting.

Fig. 8-52

Fig. 8-53 Uplighting was easily added to the trees by selecting a large mass of uplit leaves from a digital photograph of a tree illuminated from below. The *Magic Wand Tool* was used to select the lighted area, thereby maintaining its holes and ragged edges, a process very similar to that used to copy tree shadows in figures 8-59 through 8-62.

Once the lighted leaves were selected, they were copied and pasted over the darkened trees, then repeatedly copied, pasted, and scaled using the *Transform* command. Some of the copies were reversed (Edit > Transform > Flip Horizontal) to reduce the appearance of uniform repetition.

Fig. 8-53

Fig. 8-54 Next, the date palm trees in the median were illuminated. A new layer was created, this time with its blending mode set to "Normal." This kept the color application opaque, making it more vivid. The trunks were selected and color was applied with the *Pencil Tool*, using a small, hard round brush. While the trunk selection was initially time consuming, a variety of colors could be applied quickly, using rapid, horizontal strokes. The color stayed, of course, within the boundaries of the trunk selection outline. A variety of "trunk colors" were applied, with progressively lighter colors used closer to the ground—the source of the tree uplighting. The horizontal stroke was used to suggest the texture of the trunk. When completed, the trunks were de-

Fig. 8-54

selected. The tree canopies were colored freehand, using the *Brush Tool* and a larger hard round brush.

As a final touch, another layer was created (blending mode "Normal") and the faint cones of uplight applied with the *Gradient Tool*. A conical area was

delineated for the first few foreground palm trunks with the *Polygonal Lasso Selection Tool*. The gradient was set to "Foreground to Transparent" and the opacity of the gradient to 50%. The layer's *Opacity* slider was used to make final adjustments, which kept the uplit

cones from appearing too opaque.

Note that, as the drawing progressed, this layer was kept toward the top so that its effects would not be diminished by the color applied to the buildings and trees behind the palms.

Fig. 8-55 The building lights were applied on a new layer using the "Normal" blending mode. This layer was placed beneath the layers used to illuminate the trees. The ground-level lighted window color was applied with the *Pencil Tool* and a small, hard round brush, using whites, yellows, and touches of blue and red.

A somewhat different approach was used to create most of the buildings' lighted upper windows. These window areas were first selected with the *Polygonal Lasso Selection Tool*. The airbrush capability of the *Brush Tool*, using a soft round brush, was used to splash pale blues, yellows, reds, and white over the selected window areas at random, using an opacity setting of 50% (set on the

Fig. 8-55

options bar). Touches of white were added with the *Pencil Tool* and a hard round brush, set at 100% opacity. Finally, black window mullions were added with the *Line Tool*. The resulting effect is that

of an office interior with some depth and highlight, but less highly illuminated than the first-floor retail windows.

The *Pencil Tool*, with a small, hard round brush was used to add the aircraft

warning lights at the buildings' top corners. The *Brush Tool's* airbrush capability, set at 10% opacity, was use to create the faint glow of both the retail lighting and the aircraft warning lights.

Fig. 8-56

Fig. 8-56 The pylon lights, used to illuminate the pedestrian walkway areas, were introduced by copying and pasting one from another illustration. It was scaled to the correct size using the *Transform* command. The lights were repeatedly copied and scaled in this manner, using the help lines to ensure they conformed to the illustration's perspective. A new layer was created, its blending mode set to "Normal," and an elliptical area selected that centered on the closest pylon light. A "Foreground to Transparent" radial gradient was made using the *Gradient Tool*, centered on the pylon light. These pools of light were repeatedly copied and scaled to create the light pools for those pylon lights in the distance.

Note that the layers for both the pylon lights and their pools of light were placed beneath the tree layers. This created the visually expected partial obstruc-

tion of the lights and their light pools by the tree trunks, making it unnecessary to erase or delete them manually.

Another layer was made for the car headlights and taillights, using "Normal" blending mode. White and red were applied with the *Pencil Tool* and a small, hard round brush. The streaking taillights were made by first delineating the streak with the *Polygonal Lasso Selection Tool*, then applying a "Foreground to Transparent" linear gradient. Then the *Brush Tool*, set to its airbrush capability, was used to apply a subtle glow to the lights. The *Flow* was set to 10% in the options bar and applied with one of the larger soft round brushes.

Yet another layer was created to add the roadway reflections. The *Brush Tool*, with a soft round brush, was used to create the reflections with horizontal strokes, using the same colors as those reflected. Its *Flow* was set to 25%.

Fig. 8-57 Highlights were added to the large, polished stainless steel arches that span the street. A new layer was created for each color of highlight—black, white, green, and red. The *Elliptical Marquee Selection Tool* was used to trace the shape of the arch. Once the elliptical selection was approximately the same as that of the arch, the selection was rotated and manipulated as necessary with the *Transform* command (Select > Transform Selection). The color desired for the reflection was then sampled with the *Eyedropper Tool* from the trees, taillights, etc., then "stroked" onto the elliptical selection (Edit > Stroke . . . ; Width = 6 px [pixels], Location = Center, Blending = Normal, Opacity = 100%.). The color was then erased from where it was not wanted with the *Eraser Tool*.

Along the arch itself, gaps were erased into the stroked color. Each of

Fig. 8-57

the four highlight colors was applied to the arch in a similar way. Since each was on a separate layer, each could be selectively erased independently without affecting the others. When completed, the arch highlight layers were merged into a single layer. On this resultant layer, small white dots of specular

reflection were added to the cars.

The layer with the figures on it was turned on and darkened sufficiently (Image > Adjustments > Brightness/Contrast . . .) so the figures appeared silhouetted against the illuminated sidewalk. In order to create an adequate silhouette, this layer was moved to a

position in the *Layers Palette* above that of both the sidewalk and the glow from the pylon lights. The *Brush Tool* and a small, soft round brush were used to add white highlights and a shadow to the figure crossing the street, since it is illuminated by the oncoming car.

Fig. 8-58 When the illustration was completed, the image was duplicated (Image > Duplicate . . .), named, and flattened. The *Dry Brush* filter was applied (Filter > Artistic > Dry Brush Size = 2, Brush Detail = 8, Texture = 1) to give the illustration a more relaxed character.

A levels adjustment layer was created (Layer > New Adjustment Layer > Levels . . .) and the sliders beneath the histogram were manipulated. The left slider was moved slightly to the right, while the slider on the right was moved slightly to the left. This lightened the image somewhat, while giving it some additional contrast and "punch."

Fig. 8-58

Easy Tree Shadows

The shadows of leafy trees that "fall" on the pavement, streets, buildings, and even on people, impart a dappled pattern of light and dark that has a character all its own. We have many conscious and subconscious associations with these particular kinds of shadows; it is important to illustrate them successfully.

They can, of course, be drawn either with hand media or by using Photoshop's drawing tools. In fact, they *should* be hand drawn if it is important that your illustration maintain a strictly hand-drawn character. However, sometimes drawing them can be time consuming, depending on the amount of shadow and the orientation of the surfaces they fall on.

Fortunately, when a hand-drawn character is less important, these kinds of shadows are also easily "stolen." Not literally, of course. But they can be copied from an appropriate digital photograph in your collection and pasted into an illustration. There are a couple of advantages to doing this. First, it is very fast—a basic copy, paste, transform, and adjust operation. Second, by copying this kind of shadow, you will preserve its character—its density, proportion of light to dark and, for the most part, the shapes of its light areas, dark areas, and edges.

The procedure for "stealing" a shadow and applying it to an illustration is demonstrated in figures 8-59 through 8-62.

Fig. 8-59

Fig. 8-60

Fig. 8-59 An appropriate photograph of a tree shadow was located. The best photos are those taken from the same viewpoint as the intended destination of the shadow—in this case, eye level—and in which the shadow is falling on a smooth, even surface, such as a street. The photo was then opened in Photoshop.

Fig. 8-60 The *Magic Wand Tool* was used to select the shadow by clicking on it. This tool can be used to select the outline of an area of a consistent color without having to laboriously trace that outline. In the options bar, "New Selection" was enabled in the row of four buttons on the left side. The *Tolerance* was set to 32.

The Shift key was held down while clicking with the *Magic Wand Tool* on areas of shadow not included in the first attempt at selection in order to add them to the selection; the Option key (for Mac) or Control key (for Windows) was held while clicking the *Magic Wand Tool* on patches of sunlight that should have been excluded from the selection. You may have to experiment with the *Tolerance* setting in order to obtain an adequate sampling of the shadow: Lower the number to select shadow colors more similar to the original pixel color you click; raise the number to broaden the range of colors. Remember that whatever sampling you obtain, it can be manipulated later to fit the requirements of the illustration.

Fig. 8-61

Fig. 8-62

Fig. 8-61 Once the shadow was selected, it was copied (Edit > Copy). The destination illustration was then activated and the shadow was pasted into that illustration (Edit > Paste). Once pasted, the shadow formed its own layer; its blending mode was changed from "Normal" to "Multiply," changing the shadow from opaque to transparent.

The *Transform* command (Edit > Free Transform) was used to scale down the shadow to the appropriate size.

Fig. 8-62 The *Move Tool* was used to drag the shadow into place under the tree in the right foreground. The *Lasso Tool* was used to delineate a more jagged outline for the shadow's squared-off left edge and, after completing the selection, the excess shadow was deleted. The shadow was then repeatedly copied, pasted, and scaled as further described in the caption for figure 8-47.

USING FILTERS IN DIGITAL COLOR DRAWING

Photoshop has a variety of special effects, called *filters,* with which you can add certain textures to color drawings—even if that drawing is not digital in origin. The term "filter" comes from photography, which uses specially treated transparent glass or plastic covers placed over a camera lens in order to alter the resulting image.

There are a wide variety of filters built into Photoshop, and many more available as freeware online, but only a very few are consistently useful for color drawing. They are used to soften and add texture to consistent lines and planes of color, making illustrations—usually those generated digitally—appear similar to those created by hand media. If you intend to use a filter on a low-resolution image (72 dpi or so), you may find you first have to increase the resolution of the image to about 150 to 220 pixels per inch (Image > Image Size . . .) in order to allow the filter to work to maximum effect.

Filters can be applied to all or a selected part of a flattened image, or to certain layers of a multilayered image. They should be applied with an eye to the continued legibility of your drawings, since filters can both darken an image and obscure important details. However, you can reduce the effect of any filter with the *Fade* command. After applying a filter, immediately select the *Fade* command from the *Edit* menu in the menu bar. This will bring up the *Fade* dialog box, in which you can adjust the opacity of the filter's effect. (Note that you can also adjust the opacity and blending mode of any painting tool, the *Eraser Tool,* or an adjustment command, by using the *Fade* command as well.)

Some filters can be memory intensive, and their use may increase the file size of your illustration. You will also find that certain filters only work when the file is in RGB mode. To check or change modes, select *Mode* from the *Image* menu in the menu bar. Click on "RGB Color" to access all the filters. If your printer is set up for CMYK color, be sure to change the mode back to CMYK color before printing.

Spatter Filter

The *Spatter* filter is most useful in color drawing for roughening digitally generated linework, making it appear more similar to hand-drawn lines (8-63, 8-64). It is located under the *Brush Strokes* filter (Filter > Brush Strokes > Spatter . . .).

After you access the *Spatter* filter, use the *Spray Radius* and *Smoothness* sliders to control the character and amount of line "shakiness." You will find that if the *Smoothness* slider is set too low, your lines become too fuzzy as you increase the *Spray Radius* slider. To make the lines appear similar to hand-drawn lines, move the sliders somewhere near their respective midpoints. Then, use the *Fade* adjustment to more precisely control the resulting line quality.

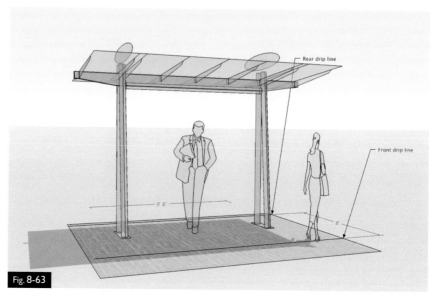

Fig. 8-63

Fig. 8-63 This transit shelter study uses the typical smooth, even lines of a digital image.

Fig. 8-64 A closer view of the image shown in 8-63, after the *Spatter* filter has been applied (Filter > Brush Strokes > Spatter . . .). The *Spray Radius* and *Smoothness* settings are shown in the slider readout windows. The preview window shows an initial result in which the lines are rougher than the finished image, since the *Fade* command was used to reduce the effect to 70% of the original. Note that the character of the color areas remains unaffected.

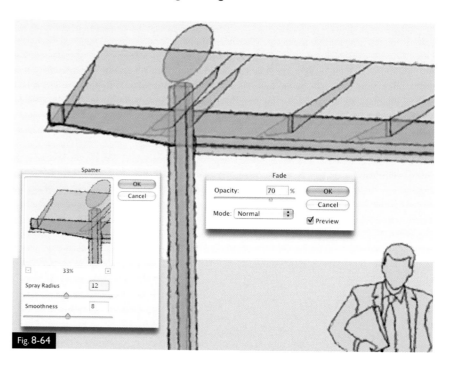

Fig. 8-64

Noise Filter

If you want to introduce a level of texture or grain to all or part of your color drawings, you may find the *Noise* filter useful (Filter > Noise > Add Noise . . .). This filter adds randomly colored pixels to a selected area or layer; it can quickly add texture to such elements as ground covers, plant materials, gravel paths, and rugs (8-65, 8-66). Its effect can range from quite subtle to very obvious, depending on the amount of noise you add. This filter works in both the RGB and CMYK color modes.

Within the *Noise* filter's control box you can choose "Normal" or "Gaussian" distribution. "Normal" distribution gives you a more subtle effect, while "Gaussian" distribution enables you to create a more obvious, speckled effect. You can also choose whether you want either effect to be colored or monochromatic. Remember, too, that you can always adjust the amount of noise you add to an image by using the *Fade* command (Edit > Fade Add Noise).

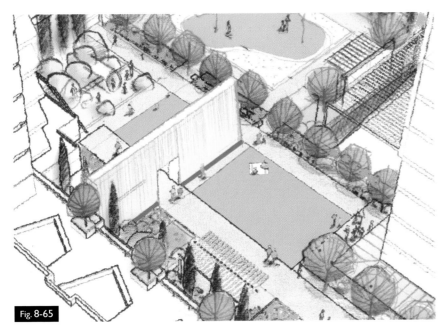

Fig. 8-65

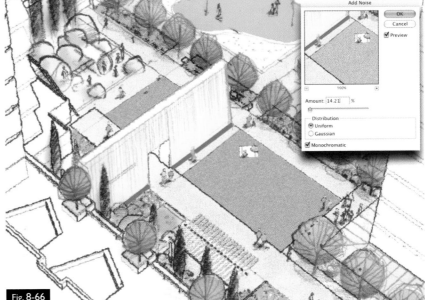

Fig. 8-66

Fig. 8-65 In this study, the grass areas in the center are smooth areas of color, applied with the *Paint Bucket Tool*.

Fig. 8-66 In order to give the grass areas more character, they were selected and a little over 14% monochromatic noise was applied to them with the *Noise* filter, using *Uniform Distribution* (Filter > Noise > Add Noise . . .). The *Fade* command (Edit > Fade Add Noise . . .) was then used to reduce the noise to 60% of its original level. Before the grass area was deselected, the *Hue/Saturation* adjustment (Image > Adjustments > Hue/Saturation . . .) was used to make them slightly darker, as well as increase their chroma via the *Saturation* slider.

Dry Brush Filter

The *Dry Brush* filter (Filter > Artistic > Dry Brush . . .) imparts an impressionistic quality to an illustration, vaguely reminiscent of the character seen in the oils of, say, Claude Monet or Edgar Degas (8-67 through 8-69). It does this by giving the myriad shapes in an illustration softer edges and a simplified range of colors. Digital images appear more painterly and "hand done" in character. This is especially useful for unifying the appearance of an illustration, particularly when it hosts a variety of image types, such as those generated by computer, photography, and hand drawing.

Since the *Dry Brush* filter can obscure detail, consider isolating areas of desirable detail from the effects of the filter with your selection tools. Remember, too, that this filter only works when the image is in RGB color mode.

Fig. 8-67 This design study for a project entry uses a digital photograph over which layers of scanned, hand-drawn elements (sign wall, lanterns) as well as additional digital images (conifer trees, car) have been placed using Photoshop. The foreground grasses were added over the digital photo base using the *Pencil Tool*.

Fig. 8-67

Fig. 8-68

Fig. 8-68 Once flattened, the *Dry Brush* filter was applied to the image (**Filter > Artistic > Dry Brush; Brush Size = 2, Brush Detail = 8, Texture = 1**). Note the painterly quality imparted to the tree images in the distance and, especially, how the filter significantly relaxed the detailed conifer trees behind the sign wall. Note, too, how the filter obliterated the details of the lanterns and sign elements, making the project name illegible.

Fig. 8-69

Fig. 8-69 This image is the same as that in 8-68, with one exception: The lanterns, sign face, and elliptical logo panel were selected using the *Polygonal Lasso Selection Tool* and the *Elliptical Marquee Selection Tool*. The selections were then inverted (**Select > Inverse**) so that everything *except* the selected areas was subjected to the effects of the *Dry Brush* filter. This preserved the original detail of these important elements, allowing them to remain visible in the final, filtered image.

Combined Filters

There are circumstances in which you may find it useful to employ more than one filter on an illustration in order to combine and expand their individual effects. In figures 8-70 through 8-74, the filters discussed above were used together to give a digital model image a more relaxed character.

Fig. 8-70

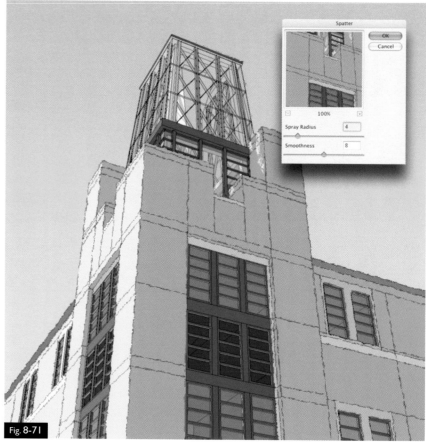

Fig. 8-71

Fig. 8-70 This is a **SketchUp** study model image of the tower for the building shown in figure 3-50. The model had been made to study the viability of proposed dichroic glass strips, visible here as red-purple diagonal elements inside the enclosure glass of the tower top.

Fig. 8-71 As a first step, the linework was loosened up by applying the *Spatter* filter (Filters > Brush Strokes > Spatter . . . ; Spray Radius = 4, Smoothness = 8) to everything in the image *except* the glass tower top and the windows, in order to preserve their detail and "machined" character. These parts were selected, then inverted, so the filters would not apply to them (Select > Inverse).

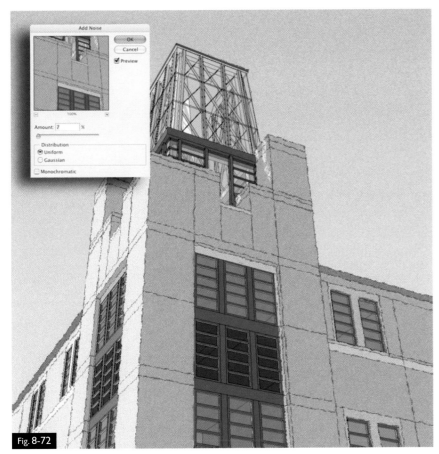

Fig. 8-72

Fig. 8-73

Fig. 8-72 Maintaining the selection as described in the previous step, the *Noise* filter was then applied to the image (Filter > Add Noise . . . ; Amount = 7%, Uniform Distribution). This provided additional, though subtle, character to the sandstone walls of the building and the sky. Note that the tower top and windows remain unaffected.

Fig. 8-73 In the final step, the building was deselected, leaving only the sky selected. The *Dry Brush* filter was then applied to the sky (Filter > Artistic > Dry Brush . . . ; Brush Size = 0, Brush Detail = 8, Texture = 1). The result shows the unique effect the *Dry Brush* filter has on the *Noise* filter: a texture not unlike that seen when using watercolor on rough paper.

Fig. 8-74 The result is an illustration with much more textural interest, ranging from refined to rough, but one that still allows the viewer to easily discern the detail at the tower top.

Fig. 8-74

GLOSSARY

adjustment layer A layer that adjusts the color of only the layers beneath it in a Photoshop file. The adjustment controls of an adjustment layer can be reopened and the layer readjusted.

aerial perspective A view from above, created by making a drawing below its horizon line. This kind of perspective is also known as a "bird's-eye perspective" (see also atmospheric perspective).

afterimage The imagery seen floating before one's eyes after the stimulus has been withdrawn.

analogous hues Hues related to one another owing to their side-by side relationship on the color wheel.

aniline dye The dye used as the colorant in markers. Aniline dye is sensitive to ultraviolet light, and drawings using markers should be archived by color slides. If such a drawing is to be displayed, make a color bubble-jet photocopy for display purposes and store the original in a dark place.

atmospheric perspective The pronounced illusion of distance caused by the progressive changes in colors as they recede in space. Generally, colors become weaker in chroma, higher in value, and shift in hue toward the purple and purple-blue range. Artists sometimes call this effect "aerial perspective."

background (of a drawing) The part of a drawing that occurs behind the center of interest.

balance The quality of a drawing whereby its various parts appear to be in proper proportion to one another.

base, marker base The initial application of color to a drawing, often made with marker.

blending mode In Photoshop's *Layers Palette,* the blending mode is the drop-down options bar located on the upper left. You will usually see it set on "Normal." It controls how a painting or editing tool affects the pixels in an image. One of its most useful modes for color drawing is "Multiply." When a line drawing is imported as a layer on top of a Photoshop image, using the "Multiply" mode makes all but the lines of the drawing transparent. The result is that the drawing looks like part of the underlying Photoshop image.

bond paper An inexpensive white paper used in most black-and-white photocopiers. Use 24 lb. or heavier bond paper for color drawings if possible.

brilliance Another word for the chroma of a color, also called "intensity," "saturation," or "purity."

Bristol paper A high-quality white paper often used for presentation-quality color drawings. This paper has excellent tooth and shows marker, color pencil, and pastel very well. The two-ply "vellum" finish is the best to use for the types of drawing shown in this book and easily takes a black-and-white photocopy image.

Brush Tool A tool in Photoshop that uses the foreground color in the *Color Picker* to apply soft-edged strokes to an image. A variety of brush types can be found in the *Brushes Palette.* An airbrush capability is available in the options bar.

Canson paper A high-quality textured drawing paper that shows marker, color pencil, and pastel well. It can also receive images from a photocopier, although it may need to be sprayed with a fixative such as Krylon Crystal Clear spray acrylic, as the toner from the photocopier may not completely fuse to the paper because of its texture. Canson is part of the Mi-Tienes line of paper made by Canson-Talens.

Character Palette A palette found on the options bar when the *Type Tool* is selected in Photoshop. This palette allows the user to customize a variety of text attributes.

chiaroscuro The light-to-dark shading of an illustrated form, used to make it appear three-dimensional.

chroma The strength of a color, which can range from weak (almost gray) to strong (pure). Other names for chroma include "saturation," "purity," "brilliance," and "intensity."

Clone Stamp Tool A tool that allows the user to copy one area of a Photoshop image into another, using a selected brush.

Color Picker In Photoshop, enables the selection and customization of a color for use with the editing tools.

color wheel A circular arrangement of hues based on the side-by-side relationship of colors seen in visible light when it is refracted. The circular arrangement is useful to designers and artists because it makes the relationships between the hues more readily visible.

complementary hues Hues that are diametrically opposite each other on the color wheel. When these hues are placed side by side, each makes the other appear its most intense.

composition An arrangement of elements intended to be seen together, as a whole.

contrast A perceivable difference between two parts of the same color dimension. This difference can range from subtle to strong.

cool gray A gray that is very slightly bluish.

cool hue, cool color A hue or color that is associated with cool temperatures. Blue green, blue, purple blue, and purple are the cool hues on the Munsell color wheel (see figure 6-2). Green and red purple form the border between the warm and cool colors on the color wheel and can be made to be either warm or cool.

Crop Tool A Photoshop tool that uses adjustable boundaries to allow the user to trim the edges of an image.

design drawing Exploratory drawing used to manifest early design ideas for oneself and to communicate those ideas to others.

design mind That part of one's mind that is thinking ahead to the design implications of what one is drawing and, usually, making adjustments in the drawing accordingly. Likewise, drawing an idea may also require making corresponding adjustments to the design.

diffuse shadow edge A shadow edge that gradually changes from shadow to light and forms no distinct boundary.

dimension of color A perceivable, measurable quality of a color. A color has three dimensions—hue, value, and chroma—and each may be theoretically altered without affecting the others.

distinct shadow edge A shadow edge that forms a distinct boundary between shadow and light.

document window The main image window in Photoshop. While more than one document window may be open, the active window is always in the foreground.

dominant, dominance Relates to that which perceptibly occupies most of the area in a drawing; usually used in reference to the presence of a particular dimension of color in a composition.

dpi, dots per inch The number of pixels per linear inch in a digital image. The more dots per inch an image has, the higher its resolution. A holdover term from nondigital printing, "dots per inch" and "pixels per inch (ppi)" are terms that are now usually used interchangeably.

entourage Elements that are added to a design drawing, such as figures and automobiles, that help give the drawing scale and context.

Eraser Tool A tol used to erase or delete pixels in a Photoshop image.

even wash A coating of color, usually by color pencil, that does not vary over the area to which it is applied.

extension The overcrossing of lines that form a corner in a drawing. Line extension can help to visually strengthen the corners of forms and shapes.

eyeball perspective Perspective drawing without the aid of perspective measuring systems or devices. Eyeball perspective is an extremely useful design drawing tool that, once mastered through practice, allows the designer to visualize three-dimensional forms and spaces by estimation.

Eyedropper Tool A tool used to sample a color from an image in Photoshop. The sampled color becomes the foreground color in the toolbox's *Color Picker*.

fixative A sprayed coating that helps to keep powdery color media, such as pastel, from smearing. Fixatives should be used with care, as they can somewhat deaden the brilliance of pastels.

flavoring A wash that imparts only a subtle hint of color, usually with color pencil.

forcing the shadow The act of grading a shadow darker toward its boundary, so the illuminated surface next to it appears brighter by contrast. This term also includes the converse, whereby an illuminated surface is made lighter next to a shadow.

foreground That part of a drawing that lies in front of the center of interest. Foreground elements are often used compositionally to make the middle ground appear more luminous and to help "frame" the center of interest.

French gray Grays that are very slightly yellowish or yellow reddish.

Golden Mean A guide to proportional relationships between two parts of a thing, developed by the Greeks, whereby the relationship of the smaller part to the larger part is the same as the larger part's relationship to the whole.

gouache An opaque watercolor paint.

gradation A gradual change in the dimensions of color over a given surface. A gradation can occur in one, two, or all three dimensions of a surface's color simultaneously.

graded wash A wash of color, applied with marker, pencil, or pastel, whose dimensions are made to change over a given surface.

gradient The blend or transition of one color or value into another.

Gradient Tool A tool used to create a blend of two or more colors within a selected area of a Photoshop image. The *Gradient Editor* in the options bar allows you to control the extent and graduation of the gradient.

grain The texture of a paper, also known as its "tooth." A fine-grain paper, such as Bristol, has less apparent "tooth" than a coarse-grain paper, such as Canson.

highlight The lightest spot or area of a surface, usually created by a light source or specular reflection.

histogram A graph of the value range of your image found when you open the *Levels Adjustment* command in Photoshop. It is divided into 256 levels, ranging from pure black at level 0 on the left, to pure white at level 255 on the right. The vertical range shows how many pixels are at each value.

History Palette A palette in Photoshop that tracks the steps used to create an image.

hue The name of a color and one of its three dimensions.

hue chart A chart of orderly samplings of a hue that displays its range of value and chroma. The extent of the ranges depends on the color medium used.

hue scheme A set of hues intended for a composition that are chosen for their particular relationship on the color wheel.

hybrid drawing A drawing created using both hand and digital techniques.

indistinct shadow edge See *diffuse shadow edge.*

illumination A term used in this book to describe lighting effects that come from sources of light other than direct sunlight. An interior is usually illuminated by a variety of light sources, including reflected sunlight.

key A closely related group of values that dominate the colors of a composition. Light values dominate a "high-key" composition, and dark values dominate a "low-key" composition.

Lasso Selection Tool A tool used to create free-form selections in Photoshop.

Layers Palette A Photoshop palette that allows the user to keep track of the layers used to create an image. It can create, hide, merge, duplicate, link, lock, and delete layers. Adjustment layers and layer styles (drop shadows, etc.) can be generated from this palette. It can also control the blending mode and the opacity of a layer.

lightness The degree to which the value of a color approaches white.

line control Disciplined movement and the use of the line media characteristic of hand-drawn linework.

line quality The character of linework in a drawing, usually used in reference to hand-drawn lines. Good line quality can include line control, an intelligent use of line weights, extensions, and line snap. It also can provide a window into the attitudes and characteristics of the designer.

line snap A slight darkening of the end of a hand-drawn line, often used to emphasize the intersection of lines at corners of shapes.

Line Tool A tool used to create straight lines in Photoshop. The selection of line weight and arrowheads occurs in the options bar.

line weight A line's degree of darkness and thickness.

local tone The inherent value of an object, regardless of its illumination.

lowlights Small areas of shade, shadow, or very dark reflection on an object that usually also contain highlights.

luminosity The appearance of giving off light.

Magic Wand Tool A Photoshop tool used to quickly select areas of similar colors.

marker A color application device that has a chisel-shaped tip made of an absorbent proprietary plastic. The coloring medium is composed of a carrier and a dye. The carrier is either alcohol or xylene, and the colorant is aniline dye. The colors are transparent and dry very quickly upon application.

Marquee Selection Tools Tools that allow the easy selection of orthogonal, circular, and elliptical shapes in a Photoshop image.

Measure Tool Used to measure distances and angles in a Photoshop image. The readouts can be found either in the options bar or on the *Info Palette.*

medial mixture The color created as the result of a visual averaging or mixing of several separate colors.

menu bar Contains all of the menus available in Photoshop. It is located at the very top of the Photoshop window.

mingling Creating a mixture of different colors in which each color retains some of its original identity. Mingling is often used in watercolor illustrations, and similar effects can be achieved with markers, with color pencils, and with pastels.

monochromatic Having or consisting of a single hue. In a monochromatic hue scheme, the dimensions of value and chroma may vary, but only one hue is used.

Move Tool A tool that allows you to move a layer or selection in a Photoshop file by clicking and dragging with your pen-tablet pen or mouse.

Munsell Student Charts A series of 10 hue charts and a chart containing the Munsell color wheel, a value scale, and a sample chroma scale. These charts are useful references for color composition work and can be obtained from Fairchild Books, 7 West 34th Street, New York, NY 10001; (800) 932-4724. They can also be ordered from Amazon.com.

Munsell System of Color A system in which color is organized visually rather than according to the mixture of pigments or dyes. It was originated by Albert H. Munsell in 1898, and the Munsell Color Company was formed shortly before his death in 1918. This system, like all color systems, originated from the need to describe colors in definite terms.

Navigator Palette A Photoshop palette that can be used to quickly show any part of an enlarged image in the document window by moving an outline of the document window over a thumbnail image of the document. This palette also includes a slider for enlarging or reducing the image.

neutral color A color that has no hue or chroma; white, black, and the grays.

Office Method, Common Method (of perspective drawing) A once-popular method of two-point perspective construction that utilized a plan and elevation to construct a perspective view. The method used the intersection of imaginary lines with a "picture plane" drawn from a station point to corners of the plan view. Additional lines were extended from this intersection to form the vertical corners of the three-dimensional image. The elevation was used to provide the necessary height information.

Opacity slider A slider in the Photoshop *Layers Palette* that controls the degree of a layer's opacity, ranging from completely opaque to completely transparent.

options bar A strip exhibiting controls that can be used to modify an active tool in Photoshop. The options bar is located directly beneath the menu bar.

Paint Bucket Tool Used to fill a selected area in a Photoshop file with the foreground color shown in the *Color Picker*.

palette A selection of colors used for a particular purpose or series of similar purposes.

paraline drawing A drawing that uses parallel lines to create three-dimensional images. Isometric, dimetric, axonometric, and oblique drawings are all types of paraline drawing.

pastel A color stick made by combining dry pigment with a methylcellulose binder.

pastel "quickie" A color drawing created very quickly with the use of pastel.

pen and pen tablet A digital device that can be used to control the movement of the cursor on the computer screen instead of a mouse. It is especially useful when using Photoshop and other digital drawing applications because it approximates the shape and feel of a pencil and paper; it is therefore more comfortable than a mouse, and affords more precision, facility, and pressure sensitivity when drawing.

Pencil Tool Used for drawing hard-edged lines in Photoshop. The width and character of the line can be controlled using the settings on the options bar, including the *Brush Preset Picker*.

perspective The representation of a three-dimensional form or space on a two-dimensional surface. It came into use in the fourteenth century.

plotter A color printing device, which can be connected to a single computer or network, that is used to generate large-format prints, usually on paper.

poché (n.) The shading of that part of an architectural drawing representing a section cut; (v.) to shade a section cut, usually with pencil or pen.

Polygonal Lasso Selection Tool A tool used to create selections bounded by straight lines in Photoshop.

presentation drawing A drawing used to communicate design ideas in a presentation situation. In addition to communicating design content, presentation drawings are also prepared as compositions in their own right.

proportion The relationship between the various parts of a thing.

punch Visual impact in a drawing, usually created by value contrast.

reflection mass A group of objects reflected in a window or series of windows that are so dark as to appear in the reflection as a single mass.

refract To break white light into its component colors, usually by a prism or in a rainbow. The component colors of white light are red, orange, yellow, green, blue, indigo, and violet.

repetition A form of rhythm in which a characteristic is repeated throughout a drawing.

retrocolor The application of color to the back of a drawing on a translucent sheet, such as white tracing paper.

retrocolor hybrid A retrocolor drawing whose front-side image is created by both computer and hand drawing.

reversal An image in which the typical black-line-on-white-background is reversed, exhibiting white lines on a black background. A reversal is most easily made with the use of a color copier (most color copiers have a function to provide this kind of image). To produce the drawing surface for figures 4-76 through 4-78, the reversed image was again photocopied, using a black-and-white photocopier to transfer it to frosted mylar. The frosted mylar reversal was subsequently printed on blackline diazo paper, with the machine at *normal* speed.

rhythm Flow or apparent movement characterized by regular recurrence of elements or features. In color drawing, rhythm can be introduced with such things as gradations and repetition.

rulers Used to visually measure the size of a Photoshop image in the document window. The scale of the rulers change with an image's size (Image > Image Size . . .). The rulers can be turned on or off using the *View* menu (View > Rulers).

saturation The chroma of a color; its degree of purity, which can range from weak, or grayish, to strong or vivid.

setup An image that provides the basic guidelines for a drawing, usually a perspective view. Setups can be rough hand-drawn layouts, computer wireframes, real-life photographs, or photographs of models.

shade The diminished light on a surface as a result of its facing away from the source.

shadow The absence of direct light on a surface caused by an intervening object.

simultaneous contrast The effect created by placing complementary hues in proximity to each other. Each makes the other appear its most vivid. It can also mean the phenomenon whereby the eye conjures up the complement of a color it is seeing, even if that complement is not present.

sketch A quick, loose drawing used to depict an idea, usually preliminary in nature.

sketchpack A collection of exploratory design drawings that are assembled into a uniform, manageable size for subsequent review, usually 11" x 17". This term originated at CommArts.

SketchUp An easy-to-use application for digitally creating, viewing, and modifying three-dimensional forms and spaces.

source file A file of color photographs and clippings that is used as a reference for drawing elements, materials, and finishes.

spatial interest "The anticipated experience of a variety of spaces and vistas [seen in a drawing] which [promise to] become available as we move through the space" (from *Drawing as a Means to Architecture,* Revised Edition, by William Kirby Lockard. 1977. Tucson: Pepper Publishing).

spectrum value The value of a color when it is shown at its strongest chroma.

splice A revised portion of a drawing that is cut into the original or a reproduction of the original.

stipple The addition of small dots to a drawing, usually with pen or pencil, to create a texture.

subordinate That part of a color composition that does not possess the dominant qualities of the composition.

Swatches Palette A palette in Photoshop that allows you to name and store colors and gradients for easy access.

toned paper A paper that is not white, but has a gray or colored surface. The toned papers most commonly used for color design drawing are ink-jet paper with a toned or gradient background, Canson paper, and white roll tracing paper backed with colored or kraft paper.

toolbox A Photoshop palette containing all the tools for working on image files. A small triangular arrow in the bottom right corner of a tool's icon indicates there are additional options available for that tool.

tooth See *grain.*

triad Any three hues that are approximately equidistant on a color wheel.

Type Tool The tool used to create horizontal or vertical type in Photoshop images.

unity The quality of a composition whereby the various parts act together to form a single idea.

value The lightness or darkness of a color or colorless area.

value strategy Plan for arranging the major values of a drawing that best serves the ideas shown therein.

value study A small, quick study used to create and test possible arrangements of the major values for a presentation drawing. The chosen study is an effective guide in creating the final drawing.

values, major Large, contiguous areas of similar values in a drawing.

vellum A translucent drawing paper, heavier than white roll tracing paper. A common type is Clearprint 1000H.

vellum finish A lightly textured finish, characteristic of Bristol paper. Bristol can also be obtained in a very smooth "plate" finish, typically better suited for certain types of media such as graphite pencil.

vision sketch An attempt, early in the design process, at creating a three-dimensional design drawing of an idea, drawn directly from the designer's imagination onto paper. No setup—horizon lines, vanishing points, or scale figures—are included. These drawings are usually very rough and are used for personal reference.

visual mixture The color resulting from the blending by eye of several different colors (see also *medial mixture*).

warm gray A gray that is very slightly reddish.

warm hue A hue that is associated with warm temperatures. Red, yellow red, yellow, and green yellow are warm hues on the Munsell color wheel (see figure 6-2). Green and red purple form the boundary between warm and cool hues and can be made to be either warm or cool.

wash A coating of color, usually color pencil, but can also be created by marker, pastel, or by using the *Paint Bucket Tool* or the *Gradient Tool* in Photoshop.

xylene A fast-drying organic solvent used as a carrying agent for the aniline dye in markers. Markers containing xylene should be used in a well-ventilated place.

Zoom Tool A tool used to enlarge an image in Photoshop by a preset amount. To reduce magnification, hold down the Option key (Mac) or the Alt key (Windows) while clicking on the image.

BIBLIOGRAPHY

Ackerman, Diane. 1991. *A Natural History of the Senses.* New York: Vintage.

Albers, Josef. 1963. *Interaction of Color.* New Haven, Conn.: Yale University Press.

American Society of Architectural Perspectivists. 1996. *Architecture in Perspective: 11th Annual International Competition of Architectural Illustration.* Rockport, N.Y.: Rockport Publishers.

Birren, Faber. 1965. *History of Color in Painting.* New York: Reinhold.

Birren, Faber. 1982. *Light, Color and Environment.* New York: Van Nostrand Reinhold.

Conran, Terence. 1993. *The Kitchen Book.* Woodstock, N.Y.: Overlook Press.

Davis, Jack. 2003. *The Photoshop 7 Wow! Book.* Berkeley: Peachpit Press. This book covers both the basics as well as advanced Photoshop techniques. While its examples are geared more toward graphic designers, it has plenty of in-depth information for those who use Photoshop for digital color design drawing.

Doyle, Michael E. 1999. *Color Drawing.* 2d. ed. New York: John Wiley & Sons.

Drucker, Mindy, and Pierre Finkelstein. 1990. *Recipes for Surfaces.* New York: Fireside.

Feldman, Edmund Burke. 1987. *Varieties of Visual Experience.* New York: Abrams.

Goldstein, Nathan. 1977. *The Art of Responsive Drawing.* 2d ed. Englewood Cliffs, N.J.: Prentice-Hall.

Graham, Donald W. 1970. *Composing Pictures.* New York: Van Nostrand Reinhold.

Grice, Gordon, ed. 1997. *The Art of Architectural Illustration.* New York: McGraw-Hill.

Hale, Jonathan. 1994. *The Old Way of Seeing.* Boston: Houghton Mifflin.

Hope, Augustine, and Margaret Walch. 1990. *The Color Compendium.* New York: John Wiley & Sons.

Itten, Johannes. 1973. *The Art of Color.* New York: John Wiley & Sons.

Kautzky, Theodore. 1947. *Pencil Pictures: A Guide to Their Pleasing Arrangement.* New York: Van Nostrand Reinhold. This short book contains some of the most spectacular pencil demonstrations of value arrangement and drawing virtuosity ever published.

Lockard, William Kirby. 1998. *Drawing As A Means To Architecture.* 2d. rev. ed. Mississauga, Ontario: Crisp Learning.

Macbeth. 1996. *Munsell Color: The Universal Language* (brochure). New Windsor, N.Y.: Macbeth.

Martin, C. Leslie. 1968. *Design Graphics.* 2d. ed. New York: Macmillan Publishing. This book contains all the secrets of perspective and shade and shadow construction. It also has a short but effective section on the principles of rendering, including pencil, pen and ink, wash, watercolor, and tempera (gouache) rendering. It includes some terrific black-and-white images of 1950s and 1960s illustrations.

Neumeier, Marty. "Secrets of Design: Draftsmanship." *Critique* 6 (Autumn 1997): 18–27.

Simon, Hilda. 1980. *Color in Reproduction.* New York: Viking.

Spies, Werner. 1970. *Albers.* New York: Abrams.

Street-Porter, Tim. 1989. *Casa Mexicana.* New York: Stewart, Tabori & Chang.

The Editors of *Réalités.* 1973. *Impressionism.* Secaucus, N.J.: Chartwell Books.

DESIGN CREDITS

Fig. 1-5. Transit Shelter, Uptown Houston. CommArts, designers, with SWA Group, Houston, for The Metropolitan Transit Authority of Harris County and Harris County Improvement District #1.

Fig. 1-6. East Baltimore Development RFP, Baltimore (design study). Commarts, designers, with SMWM, Elkus Manfredi, and Michael Marshall Architects, for Forest City Enterprises.

Fig. 1-8. After a photograph in *Casa Mexicana* by Tim Street-Porter. 1989. New York: Stewart, Tabori & Chang, Inc.

Fig. 1-9. After a photograph in *The Kitchen Book* by Terence Conran. 1993. Woodstock, New York: Overlook Press. The photograph is credited: "Rodney Hyett/Elizabeth Whiting and Associates (B. B. P. Architects, Melbourne, Australia)."

Fig. 1-14. West Marine Store, Piers 27-31, San Francisco (facade study). Comm Arts, designers, with D'Agostino Izzo Quirk Architects, Inc., for The Mills Corporation.

Fig. 1-15. Uptown Houston, Houston (lighting study). CommArts, designers, with SWA Group, Houston, for Harris County Improvement District #1.

Fig. 1-16. Hotel Teatro, Denver (illustration). CommArts, illustrator, with Carney Architects, for Jeff Selby, Hotel Teatro, L.L.C.

Fig. 2-11. Dolphin Mall, Miami (interior study). CommArts, designers, for the Taubman Company.

Fig. 2-12. Plaza las Fuentes, Pasadena. CommArts, modification designers, for Maguire Thomas Partners. Building architect was Moore Ruble Yudell.

Fig. 2-13. Houston Uptown, Houston. CommArts, designers, with Slaney Santana Group, landscape architects, for the Harris County Improvement District #1.

Fig. 2-17. St. Louis Union Station, St. Louis. CommArts, designers, with HOK, architects, for the Rouse Company.

Fig. 2-18. Restaurant study, California. CommArts, designers, with the Sterling Rice Group, for Cocos and Carrows Restaurants.

Fig. 2-19. Uptown Houston, Houston. CommArts, designers, with SWA Group, Houston, for The Harris County Improvement District #1.

Figs. 3-10 to 3-13. Pinecrest Mountain, Evergreen, Colorado (residential duplex design study). Commarts, designers, with DHM Design, for Pyramid Properties.

Figs. 3-25, 3-26. Tokyo Midtown, Tokyo (atrium study). CommArts, (commercial design architect), with SOM, New York (master plan and master design architect) and Nikken

Sekkei, LTD, Tokyo (architect of record), for Mitsui Fudosan.

Figs. 3-28, 3-30. Colorado Building, Boulder, Colorado (remodel). CommArts, designers, with Zimmerman Architects, for Colorado Building Management and Dr. Henry Eaton.

Figs. 3-31, 3-32. Pinecrest Mountain, Evergreen, Colorado (chapel study). Commarts, designers, with DHM Design, for Pyramid Properties.

Figs. 3-34, 3-35. Building for the Alliance for Learning, Technology, and Society (ATLAS), Boulder, Colorado (café design). CommArts, designers, with DTJ Design, for the University of Colorado.

Figs. 3-37, 3-38, 3-40. Restaurant study, California. CommArts, designers, with the Sterling Rice Group, for Cocos and Carrows Restaurants.

Figs. 3-41, 3-42. Pinecrest Mountain, Evergreen, Colorado (entry study). Commarts, designers, with DHM Design, for Pyramid Properties.

Fig. 3-47. Uptown Houston, Texas. CommArts, designers, with SWA Group, Houston, for The Harris County Improvement District #1.

Fig. 3-48. Crossroads Mall, Boulder, Colorado (remodel study). CommArts, designers, for the Macerich Company.

Fig. 3-49. The Alliance for Learning, Technology, and Society (ATLAS), Boulder, Colorado. CommArts, designers, with DTJ Design, project architects, for the University of Colorado.

Fig. 3-50. Downtown Boulder Mall, Boulder, Colorado (lighting study). CommArts, designers, for the City of Boulder.

Fig. 3-51. Proposed modifications to stairway in the former location of the Angel's Flight funicular railway, Los Angeles. Stairway by Lawrence Halprin and Associates. Proposal for Maguire Thomas Partners.

Fig. 3-52. Uptown Houston, Houston, Texas (streetscape study). CommArts, designers, with SWA Group, Houston, for The Harris County Improvement District #1.

Figs. 3-53 through 3-58. Fashion Place, Salt Lake City. CommArts, designers, with Feola Carli Archuleta, architects, for the Hahn Company.

Fig. 3-59. Grand Park, Winter Park, Colorado (building massing and streetscape study). CommArts, designers, for Cornerstone Holdings, LLC.

Fig. 3-60. Aspen, Colorado (streetscape design study). CommArts, designers, for the town of Aspen.

Fig. 3-61. Minneapolis-St. Paul International Airport (design study). CommArts, designers, for Host Mariott.

Fig. 3-62. Uptown Houston, Houston, Texas (streetscape study). CommArts, designers, with SWA Group, Houston, for The Harris County Improvement District #1.

Figs. 4-1, 4-2. After a design by Frederick Biehle and Erika Hinrichs, Via Architecture Studio, for Lizden Industries.

Figs. 4-3 to 4-6. Restaurant study, California. CommArts, designers, with the Sterling Rice Group, for Cocos and Carrows Restaurants.

Figs. 4-14, 4-15. Pearlridge Mall, Honolulu. CommArts, designers, with Feola Carli Archuleta, architects, for Northwestern Mutual Life and E. Phillip Lyon Co.

Figs. 4-16, 4-17. The Prudential Center, Boston. CommArts, designers, with Sikes, Jennings, Kelly and Brewer, architects, for the Prudential Property Company.

Figs. 4-18, 4-19. Brothers Coffee, New York. CommArts, designers, for the Gloria Jean Coffee Company.

Fig. 4-55. Perimeter Mall, Atlanta. CommArts, designers, with D'Augostino, Izzo, Quirk, architects, for the Rouse Company.

Fig. 4-86. Pearlridge Mall, Honolulu. CommArts, designers, with Feola Carli Archuleta, architects, for Northwestern Mutual Life and E. Phillip Lyon Co.

Fig. 4-106. Houston Uptown, Houston. CommArts, designers, with Slaney Santana Group, landscape architects, for the Harris County Improvement District #1.

Fig. 4-135. Boulder County Courthouse Lawn Study, Boulder, Colorado. Comm Arts, designers, for Boulder County Commissioner Heath.

Fig. 4-150. The Maxim Building, Boulder, Colorado. CommArts, designers, with the Hunter Group, architects, for 901 Walnut Street, L.L.C.

Fig. 4-152. Westminster Promenade, Westminster, Colorado. CommArts, designers, with Martin and Martin Engineers, for the City of Westminster.

Figs. 4-157, 4-163. Colorado Building, Boulder, Colorado (remodel). CommArts, designers, with Zimmerman Architects, for Colorado Building Management and Dr. Henry Eaton.

Figs. 4-168 through 4-178. The Maxim Building, Boulder, Colorado. CommArts, designers, with the Hunter Group, architects, for 901 Walnut Street, L.L.C.

Figs. 4-182 through 4-187. Uptown Houston, Houston, Texas (streetscape study). CommArts, designers, with SWA Group,

Houston, for The Harris County Improvement District #1.

Fig. 4-217. Uptown Houston, Houston, Texas (streetscape study). CommArts, designers, with SWA Group, Houston, for The Harris County Improvement District #1.

Fig. 4-227. Pinecrest Mountain, Evergreen, Colorado (residential duplex design study). Commarts, designers, with DHM Design, for Pyramid Properties.

Fig. 4-248. Uptown Houston, Houston, Texas (streetscape study). CommArts, designers, with SWA Group, Houston, for The Harris County Improvement District #1.

Fig. 5-1. Citywalk, Los Angeles. CommArts, designers, with Houston / Tyner, architects, for Universal Studios, Hollywood.

Fig. 5-2. Uptown District of Houston (proposed modifications). CommArts, designers, for Houston Metro.

Fig. 5-3. Hollywood Athletic Club, Los Angeles (proposed modifications). CommArts, designers, for Hollywood Athletic Club.

Fig. 5-6. Brothers Coffee, New York. CommArts, designers, for the Gloria Jean Coffee Company.

Fig. 5-16. The Maxim Building, Boulder, Colorado. CommArts, designers, with the Hunter Group, architects, for 901 Walnut Street, L.L.C.

Fig. 6-1. The San Diego Exposition. Bertram Goodhue, architect. Illustration by Birch Burdette Long, from *Color in Sketching and Rendering* by Arthur Guptill. 1935 New York: Reinhold Publishing.

Fig. 6-3. The Seasons at Avon, Avon, Colorado. CommArts, designers, with Victor Mark Donaldson, architects, for the Gart Companies.

Fig. 6-8. United States Embassy Competition, Berlin. Moore Ruble Yudell Architects. Watercolor over pencil, 18" x 24". Illustration by Douglas E. Jamieson.

Fig. 6-9. The United States Embassy, Cairo. The Architects Collaborative (TAC), architects. Watercolor. Frank M. Costantino, illustrator.

Fig. 6-10. Proposed Plaza, Olympics 2000, Istanbul, Turkey. Thomas W. Schaller, AIA, with Stang & Newdow / Atlanta. Watercolor, 36" x 24". Illustration by Thomas W. Schaller, Schaller Architectural Illustration.

Fig. 6-12. Millenium Square, London. CommArts, designers, with Barr Gazetas, architects, for Meridian Delta, Ltd., Anschutz Entertainment Group Europe, and English Partnerships.

Fig. 6-13. The Maxim Building, Boulder, Colorado. CommArts, designers, with the Hunter Group, architects, for 901 Walnut Street, L.L.C.

Fig. 6-14. Teltow Housing Masterplan, Zeidler Roberts Partnership. Watercolor over pencil, 6½" x 8½". Illustration

by Douglas E. Jamieson.

Fig. 6-15. Art Museum, self-comissioned. Mixed media. Illustration by Ronald J. Love, Ronald J. Love Architectural Illustration, 3891 Bayridge Avenue, West Vancouver, BC V7V3J3, Canada (604-922-3033).

Fig. 6-16. From *The City*. Watercolor, 30" x 22". Illustration by Thomas W. Schaller, Schaller Architectural Illustration, 2112 Broadway, Suite 407, New York, NY 10023 (212-362-5524).

Fig. 6-17. Display window study for Gas Company Tower, Los Angeles. CommArts, window designers, for Maguire Thomas Partners.

Fig. 6-18. Proposed Hydroponics Research Center, Uruguay. Thomas W. Schaller, AIA, architect. Watercolor, 18" x 24". Illustration by Thomas W. Schaller, Schaller Architectural Illustration, 2112 Broadway, Suite 407, New York, NY 10023 (212-362-5524).

Fig. 6-19. Study for Old Orchard, Chicago. CommArts, designers, for Equity Properties.

Fig. 6-20. The Rattlesnake Club, Denver. CommArts, designers, for the Rattlesnake Club Associates.

Fig. 6-21. Naples Beachfront Cottages, Architectural Design Group, architects. Illustration by Curtis James Woodhouse.

Fig. 6-22. Illustration by Edward Dixon McDonald, from *Color in Sketching and Rendering* by Arthur Guptill. 1935. New York: Reinhold Publishing.

Fig. 6-23. Uptown Houston, Houston, Texas (streetscape study). CommArts, designers with SWA Group, Houston, for The Harris County Improvement District #1.

Fig. 7-12. Santa Monica Place (renovation), Santa Monica. CommArts, designers, with Ray Bailey Architects, for the Rouse Company.

Fig. 7-6 Houston Uptown, Houston. CommArts, designers, with Slaney Santana, landscape architects, for Harris County Improvement District #1.

Fig. 7-7. Madison Square Garden, New York. CommArts, designers, with Gensler, architects, for Madison Square Garden.

Fig. 7-14. Perimeter Mall, Atlanta. CommArts, designers, with D'Augustino, Izzo, Quirk, architects, for the Rouse Company.

Fig. 7-21. Park Meadows, Denver. CommArts, designers, with Anthony Belluschi Architects, for TrizecHahn.

Fig. 7-24, 7-28. Uptown Houston, Houston (streetscape study). CommArts, designers, with SWA Group, Houston, for The Harris County Improvement District #1.

Fig. 7-34. Uptown Houston, Houston (park study). CommArts, designers, with SWA Group, Houston, for The Harris County Improvement District #1.

Fig. 7-41. World Trade Center, New York (renovation

competition). CommArts, designers, with HOK New York, architects, for LCOR, Inc., and the Port Authority of New York and New Jersey.

Figs. 7-48, 7-54. The Maxim Building, Boulder, Colorado. CommArts, designers, with the Hunter Group, architects, for 901 Walnut Street, L.L.C.

Figs. 7-55, 7-61 Grand Park, Winter Park, Colorado (building massing and streetscape study for a new town center). CommArts, designers, for Cornerstone Holdings, LLC.

Fig. 7-62. Faneuil Hall Marketplace, Boston. Benjamin Thompson Associates for the Rouse Company.

Fig. 7-63 South Waterfront Central District, Portland, Oregon (courtyard study for Block 30). CommArts, designers, with GBD Architects and Walker Macy, for Williams & Dame Development.

Fig. 7-64. Uptown Houston, Houston, Texas (lighting study). CommArts, designers, with SWA Group, Houston, for The Harris County Improvement District #1.

Fig. 8-1 to 8-5. Stanford Shopping Center, Palo Alto, California (design study). CommArts, designers, for Simon Property Group, Inc.

Fig. 8-6 to 8-12. The District at Northridge, Northridge, California. CommArts, designers, with Johnson Fain, architects, for New Urban West, Inc.

Fig. 8-13 to 8-24. Grand Park, Winter Park, Colorado (building massing and streetscape study for a new town center). CommArts, designers, for Cornerstone Holdings, LLC.

Fig. 8-25 to 8-34 Fidenza Design Center, Fidenza, Italy. Lockard Creative, designer, with Kaplan McLaughlin Diaz, architects, for Value Retail.

Fig. 8-35 to 8-41 Shenzhen Swimming and Diving Halls, Shenzhen, China. LHP (Lockard He Pan) Design, designers, for the municipality of Shenzhen, China.

Fig. 8-42 to 8-62 Uptown Houston, Houston (streetscape study). CommArts, designers, with SWA Group, Houston, for The Harris County Improvement District #1.

Fig. 8-65, 8-66. South Waterfront Central District, Portland, Oregon (courtyard study for Block 30). CommArts, designers, with GBD Architects and Walker Macy, for Williams & Dame Development

Fig. 8-67 to 8-69. Pinecrest Mountain, Evergreen, Colorado (project entry design study). Commarts, designers, with DHM Design, for Pyramid Properties.

Fig. 8-70 to 8-74. The Alliance for Technology, Learning, and Society (ATLAS), Boulder, Colorado. CommArts, designers, with DTJ Design, project architects, for the University of Colorado.

INDEX